March29–April1, 2015
Monterey, CA, USA

**Association for
Computing Machinery**

Advancing Computing as a Science & Profession

ISPD'15

Proceedings of the ACM

International Symposium on Physical Design 2015

Sponsored by:

ACM SIGDA

Supported by:

Altera, ATopTech, Cadence, IBM Research, Intel Corporation, Mentor Graphics, Oracle, Qualcomm, and Synopsys

**Association for
Computing Machinery**

Advancing Computing as a Science & Profession

The Association for Computing Machinery
2 Penn Plaza, Suite 701
New York, New York 10121-0701

ISBN: 978-1-4503-3399-3

Additional copies may be ordered prepaid from:

ACM Order Department
PO Box 30777
New York, NY 10087-0777, USA

Phone: 1-800-342-6626 (USA and Canada)
+1-212-626-0500 (Global)
Fax: +1-212-944-1318
E-mail: acmhelp@acm.org
Hours of Operation: 8:30 am – 4:30 pm ET

ACM Order #: 477155

Printed in the USA

Foreword

On behalf of the organizing committee, we are delighted to welcome you to the 2015 ACM International Symposium on Physical Design (ISPD), held at Monterey, California. Continuing the great tradition established by its twenty-three predecessors, which includes a series of five ACM/SIGDA Physical Design Workshops held intermittently in 1987-1996 and eighteen editions of ISPD in the current form since 1997, the 2015 ISPD provides a premier forum to present leading-edge research results, exchange ideas, and promote research on critical areas related to the physical design of VLSI and other related systems.

We received 44 abstract submissions and 37 full submissions from all around the world. After a rigorous, month-long, double-blind review process, the Technical Program Committee (TPC) met face-to-face to select papers to be included in the technical program based on 185 reviews provided by 18 TPC members and 39 external reviewers. Finally, the committee accepted 14 papers to be presented in the symposium. These papers exhibit latest advancements in a variety of topics in placement, routing, 3D integration, clocking, power network planning, design for manufacturability, and physical design with latest machine learning approaches.

The ISPD 2015 program is complemented by two keynote addresses, seven invited talks and an invited session on FreePDK library, all of which are delivered by distinguished researchers in both industry and academia. Dr. Karim Arabi, Vice President, Engineering at Qualcomm will present in the Monday keynote speech, challenges and opportunities in scalable integration of 3D VLSI. Dr. Rob Rutenbar, Abel Bliss Professor and Head of the Department of Computer Science in the University of Illinois at Urbana-Champaign will present in the Tuesday keynote speech on analog circuit and layout synthesis. A commemorative session on Tuesday afternoon pays a tribute to Dr. Kurt Antreich. His collaborators will share with us Dr. Antreich's exceptional contributions to EDA research, including his pioneering effort in analytical circuit placement, which still has significant impact on various placement methods today. The other invited talks will be interspersed with the presentations of accepted papers. The topics of the invited papers range from emerging technologies like directed self-assembly circuits, monolithic 3D ICs, to modern challenges in analog IC layout and applications of machine learning in physical design.

Since 2005, ISPD has organized highly competitive contests to promote and advance research in placement, global routing, clock network synthesis, and discrete gate sizing. This year's contest is on detailed routing-driven placement and is organized by Mentor Graphics. Specifically, this is the second year of this topic and the problem is made even more challenging by imposing constraints of fence regions and placement blockages, besides the detailed pin, cell and wire geometry constraints in 2014. The contest evaluates the quality of a placement with a commercial detailed router in order to motivate research to address significant complexity of routing-design rules in sub-20nm nodes. Continuing the tradition of all the past contests, a new large-scale real-world benchmark suite will be released in industry-standard formats including LEF, DEF, and Verilog description in the ISPD website: http://www.ispd.cc

We would like to take this chance to express our gratitude to the authors, the presenters, the keynote/invited speakers for contributing to the high-quality program, and the session chairs for moderating the sessions. We would like to thank our program committee and external reviewers, who provided insightful constructive comments and detailed reviews to the authors. We greatly appreciate the exceptional set of invited talks put together by the Steering Committee, which is chaired by Cliff Sze. We also thank the Steering Committee for selecting the best paper. Special thanks go to the Publications Chair Mustafa Ozdal and the Publicity Chair Chris Chu for their tremendous services. We would like to acknowledge the team organizing the contest led by Ismail Bustany. We are also grateful to our sponsors. The symposium is sponsored by the ACM SIGDA (Special Interest Group on Design Automation) with technical co-sponsorship from the IEEE Circuits and Systems Society. Generous financial contributions have also been provided by (in alphabetical order): Altera, ATopTech, Cadence, IBM Research, Intel Corporation, Mentor Graphics, Oracle, Qualcomm and Synopsys. Last but not least, we thank Lisa Tolles of Sheridan Communications for her expertise and enormous patience during the production of the proceedings.

The organizing committee hopes that you will enjoy ISPD. We look forward to seeing you again in future editions of ISPD.

Azadeh Davoodi
ISPD 2015 General Chair

Evangeline Young
Technical Program Chair

Table of Contents

Keynote Address
Session Chair: Azadeh Davoodi *(University of Wisconsin - Madison)*

Advanced Placement and Analog Design
Session Chair: Jackey Yan *(Cadence)*

Learning Physical Design
Session Chair: Hung-Ming Chen *(National Chiao Tung University)*

DFM
Session Chair: Hongbo Zhang *(Synopsys)*

Dinner Banquet
Session Chair: Noel Menezes *(Intel)*

Tuesday Keynote Address

Session Chair: Patrick Groeneveld *(Synopsys)*

Clocking and Power

Session Chair: Aiqun Cao *(Synopsys)*

Physical Design and Beyond

Session Chair: Dwight Hill *(Synopsys)*

Commemoration for Prof. Kurt Antreich

Session Chair: Andrew Kahng *(University of California, San Diego)*

Placement and Contest

Session Chair: Yuyen Mo *(Oracle)*

FreePDK

Session Chair: David Chinnery *(Mentor Graphics Corporation)*

ISPD 2015 Symposium Organization

General Chair: Azadeh Davoodi *(University of Wisconsin - Madison)*

Technical Program Chair: Evangeline Young *(The Chinese University of Hong Kong)*

Past Chair: Cliff Sze *(IBM Research)*

Steering Committee Chair: Cliff Sze *(IBM Research)*

Steering Committee: Ismail Bustany *(Mentor Graphics)*
Yao-Wen Chang *(National Taiwan University)*
Patrick Groeneveld *(Synopsys)*
Inki Hong *(Cadence)*
Cheng-Kok Koh *(Purdue University)*
Malgorzata Marek-Sadowska *(University of California, Santa Barbara)*
Noel Menezes *(Intel)*

Program Committee: Aiqun Cao *(Synopsys)*
David Chinnery *(Mentor Graphics)*
Stephan Held *(University of Bonn)*
Dwight Hill *(Synopsys)*
Tsung-Yi Ho *(National Cheng Kung University)*
Andrew Kennings *(University of Waterloo)*
Jens Lienig *(Dresden University of Technology)*
Guojie Luo *(Peking University)*
Yu-Yen Mo *(Oracle)*
Sherief Reda *(Brown University)*
William Swartz *(TimberWolf Inc.)*
Atsushi Takahashi *(Tokyo Institute of Technology)*
Natarajan Viswanathan *(IBM)*
Alexey Volosskiy *(AMD)*
Jackey Yan *(Cadence)*
Hailong Yao *(Tsinghua University)*
Evangeline Young *(Chinese University of Hong Kong)*
Cheng Zhuo *(Intel)*

Publication Chair: Mustafa Ozdal *(Intel)*

Publicity Chair: Chris Chu *(Iowa State University)*

Contest Chair: Ismail Bustany *(Mentor Graphics)*

Additional Reviewers:

Sarvesh Bhardwaj
Steve Bigalke
Ismail Bustany
Duo Chen
Song Chen
CK Cheng
Jerrica Gao
Tao Huang
Myung-Chul Kim
Johann Knechtel
Chikaaki Kodama
Yukihide Kohira
Andreas Krinke
Wen Hao Liu
Jingwei Lu
Tetsuaki Matsunawa
Shigetoshi Nakatake
Sergii Osmolovskyi
Weikang Qian
Anand Rajaram

Ramoji Rao
Chiu-Wing Sham
Minghua Shen
Yiyu Shi
Joseph Shinnerl
Satoshi Tanaka
Matthias Thiele
Ting-Chi Wang
Dean Wu
Pei-Ci Wu
Steve Wu
Chang Xu
Yue Xu
Guo Yu
Wentai Zhang
Yanheng Zhang
Min Zhao
Wenxing Zhu
Hao Zhuang

ISPD 2015 Sponsor & Supporters

Sponsor:

Technical Co-sponsor:

Supporters:

3D VLSI: A Scalable Integration Beyond 2D

Karim Arabi, Kambiz Samadi and Yang Du
Qualcomm Research, San Diego, CA

ABSTRACT

As the semiconductor industry faces serious challenges extending the CMOS roadmap, traditional cost reduction benefits that accompanied power/performance/area (PPA) advantages of successive technology nodes have decreased due to a myriad of process integration challenges and increased variability, reliability, power and thermal constraints. 3D integration technologies have been pursued as a potential solution to help integrate more functions within a confined available dimensions of advanced mobile devices. 3D VLSI (3DV) is an emerging 3D integration technology that unlike packaging-driven 3D technologies (e.g., 2.5D, TSV-based 3D, etc.) can deliver orders of magnitude more integration densities due to extremely small sizes of vertical vias. In this paper, we describe the 3DV technology and its current benefits and challenges. We also survey recent literature that show the potential of 3DV to help continue Moore's law trajectory beyond 2D.

Categories and Subject Descriptors

B.7.2 [**Integrated Circuits**]: Design Aids

General Terms

Algorithms, Design, Integration

Keywords

3D VLSI; Placement; Routing; Computer-aided Design

1. INTRODUCTION

Semiconductor and electronics industries have enjoyed tremendous growth and innovations over the past 50 years thanks largely to a self-fulfilling prophecy, called Moore's law. Moore's law is a scaling phenomenon that historically has been a metric for density or functionality, and performance; however, in reality it has been a proxy for cost-effective integration. International Technology Roadmap for Semiconductors (ITRS) provides a taxonomy of traditional "More Moore" scaling which can be categorized into (1) geometrical scaling (refers to continued shrinking of horizontal and vertical physical feature sizes), (2) equivalent scaling (refers to 3D device structures) and (3) design equivalent scaling (refers to design technologies that enable improved power, performance and cost envelopes) [1]. As the semiconductor industry is heading towards the physical limits of Silicon, the economies of Moore's law is diminishing, and hence the success of the semiconductor lies on the scaling of different elements than the "More Moore".

One of the new elements of scaling is integration and a viable way of achieving it is to use the third dimension. 3D integration has been emerging as a viable solution to enable integration of more devices to create designs with better overall power and performance envelope. Historically, there has been an ever growing gap between transistor and wire performances as technology scales with majority of the innovation focusing on transistor performance scaling. In older generation designs, this was not much of a problem as designers insert enough buffers to compensate for the lagging wire performance, i.e., making the design cell dominated in order to meet design timing. However, as industry started to hit the thermal limits every bit of power counts. One way to cope with these challenges is to reduce the interconnect-related power and latency and that is a major benefit of 3D integration. Traditionally, 3D IC has been used to refer to packaging-driven techniques, e.g., flip-chip (FC), package-on-package (PoP), and more recently, through-silicon via (TSV)-based 3D. Even though technically all these approaches integrate devices in the third dimension in one way or another, they do not offer enough integration that can scale performance or power. These techniques have been devised primarily to cope with the cost of scaling and limited physical space in mobile devices.

Recently 3D VLSI (3DV) has been emerging as an alternative to the packaging-driven 3D integration technologies. 3DV is described as a foundry-driven wafer-level 3D integration process that can further be categorized into sequential face-to-back (F2B) and parallel F2B/face-to-face (F2F) integration technologies. 3D VLSI technologies can offer orders of magnitude more integration density than the existing packaging-driven 3D technologies. The abundance of vertical interconnects in 3DV is the key enabler to achieve significant power and performance improvements through shorter interconnect and less interconnect buffers.

On the other hand, functional diversification is defined as incorporation of functionalities that do not necessarily scale with Moore's law, but provide additional value to the end user [1]. 3DV enables such value scaling by providing a single-chip solution that migrates non-digital functionalities such as RF communication, power management, sensors, etc. onto a system-on-chip (SoC) solution as shown in Figure 1. In addition, 3DV creates numerous opportunities at architecture / system levels for new innovations that can take us through a period of architecture- / system-level scaling instead of device-level scaling.

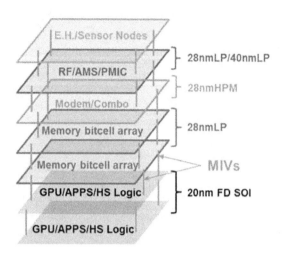

Figure 1: An example single-chip solution with various components integrated in 3D.

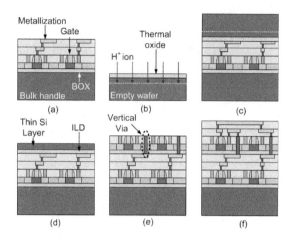

Figure 2: The fabrication process of sequential F2B 3D-ICs. (a) The bottom tier is created the same way as 2D-ICs. (b,c,d) Attachment of thin layer of silicon to the top of the bottom tier. (e) FEOL of top tier and creation of vertical via and top-tier contacts, and (f) BEOL processing of top-tier [5].

In this paper, after describing the 3DV technology options, we survey couple of the state-of-the-art design techniques that can show 3DV's potential in improving design power/performance envelope. The rest of this paper is organized as follows. Section 2 describes sequential integration and parallel wafer bonding technologies. Section 3 describes 3DV implementation options, e.g., block-level, gate-level, etc. with their corresponding power reduction implications. Section 4 describes a block-level 3D implementation flow to mitigate the impact of transistor performance mismatch in sequential integration. Section 5 describes a gate-level 3D implementation flow for both sequential and parallel 3D integrations. In Section 6, we provide a list of electronic design automation (EDA) requirements to enable more effective utilization of the 3DV benefits. Finally, Section 7 concludes the paper.

2. 3DV FABRICATION PROCESS AND ISSUES

As mentioned earlier, 3D VLSI can be categorized into (1) sequential F2B and (2) parallel F2B/F2F integration technologies. Sequential F2B process is described in [2] and the entire fabrication process is shown in Figure 2. First, the bottom-tier is fabricated exactly like a conventional 2D-IC (Figure 2(a)). Next, a thermal oxide is grown on an empty wafer, and hydrogen ions are implanted just below the silicon surface at a constant depth (Figure 2(b)). This empty wafer is then flipped and bonded to the top of the bottom tier using low temperature molecular bonding (Figure 2(c)). The silicon is then sheared off at the H^+ ion line and polished to give a high quality silicon layer (Figure 2(d)). The gates are formed on the top tier, and the vertical via are created with the contact mask of the top tier (Figure 2(e)). Finally, the metallization of the top tier is created as usual (Figure 2(f)). This process is repeated to obtain more tiers [5].

The main challenge facing sequential F2B 3D-ICs is that the transistors on the top tier need to be fabricated at a low temperature to avoid damaging the FEOL and BEOL of the bottom tier. This implies that the performance of the top tier may not be the same as that of the bottom tier. Recently, [3] quantifies the maximum thermal budget of in-situ doped source / drain fully depleted silicon-on-insulator (FDSOI) MOSFET transistors to ensure transistor stability in sequential F2B integration. Due to silicide stabil-

ity improvement, the top MOSFET temperature could be relaxed up to 500°. In addition, laser anneal is shown to be a promising candidate for junction activation for high-performance 3D VLSI integration. Overall, it seems that process challenges of sequential F2B can be addressed in the near future.

Another 3DV technology is precision wafer-level hybrid bonding for fine-grained 3D integration. Figure 3 shows an example F2F fabrication process. First, bond pads (BPs) are formed on both wafers. Then, both wafers are bonded using metal / adhesive hybrid bonding process. Next, top wafer is thinned to expose the TSVs followed by the backside metallization [4]. Bond pads construct vertical vias and the adhesive material provides necessary mechanical stability to withstand the wafer thinning and subsequent processes.

Similar to sequential F2B, in F2F integration, the integration density is a function of vertical via sizes. Hence, for F2F integration the upperbound on integration density depends on the misalignment control during bonding process whereas in sequential F2B vertical vias can technically be similar to the existing back-end-of-line (BEOL) vias. However, recent developments in wafer bonding alignment demonstrated possibility of sub-$0.25\mu m$ alignment accuracy that can lead to $0.5\mu m$ pad size with the pitch as low as $1\mu m$, i.e., 1 million vertical vias per mm^2 which can provide enough integration density to significantly reduce BEOL-related power. Other wafer bonding technology challenges include wafer bonding uniformity due to wafer warping and potential problems of wafer thinning. Various process solutions are in place to solve these issues. In addition, more integration, less latency and power can open up various opportunities to further improve the design power, performance and area envelope by changing the existing circuit / architecture. Furthermore, parallel integration does not have similar low-temperature process requirements as sequential integration so it can be an effective short-term solution to scaling challenges. Nonetheless, the best scalable solution in 3D integration remains to be the sequential F2B integration as long as all tiers can provide high-performance transistors.

3. 3DV IMPLEMENTATION OPTIONS

Conceptually, 3D partition can be realized at different abstraction levels, i.e., (1) package-level, (2) chip-level, (3) core-level,

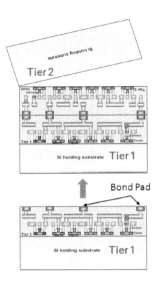

Figure 3: The fabrication process of F2F wafer-level bonding.

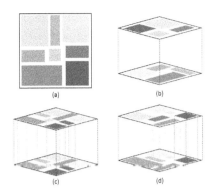

Figure 4: An example of (a) 2D block partitioning and floorplanning (b) 2D block partitioning with 3D floorplanning (c) 3D block partitioning with 2D floorplanning and (d) combination of 2D and 3D block partitioning with 3D floorplanning [7].

(4) block-level, (5) gate-level and (6) transistor-level. Examples of package-level, chip-level and core-level 3D partition are flip chip and package-on-package, 2.5D interposer and TSV-based 3D, respectively. Due to shortcomings of packaging-driven 3D integration technologies, only limited vertical integration is feasible and as a result fine-grained partitioning is not an option. On the other hand, 3DV provides orders of magnitude more integration density that enables designers to rethink existing intellectual property (IP) partitioning in order to improve overall design power and performance envelope. Hence, 3DV designs can be realized at more fine-grained levels such as block-level, gate-level and transistor-level to provide appropriate scaling of integration.

Transistor-level integration is the most fine-grained implementation option. However, since vertical vias are required in each standard cell, there is an increase in total cell area which leads to overall design area overhead. In addition, each cell will need to be redesigned and characterized. In gate-level integration, there is no area overhead as existing 2D-IC cells are used. However, since vertical vias can be placed anywhere in between cells, higher integration density is achieved which leads to significant power and performance improvements. On the other hand, in block-level integration since each block is the same in 2D and 3D, the potential power and performance benefits are limited; however, it does not incur the redesign overhead as in transistor- and gate-level approaches [5]. One form of block-level 3D partitioning that has a lot of potential is memory and logic stacking as it could effectively improve the communication bandwidth between logic and memory blocks. From a physical design implementation perspective, with the granularity of gate-level 3D integration, we can realize three partitioning / floorplanning schemes for any given design: (1) 2D block partitioning with 3D floorplanning, (2) 3D block partitioning with 2D floorplanning and (3) combination of 2D and 3D block partitioning with 3D floorplanning as shown in Figure 4 [6].

Each of the above design styles provides a tradeoff between improvement in power and performance envelope versus additional redesign efforts. In conclusion, gate-level 3D integration and block level memory and logic stacking offer the greatest balance between integration density and reuse of existing libraries. However, other block-level partitioning approach should be used to reduce redesign overhead as long as it does not hamper the power, performance and area gains. In addition, transistor-level integration could help in certain custom circuits.

In the next two sections, we survey two recent block-level and gate-level design methodologies [5, 6] for 3DV sequential F2B and parallel F2F/F2B that highlight the power, performance benefits of the 3DV integration. Note that these are preliminary efforts in this domain and the improvements will become more substantial once appropriate 3D design infrastructures (i.e., EDA support, etc.) is in place.

4. BLOCK-LEVEL 3DV IMPLEMENTATION

As mentioned in Section 3, logic block-level 3D integration gives relatively less power, performance benefits compared to gate-level 3D; however, it does not incur redesign efforts as all the blocks are 2D. In this section, we discuss a recent block-level 3D methodology [5] specifically for sequential F2B, but can be applicable to parallel F2F/F2B as well. In Section 2, we described that the main challenge for sequential F2B is to achieve high-performance transistors across all tiers within a low-thermal fabrication process. However, we have to point out that despite technical challenges, promising solutions are under development as was recently presented [3].

4.1 Overall Methodology

There are two scenarios in realizing a sequential F2B 3D design. (1) We use a low-thermal process that degrades the top-tier transistors performance. (2) We use conventional process, but replace the bottom tier BEOL with Tungsten to withstand the temperature. To enable an infrastructure to evaluate both scenarios a performance-aware 3D block-level floorplanner is needed. Three scenarios should be considered, (1) top-tier transistors performance is 10% degraded w.r.t. nominal ($TTm10p$), (2) top-tier transistors performance is 20% degraded w.r.t. nominal ($TTm20p$) and (3) bottom-tier BEOL is Tungsten instead of copper (TT_W).

An overview of the flow is shown in Figure 5. Once the design is synthesized, it is sent to the performance-aware floorplanner, which gives the outlines of all the blocks in the 3D space. Next, vertical via planning is performed to determine all the via locations. With these locations, each block and tier is placed and routed (P&R) separately. At this stage, wire-load models are extracted and used to run synthesis to achieve a better result. Once the P&R is complete, we proceed to 3D timing and power analysis.

The floorplanner is timing driven to appropriately handle performance degradation of either (1) top-tier transistors or (2) bottom-tier BEOL. This is achieved by weighting each inter-block net by the longest path delay through it. In most designs, not every block

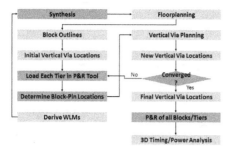

Figure 5: The 3D block-level design. Orange indicates 3D specific steps [5].

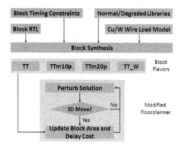

Figure 6: Performance-driven 3D floorplanner [5].

is timing critical. The non-timing critical blocks can in theory operate faster, but they are synthesized at the frequency of the critical block to save area and power. Therefore, even with degraded transistors, these blocks can be synthesized to operate at the frequency of the critical block, albeit with a larger area. As long as the critical blocks do not operate with slower transistors or interconnects, the chip can still meet timing. This is utilized in the 3D floorplanner.

An overview of the performance-aware 3D floorplanner is shown in Figure 6. First, given the block RTL and timing constraints, four different flavors of each block is synthesized: One for the nominal corner, and one for each of the degraded libraries. In the case of Tungsten interconnects, the resistivity of the wire-load models are modified to accurately drive synthesis. For each version of the block, the corresponding area and longest path delay (LPD) through it is recorded.

Given that the design has inter-tier variations, each block will have a different area and LPD depending on the tier in which it lies. If $LPD(b_i)$ is the tier-dependant longest path delay of a block b_i, then the modified cost function of the floorplanner is defined as:

$$Cost_{VA} = \alpha.WL + \beta.Area + \gamma \sum_{i=1}^{N_{Block}} LPD(b_i) \quad (1)$$

In the above equation, WL refers to the wirelength. The area of a block is also dependent on its tier. Therefore, whenever a 3D move is made, the area of all the blocks that have changed their tier are updated. The third term in the above equation will try to place the timing critical blocks in the faster tier, and push the non-timing critical blocks to the slower tier.

4.2 3D Timing and Power Analysis

To demonstrate the timing and power benefits of block-level sequential 3D versus 2D, the authors of [5] have used three open-source benchmarks implemented in 45nm as shown in Table 1.

First, the assumption is that both tiers in 3D have identical transistors and interconnects. This represents an ideal manufacturing

Table 1: Benchmarks used in the 3D block-level evaluation [5].

Benchmark	#Blocks	#Gates	#Inter-Block Nets
des3	55	63,194	6,138
b19	55	78,852	14,223
mul128	63	253,867	12,447

process, and represents the best possible case for block-level 3D. In addition to these two 2D and 3D flavors, an "ideal" block-level implementation is also considered. This implementation is obtained by assuming that all the inter-block nets have zero length and parasitics. During the block implementation, the output load of the blocks are set to zero and the inputs are driven by ideal drivers. This is the theoretical lower bound on any block-level implementation of this design, given the same set of blocks, and the constraint that each block is implemented in 2D.

In order to get the numbers for the ideal implementation, all inter-block nets parasitics is forced to be zero during static timing analysis. In addition to the nominal V_{DD} of 1.1V, the stdard cell libraries are characterized at four additional V_{DD} values covering ±10% of nominal V_{DD} (1.00V, 1.05V, 1.10V, 1.15V, 1.20V). Then, the power and frequency at each of the V_{DD} values are measured. These curves are plotted in Figure 7. From this figure, it is shown that 3D usually offers a performance advantage (at the same power) over 2D, and it closes the gap to ideal by up to 50%. This additional performance can be traded for power savings to meet the 2D frequency, leading to a 16.1% reduction in power.

Next, the power-performance trade-off curves for the degraded transistors and interconnects are shown in Figure 8. These are shown as solid lines. For the sake of comparison, the results of degraded transistors and interconnects on top of a non-performance aware floorplanning solution is also shown. These are shown as dashed lines. As observed from this figure, the performance-aware floorplanner always outperforms the non-performance aware one. It is shown that except in the case of "mul128", the top tier having $TTm20p$ transistors is worse than 2D, even with performance-aware floorplanner. Is it also observed that the top tier with $TTm10p$ transistors is always better than 2D. Finally, the observation is that Tungsten interconnects on the bottom tier are by far the best option, and although there is negligible timing degradation compared to the identical tiers case, some power overhead exists. In conclusion, even with Tungsten interconnects on the bottom tier, the gap to the ideal block-level implementation can be closed by up to 50% w.r.t. performance and 36% w.r.t. power.

5. GATE-LEVEL 3DV IMPLEMENTATION

As mentioned in Section 3, gate-level 3D integration gives the best savings in terms of power, performance and area; however, requires redesign of all the 2D blocks. In this section, we discuss a recent gate-level 3D methodology, called "Shrunk 2D", that builds on top the existing commercial 2D placement and routing (P&R) engines [6]. The premise of this methodology is that the z-dimension is negligible in 3DV (less than a few μm), and hence an existing 2D placer can be used to first to find optimum x and y solutions, and then the z location can be determined as a post-process, i.e., through some partitioning scheme.

5.1 Overall Methodology

"Shrunk 2D" methodology is contingent on the ability of a given 2D placer to place all the cells in a given 3D footprint area, which is half the footprint area of the counterpart 2D. This requires either the placement supply doubles (allowing for cell overlap) or cells dimensions and routing resources shrink accordingly. To utilize the

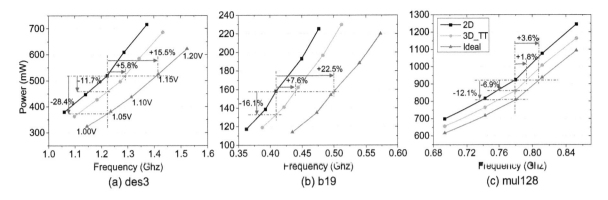

Figure 7: Power-performance trade-off curves assuming that both the tiers have identical transistors and interconnects [5].

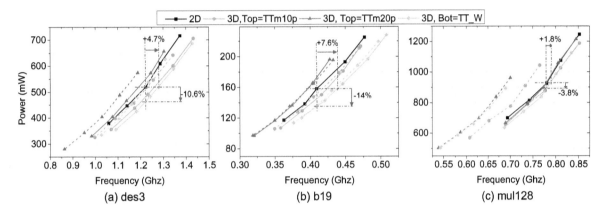

Figure 8: Power-performance trade-off curves assuming degraded transistors and interconnects. Dashed lines represent non performance-aware floorplanning and solid lines represent performance-aware floorplanning [5].

existing 2D tools to handle standard cell placement in a reduced footprint area, the authors of [6] use the latter approach, i.e., to scale appropriate technology files and memory macros.

In general, Shrunk 2D methodology has three major steps, (1) memory macro handling, (2) Shrunk 2D P&R and (3) 3D partitioning and final tier-by-tier implementation. Since no standard cell can be placed in the location where a memory is pre-placed, simply shrinking the memory is not an option. A memory macro can be represented by a placement blockage and memory pin locations. The placement blockage prevents standard cells from being placed over the memory area and the memory pins serve as anchors for standard cell placement. In a given 3D design, the following memory placement scenarios can occur: (1) regions with memories overlapping across the tiers (2) regions where the memories do not overlap across the tiers. In Scenario (1), after 3D partitioning, neither tier can contain standard cells in this region. Therefore, full placement blockages are inserted in these regions to avoid cell placement. In Scenario (2), the tier that does not contain memory can have cells; however, the supply of such regions need to be halved during the Shrunk 2D placement. Therefore, partial placement blockages are inserted in these regions with a maximum density than the rest of the chip. Figure 9 shows how corresponding placement blockages are inserted given different memory placement scenarios.

The second step is Shrunk 2D placement and routing. The objective of this step is to place all the cells into half the area footprint. This is achieved by shrinking the area of each standard cell by 50%, i.e., scaling the width, height and location of all the pins within the

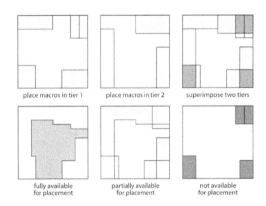

Figure 9: Memory macro handling in Shrunk 2D methodology.

cell by $1/\sqrt{2}$. In addition, the chip width and height are scaled by 0.707 to reduce the 2D footprint area by half. This results into a theoretical HPWL improvement of 29.3%. Next, to make the routing in Shrunk 2D to correctly represent the routing in 3D, metal width and pitch of each metal layer are also scaled by 0.707.

This is done to make sure that total routing track length does not change between 2D and Shrunk 2D as well as 3D once the design is partitioned. To correctly represent timing behavior of the design in 3D neither timing liberty files nor the wire RC per-unit-length are changed. Finally, scaled technology and standard cell libraries along with the memory pins and corresponding placement block-

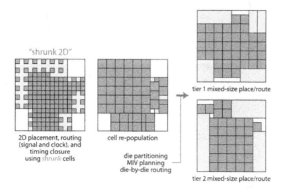

"shrunk 2D"

2D placement, routing (signal and clock), and timing closure using shrunk cells

cell re-population

die partitioning
MIV planning
die-by-die routing

tier 1 mixed-size place/route

tier 2 mixed-size place/route

Figure 10: Shrunk 2D P&R, 3D partitioning and final tier-by-tier implementation steps.

age sites are fed into the 2D P&R tool. The commercial tool is then used to run all the design stages such as placement, post-placement optimization, clock tree synthesis (CTS), routing and post routing optimization. Unlike conventional 3D flows, Shrunk 2D avoids the problem of tier-by-tier timing optimization; hence the tool can see the entire 3D path and will insert appropriate buffers given the shorter interconnect length.

The third step is to split the post-route Shrunk 2D design into two tiers ensuring minimum perturbation to the solution. This is done by modifying an existing move-based min-cut partitioner such that it checks for area balance during partitioning. To ensure minimum perturbation to the Shrunk 2D solution, first placement bins (e.g., $15 \times 15 \mu m$) are created, and then the design is partitioned such that approximately half of the cells in each bin are in each tier. Once this is done, existing 3D routers can be used to determine the location of vertical vias. Finally, new netlist and DEF files are generated for each tier followed by a tier-by-tier refine placement and routing. There are a few other techniques to improve the quality of CTS as well as overall wirelength which are described in [6]. Note that the Shrunk 2D flow is not limited to a given commercial P&R tool and can be wrapped around any existing 2D P&R engine.

5.2 2D vs. 3D Power Tradeoffs

To demonstrate the power benefits of sequential F2B and fine-grain F2F 3D versus 2D, OpenSPARC T2 single core is used as the benchmark. The core is implemented in 28nm with a clock frequency of $1GHz$. The vertical via pitch is assumed to be $0.2\mu m$ and $1\mu m$ for sequential F2B and F2F implementations, respectively.

Using the Shrunk 2D flow, a comparison of sequential F2B and F2F 3D with the corresponding 2D implementation is shown in Table 2. From this table, it is observed that Shrunk 2D reduces the wirelength by 27.05% compared to 2D. This is very close to the 29.3% HPWL bound. The improvement number goes down for both sequential F2B and F2F, which is to be expected. In addition, F2B has slightly higher WL compared to F2F because the vertical vias are limited to whitespace, while F2F vertical vias are not. Next, it is observed that the 3D implementations reduce the buffer count by 22.3%, which translates to a 8.03% reduction in total gate count. Since F2B and F2F designs are obtained by simply splitting the Shrunk 2D design, all three have the same gate counts. The reduced wirelength and gate count lead to a total power reduction of 15.57% and 15.27% for F2B and F2F respectively. It is also shown that both F2B and F2F power numbers are quite close to the Shrunk 2D numbers, which shows that the Shrunk 2D design is a good estimate of sequential F2B and parallel F2B/F2F 3D technologies.

6. EDA REQUIREMENTS

Current studies of 3DV benefits have been performed using existing 2D-IC tools. Even though significant improvements have been shown, we need to have appropriate 3D design infrastructure, i.e., methodologies, tools, etc. The following is a short list of existing design stages / analyses that need to be rethought for appropriate 3D implementation.

- **Synthesis.** Existing 3D physical implementation flows, including the ones we discuss in this paper, start from a 2D synthesized netlist which is oblivious to the existence of the third dimension. Synthesis is the first step in the physical implementation flow and its quality of result (QoR) significantly affects the final signoff design QoR. 3D synthesis tools should be aware of the vertical vias and available integration layers.

- **Floorplanning.** 3D floorplanning is necessary to ensure that we appropriately utilize architecture-level benefits of 3D, e.g., relative placements of micro-architectural units such that certain power / performance metrics are achieved. In addition, 3D floorplanning is an essential step in which we can appropriately mitigate thermal challenges in 3D designs. In addition to improve area and wirelegnth metrics, 3D floorplanner should also avoid placement of high-power consuming blocks on top of each other. Recently, [7] shows that appropriate 3D floorplanning can improve thermal profile of 3D designs beyond the counterpart 2D designs.

- **Placement / Timing Optimization.** Placement is probably the step in which we really need to enhance to take advantage of the 3DV benefits. Existing placement solutions consider a single placement layer and find optimum x, y locations. Current 3D timing optimization methodologies rely on timing budgeting technique to define the timing of each tier; however, this degrades the timing quality of the 3D design and diminish its advantages. Hence, an effective 3D placement (i.e., placement algorithm that considers more than one placement layer) coupled with an optimization engine is required.

- **Clock Tree Synthesis (CTS).** Clock tree is a major portion of today's synchronous designs and its quality significantly affects overall design power and performance envelope. Clock trees of high-performance designs have many clock cells (e.g., clock gating, dividers, etc.) to achieve aggressive clock gating and required performance across a wide range of operating modes. In addition, in advanced nodes CTS becomes more challenging due to on-chip variations (OCV) effects. For 3D CTS, the issues to be addressed are whether to have a single clock tree backbone or break it across all tiers, whether to spread clock sinks across all tiers or confine them into a single tier (i.e., to control the effect of variation), etc. Hence, to maximize the overall power and performance benefits, true 3D CTS needs to be developed.

- **Routing.** Routing is an important step in physical design as it has to take various constraints into account to come up with the optimum solution. However, existing routers are 3D in the sense that they can connect pins on different metal layers. Hence, we can utilize existing 3D routers and only have to update their cost models. E.g., how to account for going from a thick metal to another thick metal (in F2F) versus going from thick metal to thin metal (in F2B).

Table 2: Overall comparisons between 2D and different 3D implementation styles [6].

	Encounter 2D	Shrunk 2D		Sequential F2B		Fine-grained F2F	
Total WL(m)	17.96	13.10	(-27.05%)	14.29	(-20.40%)	13.89	(-22.65%)
# MIV/F2F	-	-		235,394		235,394	
# Buffers	164,917	128,098	(-22.33%)	128,098	(-22.33%)	128,098	(-22.33%)
#Total Gates	458,824	421,959	(-8.03%)	421,959	(-8.03%)	421,959	(-8.03%)
Total Power (mW)	**618.40**	**514.40**	**(-16.82%)**	**522.10**	**(-15.57%)**	**524.00**	**(-15.27%)**
Cell Power (mW)	135.60	126.80	(-6.49%)	126.10	(-7.01%)	126.40	(-6.78%)
Net Power (mW)	356.30	274.30	(-23.01%)	282.70	(-20.66%)	284.30	(-20.21%)
Leakage Power (mW)	126.50	113.30	(-10.43%)	113.30	(-10.43%)	113.30	(-10.43%)
Memory Power (mW)	49.00	45.10	(-7.96%)	45.10	(-7.96%)	45.00	(-8.16%)
Combinational Power (mW)	385.10	300.00	(-22.10%)	305.30	(-20.72%)	306.80	(-20.33%)
Clock Tree Power (mW)	62.50	46.90	(-24.96%)	48.00	(-23.20%)	48.50	(-22.40%)
FF Clock Pin Power (mW)	9.70	9.90	(+2.06%)	9.60	(-1.03%)	9.70	(0.00%)
Register Power (mW)	112.10	112.50	(+0.36%)	114.00	(+1.69%)	114.00	(+1.69%)

- **Power Delivery Network (PDN).** As number of devices per unit area increases, design of a reliable power delivery network becomes challenging due to increase in current demand. This challenge is exacerbated in 3D since (1) power density is even more than that of 2D and (2) PDN competes with vertical signal routing. The latter becomes a challenge especially for designs with finer granularity of integration, i.e., due to increase in vertical connections. Hence, appropriate 3D PDN analyses should be performed and maybe relevant constraints passed down to the router.

- **Design-For-Test.** Assuring an acceptable defect per million (DPM) in line with traditional 2D solutions is a key metric for adopting 3D solutions. New DFT solutions are needed to provide required production quality at target cost and enough controllability and observability to enable a fast yield ramp. DFT solutions should enable isolating various integration layers to be tested individually and as part of the entire system. It is also important to provide adequate stuck-at and timing fault coverage of all inter-layer vias.

- **Verification, Signoff Analyses.** In addition to the above tool enhancements or additional features, we also need to figure out ways of verifying the correctness of 3D designs, e.g., layout-vs-schematic (LVS), etc. Furthermore, appropriate 3D extractions need to be performed to correctly account for new elements of parasitics that are inherent in the way we integrate tiers on top of each other. Finally, variability issues need to be carefully addressed in order to develop appropriate 3D signoff methodologies as they significantly affect the actual achievable power, performance envelope that we can extract out of the technology.

7. CONCLUSIONS

As semiconductor industry faces serious challenges to extend Moore's law, alternative solutions are being investigated. 3D VLSI (3DV) is an emerging foundry-driven 3D integration technology that achieves orders of magnitude more inter-layer via integration density than the existing packaging-driven 3D solutions. 3DV provides scaling of both integration and value to complement conventional "More Moore" scaling approaches. Taking advantage of high inter-layer via integration density provided by 3DV, we can significantly improve the interconnect-related power and performance metrics. In fact, 3DV enables appropriate wire scaling as opposed to a device-only scaling paradigm. Furthermore, in addition to physical implementation benefits, 3DV opens an array of opportunities at circuit and architecture level innovations that can

further help extending Moore's law. In this paper, we introduced 3DV technology and described its integration styles: (1) sequential F2B and (2) parallel F2B/F2F, where parallel F2B/F2F is regarded as short-term solution, and sequential F2B as the ultimate integration solution. We also surveyed two state-of-the-art 3D physical implementation flows. In the block-level flow, we observe that 3D integration shows significant inter-block interconnect performance improvement (up to 50%); this is a significant improvement given today's large system-on-chips (SoCs). In the gate-level flow, we observe significant power reduction improvement that can be a great knob to reduce overall SoC power envelope. With parallel F2B/F2F integration style of 3DV being available and signs of further process improvements in near future, the challenge now lies on creating an efficient design infrastructure and EDA tool suit that can fully utilize all the 3DV benefits. In this paper, we short listed a few improvements that seem necessary for short-term; however, a lot more opportunities for design and exploration efforts lies ahead.

8. ACKNOWLEDGMENTS

We would like to thank members of 3D project at Qualcomm Research for their support, GTCAD laboratory at Georgia Institute of Technology and CEA LETI 3D team for their collaboration and contributions to this work.

9. REFERENCES

[1] A. B. Kahng, "Scaling: More than Moore's law," *IEEE D&T of Computers*, 27(3) 2010, pp. 86–87.

[2] P. Batule et al., "Advances in 3D CMOS Sequential Integration," *Proc. IEEE IEDM*, 2009, pp. 1–4.

[3] C. Fenouillet-Beranger, et al., "New Insights on Bottom Layer Thermal Stability and Laser Annealing Promises for High Performance 3D Monolithic Integration," *IEEE IEDM*, 2014.

[4] C.-T. Ko et al., "Wafer-to-Wafer Hybrid Bonding Technology for 3D IC," *Proc. IEEE ESTC*, 2010, pp. 1–5.

[5] S. Panth, K. Samadi, Y. Du and S. K. Lim, "Power-Performance Study of Block-Level Monolithic 3D-ICs Considering Inter-Tier Performance Variations," *Proc. ACM/IEEE DAC*, 2014, pp. 1–6.

[6] S. Panth, K. Samadi, Y. Du and S. K. Lim, "Design and CAD Methodologies for Low Power Gate-Level Monolithic 3D ICs," *Proc. IEEE ISLPED*, 2014, pp. 171–176.

[7] M. Saeidi, K. Samadi, A. Mittal and R. Mittal, "Thermal Implications of Mobile 3D-ICs," *IEEE 3DIC*, 2014.

BonnPlace: A Self-Stabilizing Placement Framework

Ulrich Brenner, Anna Hermann, Nils Hoppmann, Philipp Ochsendorf
Research Institute for Discrete Mathematics, University of Bonn
Lennéstr. 2, 53113 Bonn, Germany
{brenner, hermann, hoppmann, ochsendorf}@or.uni-bonn.de

ABSTRACT

We present a new algorithm for VLSI placement. Our tool BonnPlace incorporates a partitioning-based legalization into a force-directed loop by iteratively pulling circuits towards their positions in a legalized placement. This self-stabilizing algorithm combines the accuracy of partitioning-based methods with the stability of force-directed placement strategies. Using information from earlier iterations, it is capable of improving netlength as well as more involved objective functions like routability and timing behavior. In contrast to previous techniques, we legalize with higher effort, which allows us to reduce the number of iterations. Performance is further improved by adapting a clustering heuristic that takes into account the current cell positions, both for clustering and unclustering. We tested our tool on recent instances from industry and on publicly available benchmark suites. In particular on the routability-driven placement instances of the DAC 2012 contest, our algorithm produces the best known results.

Categories and Subject Descriptors

B.7.2 [**Integrated Circuits**]: Design Aids—*Placement and routing*

Keywords

VLSI placement; clustering; force-directed placement

1. INTRODUCTION

Global placement is a crucial step in the physical design of VLSI chips. The quality of the placement has far-reaching effects on the whole design process. Placement tools typically minimize the total interconnect length. In addition, they have to guarantee routability of their placements while meeting tight timing constraints on individual signals.

Most state-of-the-art placement tools are analytical algorithms. They start off with a placement minimizing a smoothened approximation of the total half-perimeter wirelength,

but allowing cells to overlap. Afterwards, the task is to reduce the overlapping of cells.

There are different ways to work towards an overlap-free placement. In partitioning-based algorithms, the chip area is divided into bins and the algorithm ensures that no bin contains more cells than fit into it. While those approaches are highly efficient and meet density constraints very accurately, they are usually not robust against small changes in the input as they are faced with a huge amount of discrete decisions.

Other approaches iteratively apply artificial forces pulling cells from over-crowded areas of the chip towards free space. Those force-directed placers vary widely in their force computation and modulation. Usually, they need dozens of iterations in order to obey the density constraints and to achieve a placement without overlaps. In contrast to partitioning-based algorithms, though, they are very stable.

We seek to unite those elementary different placement strategies maintaining their respective strengths. These are the main contributions of this paper:

- We present a placement framework that uses an efficient partitioning-based placement algorithm as a subroutine of a force-directed loop. Our approach allows more running time for one single legalization and thus can reduce the number of iterations drastically.

- We present position-based clustering and unclustering algorithms that examine the placement of the local neighborhood of clusters. The combination of both algorithms allows us to dissolve clusters in later placement stages compared to previous approaches.

- We show how the framework can interact with optimization steps for timing and routability. For the congestion-driven mode of our tool, we present a heuristic which dynamically adapts the threshold used to estimate the criticality of a routing edge. This allows us to compute routable placements on very critical instances while, on less critical instances, fewer congestion-avoiding detours are necessary.

- In an experimental study, we demonstrate on recent industrial instances how BonnPlace is able to improve timing results. Moreover, on the benchmarks of the DAC 2012 contest [25] for congestion-driven placement, our algorithm is able to produce the best known results.

This paper is organized as follows. In Section 2, we review background and previous work before we describe our placement algorithm in Section 3. In Section 4, we present our clustering techniques. Experimental results in Section 5 demonstrate how our algorithm performs concerning the three objectives netlength, timing behavior and routability. Section 6 contains some concluding remarks.

2. PREVIOUS WORK

Analytical placement tools start with an arrangement of cells which is best-possible with respect to a smooth approximation of the resulting interconnect netlength if all constraints are ignored. In particular, cells will overlap in the obtained initial solution. Now, the goal is to find a legal placement which is almost as good as the initial arrangement – with respect to classical netlength, routability or even timing properties.

Force-directed placers perform multiple placement iterations and apply successively increasing forces pulling cells out of overfull areas of the chip in order to achieve legality. In RQL [26] as well as in SIMPL [16] (including its subsequent evolutions SIMPLR [15], RIPPLE [12], COMPLX [17] and MAPLE [18]), a rough legalization is computed and each cell is pulled towards its legalized position. Different to Lagrangian multipliers, forces do not penalize illegality directly but punish the difference to one particular legal placement which has been computed previously. Hence, the quality of the overall algorithm depends on legalization itself. The legalization which is applied in these papers based on SIMPL is fast but not very sophisticated. As a result, cells can be pulled only slightly towards their former legal positions making a large number of iterations necessary.

Self-stabilizing BonnPlace also consists of a force-directed loop based on SIMPLR. In comparison to other placers, we perform a very elaborate and thus reliable legalization allowing us a steeper increase of forces.

All algorithms mentioned so far introduce forces as artificial connections subsequently smoothened by the respective analytical interconnect minimizer. Other force-directed approaches directly incorporate smooth approximations for the opposing placement goals density, legality and routability. In MPL [7], density constraints are globally smoothened using the Helmholtz equation. NTUPLACE4 [13] uses quadratic functions to penalize violations of a locally smoothened density function and of a smoothened congestion estimation. More recently, EPLACE [20] successfully models placement instances as electrostatic systems translating density violations to the system's potential energy.

In contrast to those ideas, partitioning-based algorithms recursively subdivide the chip area while assigning circuits to the respective regions. This can be done minimizing the induced cut in the netlist hypergraph (see CAPO 10.5 [23]). Xiu and Rutenbar [28] iteratively determine a non-uniform grid that optimizes density violations and scale these assignments into a regular grid.

In our algorithm, we use partitioning-based BonnPlace [24] as legalization for the force-directed loop. This tool uses flow-based partitioning to determine the cells' bin assignments. Our loop relies on those competitive placements and spreads cells accordingly during analytical placement.

In order to improve runtime and solution quality, we incorporate a position-based clustering that suits our force-directed loop. Location-oriented clustering has previously been used by the algebraic multigrid solver [8], MFAR [14], FASTPLACE 3.0 [27] and SafeChoice [29].

Similar as in FASTPLACE 3.0, we adapt the BestChoice clustering algorithm from [3], which iteratively clusters cells

---

Algorithm 1: SELF-STABILIZING BONNPLACE

Input: placement area A_P, cells $\mathcal{C}$
Output: positions $\mathsf{pos}(c)$ for all cells $c \in \mathcal{C}$

1 iter $\leftarrow 0$
2 foreach $c \in \mathcal{C}$ do $\mathsf{pos}(c) \leftarrow 0$ while not BreakCondition(pos, iter) do
3   foreach $c \in \mathcal{C}$ do
4   Connect c to a new pin at position $\mathsf{pos}(c)$ via a virtual net of weight $0.01 \cdot$ iter.
5   Partitioning-based GLOBALPLACEMENT with position-based clustering and unclustering
6   LEGALIZATION
7   Delete virtual nets
8   if timing_optimization_enabled then
9   LAYERASSIGNMENT
10   REFINEPLACE
11   NETWEIGHTUPDATE
12   if routability_driven_placement_enabled then
13   CONGESTIONAVOIDANCE
14   foreach $c \in \mathcal{C}$ do Store current location in $\mathsf{pos}(c)$ iter $\leftarrow$ iter $+ 1$

---

according to their netlist connectivity and size. However, whereas FASTPLACE 3.0 merely rejects clustering circuits that are too far apart, we additionally incorporate distances of circuits into the BestChoice clustering score function. Physical clustering in MFAR works similar as in FASTPLACE 3.0, but a different function is used to determine netlist connectivity. In [8], another greedy algorithm iteratively clusters circuits depending on current cell positions and cell sizes only, and thus regarding cell connectivity only implicitly. The concept of SafeChoice [29] is to reject clusters that would degrade optimum netlength. Practically, they also use BestChoice with a modified clustering score function that trades off safety against size of the arising clusters.

All four placers do not mention whether their unclustering methods also take cell positions into account.

For many placement tools, there is a version that optimizes routability rather than netlength, e.g., SIMPLR [15] and RIPPLE [12] as routability-driven versions of SIMPL [16] and NTUPLACE4 [13] as a congestion-driven NTUPLACE3 [9]. In NTUPLACE4 [13], congestion is incorporated into the overall smoothened objective function. Most congestion-driven placement tools call a fast routing estimation and inflate cells in routing-critical areas in order to reduce placement density locally (e.g. [6], [12], [15]). The congestion-driven version of self-stabilizing BonnPlace is similar to [6] but contains two improvements. On the one hand, we use BONNROUTEGLOBAL [21] for congestion estimation; on the other hand, we dynamically adapt inflation of cells during our force-directed loop (see Section 3.3).

3. OUR ALGORITHM

Our placement algorithm combines the force-directed approach with partitioning-based global placement. Essentially, we perform multiple *iterations* of a partitioning-based global placement followed by a legalization, whereby in each iteration, forces pull cells towards their previously legalized positions. Each partitioning-based placement is performed using a position-based clustering method which also respects previous locations and thus suits our force-directed loop.

Besides netlength optimization, our framework is able to handle different objectives like timing and routability behavior. Therefore, each iteration of our algorithm also contains routing and timing optimization steps.

Algorithm 1 gives an overview of our placement strategy. In the following sections, we will describe single steps of the algorithm in detail.

3.1 Partitioning-Based Global Placement

A key ingredient of our tool is a partitioning-based global placement algorithm (Algorithm 1, line 5) which has been described in [24]. This algorithm covers the chip area by a grid and assigns cells to grid bins. Iteratively refining the grid defines different *levels* of partitioning. In order to place cells inside grid bins, we solve a quadratic program (QP) minimizing the total weighted bounding box netlength. The chosen approach for our QP is a combination of the bound-2-bound net model (B2B) with a super-linear distance scaling factor. As of iteration one, we use the current placement to determine the outer pins of nets for the B2B net model. Thus, we do not have to run multiple QPs with B2B in order to stabilize the solution.

Based on the subdivision of the placement area and the quadratic placement solution, cells are assigned to bins of the refined grid. This assignment must satisfy a given target density for each bin.

The resulting placement in the last level of our partitioning is of high quality as shown in [24]. It strictly obeys density limits in each bin. Hence, the partitioning solution can be legalized easily by a minimum quadratic movement legalization from [5] (Algorithm 1, line 6). Moreover, an integration of clustering into the partitioning-based algorithm as presented in Section 4 improves the runtime without impairing the quality of the solution.

In the first iteration of our self-stabilizing global placer, partitioning is executed without using any forces. Afterwards, the forces presented in the next section are respected in each partitioning level, i.e., they affect the solution in each level and not only the global quadratic placement at the beginning.

3.2 Forces

In our placement algorithm, forces are used to transfer information and to stabilize the placement procedure. The higher the quality of information that we get from earlier iterations, the greater is the efficiency of forces. Due to the effort we spend in legalizing our placement, the quality of the collected information is high, which makes forces effective. During each higher placement iteration iter > 0, there is exactly one force pulling at each cell.

Forces are modeled as virtual nets, i.e., nets that affect the distribution of cells during the QPs, but have no influence on other steps. For each cell c in the set of circuits $\mathcal{C}$, an artificial net connects the cell's center with the placement position of c in the previous iteration, which is called the *target point* of the force pulling at c. We add forces at the beginning of each iteration iter > 0 (Algorithm 1, lines 3 and 4). For constructing forces, the placement information stored at the end of the previous iteration iter -1 is used (Algorithm 1, line 14).

The weight of force nets increases in each iteration to stabilize the placement. Higher stability is expressed by decreasing cell movement between two consecutive iterations (cf. Section 5.3). On the one hand, forces have to be ef-

---

Algorithm 2: CONGESTIONAVOIDANCE

Input: Grid G, cells $\mathcal{C}$, placement pos(c) for $c \in \mathcal{C}$,
  target wire density tgt, critical wire density crit

1 Use BONNROUTEGLOBAL as congestion estimation on G
2 **while** congested_edge_percentage $< 10\%$ **and** crit $>$ tgt
   do
3   crit $\leftarrow \max\{$tgt, crit $- 5\%\}$
4 **foreach** *region* R $\in G$ **do**
5   Compute criticality(R) w.r.t. crit
6 Choose $a \in [0, 1]$
7 **foreach** *region* R $\in G$ **do**
8   **foreach** *cell* $c \in$ R **do**
9   **if** criticality(R) > 0 **then**
10   size(c) $\leftarrow$ size(c) $+ a \cdot$ inflate(c, R)
11   **else if** criticality(R) ≤ 0 **then**
12   size(c) $\leftarrow$ size(c) $+$ shrink(c, R)

---

fective. In particular, information from previous iterations should induce a significant cell spreading especially in lower levels of partitioning. On the other hand, force weights need to be chosen such that they do not dominate the instance. Hereby, we guarantee that the partitioning-based global placer remains flexible. We start with a weight of 1% of the average non-virtual net weight and increase this by another percent in each iteration.

The impact of forces to the quadratic placement is shown in Figures 1 and 2 on two designs of the DAC 2012 placement contest [25]. We see the placement computed in the first level of partitioning, where we only have one bin representing the whole chip area. We show the QP solutions in iterations zero to three. The spreading is already significant, but far from giving a legal solution. This shows that, although we increase spreading and thus stability, we still leave considerable freedom to partitioning.

After partitioning and legalization, we delete the forces (Algorithm 1, line 7). In the following iteration, new forces are computed.

The general breaking condition for the overall loop is a predefined maximum number of iterations (typically between 4 and 10). Other criteria to end our algorithm prematurely, e.g. based on the cells' movement, are possible.

3.3 Routability-Driven Placement

Besides minimizing netlength, our placer is able to improve the routability of a chip. The main idea is to dynamically distribute additional area (*inflations*) to the cells. Inflations are intended to lower the placement density in routing-critical (*congested*) regions. In contrast to the force computation, we adjust inflation values only preserving information of previous iterations.

Our CONGESTIONAVOIDANCE routine (cf. Algorithm 2) is called at the end of each iteration (Algorithm 1, line 13). In Algorithm 2, line 1, we estimate the congestion induced by our placement with a call of BONNROUTEGLOBAL [21] (used in [11], [1]) first. Afterwards, we assign congestion criticalities to the grid bins based on the congestion of incident global routing edges (lines 4, 5). For each of these regions, criticality in conjunction with local pin density determines the contained cells' inflations (lines 7 - 12).

The distribution of inflations is performed in analogy to [6], which we briefly recapitulate: Inflation criticalities are

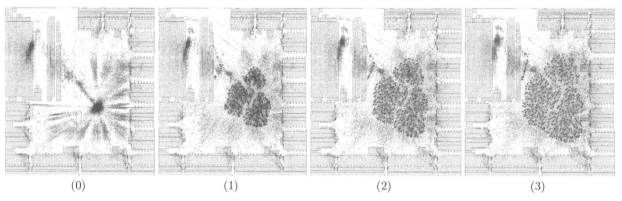

Figure 1: Spreading of cells on superblue16 after global QP throughout iterations (0) to (3).

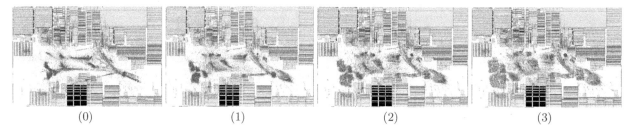

Figure 2: Spreading of cells on superblue3 after global QP throughout iterations (0) to (3).

in the interval $[0,1]$ and derived by a linear interpolation. We map a routing congestion of crit to 0 and a congestion of at least 130% to 1. For the exact cell inflation, 80% emerge from criticality; the remaining 20% are due to pin density. Inflations can not only be increased, but also reduced. In order to downsize cells in a bin, none of the bin's adjacent edges may be congested. This way, we are able to recover space in totally uncongested regions. Of course we make sure the inflated instance is not too dense as we scale inflations by a maximum $a \in [0,1]$ s.t.

$$\sum_{c \in \mathcal{C}} \text{size}(c) \leq 95\% \cdot \text{free\_placement\_area}.$$

Improving [6], Self-Stabilizing BonnPlace adapts its thresholds on wire-densities leading to more cautious and targetted inflations. CONGESTIONAVOIDANCE aims at meeting a given target density tgt at the end of our placement scheme. Usually, the target density is chosen to be at 80% or 90%. During the execution of the algorithm, we allow a possibly higher density crit $\geq$ tgt. Initially, crit is set to 100% and is iteratively reduced by 5% if the percentage of congested edges is below 10% and (crit $- 5\%$) $\geq$ tgt.

Reducing congestion even below 100% is crucial: Barely routable chips make detours inevitable, which has a negative effect on other design objectives. Hence, it is important to adapt the critical congestion crit dynamically.

3.4 Timing-Aware Placement

Apart from routability, the most important objective for placement is timing optimization. Our framework applies two different methods to resolve timing problems: In each iteration, a timing estimation and a local timing optimization are performed. Afterwards, if there are still timing critical paths, the nets on these paths obtain higher weights in the next iteration of our self-stabilizing loop.

For timing estimation, we apply a linearized timing model which assumes that all nets can be buffered optimally (cf. [22] and [2] for a description of such models). For the optimization, we first run a layer assignment that assigns critical nets to higher layers with smaller resistance (Algorithm 1, line 9). After that, the local timing optimization REFINE-PLACE [4] relocates a predefined ratio of cells in critical nets in order to decrease the overall timing criticality. In this step, cells are moved such that critical paths are shortened and detours are removed. The force target points in the next iteration are set to the refined positions. Furthermore, force weights of moved cells are chosen higher (at most by 50%) than the iteration's standard force weight. This increases the importance of the positions found by REFINEPLACE and improves the timing behavior of subsequent placement solutions. The force weight increase of relocated cells will be transferred to all following iterations. After REFINEPLACE, cells may overlap. However, the total overlap is low because only a small ratio of cells is moved.

In addition to local optimization by REFINEPLACE we tackle global timing problems by updating net weights (Algorithm 1, line 11). We increase net weights of the 2% most critical nets. The weight increment is determined based on nets' criticality percentile such that a fixed amount of net weight is introduced in total.

Typically, REFINEPLACE can shorten critical paths significantly if it is sufficient to move only some of the cells. Net weights can help to improve timing in the case that larger groups of cells have to be moved closer to each other. That is why the combination of both techniques is quite powerful.

It proved advantageous to perform ten iterations of timing-driven BonnPlace, whereby net weight update is applied in any iteration, REFINEPLACE starts in iteration two and forces are incorporated as of iteration three. Net weight updates of the most critical nets can affect the placement considerably. Thus, we allow our algorithm to react on net weight updates most flexibly by not applying forces before iteration three. As a result, we do not need to execute REFINEPLACE before iteration two because the information gained by REFINEPLACE cannot be transferred to subsequent iterations without the use of forces.

4. CLUSTERING

In order to reduce the number of circuits, nets and pins considered during our partition-based global placement subroutine 3.1, we simplify the netlist by clustering cells. We can benefit from the positions determined in previous iterations of our loop, both during clustering and unclustering.

We develop a position-based clustering technique evolving BestChoice [3] for the context of our self-stabilizing loop. Additionally, we introduce a refined unclustering respecting former positions which allows us to maintain circuits clustered for a greater number of placement levels.

4.1 Position-Based Clustering

Recall that BestChoice [3] iteratively clusters neighboring circuits u and v until the resulting netlist is sufficiently coarse. The pair of neighbors is chosen to maximize a *clustering score* $d_c(u, v)$ that is defined as

$$d_c(u, v) := \sum_{N: u, v \in N} \frac{1}{|N|} \cdot \frac{1}{a(u) + a(v)},$$

where $a(x)$ denotes the area of the cells already clustered within x. This clustering score d_c merely depends on netlist connectivity and circuit area. Therefore, many pairs of cells usually share the same score, which defers a great number of clustering choices to the actual implementation. It is likely that this impacts placement quality in a negative way.

We improve clustering choices by looking upon the cells' current positions. Let $BB(u, v)$ denote the half perimeter of the bounding box containing all cells previously clustered within u or v. In two different ways, we respect $BB(u, v)$ in our new clustering score.

First, we strictly refuse to cluster u and v if their positions differ significantly, i.e., $BB(u, v)$ is large. Secondly, we directly incorporate the positions into the connectivity clustering score function d_c. Thus, we rather cluster circuits that lie close together, but still prefer clustering distant circuits if their netlist connectivity is extremely high. Altogether, we obtain the *position-based clustering score*

$$d_p(u, v) := \begin{cases} d_c(u, v)/(BB(u, v) + s) & \text{if } BB(u, v) \leq h, \\ 0 & \text{otherwise}. \end{cases}$$

The bound h and the scaling value s are constants depending on the respective chip domain.

The bounding box is chosen for measuring the distance between u and v since we even want to prevent u to be clustered with v if a single circuit within v has a significantly distinct position. We tested various alternatives based on centers of gravity of the cells within u and v. In experiments, those approaches led to further spread clusterings and increased netlength.

4.2 Position-Based Unclustering

Repeatedly unclustering to finer netlists is essential when dealing with density constraints of bins whose sizes decrease during time. Usually, the maximum size of each cluster is therefore upper bounded depending on the bins' capacity. Whenever a clustered cell exceeds this bound, it is dissolved.

We call this *unclustering by size*. This technique often leads to drastic netlist changes for certain bin-levels. We develop a supplementary criterion that, in conjunction with unclustering by size, weakens this effect and allows to preserve clusters longer.

We judge a clustered cell by the closeness of the preferred locations of its members. Given the clustered cell $\{u, v\}$, we determine optimum positions for both u and v assuming fixed positions for other circuits. We will preserve the cluster $\{u, v\}$ for the subsequent level of our PARTITIONINGBASED-PLACEMENT subroutine if and only if the desired positions are close. To measure proximity, we bound the distance of the optimum positions for u and v related to the current location of $\{u, v\}$. We call this *unclustering by positions*.

We invoke unclustering by positions before using the standard unclustering by size with increased bounds. Doing so can preserve larger clusters of cells with similar desired positions while dissolving netlength critical clusters. This is why we can relax the influence of unclustering by size. Our proposed unclustering can be implemented to run in linear time with respect to the number of involved pins. Since the unclustering processes of two distinct clusters are independent from each other, unclustering can be parallelized efficiently.

5. EXPERIMENTAL RESULTS

We examined our tool by experiments both on recent real-world instances from industry and on benchmark chips.

5.1 Clustering Experiments

We first want to demonstrate the impact of the position-based (un-)clustering methods proposed in Section 4 upon the netlength of a single chip from industry. To this end, we performed experiments on the industrial 22 nm-chip Meinolf with 393 324 cells. Table 1 summarizes our results. We ran ten iterations of our self-stabilizing loop with the standard parameters (cf. Section 5.4), testing different (un-)clustering methods against our position-based techniques. We compare half-perimeter wirelength (WL) in meters for the following three clustering strategies, each clustering the netlist down to 15 % of its original size:

- BestChoice clustering with connectivity clustering score function; position-based unclustering (Conn & Pos)

- Position-based BestChoice clustering; size-based unclustering (Pos & Size)

- Position-based BestChoice clustering; position-based unclustering (Pos & Pos)

In the zeroth iteration, we always ran the connectivity-based BestChoice algorithm with the given unclustering strategy. For comparison, we also show results for a run of BonnPlace without clustering. The percentages in the last column are relative to the run without clustering.

We see that the run "Pos & Pos" with position-based clustering and unclustering methods was the only run that outperformed the run without clustering in each of the iterations one up to nine. The netlength in this run improved upon that in the run without clustering by about 1.6 %. In each iteration, the runs "Conn & Pos" respectively "Pos & Size" with clustering respectively unclustering versions not considering positions performed worse than the run without clustering. If we do not consider positions at all, results worsen further. The unclustering method based on cell sizes

Clustering Method	WL [m] after iteration										Final WL [m, %]	
	0	1	2	3	4	5	6	7	8	9		
No Clustering	7.226	7.068	7.015	6.982	6.958	6.930	6.918	6.905	6.891	6.884	6.870	100.00
Conn & Pos	7.259	7.101	7.048	7.020	7.006	6.992	6.983	6.975	6.967	6.960	6.931	100.89
Pos & Size	7.480	7.148	7.055	7.015	6.979	6.954	6.942	6.929	6.915	6.912	6.881	100.16
Pos & Pos	7.259	6.981	6.905	6.866	6.847	6.824	6.801	6.784	6.783	6.775	6.758	98.37

Table 1: Experimental netlength results with various clustering methods on the industrial chip Meinolf.

Clustering Method	Runtime [s] of GLOBALPLACEMENT in iteration										Total runtime [s, %]	
	0	1	2	3	4	5	6	7	8	9		
No Clustering	1075	1144	1147	1039	1043	1046	1029	1032	1024	1046	10625	100.00
Conn & Pos	794	872	905	937	942	875	886	875	883	884	8854	83.33
Pos & Size	755	854	835	842	854	829	840	840	810	802	8260	77.74
Pos & Pos	749	861	897	838	847	859	839	841	830	805	8368	78.76

Table 2: Experimental runtime results with various clustering methods on the industrial chip Meinolf.

only can be tuned to obtain better results if we use a stricter bound on cell sizes compared to the window sizes (cf. Section 4.2). However, this diminishes the positive effect of clustering on the numbers of cells during the levels of our partition-based placement. In the run "Pos & Pos", however, we obtain good netlength results while keeping the number of cells of the clustered netlist below 18 % until the fifth level, below 43 % until the seventh level and uncluster completely in the eighth of ten levels.

In Table 2, we picture the execution time of these runs in seconds. Each of the runs with clustering improved the running time of the run without clustering by about 20 %. In lower levels of each iteration, our runtime gain was much higher (about 50%), but since the last two levels, that are most time consuming, are always calculated on the completely unclustered netlist, the total gain was smaller.

5.2 Timing Results

Due to the lack of publicly available testbeds for timing-aware placement, we present our results on industrial designs. Our timing-aware self-stabilizing global placer introduced in Section 3.4 was run ten iterations without routability optimization.

Contrary to the previous setup, we used a combination of the clique and star net model. Minimizing super-linear netlength proved beneficial while optimizing timing.

At the end of each iteration, net weights were updated and layer assignment was done. The REFINEPLACE routine was executed in iterations two to nine. All results were gathered after timing optimization.

In Table 3, we illustrate our timing-aware placement results on four 22 nm-designs from industry. To evaluate the timing behavior, we list the worst slack (WS in ps) and the sum of negative endpoint slacks (SNES in ps). The SNES is measured with respect to a slack target of 5 ps. Thus, SNES may still be negative although the WSL is positive. Furthermore, we list the development of half-perimeter wirelength (WL in m) for each iteration. The results show that over the course of iterations, we are able to improve timing behavior significantly. From iterations zero to nine, we were able to reduce SNES by 90.4 % on average over the four chips. From iterations one to nine, we still improved SNES by more than 78.8 %. The half-perimeter wirelength in iteration nine is on average increased by less than 2.75 % compared to it-

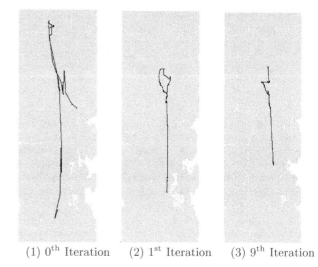

(1) 0th Iteration (2) 1st Iteration (3) 9th Iteration

Figure 3: The most critical path shown on part of our industrial design Benedikt at the end of iterations zero, one and nine.

eration zero and by less than 1.5 % compared to iteration one. Hence, compared to the huge improvements in timing behavior, the increase in wirelength is moderate.

The remaining negative slack is often related to local minima that our REFINEPLACE engine is not capable of overcoming. The usual development of the worst paths is exemplary depicted in Figure 3 on the industrial design Benedikt. The shortened path after the first iteration is due to our net weight update based on timing criticality. Further improvements are due to the good solutions of REFINEPLACE which we are able to preserve in our self-stabilizing framework. The figures show the same critical path becoming shorter while straightening.

5.3 Self-Stabilizing Behavior

In Figure 4, we demonstrate the self-stabilizing behavior of timing-driven BonnPlace on the timing testbed (cf. Section 5.2 and Table 3). For each chip, there is a graph displaying the linear movement between the final placements of any two consecutive iterations of our algorithm.

We can see how drastically movement decreases throughout Self-Stabilizing BonnPlace. This holds for congestion-

| It. | Ida (20 617 circuits) | | | Leo (31 590 circuits) | | | Antonio (103 795 circuits) | | | Benedikt (370 210 circuits) | | |
	WS [ps]	SNES [ps]	WL [m]	WS [ps]	SNES [ps]	WL [m]	WS [ps]	SNES [ps]	WL [m]	WS [ps]	SNES [ps]	WL [m]
0	-143	-13681	0.42	-500	-889402	2.49	-278	-724535	2.61	-1949	-7248451	9.43
1	-91	-8856	0.43	-206	-107260	2.52	-129	-136805	2.63	-495	-463030	9.47
2	-63	-7367	0.46	-85	-95132	2.58	-36	-26371	2.72	-26	-815	9.60
3	-57	-5992	0.47	-54	-26691	2.56	-35	-35599	2.71	-11	-245	9.47
4	-51	-5635	0.47	-41	-27536	2.57	-33	-29448	2.71	-21	-618	9.45
5	-58	-5769	0.47	-41	-28872	2.54	-66	-38683	2.74	-21	-661	9.37
6	-54	-5316	0.47	-41	-26569	2.55	-27	-28277	2.74	-12	-205	9.34
7	-57	-4901	0.47	-41	-23429	2.54	-25	-23048	2.70	-18	-417	9.30
8	-54	-4828	0.47	-41	-23400	2.55	-38	-24470	2.67	-3	-38	9.25
9	-52	-4622	0.46	-41	-25173	2.54	-19	-11973	2.65	5	0	9.23

Table 3: Experimental timing and netlength results on industrial 22 nm-designs. We compare the worst slack WS [ps], the overall sum of negative endpoint slacks SNES [ps] and the HPWL [m].

driven and netlength-minimization setups as well, during which movement diminishes even more steadily. The increased movement between iterations 1 and 2 on Benedikt and Antonio is a side-effect of our emphasis on timing optimization (cf. Table 3, recall that the timing-driven mode of our algorithm 3.4 uses forces as of iteration 3). Thus, Figure 4 documents a significant decrease in movement whenever forces are used.

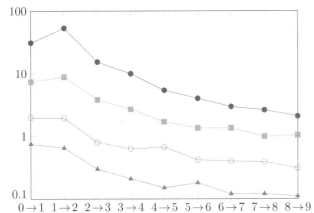

Figure 4: Linear movement [m] between iterations on Ida (—▲—), Leo (—○—), Antonio (—■—) and Benedikt (—●—). Note the logarithmic scaling.

5.4 DAC 2012 Placement Contest

We compare our placement tool to other state-of-the-art placers on the DAC 2012 placement contest benchmark suite [25]. All our final placements are routed by the official contest router NCTUgr [19] in regular mode with default parameters. We compare the official contest metric, i.e., the scaled wirelength sWL defined as

$$sWL := HPWL \cdot \left(1 + \frac{3}{100}(RC - 100)\right).$$

Here, the *routing congestion RC* is defined as $RC := \max\left\{\frac{1}{4}(ACE(0.5) + ACE(1) + ACE(2) + ACE(5)), 100\right\}$ and $ACE(x)$ is the average congestion of the $x\%$ of the most congested global routing edges. HPWL denotes the (unscaled) linear half-perimeter wiring length. We report the (scaled) wirelengths and routing congestions as determined by the official benchmark evaluation scripts.

All benchmarks were placed with identical parameter settings. We ran our placer with a target density of 90 % for

four iterations. Clustering condensed the netlist to 15 % of its original size from the second iteration on using the techniques described in Section 4. After each iteration, we updated our inflations limiting the cell size increment to 50 % of the original cells' size for each grid bin separately.

The results are summarized in Table 4. We compare ourselves to NTUPLACE4 [13], the best participant of the contest, and to the tool of Cong et al. [10] which achieved the best results on these benchmarks so far. We report the scaled wirelength (sWL) both as an absolute value and as the percentage of the scaled wirelength produced by our algorithm. Moreover, for NTUPLACE4 and our tool, we report the routing congestion (RC). Note that the routing congestion of Cong et al. [10] has not been published.

NTUPLACE4 produces 4.04 % more scaled wirelength than our tool while the algorithm of Cong et al. [10] produces 3.59 % more wirelength. We get the best published results on six out of the ten benchmark designs. Moreover, we reduce the routing congestion RC on all chips attaining the minimum possible in eight out of ten cases.

If we disable clustering, our results worsen by 0.23 % with respect to sWL while RC stays the same and the running time increased by 16.54 %. Our congestion mitigation technique is indeed very careful; the scaling factor a (cf. Section 3.3) is consistently at $a = 1.0$. We inflate the movable cells' area by 30.72 % on average. This, of course, increases HPWL by 3.84 % on average over the course of our iterations. Despite of this, we are able to rapidly accomplish a drastically improved routability and hence to advance upon this dominating and essential placement objective.

It is not trivial to compare running times properly. The official benchmark was performed on 64-bit Intel Xeon CPU X7560 running at 2.27 GHz in single threaded mode. Our machines are about 45 % faster and our placer is implemented to run highly parallel. In this setting, the former best placer by Cong et al. [10] needed on average more than 225 % of our runtime on eight threads. Our runtime includes the invocations of BONNROUTEGLOBAL.

6. CONCLUSION

We have presented a self-stabilizing placement framework. It combines force-directed with partitioning-based placement making use of an appropriate clustering. We have demonstrated that our flexible approach can optimize routing congestion as well as timing behavior on academic and industrial designs.

| Chip | NTUPLACE4 [13] | | | Cong et al. [10] | | Self-Stabilizing BonnPlace | | | |
	sWL [$\times 10^8$, %]	RC [%]		sWL [$\times 10^8$, %]		sWL [$\times 10^8$, %]	RC [%]	Inflation [%]	
superblue2	6.24	103.14	100.68	6.14	101.49	6.05	100.00	100.17	46.42
superblue3	3.62	112.26	103.53	3.60	111.64	3.22	100.00	100.00	58.03
superblue6	3.42	101.54	101.21	3.40	100.81	3.37	100.00	100.00	31.77
superblue7	3.99	97.90	100.68	3.95	97.04	4.07	100.00	100.00	19.23
superblue9	2.55	108.25	102.48	2.50	106.31	2.35	100.00	100.00	26.51
superblue11	3.42	99.38	100.02	3.40	98.75	3.44	100.00	100.02	15.97
superblue12	3.12	111.21	100.02	3.04	108.38	2.80	100.00	100.01	41.57
superblue14	2.26	99.74	100.07	2.45	108.32	2.26	100.00	100.00	15.53
superblue16	2.80	105.79	102.39	2.74	103.38	2.65	100.00	100.00	31.85
superblue19	1.53	101.18	100.61	1.51	99.79	1.51	100.00	100.00	20.30
average		104.04	101.17		103.59		100.00	100.02	30.72

Table 4: Results on the DAC 2012 placement contest benchmark suite [25]. We analyze the official contest metrics scaled wirelength sWL as well as routing congestion RC. Inflation denotes the size increase we impose on cells relative to the initial areas.

7. REFERENCES

[1] M. Ahrens, M. Gester, N. Klewinghaus, D. Müller, S. Peyer, C. Schulte, and G. Téllez: Detailed routing algorithms for advanced technology nodes. To appear in TCAD.

[2] C.J. Alpert, J. Hu, S.S. Sapatnekar, C.N. Sze: Accurate estimation of global buffer delay within a floorplan. TCAD (2006), 25, 6, 1140–1146.

[3] C.J. Alpert, A.B. Kahng, G.-J. Nam, S. Reda, P.G. Villarrubia: A semi-persistent clustering technique for VLSI circuit placement. ISPD (2005), 200–207.

[4] A. Bock: Postoptimierung durch Umplatzierung und Gate Sizing. Diploma Thesis, University Bonn (2010).

[5] U. Brenner: VLSI legalization with minimum perturbation by iterative augmentation. DATE (2012), 1385–1390.

[6] U. Brenner, A. Rohe: An effective congestion-driven placement framework, TCAD (2003), 22, 4, 387–394.

[7] T.F. Chan and J. Cong and J.R. Shinnerl and K. Sze and M. Xie: mPL6: Enhanced multilevel mixed-size placement. ISPD (2006), 212–214.

[8] H. Chen, C.-K. Cheng, N.-C. Chou, A.B. Kahng, J.F. MacDonald, P. Suaris, B. Yao, Z. Zhu: An algebraic multigrid solver for analytical placement with layout based clustering. DAC (2003), 794-799.

[9] T.-C. Chen, Z.-W. Jiang, T.-C. Hsu, H.-C. Chen, Y.-W. Chang: NTUplace3: An analytical placer for large-scale mixed-size designs with preplaced blocks and density constraints. TCAD (2008), 27, 7, 1228–1240.

[10] J. Cong, L. Guojie, K. Tsota, X. Bingjun: Optimizing routability in large-scale mixed-size placement. ASP-DAC (2013), 441–446.

[11] M. Gester, D. Müller, T. Nieberg, C. Panten, C. Schulte, J. Vygen: BonnRoute: Algorithms and data structures for fast and good VLSI routing. TODAES 18 (2013), Article 32.

[12] X. He, T. Huang, L. Xiao, H. Tian, G. Cui, E.F.Y. Young: Ripple: An effective routability-driven placer by iterative cell movement. ICCAD (2011), 74–79.

[13] M.-K. Hsu, S. Chou, T.-H. Lin, Y.-W. Chang: Routability-driven analytical placement for mixed-size circuit designs. ICCAD (2011), 80–84.

[14] B. Hu, M. Marek-Sadowska: Multilevel fixed-point-addition- based VLSI placement. TCAD (2005), 24, 8, 1188–1203.

[15] M.-C. Kim, J. Hu, D.-J. Lee and I.L. Markov: A SimPLR method for routability-driven placement. ICCAD (2011), 67–73.

[16] M.-C. Kim, D. Lee, I.L. Markov: SimPL: An effective placement algorithm. TCAD (2012), 31, 1, 50–60.

[17] M.-C. Kim and I.L. Markov: ComPLx: A competitive primal-dual Lagrange optimization for global placement. DAC (2012), 747–752.

[18] M.-C. Kim, N. Viswanathan, C.J. Alpert, I.L. Markov, S. Ramji: MAPLE: Multilevel adaptive placement for mixed-size designs. ISPD (2012) 193–200.

[19] W.-H. Liu, W.-C. Kao, Y.-L. Li, K.-Y. Chao: Multi-threaded collision-aware global routing with bounded-length maze routing. DAC (2010) 200–205.

[20] J. Lu, P. Chen, C.-C. Chang, L. Sha, D. J.-H. Huang, C.-C. Teng, C.-K. Cheng: ePlace: Electrostatics based placement using Nesterov's Method. DAC (2014), 1–6.

[21] D. Müller, K. Radke, J. Vygen: Faster min-max resource sharing in theory and practice. MPC 3 (2011), 1-35.

[22] R.H.J.M. Otten: Global wires: harmful? ISPD (1998), 104–109.

[23] J.A. Roy, S.N. Adya, D.A. Papa, I.L. Markov: Min-cut floorplacement. TCAD (2006), 1313–1326.

[24] M. Struzyna: Sub-quadratic objectives in quadratic placement. DATE (2013), 1867–1872.

[25] N. Viswanathan, C.J. Alpert, C.N. Sze, Z. Li, Y. Wei: The DAC 2012 routability-driven placement contest and benchmark suite. DAC (2012), 774–782.

[26] N. Viswanathan, G.-J. Nam, C.J. Alpert, P.G. Villarrubia, H. Ren, C. Chu: RQL: Global placement via relaxed quadratic spreading and linearization. DAC (2007), 453–458.

[27] N. Viswanathan, M. Pan, C.C.N Chu: FastPlace 3.0: A fast Multilevel quadratic placement algorithm with placement congestion control. ASP-DAC (2007), 135-140.

[28] Z. Xiu, R.A. Rutenbar: Mixed-size placement with fixed macrocells using grid-warping. ISPD (2007), 103–110.

[29] Yan, J.Z.,C.C.N. Chu, W.-K. Mak: SafeChoice: A novel approach to hypergraph clustering for wirelength-driven placement. TCAD (2011), 30, 7, 1020–1033.

Coarse-grained Structural Placement for a Synthesized Parallel Multiplier

Sungmin Bae[*]
sungmin1.bae@samsung.com

Hyung-Ock Kim[*]
ho79.kim@samsung.com

Jungyun Choi[*]
jungyun74.choi@samsung.com

Jaehong Park[*]
jaehongp@samsung.com

[*]Design Technology
Samsung System LSI.
South Korea

ABSTRACT

We propose a new coarse-grained structural placement methodology tightly coupled with logic synthesis to exploit inherent structure of a synthesized parallel multiplier. The proposed method takes advantage of both benefits of logic optimizations and remaining regularity in the synthesized netlist. This is achieved by using a structural template of the multiplier, which is considered to be provided by dedicated datapath generators in the logic synthesis. The template includes primary input and output nets and structural specification of the multiplier, which is used to infer structural relative locations of a partial netlist and then structurally map the partial cells to guide structural placement of the rest of the module. Comparing to a conventional P&R (Place and Route) methodology, it improves the critical path delay, the total negative slacks, and the total wirelength by 2%, 42%, and 2%, respectively, on datapath intensive industrial designs.

1. INTRODUCTION

Due to tight schedules of designing today's ever more complex application specific integrated circuits (ASICs), even high-performance microprocessors are implemented using standard cell based P&R methodologies. However, structure-unaware wirelength minimization objectives of placement algorithms often mislead placers for optimizing such datapath-intensive designs, which may result in sub-optimal implementation qualities [8, 13]. To close the sub-optimality gap, one may manually map the standard-cell based datapath designs by skipping the logic minimization and manually perform the technology mapping to keep the structural regularity. However, it is often very human-effort demanding and can be undesirable, since potential benefits from the logic optimizations may outweigh benefits of the fully regularly mapped placement [6].

There have been several approaches to automate this manual structural placement process, where it can be mainly

ISPD'15, March 29–April 1, 2015, Monterey, CA, USA.
Copyright © 2015 ACM 978-1-4503-3399-3/15/04 ...$15.00.
http://dx.doi.org/10.1145/2717764.2717775.

categorized into logic synthesis, regularity extraction, and structure-aware placement. Firstly, datapath-aware logic synthesis can be used to preserve regularity by performing selective logic transformation and globally guiding the synthesis process [6]. Secondly, regularity is typically extracted by identifying a set of structural logic cell similarity in the netlist by various techniques. Using high fan-out nets as initial searching seeds, [3] performed breadth-first search to distinguish a set of similarly structured logics within the netlist. Similarly, [7] performed searching for groups of neighboring logics sharing similarity in stage-by-stage manner to extract two-dimensional regularity. [4] proposed template mapping to cover a circuit in high-level synthesis. [11] used a machine-learning based datapath identification method to distinguish datapath from random logic. Thirdly, the extracted regularity is used as alignment constraints during placement to guide datapath-aware placement. [3] achieved structure aware placement for a datapath module through a nonlinear HPWL (Half-Perimeter Wire Length) minimization and a sigmoid based density model, where the regularly placed module is treated as a macro block and placed with other random logic with a mixed size placement algorithm. [12] used a unified placement flow that simultaneously places random and datapath logics to minimize possible overly constraining random logic placement due to the datapath logics, where alignment constraints were integrated into a force-directed placer. [7] used finding partial correspondence between the cells between the cells of a netlist before and after logic optimization by detecting equivalent nets using binary decision diagrams (BDDs) [9]. Then the un-optimized netlist, which has a a known regular placement, provides structural placement information to the cells with the matching nets in the optimized one.

In this work, we propose a new structure-aware placement methodology tightly coupled with logic synthesis to guide structural placement of a synthesized parallel multiplier. This method exploits inherent regularity in the synthesized netlist after passing through local cell regularity destroying logic minimization and technology mapping [6], where it is likely to have sufficient inherent regularity to benefit from it using structural placement especially for arithmetic circuits [7]. Unlike other indirect logic cell similarity based extraction methods, our method extracts inherent structure from the local regularity destroyed netlist by using explicit structural information and the primary input and primary output nets of the multiplier, which are considered to be provided by dedicated datapath generators in a logic synthesis tool [15] [1]. We extract and structurally place only a few structurally significant portions of the multiplier, which are the parts of the partial product generator and final carry propagating adder. This is not to too overly constraining placement for local regularity destroyed datapath circuits. They are chosen to guide bit-slice aligned placement of the multiplier by compensating low fidelity of the HPWL metric of a wirelength driven placer especially for the partial product generator with high fanout structures. An approach in [7] is similar to our methodology in terms of using partial structural placing of guiding cells to lead structure placement of the rest of the cell of a synthesized netlist. However, the regularity extraction and mapping methods are different from our method, where we use explicit structural information to efficiently extract regularity by topologically traversing a netlist and also can be less ambiguous in the extraction.

The remainder of this paper is organized as follows. Section 2 introduces the overall concept of the methodology and its design flow. In section 3, we explain the architectures of parallel multipliers in brief and our proposed methodology in details. Results on several benchmark designs are presented in section 4, followed by conclusions in section 5.

2. DESIGN FLOW

Our design flow is depicted in Figure 1, where the key differences between a conventional P&R flow and ours are shaded.

Firstly, the datapath generator provides an explicit structural template of a synthesized arithmetic datapath to the structural extraction stage. The template contains structural placement guiding nets, which can be cells instead, to extract the cells in the some selected parts of the datapath to guide structural placement, and algorithmic methods specifically built for the arithmetic datapath, to form structural relative placement of the cells. In this work, we only propose a methodology for a parallel multiplier, however, we believe it can be extended to other datapath modules generated from the datapath generator. Secondly, structural location inference [2] and cell mapping of the cells are performed based on the template. Thirdly, the cell mapping and an estimated dataflow direction [3] are fed to the physical aware bit-slice alignment of the cell mapping to generate bit-slice aligned relative placement directives. Lastly, the directives form relative placement blocks, where they are placed with the rest of the datapath using mixed-size placement techniques to guide structure aware placement of the datapath. The relative placement directives are removed after finishing global placement to cope with locally optimizing legalization and detailed placement. The later design stages are then evaluated as usual, if the design objectives and constraints are satisfied.

3. STRUCTURAL PLACEMENT FLOW FOR A SYNTHESIZED PARALLEL MULTIPLIER

To exploit the underly regularity of a synthesized arithmetic datapath, the proposed methodology structurally places

[1] A commercial logic synthesis tool synthesizes arithmetic operations in an RTL code into a standard-cell netlist using dedicated datapath generators [15].

[2] We use "extraction" and "inference" interchangeably throughout the paper.

[3] One can estimate it by inspecting relative locations of the input and output portions of the datapath from a global placement.

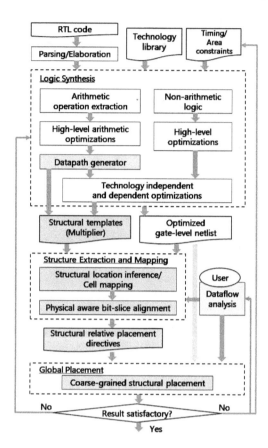

Figure 1: Design flow

the placement guiding cells to lead the non-guiding cells to be placed closely to the inherent structure of the datapath. This is acquired by inferencing structural locations of the guiding cells, mapping them according to the inferred locations based on the structural template, and then bit-slice aligning them considering their physical dimensions to finally get structural relative placement directives to be used in global placement.

This section describes the methodology specifically built for a parallel multiplier, where the guiding cells are part of the partial product generator and final carry propagating adder. They are chosen to guide bit-slice aligned placement for the multiplier, while avoiding overly constrained placement. The template includes corresponding input and output nets of the multiplier to retrieve the guiding cells, and the structural information and algorithmic methodd to extract the structural locations and mapping the cells according to them.

In this section, we briefly review the basic architectures of a parallel multiplier, then explain the details of the methodology.

3.1 Parallel Multiplier Structures

A parallel multiplier can be divided into three stages of partial products generation stage, partial product reduction stage, and the final adder stage (see figure[4] 2). Firstly, the multiplicand and the multiplier are multiplied bit by bit to generate the partial products, where modified booth encoding (MBE) scheme can be used to reduce the number of

[4] The dot-notation can vary with the partial product generation scheme and the sign representation used

partial products by a factor of two. Secondly, carry-save adder (CSA) tree is usually used to add the partial products in a tree-like fashion to produce two rows of the partial products. Finally the two rows are fed to the last stage of a high-speed final carry propagating adder to generate the final output.

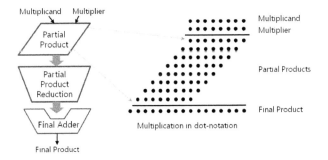

Figure 2: Architecture of the multiplier

3.1.1 Partial Product Generation

The partial-product generation stage generates a set of binary number rows whose sum equals the product of the positive or negative multiplicand and multiplier. The way that the partial products are generated is the difference between the different architectures of various multipliers optimized for their design contexts, such as high clock speeds, less area occupation, or low power, which can be largely divided into non-Booth and Booth schemes.

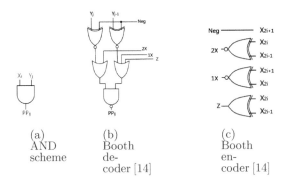

Figure 3: Partial product generators

Non-Booth scheme.

Figure 3(a) shows a simple example of the partial product generation in parallel by the bitwise ANDing of multiplicand and multiplier bits. The Baugh-Wooley method can be used for signed partial product generations [2]. This scheme is good for small word lengths of 8-16 bits [15].

Modified Booth recoding (Radix-4).

It is an efficient encoding technique in parallel multipliers which can reduce the number of partial product rows by a factor of two [5], thereby improving the multiplier per-

---

[5]Without loss of generality, we only demonstrate for Radix-4 modified Booth scheme. This method can be similarly applied to higher Radix Booth schemes with the different reduction factors.

formance. The method of encoding starts by decomposing the multiplier bits into overlapping 3-bit segments, which is shown in figure 4 ("0" is added to right of the LSB of multiplier.). The segments are encoded into one of -2, -1, 0, 1, 2 by the the encoding logic shown in figure 3(c). The Booth decoder generates the partial products from the encoded signals as shown in 3(b).

Figure 4: Grouping of the multiplier term for Booth encoding

3.1.2 Partial Product Reduction

The partial product reduction stage reduces the partial-product bits by reducing every column of input bits down to 2 output bits. The partial product column compression technique is performed using compressor cells, such as half-adders (2:2 compressor), full-adders (3:2 compressor) and 4:2 compressors etc., where the compressor cells are arranged in a tree-like structure (e.g. Wallace tree [10]). Figure 5 shows a part of a CSA adder tree with a 3:2 compressor cell which takes three input bits with the same weight and produce two output bits of sum and carry-out. The sum is the same weight as the input bits, while the carry has twice the weight of the sum and inputs.

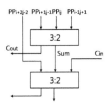

Figure 5: Partial product reduction with 3:2 compressor cells

3.1.3 Final carry propagating adder

The two-row outputs of the tree are added typically using a final carry propagating high-speed adder to generate multiplication output. However, various adding schemes can be used to meet different requirements in terms of timing, area, and power etc. For example, a ripple carry adder can be used to reduce the area of the adder at the cost of degraded timing, while carry-lookahead or carry-select adder can be used to increase the speed of the adder at the cost of the area.

3.2 Structural Location Inference for a Parallel Multiplier

The structural placement guiding cells are categorized into primary input (PI) and primary output (PO) cells, which are part of the partial product generator and final carry propagating adder, respectively. The cells are extracted by collecting immediate fan-out (PI cells) or fan-in (PO cells) cone cells of a given set of nets, where they are consist of the multiplicand and multiplier inputs, and result output nets. We assumed the nets are given in this work. In [5, 7], it is explained how to find corresponding nets of an optimized netlist to the nets of the un-optimized one, or it can be extracted from the functional hierarchy. The structural locations of the cells are inferred by analyzing their nets and topological relations with the template of the multiplier.

3.2.1 PI Cell Structural Location Inference

A set of nets that to collect the PI cells differs depending on the type of the partial product generator. A non-Booth multiplier uses multiplicand and multiplier input nets. Yet a modified Booth recoded multiplier uses only multiplicand nets. Since multiplier nets mainly connect to the Booth encoder cells where their optimal locations can be better dealt with high fan-out synthesis algorithms. Furthermore, their cell clumping impact is likely to be minimized by fixing some of the booth decoding cells in their structural locations. After collecting the PI cells, their two dimensional locations on a partial product generator are decided by the horizontal partial product row and the vertical bit-slice column. Algorithm 1 denotes the structural location inference method, and the explanation is as follows.

Partial Product Generator Row Inference.

The partial product generator row of the cell is inferred by its topologically closest multiplier bit as shown in Algorithm 2. For example, as shown in figure 3, the partial product output of PP_{ij} is generated from the input of Y_j and X_i for a non-Booth, and the Y_j, Y_{j-1}, X_{2i-1}, X_{2i}, and X_{2i+1} bits for a modified Booth recoded multiplier [6]. The i indicates the ith row of the partial product generator. For a modified Booth generator, the PI cells belong to PP_{ij} mostly have the closest multiplier bit of $2i+1$ which can be divided by 2 and floored to get i. When the bit is $2i-1$, the inference error can be a row difference. However, this does not significantly impact QoR (Quality of Result), since our guidance method does not rely on exact location of each cell. If no closest multiplier bit exists, the row number can be estimated by subtracting multiplicand bit number from the bit-slice column number and multiplicand bit number.

$$PI_{row}(C_k) = \begin{cases} PI_{col}(C_k) - B_{md}(C_k), & B_{mr}(C_k) = \varnothing \\ \lfloor \frac{B_{mr}(C_k)}{2} \rfloor, & PP_{type} = Booth \\ B_{mr}(C_k), & PP_{type} = \overline{Booth} \end{cases} \quad (1)$$

Equation 1 depicts the aforementioned inference methods, where $PI_{row}(C_k)$ indicates the row number of the PI cell C_k, $PI_{col}(C_k)$ indicates the column number of the PI cell C_k, $B_{md}(C_k)$ is the closest multiplicand bit of C_k, $B_{mr}(C_k)$ is the closest multiplier bit of C_k, PP_{type} is the partial product type, and $Booth$ and $\overline{Booth}$ are the modified Booth recoded and non-Booth partial product generator, respectively. This assumes the structural templates are based on the architectures in figure 3. Different architectures may use different templates.

Partial Product Generator Column (Bit-slice) Inference.

The partial product generator column (bit-slice) can be derived by discovering the topologically closest and bit-slice aligned result bit to the PI cell. However, only considering the topological closeness does not guarantee to find the proper result bit, since there is an ambiguity in the column inference shown in figure 6. The blue compressor has two connections with the same topological depth toward to the $Column[i+1]$ and $Column[i]$ from the carry-out and sum, respectively, where the same weighted column is along the $Column[i]$. Thus, another structural characteristic is exploited to accurately determine the bit-slice aligned column. The topological ordering propagation is restricted to

only follow the same weighted bit-slice along the CSA tree. This can be achieved by ignoring the carry-out pin during the propagation, hence it goes along the sum output of the compressor shown in figure 5. We assumed the CSA tree is synthesized with dedicated compressor cells, since industrial designs use a rich set of design libraries that typically has the datapath cells [7]. Similarly, when propagating through the final carry propagating adder, we omit the carry-out pin to reach the closest yet bit-slice aligned result bit. Algorithm 3 describes the aforesaid method.

Algorithm 1 PI cell structural location inference

Input: $PI_{multiplicand}, PI_{multiplier}$ **Output:** PI_{cell}
  procedure $StructuralLocationInference(\forall Input)$
    if $M_{type} == Booth$ **then**
      $PI_{net} \leftarrow PI_{multiplicand}$
    else
      $PI_{net} \leftarrow PI_{multiplicand}, PI_{multiplier}$
    end if
    for each net PI_i in PI_{net} **do**
      $cell_{fanout} \leftarrow GetImmediateFanoutConeCells(PI_i)$
      for each cell $cell_{PI}$ in $cell_{fanout}$ **do**
        $PI_{closest}, depth \leftarrow RowInference(cell_{PI})$
        $PO_{closest}, depth \leftarrow ColumnInference(cell_{PI})$
        $column \leftarrow GetBitNumber(PO_{closest})$
        if $PI_{closest} == \varnothing$ **then**
          $row \leftarrow column - GetBitNumber(PI_i)$
        else if $M_{type} == Booth$ **then**
          $row \leftarrow \lfloor \frac{GetBitNumber(PI_i)}{2} \rfloor$
        else
          $row \leftarrow GetBitNumber(PI_i)$
        end if

        Tag row and column bits to $cell_{PI}$
        Add $cell_{PI}$ *to* PI_{cell}
      end for
    end for
    return PI_{cell}
  end procedure

Algorithm 2 PI cell row inference

Input: $cell_{PI}$ **Output:** $PI_{closest}, depth_{min}$
  procedure $RowInference(\forall Input)$
    $PI_{closest} \leftarrow \varnothing$
    $depth_{min} \leftarrow MAX_{DEPTH}$
    for each input pin p_i of $cell_{PI}$ **do**
      if p_i is connected to a $PI_{multiplier}$ **then**
        $depth \leftarrow 1$
        $PI \leftarrow PI_{multiplier}$
      else if $row(p_i) == empty$ **then**
        $cell_{driver} \leftarrow GetDriverCell(p_i)$
        $PI, depth \leftarrow RowInference(cell_{driver})$
      else
        $PI, depth \leftarrow row(p_i)$
      end if
      if $depth_{min} > depth + 1$ **then**
        $PI_{closest} \leftarrow PI$
        $depth_{min} \leftarrow depth + 1$
      end if
    end for
    return $PI_{closest}, depth_{min}$
  end procedure

3.2.2 PO Cell Extraction

The PO cells are the output cells of the final carry propagating adder. They are trivially extracted by retrieving an

---

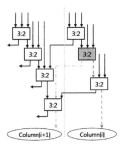

Figure 6: Possible misaligned bit-slice inference for a Wallace tree

---

Algorithm 3 PI cell column inference

Input: $cell_{PI}$
Output: $PO_{closest}, depth_{min}$

   procedure $ColumnInference(\forall Input)$
      $depth_{min} \leftarrow MAX_{DEPTH}$
      for *each output pin* p_o *of* $cell_{PI}$ **do**
         if $cell_{PI}$ *is a compressor cell* **then**
            if p_o *is carryout pin* **then**
               continue
            end if
         else if p_o *is connected to a* PO_{result} **then**
            $depth \leftarrow 1$
            $column(p_o) \leftarrow PO_{net}, depth$
         else if $column(pin_{out}) == empty$ **then**
            $cell_{receiver} \leftarrow GetReceiverCell(p_o)$
            $depth'_{min} \leftarrow MAX_{DEPTH}$
            for *each cell* $cell_r$ *in* $cell_{reiver}$ **do**
               $PO, depth \leftarrow ColumnInference(cell_r)$
               if $depth'_{min} > depth + 1$ **then**
                  $PO'_{closest} \leftarrow PO$
                  $depth'_{min} \leftarrow depth + 1$
               end if
            end for
            $column(p_o) \leftarrow PO_{closest}, depth_{min}$
         end if
         if $depth_{min} > depth'_{min}$ **then**
            $PO_{closest} \leftarrow PO'_{closest}$
            $depth_{min} \leftarrow depth'_{min}$
         end if
      end for
      return $PO_{closest}, depth_{min}$
   end procedure

---

immediate fan-in cone cell of each given result net and tagging the result bit to the cell as in Algorithm 4. The cells will later be bit-slice aligned to guide the placement of the multiplier.

3.3 Structural Cell Mapping

After extracting the PI and PO cells, we perform cell mapping to assign PI and PO cells according to their inferred structural locations.

3.3.1 Partial Product Generator Mapping

The PI cells are then mapped onto a 2-D array according to the partial product generator structure of the multiplier, where there are row spacing [8] between the rows in the array to allow other non guiding cells to be placed close to their inherent structural locations. The partial product generator structure has two types of alignments, namely, vertical (partial product generator column) and horizontal (partial

---

[8]The number of spacing rows is multiplier architecture and technology dependent.

Algorithm 4 PO cell extraction algorithm

Input: net_{result}
Output: PO_{cell}

   procedure $POCellExtraction(\forall Input)$
      for *each net* net_i *in* net_{result} **do**
         $cell_{PO} \leftarrow GetImmediateFaninConeCell(net_i)$
         Tag result bit of net_i *to* $cell_{PO}$
         Add $cell_{PO}$ *to* PO_{cell}
      end for
      return PO_{cell}
   end procedure

---

product generator row) alignments. To vertically and horizontally align the cell mapping, we utilize the inferred row and column numbers of each PI cell.

The number of cells that have the same inference location is very likely to be uneven due to the local nature of logic synthesis optimization algorithms. Thus if all the cells are allowed to map to their inferred locations by allocating enough slots at the locations, the cell mapping slots may have uncontrollable aspect ratio which may significantly span horizontally and result in QoR (Quality of Result) degradation. Thus, our cell mapping method minimizes mis-mapping of them within 2-D mapping array dimensional constraints. In addition, to compensate for net-connection blindness of the purely alignment based optimization, weighted alignment and HPWL optimizations are simultaneously performed.

The cell mapping problem is formulated as equation 2, which can be stated as follows. All the PI cells are mapped to a constrained 2-D mapping array by minimizing the weighted sum of mis-mapping cost of cell c_i $Cost_{MA}(c_i)$ and half perimeter wire length cost of net n_i $Cost_{HPWL}(n_i)$, where $0 < \alpha \leq 1$. The $Cost_{HPWL}(n_i)$ is considered to closely placing related cells to minimize net length, since $Cost_{MA}(c_i)$ is purely mapping cost based on the inference location of c_i. The dimension constraints consist of a fixed number of row slots ($|PP_{row}|$) and the maximum number of available column slots ($|PP_{column}|$).

$$\min \quad \alpha \cdot \sum_{c_i \in C} Cost_{MA}(c_i) + (1-\alpha) \cdot \sum_{n_i \in N} Cost_{HPWL}(n_i)$$
$$\text{s.t.} \quad |C_{unmapped}| = 0$$
$$|PP_{column}| \leqq MAX_{column}$$
$$|PP_{row}| = NUM_{row}$$
$$(2)$$

Our method for the problem builds upon the linear programming formulations of min-cost max-flow (MCF) for $Cost_{MA}(c_i)$ and HPWL minimization for $Cost_{HPWL}(n_i)$ as in Algorithm 5. Initially, it builds a 2-D slot array which may not fully contain all the cells to allow empty slot sharing between adjacent bit-slice columns. Then, it iteratively solves the problem by allocating a column of slots (DummySlot) in the place having the worst mis-mappings, which is a column that has the maximum sum of the mis-mapping costs of adjacent bit-slice columns. This iteration runs until the maximum mis-mapping cost is under a threshold ($Threshold_{MA}$) or the number of the columns exceeds the maximum number (MAX_{column}). These threshold and weight variables are technology dependent, which may depend on wiring parasitics and library characteristics etc.

Algorithm 6 builds a MCF graph and HPWL minimization constraints and optimize the constraints via linear pro-

Algorithm 5 PI cell mapping

Input: $PI_{cell}, NUM_{row}, Threshold_{MA}$
Output: MAP_{cell}

> **procedure** $PICellMapping(\forall Input)$
>> ▷ Initialize a 2-D slot array
>> **for** *each cell group of bit-slice* $PI_{cell}[i]$ *in* PI_{cell} **do**
>>> $Num_{col}[i] \leftarrow \lfloor PI_{cell}[i]/Num_{row} \rfloor$
>> **end for**
>> ▷ Inserting a column of dummy slots
>> **do**
>>> $MAP_{cell}, PI_{cost} \leftarrow MIN_{MAP}(PI_{cell}, PI_{array})$
>>> ▷ Searching the worst mis-mapped bit-slice column
>>> $COST_{max} \leftarrow 0$
>>> **for** *each* $PI_{cost}[i]$ *in* PI_{cost} **do**
>>>> **if** $COST_{max} < PI_{cost}[i] + PI_{cost}[i+1]$ **then**
>>>>> $COST_{max} \leftarrow PI_{cost}[i] + PI_{cost}[i+1]$
>>>>> $DummySlotCol \leftarrow i$
>>>> **end if**
>>> **end for**
>>> $InsertDummySlot(DummySlotCol)$
>> **while** $COST_{max} > Threshold_{MA}$ & $NUM_{col} < MAX_{col}$
>> **return** MAP_{cell}
> **end procedure**

Algorithm 6 MCF and HPWL based PI cell mapping

Input: PI_{cell}, PI_{array}
Output: MAP_{cell}, PI_{cost}

> **procedure** $MIN_{MAP}(\forall input)$
>> ▷ Build slot constraints
>> **for** *each slot* S_i *in* PI_{array} **do**
>>> *Connect* S_i *to Sink with flow capacity* $cap(S_i)$
>> **end for**
>> **for** *each cell* C_i *in* PI_{cell} **do**
>>> *Connect* C_i *to Source with flow capacity* 1
>>> $edge_{cost} \leftarrow MCFcost(C_i, PI_{array})$
>>> **for** *each edge cost of* $edge_{cost}(i)$ *in* $edge_{cost}$ **do**
>>>> *Add* $edge_{cost}(i)$ *to* MCF_{CNST}
>>> **end for**
>> **end for**
>> ▷ Build HPWL constraints
>> $HPWL_{CNST} \leftarrow HPWLcost(PI_{cell})$
>> ▷ Minimize weighted sum of MCF and HPWL
>> $MAP_{cell}, PI_{cost} \leftarrow LPSolve(MCF_{CNST}, HPWL_{CNST})$
>> **return** MAP_{cell}, PI_{cost}
> **end procedure**

Algorithm 7 MCF cost

Input: C_i, PI_{array}
Output: $COST_{MCF}$

> **procedure** $MCFcost(\forall input)$
>> $row_{cell} \leftarrow GetRow(C_i)$
>> $col_{cell} \leftarrow GetColumn(C_i)$
>> **for** *each column index* i *in* $-1, 0, +1$ **do**
>>> **if** $i == 0$ **then**
>>>> $\gamma \leftarrow \gamma_{own}$
>>> **else if** $DummySlot[col_{cell} + i] == \varnothing$ **then**
>>>> $\gamma \leftarrow \gamma_{dummy}$
>>> **else**
>>>> $\gamma \leftarrow \gamma_{shared}$
>>> **end if**
>>> **for** *each slot* S_j *in* $PI_{array}[col_{cell} + i]$ **do**
>>>> $row_{slot} \leftarrow GetRow(S_j)$
>>>> $COST_{row}(C_i, S_j) \leftarrow \gamma \cdot |row_{cell} - row_{slot}|$
>>>> *Add* $COST_{row}(C_i, S_j)$ *to* $COST_{MCF}$
>>> **end for**
>> **end for**
>> **return** $COST_{MCF}$
> **end procedure**

gramming and returns the cell mapping MAP_{cell} and mis-mapping cost PI_{cost} of the optimization. Figure 7 and Algorithm 7 denote the MCF constraints. It adds an edge with a flow capacity constraint $cap(S_i)$, which is the available number of slots, to each slot connecting to the sink. Then, each cell gets connected to the source with flow constraint of 1, and the mapping cost edges are connected to mappable slots.

The details of the mapping cost edges in Algorithm 7 are as follows. Each cell in a bit-slice group has edges with flow costs according to possible mapping locations. In bit-slice wise, there are three types of mappings with different mapping costs. Firstly, it can map to the inferred bit-slice column, which has the least cost discrimination of γ_{own}. Secondly, it can map to dummy slot columns with the cost discrimination of γ_{dummy}, where they are inserted to be shared between two adjacent bit-slices to improve mis-mapping costs. Finally, it can map to shared slot columns, which are some portions of the adjacent bit-slice columns with the cost discrimination of γ_{shared}. If there are dummy columns in between the adjacent bit-slice columns, no columns are shared between them. The bit-slice alignment cost γ is used to modulate the row displacement cost of $|row_{cell} - row_{slot}|$.

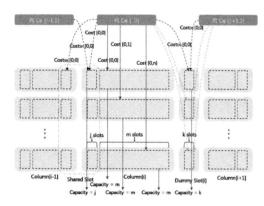

Figure 7: Minimum cost flow formulation

In addition to the MCF constraints above, we minimize

HPWL as in Algorithm 8. This is done by formulating linear HPWL constraints of $max_{i,j \in c_{n_i}} |C_i - C_j|$ and $max_{i,j \in c_{n_i}} |R_i - R_j|$ for each net, where the c_{n_i}, C, and R are cells connected to net n_i, column, and row number, respectively.

3.4 Bit-slice Alignment

The logically mapped PI and PO cells are then bit-slice aligned with respect to their physical dimensions.

To bit-slice align them, a strict bit-slice align method may be used as shown in Figure 8(a). It ensures each cell in a bit-slice column is strictly aligned to the other cells in the column, where a column width is decided by the widest cell among them. [9] This can ensure fully bit-slice aligned cell mapping, however, this comes with a disadvantage of uncontrollable cell alignment sizes. Conversely, a compression method clusters each row without any spacing between the cells in Figure 8(b). This generates a compact cell cluster, however, it cannot insure vertical bit-slice alignment especially with the presence of empty slots like $(i-1, j-1)$ and

---

[9]We assumed that the strict alignment in Figure 8(a) is based on the left edges of the cells, while it can be their certain pins.

Algorithm 8 HPWL cost
***
Input: PI_{cell}, PI_{array}
Output: $COST_{HPWL}$

   procedure $HPWLcost(\forall input)$
     $net_{all} \leftarrow GetNets(PI_{cell})$
     for *each net* n_i *in* net_{all} **do**
       $cell_{n_i} \leftarrow GetCells(n_i)$
       $C, R \leftarrow GetColRow(cell_{n_i})$
          ▷ LPC means Linear Programming Constraint
       $HPWL_{col}(n_i)$ gets LPCs of $max_{i,j \in c_{n_i}}|C_i - C_j|$
       $HPWL_{row}(n_i)$ gets LPCs of $max_{i,j \in c_{n_i}}|R_i - R_j|$
       $HPWL_{CNST} \leftarrow HPWL_{col}(n_i), HPWL_{col}(n_j)$
     end for
     return $HPWL_{CNST}$
   end procedure
***

$(i - 2, j - 1)$.

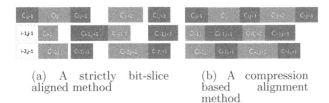

(a) A strictly bit-slice aligned method

(b) A compression based alignment method

Figure 8: Bit-slice alignment method examples

3.4.1 Bit-slice Alignment Method

Our method combines the advantages of the above methods of bit-slice alignment and cell spacing compression. It performs bit-slice misalignment minimization while ensuring a maximum alignment width, where the bit-slice misalignment is defined as the difference between the left-most and right-most cell in a column regarding their alignment references. Figure 9 depicts and Equation 3 formulates the alignment objective and the constraints of the method.

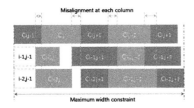

Figure 9: Bit-slice alignment objective and constraints

$$\min \quad \sum_{c_k \in Col} \max_{r_i, r_j \in c_k} |X(c_k, r_i) - X(c_k, r_j)|$$

$$\text{s.t.} \quad \max_{r_i \in Row} \sum_{c_k \in r_i} (W_C(c_k, r_i) + W_S(c_k, r_i)) \leqq W_{MAX}$$

$$(3)$$

This alignment problem can be restated as finding proper spacing width in between every cell. Algorithm 9 details the method. Firstly, it merges the 1-D array of the PO cells at the bottom of the 2-D PI cell mapping array to align

them together. And it doubles the number of the merged 2-D mapping array column and assigns spacing variable W_S in between every cell. The spacings are inserted to the left of the cells, since the cells will be compressed to the left. Secondly, it assigns optimal spacings to minimize the misalignment by using linear programming with the maximum width constraints in Equation 3.

Algorithm 9 Bit-slice alignment
***
Input: $MAP_{cell}, PO_{cell}, W_{MAX}$
Output: W_S

   procedure BIT-SLICE ALIGNMENT$(\forall input)$
     Merge PO_{cell} *at the bottom of* MAP_{cell}
     Double the number of MAP_{cell} *column for* W_S
     for *each column* c_k *in* Col **do**
       for *each row* r_i *in* RoW **do**
         $MAP_{cell}(2 \cdot c_k - 1, 2 \cdot r_i - 1) \leftarrow W_S(c_k, r_i)$
       end for
     end for
     $BS_{CNST} \leftarrow BitSliceConst(MAP_{cell}, W_{MAX})$
     $W_S \leftarrow LPSolve(BS_{CNST})$
     return W_S
   end procedure
***

3.5 Structural Relative Placement Directives Generation

After the bit-slice alignment, the structural locations and the cell spacings are transformed into structural relative placement directives. An estimated dataflow direction is used to set the initial orientations of the cell arrays for global placement. To accommodate the cell spacings, the number of array columns of the directive is set to twice the number of the initial array column for the structural cell mapping. And the number of array rows includes the row spacing. The PI and PO cell arrays are separated to freely follow dataflow during the placement. The cell spacing and row spacing slots are set as empty spaces to lower the cell density at the locations allowing non-guiding cells to be placed close to their guiding cells. Once the placement directives are generated, the compression based alignment method is used to align the cell regarding the cell dimensions and spacings during mixed-size global placement.

4. EXPERIMENTAL RESULTS

We implemented the proposed methodology in Tcl and used CLP [1] as a linear program solver. We used commercial logic synthesis and P&R tools to conduct the experiments.

Figure 10 shows the effectiveness of our approach to extract and structurally place the guiding cells according to the inherent structure of a 32-by-16 synthesized parallel multiplier with Radix-4 modified Booth scheme. The PI and PO cells respectively forming the parallelogram and line are corresponding to the partial product generator and the final carry propagating adder, respectively. There are two rows of spacing in between every partial product row to accommodate non-guiding partial product cells to be placed near the guiding cells. The colors show bit-slice alignment of the guiding cells. Every color is a group of 7 bit-slices, the LSB and MSB are in red and purple, respectively.

To empirically validate its effectiveness in QoR improvement, we designed an experimental flow and compared the results in terms of the critical path delay (CPD), the total negative slacks (TNS), and the total wiring length. We tested the method with 11 datapath-intensive industrial designs. The baselines were implemented with the same design

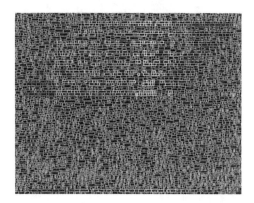

Figure 10: Coarse-grained structural placement for a synthesized parallel multiplier

Table 2: Experimental results

Design	#Mults	Area ratio	CPD	TNS	Wirelength
D1	7	0.49	0.94	0.02	0.99
D2	8	0.17	1.00	0.82	0.98
D3	6	0.33	1.00	0.74	0.95
D4	4	0.32	0.97	0.00	0.98
D5	3	0.30	0.99	0.97	1.00
D6	1	0.25	0.98	0.91	0.95
D7	9	0.21	0.98	0.28	0.94
D8	2	0.21	0.99	0.82	0.99
D9	8	0.18	0.99	0.58	1.00
D10	16	0.09	0.96	0.14	0.99
D11	1	0.40	1.03	1.10	1.02
Ave.	6	0.27	**0.98**	**0.58**	**0.98**

flow except without using the structural relative placement directives during global placement. To compensate randomness in the P&R algorithms, every benchmark ran twice and the results were averaged. The experimental parameters are reported in Table 1. The types of the multipliers in the designs were given from logic synthesis, where the nets of the template were extracted from functional hierarchies of the multipliers. Moreover, dataflow was estimated by examining the PI and PO cells relative locations in a global placement. Table 2 reports baseline normalized results after routing and timing optimization stages; "#$Mults$" and "$Area\ ratio$" are the number of multipliers and their area ratios in the designs, respectively. It shows that the method obtains significantly better TNS than the conventional P&R flow, which was improved by about 42%, In addition, the critical path delay and the total routing length equally improved by about 2%. However, $D11$ degraded the quality metrics. The design had a 32x32 multiplier whose inputs were pruned by about 25% because of constant propagation, consequently, it was not sufficiently regular for the approach.

5. CONCLUSIONS

In this work, we propose a new coarse-grained structural placement methodology tightly coupled with logic synthesis to exploit inherent regular structure of a synthesized parallel multiplier. We presented efficient regularity extraction and structural cell mapping methods of the synthesized multiplier by using its explicit structural information. These methods take advantage of both benefits of logic optimizations and remaining regularity in the synthesized netlist. Our results showed that the methods were effective in enhancing QoR of the datapath oriented designs, which improved the critical path delay, the total negative slacks, and the total wirelength by 2%, 42%, and 2%, respectively.

The future works will focus on developing regularity measures to avoid structurally placing insufficiently regular multipliers, and extending the methodology for other generated datapath circuits.

6. REFERENCES

[1] http://www.coin-or.org/Clp/.

[2] C. R. Baugh and B. A. Wooley. A two's complement parallel array multiplication algorithm. *IEEE Trans. Comput.*, 22(12):1045–1047, Dec. 1973.

[3] S. Chou, M.-K. Hsu, and Y.-W. Chang. Structure-aware placement for datapath-intensive circuit designs. DAC '12, pages 762–767, New York, NY, USA, 2012. ACM.

[4] M. Corazao, M. Khalaf, L. Guerra, M. Potkonjak, and J. Rabaey. Performance optimization using template mapping for datapath-intensive high-level synthesis. *Computer-Aided Design of Integrated Circuits and Systems, IEEE Transactions on*, 15(8):877–888, Aug 1996.

[5] C. A. J. v. Eijk and G. Janssen. Exploiting structural similarities in a bdd-based verification method. In *Proceedings of the Second International Conference on Theorem Provers in Circuit Design - Theory, Practice and Experience*, TPCD '94, pages 110–125, London, UK, UK, 1994. Springer-Verlag.

[6] T. Kutzschebauch and L. Stok. Regularity driven logic synthesis. In *Computer Aided Design, 2000. ICCAD-2000. IEEE/ACM International Conference on*, pages 439–446, Nov 2000.

[7] R. X. T. Nijssen and C. A. J. van Eijk. Regular layout generation of logically optimized datapaths. In *Proceedings of the 1997 International Symposium on Physical Design*, ISPD '97, pages 42–47, New York, NY, USA, 1997. ACM.

[8] D. A. Papa, S. N. Adya, and I. L. Markov. Constructive benchmarking for placement. In *Proceedings of the 14th ACM Great Lakes Symposium on VLSI*, GLSVLSI '04, pages 113–118, New York, NY, USA, 2004. ACM.

[9] C. van Eijk and G. L. J. M. Janssen. Exploiting structural similarities in a bdd-based verification method. In *in Theorem Provers in Circuit Design. 1994, number 901 in Lecture Notes in Computer Science*, pages 110–125. Springer-Verlag, 1994.

[10] C. S. Wallace. A suggestion for a fast multiplier. *Electronic Computers, IEEE Transactions on*, EC-13(1):14–17, Feb 1964.

[11] S. Ward, D. Ding, and D. Pan. Pade: A high-performance placer with automatic datapath extraction and evaluation through high-dimensional data learning. In *Design Automation Conference (DAC), 2012 49th ACM/EDAC/IEEE*, pages 756–761, June 2012.

[12] S. Ward, M.-C. Kim, N. Viswanathan, Z. Li, C. Alpert, E. Swartzlander, and D. Pan. Structure-aware placement techniques for designs with datapaths. *Computer-Aided Design of Integrated Circuits and Systems, IEEE Transactions on*, 32(2):228–241, Feb 2013.

[13] S. I. Ward, D. A. Papa, Z. Li, C. N. Sze, C. J. Alpert, and E. Swartzlander. Quantifying academic placer performance on custom designs. In *Proceedings of the 2011 International Symposium on Physical Design*, ISPD '11, pages 91–98, New York, NY, USA, 2011. ACM.

[14] W.-C. Yeh and C.-W. Jen. High-speed booth encoded parallel multiplier design. *Computers, IEEE Transactions on*, 49(7):692–701, Jul 2000.

[15] R. Zimmermann. Datapath synthesis for standard-cell design. In *Computer Arithmetic, 2009. ARITH 2009. 19th IEEE Symposium on*, pages 207–211, June 2009.

Table 1: Experimental parameters

Type	α	MAX_{column}	W_{MAX}	# shared slots	# spacing rows
Booth (non-Booth)	0.9	$2 \cdot result_{width}$	$1.2 \cdot \max_{r_i \in Row} \sum_{c_k \in r_i} W_C(c_k, r_i)$	2	2 (1)
Type	$Threshold_{MA}$	γ_{own}	γ_{dummy}	γ_{shared}	# PPG row slots
Booth (non-Booth)	NUM_{row}	1	1.25	1.5	2 (1)

Common-Centroid FinFET Placement Considering the Impact of Gate Misalignment[*]

Po-Hsun Wu[1], Mark Po-Hung Lin[2], X. Li[3], and Tsung-Yi Ho[4]

[1]Department of Computer Science and Information Engineering, National Cheng Kung University, Tainan, Taiwan
[2]Department of Electrical Engineering and AIM-HI, National Chung Cheng University, Chiayi, Taiwan
[3]Department of Electrical and Computer Engineering, Carnegie Mellon University, Pittsburgh, PA 15213, USA
[4]Department of Computer Science, National Chiao Tung University, Hsinchu, Taiwan
devilangel@eda.csie.ncku.edu.tw; marklin@ccu.edu.tw; xinli@cmu.edu; tyho@cs.nctu.edu.tw

ABSTRACT

The FinFET technology has been regarded as a better alternative among different device technologies at 22nm node and beyond due to more effective channel control and lower power consumption. However, the gate misalignment problem resulting from process variation based on the FinFET technology becomes even severer compared with the conventional planar CMOS technology. Such misalignment may increase the threshold voltage and decrease the drain current of a single transistor. When applying the FinFET technology to analog circuit design, the variation of drain currents will destroy the current matching among transistors and degrade the circuit performance. In this paper, we present the first FinFET placement technique for analog circuits considering the impact of gate misalignment together with systematic and random mismatch. Experimental results show that the proposed algorithms can obtain an optimized common-centroid FinFET placement with much better current matching.

Categories and Subject Descriptors

B.7.2 [Integrated Circuits]: Design Aids - Placement and Routing; Layout.

General Terms

Algorithms, Design.

Keywords

Analog placement; FinFET; gate misalignment; common centroid.

1. INTRODUCTION

In modern system-on-chip (SoC) design, the voltage of a transistor has been aggressively operated from the traditional super-threshold region to the sub/near-threshold region to effectively reduce power consumption of integrated circuits [4]. As the conventional planar CMOS technology scales down to the $22nm$ node and beyond, it becomes more and more challenging to effectively control short channel effects (SCEs) [1]. As a result, high leakage

current and threshold voltage variation will significantly affect the circuit performance, power dissipation, and reliability of circuits.

To overcome the difficulty of planar CMOS scaling, several new device technologies have been developed as alternatives of the bulk-silicon MOSFET structure for improved reliability. Among those device technologies, the Fin Field Effect Transistor (FinFET) has been regarded as one of the most promising technologies to substitute the bulk-silicon MOSFET for ultimate scaling [2]. As the three-dimensional (3-D) structure of FinFETs can better control the drain-source channel, the leakage current can be significantly reduced due to the alleviation of SCEs. In addition, the threshold voltage variation can also be reduced by near-intrinsic channel doping due to random dopant fluctuations [21]. Owing to the reduction of both leakage current and threshold voltage based on the FinFET technology, it had been suggested to design analog integrated circuits with FinFETs for greater improvement of power, performance, and chip area [25].

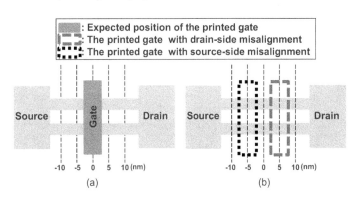

Figure 1: An example of gate misalignment of a FinFET [24]. (a) An ideal FinFET without gate misalignment. (b) A real FinFET with either drain-side or source-side gate misalignment.

Although the FinFET technology can effectively minimize the impact from SCEs and benefit power, performance, and chip area of integrated circuits, some lithography-induced process variation, such as gate misalignment, becomes even more severe. Due to the gate misalignment, the position of the printed gate of a FinFET may be deviated from the expected position after a set of lithography processes, which will increase the threshold voltage and decrease the drain current of the FinFET [5, 23, 24]. Figure 1 illustrates an example of gate misalignment. Ideally, the gate of a FinFET is expected to be located at the center between source and drain, as shown in Figure 1(a). However, the printed gate is usually misaligned due to process variation, as shown in Figure 1(b). Accord-

---

[*]This work was partially supported by the Ministry of Science and Technology of Taiwan, under Grant No's. NSC 102-2220-E-194-006, NSC 102-2221-E-194-065-MY2, and NSC 103-2917-I-006-086.

ing to [24], the misaligned distance can be as large as $5nm$ either to the source side or the drain side for a $10nm$ process technology.

Sarangia *et al.* [23] reported that the threshold voltage of a Fin-FET, V_{th}, is more sensitive with source-side misalignment than with drain-side misalignment. When the gate is misaligned to the drain side of a FinFET by $5nm$ in the worst case, V_{th} will be increased by 0.01V. On the other hand, when the gate is misaligned to the source side a FinFET by $5nm$, V_{th} will be increased by 0.05V. Such increment will significantly degrade the drain current of the FinFET by 40% with a supply voltage of 1V. As most of the analog building blocks, such as current mirrors and differential pairs, are very sensitive to the current variation or current mismatch, it is essential to consider the impact of gate misalignment during the layout design of those building blocks. It should be noted that during IC fabrication, the direction and distance of gate misalignment of different FinFETs on the same chip are usually the same. What designers need to do is to carefully arrange the orientations of all FinFETs within a current mirror or a differential pair such that the ratio of the drain current among different transistors in a current mirror or a differential pair can be perfectly matched [5].

To generate a matched layout of the transistors in a current mirror or a differential pair, all the previous works [13, 14, 16, 18, 19, 26, 27, 28] simply followed the general common-centroid rules, including coincidence, symmetry, dispersion, and compactness [6]. None of them considered the impact of gate misalignment arising from the FinFET technology. Although Long *et. al.* [16] mentioned the chirality condition of transistors within a common-centroid structure, such chirality condition cannot achieve the best current matching with the impact of gate misalignment. Other recent works [7, 8, 9, 10, 11, 12] focus on the optimization of common-centroid capacitor placement, but the capacitors in these works are still not associated with the FinFET technology.

Different from all the previous works, we present the *first* problem formulation in the literature for common-centroid FinFET placement with the consideration of the impact of gate misalignment. Our contributions are summarized as follows:

- We propose a novel common-centroid FinFET placement formulation which simultaneously considers all the conventional common-centroid rules, including coincidence, symmetry, dispersion, and compactness, and the impact of gate misalignment for next generation analog layout design.

- We derive a new quality metric for evaluating the matching quality of drain currents of different transistors in a current mirror on the existence of gate misalignment within a common-centroid FinFET array.

- Based on the quality metric and the spatial correlation model, we present the common-centroid FinFET placement flow and algorithms to optimize the orientations of all sub-transistors and maximize the dispersion degree of a common-centroid FinFET array.

- Our experimental results show that the proposed common-centroid FinFET placement approach can achieve much better current matching among transistors in a current mirror on the existence of gate misalignment while maintaining high dispersion degree.

The rest of this paper is organized as follows: Section 2 introduces the common-centroid FinFET placement of a current mirror, and reviews the spatial correlation model for evaluating the dispersion degree of a common-centroid FinFET placement. Section 3 demonstrates the current mismatch resulting from the impact of gate misalignment. Section 4 details the proposed common-centroid FinFET placement algorithms. Section 5 shows the experimental results, and Section 6 concludes this paper.

2. PRELIMINARIES

A current mirror, as shown in Figure 2(a), is one of the most important basic building blocks in many analog circuit components. It produces a constant replicated current, I_{Copy}, flowing through a scaled transistor regardless of its loading by copying the reference current, I_{Ref}, flowing through another reference transistor. If the size, or the channel width, of the scaled transistor is n times larger than that of the reference transistor, I_{Copy} will be also scaled by a factor of n with respect to I_{Ref}. A current mirror may have several replicated currents with different scaling factors.

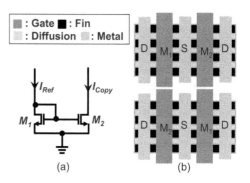

Figure 2: (a) A current mirror, where the size of the transistors, M_1 and M_2, are the same. (b) An example common-centroid FinFET placement of the current mirror in (a), where M_1 and M_2 are split into two sub-transistors with the same number of fins, respectively.

When generating a common-centroid placement of a current mirror, it is required to optimize the matching quality among the reference transistor and all the other scaled transistors for accurate scaling factors. According to [10], the mismatch occurs due to process variation can be divided into two categories: systematic mismatch and random mismatch. To reduce systematic mismatch, each transistor is split into several smaller sub-transistors of the same size, and each sub-transistor should be placed symmetrically with respect to a common center point, as shown in Figure 2(b), where each transistor in Figure 2(a) is divided into two sub-transistors.

On the other hand, random mismatch is mainly related with statistical fluctuations in processing conditions or material properties. Because these fluctuations are in random mechanisms, all sub-transistors of each transistor should be distributed throughout a layout to reduce random mismatch. In other words, all sub-transistors should exhibit the highest degree of dispersion in a common-centroid sub-transistor array [22]. A spatial correlation model [10, 17] had been proposed in the literature to measure the dispersion degree of a common-centroid placement.

Assume that a set of sub-transistors of all transistors are arranged in an $r \times c$ matrix. For any two sub-transistors, st_i and st_j, which are located at the entries in the r_i^{th} row and c_i^{th} column and the r_j^{th} row and c_j^{th} column, their correlation coefficient ρ_{ij} is defined in Equation (1).

$$\rho_{ij} = \rho_u^{D(i,j)}, \tag{1}$$

where $0 < \rho_u < 1$, and $D(i,j) = \sqrt{(r_i - r_j)^2 + (c_i - c_j)^2} \times l$. l depends on process and size of transistors. According to [17], they assume that $\rho_u = 0.9$ and $l = 1$ to observe the relation between correlation and mismatch.

Let L denotes the overall correlation coefficient, or the dispersion degree, of a common-centroid placement. For n transistors, L is the summation of all correlation coefficients of a pair of transistors and is defined as Equation (2).

$$L = \sum_{i=1}^{n-1} \sum_{j=i+1}^{n} R_{ij}, \qquad (2)$$

where R_{ij} is the correlation coefficient of two transistors, t_i and t_j. Assume that t_i consists of n_i sub-transistors and t_j consists of n_j sub-transistors. R_{ij} can be calculated by Equation (3).

$$R_{ij} = \frac{\sum_{a=1}^{n_i} \sum_{b=1}^{n_j} \rho_{ab}}{\sqrt{X \times Y}}, \qquad (3)$$

where $X = n_i + 2 \sum_{a=1}^{n_i-1} \sum_{b=a+1}^{n_i} \rho_{ab}$,
and $Y = n_j + 2 \sum_{a=1}^{n_j-1} \sum_{b=a+1}^{n_j} \rho_{ab}$.

Based on the above mathematical model, we want to generate common-centroid placement with larger L for higher dispersion degree.

3. CURRENT MISMATCH DUE TO GATE MISALIGNMENT

As mentioned in Section 1, the gate misalignment problem based on the FinFET technology may have great impact on drain currents among different transistors in a current mirror. In addition to maximizing the dispersion degree of a common-centroid placement for minimizing random mismatch, it is required to study how to evaluate the matching quality of current ratios resulting from a common-centroid placement with known orientations of all sub-transistors within a common-centroid FinFET array on the existence of gate misalignment.

In this section, we will first derive the quality metric for evaluating the current mismatch of a current mirror on the existence of gate misalignment within a common-centroid FinFET array, and then give a case study to show the importance of determining the orientation of each transistor during common-centroid placement for minimizing the impact of gate misalignment.

3.1 Evaluation of Current Mismatch

We are given a set of k transistors and each transistor, t_i, contains n_i sub-transistors with determined orientations. Due to the impact of gate misalignment, the threshold voltage of the sub-transistors with drain-side misalignment is V_{th}^d and the threshold voltage of the sub-transistors with source-side misalignment is V_{th}^s. The resulting current ratio, $I_{n_1} : I_{n_2} : \ldots : I_{n_k}$, of these transistors with the impact of gate misalignment can be expressed, as given in Equation (4):

$$
\begin{aligned}
I_{n_1} : I_{n_2} : \ldots : I_{n_k} &= n_1 : n_2 : \ldots : n_k = \\
&(n_1^d \times f(V_{th}^d) + n_1^s \times f(V_{th}^s)) : \\
&(n_2^d \times f(V_{th}^d) + n_2^s \times f(V_{th}^s)) : \ldots : \\
&(n_k^d \times f(V_{th}^d) + n_k^s \times f(V_{th}^s)),
\end{aligned}
\qquad (4)
$$

where n_i^d denotes the number of sub-transistors of t_i with drain-side misalignment, and n_i^s denotes the number of sub-transistors of t_i with source-side misalignment (i.e., $n_i = n_i^d + n_i^s$), and $f(x)$ is a function of drain current based on given voltage x.

Based on the multiplication property of equality, we can derive the expression in Equation (5):

$$
\begin{aligned}
&\frac{1}{n_1} \times (n_1^d \times f(V_{th}^d) + n_1^s \times f(V_{th}^s)) = \\
&\frac{1}{n_2} \times (n_2^d \times f(V_{th}^d) + n_2^s \times f(V_{th}^s)) = \ldots = \\
&\frac{1}{n_k} \times (n_k^d \times f(V_{th}^d) + n_k^s \times f(V_{th}^s)).
\end{aligned}
\qquad (5)
$$

After splitting the Equation (5), we can obtain a set of $k \times (k-1)$ equalities, as shown in Equation (6):

$$
\begin{aligned}
&\frac{1}{n_1} \times (n_1^d \times f(V_{th}^d) + n_1^s \times f(V_{th}^s)) = \\
&\quad \frac{1}{n_2} \times (n_2^d \times f(V_{th}^d) + n_2^s \times f(V_{th}^s)), \\
&\frac{1}{n_1} \times (n_1^d \times f(V_{th}^d) + n_1^s \times f(V_{th}^s)) = \\
&\quad \frac{1}{n_3} \times (n_3^d \times f(V_{th}^d) + n_3^s \times f(V_{th}^s)), \ldots, \\
&\frac{1}{n_{k-2}} \times (n_{k-2}^d \times f(V_{th}^d) + n_{k-2}^s \times f(V_{th}^s)) = \\
&\quad \frac{1}{n_k} \times (n_k^d \times f(V_{th}^d) + n_k^s \times f(V_{th}^s)), \\
&\frac{1}{n_{k-1}} \times (n_{k-1}^d \times f(V_{th}^d) + n_{k-1}^s \times f(V_{th}^s)) = \\
&\quad \frac{1}{n_k} \times (n_k^d \times f(V_{th}^d) + n_k^s \times f(V_{th}^s)).
\end{aligned}
\qquad (6)
$$

By substituting $n_i = n_i^d + n_i^s$ into the above equalities and simplifying the equalities, a set of equations can be derived, as shown in Equation (7):

$$
\begin{aligned}
&\frac{|f(V_{th}^s) - f(V_{th}^d)| \times |n_1^d \times n_2^s - n_2^d \times n_1^s|}{n_1 \times n_2} = \epsilon_{1-2}, \\
&\frac{|f(V_{th}^s) - f(V_{th}^d)| \times |n_1^d \times n_3^s - n_3^d \times n_1^s|}{n_1 \times n_3} = \epsilon_{1-3}, \ldots, \\
&\frac{|f(V_{th}^s) - f(V_{th}^d)| \times |n_{k-1}^d \times n_k^s - n_k^d \times n_{k-1}^s|}{n_k \times n_{k-1}} = \epsilon_{(k-1)-(k)},
\end{aligned}
\qquad (7)
$$

where ϵ_{i-j} denotes the current mismatch between two transistors, t_i and t_j, and $0 \le \epsilon_{i-j} \le 1$. If the resulting current ratio equals to the expected current ratio (i.e., no current mismatch), ϵ_{i-j} will be equal to 0.

Consequently, the overall current mismatch among different transistors in a current mirror, ϵ, can be obtained by summing up all ϵ_{i-j}, as seen in Equation (8):

$$
\begin{aligned}
\epsilon &= \epsilon_{1-2} + \epsilon_{1-3} + \ldots + \epsilon_{(k-1)-(k)} \\
&= \sum_{i=1}^{k-1} \sum_{j=i+1}^{k} \epsilon_{i-j} \\
&= \sum_{i=1}^{k-1} \sum_{j=i+1}^{k} \left(\frac{|f(V_{th}^d) - f(V_{th}^s)| \times |n_i^d \times n_j^s - n_j^d \times n_i^s|}{n_i \times n_j} \right).
\end{aligned}
\qquad (8)
$$

3.2 A Case Study

We conduct a case study, as demonstrated in Figure 3, for the following purposes: (1) comparing different common-centroid placements with and without considering the impact of gate misalign-

Table 1: Comparisons of the simulated current ratios, current mismatch (ϵ) and dispersion degree (L) for different common-centroid placements in Figures 3(b)–(d).

Test Case	# of Sub-transistors	Simulated Current Ratio	ϵ	L
Figure 3(b)		$1.00 : 0.93 : 2.07 : 4.00$	0.16	5.6827
Figure 3(c)	2, 2, 4, 8	$1.00 : 0.93 : 1.93 : 4.14$	0.17	5.7338
Figure 3(d)		$1.00 : 1.00 : 2.00 : 4.00$	0.00	5.7459

ment and dispersion, (2) evaluating the resulting current mismatch and dispersion degree of each common-centroid placement, and (3) justifying the correctness of Equation (8) based on circuit simulation.

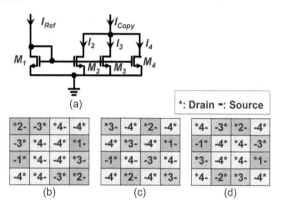

Figure 3: Comparisons of different common-centroid FinFET placements. (a) A current mirror with the idea current ratio, $I_{Ref} : I_2 : I_3 : I_4$ is $1 : 1 : 2 : 4$. (b) A common-centroid FinFET placement for the current mirror in (a) without considering both gate misalignment and dispersion. (c) A common-centroid FinFET placement for the current mirror in (a) with the consideration of dispersion. (d) A common-centroid FinFET placement for the current mirror in (a) with the considerations of both gate misalignment and dispersion.

The current mirror in Figure 3(a) consists of four transistors. The reference current, I_{Ref}, flows through the reference transistor, M_1, and the replicated currents, I_2, I_3, and I_4, are copied from I_{Ref} to other three transistors, M_2, M_3, and M_4 with different scaling factors. The scaling factors, or the number of sub-transistors of M_1, M_2, M_3, and M_4 are 2, 2, 4, and 8, respectively, so the ideal current ratio, $I_{Ref} : I_2 : I_3 : I_4$, is $1 : 1 : 2 : 4$. Figures 3(b)–(d) give three different common-centroid FinFET placements for the current mirror in Figure 3(a) with and without considering gate misalignment and dispersion.

For each common-centroid placement in Figure 3, we evaluate the dispersion degree and current mismatch based on Equations (2) and (8), and observe the resulting drain current of each transistor by performing SPICE simulation based on the BSIM-CMG model [15]. Without loss of generality, we assume that the printed gates of all sub-transistors in each common-centroid placement are misaligned to the right side, so the printed gate of a sub-transistor will have either drain-side or source-side misalignment according to its orientation. As mentioned in Section 1, in the worst case, V_{th} is increased by 0.01V with drain-side misalignment and increased by 0.05V with source-side misalignment based on a $10nm$ FinFET technology with 1V supply voltage, and hence the function, $|f(V_{th}^d - f(V_{th}^s)|$, in Equation (8) is equal to 0.069 (A). We also adopt these settings to adjust the threshold voltage of each sub-transistor for SPICE simulation.

Table 1 reports the resulting simulated current ratio, current mismatch (ϵ), and dispersion degree (L) for each common centroid placement in Figures 3(b)–(d). According to the Table 1, the common-centroid FinFET placement in Figure 3(b) without considering both gate misalignment and dispersion results in worse dispersion degree and current ratio matching. The common-centroid FinFET placement in Figure 3(c), with the only consideration of dispersion and without considering the impact of gate misalignment, results in better dispersion degree, but the worst current ratio matching. The common-centroid FinFET placement in Figure 3(d) with the considerations of both gate misalignment and dispersion results in the best dispersion degree and current ratio matching. Consequently, it is very important to consider both gate misalignment and dispersion to effectively reduce the current mismatch and to maximize the dispersion degree. The current mismatch due to gate misalignment can be eliminated if the orientation of each sub-transistor is carefully arranged.

4. COMMON-CENTROID FINFET PLACEMENT ALGORITHMS

Based on the evaluation metrics of dispersion degree and current mismatch in Equations (2) and (8), in this section, we propose our algorithms to generate an optimized common-centroid FinFET placement with the considerations of the impact of gate misalignment and dispersion. Our approach starts with the determination of sub-transistor orientations, which is detailed in Section 4.1. Based on the determined orientations, an initial common-centroid FinFET placement is then generated by maximizing diffusion sharing and dispersion degree in each row, which is illustrated in Section 4.2. A final placement refinement is done by a shortest path formulation for maximizing the dispersion degree among sub-transistors in different rows, which is described in Section 4.3.

4.1 Determination of Sub-transistor Orientations

As explained in the previous section, to reduce the current mismatch, the orientation of the sub-transistors must be properly determined. We formulate the problem as finding the minimum-weight clique [3] in an undirected graph to simultaneously determine the orientation of all sub-transistors. Each vertex in the graph represents one configuration of the sub-transistor orientations of a transistor, t_i, which has n_i^s sub-transistors with source-side misalignment and n_i^d sub-transistors with drain-side misalignment, respectively. There exists an edge between two vertices if the vertices correspond to two different transistors, t_i and t_j. The edge weight, ϵ_{i-j}, which can be calculated by Equation (7), denotes the current mismatch between t_i and t_j based on the configurations of sub-transistor orientations represented by the vertices. We enumerate all possible configurations (i.e., a k-finger FinFET have $k+1$ configurations whose orientations are the combination of source-side misalignment and drain-side misalignment) of sub-transistor orientations for each transistor in the graph. Figure 4 shows an minimum-weight-clique formulation for a current mirror with three transistors, A, B, and C, where each transistor has 2, 2, and 3 possible configurations of sub-transistor orientations, respectively. By finding the minimum-weight clique in the undirected graph, the best configuration of sub-transistor orientations for each transistor can be determined such that the minimum current mismatch can be achieved.

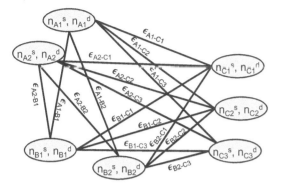

Figure 4: An example minimum-weight-clique formulation for a current mirror with three transistors, A, B, and C, where each transistor has 2, 2, and 3 possible configurations of sub-transistor orientations, respectively.

4.2 Common-Centroid FinFET Placement Considering Dispersion and Diffusion Sharing

After determining the sub-transistor orientations, we want to generate a common-centroid FinFET placement while maintaining the sub-transistor orientations and maximizing the dispersion degree. When generating an m-row common-centroid FinFET placement, we first evenly distribute all sub-transistors of each transistor to the m rows such that the dispersion degree of a common-centroid FinFET placement can be effectively maximized in the subsequent steps. Given a set of n_i sub-transistors of a transistor, t_i, we assign $\frac{n_i}{m}$ sub-transistors into each row. If n_i is less than m, we randomly assign the sub-transistors into different rows while keeping the numbers of sub-transistors in different rows the same.

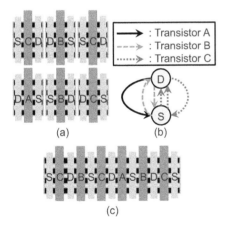

Figure 5: An example of constructing the diffusion graph. (a) A set of sub-transistors with fixed orientation. (b) The corresponding diffusion graph of (a). (c) The generated row placement by searching the diffusion graph in (b).

Once all sub-transistors are assigned into different rows, we should consider the diffusion-sharing for transistors. We construct the dif-

fusion graph of the sub-circuit in each row, and then we find the Euler paths on the diffusion graph [20]. However, the diffusion graph we used in this paper is different from [20]. As described in the previous subsection, we have determined the orientation of all sub-transistors. To avoid degrading the current mismatch, the orientations of all sub-transistors cannot be changed during searching the Euler path. Therefore, the constructed diffusion graph is a directed graph instead of a undirected graph used in [20], where the number of directed edges originated from source node (S) to drain node (D) equals to the number of sub-transistors with drain-side misalignment, and vice versa. For example, given a set of sub-transistors with fixed orientation as shown in Figure 5(a), a directed diffusion graph can be created as given in Figure 5(b). In this example, for simplification, we assume that the source terminal/drain terminal of different sub-transistors can be merged. If the source/drain terminals of some sub-transistors cannot be merged, extra source/drain nodes in the diffusion graph is created.

According to the spatial correlation model in Section 2, to effectively maximize the dispersion degree of a common-centroid FinFET placement, all sub-transistors belonging to the same transistor should be properly separated while the sub-transistors belonging to different transistors should be as close as possible. For clear presentation, we define different kinds of sub-transistors in Definition 1.

DEFINITION 1. *Two sub-transistors are called* **unrelated transistors** *(***related transistors***), if they belong to different transistors, t_i and t_j (the same transistor, t_i).*

To effectively maximize the dispersion degree of a common-centroid FinFET placement, we set a maximum separation (minimum separation) constraint, as defined in Definition 2, for two unrelated transistors (related transistors) to constrain the selection of edge during finding the Euler paths such the dispersion degree can be effectively maximized.

DEFINITION 2. *A* **maximum separation constraint** *(***minimum separation constraint***) is the maximum (minimum) allowable distance between two neighboring unrelated transistors (related transistors) when finding the Euler paths, which is denoted by D_{max_sep} (D_{min_sep}). The distance between two neighboring sub-transistors refers to the number of sub-transistors between the neighboring sub-transistors.*

During searching the Euler path, we only choose the edge satisfying both maximum and minimum separation constraints to properly distribute different sub-transistors while maximizing the dispersion degree. Initially, D_{min_sep} is set to 0 and D_{max_sep} is set to the number of sub-transistors in the row to start the procedure of searching the Euler paths. By iteratively increasing D_{min_sep} and decreasing D_{max_sep} during the procedure of searching the Euler path until an extra diffusion gap is required, the dispersion degree of the resulting row placement can be effectively maximized. After obtaining the Euler paths, the sub-transistors on the same Euler path are merged with diffusion sharing. For example, starting from the source node, as seen in Figure 5(b), an optimized row placement, as shown in Figure 5(c) can be obtained by iteratively searching the Euler paths with decreasing the maximum separation constraint and increasing the minimum separation constraint. In this example, the iteration stops when $D_{max\_sep} = 3$ and $D_{min\_sep} = 1$, which does not incur an extra diffusion gap.

Since the sub-transistors in $(m-i+1)^{th}$ row are symmetrical to that in i^{th} row for a m-row common-centroid FinFET placement, its placement can be derived by placing merged sub-transistors in $(m-i+1)^{th}$ row in the reverse order of that in i^{th} row. By performing the above steps for each row, we can obtain a final common-centroid FinFET placement such that the diffusion sharing and the dispersion degree among all sub-transistors in each row is maximized.

4.3 Dispersion Degree Maximization

After obtaining an initial common-centroid FinFET placement with optimized diffusion sharing and dispersion degree of the sub-transistors in each row, we further maximize the dispersion degree of sub-transistors in different rows by adjusting the relative positions of different sub-transistors among different rows. We first perform placement rotation for each row by iteratively moving the sub-transistor at the end of the row to the beginning of the row. For example, given a row placement, as shown in Figure 6(a), after iteratively moving the sub-transistor at the end of the row to the beginning of the row, we can derive other three row placements, as shown in Figure 6(b)–(d).

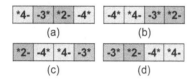

| *4- | -3* | *2- | -4- | | -4* | *4- | -3* | *2- |
(a)   (b)

| *2- | -4* | *4- | -3* | | -3* | *2- | -4* | *4- |
(c)   (d)

Figure 6: An example of placement rotation in a row. (a) An initial row placement. (b)–(d) Three derived row placements after placement rotation.

After performing placement rotation for each row, we need to determine the best placement of each row with the largest dispersion degree of the sub-transistors in different m rows. The simultaneous selection of the best placement of different rows can be formulated as the shortest path (SP) problem. Initially, a source node (S) and a sink node (T) are created, respectively. For a respective row, a group node is created, where a set of element nodes representing the possible row placements are contained in the group node, as demonstrated in Figure 7. Once the group nodes and element nodes are created, we then add a set of directed edges from S to each element node in the group node corresponding to the first row, and a set of directed edges from each element node in the group node corresponding to the last row to T, where the weight of these edges are all zero.

For two adjacent rows, there is a directed edge from an element node in the group node corresponding to the ith row to an element node in the group node corresponding to the $(i+1)^{th}$ row, where $1 \leq i < m$. The weight of each edge is calculated based on Equation (8), which indicates the current mismatch. By finding the shortest path from S to T, the best placement of each row can be determined and the dispersion degree of the whole common-centroid FinFET placement can be further maximized.

Figure 7 shows an example of the SP formulation for a 4-row common-centroid FinFET placement. Each row has three possible row placements after placement rotation. After solving the SP problem, the 2nd, 1st, 3rd, and 2nd placements of the 1st, 2nd, 3rd, and 4th rows are selected to achieve the best common-centroid FinFET placement with the maximum dispersion degree.

5. EXPERIMENTAL RESULTS

We implemented the proposed common-centroid FinFET placement methodology in the MATLAB programming language on a 3.4GHz Windows machine with 16GB memory. To demonstrate the effectiveness of our approach, we created a set of testcases of current mirrors, CM1, CM2, ..., CM8, with different width ratios of the transistors as shown in the second column of Table 2.

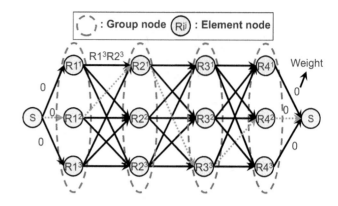

Figure 7: An example of the shortest-path (SP) formulation for a 4-row common-centroid FinFET placement.

We compared our approach with Lin *et al.*'s approach [14], which is known to be the most recent work in the literature handling common-centroid transistor placement with the considerations of diffusion sharing and dispersion. For each common-centroid FinFET placement generated by both approaches, we performed SPICE simulation based on the BSIM-CMG model [15] to obtain the drain current of each transistor in the current mirror. We also evaluate the current mismatch based on Equation (8) and the dispersion degree based on Equation (2).

TABLE 3 show the experimental comparisons of Lin *et al.*'s approach and ours. The results show that our approach results in much better current matching and even better dispersion degree in all test cases. We did not compare the placement area because the area resulting from both approaches for each test case is the same. The runtime based on our approach is longer because we additionally optimize sub-transistor orientations for minimizing the impact of gate misalignment. Consequently, it is very important to consider the impact of gate misalignment and dispersion during common-centroid FinFET placement.

Table 2: Benchmark statistics.

Circuits	# of Sub-transistors
CM1	1, 1
CM2	1, 1, 2
CM3	1, 1, 2, 4
CM4	1, 1, 2, 4, 8
CM5	1, 1, 2, 4, 8, 16
CM6	1, 1, 2, 4, 8, 16, 32
CM7	1, 1, 2, 4, 8, 16, 32, 64
CM8	1, 1, 2, 4, 8, 16, 32, 64, 128

6. CONCLUSIONS

In this paper, we have introduced the impact of gate misalignment to the drain current of different common-centroid FinFET placements. We have proposed a novel common-centroid FinFET placement approach to generate the common-centroid FinFET placements while considering the impact of gate misalignment and dispersion. Experimental results show that the proposed common-centroid FinFET placement methodology can effectively reduce the

Table 3: Comparisons of simulated current ratios, current mismatch (ϵ), and dispersion degree (L), based on Lin _et al._'s and our approaches.

Circuits	Lin _et al._'s approach [14]			Our approach			Comparison (%)	
	Simulated Current Ratio	ϵ / L	Time (s)	Simulated Current Ratio	ϵ / L	Time (s)	ϵ / L	Time
CM1	1 : 0.93	0.07 / 0.90	0.01	1 : 1	0.00 / 0.90	0.01	-100/0.00	0.00
CM2	1 : 1.85	0.14 / 2.73	0.02	1 : 1 : 2	0.00 / 2.73	0.02	-100/0.00	0.00
CM3	1 : 1 : 1.85 : 3.92	0.22 / 5.55	0.03	1 : 1 : 1.93 : 3.86	0.12 / 5.58	0.04	-46.14/0.61	33.10
CM4	1 : 1 : 1.85 : 3.92 : 4.00	0.35 / 9.19	0.04	1 : 1 : 1.93 : 3.93 : 7.63	0.24 / 9.48	0.05	-30.00/3.18	25.13
CM5	1 : 1 : 1.85 : 3.77 : 8.00 : 15.11	0.41 / 13.69	0.07	1 : 1 : 1.93 : 3.86 : 7.78 : 15.48	0.28 / 14.23	0.11	-32.29/3.94	71.45
CM6	1 : 0.93 : 1.92 : 3.85 : 7.48 : 15.11 : 31.26	0.60 / 19.09	0.20	1 : 1 : 1.93 : 3.93 : 7.63 : 15.33 : 30.89	0.45 / 19.91	0.55	-25.72/4.31	180.87
CM7	1 : 1 : 1.85 : 3.85 : 7.92 : 15.63 : 31.11 : 60.95	0.79 / 25.23	0.75	1 : 1 : 1.93 : 3.86 : 7.71 : 15.26 : 30.81 : 61.77	0.48 / 26.36	3.38	-38.83/4.47	351.26
CM8	1 : 0.93 : 1.85 : 3.85 : 7.55 : 15.48 : 31.26 : 61.77 : 122.70	0.93 / 32.13	3.44	1 : 1 : 1.93 : 3.86 : 7.71 : 15.48 : 30.96 : 61.92 : 122.60	0.54 / 33.62	5.10	-41.86/4.63	48.19

impact of gate misalignment to the drain current and maximize the dispersion degree of a common-centroid FinFET placement.

7. REFERENCES

[1] International Technology Roadmap for Semiconductors, 2012.

[2] T. Chiarella, L. Witters, A. Mercha, C. Kerner, M. Rakowski, C. Ortolland, L.-ÃÉ. Ragnarsson, B. Parvais, A. De Keersgieter, S. Kubicek, A. Redolfi, C. Vrancken, S. Brus, A. Lauwers, P. Absil, S. Biesemans, and T. Hoffmann. Benchmarking SOI and bulk FinFET alternatives for PLANAR CMOS scaling succession. _Solid-State Electron._, 54(9):855–860, Sept. 2010.

[3] T. H. Cormen, C. E. Leiserson, R. L. Rivest, and C. Stein. _Introduction to Algorithms._ MIT Press and McGraw-Hill Book Co., 2 edition, 2001.

[4] R. Dreslinski, M. Wiekowski, D. Blaauw, D. Sylvester, and T. Mudge. Near-threshold computing: reclaiming MooreâĂŹs law through energy efficient integrated circuits. In _Proceedings of the IEEE_, pages 253–266, 2010.

[5] M. Fulde, A. Mercha, C. Gustin, B. Parvais, V. Subramanian, K. von Arnim, F. Bauer, K. Schruefer, D. Schmitt-Landsiedel, and G. Knoblinger. Analog design challenges and trade-offs using emerging materials and devices. In _Proceedings of IEEE European Solid State Device Research Conference_, pages 123–126, 2007.

[6] A. Hastings. _The Art of Analog Layout._ Prentice Hall, 2 edition, 2006.

[7] C.-C. Huang, C.-L. Wey, J.-E. Chen, and P.-W. Luo. Optimal common-centroid-based unit capacitor placements for yield enhancement of switched-capacitor circuits. _ACM T DES AUTOMAT EL_, 19(1):7:1–7:13, Dec. 2013.

[8] Y. Li, Z. Zhang, D. Chua, and Y. Lian. Placement for binary-weighted capacitive array in SAR ADC using multiple weighting methods. _IEEE Trans. Comput.-Aided Design Integr. Circuits Syst._, 33(9):1277–1287, Sept. 2014.

[9] C.-W. Lin, C.-L. Lee, J.-M. Lin, and .-J. Chang. Analytical-based approach for capacitor placement with gradient error compensation and device correlation enhancement in analog integrated circuits. In _Proceedings of IEEE/ACM International Conference on Computer-Aided Design_, pages 635–642, 2012.

[10] C.-W. Lin, J.-M. Lin, Y.-C. Chiu, C.-P. Huang, and S.-J. Chang. Mismatch-aware common-centroid placement for arbitrary-ratio capacitor arrays considering dummy capacitors. _IEEE Trans. Comput.-Aided Design Integr. Circuits Syst._, 31(12):1789–1802, Dec. 2012.

[11] M. P.-H. Lin, Y.-T. He, V. W.-H. Hsiao, R.-G. Chang, and S.-Y. Lee. Common-centroid capacitor layout generation considering device matching and parasitic minimization. _IEEE Trans. Comput.-Aided Design Integr. Circuits Syst._, 32(7):991–1002, July 2013.

[12] M. P.-H. Lin, V. W.-H. Hsiao, and C.-Y. Lin. Parasitic-aware sizing and detailed routing for binary-weighted capacitors in charge-scaling DAC. In _Proceedings of ACM/IEEE Design Automation Conference_, pages 1–6, 2014.

[13] M. P.-H. Lin, H. Zhang, M. D. F. Wong, and Y.-W. Chang. Thermal-driven analog placement considering device matching. In _Proceedings of ACM/IEEE Design Automation Conference_, pages 593–598, 2009.

[14] M. P.-H. Lin, H. Zhang, M. D. F. Wong, and Y.-W. Chang. Thermal-driven analog placement considering device matching. _IEEE Trans. Comput.-Aided Design Integr. Circuits Syst._, 30(3):325–336, Mar. 2011.

[15] W. Liu, X. Jin, J. Chen, M-C. Jeng, Z. Liu, Y. Cheng, K. Chen, M. Chan, K. Hui, J. Huang, R. Tu, P.K. Ko, and Chenming Hu. Bsim 3v3.2 mosfet model users' manual. Technical Report UCB/ERL M98/51, EECS Department, University of California, Berkeley, 1998.

[16] D. Long, X. Hong, and S. Dong. Optimal two-dimension common centroid layout generation for MOS transistors unit-circuit. In _Proceedings of the IEEE International Symposium on Circuits and Systems_, pages 2999–3002, 2005.

[17] P.-W. Luo, J.-E. Chen, C.-L. Wey, L.-C. Cheng, J.-J. Chen, and W.-C. Wu. Impact of capacitance correlation on yield enhancement of mixed-signal/analog integrated circuits. _IEEE Trans. Comput.-Aided Design Integr. Circuits Syst._, 27(11):2097–2101, Nov. 2008.

[18] Q. Ma, L. Xiao, Y. C. Tam, and E. F. Y. Young. Simultaneous handling of symmetry, common centroid, and general placement constraints. _IEEE Trans. Comput.-Aided Design Integr. Circuits Syst._, 30(1):85–95, Jan. 2011.

[19] Q. Ma, E. F. Y. Young, and K. P. Pun. Analog placement with common centroid constraints. In _Proceedings of ACM/IEEE International Conference on Computer-Aided Design_, pages 579–585, 2007.

[20] R. Naiknaware and T.S. Fiez. Automated hierarchical CMOS analog circuit stack generation with intramodule connectivity and matching considerations. _IEEE J. Solid-State Circuits_, 34(3):304–303, Mar. 1999.

[21] S. H. Rasouli, K. Endo, and K. Banerjee. Variability analysis of FinFET-based devices and circuits considering electrical confinement and width quantization. In _Proceedings of IEEE/ACM International Conference on Computer-Aided Design_, pages 505–512, 2009.

[22] B. Razavi. _Design of Analog CMOS Integrated Circuits._ McGraw-Hill Book Co., 2000.

[23] S. Sarangia, S. Bhushana, A. Santraa, S. Dubeyb, S. Jitb, and P. K. Tiwari. A rigorous simulation based study of gate misalignment effects in gate engineered double-gate (DG) MOSFETs. _Superlattices Microstruct._, 60(0):263–279, Aug. 2013.

[24] R. Valin, C. Sampedro, M. Aldegunde, A Garcia-Loureiro, N. Seoane, A Godoy, and F. Gamiz. Two-dimensional monte carlo simulation of DGSOI MOSFET misalignment. 59(6):1621–1628, June 2012.

[25] P. Wambacq, B. Verbruggen, K. Scheir, J. Borremans, M. Dehan, D. Linten, V. De Heyn, G. Van der Plas, A Mercha, B. Parvais, C. Gustin, V. Subramanian, N. Collaert, M. Jurczak, and S. Decoutere. The potential of FinFETs for analog and RF circuit applications. _IEEE Trans. Circuits Syst. Regul. Pap._, 54(11):2541–2551, Nov. 2007.

[26] L. Xiao and E. F. Y. Young. Analog placement with common centroid and 1-D symmetry constraints. In _Proceedings of ACM/IEEE Asia and South Pacific Design Automation Conference_, pages 353–360, 2009.

[27] T Yan, S. Nakatake, and T. Nojima. Formulating the empirical strategies in module generation of analog MOS layout. In _Proceedings of the IEEE Computer Society Annual Symposium on Emerging VLSI Technologies and Architectures_, pages 44–49, 2006.

[28] L. Zhang, S. Dong, Y. Ma, and X. Hong. Multi-stage analog placement with various constraints. In _Proceedings of IEEE International Conference on Communications, Circuits and Systems_, pages 881–885, 2010.

Automation of Analog IC Layout – Challenges and Solutions

Juergen Scheible
Robert Bosch Center for Power Electronics
Reutlingen, Germany
juergen.scheible.de@ieee.org

Jens Lienig
Dresden University of Technology
Dresden, Germany
jens@ieee.org

ABSTRACT

Physical analog IC design has not been automated to the same degree as digital IC design. This shortfall is primarily rooted in the analog IC design problem itself, which is considerably more complex even for small problem sizes. Significant progress has been made in analog automation in several R&D target areas in recent years. Constraint engineering and generator-based module approaches are among the innovations that have emerged. Our paper will first present a brief review of the state of the art of analog layout automation. We will then introduce active and open research areas and present two visions – a "continuous layout design flow" and a "bottom-up meets top-down design flow" – which could significantly push analog design automation towards its goal of analog synthesis.

Categories and Subject Descriptors

B7.2[**Integrated Circuits**]: Design Aids

General Terms

Algorithms, Design, Verification.

Keywords

Analog design; layout; constraint engineering; design methodology; physical design; analog layout automation

1. INTRODUCTION

While physical design automation of analog IC design has seen significant improvement over the past decade, it has not advanced at anything like the rate of its digital counterpart. This shortfall is primarily rooted in the analog IC design problem itself, which is very much more complicated even for small problem sizes: it deals with a large number of specific circuit classes; it requires a customized design approach for each circuit class; and analog circuits are very susceptible to noise and process variations. In particular, the work and costs involved in producing analog layout is a serious bottleneck in IC design, despite numerous attempts at automating the process. Furthermore, the analog design problem lacks a suffi-

ISPD'15, March 29–April 1, 2015, Monterey, CA, USA.
ACM 978-1-4503-3399-3/15/03.
http://dx.doi.org/10.1145/2717764.2717781

ciently comprehensive and exact descriptiveness in conventional CAD approaches [1-3].

Advances in analog layout automation have been made however in recent years in many R&D target areas, such as generator-based module approaches [8,9,11-13,16]; and we have witnessed the emergence of constraint engineering to support top-down design styles [2,6,10,18,19,24].

Unfortunately, achievements made thus far fall way short of meeting the needs of advanced analog layout automation. Active new research areas needed to bridge this deficiency gap include

- The next generation of constraint engineering approaches;
- Context-aware layout design;
- Advanced methods for assisted layout design;
- The development of top-down design approaches, tailored for analog circuits, and very powerful bottom-up design procedures, such as module-generator-based and template-based design.

The purpose of this paper is to give an up-to-date overview of analog design automation, highlighting physical design, its specific characteristics and its current research areas from both an industrial and an academic perspective. Specifically, we will first review the analog layout design problem itself and discuss various aspects of today's design flows. We then introduce active and open research areas and finally present two visions, a *continuous layout design flow* and a *bottom-up meets top-down design flow*. It is our hope that these new design paradigms will significantly enhance analog design automation and bring us one step closer to the long-awaited goal of analog synthesis.

2. THE LAYOUT OF ANALOG CIRCUITS

2.1 Sources of Complexity

The majority of today's ICs are mixed signal designs, i.e., they consist of analog and digital circuits (blocks, partitions). Both analog and digital designers claim their design tasks are "highly complex", and in fact both are right, but in a different sense.

Analog designs are characterized by a much richer and more complex set of design constraints that need to be considered simultaneously and which may span several domains (e.g., electrical, electro-thermal, electro-mechanical, technological, geometrical domain). Therefore, in typical mixed signal ICs, the effort needed to design the analog part often matches or even exceeds the effort for the digital part by far. This is true despite the fact that analog modules typically contain only a small number of devices compared to digital ones.

Therefore, when talking about complexity, we prefer to distinguish between (1) *quantitative* complexity, as observed in digital designs, referring mainly to the number of design elements ("More Moore"), and (2) *qualitative* complexity. The latter is rooted in the diversity of the requirements to be considered ("More than Moore"), as found in analog designs.

2.2 Problem Description

Any physical design process can be understood as a course of actions that aim at optimizing a layout with regard to design objectives while meeting *design constraints*. Constraints generally belong to one of the following four categories:

(1) *technological constraints* that enable the fabrication and are derived from technological restrictions,

(2) *functional* (or: *electrical*) *constraints* that ensure the desired electrical behavior of the design,

(3) *geometric* (or: *design-methodical*) *constraints* that are introduced to reduce the overall complexity of the design process, thus facilitating or even enabling the use of design tools, and

(4) *commercial constraints* that arise from chip area or packaging requirements, and the like.

Whereas technological and functional constraints are mandatory, geometric constraints are in principal optional (depending on the layout design tools in use). Any given constraint can be assigned to a *constraint type* that defines the algorithms for its consideration in the design.

A constraint can be *implicit* or *explicit*. An implicit constraint is not clearly expressed: it may be a plain textual note; or it may arise from assumptions intrinsically built into circuit descriptions or layout generators. Explicitly defined constraints are visible and accessible to design algorithms.

Explicitly defined functional constraints are the primary means for describing the designer's intent. On average, each design object (instance, net, path, etc.) in an analog IC design must comply with a larger and more comprehensive set of functional constraints to fulfill its intended function than is the case with digital design. The primary reason for this observation is the higher level of functional abstraction achievable (and offered) in digital designs. This allows for more robust operation requiring fewer constraints to assure the intended function, compared to the quasi low-level mode of operation in analog designs.

In addition, many constraints may still be unknown when the analog design process begins, due to the qualitative complexity described above. This often renders traditional automatic top-level design planning for analog IC designs impossible. It is one of the reasons that highly skilled design engineers are needed to plan and implement top-level design manually.

This constraint-related problem also makes algorithm and tool development for analog IC design much more difficult as the number of specific design algorithms needed may increase with each new constraint type. Considering today's conventional design algorithm development approach (one constraint type and one algorithm to handle it), its weakness becomes all too apparent when faced with new complex constraints affecting multiple design parameters simultaneously and vastly outnumbering simple constraints. This is one of the primary reasons why conventional analog design automation still lags behind its digital counterpart. We will make some suggestions on how to overcome this bottleneck in Sec. 5.

Considering and verifying all mandatory constraints in analog design automatically is currently not possible, mainly for three reasons. First, the constraints are often used implicitly, i.e., based on the designer's experience (expert knowledge), due to the lack of identical tool representation. Second, analog designers are constantly confronted with new requirements that are application specific and cannot be translated "on the fly" into functional constraints. Third, the number of constraints as well as the correlations between them are increasing continuously with more and more contradictory constraints that cannot be met simultaneously. Sections 5.1 and 5.2 suggest new design flows that address this issue of incorporating complex and conflicting constraints.

2.3 Today`s Analog Physical Design

2.3.1 Design Flow: Digital vs. Analog

While the design steps for digital circuits are mostly separated from each other and are performed sequentially, analog design steps typically overlap and several steps are performed simultaneously. For example, device generation, module placement and routing are usually executed simultaneously (Fig. 1).

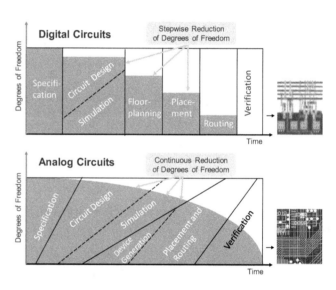

Figure 1. Simplified design flow for digital circuits (above) and for analog IC design (below) where steps typically overlap and are tightly linked. Both flows are also characterized by a reduction in the design freedom throughout the process.

Any design flow is also characterized by a chronological reduction in the *design freedom* which is reduced stepwise in digital designs and continuously reduced in analog circuit designs (see Fig. 1). In general, a feasible solution for a specific design problem is obtained by sequentially removing all degrees of design freedom by sequentially transforming functional representations with many degrees of design freedom into equivalent ones with fewer degrees. For example, one may transform a given functional specification into a netlist, which is subsequently transformed into a floorplan, a placement order, a wired layout and finally into a physical mask layout which contains no further degree of design freedom.

2.3.2 Design Evolution:
Schematic-Driven vs. Constraint-Driven

Despite the advances that have been made over the past 10 years or so, current analog design tools cannot fully cover the entire design process for analog or mixed-signal circuits. They are either restricted to specific parts of the design flow or require the intervention of an expert designer. Thus, most analog circuits are currently designed interactively, in terms of schematics, followed by layout design ("schematic-driven") and several (iterative) verification steps.

Many experts agree that the ultimate goal of fully automated analog design (analog design automation) can only be achieved if the current schematic-driven layout (SDL) methodology first evolves into a *constraint-driven design paradigm* as a necessary intermediate step [4-7]. This is based on the belief that we first need a methodology that enables the inclusion of "expert knowledge" in the form of constraints (i.e., specifying requirements). Secondly, based on this we need the ability to verify them (i.e., checking requirements). Only then (in a third step) will we be able to tackle the task of analog layout synthesis (i.e., fulfilling requirements) in a comprehensive and consistent manner. In other words, "analyzing" and "verifying" capabilities are a precondition for "synthesizing" [4] (Fig. 2).

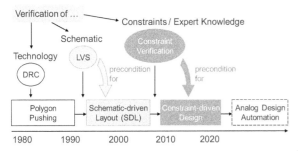

Figure 2. The evolution of analog physical design methodologies towards the goal of a fully automated analog design flow.

2.3.3 Design Styles: Top-Down vs. Bottom-Up

The existing layout design styles can be divided into "top-down" and "bottom-up".[1] A *top-down design* approach addresses the design problem from a high-level strategic perspective. Here it is assumed that each design object itself is (mainly) independent of its design context such as neighboring design elements and context-specific design rules. Thereby, explicitly defined design constraints are often used to enforce the designer's intent. Whenever the requirements of a design problem can be completely described by such a set of constraints, this top-down approach is the preferred design style. Examples are simple standard analog circuits, such as current mirrors, cascodes, and bandgaps.

There are however many cases where this approach doesn't lead to viable solutions. Designs that depend on design context information, such as RF designs, signal sensing designs, power-stage designs and the majority of advanced node designs, are required to embrace a *bottom-up design* style in order to include necessary external information during layout implementation. A bottom-up

design approach addresses the design problem from a more tactical perspective while assuming that multiple design objects are required to cooperate in concert to achieve a desired design result. Today, these designs primarily rely on expert knowledge and manual work while using implicit constraints.

Commercial tool chains address both design styles. For example, while schematic-driven layout (SDL) tools are top-down approaches, the widely used concept of parameterized cells (see Sec. 2.3.4) uses the bottom-up style.

2.3.4 Design Automation:
Optimization vs. Procedures

As already indicated, design automation of analog circuits is currently characterized by two different design styles – top-down vs. bottom-up. Both represent different paths towards fully automated analog design: an optimizing approach vs. a procedural approach. While so-called "optimizers" perform design automation top-down, the procedural approaches ("procedures") generate the final layout with the bottom-up style.

As illustrated in Fig. 3, the top-down approach makes use of optimization-based tools similar to conventional digital flows. Their overall structure is given by an optimization engine generating solution candidates and an evaluation engine selecting the "best" candidates based on design objectives in a loop-wise manner [23]. An optimizer is capable of producing new (genuine) design *solutions*.

In contrast, procedures re-use expert knowledge with the *result* of solutions previously conceived and captured in a procedural description by a human expert, thus imitating the expert's decisions in a straight-forward manner. Typical examples are the widely used concepts of parameterized cells as provided by Cadence's PCells [14] or Synopsys' PyCells [15].

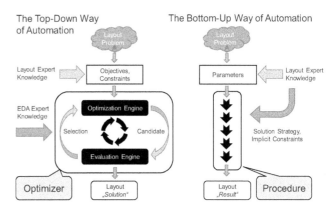

Figure 3. Top-down optimization vs. bottom-up procedures. The top-down approach makes use of optimization-based tools similar to conventional digital flows. The bottom-up way of automation reproduces a design solution previously conceived and captured in a procedural description by a human expert. The grey arrows indicate the data flow of the layout design process. Whereas optimizers are built by EDA experts, procedures are built by layout experts (blue arrows).

Most of the attempts at automatizing analog designs focus on migrating digital design strategies into the analog world. Hence, the above-mentioned top-down "optimizing approach" – successfully applied in digital designs – has been modified and deployed to address analog requirements. However, despite various initia-

---

[1] In this context the term "top-down" is not used in the usual sense of relating to a design hierarchy, but to denote the approach to a design solution.

tives, no viable "analog synthesis solution" has emerged as yet. In our opinion, this is mainly due to the fact that analog "expert knowledge" cannot be translated into formal expressions of high-level, abstract design requirements (constraints). Hence, we believe "bottom-up automation" based on the above mentioned procedural approach is an indispensable element in any future "analog synthesis flow" (see Sec. 5).

3. ACTIVE RESEARCH AREAS

In this section we describe some current research areas in analog design automation. We focus on aspects which we believe to have the largest impact on urgently needed improvements.

3.1 Constraint Engineering

The specification step in a design process defines certain design requirements, such as the operating frequency of a circuit or a symmetry requirement for a current mirror bank. Subsequently, these requirements are expressed as specific functional constraints. These functional constraints then have to be translated into geometric constraints in order to consider them properly in the layout design step. The required operating frequency could result in a maximum RC value, for example, which is subsequently translated into a maximum wire length of a net. The symmetry requirement for a current mirror bank would lead to a (preferably quantified) matching constraint attached to the set of related elements.

The formal constraint representation is a key requirement for a constraint-driven design flow and – as the examples have shown – extra resources are needed to transform constraints automatically from the electrical to the physical domain.

Specifically in the physical domain, the consideration of geometric constraints, such as alignment, placement pattern, orientation, during design implementation has steadily improved over the last couple of years [6,10,19]. Unfortunately, despite this progress, we are still a far cry from advanced analog layout automation. Additionally, methods for checking the completeness of a set of constraints, their self-consistency as well as the verification coverage achieved, need to be developed further to assure IC functionality, reliability, robustness, etc. [5,6].

Other key enabling research areas are improved methods for constraint handling throughout hierarchies (transistor – block – chip levels) [25] and design domains (chip – board – system levels) [26]. Given that design domains today are characterized by different and almost independent tool environments, we are convinced that this requires tool-independent constraint data management to achieve consistency over the above domain levels (*constraint propagation*) [18,24].

3.2 Context-Aware Physical Design

As in digital design, analog circuits face multiple design for manufacturability (DFM) issues due to reduced structural dimensions. Examples are context-dependent design rules, layout-dependent effects and reliability problems caused by electromigration and electrical overstress. These issues can be addressed at the design implementation stage (1) by introducing *context awareness* to the layout generation tools and (2) by using *query functionality* to identify critical structures. For instance, a PCell placing a set of matching transistors might obtain its context (e.g., the distance to the trench) as a parameter value and then act accordingly to assure device matching (e.g., by adjusting the space between the set and the trench in order to avoid local proximity effects).

3.3 Module Generators

It is widely agreed that bottom-up layout design based on module generators is well suited for basic analog circuitry. Module generators, such as the PCells concept, should therefore be upgraded to include "higher-up" design levels.

Basic layout devices are usually available as *device generators* that procedurally create the appropriate device layout based on device parameters. Augmenting this purpose, extensive research is going into the development of higher-level parameterized *module generators*. These are able to generate entire layouts for basic analog circuits by hierarchically employing other generators and creating in-between interconnections [8,11,16].

While this represents a smart way of incorporating valuable expert knowledge in the layout automation, it implies a trade-off between module re-usability and generator development effort. Thus, there are many on-going studies into improving the techniques for creating complex generators that have brought forth powerful new tools for PCell development such as PCell Designer [12,13] and others [8,11]. Accompanying this intention in the layout domain, complex procedural circuit generators have also emerged on the schematic side for circuit generation [17] and testbench generation, along with sophisticated novel approaches for their development [8,9].

The advancement of module generator approaches is essential to achieve the overarching goal of elevating the seamless schematic-driven-layout design flow to higher levels of abstraction (Fig. 4). This move accommodates a designer's way of engineering circuit functions beyond that of basic devices. It also mirrors the level of functional abstraction achieved to date in the digital domain. Providing consistent module generators both in schematic and layout not only yields an immediate increase in design productivity in both domains, but also allows for the consideration of layout parasitics when initially sizing a schematic circuit, thus obviating the need for costly design recursions.

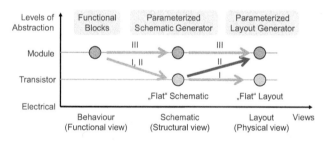

Figure 4. Analog design flows illustrated by design views and compared by levels of abstraction. (I) Today's schematic-driven flow: schematic and layout design at transistor level. (II) Layout module generators (e.g., "module-PCells") improve automation in layout design but encounter a second hierarchical break in the flow. (III) Schematic module generators improve automation in circuit design; additionally they eliminate hierarchical breaks by elevating the entire flow to a higher level of abstraction.

Further works in this context focus on the task of migrating module generators to other semiconductor technologies using templatization [11]. This effort addresses the challenges of incorporating high-level layout generators into the SDL-design flow by means of circuit structure recognition [27], and by combining PCells with other automation approaches. A particular problem with hierarchical module generators is the necessity to verify input parameters for sub-entities of the module at the module level and efficiently pass them down through the hierarchy [13].

3.4 Assisted Physical Design

As previously mentioned, algorithmic approaches aiming for fully automated layout synthesis have not established themselves to any great extent in an industrial setting to date. Nevertheless there is great interest in algorithmic approaches that assist the layout designer in his or her daily routine. Some promising approaches are described below.

Online DRC support is already widely used. Current development efforts are aimed at improving calculation speed and functionality. Selected applications of these solutions focusing on specific design steps lead to guided placement (e.g., [20]) and guided routing (e.g., [21]) with automatic recognition of relevant design rules and constraints.

Closely related to guided placement is interactive compaction. Although online compactors already exist, there is a demand for further improvements because, as mentioned in Sec. 3.2, the distance rules are getting more and more complicated. Improving the state of the art could also lead to sophisticated decompactors which can repair incorrect layout distances or overlaps.

Although powerful routing engines are available in analog layout environments, the use of these "autorouters" is not very popular in the analog community. One reason is that they are incapable of calculating the net segments to comply with current density requirements. On-going developments aim at improving routing algorithms to understand current constraints, thus enabling *current-driven routing* [22].

Assisted physical design leads to a growing number of "assistant functions"; this tendency may worsen user-friendliness. This, in turn, requires improvements in the human-machine (HM) interface in order to keep the resulting increases in tool functionality in sync with tool usability. A solution could be the application of interactive user interfaces commonly found in other domains, such as tablet computers.

4. OPEN RESEARCH ISSUES

Analog design automation is a very vibrant research topic. In our opinion, the open research issues cited below are just a few of the issues that will have the greatest impact on design automation in the future.

Pursuing the goal of constraint-driven design [4,6,7], EDA research has put considerable research effort into constraint engineering over the past decade. Most elementary to this is the question of constraint data management, which basically specifies how constraints can be described in an abstract and uniform manner. Next-generation design flows need to drive this generalization towards the coalescence of circuit, layout and constraint data, such that constraints can be consistently used across various domains, between different applications, and throughout all design steps in the flow [6,18,24,25].

In addition to the generalization of constraints there is a need for further constraint standardization to enhance algorithmic verifiability. This is analogous with design rule checking (DRC), where all rules must be described such that they can be verified with a predefined set of graphical functions. Thus, the constitution of these functions defines the description format of the rules. Equiva-

lently, the description format for constraints is best developed in absolute compliance with the methods that will be available for their verification. For example, [5] contributes a meta-verification environment where constraints are represented with a formal description based on Horn clauses.

Another topic in this context is the universality of constraint-description formats for the purpose of constraint extensibility. In order to promote a resolute usage of constraints in day-to-day design, designers ask for the means to introduce new, proprietary constraint types on their own account. This not only implies sufficiently flexible constraint formalization, as presented in [24], for example, but also the availability of appropriate, user-friendly tool interfaces with intuitive constraint definition capabilities.

Technological and functional constraints associated with layout solutions are verified with automated tools like DRC and LVS, which use graphical layout data. Therefore layout generators, which are in fact software, are verified by checking their layout results with these tools. For parameterized generators (e.g., PCells), a large number of instances are created for this verification purpose, each with a differently permuted set of parameter values. However, an issue arising here is that the full parameter space of a layout generator cannot be explored; hence, the extent of test coverage is unknown. Against the backdrop of the ever-increasing complexity of layout generators[2], there is an urgent need for new approaches to solve this issue. The generator's code could be investigated, for example, as part of a solution. Another approach could be to model the behavior of generators in order to efficiently find critical parameter value sub-spaces.

5. TWO VISIONS OF ANALOG LAYOUT

The aforementioned open research issues are derived from a careful analysis of the state of the art in industrial analog design. In the following, we would like to expand on this analysis by adding two visions. While the first suggestion for a continuous layout design flow could significantly enhance the current interactive layout style (Sec. 5.1), the second vision conflates the advantages of the top-down and bottom-up design styles (Sec. 5.2).

5.1 A "Continuous" Layout Design Flow

5.1.1 A Blind Spot in Today's Analog Layout Flow

As mentioned in Sec. 2.3.1 and illustrated in Fig. 1, the reduction of *degrees of design freedom* in today's interactive analog layout design style seems to occur in a continuous way. Unfortunately however, this observation is *not* an intrinsic capability of this flow, rather it is the result of a vast number of recursions! These recursions result from repeating the same design steps, notably placement, routing and device generation, again and again in order to make necessary modifications. Previously determined parameters, such as the folding characteristic of a transistor or the width of a wiring segment, have to be updated due to constraints which emerge at a later stage in the design process and therefore cannot be foreseen. These modifications account for the greatest amount of time and effort in analog layout work. The efficiency of the widely used interactive layout style can therefore be greatly improved by reducing the number of these recursions.

---

[2] Module generators with up to 50 parameters are in use in the automotive electronics industry of today.

Before outlining our proposal for a solution we need to discuss the root cause of this problem, which is that the *edit commands* used in today's layout editors are simple implementations of *design steps* for the purpose of interactive usage. The problem arising from this similarity can be best explained by looking at how the editor commands affect the degrees of design freedom.

Each design parameter (i.e., the property of a design element such as a wire width) can be regarded as a degree of design freedom. When assigning a value to a design parameter, the related degree of freedom is eliminated. Two typical layout tasks and their corresponding editor commands shall be considered next to exemplify their impact on the degrees of design freedom.

The task "routing a net" is usually performed by drawing paths. A path command simultaneously eliminates all degrees of freedom an electrical connection can have (i.e., layer assignment, x- and y-coordinates, Steiner nodes, wire width, and so on). This is an inevitable consequence of the command itself. The same thing happens when "placing" a device, where all related degrees of freedom (i.e., x-, y-coordinates of absolute position, orientation and, implicitly, all relations to other elements as well) are eliminated with one single mouse click.

The underlying reason for the recursions mentioned above is given by this "design-step-like" behavior of today's layout editors, which only allows combined handling of the degrees of freedom resulting in their *implicit* elimination. Thus a designer is permanently forced to make implicit decisions concerning the degrees of freedom without having the appropriate information at the decision time. This tends to lead to an unavoidable "trial and error mode" resulting in the said recursions.

Despite this deficiency, this aspect of today's layout editors is accepted by the analog-designer community as this behavior feels "natural" and everyone has got accustomed to it. We would like to raise awareness to this "blind spot" and outline a proposal for a new *continuous layout design flow* that addresses this issue.

5.1.2 Direct Access to Degrees of Design Freedom

One solution to this problem would be to sequentially remove only those degrees of design freedom that are fully defined at the current design stage. This would require that functions like place and route are decoupled from their respective *fixed* degrees of freedom such that these degrees can be accessed directly and thus managed independently. Hence, they are now eliminated *continuously* during the layout process, but, each one only when it is necessary and appropriate according to its "definition status". This intrinsic capability of the flow is performed until we reach the physical mask layout which contains no further degree of design freedom. In such a *continuous layout design flow* the layout would be generated first in an almost symbolic manner before getting more and more detailed with actual physical parameters until it finally "crystallizes" to a real physical design.

For example, a net is laid out like this: First the net routing region is assigned, afterwards the preferred routing layer is determined, and at a later stage, when the current flows are known, the appropriate wire widths are assigned to their associated net sections.

5.1.3 Constraint Handling and Re-Use Capabilities

A continuous design flow would also deliver real benefits for constraint handling, and new ways of constraint recognition. With the direct access to the degrees of freedom, a detailed representation of the dependency of the layout-specific degrees of freedom on the functional constraints becomes possible. Hence, constraint

verification and, thus, constraint-driven design (Sec. 2) become viable options.

The re-use of previous layout solutions in current designs is a well-known problem. Some reasons are that (1) the design is too application-specific, (2) even small changes to the circuit may require large changes in layout, (3) a new technology node is used, and (4) the shape of a layout module does not fit. However, careful consideration reveals that the underlying reason is that the layout view does not encompass any remaining degrees of freedom.

This problem can be addressed in an elegant manner in a continuous design flow by re-using a layout at a *symbolic stage* defined as follows: A re-usable design may only contain design freedoms that do not impact constraints; hence, the remaining design freedoms are *unconstrained*. In turn, the absence of constrained degrees of freedom indicates that all constraints are met. In other words, all design decisions induced by fulfilling a constraint are maintained, which is in fact the (long-sought-after) re-use of the implemented expert design knowledge (Fig. 5).

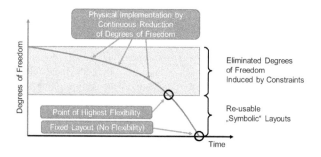

Figure 5. In the proposed design flow, the degrees of design freedom are continuously reduced. Re-using unfinished layout (i.e., symbolic level) supports the adjustment to new project-specific requirements because the symbolic level still contains degrees of design freedom needed for the adjustment.

The remaining degrees of freedom help modify the design for re-use to meet project-specific requirements, thus overcoming the problems mentioned above. The greater the number of remaining degrees of freedom, the higher the remaining flexibility, and thus, the higher the "re-usability". And the more the design problem to be solved resembles the re-use candidate, the fewer the remaining degrees of freedom that are needed for modifications and the less work is involved. This is a major advantage over current re-use methodologies which lack this ability to modify a design to suit a particular project.

5.2 A "Bottom-Up Meets Top-Down" Layout Design Flow

5.2.1 The Dilemma of Top-Down Automation

Analog layout automation has been studied and investigated intensely by EDA for over 30 years now, and almost exclusively in an attempt to solve the analog layout problem with techniques similar to those successfully deployed in the digital domain. These optimization-based "top-down" approaches require an abstraction of the design problem as a formalized mathematical model to which optimizing algorithms can be easily applied. Despite occasional successes, an industry-wide breakthrough of optimization-based approaches in the analog domain has not emerged so far.

This is due to the fact that the solutions generated by optimizers (see Fig. 3) suffer from either a weakness of the optimizing engines (if the modeling is at a low level of abstraction, which is done in an attempt to mirror physical reality as closely as possible) or from the weakness of the modeling approach (done to enable the use of efficient algorithms).

Fig. 6 illustrates this dilemma. The efficiency of optimizing algorithms, often measured in speed and the ability to find a global optimum, is generally inversely proportional to the accuracy of the underlying mathematical model which is derived from the physical world. Designs of high qualitative complexity demand high modeling accuracy while those of high quantitative complexity require high algorithmic efficiency. Hence, only design problems located below the curve can be satisfactorily solved by optimizers.

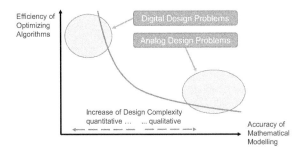

Figure 6. Illustration of the efficiency of optimizing algorithms, which is generally inversely proportional to the accuracy of the underlying mathematical model (blue curve). Analog designs of high qualitative complexity demand high modeling accuracy. Digital designs that are usually of high quantitative complexity require high algorithmic efficiency. Only design problems located below the curve can be satisfactorily solved by optimizers – which thus excludes most analog design problems.

This observation leads to the conclusion that top-down automation alone cannot solve the analog layout problem in its entirety.

5.2.2 Automated Delegation of Design Tasks to Procedures

The obvious approach to overcome the deficiencies in top-down optimization strategies is to complement them with appropriate bottom-up procedures (e.g., PCells). This is based on our observation that bottom-up procedures have the potential to provide the missing features in optimization-based approaches. A common issue with top-down automation is that algorithmically "invented" layout solutions are rejected by expert designers because they do not meet their expectations. Thus, designers prefer to re-use existing, silicon-proof design solutions which usually incorporate years of design knowledge, both from a human expert's personal experience and a company's design group portfolio.

In that regard, a particular strength of bottom-up automation is its intrinsic ability to augment the re-use of singular design solutions (i.e., "copy-paste") to a more sophisticated manner of re-using design solution strategies. This is why novel techniques are needed that enable circuit and layout designers to efficiently translate their design strategies into new automatic procedures. Only then will we see real progress with bottom-up procedures. The closer these techniques match the designer's way of thinking and the better they are adapted to his/her work style, the easier the techniques will capture the valuable expert knowledge, skills and

creativity that are mainly absent from mere top-down automatisms. We believe that these techniques must be more than just novel description languages or tool wizards: They should be "schematic-like" for a circuit designer and "layout-editor-like" for a physical designer.

As mentioned above, analog design automation is severely handicapped by the qualitative complexity of analog constraints (expert knowledge). By restricting top-down optimization to "strategic constraints", such as high level design requirements, and by delegating the remaining constraints to bottom-up procedures, this problem could be eliminated. The ability of bottom-up procedures to make use of implicitly integrated expert knowledge is an ideal supplement to optimization approaches. In this regard the optimizers can be regarded as "senior tools", which delegate special tasks to their "subordinate" procedural tools.

An important step in this direction is the development of context-aware generators and of parameterized module generators as introduced in Secs 3.2 and 3.3. Context-aware generators, in particular, have the potential to play a central role, because their "sensing ability" brings a new kind of intelligence to procedural generators, which is notably helpful when taking over tasks from (senior) tools rather than from human designers.

5.2.3 Bridging the Gaps

Despite the widely held assumption that procedural automation is just a matter of handcraft and thus of little interest to academia, we are convinced that developing the techniques mentioned above is an academically appealing and practically profitable challenge for future EDA research. Conflating the resulting bottom-up procedures with existing top-down automation may be the key to finally achieving the full analog synthesis flow that has been pursued for over three decades now.

To make this vision a reality, we need at least two kinds of "bridges": Firstly, sophisticated techniques need to be developed that enable human design experts to capture easily their design know-how in bottom-up automation procedures. Secondly, technical concepts are needed that intelligently combine the different automation paradigms of optimization-based (top-down) and procedural (bottom-up) approaches.

6. SUMMARY AND OUTLOOK

In this paper we presented an overview of the analog layout design problem and the state of the art of analog layout automation with respect to active and future research areas. Despite enormous research effort in analog design automation, little progress has been made towards a fully automated design flow. We discussed some of the reasons for this, for example, the lack of uniform representation of design constraints in the analog design flow context. Thus, most of the constraints in today's analog designs are still specified and considered manually by expert designers (expert knowledge). Furthermore, analog constraints are often used implicitly (i. e., based on a designer's experience) rather than being explicitly defined – thereby preventing their effective use in design automation.

We also identified key factors relating to the next generation of analog design automation. Among them are techniques that reduce the degree of design freedom gradually rather than abruptly by providing direct and independent access to each degree of design freedom (*continuous layout design flow*). Another vision is to exploit the full potential of both bottom-up and top-down design styles. Conflating both styles to one *bottom-up meets top-down* design *flow* should enable us to incorporate the aforementioned expert knowledge while also addressing high-level design requirements.

While breaking with conventional design approaches, these two proposed paradigm changes could lead to a new class of (higher level) design techniques that brings us one step closer to the goal of full-scale analog design automation.

ACKNOWLEDGEMENTS

We would like to thank Daniel Marolt, Andreas Krinke, Vinko Marolt and Göran Jerke for the numerous fruitful discussions related to the topic of this paper.

REFERENCES

[1] H. Chang, E. Charbon, U. Choudhury, et al. *A Top-down, Constraint-driven Design Methodology for Analog Integrated Circuits*, Springer Verlag, Norwell, MA (1997) ISBN: 978-0792397946.

[2] E. Malavasi, E. Charbon, E. Felt, A. Sangiovanni-Vincentelli, "Automation of IC layout with analog constraints," *IEEE Trans. CAD of Integr. Circuits and Systems*, 15, 8 (1996) 923–941. DOI= http://dx.doi.org/10.1109/43.511572

[3] R. Rutenbar, J. Cohn, "Layout tools for analog ICs and mixed-signal SoCs: a survey," *Proc. Int. Symp. on Physical Design* (ISPD) (2000) 76–83. DOI= http://dx.doi.org/10.1145/332357.332378

[4] J. Scheible, "Constraint-driven Design – Eine Wegskizze zum Designflow der nächsten Generation," *Proc. of ANALOG '08*, 2008, VDE Verlag, Berlin, Offenbach (2008) ISBN 978-3800730834.

[5] J. Freuer, G. Jerke, J. Gerlach, W. Nebel, "On the verification of high-order constraint compliance in IC design," *Proc. Design, Automation and Test in Europe* (DATE) (2008) 26–31. DOI= http://dx.doi.org/10.1109/DATE.2008.4484655

[6] G. Jerke, J. Lienig, J. B. Freuer, "Constraint-driven design methodology: A path to analog design automation," *Analog Layout Synthesis — A Survey of Topological Approaches* H. Graeb (ed.) Springer Verlag, New York, ISBN 978-1-4419-6931-6, (2011) 271-299. DOI= http://dx.doi.org/10.1007/978-1-4419-6932-3_7

[7] G. Jerke, J. Lienig, "Constraint-driven design — the next step towards analog design automation," *Proc. of the Int. Symp. on Physical Design* (ISPD) (2009) 75–82. DOI= http://dx.doi.org/10.1145/1514932.1514952

[8] J. Crossley, et al., "BAG: A designer-oriented integrated framework for the development of AMS circuit generators," *Proc. IEEE/ACM Conference on Computer-Aided Design (ICCAD)* (2013) 74-81. DOI= http://dx.doi.org/10.1109/ICCAD.2013.6691100

[9] D. Marolt, J. Scheible, G. Jerke, "PCDS: A new approach for the development of circuit generators in analog IC design," *Proc. 22nd Austrian Workshop on Microelectronics (Austrochip)* (2014). DOI= http://dx.doi.org/10.1109/Austrochip.2014.6946310

[10] V. Meyer zu Bexten, M. Tristl, G. Jerke, H. Marquardt, D. Medhat, "Physical verification flow for hierarchical analog IC design constraints," *Proc. Asian and South Pacific Design Automation Conference (ASPDAC)* (2015).

[11] IPGen 1Stone, *Internet:* http://ipgenme.de/

[12] G. Jerke, T. Burdick, P. Herth et al. "Visual PCell programming with Cadence PCell Designer," *Proc. CDNLive! EMEA 2013*, Munich, 2013.

[13] G. Jerke, T. Burdick, P. Herth et al. "Hierarchical module design with Cadence PCell Designer," *Proc. CDNLive! EMEA 2015*, Munich, 2015.

[14] R. Arora, A. Ginetti, R. Bishop, G. Lamant, S. Gangwar, "Virtuoso Express Pcells for better interoperability and performance on OA," *Proc. CDNLive! India 2007*. Internet: http://www.cadence.com/rl/Resources/conference_papers/4.5_presentationIndia.pdf

[15] Synopsys, "PyCell Studio," Internet: http://www.synopsys.com/cgi-bin/pycellstudio/req1.cgi

[16] D. Marolt, J. Scheible, G. Jerke, "A practical layout module pcell concept for analog IC design," *Proc. CDNLive! EMEA 2013*, Munich, Germany, paper nr. CUS01. Internet: http://www.cadence.com/cdnlive/eu/2013/pages/proceedingssummary.aspx

[17] P. Bhushan, R. Mitra, "Schematic Pcell implementation in Virtuoso platform," *Proc. of International Cadence Users Group Conference*, Santa Clara, 2004.

[18] A. Krinke, M. Mittag, G. Jerke, J. Lienig, "Extended constraint management for analog and mixed-signal IC design," *Proc. of the 21th European Conf. on Circuit Theory and Design (ECCTD)* (2013) 1-4. DOI= http://dx.doi.org/10.1109/ECCTD.2013.6662319

[19] A. Nassaj, J. Lienig, G. Jerke, "A new methodology for constraint-driven layout design of analog circuits," *Proc. of the 16th IEEE Int. Conference on Electronics, Circuits and Systems* (ICECS) (2009) 996-999. DOI= http://dx.doi.org/10.1109/ICECS.2009.5410838

[20] K. Krishnamoorthy, S. C. Maruvada, F. Balasa, "Topological placement with multiple symmetry groups of devices for analog layout design," *IEEE Int. Symp. Circuits and Systems.* (2007) 2032–2035. DOI= http://dx.doi.org/10.1109/ISCAS.2007.378437

[21] P.-C. Pan, H.M. Chen, Y-K. Cheng, J. Liu, W. Yi Hu, "Configurable analog routing methodology via technology and design constraint unification," *IEEE/ACM Int. Conf. Comput.-Aided Design*, (2012) 620–626.

[22] J. Lienig, "Electromigration and its impact on physical design in future technologies," *Proc. of the ACM 2013 Int. Symposium on Physical Design* (ISPD'13), Stateline, Nevada, (2013) 33-40. DOI= http://dx.doi.org/10.1145/2451916.2451925

[23] R. Rutenbar, "Design automation for analog: The next generation of tool changes," *1st IBM Academic Conf. on Analog Design, Technology, Modelling and Tools* (2006).

[24] A. Krinke, G. Jerke, J. Lienig, "Adaptive data model for efficient constraint handling in AMS IC design," *Proc. of the 20th IEEE Int. Conf. on Electronics, Circuits and Systems* (ICECS), (2013) 285-288. DOI= http://dx.doi.org/10.1109/ICECS.2013.6815410

[25] M. Mittag, A. Krinke, G. Jerke, W. Rosenstiel, "Hierarchical propagation of geometric constraints for full-custom physical design of ICs," *Proc. of Design, Autom. & Test in Europe Conf. (DATE)* (2012) 1471-1474. DOI= http://dx.doi.org/10.1109/DATE.2012.6176599

[26] C. Katzschke, M.-P. Sohn, M. Olbrich, V. Meyer zu Bexten, M. Tristl, E. Barke, "Application of mission profiles to enable cross-domain constraint-driven design," *Proc. of Design, Autom. & Test in Europe Conf. (DATE)*, (2014) 1-6. DOI= http://dx.doi.org/10.7873/DATE.2014.079

[27] D. Marolt, J. Scheible, "The Application of layout module generators upon circuit structure recognition," *Proc. CDNLive! EMEA 2011*, Munich, Germany, paper nr. AC13. Internet: http://www.cadence.com/cdnlive/eu/2011/pages/proceedings.aspx

Q-Learning Based Dynamic Voltage Scaling for Designs with Graceful Degradation

Yu-Guang Chen
Dept.of CS, National Tsing Hua University, HsinChu, Taiwan
andyron75@yahoo.com.tw

Wan-Yu Wen
Dept. of CS, National Tsing Hua University, HsinChu, Taiwan
sapphirefreshman@gmail.com

Tao Wang
Dept.of ECE, Missouri University of Science and Technology, Rolla, Mo, USA
wt2pku@gmail.com

Yiyu Shi
Dept.of ECE, Missouri University of Science and Technology, Rolla, Mo, USA
yshi@mst.edu

Shih-Chieh Chang
Dept.of CS, National Tsing Hua University, HsinChu, Taiwan
scchang@cs.nthu.edu.tw

ABSTRACT

Dynamic voltage scaling (DVS) has been widely used to suppress power consumption in modern designs. The decision of optimal operating voltage at runtime should consider the variations in workload, process as well as environment. As these variations are hard to predict accurately at design time, various reinforcement learning based DVS schemes have been proposed in the literature. However, none of them can be readily applied to designs with graceful degradation, where timing errors are allowed with bounded probability to trade for further power reduction. In this paper, we propose a Q-learning based DVS scheme dedicated to the designs with graceful degradation. We compare it with two deterministic DVS schemes, i.e., a stepping based scheme and a statistical modeling based scheme. Experimental results on three 45nm industrial designs show that the proposed Q-learning based scheme can achieve up to 83.9% and 29.1% power reduction respectively with 0.01 timing error probability bound. To the best of the authors' knowledge, this is the first in-depth work to explore reinforcement learning based DVS schemes for designs with graceful degradation.

Categories and Subject Descriptors

B.8.2 [PERFORMANCE AND RELIABILITY]

General Terms

Performance

Keywords

Graceful Degradation; Dynamic Voltage Scaling; Q-Learning.

ISPD'15, March 29 - April 01, 2015, Monterey, CA, USA
Copyright is held by the owner/author(s). Publication rights licensed to ACM.
ACM 978-1-4503-3399-3/15/03...$15.00
http://dx.doi.org/10.1145/2717764.2717765

1. INTRODUCTION

The relentless scaling of semiconductor technologies has led to a drastic increase in power density, which poses severe threats to modern IC designs. First, excessive heat dissipation can jeopardize the circuit performance, and reliability. Second, for energy constrained applications such as portable devices and remote sensors, the battery capacity cannot grow at par with the power density, resulting in lifetime degradation.

To address these problems, various low power design methodologies have been proposed [19]. Dynamic voltage scaling (DVS) is one of the most popular schemes to efficiently reduce operating power and address timing violation caused by workload, process, and environment variations. DVS schemes dynamically switch operating voltage and/or operating frequency to appropriate levels that can just meet performance requirement [31]. Moreover, the adaptability of DVS can reduce design margins.

The key concept of DVS is to decide the optimal operating voltage for different scenarios that may appear at runtime. Towards this, much literature has provided various DVS schemes on different designs [1][6][13][18][23][26]. Most of them take information that can be monitored at runtime such as current performance, workload, slack, and/or temperature as inputs (states) to decide the optimal operating voltage policy, usually in the format of a state table. The state table is constructed offline based on various statistical analyses. During circuit operation, the optimal voltage will be configured according to the real-time sensor/software feedback and the state table [21]. In this paper, we call such DVS schemes as deterministic. As will be shown in Section III.A, the quality of deterministic DVS schemes heavily depends on the accuracy of the statistical modeling, which is hard for two reasons: many uncertainties are non-Gaussian and tightly correlated [5]; and much information may not be known a priori.

To tackle this issue, a few reinforcement learning based DVS schemes have been proposed [25][14]. Instead of deciding the optimal voltage policy offline through statistical analyses, they dynamically adjust the policy at runtime based on the system performance through various learning procedures. Some initial studies on learning based DVS emerged in [7], with a few improvements or variations later [1][14][16]. However, all these schemes either implicitly or explicitly require a model of the environment, which has a huge impact on the outcome of learning.

Recently, several studies have shown the success on the adoption of Q-learning in circuit designs [6][27][30]. Q-learning is a model-free reinforcement learning technique that can be used to find an optimal action-selection policy for any given (finite) Markov decision process (MDP) [24]. It is proven that Q-learning can find optimal solution for any finite MDP. The authors in [25] proposed a low overhead Q-learning based DVS scheme to explore trade-off between temperature, performance, and energy space.

An implicit assumption of all the existing learning based DVS schemes is that the timing requirements of the system must be guarded (i.e., no timing error allowed). Accordingly, they cannot be directly applied to the designs with graceful degradation [2][17]. As will be shown in Section II.B, by allowing timing errors to occur with a low probability, the chip operating power can be significantly reduced. The errors can be detected and corrected by mechanisms such as DeCoR [11]. For designs with graceful degradation, timing violation should no longer be simply treated as a penalty term. How the limited tolerance of timing error, specified as timing error probability (TEP 1) bound, is incorporated into the learning framework can greatly affect the resulting efficacy and efficiency. Yet it remains an open problem in the literature.

In this paper, we propose a novel Q-learning based DVS scheme dedicated to the designs with graceful degradation. By applying recent advances in on-chip critical path monitor (CPM) [8][20] to obtain timing information, the Q-learning based scheme can yield the optimal operating voltage with a TEP bounded specified by the designer. Similar to the operations of other learning based DVS schemes, it needs a few cycles to learn and adopt a new policy when workload or environment pattern changes abruptly. Under stable patterns, however, the policy converges and remains effective, allowing immediate decision of optimal voltage. We compare the proposed Q-learning based scheme with two deterministic schemes, i.e., a stepping based scheme and a statistical modeling based scheme. Experimental results on three 45nm industrial designs show that the proposed Q-learning based scheme can achieve up to 83.9% and 29.1% power reduction respectively with 0.01 timing error probability bound. To the best of the authors' knowledge, this is the first in-depth work to explore reinforcement learning based DVS schemes for designs with graceful degradation.

The remainder of this paper is organized as follows. Section II describes the basic concepts of critical path monitor and graceful degradation. Section III provides the motivation and problem formulation of this work. Section IV details the Q-learning based scheme. Experimental results are presented in Section V and concluding remarks are given in Section VI.

2. PRELIMINARIES

In this section, we review the concepts of critical path monitor (CPM) and graceful degradation; both are crucial in this work.

2.1 Critical Path Monitor

In 2007, IBM first proposed the concept of CPM [8], which measures critical path delays and reflects the influence of process and temperature variations dynamically. The simple block of a CPM design is shown in Figure 1, which is composed of an edge-triggered pulse generator, a critical path synthesis block, and an edge detector.

The CPM works as follows: In each clock cycle, an edge is launched from the pulse generator into critical path synthesis block which synthesizes critical path delays. After passing through the critical path synthesis block, the edge is latched in the edge detector on the next clock edge and then provides dynamical timing information. As long as the CPMs are placed in multiple locations across the chip, they will respond to process and temperature variations in a similar fashion as the real critical paths and act as effective timing monitors [8][20].

In this paper, our DVS scheme partially relies on the delay measured by the CPMs. It is understood, however, that any other designs that can measure critical timing at runtime can also be used.

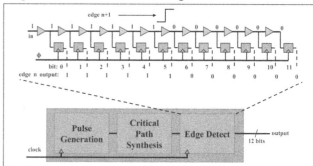

Figure 1. The structure of a Critical Path Monitor (CPM) design.

2.2 Graceful Degradation

It is well known that the impact of workload, process and environment uncertainties on chip performance and reliability is becoming bigger with the scaling of technology. A significant increase in power and area is expected to guarantee success in worst-case conditions, which can be very rare. The concept of graceful degradation, also called Better-than-worst-case (BTWC), is proposed to trade-off reliability with area/power by avoiding unnecessary stick requirement for worst-case operating conditions [1]. Circuits are designed with bounded error probability conditions to reduce power and area, and a reliable checker mechanism is employed to detect and correct any error that occurs [11].

Figure 2 shows the relationship between TEP (obtained from 10K Monte Carlo simulations) and the operating voltage (VDD) for a 45nm industrial design. It is obvious that with only 0.02 TEP, the

---

1 TEP is defined as the probability that the chip slack becomes negative.

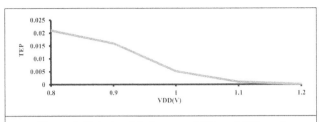

Figure 2. Relationship between TEP and different operating voltages.

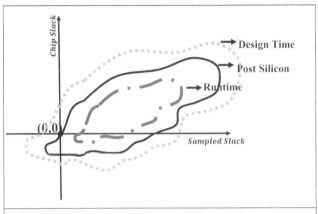

Figure 3. JPDF of chip slacks and sampled slacks at design time, post-silicon and runtime.

operating voltage can be reduced from 1.1V to 0.8V, leading to a 47.1% power reduction.

Most recently, the authors in [5] proposed a deterministic joint probability density function (JPDF) based DVS scheme for graceful degradation in sub-threshold designs. In this research, considering workload, process and temperature variations, the authors model the chip slack and the sampled slack obtained from CPMs as non-Gaussian random variables. The JPDF of both slacks are constructed through Monte Carlo simulations. Then an intuitive approach and an exact approach are delivered for finding the optimal switching thresholds through the JPDF with a given TEP bound. The biggest challenge for this approach is the need to construct the JPDF accurately, as will be detailed in Section III.A.

3. MOTIVATION and PROBLEM FORMULATION

In this section, we will first present the motivation of our work and then formulate the problem to be solved.

3.1 Motivation

As discussed in Section II.B, the deterministic JPDF based DVS scheme [5] for graceful degradation needs to construct the JPDF of the sampled slack and the chip slack through Monte Carlo simulations. At design time, the uncertainties in workload, process and temperature all have to be considered to obtain the JPDF. However, once a chip is fabricated, the process conditions of it are fixed. As such, only the uncertainties in workload and temperature come into play. This will result in a different JPDF. During runtime,

the workload and temperature information can also be revealed (at least partially), so the JPDF will again change. Since the decision of optimal switching thresholds depend on the JPDF, it can be anticipated that the thresholds decided at design time may not work best at runtime. Unfortunately, the workload, process and temperature uncertainties are very hard, if impossible, to rule out at design time.

An illustration of the contour lines of the JPDFs obtained at design time, post-silicon and runtime are shown in Figure 3, all corresponding to the same joint probability density. The contour line gets narrower as fewer uncertainties are involved.

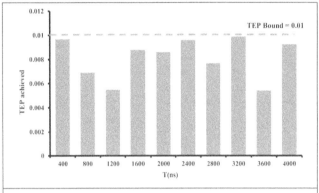

Figure 4. TEP achieved at different timing windows for a specific design (TEP bound = 0.01).

To observe this issue, we apply the deterministic JPDF based DVS scheme to a 45 nm industrial design with TEP bound of 0.01. We use the design-time JPDF, simulated from a given set of workload, process, and temperature distributions, to decide the optimal switching thresholds. We then apply them to a single chip with a particular workload pattern under a constant temperature, all sampled from the given distributions. We record the TEP at a few consecutive timing windows, and the results are shown in Figure 4. From the figure we can see that the bound is not achieved most of the times, leaving space for further power reduction.

Apparently, the only possible way to address this problem is to avoid fixing the switching thresholds offline, which calls for learning based DVS schemes.

3.2 Problem Formulation

Before we formally formulate the problem, it is necessary that we start our discussion by laying the assumptions we make in this paper.

First, only some specific and discrete operating voltages (i.e., operating voltage candidates) are available, which are pre-determined by the designer. Similar assumption is used in [5][31]. The selection of these voltage candidates can of course affect the amount of power reduction that can be achieved, and we will leave this as our future work.

Second, the CPM can only return discrete delay values, and its resolution (maximum reading error) depends on the delay of each buffer. However, in our scheme, we assume the delay reading is always accurate. The impact of the noise introduced will be studied in the experiments.

Third, since we can easily convert delay data from the CPM to slack, for the simplicity of discussion we directly take slack as the output of the CPM. Since the delay data from CPM is discrete, so is the slack.

Fourth, for designs with graceful degradation a TEP bound is required to control the trade-off between the power reduction and the performance loss. It can be set to any reasonable value between 0 and 1 depending on different applications. In addition, the TEP has to be measured over a timing window, within which the circuit keeps track of the number of timing errors. We assume that both the TEP bound and the timing window lengths are given as inputs to the scheme.

Fifth, as the temperature of a chip only changes gradually with a large time constant compared with the period of DVS scaling, we will only consider temperature implicitly in our learning scheme.

Finally, the workload of a circuit tends to exhibit patterns, although such patterns may change over time. This can be caused by loop instructions or limited operation modes/functionalities, as have been shown in [10][29]. It is this property that makes learning based DVS schemes beneficial.

Based on the above assumptions, our problem can be stated as follows:

Formulation 1 (Optimal Operating Voltage Decision Problem) Given (i) a chip with CPM placed, (ii) the voltage candidates for DVS, (iii) a TEP bound and a timing window length for TEP measurement, determine the optimal operating voltages at runtime based on the sampled slack from the CPM so that the operating power is minimized.

4. Q-LEARNING BASED DVS SCHEME

In this section, we first deliver the top view of our proposed scheme. We will then detail the learning procedure based on Q-Learning.

4.1 Framework

In our DVS scheme, a two-dimensional state table will be constructed and kept track of at runtime. Each element in the table is the "score" for the corresponding combination of operating voltage and sampled slack from CPM. Each row corresponds to a particular operating voltage candidate and each column corresponds to a particular reading from the CPM. The size of the table is apparently $M \times N$, where M is the number of voltage candidates and N is the number of possible discrete readings from the CPM. This table is initialized with all zeros.

When the circuit starts to run, at the beginning of each cycle the DVS controller will sample the slack reading s from the CPM. It then looks up the state table and identifies the voltage candidate V with the highest score in the column corresponding to the sampled slack. If two or more voltage candidates have the same score, the lowest one will be selected for maximum power reduction. The controller

will then change the operating voltage to V if it is different from the current voltage.

At the end of the cycle, the controller will update the TEP of the circuit based on the accumulated errors within the timing window of the designer-specified length that ends at the current time. Based on the TEP and the designer-specified TEP bound, the controller then updates the scores in the state table that corresponds to s and v according to some policies.

The same process repeats and with a properly designed score update scheme, it should remain constant converge quickly if the workload pattern does not change significantly. We can easily find that the proposed framework is very similar to that of Q-learning, which will shed light on the decision of score update policies and the convergence of the scheme.

4.2 Q-learning

Q-learning [30] is one of the first algorithms for reinforcement learning [27] specifically designed to maximize long-term rewards. It can be proven that the algorithm can converge with probability one to a close approximation of the action-value function for an arbitrary target policy [28]. It applies to Markov decision problems with unknown costs and transition probabilities.

In the interest of space, we will not elaborate the details of Q-learning algorithms. Interested readers are referred to [27][28] for a complete review of them. Briefly speaking, an agent operates on a set of states among which it needs to decide an optimal one based on some varying conditions. An action is defined as a transition from one state to another that is allowed. Q-learner maintains a Q-table, which stores a value for each state-action pair. In each state, for each action, the Q-value represents the expected pay-off that the agent receives from choosing the given action from that state. The Q-values are updated through reward and penalty policies. The agent then select actions in future states to maximize the expected payoff. Below we will explain the possible mapping from our framework in Section IV.A to Q-learning.

Apparently, the most critical parts in a Q-learning scheme are to define states and actions, and then to construct a Q-table with the corresponding reward and penalty policy based on the actions between states. It is straightforward to define a state as a combination of an operating voltage and a sampled slack. We can then define an action as a voltage transition under the same sampled slack. Note that it is never possible to transit to a state with different sampled slacks. As such, we can directly map the state table mentioned in Section IV.A to a Q-table, and the score to Q-value. The only missing part now is to define the reward and penalty policies.

It should be expected that the reward is associated with the power reduction from voltage scaling. To simplify the discussion, we denote $T_{ik} = (V_i, S_k)$ as the state with operating voltage V_i and sampled slack S_k. Also we donate $A_{ijk} = (T_{ik}, T_{jk})$ as the action of voltage scaling from V_i to V_i with sampled slack S_k. Then an entry of Q-table Q_{ik} contains a Q-value for switching from T_{ik} to state T_{jk}. As such, an intuitive reward for action A_{ijk} can be evaluated as

$$R\left(A_{ijk}\right) = Norm\left(\Delta PR\left(A_{ijk}\right)\right)$$
$$= \left(\frac{V_i{}^2 - V_j{}^2}{V_{max}{}^2 - V_{min}{}^2}\right) \qquad (1)$$

where $\Delta PR\left(A_{ijk}\right)$ is the power reduction from action A_{ijk}, and then applied with a normalization function $Norm$. V_{max} and V_{min} denote the maximum and minimum operating voltage candidates, respectively. The reward is normalized between 0 and 1 so that it is in line with the penalty to be discussed in the following.

The penalty is set to prevent TEP from exceeding the TEP bound. It is related to the relative relationship between TEP and TEP bound. We denote Eb and Ec as the TEP bound and the current TEP, and $P\left(A_{ijk}\right)$ as the penalty of A_{ijk}. We use two different types of penalty functions in this paper, an abrupt one and a linearly graded one. For abrupt penalty a constant and large penalty, which is set to $\sigma R\left(A_{ijk}\right)$, is assigned if Ec exceeds $E_b - \rho$, where ρ is a small positive constant set as a margin and σ is a constant. As the learning process has latency, a too small ρ will cause E_c to exceed E_b. On the other hand, a too large ρ will result in unnecessary loss in power reduction. For linearly graded penalty, we linearly increase the penalty based with the increase of E_c with a constant grading factor (i.e., slope) until it reaches $E_b - \rho$, and then remains constant. With the same TEP bound, σ should be a function of γ, i.e., $\sigma(\gamma)$ In our experiments, we find that setting $\rho = \frac{1}{3}E_b$ works well. Mathematically, the above two penalty functions can be expressed as

$$P\left(A_{ijk}\right) = Norm\left(\begin{cases} \varepsilon, if\ E_c < E_b - \rho \\ \sigma R\left(A_{ijk}\right), if\ E_c \geq E_b - \rho \end{cases}\right) \qquad (2)$$

for abrupt penalty and

$$P\left(A_{ijk}\right) = Norm($$
$$\begin{cases} \varepsilon, if\ E_c < \frac{\varepsilon - \sigma(\gamma)R(A_{ijk})}{\gamma} + (E_b - \rho) \\ -\gamma[(E_b - \rho) - E_c] + \sigma(\gamma)R(A_{ijk}), if\ \frac{\varepsilon - \sigma(\gamma)R(A_{ijk})}{\gamma} + (E_b - \rho) \leq E_c < E_b - \rho \\ \sigma R(A_{ijk}),\ if\ E_c \geq E_b - \rho \end{cases}$$
$$)$$

$$(3)$$

for linearly graded penalty. ε is a small constant, and γ is grading factor. A graphical illustration of the two penalty types is shown in Figure 5. Their performance will be compared in Section V.

Finally, the update policy of Q-values for voltage switching from V_i to V_j with slack S_k can be expressed as

$$Q_{ik} = (1 - \alpha)Q_{ik} + \alpha[R\left(A_{ijk}\right) - P + Q_{jk}] \qquad (4)$$

where α denotes the learning rate, which reflects the learning weight between the original and the new Q-values, which will be studied in Section V. P is defined as

$$P = \begin{cases} 0, if\ S_{k\prime}\ of\ T_{jk\prime} > 0 \\ P\left(A_{ijk}\right), if\ S_{k\prime}\ of\ T_{jk\prime} \leq 0 \end{cases} \qquad (5)$$

where $S_{k\prime}$ is the sampled slack after voltage scaling.

To summarize, we list all the steps of our Q-learning based DVS scheme as follows:

Step 1: When the Q-learning process starts, initialize all the Q-values in the Q-table to 0.

Step 2: Denote the current state as T_{ik}. Find an action A_{ij_0k} with the highest Q_{jk} for all the eligible j's. Switch to V_{j_0}.

Step 3: Evaluate and update TEP. Calculate the corresponding reward $R\left(A_{ijk}\right)$ and penalty $P\left(A_{ijk}\right)$ using (2) and (3). Then update Q_{ik} using (4).

Step 4: Set the current state as $T_{jk\prime}$, and go to Step.2 when the next cycle starts.

Finally, we would like to emphasize that the Q-table will remain constant or converge quickly if the workload pattern does not change significantly, allowing a quick voltage setting and maximum power reduction. This will be validated by our experimental results.

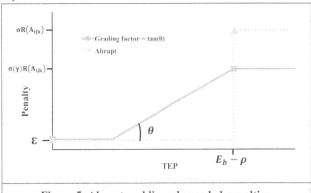

Figure 5. Abrupt and linearly graded penalties.

5. EXPERIMENTAL RESULTS

In this section, experimental results are presented to demonstrate the efficacy of the proposed Q-learning based scheme. We performed our experiments on an 8-core, 2.40GHZ, Intel Xeon E5620 CPU, with 32GB memory, CentOS release 5.9 machine. Three industrial designs with 45nm library are used as our benchmarks. The voltage candidates are set to 0.8V, 0.9V, 1V, 1.1V, 1.2V, and the operating temperature varies from 20oC to 35oC. We obtain the delay and power information by SPICE simulations, and implement our Q-learning based DVS scheme in Matlab. All the sources and variations used in the experiments are simulated based on foundry rules for this technology.

We start our experiments with the impact of the penalty functions on the power reduction. For linearly graded penalty function, we also try different grading factor γ. We use Design one as an example. The learning rate α is set to 0.1; σ is set for each individual γ so that TEP attains but not exceeds the TEP bound. ε is set to 0.05. The results for TEP bounds 0.0001, 0.001, 0.01 and 0.02 are shown in Figure 6. From the figure we can see that the maximum power reduction is always achieved when the grading factor is 1.5 for all the TEP bounds. In the following experiments, we will always apply linearly graded penalty function and set the grading factor to 1.5.

Table 1. Operating power (in μW) and power reduction (in %) for the stepping based, JPDF based, and Q-learning based schemes.

	Stepping Based								JPDF Based								Q-Learning							
TEP bound	0.0001		0.001		0.01		0.02		0.0001		0.001		0.01		0.02		0.0001		0.001		0.01		0.02	
Operating Power	Max.	Avg.	Max.	Avg.	Max.	Avg.	Max.	Avg.	Max.	Avg.	Max.	Avg.	Max.	Avg.	Max.	Avg.	Max.	Avg.	Max.	Avg.	Max.	Avg.	Max.	Avg.
Design One	25100	11100	20700	10200	19346	9107	19300	8810	6481	4016	4575	3070	3519	2362	3250	1707	4680	3540	4570	2390	3250	1707	3250	1707
Power Reduction (%)	--	--	--	--	--	--	--	--	66.4	54.4	76.3	65.2	81.8	73.2	83.2	80.6	81.4	68.1	77.9	76.6	83.2	81.3	83.2	80.6
Design Two	74000	20500	52500	19700	51120	18585	50400	17900	21290	9450	15790	6650	13158	5115	12840	3540	16253	7559	14630	5050	12840	3540	12840	3540
Power Reduction (%)	--	--	--	--	--	--	--	--	57.8	47.2	68.7	62.8	73.9	71.4	74.5	80.2	78.0	63.1	72.1	74.4	74.9	81.0	74.5	80.2
Design Three	155000	60400	129500	57600	124716	54340	122900	53300	40210	26280	26900	17380	20534	13369	20130	10520	28500	20400	26900	13990	20130	10520	20130	10520
Power Reduction (%)	--	--	--	--	--	--	--	--	67.3	50.7	78.1	67.4	83.3	74.9	83.6	80.3	81.6	66.2	79.2	75.7	83.9	80.6	83.6	80.3

We then observe the relationship between the learning rate α and the power reduction in the Q-learning based scheme. We take the same benchmark and follow the same parameter setting as used in Figure 6. The results are depicted in Figure 7. From the figure it is obvious that the maximum power reduction can be achieved with $\alpha = 0.1$ for all the TEP bounds. Therefore, we will always set the learning rate to 0.1 in the following experiments.

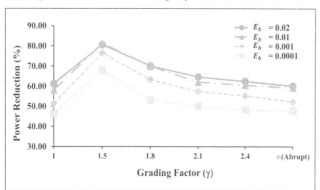

Figure 6. Power reduction versus grading factor (γ) at different TEP bounds.

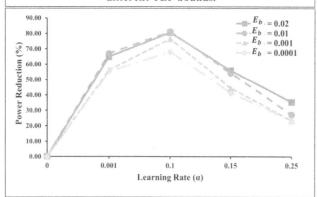

Figure 7. Power reduction versus learning rate (α) at different TEP bounds.

After studying the impact of different settings in Q-learning, we would like to see its performance as compared with other schemes. Since our scheme is the first learning based DVS scheme for designs with graceful degradation, we compare it with two deterministic schemes: a stepping based one modified from [19], which greedily steps down the operating voltage when allowed and

steps up if TEP bound is achieved, and a JPDF based one as discussed in Section II.B.

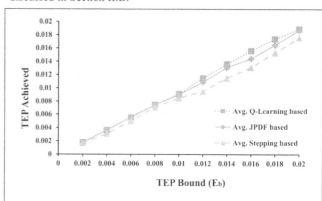

Figure 8. TEP achieved versus different TEP bounds (Eb) on the stepping bases, JPDF based, and Q-learning based schemes.

It is interesting to see the relationship between the TEP bound and the actual TEP achieved. Again, we take the same benchmark and settings as previous. We apply the three schemes and run SPICE simulations with 10K chips of Design One under different workload, process and temperature settings. The results of average TEPs achieved from all the schemes are shown in Figure 8. From the figure we can find that with different TEP bounds, the TEP achieved for all the schemes are below the bound. Moreover, the TEP achieved by the Q-learning based scheme has the smallest gap to the TEP bounds, which implies that it can save more power than the other two.

Table 1 further shows the maximum/average operating power (in μW) of the three designs when applying the three schemes under different TEP bounds. The same settings as previous are used. Column 1 of the table shows benchmark distinction, while column 2 to column 9 show the maximum/average operating power for the stepping based scheme, with the TEP bounds set to 0.0001, 0.001, 0.01, and 0.02, respectively. The results for the JPDF based scheme are shown in column 10 to column 17, while those for the Q-learning based scheme are shown in column 18 to column 25. The power reduction of the JPDF based and Q- learning based schemes with respect to the stepping based one is also shown in the table. We can see that up to 83.9% and 29.1% power reduction can be

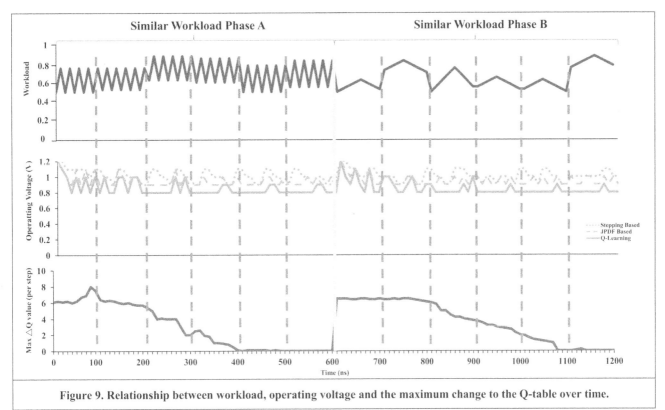

Figure 9. Relationship between workload, operating voltage and the maximum change to the Q-table over time.

achieved by the Q-learning based scheme compared with the stepping based and JPDF based ones, respectively.

To further investigate how the Q-learning based scheme reacts to various workloads, we perform the three schemes on Design One with 0.01 TEP bound. We depict the waveforms of workload and operating voltage as well as the maximum change to the Q-table over time in Figure 9. The waveform on the top is the workload (normalized total operating current), while that in the middle is the operating voltage for the three schemes. The waveform on the bottom records the maximum change to the Q-table (Max ΔQ). Apparently the workload can be divided into two different patterns. For each pattern, the Q-learning based scheme always gives the lowest operating voltage. The waveform on the bottom records the maximum change to the Q- table (Max ΔQ). As expected, the learning process converges after the same pattern repeats a couple

of times, as can be seen from t >400 ns in Phase A and t >1080 ns in Phase B. In these time periods, the Q-learning based scheme can immediately provide the best operating voltage, thus showing the biggest difference compared with the other two schemes.

Finally, we study the influence of the noise, which can be from CPM measurements (due to limited resolution) on the power reduction and the TEP achieved. We inject random noise from 1% to 3% of the average sampled slack to mimic the effect. We use Design One as an example with the same setting as used in Figure 7 and the TEP bound is 0.02. The relationships between the noises injected, the average power reduction, and the TEP achieved for the Q-learning based scheme are shown in Figure 10. From the figure we can observe that both the power reduction and the TEP achieved decrease with the increased noise. However, even with 3% noise, only 16% degradation appears in the average power reduction. This indicates the influence of the noise in our scheme is slight.

6. CONCLUSIONS

In this paper, we have proposed a Q-learning based DVS scheme dedicated to the designs with graceful degradation. Experimental results on three 45nm industrial designs show that compared with the stepping based scheme and the statistical modeling based scheme, both of which are deterministic, the proposed Q-learning based scheme can achieve up to 83.9% and 29.1% power reduction respectively with 0.01 TEP bound. To the best of the authors' knowledge, this is the first in-depth work to explore reinforcement learning based DVS schemes for designs with graceful degradation.

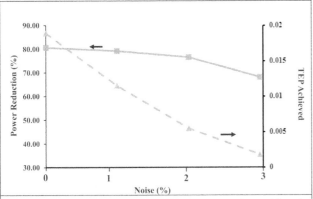

Figure 10. Noise versus power reduction and TEP achieved at the TEP bound 0.02.

7. ACKNOWLEDGEMNET

This work is supported in part by Ministry of Science and Technology of Taiwan under Grant NSC 101-2221-Z-007-119-MY3 and MOST 103-2218-E-007-016, and the University of Missouri Research Board, and NOVATEK Fellowship.

8. REFERENCES

[1] N. AbouGhazaleh, A. Ferreira, C. Rusu, R. Xu, F. Liberato, B. Childers, D. Mosse, R. Melhem, "Integrated CPU and l2 cache voltage scaling using machine learning," in *Proc. of conference on Languages, compilers, and tools for embedded systems*, pp.41-50, 2007.

[2] T. Austin, V. Bertacco, D. Blaauw and T. Mudge, "Oppotunities and Challenges for Better Than Worst-Case Design", in *Proc. Asia and South Pacific Design Automation Conf.*, 2005, pp. 2-7.

[3] T.D. Burd and R.W. Brodersen, "Design issues in dynamic voltage scaling," in *Proc. of the IEEE International Symposium on Low Power Electronics and Design*, pp. 9–14, 2000.

[4] L. N. Chakrapani, B. E. S. Akgul, S. Cheemalavagu, P. Korkmaz, K. V. Palem and B. Seshasayee, "Ultra-Efficient (Embedded) SOC Architectures Based on Probabilistic CMOS (PCMOS) Technology", in *Proc. Design Automation and Test in Europe*, 2006, pp. 1110-1115.

[5] Y.G. Chen, T.Wang, K.Y. Lai, W.Y. Wen, Y. Shi, and S.C. Chang, "Critical path monitor enabled dynamic voltage scaling for graceful degradation in sub-threshold designs," in *Proc. of 51st ACM/EDAC/IEEE Design Automation Conference (DAC)*, pp.1-6, June 2014.

[6] D. Chinnery, "High performance and low power design techniques for ASIC and custom in nanometer technologies," in *Proc. of the 2013 ACM international symposium on International Symposium on Physical Design (ISPD)*, pp.25-32. 2013.

[7] G. Dhiman and T. S. Rosing, "Dynamic voltage frequency scaling for multi-tasking systems using online learning," in *Proc. of 2007 ACM/IEEE International Symposium on Low Power Electronics and Design (ISLPED)*, pp.207-212, Aug. 2007.

[8] A. Drake, R. Senger, H. Deogun, G. Carpenter, S. Ghiasi, T. Nguyen, N. James, M. Floyd, and V. Pokala, "A Distributed Critical-Path Timing Monitor for a 65nm High-Performance Microprocessor," in *IEEE International Solid- State Circuits Conference (ISSCC)*, pp.398–399, 2007.

[9] F. Farahnakian, M. Ebrahimi, M. Daneshtalab, J. Plosila and P. Liljeberg, "Optimized Q-learning Model for Distributing Traffic in On-Chip Networks", in *Proc. IEEE International Conference on Networked Embedded Systems for Every Application (NESEA)*, 2012.

[10] M.E. Gomez, V. Santonja, "Self-similarity in I/O workload: analysis and modeling", in *Proc. of Workload Characterization: Methodology and Case Studies*, pp.97 - 104, 1999.

[11] M.S. Gupta, K.K. Rangan, M.D. Smith, G.Y. Wei, and D. Brooks, "DeCoR: A Delayed Commit and Rollback mechanism for handling inductive noise in processors," in *Proc. of IEEE International Symposium on High Performance Computer Architecture (HPCA)*, pp.381–392, Feb 2008.

[12] R. Hegde and N. R. Shanbhag, "Energy-Efficient Signal Processing via Algorithmic Noise-Tolerance", in *Proc. International Symposium on Low Power Electronics and Design (ISLPED)*, 1999, pp. 30–35.

[13] R. Jejurikar, C. Pereira, and R. Gupta, "Leakage aware dynamic voltage scaling for real-time embedded systems," in *Proc. of 41st annual Design Automation Conference (DAC)*, pp.275-280.

[14] D. C. Juan, D. Marculescu, "Power-aware performance increase via core/uncore reinforcement control for chip-multiprocessors," in *Proc. of 2012 ACM/IEEE International Symposium on Low Power Electronics and Design (ISLPED), pp.97-102, Aug. 2012.*

[15] D. C. Juan, S. Garg, J. Park, D. Marculescu, "Learning the optimal operating point for many-core systems with extended range voltage/frequency scaling," in *Proc. of the Ninth IEEE/ACM/IFIP International Conference on Hardware/Software Codesign and System Synthesis*, pp.01-10.

[16] H. Jung and M. Pedram, "Supervised learning based power management for multicore processors," in *Proc. of IEEE Transactions on Computer-Aided Design of Integrated Circuits and Systems*, Vol. 29, Issue 9, pp.1395-1408, Sep. 2010.

[17] A.B. Kahng, S. Kang, R. Kumar, and J. Sartori, "Slack redistribution for graceful degradation under voltage overscaling," in *Proc. of Asia and South Pacific Design Automation Conference (ASP-DAC)*, pp.852–831, Jan. 2012.

[18] J.T. Kao, M. Miyazaki, A.P. Chandrakasan, "A 175-mV multiply-accumulate unit using an adaptive supply voltage and body bias architecture," in *IEEE Journal of Solid-State Circuits*, Vol.37, pp.1545–1554, 2002.

[19] M. Keating, D. Flynn, R. Aitken, A. Gibbons, and K. Shi, *Low Power Methodology Manual*, For System-on-Chip Design, Springer, 2007.

[20] C.R. Lefurgy, A.J. Drake, M.S. Floyd, M.S. Allen-Ware, B. Brock, J.A. Tierno, and J.B. Carter, "Active management of timing guardband to save energy in POWER7," in *Proc. of the 44th Annual IEEE/ACM International Symposium on Microarchitecture*, pp.1–11, 2011.

[21] J. M. Levine, E. Stott and P. Y. K. Cheung, "Dynamic Voltage & Frequency Scaling with Online Slack Measurement," in *Proc. of ACM/SIGDA international symposuium on Fild-Programmable Gate Arrays*, 2014.

[22] P. Pillai and K. G. Shin, "Real-time dynamic voltage scaling for low-power embedded operating systems," in *Proc. of eighteenth ACM symposium on Operating systems principles*, pp.89-102, 2001.

[23] J. Pouwelse, K. Langendoen, and H. Sips, "Dynamic voltage scaling on a low-power microprocessor," in *Proc. of the 7th annual international conference on Mobile computing and networking*, PP.251-259.

[24] C.A. Rummery and M. Niranjan, "On-Line Q-Learning Using Connectionist System", in *Technical Report CUED/F-INFENG/TR 166*, Cambridge University, Cambridge, UK.

[25] H. Shen, J. Lu and Q. Qiu, "Learning based DVFS for simultaneous temperature, performance and energy management", in *Proc. of 13th International Symposium on Quality Electronic Design (ISQED)*, pp.747-754, March 2012.

[26] T. Simunic, L. Benini, A. Acquaviva, P. Glynn, and G. D. Micheli, "Dynamic voltage scaling and power management for portable systems," in *Proc. of the 38th annual Design Automation Conference*, pp.254-529.

[27] R.S. Sutton and A.G. Barto, "Reinforcement Learning. An Introduction", MIT Press, Cambridge, MA, 2000.

[28] J. N. Tsitsiklis. Asynchronous stochastic approximation and Q-learning. Machine Learning, 16(3):185–202, 1994.

[29] F. Vandeputte and L. Eeckhout, "Finding Stress Patterns in Microprocessor Workloads," in *Proc. of 4th International Conference on High Performance Embedded Architectures and Compilers*, pp.153-167, 2009

[30] C. J. C. H. Watkins and P. Dayan, "Q-Learning", in *Proc. Machine Learning*, pp.279-292, 1992.

[31] L. Yuan and G. Qu, "Analysis of energy reduction on dynamic voltage scaling-enabled systems," in *Proc. of IEEE Transactions on Computer-Aided Design of Integrated Circuits and Systems*, Vol. 24, pp.1827–1837,Dec.200

SVM-Based Routability-Driven Chip-Level Design for Voltage-Aware Pin-Constrained EWOD Chips[*]

Qin Wang[1], Weiran He[1], Hailong Yao[1], Tsung-Yi Ho[2], and Yici Cai[1]

Tsinghua National Laboratory for Information Science and Technology

1. Department of Computer Science & Technology, Tsinghua University   2. National Chiao Tung University

woodylhu@163.com, hewr2010@gmail.com, hailongyao@tsinghua.edu.cn
ho.tsungyi@gmail.com, caiyc@mail.tsinghua.edu.cn

ABSTRACT

The chip-level design problem is critical in pin-constrained electrowetting-on-dielectric (EWOD) biochips, which not only affects the number of control pins and PCB routing layers from the manufacturing cost point of view, but also determines the functional reliability induced by excessive applied voltage. Existing works either greedily minimize the number of control pins with degraded routability, or disregard the differences in driving voltages on the electrodes, where the trapped charge due to excessive applied voltage causes significant reliability issue. This paper presents the first SVM-based classifier for electrode addressing in chip-level design stage, which simultaneously optimizes the number of control pins, routability, as well as reliability. Experimental results on both real-life chips and synthesized benchmarks show that, compared with the state-of-the-art method, the SVM-based electrode addressing method obtains significant improvements in both routability and reliability.

Categories and Subject Descriptors

B.7.2 [**Integrated Circuits**]: Design Aids

General Terms

Algorithm, Performance, Design

Keywords

Digital microfluidic biochips, Electrowetting-on-dielectric, Chip-level design, Electrode addressing, SVM

1. INTRODUCTION

Based on the electrowetting-on-dielectric (EWOD) technology, digital microfluidic biochips (DMFBs) are revolutionizing

[*]The work of H. Yao was supported in part by the National Natural Science Foundation of China (61106104), Doctoral Fund of Ministry of Education of China (20111011328), and Tsinghua University Initiative Scientific Research Program (20121087997). The work of T.-Y. Ho was supported in part by the Taiwan Ministry of Science and Technology under grant no. MOST 102-2221-E-009-194-MY3, 103-2220-E-009-029, and 103-2923-E-009-006-MY3. The work of Y. Cai was supported by the National Natural Science Foundation of China (61274031).

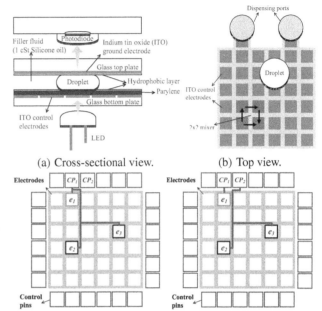

(a) Cross-sectional view.   (b) Top view.

(c) Broadcast addressing.   (d) Avoid trapped charge.

Figure 1: Schematic of a digital microfluidic biochip [2, 5] and broadcast addressing considering the trapped charge problem. (a) Cross-sectional view of the EWOD chip. (b) Top view of the droplet routing layer. (c) Broadcast addressing without considering the trapped charge problem. (d) Better electrode addressing considering trapped charge for improved reliability.

toward miniaturization for the automation of laboratory, i.e., Lab-on-a-Chip (LoC) [1–5]. In such an LoC platform, droplets are manipulated by a 2-D array of electrodes using the electrowetting technology [5]. LoC integrates different biochemical analysis modules, such as dispenser, filter, mixer, separator, detector, etc., into a single small chip, and hence reduces sample/reagent droplets to microliter or even nanoliter scale [6]. Compared with the traditional laboratory procedures, LoC greatly improves the sensitivity, precision, and throughput, as well as reduces the analysis time and sample/reagent consumption [7]. DMFBs have many promising biochemical applications including enzymatic assays, DNA sequencing, cell-based assays, immunoassays, environmental monitoring, and clinical diagnosis [5, 8–15].

Figures 1(a) and (b) show the schematic of a DMFB based on the EWOD technology [5, 8], which controls the wetting behavior of a polarizable or conductive liquid droplet by an electric field, so as to control the movement of the droplet. Figure 1(a) shows the cross-sectional view of the DMFB. By applying a series of voltages to adjacent control electrodes, the droplets between the top and bottom plates will move to different cells as expected.

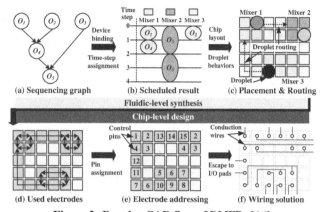

Figure 2: Regular CAD flow of DMFBs [16].

Here, a *cell* refers to the square room of a control electrode. Utilizing this electrowetting technology, automatic biochemical experiments can be performed. Different sample and reagent droplets can be transported to the same cell for mixing and then transported to another cell for detection. Figure 1(b) shows the 2-D electrode array. The dispensing ports are used to input/output the droplets. There are also other modules in DMFB for the biochemical experiments [2], such as mixers of different sizes, the storage cell, etc.

Figure 2 shows the typical CAD flow for DMFBs, which consists of two main stages: (1) fluidic-level synthesis, and (2) chip-level design [16]. In the past decade, there have been noticeable advances in computer-aided design (CAD) methodology for fluidic-level synthesis, including resource binding, operation scheduling, module placement, as well as washing and functional droplet routing [17–35]. Typical objectives are to minimize the assay execution time and the number of used cells, such that the driving electrodes can be minimized for power and interconnection savings. However, chip-level design is also of great importance, which directly determines the PCB (printed circuit board) fabrication cost and reliability. If the wires for electrode addressing fail to be routed, additional PCB routing layers are needed, which will unavoidably increase the fabrication cost. Besides, chip-level design significantly affects DMFB's reliability, which is a critical issue in future portable point-of-care devices. Therefore, this paper mainly addresses the routability and reliability challenges in the chip-level design stage.

To control the movement of the droplets in a programmable way, the underlying electrodes need to be connected to the peripheral electrical pads via *control pins*, where the time-varying voltages are injected by the controller. The controller generates the *actuation sequences* to the control pins for driving the electrodes, which are essentially sequences of voltage values: (1) value "1" for logic high value, (2) value "0" for logic low value, and (3) "X" denotes a don't-care value which can either be "1" or "0" without affecting the designated droplet movements. For correctly controlling the movement of the droplets, each electrode along the droplet paths is assigned an actuation sequence.

The mapping between the electrodes and the control pins is called *electrode addressing*. There are two types of electrode addressing schemes: (1) *direct addressing*, and (2) *broadcast addressing*. DMFBs in early stages use direct addressing, where each electrode is driven by an independent control pin. However, the large chip size nowadays makes direct addressing infeasible due to large number of electrodes and limited number of control pins. The DMFBs with constrained number of control pins are called *pin-constrained DMFBs (PDMFBs)*. Broadcast addressing scheme is required for PDMFBs, where each control pin may drive multiple

electrodes as long as the assay executes correctly [36]. In [36], Xu et al. presented a compatible graph to model the compatibility in actuation sequences between electrodes, and then performed clique partitioning on the graph to find compatible electrodes for sharing the same control pin.

Figures 1(c) shows an example of broadcast addressing. Assume the actuation sequences (s for short) are as follows: (1) $s(e_1) =$ "01X01X110X", (2) $s(e_2) =$ "0X00111X01", (3) $s(e_3) =$ "01X0X111X1". Then the three electrodes are compatible with each other, and a single control pin with actuation sequence "0100111101" can correctly drive all the three electrodes simultaneously. Therefore, control pin CP_1 is introduced to drive the three electrodes (e_1, e_2, and e_3). Manhattan wires are routed for connecting the control pin and the electrodes on the *escape routing layer*, which actually form a Steiner tree. Please note that there is typically a single escape routing layer, and hence wires cannot cross each other. When there are routing failures, an additional routing layer will be required with increased fabrication cost. Therefore, the electrode addressing and routing is critical in reducing the total manufacturing cost.

Another critical issue with broadcast addressing is the trapped charge problem [37–39]. Different electrodes require different driving voltages for different types of droplet operations, e.g., droplet dispensing from input reservoir may require 60-80 volts, while droplet transportation may require at least 10-20 volts [40]. If a control pin drives two electrodes, one for droplet dispensing and one for transportation, then the minimum driving voltage needs to be 60-80 volts for effectively driving both the two electrodes. In that case, charge is trapped in the dielectric insulating layer around the electrode for droplet transportation, due to excessive applied voltage. The trapped charge reduces the electrowetting force, and thus causes wrong assay results and even permanent dielectric breakdown. For applications such as patient health monitoring, clinical diagnosis, etc., reliability is of great importance [41]. The reliability issue is even more critical in future portable point-of-care devices. Therefore, the trapped charge issue should be avoided in broadcast addressing, i.e., electrodes with different preferred driving voltages should avoid sharing the control pin as much as possible. Figures 1(d) shows an example of electrode addressing to avoid the trapped charge problem. Assume electrode e_1 needs to be driven by much higher voltage than e_2 and e_3. Then the three electrodes must not be driven by a single control pin. Therefore, another control pin CP_2 is used to drive e_2 and e_3, and e_1 is driven independently by CP_1. Please note that e_1 may also share the control signal with other electrodes requiring high voltages for minimized number of control pins.

Regarding the reliability issue, Huang et al. presented a method to optimize the maximum actuation time on the electrodes for better reliability [15]. However, high actuation time is not critical and will not cause the reliability issue with appropriate actuation voltage. Yeh et al. presented the first work to address the trapped charge issue with the minimum cost maximum flow formulation [39], which is an extension of [14]. The presented network flow algorithm greedily reduces the number of control pins without appropriate prediction of the routing demand. Thus, routability is a big issue in their presented method. The works in [14] and [43] presented to improve routability by simultaneous electrode addressing and wire routing. And the work in [42] presented to use decluster and re-route approach rather than ripup and re-route to improve the routability, which, to the best of our knowledge, is the latest work for routability enhancement with best reported results. However, the above works do not consider the reliability issue, and thus are not practical for real applications.

This paper presents the first routability- and reliability-driven chip-level design method based on the SVM (Support Vector Machine) classifier. The SVM-based classifiers effectively improve routability in two aspects: (1) routability between the electrodes in each cluster, and (2) routability between the clusters and the control pins. Experimental results show that the presented method obtains 100% routing completion rate for all the benchmarks. Moreover, the reliability issue induced by the trapped charge problem is also effectively addressed. Major contributions of the paper are as follows.

- The first SVM-based electrode addressing methods are presented, which obtain significant routability improvements compared with the state-of-the-art method.
- Our SVM-based electrode addressing methods can effectively improve the reliability induced by the trapped charge problem.
- Effective ripup and rerouting methods are adopted, with declustering functionality, for improving the routability.

The rest of the paper is organized as follows. Section 2 presents the problem formulation. Section 3 presents the overview of the whole chip-level design flow. Section 4 presents the SVM-based electrode addressing method. Section 5 presents the escape routing method along with ripup and rerouting technique. Section 6 presents the experimental results. Finally, conclusion is drawn in Section 7.

2. PROBLEM FORMULATION

This paper addresses two major problems in chip-level design, which need to be considered early in the electrode addressing stage. (1) Routability: Routing is not a trivial task because there is typically a single routing layer. Routing failures will unavoidably increase the number of routing layers, which may dramatically increase the fabrication cost. (2) Reliability (trapped charge problem): When the electrode is driven by excessive applied voltage, due to inappropriate control signal sharing in broadcast addressing, chip malfunction or even dielectric breakdown may occur. Thus, the trapped charge problem must be addressed during electrode addressing.

The routability and reliability driven chip level design problem can be stated as follows.

Given: (1) A set of electrodes $E = \{e_1, e_2, \ldots, e_n\}$, (2) the actuation sequences $S = \{s_1, s_2, \ldots, s_n\}$ corresponding to the electrodes in E, (3) the preferred voltage values $V = \{v_1, v_2, \ldots, v_n\}$ corresponding to the electrodes in E, (4) a threshold voltage value V_{th}, above which the driving voltage tends to cause the trapped charge problem, (5) the maximum number of allowed control pins C_{max} for external controller, and (6) the control layer design rules.

Find: A feasible routing solution from all the electrodes in E to the control pins with minimized total routing cost.

Subject to: (1) Control pin constraint: the number of used control pins must be less or equal to C_{max}, (2) Routing constraint: each electrode is successfully routed to a control pin without any design rules violations, (3) Broadcast-addressing constraint: the actuation sequences of the electrodes within the same cluster must be compatible with each other, and (4) Voltage constraint: for each cluster of electrodes, the driving voltage at the corresponding control pin should not be less than the preferred voltage of any member electrode.

For the trapped charge problem, we use the same measurement model as [39]. In the model, a variable TC_i is introduced to

represent the trapped charge on electrode e_i due to excessive driving voltage. TC_i is defined as

$$TC_i = \begin{cases} v_i^* - max(V_{th}, v_i), & v_i^* \geq V_{th} \\ 0, & v_i^* < V_{th} \end{cases} \quad (1)$$

where v_i^* and v_i represent the actual driving voltage and the preferred voltage for electrode e_i, respectively. TC_i represents the trapped charge on e_i due to excessive driving voltage.

Based on Equation (1), the overall cost of the trapped charge problem, denoted as TC, is computed as

$$TC = max\{TC_i | e_i \in E\} \quad (2)$$

Then the total routing cost considering the trapped charge problem is computed as

$$C = \alpha \cdot |CP| + \beta \cdot WL + \gamma \cdot TC \quad (3)$$

where $|CP|$ represents the total number of used control pins, WL represents the total wire length, and TC is for trapped charge as defined above. Here, α, β and γ are user-defined parameters.

In the above problem formulation, the electrode addressing stage is not included. However, the electrode addressing process is of great importance, which greatly affects all the three optimization items (i.e., $|CP|$, WL, and TC), and hence determines total routing cost. Therefore, this paper mainly focuses on the electrode addressing problem targeting for enhanced routing solution with minimized total cost.

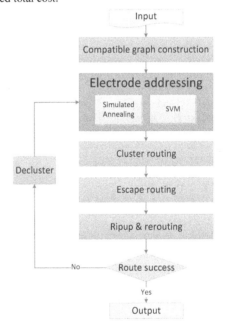

Figure 3: Design flow of our approach.

3. OVERVIEW

Figure 3 presents the overall flow of our chip-level design method. There are five major steps, i.e., compatible graph construction, electrode addressing, cluster routing, escape routing, and ripup and rerouting. First of all, we construct a compatible graph according to the actuation sequences of electrodes. In the following stages, we interconnect the electrodes within each cluster first, and then route them to the control signals by escape routing. When necessary, ripup and rerouting along with declustering are performed to improve the routing completion rate.

We propose the SVM-based strategy in electrode addressing module. The SVM-based strategy randomly generates a set of candidate clustering solutions first. Then a ranking model based on SVM is used to obtain a set of clustering solutions with higher ranking score. Table 1 presents the variables used in the following sections and their meanings.

Table 1: Notations used in our approach.

Notations	Meaning
C_N	Number of clusters in a clustering solution
C_{N_i}	Number of clusters belong to quadrant i
$\lvert E \rvert$	Number of electrodes for a benchmark
C_S	Total area of a chip
P_C	Number of clusters which have only one electrode
T_B	Total bounding box area for the whole chip
T_{B_i}	Bounding box area for quadrant i
T_O	Total area of bounding box overlap for the whole chip
T_{O_i}	Area of bounding box overlap for quadrant i
T_{P_i}	Number of electrodes in cluster i
B_{P_i}	Number of electrodes on the edge of the chip in cluster i
O_{L_i}	Area of bounding box overlap for cluster i
B_{B_i}	Area of bounding box for cluster i
$v_{C_i}^*$	Actual driving voltage for cluster i
v_i	Preferred voltage for electrode e_i
V_{th}	Threshold voltage given by benchmarks

4. SVM-BASED CLUSTERING

There are two key steps in chip-level design flow, i.e., electrode addressing and routing. There is a big design gap between the two steps, which results in many routing iterations and waste of time. What's more, sometimes the electrode addressing cannot find an feasible solution for successful routing even after many iterations. In order to minimize this gap, we propose a routing prediction model to find a electrode addressing solution with enhanced routability and reliability. The core idea of our prediction model is based on SVM (Support Vector Machine). Figure 4 gives the fundamental principle of SVM [44]. In order to discriminate the two classes, we need to find a decision boundary, which should be far away from the data of both classes. Thus, we should maximize the margin m, which is computed as

$$m = \frac{2\gamma}{\lVert W \rVert} \tag{4}$$

where W is the normal vector of decision boundary, and γ is a parameter related to the intercept of the line.

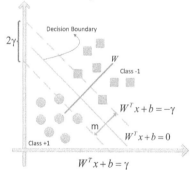

Figure 4: Fundamental principle of SVM [44].

SVM classifies sample vectors by generating a boundary with maximum margin of different classes. The vectors forming boundaries are called support vectors. By transforming the original problem into binary classification, multi-class classification and ranking problems can also be solved by SVM. In this paper, we use the SVM kernel in [45].

Figure 5 presents the flow of the training part in the SVM-based electrode addressing method. In this flow, the clustering module

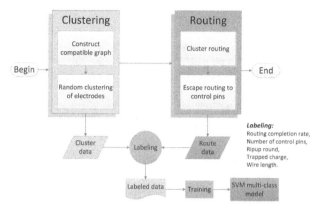

Figure 5: Training flow of our method.

first computes the compatible graph, and then randomly generates a set of clustering solutions according to the compatible graph. Then the routing module computes the routing solutions for each clustering solution, which includes two major steps: (1) cluster routing for each cluster, and (2) escape routing from clusters to control pins. In the clustering module, SVM features for each clustering solution are extracted as *cluster data*. When the *route data* are obtained from the routing module, the *cluster data* are labeled by the *route data*. The labeling data includes wire length, routing congestion rate, number of used control pins, trapped charge etc. We use the Equation (18) to evaluate the quality of a clustering solution. And we classify the quality of electrode clustering solutions into several levels according to the value of *Score*. Then the *training set* is obtained for the SVM classifier. Finally, we learn a SVM multi-class classifier based on the training set using the SVM kernel in [45].

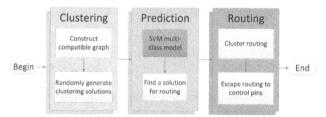

Figure 6: Testing flow of our method.

Figure 6 shows the SVM testing flow. After the training stage, we obtain the SVM-based multi-class classifier, which is used for the prediction module. In clustering module, a certain number of clustering solutions are generated randomly. Then the SVM classifier in prediction module is applied to obtain several clustering solutions with top ranking scores from the set of candidate clustering solutions. In the experiments, around 5 percent of the original candidate solutions are chosen. Finally the routing solution is obtained from the routing module.

Feature extraction is one of the most important step in the approach based on machine learning. In our approach, we obtain the features empirically with experimental calibration. To be brief, we divide these features into three parts: (1) general features, (2) context features, and (3) cluster features. The general features describe a clustering solution in the global view. These features are overall characteristics of a clustering solution. The context features are used to represent the routing resource information and congestion information when the clustering solution is determined. Finally, we extract each cluster's features of a solution to record some detail information includes the proportion of electrodes on the edge of the chip, bounding box area and bounding box overlap area for each cluster.

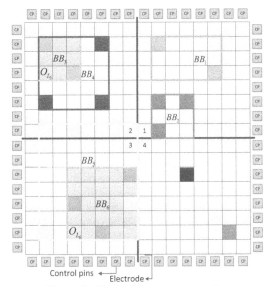

Control pins ← Electrode ←

Figure 7: Context features extraction.

First of all, our approach calculates the bounding box for each cluster. Then we obtain some basic information of a clustering solution: (1) number of clusters, (2) total area of bounding boxes, (3) number of clusters with a single electrode, and (4) total area of bounding box overlaps. Here we use vector $G = (g_1, g_2, g_3, g_4)$ to represent the above general features. In addition, the area of the chip and number of electrodes are used for normalization. In this way, our model can be applied to different types of benchmarks with various. The definitions of the above features are as follows:

$$g_1 = \frac{C_N}{|E|}, \quad g_2 = \frac{C_S}{T_B}, \quad g_3 = \frac{P_C}{C_N}, \quad g_4 = \frac{C_S}{T_O} \quad (5)$$

Figure 7 presents an example of context features extraction. In order to obtain the context features, we propose the following model. We first compute the bounding box for each cluster, then we divide the whole chip into four quadrants. If the center point of a bounding box is in quadrant $i\{i \in (1,2,3,4)\}$, we define that this cluster belongs to this quadrant. Each quadrant collects the information of clusters belong to itself. In Figure 7, where the whole chip is partitioned into 4 quadrants, the electrodes with the same color belong to the same cluster. Then each quadrant calculates the bounding box area and bounding box overlap area separately. In this example, bounding boxes BB_1 and BB_2 belong to quadrant 1. Bounding boxes BB_3, BB_4 and bounding box overlap O_{L_3} belong to quadrant 2. Quadrant 3 has BB_5, BB_6 and bounding box overlap O_{L_6}. Quadrant 4 has two clusters with only one electrode. Finally, the data of the four quadrants forms a context feature vector, denoted as vector $C = (P, R, N)$. It contains three vectors, which are represented as follows:

$$P = (p_1, p_2, p_3, p_4), \quad p_i = \frac{C_{N_i}}{C_N} \quad (6)$$

$$R = (r_1, r_2, r_3, r_4), \quad r_i = \frac{T_{B_i}}{T_B} \quad (7)$$

$$N = (n_1, n_2, n_3, n_4), \quad n_i = \frac{T_{O_i}}{T_O} \quad (8)$$

where p_i denotes the proportion of clusters belonging to quadrant i. r_i records the proportion of bounding box area in quadrant i, and n_i represents the proportion of overlap area in quadrant i.

Cluster features describe a clustering solution in detail, which are helpful to routability especially for escaping routing from cluster to control pins. Vector $D = (B, O, A)$ represents the cluster features, where B, O, and A are defined as follows:

$$B = (b_1, b_2, b_3, b_4, b_5) \quad (9)$$

$$b_i = \frac{(\sum_{j=1}^{C_N} \mathcal{P}(\frac{B_{P_j}}{T_{P_j}}))}{C_N} \quad (10)$$

$$O = (o_1, o_2, o_3, o_4, o_5) \quad (11)$$

$$o_i = \frac{(\sum_{j=1}^{C_N} \mathcal{P}(\frac{O_{L_j}}{C_S}))}{C_N} \quad (12)$$

$$A = (a_1, a_2, a_3, a_4, a_5) \quad (13)$$

$$a_i = \frac{(\sum_{j=1}^{C_N} \mathcal{P}(\frac{B_{B_j}}{C_S}))}{C_N} \quad (14)$$

Here, vectors B, O, A describe the distribution of some variables. And these variables may be related to routability and reliability of a clustering solution. m_i and n_i are user-defined parameters. In Equations (10), (12), and (14), $\mathcal{P}$ is 1 when $\frac{B_{P_j}}{T_{P_j}} \in (m_i, n_i)$, $\frac{O_{L_j}}{C_S} \in (m_i, n_i)$, or $\frac{B_{B_j}}{C_S} \in (m_i, n_i)$. Otherwise, $\mathcal{P}$ is 0. In the experiment, (m_i, n_i) are set to be $(0.1, 0.3)$, $(0.3, 0.5)$, $(0.5, 0.7)$, $(0.7, 0.9)$, $(0.9, 1)$, where i is from 1 to 5. C_S is used for normalization.

To deal with the trapped charge problem, we present a feature V. We extract feature V from the definition of trapped charge problem, which is computed as

$$V = \frac{(\sum_{i=1}^{C_N} \mathcal{P}(v_{C_i}^* > V_{th}))}{C_N} \quad (15)$$

$$v_{C_i}^* = max\{v_j | e_j \in cluster \quad i\} \quad (16)$$

In Equation (15), $\mathcal{P}$ is 1 when $v_{C_i}^* > V_{th}$. Otherwise, $\mathcal{P}$ is 0.

In the routing module, our approach records the routing completion rate F_s before ripup and rerouting, and the total ripup round R_t. These two variables form variable R, which evaluates of routability of electrode addressing solution (see Equation (17)). After the routing stage, we define a function $Score$ to evaluate the quality of a clustering solution as follows:

$$R = \frac{\omega \cdot F_s}{\theta \cdot R_t} \quad (\omega + \theta = 1) \quad (17)$$

$$Score = \frac{R}{\alpha \cdot |CP| + \beta \cdot WL + \gamma \cdot TC} \cdot C_S \cdot E_C \quad (18)$$

The C_S and E_C are also used for normalization. ω and θ are user-defined parameters and their sum is 1. They are coefficients measuring the importance of the two factors. Our approach classify the clustering solutions into n classes according to the value of $Score$. In the experiments, ω is set to be 0.7, θ is set to be 0.3, α, β, γ are all set to be 1. Because we suppose that, final routing completion rate is more important than ripup rounds. But total wire length, number of used control pins, and trapped charge are equally important.

In order to obtain a SVM model with better performance, we design two different feature vectors $feature_1$ and $feature_2$. These two vectors are applied to train different SVM models, i.e., SVM_1 and SVM_2. In Section 6, we compare the experimental results of the two models. The two feature vectors can be represented as follows:

$$feature_1 = (G, C, V), \quad feature_2 = (G, C, V, D) \quad (19)$$

Vector D records the cluster data, i.e., proportion of electrodes on the edge of the chip, bounding box area of a cluster, bounding box overlap area of a cluster which are supposed to contribute to routability classify. And our experimental results show that SVM_2 has better performance than SVM_1 on routability and running time as expected.

Table 3: Results without trapped charge consideration.

Benchmark	First		Final		#Ripup		|CP|		WL		RT (s)	
	ACER	SVM_2	ACER	SVM_2	ACER	SVM_2	ACER	SVM_2	ACER	SVM_2	ACER	SVM_2
amino-acid-1	92.31	80.36	100.00	100.00	1	2	14	13	290	276	0.05	0.32
amino-acid-2	87.50	91.74	100.00	100.00	1	1	17	17	364	324	0.07	0.34
protein-1	29.63	71.67	70.97	100.00	50	6	22	37	698	727	12.60	3.52
protein-2	21.62	52.86	100.00	100.00	8	9	45	45	1135	1108	1.59	1.42
dilution	47.06	40.88	100.00	100.00	16	9	44	42	1395	1341	4.70	3.42
multiplex	83.33	85.24	100.00	100.00	6	6	50	49	1394	1411	0.46	1.29
random-1	66.67	76.30	100.00	100.00	3	2	15	11	453	458	0.21	0.33
random-2	42.11	66.75	85.71	100.00	50	4	18	21	1052	898	9.27	1.42
random-3	34.69	38.13	100.00	100.00	10	9	57	46	1926	2040	7.24	8.94
random-4	35.29	27.25	98.73	100.00	50	16	78	77	3977	4801	37.76	239.64
random-5	29.49	31.87	100.00	100.00	25	13	92	70	9039	6576	331.89	978.17
random-6	26.32	34.79	90.80	100.00	50	13	79	74	8251	8034	383.34	312.43
random-7	19.17	34.41	93.53	100.00	50	28	130	117	12976	11418	2242.50	462.60
Avg.	47.32	56.33	95.21	100.00	25	9	51	48	3304	3032	232.21	154.91

Table 2: Statistics of benchmarks.

Benchmark	Width	Height	Area	#E	Voltage(v)
amino-acid-1	6	8	1008	20	50
amino-acid-2	6	8	1008	24	50
protein-1	13	13	3136	34	50
protein-2	13	13	3136	51	50
dilution	15	15	4096	54	50
multiplex	15	15	4096	59	50
random-1	10	10	1936	20	50
random-2	15	15	4096	30	50
random-3	20	20	7056	60	50
random-4	30	30	15376	90	50
random-5	50	50	41616	100	50
random-6	50	50	41616	100	50
random-7	60	60	59536	150	50

5. ESCAPE ROUTING TO CONTROL PINS

When the clusters are generated using the above presented methods, we start the escape routing process to connect the control pins. The routing process consists of two major stages: (1) routing between the electrodes within each cluster, and (2) escape routing from the clusters to the peripheral control pins. When all the clusters are successfully routed, the number of used control pins is equal to the number of clusters. The objective of the escape routing problem is to compute the routing paths connecting clusters of electrodes with properly selected control pins for minimizing the total wire length with enhanced routing completion rate.

For routing within each cluster of multiple electrodes, the minimum spanning tree (MST) is first constructed to determine the connection topology. When the MST edges are computed, the edges are sequentially routed one by one using the A* search algorithm [46]. Using randomly determined order for MST edges, there are three different cases: (1) routing between two electrodes, (2) routing between a electrode and a partially routed path, and (3) routing between two partially routed paths. For the three different cases, we adopt different routing methods, i.e., point-to-point, point-to-path, and path-to-path A* search algorithms. The modified multi-source multi-target A* search algorithm enhances routability with reduced total wire length. For escape routing from clusters to the control pins, a similar multi-source multi-target A* search algorithm is used, which simultaneously searches from all the routing grids along the paths of the cluster to all the available control pins.

After the escape routing process, the whole routing process will be finished if all the electrodes are successfully routed. However, routing failures may occur in congested designs. As a result, the declustering and rerouting process is needed for improving the routing completion rate. In this stage, the blocking paths are identified and ripped up, which possibly declusters the original cluster into smaller ones. These smaller clusters are then routed to the control pins independently. The declustering and rerouting process is iterated, until all the electrodes are successfully routed or a predefined threshold value is reached.

6. EXPERIMENTAL RESULTS

We have implemented our routability- and reliability-driven chip-level design flow in C++, and tested it on a 2.40GHz 16-core Intel Xeon Linux workstation with 40GB memory. Only a single thread is used for the experiments.

Table 2 shows the details of the benchmarks, where "Width" and "Height" represent the size of a chip, "Area" denotes the actual routing area considering the routing grids between adjacent electrodes. There exist 3 routing grids between the adjacent electrodes. "#E" gives the number of electrodes, and "Voltage" records the threshold voltage for trapped charge issue.

To evaluate the performance of our methods, we compare the results with ACER in [42]. Due to lack of source code and executable of ACER, we implemented ACER by ourselves, and then applied it to our design flow for comparison. Because ACER does not consider the trapped charge problem, we compare the methods with and without the trapped charge consideration, respectively. Table 3 presents the experimental results of the methods without considering trapped charge problem: (1) ACER, (2) SVM_1 in Section 4, and (3) SVM_2 in Section 4. "First" gives the routing completion rate immediately after the first round of routing, without ripup and rerouting. "Final" gives the final routing completion rate after ripup and rerouting with the iteration threshold set to be 50. "#Ripup" represents the number of ripup and rerouting iterations. The above factors are used to evaluate the routability of the electrode clustering solutions. "|CP|" denotes the number of used control pins, "WL" gives the total wire length, and "RT" records the total running time. "|CP|", "WL" and "TC" (related to trapped charge in the following tables) are used to evaluate the reliability and manufacturing cost.

From Table 3, the SVM-based electrode clustering method has better performance on routability and control pin minimization

Table 4: Results with trapped charge consideration.

Benchmark	First		Final		#Ripup		|CP|		WL		TC (v)		RT (s)	
	ACER	SVM_2	ACER	SVM_2	ACER	SVM_2	ACER	SVM_2	ACER	SVM_2	ACER	SVM_2	ACER	SVM_2
amino-acid-1	92.31	83.27	100.00	100.00	1	2	14	12	290	279	19	14	0.05	0.37
amino-acid-2	87.50	90.78	100.00	100.00	1	1	17	16	364	338	18	15	0.07	0.34
protein-1	29.63	75.32	70.97	100.00	50	7	22	37	698	731	19	12	12.60	3.48
protein-2	21.62	49.66	100.00	100.00	8	9	45	44	1135	1118	19	17	1.59	1.32
dilution	47.06	50.58	100.00	100.00	16	9	44	42	1395	1373	19	18	4.70	3.52
multiplex	83.33	84.64	100.00	100.00	6	6	50	47	1394	1440	19	14	0.46	1.34
random-1	66.67	86.20	100.00	100.00	3	3	15	11	453	454	17	13	0.21	0.29
random-2	42.11	69.85	85.71	100.00	50	3	18	20	1052	889	19	11	9.27	1.32
random-3	34.69	48.16	100.00	100.00	10	9	57	45	1926	2072	19	12	7.24	8.74
random-4	35.29	47.25	98.73	100.00	50	17	78	77	3977	4829	18	16	37.76	239.64
random-5	29.49	30.37	100.00	100.00	25	12	92	69	9039	6583	19	17	331.89	982.47
random-6	26.32	39.77	90.80	100.00	50	12	79	75	8251	8054	19	12	383.34	314.13
random-7	19.17	39.21	93.53	100.00	50	27	130	115	12976	11398	19	18	2242.50	463.60
Avg.	47.32	61.16	95.21	100.00	25	9	51	47	3304	3043	19	15	232.21	155.44

than ACER, especially when the size of benchmark is large. Although the SVM-based methods consume more time for certain benchmarks, the overhead is acceptable considering the performance advantage.

Table 4 gives the experimental results considering the trapped charge problem. "TC" denotes the variable defined in Equation (2). From the results, our methods, especially SVM_2, is much better than ACER considering the reliability issue. Moreover, the routability and number of used control pins of SVM_2 are also much better than ACER.

Table 5 shows that SVM_2 obtains better solutions on routability than SVM_1. This is because SVM_2 includes more features than SVM_1, and these features are effective for routability prediction. In addition, SVM_2 is faster than SVM_1 because SVM_2 can obtain clustering solutions with better routability, and this effectively reduces the time consumption in ripup and rerouting.

7. CONCLUSION

We have presented the first SVM-based chip-level design flow considering both routability and reliability enhancements for pin-constrained EWOD biochips. Our flow features effective SVM-based electrode addressing methods. Experimental results show notable improvements over the state-of-the-art method.

8. REFERENCES

[1] F. K. Balagadde, L. You, C. L. Hansen, F. H. Arnold, and S. R. Quake, "Long-Term Monitoring of Bacteria Undergoing Programmed Population Control in a Microchemostat," *Science*, vol. 309, no. 5731, pp. 137-140, 2005.

[2] K. Chakrabarty and F. Su, "Digital Microfluidic Biochips," *CRC Press*, 2006.

[3] G. M. Whitesides, "The Origins and the Future of Microfluidics," *Nature*, vol. 442, no. 7101, pp. 368-373, 2006.

[4] P. Yager, T. Edwards, E. Fu, K. Helton, K. Nelson, M. R. Tam, and B. H. Weigl, "Microfluidic Diagnostic Technologies for Global Public Health," *Nature*, vol. 442, no. 7101, pp. 412-418, 2006.

[5] R. B. Fair, A. Khlystov, T. D. Tailor, V. Ivanov, R. D. Evans, P. B. Griffin, V. "Chemical and Biological Applications of Digital-Microfluidic Devices," *IEEE Design and Test of Computers*, vol. 24, no. 1, pp. 10-24, 2007.

[6] T. Thorsen, S. J. Maerkl, and S. R. Quake, "Microfluidic Large-Scale Integration," *Science*, vol. 298, no. 5593, pp. 580-584, 2002.

[7] D. Mark, S. Haeberle, G. Roth, F. von Stetten, and R. Zengerle, "Microfluidic Lab-on-a-Chip Platforms: Requirements, Characteristics and Applications," *Chemical Society Reviews*, vol. 39, no. 3, pp. 1153-1182, 2010.

[8] M. G. Pollack, A. D. Shenderov, and R. B. Fair, "Electrowetting-Based Actuation of Droplets for Integrated Microfluidics," *Lab Chip*, vol. 2, no. 2, pp. 96-101, 2002.

[9] V. Srinivasan, V. K. Pamula, and R. B. Fair, "An Integrated Digital Microfluidic Lab-on-a-Chip for Clinical Diagnostics on Human Physiological Fluids," *Lab Chip*, pp. 310-315, 2004.

[10] F. SU, K. Chakrabarty, and R. B. Fair, "Microfluidics-Based Biochips: Technology Issues, Implementation Platforms, and Design-Automation Challenges," *IEEE Transactions on Computer-Aided Design of Integrated Circuits and Systems*, vol. 25, no. 2, pp. 211-223, 2006.

[11] I. Barbulovic-Nad, H. Yang, P. S. Park et al., "Digital Microfluidics for Cell-based Assays," *Lab Chip*, pp. 519-526, 2008.

[12] V. Srinivasan, V. K. Pamula, P. Paik et al., "Protein Stamping for MALDI Mass Spectrometry Using an Electrowetting-based Microfluidic Platform," *Optics East*, 2004, vol. 5591, pp. 26-32.

[13] T.-Y. Ho, J. Zeng, and K. Chakrabarty, "Digital Microfluidic Biochips: A Vision for Functional Diversity and More Than Moore," *Prof. IEEE/ACM International Conference on Computer-Aided Design (ICCAD)*, 2010, pp. 578-585.

[14] T.-W. Huang, S.-Y. Yeh, and T.-Y. Ho, "A Network-Flow Based Pin-Count Aware Routing Algorithm for Broadcast-Addressing EWOD Chips," *IEEE Transactions on Computer-Aided Design of Integrated Circuits and Systems*, vol. 30, no. 12, pp. 1786-1799, 2011.

[15] T.-W. Huang, T.-Y. Ho, and K. Chakrabarty, "Reliability-Oriented Broadcast Electrode-Addressing for Pin-Constrained Digital Microfluidic Biochips," *Proc. of IEEE/ACM International Conference on Computer-Aided Design*, 2011, pp. 448-455.

[16] T.-Y. Ho, K. Chakrabarty, and P. Pop, "Digital Microfluidic Biochips: Recent Research and Emerging Challenges," *Proc. of International Conference on Hardware/Software Codesign and System Synthesis (CODES+ISSS)*, 2011, pp. 335-343.

[17] F. SU and K. Chakrabarty, "Architectural-Level Synthesis of Digital Microfluidics-Based Biochips," *IEEE/ACM International Conference on Computer Aided Design*, 2004, pp. 223-228.

[18] D. Grissom, K. O'Neal, B. Preciado, H. Patel, R. Doherty, N. Liao, and P. Brisk, "A Digital Microfluidic Biochip Synthesis Framework," *Proc. of IEEE/IFIP International Conference on VLSI and System-on-Chip (VLSI-SoC)*, 2012, pp. 177-182.

[19] M. Cho and D. Z. Pan, "A High-Performance Droplet Routing Algorithm for Digital Microfluidic Biochips," *IEEE Transactions on Computer-Aided Design of Integrated Circuits and Systems*, vol. 27, no. 10, pp. 1714-1724, 2008.

[20] M. Cho and D. Z. Pan, "A High-Performance Droplet Router for Digital Microfluidic Biochips," *Proc. of International Symposium on Physical Design*, 2008, pp. 200-206.

[21] F. SU and K. Chakrabarty, "Unified High-Level Synthesis and Module Placement for Defect-Tolerant Microfluidic Biochips," *Proc. of Design Automation Conference*, 2005, pp. 825-830.

Table 5: Comparison between SVM_1 and SVM_2.

Benchmark	First		Final		#Ripup		|CP|		WL		TC (v)		RT (s)	
	SVM_1	SVM_2	SVM_1	SVM_2	SVM_1	SVM_2	SVM_1	SVM_2	SVM_1	SVM_2	SVM_1	SVM_2	SVM_1	SVM_2
amino-acid-1	88.31	83.27	100.00	100.00	1	2	12	12	289	279	11	14	0.66	0.37
amino-acid-2	79.85	90.78	100.00	100.00	1	1	17	16	324	338	12	15	0.52	0.34
protein-1	64.80	75.32	100.00	100.00	7	7	33	37	973	731	16	12	0.63	3.48
protein-2	51.48	49.66	100.00	100.00	9	9	42	44	1190	1118	19	17	1.34	1.32
dilution	34.54	50.58	100.00	100.00	9	9	41	42	1496	1373	18	18	3.12	3.52
multiplex	88.48	84.64	100.00	100.00	6	6	48	47	1372	1440	15	14	2.05	1.34
random-1	84.60	86.20	100.00	100.00	1	3	11	11	429	454	18	13	0.25	0.29
random-2	71.48	69.85	100.00	100.00	5	3	25	20	979	889	19	11	1.86	1.52
random-3	39.89	48.16	100.00	100.00	12	9	47	45	2459	2072	18	12	38.66	8.74
random-4	27.98	47.25	100.00	100.00	9	17	54	77	3433	4829	15	16	191.26	239.64
random-5	37.95	30.37	100.00	100.00	13	12	73	69	6154	6583	18	17	1201.54	982.47
random-6	38.81	39.77	100.00	100.00	22	12	80	75	7455	8054	18	12	429.61	314.13
random-7	25.13	39.21	100.00	100.00	26	27	118	115	12331	11398	17	18	1064.34	463.60
Avg.	56.41	61.16	100.00	100.00	9	9	46	47	2991	3043	16	15	225.53	155.44

[22] F. SU, W. Hwang, and K. Chakrabarty, "Droplet Routing in the Synthesis of Digital Microfluidic Biochips," *Proc. of Design, Automation and Test in Europe*, 2006, vol. 1, pp. 1-6.

[23] T. Xu and K. Chakrabarty, "Integrated Droplet Routing in the Synthesis of Microfluidic Biochips," *Proc. of Design Automation Conference*, 2007, pp. 948-953.

[24] P.-H. Yuh, C.-L. Yang, and Y.-W. Chang, "Placement of Defect-Tolerant Digital Microfluidic Biochips Using the T-Tree Formulation," *ACM Journal on Emerging Technologies in Computing Systems (JETC)*, vol. 3, no. 3, Artical No. 13, 2007.

[25] P.-H. Yuh, C.-L. Yang, and Y.-W. Chang, "BioRoute: A Network-Flow-Based Routing Algorithm for the Synthesis of Digital Microfluidic Biochips," *IEEE Transactions on Computer-Aided Design of Integrated Circuits and Systems*, vol. 27, no. 11, pp. 1928-1941, 2008.

[26] T.-W. Huang and T.-Y. Ho, "A Two-Stage Integer Linear Programming-Based Droplet Routing Algorithm for Pin-Constrained Digital Microfluidic Biochips," *IEEE Transactions on Computer-Aided Design of Integrated Circuits and Systems*, vol. 30, no. 2, pp. 215-228, 2011.

[27] P.-H. Yuh, S. S. Sapatnekar, C.-L. Yang, and Y.-W. Chang, "A Progressive-ILP-Based Routing Algorithm for the Synthesis of Cross-Referencing Biochips," *IEEE Transactions on Computer-Aided Design of Integrated Circuits and Systems*, vol. 28, no. 9, pp. 1295-1306, 2009.

[28] Z. Xiao and E. F. Y. Young, "CrossRouter: A Droplet Router for Cross-Referencing Digital Microfluidic Biochips," *Proc. of Asia and South Pacific Design Automation Conference (ASP-DAC)*, 2010, pp. 269-274.

[29] M. Campàs and I. Katakis, "DNA Biochip Arraying, Detection and Amplification Strategies," *TrAC Trends in Analytical Chemistry*, vol. 23, no. 1, pp. 49-62, 2004.

[30] Y. Zhao and K. Chakrabarty, "Cross-contamination Avoidance for Droplet Routing in Digital Microfluidic Biochips," *Proc. Design, Automation and Test in Europe (DATE)*, 2009, pp. 1290-1295.

[31] T.-W. Huang, C.-H. Lin, and T.-Y. Ho, "A Contamination Aware Droplet Routing Algorithm for the Synthesis of Digital Microfluidic Biochips," *IEEE Transactions on Computer-Aided Design of Integrated Circuits and Systems*, vol. 29, no. 11, pp. 1682-1695, 2010.

[32] Y. Zhao and K. Chakrabarty, "Synchronization of Washing Operations with Droplet Routing for Cross-contamination Avoidance in Digital Microfluidic Biochips," *Proc. of Design Automation Conference*, 2010, pp. 635-640.

[33] C. C. Y. Lin and Y.-W. Chang, "Cross-Contamination Aware Design Methodology for Pin-Constrained Digital Microfluidic Biochips," *IEEE Transactions on Computer-Aided Design of Integrated Circuits and Systems*, vol. 30, no. 6, pp. 817-828, 2011.

[34] D. Mitra, S. Ghoshal, H. Rahaman, K. Chakrabarty, B. B.Bhattacharya, K. Chakrabarty, and B. B. Bhattacharya, "On Residue Removal in Digital Microfluidic Biochips," *Proc. of the Great Lakes Symposium on VLSI*, pp. 1-4, 2011.

[35] Q. Wang, Y. Shen, H. Yao, T.-Y. Ho, and Y. Cai, "Practical Functional and Washing Droplet Routing for Cross-Contamination Avoidance in Digital Microfluidic Biochips," *Proc. of Design Automation Conference (DAC)*, 2014, pp. 1-6.

[36] T. Xu and K. Chakrabarty, "Broadcast Electrode-Addressing for Pin-Constrained Multi-Functional Digital Microfluidic Biochips," *Proc. of IEEE/ACM Design Automation Conference*, 2008, pp. 173-178.

[37] H. J. J. Verheijen and M. W. J. Prins, "Reversible Electrowetting and Trapping of Charge: Model and Experiments," *Langmuir*, vol. 15, no. 20, pp. 6616-6620, 1999.

[38] A. I. Drygiannakis, A. G. Papathanasiou, and A. G. Boudouvis, "On the Connection Between Dielectric Breakdown Strength, Trapping of Charge, and Contact Angle Saturation in Electrowetting," *Langmuir*, vol. 25, no. 1, pp. 147-152, 2009.

[39] S.-H. Yeh, J.-W. Chang, T.-W. Huang, and T.-Y. Ho, "Voltage-Aware Chip-Level Design for Reliability-Driven Pin-Constrained EWOD Chips," *Proc. of IEEE/ACM International Conference on Computer-Aided Design*, 2012, pp. 353-360.

[40] R. Fair, "Digital Microfluidics: Is a True Lab-on-a-Chip Possible?" *Microfluid Nanofluidics*, vol. 3, no. 3, pp. 245-281, 2007.

[41] K. Chakrabarty, "Towards Fault-Tolerant Digital Microfluidic Lab-on-Chip: Defects, Fault Modeling, Testing, and Reconfiguration," *Transactions of the IRE Professional Group on Audio*, pp. 329-332, 2008.

[42] S. S.-Y. Liu, C.-H. Chang, H.-M. Chen, and T.-Y. Ho, "ACER: An Agglomerative Clustering BasedElectrode Addressing and Routing Algorithm forPin-Constrained EWOD Chips," *IEEE Trans. on CAD*, vol. 33, no. 9, pp. 1316-1327, 2014.

[43] J.-W. Chang, T.-W. Huang, and T.-Y. Ho, "An ILP-Based Obstacle-Avoiding Routing Algorithm for Pin-Constrained EWOD Chips," *Proc. of Asia and South Pacific Design Automation Conference (ASP-DAC)*, 2012, pp. 67-72.

[44] N. Cristianini and J. Shawe-Taylor, An Introduction to Support Vector Machines, *Cambridge University Press*, 2000.

[45] T. Joachims, "Making Large-Scale SVM Learning Practical," *B. Scholkopf and C. Burges, and A. Smola, Advances in Kernel Methods - Support Vector Learning, MIT-Press*, 1999.

[46] P. E. Hart, N. J. Nilsson, and B. Raphael, "A Formal Basis for the Heuristic Determination of Minimum Cost Paths," *IEEE Transactions on Systems Science and Cybernetics*, vol. 4, no. 2, pp. 100-107, 1968.

Machine Learning in Simulation-Based Analysis [*]

Li-C. Wang
University of California, Santa Barbara

Malgorzata Marek-Sadowska
University of California, Santa Barbara

ABSTRACT

This paper describes two separate learning flows for improving the efficiency of simulation-based design analysis. Machine learning concepts and methods are explained in the context of realizing the two learning flows. Experimental results are presented to demonstrate their feasibility. Generality of the proposed learning flows is illustrated using the kernel-based learning concept.

Categories and Subject Descriptors

B.7 [**Integrated Circuits**]: Design Aids

General Terms

Simulation

Keywords

Computer-Aided Design; Data Mining; Circuit Simulation

1. INTRODUCTION

Circuit simulation is indispensable for verifying the analog behavior of a design. For assessing the uncertainty of design behavior over process variations, Monte Carlo circuit simulation is one of the most popular approaches. However, circuit simulation can be time consuming. Hence, for a large and complex design, Monte Carlo circuit simulation can become prohibitively expensive.

Figure 1 depicts a functional view of the Monte Carlo style design analysis considered in this work. In this view, the design under analysis is seen as a mapping function $f()$. Inputs to the function comprise two sets of random variables. First, there are random variables modeling the input variations in the input space $\mathbf{X}$. Furthermore, there are random variables

[*]This work is supported in part by Semiconductor Research Corporation, projects 2012-TJ-2268 and 2013-TJ-2466 and by National Science Foundation Grant No. 1255818.

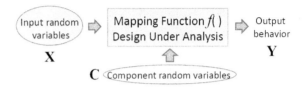

Figure 1: Functional view of a design analysis

modeling parametric variations associated with the components of the design. This component space is denoted as $\mathbf{C}$. The function $f()$ is a mapping from $(\mathbf{X}, \mathbf{C})$ to the output space $\mathbf{Y}$, i.e. $f : (\mathbf{X}, \mathbf{C}) \to \mathbf{Y}$. The function $f()$ can be computed through simulation. The objective of a Monte Carlo style design analysis is to evaluate the output variations with respect to the input variations from both the $\mathbf{X}$ space and the $\mathbf{C}$ space. For example, the analysis might be used to assess the performance yield of a design based a given process variation model.

As a specific application example, consider Monte Carlo circuit simulation of an analog design represented as a netlist of N transistors. The input space $\mathbf{X}$ comprises a set of possible input waveforms over a time period t, i.e. each sample $x_i \in \mathbf{X}$ is a waveform represented as a vector of voltage values over t time steps. Each component random variable models the size variation of a transistor, i.e. each sample $c_i \in \mathbf{C}$ is a vector of N transistor sizes. The objective of the analysis is to assess the behavior changes of the output waveforms due to the transistor size variations.

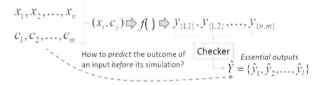

Figure 2: Formal view of the fundamental problem

Figure 2 provides a formal view of the fundamental problem considered in this research. In a Monte Carlo analysis, suppose that m samples $c_1, \ldots, c_m$ are drawn from the $\mathbf{C}$ space. Moreover, n samples $x_1, \ldots, x_n$ are derived from the $\mathbf{X}$ space. For example, these n samples can each be a waveform over the same time period $[0, t]$. As another example, circuit simulation is over a period $[0, T]$ and the period is divided into n successive time frames $[0, t_1], [t_1, t_2], \ldots, [t_{n-1}, t_n]$ where $x_1, \ldots, x_n$ are waveforms from the n time frames. In the setting of Figure 2, every *input sample*, represented as a 2-tuple (x_i, c_j), produces a corresponding output $y_{\{i,j\}}$.

Suppose that with respect to the design analysis task at hand, a subset of the l outputs $\hat{y}_1, \ldots, \hat{y}_l$ would be sufficient to represent the relevant output space. Let them be called the *essential outputs*. In Figure 2, a *checker* is applied on the $n \times m$ outputs to identify the l essential outputs. Assume $l \ll n \times m$. This assumption of having a small subset of essential outputs is usually practical. As a simple example, in a Monte Carlo style analysis of a circuit performance parameter (e.g. timing), the analysis goal could be to verify the range of the parameter. Then, among all the outputs, only two are essential: the min and the max.

Let the input samples required to produce the essential outputs be called the *important input samples*. Ideally, one desires to simulate only the important input samples to save simulation cost. This idea is only feasible if one has a way to predict the importance of an input sample or a way to predict its output. This leads to the fundamental problem:

> "How to predict the outcome (i.e. either the importance or the actual output) of an input sample *before* the sample is simulated?"

1.1 Predicting the outcome of an input sample

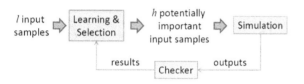

Figure 3: Learning to predict important inputs

Figure 3 and Figure 4 illustrate two approaches to the fundamental problem. Each approach is based on an iterative learning flow. In Figure 3, learning is based on the simulation results known in the current iteration, including both the known important and unimportant input samples. Once a learning model is constructed, it is used to predict the importance of input samples in the next iteration.

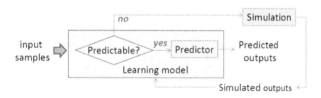

Figure 4: Learning to predict the outputs

In Figure 4, learning is for predicting the output of an input sample. The learning model comprises two parts: (1) a method to decide if an input sample is predictable, and (2) a predictor that produces the predicted output. Learning the predictor is based on the simulation results obtained so far, including the input samples simulated and their outputs. Note that while Figure 4 can be used to predict the importance of an input (by predicting its output), the learning flow can also be used to bypass simulation for those predictable inputs. This represents another way to save simulation cost. For example, given a circuit comprising multiple blocks, Figure 4 can be applied to one of the blocks and bypass simulation of some inputs to the block.

The rest of the paper is organized as follows. Section 2 introduces the related works. Section 3 states the concept of

kernel-based learning. Section 4 and Section 5 describe the details and experimental results of the two learning concepts illustrated in Figure 3 and Figure 4, respectively. Section 6 concludes this paper.

2. RELATED WORKS

Existing research for improving the efficiency of simulation based design analysis can be divided into two categories. In the first category, the analysis focuses on component variations from the $\mathbf{C}$ space without explicitly considering the variations in the $\mathbf{X}$ space. In the second category, the analysis focuses on the input variations from the $\mathbf{X}$ space and ignores the variations in the $\mathbf{C}$ space.

For example, one notable area of research is Static Statistical Timing Analysis (SSTA) [2][3]. In SSTA each delay element (equivalent to a component in Figure 1) is modeled as a random variable according to process variations. Delay elements in SSTA are usually assumed to be pin-to-pin delays of a cell [3]. Circuit timing is a function of a set of delay random variables under the worst-case assumption on the input pattern space $\mathbf{X}$. The analysis is static because variation in the input pattern space is not considered. In SSTA, $\mathbf{Y} = f(-, \mathbf{C})$ is computed by propagating the delay distributions directly through the circuit. It does not involve random sampling of the $\mathbf{C}$ space and hence, avoids the high cost of Monte Carlo simulation of random samples.

The same idea of propagating probability distributions can be applied to low-level circuit analysis where the random variables are based on basic circuit elements such as resistors and capacitors. In low-level circuit analysis, the operators involved are no longer restricted to addition and maximization as those used in SSTA. Hence, the problem becomes more complex. For example, the work in [4] applies Polynomial Chaos Theory (PCT) [5] to low-level circuit analysis. In a PCT framework, distributions are modeled with orthogonal polynomials to facilitate their propagation through the circuit equations [4].

The work in [6] retains the idea of random sampling with Monte Carlo simulation. To improve efficiency, supervised learning techniques are applied to predict the irrelevant random samples from the component space $\mathbf{C}$. These irrelevant samples are discarded from simulation. In more recent works [7][8], advanced learning techniques are applied to develop an efficient framework for statistical analysis of circuit performance parameters. The framework is intended and optimized for applications where the underlying sources of variations are mainly from the component space $\mathbf{C}$.

In Figure 1, if one takes an extreme view that the mapping function is a processor or SoC, then the input space $\mathbf{X}$ becomes extremely large. In this case, considering component variations is no longer practical. Typically, for verifying an SoC, RTL simulation is used. Simulation cost is high due to the large input space $\mathbf{X}$ which needs to be covered. In this context, an input x becomes a functional test, e.g. a sequence of vectors.

The work in [9] assumes that a functional test is a sequence of 0/1 vectors of a fixed length. Then, the input space $\mathbf{X}$ essentially can be viewed as an N-dimensional space comprising all combinations of 0/1 vectors. With such a view, the work proposes a framework for reducing simulation time by identifying and simulating only the potentially important functional tests. Unsupervised learning technique, the one-class Support Vector Machine (SVM) [10], was applied to learn and model the unimportant input subspaces to facilitate the selection of the potentially important inputs. The works in [11][12][13] extended the idea to analyze functional tests that are assembly programs.

An example to consider variations in both the $\mathbf{X}$ space and the $\mathbf{C}$ space is statistical delay testing, where the mapping function $f()$ is a gate-level circuit with w inputs. The 2^w possible input patterns constitute the $\mathbf{X}$ space. Then, component variations can be based on two sources: (1) variations of the delay elements due to process variations, and (2) variations in the delay defect sizes and locations.

Because it is not feasible to apply all 2^w input patterns, one crucial aspect of the statistical analysis is to identify the important input patterns that excite and observe delay defects under the statistical timing model. The early work in [14] is an example of an approach to this delay testing problem. However, the work relied on Monte Carlo simulation of random samples from the $\mathbf{C}$ space and no simulation time reduction was intended with respect to this space. Additionally, no statistical learning was applied.

3. KERNEL-BASED LEARNING

Figure 5 illustrates a typical dataset seen by a statistical learning algorithm (For more discussion, see e.g. [1]). When $\vec{y}$ is present and there is a label for every sample, it is called *supervised* learning [15]. In supervised learning, if each y_i is a categorized value, it is a *classification* problem. If each y_i is modeled as a continuous value, it is a *regression* problem. When $\vec{y}$ is not present and only $\mathbf{X}$ is present, it is *unsupervised* learning [15]. When some (usually much fewer) samples have labels and others have no label, the learning is called *semi-supervised* learning [16].

$$\mathbf{X} = \begin{pmatrix} \vec{x}_1 \\ \vec{x}_2 \\ \cdots \\ \vec{x}_m \end{pmatrix} = \begin{vmatrix} x_{11} & x_{12} & \cdots & x_{1n} \\ x_{21} & x_{22} & \cdots & x_{2n} \\ \cdots & \cdots & \cdots & \cdots \\ x_{m1} & x_{m2} & \cdots & x_{mn} \end{vmatrix} \quad \vec{y} = \begin{pmatrix} y_1 \\ y_2 \\ \cdots \\ y_m \end{pmatrix}$$

Features → f_1 f_2 ... f_n Vectors — Samples — Labels

Figure 5: Typical dataset for a learning algorithm

In Figure 5, each sample from $\mathbf{X}$ is assumed to be encoded with n features $f_1, \ldots, f_n$. Hence, the characteristics of each sample are described as a vector $\vec{x}_i$ of n values. Figure 5 illustrates two fundamental challenges for applying a statistical learning algorithm in the learning flows depicted in Figure 3 and Figure 4:
(1) In our application, an input sample is a 2-tuple (x_i, c_j) which might not be given as a vector as shown in Figure 5.
(2) More importantly, the output $y_{i,j}$ might not be a scalar value, e.g., outputs can be waveforms. Note that this second challenge is only relevant to Figure 4. Figure 3 can be seen as an unsupervised learning flow because outputs are not what is to be predicted. Figure 4 is a supervised learning flow because outputs are to be predicted.

3.1 The importance of similarity measure

Many modern statistical learning algorithms follow the paradigm of *kernel-based learning* [17][18]. Figure 6 illustrates the basic concept of kernel-based learning.

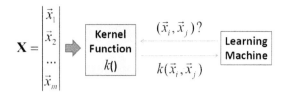

Figure 6: Kernel function vs. learning machine

In kernel-based learning, the learning machine, i.e. the learning algorithm such as a Support Vector Machine (SVM) algorithm [17], is not required to access the samples $\vec{x}_1, \ldots, \vec{x}_m$ directly. Instead, all the information required for the learning is coming from a *kernel function* $k()$ as shown in Figure 6. The kernel function measures the *similarity* between two samples based on some definition of similarity.

Kernel-based learning provides great flexibility to apply learning techniques in EDA and test applications [1], especially when the samples to be analyzed are not provided in vector formats like that shown in Figure 5. This is because from the learning perspective the representation of a sample is no longer important. What is important is how similarity between samples should be measured. This similarity measure, i.e. the kernel function, defines the space in which the learning is performed. With kernel-based learning, the challenge of having a proper input sample representation is alleviated. However, one still has the challenge of searching for a proper kernel function.

The kernel-based learning concept depicted in Figure 6 allows the separation of learning theories and methods from their specific implementation for a particular application context. To see this, consider Figure 3 and Figure 4 again. In Figure 3, we propose to develop the theories and methods to build a learning model $M_{sel}()$ to predict the importance of an input sample s by $M_{sel}(s)$. In Figure 4, we propose to develop the theories and methods to build another type of learning model $M_{pre}()$ associated with an evaluation scheme $E_{sel}()$. For a given sample s, $E_{sel}(s)$ indicates if s is predictable and $M_{pre}(s)$ provides the predicted output.

With the concept of kernel-based learning, we see that as long as a kernel function $k()$ is provided to measure the similarity between a pair of input samples s_1, s_2 as $k(s_1, s_2)$, a learning machine can operate on the similarity measures to build learning models. The actual representation of the input samples is irrelevant to the learning machine. Hence, theories and methods for learning the models $M_{sel}()$, $M_{pre}()$, $E_{sel}()$ can be based on the assumption of having the corresponding kernel functions. Then, the theories and methods are not specific to a particular type of input samples.

When the learning flows in Figure 3 and Figure 4 are applied to a particular simulation context, implementation of the specific kernel functions takes place. For example, in the context that each input x is a waveform over a time period and each component sample c is a vector of transistor sizes, one needs to implement a kernel function $k()$ such that for any pair of input samples $s_1 = (x_{i_1}, c_{j_1})$, $s_2 = (x_{i_2}, c_{j_2})$, $k(s_1, s_2)$ provides a similarity measure between them.

Without loss of generality, in the rest of discussion we assume that $0 \leq k() \leq 1$ where $k() = 1$ indicates the two samples are identical and $k() = 0$ tells that the two samples are most different. Note that one may also implement a separate kernel function $k_x()$ applied to the x samples and another function $k_c()$ applied to the c samples.

The implementation of kernel functions $k()$, $k_x()$ and $k_c()$ is application specific. The learning theories and methods to construct the learning flows in Figure 3 and Figure 4 are not. This separation allows the theories and methods developed from the proposed research to be applicable in a wide variety of different contexts.

4. PREDICTING IMPORTANT SAMPLES

Figure 2 shows that simulation of all input samples results in l *essential* output samples, $\hat{Y} = \{\hat{y}_1, \hat{y}_2, \ldots, \hat{y}_l\}$. Without loss of generality, we assume that these l output samples are those most dissimilar to each other based on a similarity measure $k_y()$. In other words, one can view these l outputs as the *representative* outputs of the space covered by all the $n \times m$ outputs based on the definition of $k_y()$. Note that this assumption is without loss of generality because we do not make any assumption on the kernel $k_y()$ itself. Hence, different definitions of $k_y()$ can be used to model different scenarios as how the essential outputs should be selected.

As a simple example, the l essential outputs can be selected with an iterative greedy method. The first essential output is selected randomly. Then, suppose the current set of essential outputs is $\hat{L} = \{\hat{y}_1, \ldots, \hat{y}_j\}$. For an output y, if $\forall \hat{y}_i \in \hat{L}$, $k_y(y, \hat{y}_i) < \delta$, then y is included as an essential output to the $\hat{L}$ set. For example, we can set $\delta = 0.8$ to mean that each essential output is different from all other essential outputs by at least 20% as measured by $k_y()$.

4.1 The essence of the learning problem

The learning flow in Figure 3 operates iteratively. In each iteration, h input samples are selected and simulated to produce h outputs. With the assumption that essential outputs are those most dissimilar to each other based on the similarity measure $k_y()$, it is intuitive to see that a feasible objective in each iteration is to select the h input samples that can produce outputs that are as much dissimilar as possible. The challenge, again, is that *before* simulation we do not know the outputs of those input samples to be selected and consequently, do not know how dissimilar their outputs would be.

For the input samples, we have another kernel function $k()$ that measures the similarity for a given pair of input samples. Suppose for every pair of input samples s_1, s_2 and their outputs y_1, y_2, we have $k(s_1, s_2) = k_y(y_1, y_2)$, i.e. input similarity = output similarity. Then, observe that in this case selecting important input samples becomes a trivial problem. This is because by selecting input samples that are most dissimilar to each other based on the kernel $k()$, we guarantee that the resulting outputs would also be equally most dissimilar to each other based on the kernel $k_y()$.

Usually, we have $k(s_1, s_2) \neq k_y(y_1, y_2)$. For example, two very different inputs can produce two very similar outputs, and vice versa. Then, the essence of the learning problem in Figure 3 can be thought of as the following: Starting from a given kernel $k()$, how to iteratively learn a kernel $k'()$ such that the similarity measures by $k'()$ are close to the similarity measures by $k_y()$?

This observation inspires the idea of *adaptive similarity measure* described below.

4.2 Iterative process with clustering

Figure 7 depicts an example of what might happen from one iteration to the next in the iterative learning flow shown in Figure 4. In this example, there are in total 14 samples. In each iteration, 3 samples are selected.

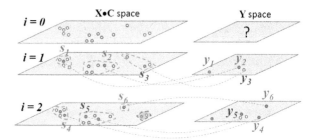

Figure 7: Iterative search for important inputs

For iteration $i = 0$, no sample is applied yet. Hence, there is no information on the $\mathbf{Y}$ space. Suppose that a kernel function $k()$ is given for measuring similarities between input samples in the input space $\mathbf{X} \bullet \mathbf{C}$. For iteration $i = 1$, three samples are selected. Because there is no information on the outputs in the $\mathbf{Y}$ space yet, in this iteration we simply cluster input samples into three groups of similar samples. Then, a representative sample is selected from each group. This is to achieve the effect that the selected three input samples are most dissimilar based on the given similarity measure function $k()$.

Suppose that the three selected inputs are s_1, s_2 and s_3, and after they are simulated, we discover that the corresponding y_1 and y_2 are essential, e.g. they are dissimilar by at least 80% based on the output kernel measure $k_y()$. But y_3 is not essential because it is similar to y_2 as shown in the figure. Then, for iteration $i = 2$, the question is, what would be a good strategy to take advantage of this new information observed in the $\mathbf{Y}$ space to help select the additional three input samples?

There are two pieces of information from simulating s_1, s_2, and s_3. First, it tells that the subspaces covered by the two clusters containing s_1 and s_2 respectively are important. Without further information, it makes sense to select additional input samples from those subspaces. Second, it tells that the subspace near s_3 is unimportant. Hence, it makes sense to exclude the subspace in the next selection.

Following these two ideas, in iteration $i = 2$, the subspace close to s_3 is blacked out. Clustering is then applied to the rest of the samples. Three samples s_4, s_5, and s_6 are selected. Samples s_4 and s_5 are selected from the same clusters as s_1 and s_2 before. Notice that s_6 is at a distance from s_3 and hence, it is not deemed unimportant because of s_3. In iteration $i = 2$, s_6 by itself forms a cluster and is selected.

4.3 Adaptive similarity measure

Figure 8 illustrates how the ideas discussed above can be accomplished without changing the clustering algorithm (for clustering algorithms, see, e.g. [22]). Given a kernel function $k()$, it implicitly defines a space where the similarity between a pair of samples is measured. In this space, clusters are formed. This is shown in the left plot of Figure 8. Suppose two clusters are formed and two samples s_1, s_2 are selected and simulated. Suppose the outcome is that s_2 produces an essential output while s_1 does not. Hence, s_2 is a known important sample and s_1 is a known unimportant sample.

The trick is that in the next iteration, a new space is created based on s_1 and s_2 and the clustering algorithm is

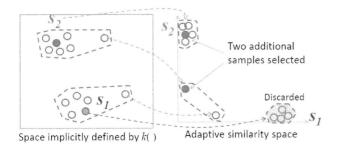

Figure 8: Adaptive similarity measure

applied to form clusters in this new space. In the new space, each sample s is placed at the coordinate $(k(s, s_1), k(s, s_2))$ in the 2-dimensional space defined by the two samples s_1 and s_2 and the given kernel function $k()$. Then, the similarity between two samples s_i and s_j in the new space is measured by $e^{-dist(s_i,s_j)^2}$ where $dist(s_i, s_j)$ calculates the distance between the two samples in the new space.

In the new space (the right plot), observe that the samples originally close to s_1 (and far from s_2) are now all close to the point $(1, 0)$ and form a cluster. This cluster is blacked out because s_1 is an unimportant sample. The samples originally close to s_2 (and far from s_1) are now close to the point $(0, 1)$ and form another cluster. One representative sample is selected because s_2 is an important sample. Furthermore, the remaining two samples form a cluster of their own and another representative sample is selected.

This simple example illustrates that without changing the clustering algorithm, by projecting the input samples into a new similarity measure space, the ideas discussed in Figure 7 can be realized. The *adaptive similarity measure* method is summarized as the following. Without loss of generality, assume that p samples s_1, ..., s_p have been simulated. Samples $s_1, \ldots, s_i$ are deemed important samples while $s_{i+1}, \ldots,$ s_p are deemed unimportant. Then, consider all input samples not yet simulated:

1. For an input sample s, for each j, $i + 1 \leq j \leq p$, if $k(s, s_j)$ is greater than $\max\{k(s, s_q)|\forall q, 1 \leq q \leq i\}$, then s is removed from consideration in the current iteration, i.e., s is more similar (or "closer") to an unimportant sample than to *any* of the important samples.

2. For all the input samples not removed, project them into the space defined by the important samples $s_1, \ldots,$ s_i and the given kernel function $k_x()$ by placing each sample s at the coordinate $(k(s, s_1), \ldots, k(s, s_i))$ in the i-dimensional space. Measure similarities using the kernel $e^{-dist()^2}$ discussed above. Find clusters in this new space to select additional representative samples.

4.4 Experimental result

To assess the feasibility of the proposed adaptive similarity measure method, we designed an experiment in the context of Monte Carlo circuit simulation for an analog design. Figure 9 shows the circuit example, an Ultra-Wideband Phase Lock Loop (UWB-PLL) design used to tune the frequency of an impulse radio ultra wideband transmitter in [19]. The UWB-PLL comprises 949 transistors. Specific design details of the PLL can be found in [19]. For our experimental purpose, the design details are not that important.

To create a dataset as shown in Figure 2, we performed Monte Carlo simulation of 100 component samples $c_1, \ldots,$ c_{100} sampled from a process variation model for the transistors. Given a fixed frequency clock as input to the PLL, 3000 time steps were simulated for each sample. In each simulation, the first 500 time steps were ignored. From the remaining 2500 time steps, 50 waveforms were extracted, each with a time period of length 50 time steps. In total, there were 5000 waveforms collected at each net.

Then, a dataset was created for each of the four selected pairs of input nets and output nets, whose locations are marked in Figure 9 as $(I_1, O_1), \ldots, (I_4, O_4)$, respectively. In each case, we applied the proposed iterative learning flow to identify important input samples (waveforms).

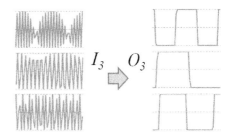

Figure 10: Input/output waveform examples

For essential output waveforms, we followed the rule discussed before that they each were at least 20% dissimilar to each other, based on a given kernel function $k_y()$. Figure 10 shows three examples of input waveforms that produce output waveforms dissimilar enough to be essential.

In	Out	Apply learning			Random	
		# Iters	# IS's	# EO's	# IS's	# EO's
I_1	O_1	4	128	31	700	31
I_2	O_2	4	222	64	2200	64
I_3	O_3	5	270	56	750	56
I_4	O_4	30	1979	50	2800	50

Table 1: Experimental results

Table 1 summarizes the results. The "# of Iters" column shows the number of iterations performed by the iterative learning flow. The "# of IS's" shows the total number of input waveforms selected as potentially important input samples. The "# of EO's" shows the total number of essential outputs covered by the selected input samples. For comparison, we also ran a process using random selection of input samples. Those results are shown in the last two columns.

As we can observe, random selection required selecting many more inputs to cover the same number of essential outputs, especially for the first three cases. This clearly demonstrates that the iterative learning flow had a positive effect on predicting the important input samples. With the fourth case, learning was not as effective as the previous three cases, because of the sequential circuit block (labeled "Counter") involved. This resulted in a sequential dependency of an input waveform at time t on the input waveforms before t, which was not modeled in the learning. This is an issue that requires further research.

4.5 Measuring similarity between two samples

In the experiments above, in each case a waveform is represented as a time-based vector of, say 50 values. In

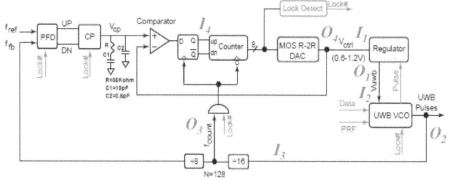

Figure 9: A UWB-PLL example circuit used in the experiments

other words, a waveform is represented as a vector $\vec{a} = [a_1, a_2, \ldots, a_{50}]$ where a_i is the amplitude value at time step i. Given two waveforms $\vec{a}$ and $\vec{b}$, one can apply popular kernel functions described in [18] to measure their similarity. For example, one can use the angle based kernel $cos(\vec{a}, \vec{b}) = (\vec{a} \cdot \vec{b})/(\| \vec{a} \| \| \vec{b} \|)$, or the distance based kernel function $e^{-dist(\vec{a}, \vec{b})}$ discussed before. For example, in the experiments we used the distance based kernel function as the output kernel function $k_y()$.

Note that in the experiments, each input waveform x_i is associated with a component sample c_j. Hence, an input sample $s_{i,j}$ should be seen as a 2-tuple (x_i, c_j). And, for two samples (x_{i_1}, c_{j_1}) and (x_{i_2}, c_{j_2}), we need a kernel function $k()$ to measure their similarity $k((x_{i_1}, c_{j_1}), (x_{i_2}, c_{j_2}))$. The way we approached this problem was by defining two separate kernels $k_x()$ and $k_c()$ and let $k() = (k_x() + k_c())/2$.

We defined $k_x()$ as the kernel function to compare two waveforms. This is similar to $k_y()$ discussed above. We then defined $k_c(c_1, c_2)$ for two component samples c_1, c_2 to be based on the output samples obtained by simulating a small number of h input waveforms based on c_1 and c_2. Given c_1 and c_2, let their corresponding output waveforms based on the same input waveforms $x_1, \ldots, x_h$ be f as $y_{1,1}, \ldots, y_{1,h}$ and $y_{2,1}, \ldots, y_{2,h}$, respectively. We then calculated $k_c(c_1, c_2) = (\sum_{i=1}^{h} k_y(y_{1,i}, y_{2,i}))/h$. In other words, $k_c(c_1, c_2)$ is calculated as the average similarity between the output waveforms observed based on the two component samples with the same input waveforms. We then calculate $k()$ as $(k_x() + k_c())/2$.

5. PREDICTING THE OUTPUTS

Next, we will discuss the learning flow proposed in Figure 4. Realization of the learning flow demands two methods. The first method evaluates the predictability of an input sample. The second method learns a predictor from simulation results.

5.1 Intuition behind predictability of SVM

The predictability of modern learning algorithms such as Support Vector Machine (SVM) [17] is explained through the statistical learning theory framework [20]. In this section we will first illustrate the intuition of the predictability notion from the SVM perspective. Then, based on the intuition, we will develop new concepts to capture the notion of predictability in the context of Figure 4.

In a learning problem setting, a set of sample points $(x_1, y_1), \ldots, (x_n, y_n)$ are given to be learned from (note: each x_i can be a vector, and each y_i is a scalar value). An SVM model is of the form [17]:

$$f(x) = (\sum_{x_i \in SV} \alpha_i k(x_i, x)) + b \qquad (1)$$

SV is a subset of the input samples. Without loss of generality, let $SV = \{x_1, \ldots, x_l\}$. Each $x_i \in SV$ is called a *support vector*. $k()$ is the kernel function. Each $k(x_i, x)$ measures the similarity between a support vector x_i and the input vector x to be predicted. The coefficient α_i is the weight associated with $k(x_i, x)$. The learning objective is usually defined for a given prediction error function. For example the error function calculates the sum of square errors: $Err(f) = \sum_{i=1}^{n}(y_i - f(x_i))^2$.

With a kernel $k()$ and an error function given, learning by an SVM algorithm means to determine the following three things: (a) the set SV, (b) the α coefficients, and (c) the constant b in equation (1) above. Because the non-support vectors $x_{l+1}, \ldots, x_n$ are not used in the calculation of the SVM model $f(x)$, they can be seen as the samples used to *validate* the model.

Conceptually, the quantity $\frac{n-l}{n}$ can be thought of as a measure for predictability of the model $f(x)$ [20]. This is because a smaller l (size of the set SV) leads to a larger number of *validation* samples. In other words, if the model can predict more validation samples (based on a given error requirement), then the dataset is more predictable.

Therefore, we make two observations: (1) The essential purpose of learning is to decide how many samples can be predicted by other samples. In a sense, it can be seen as a compression process. (2) When more samples can be predicted by other samples, the predictability for the given dataset is higher.

5.2 SVM models with two support vectors

Suppose a SVM model comprises only two support vectors x_1, x_2. The model becomes $f(x) = \alpha_1 k(x_1, x) + \alpha_2 k(x_2, x)$ (assuming $b = 0$). Assume that the kernel function $k(x, z)$ is a Gaussian kernel $k(x, z) = e^{-\|x-z\|^2}$. Figure 11 shows the behavior of three models for $x_1 = 1$, $x_2 = 2$, and $x = 1.1, 1.2, \ldots, 1.9$.

In the first case $f_1(x)$, we have $\alpha_1 = 4$ and $\alpha_2 = 4$. The predicted y values are shown. Observe that the predicted y value of a x_i is closer to $f(x_1)$ if x_i is closer to x_1. Similar

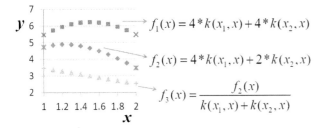

Figure 11: SVM models based on two SVs x_1, x_2

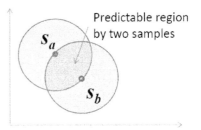

Figure 12: A predictable region

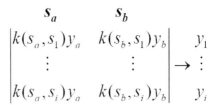

Figure 13: Local dataset to verify a pred. region

observation can be made to x_2. In the second case $f_2(x)$, we have $\alpha_1 = 4$ and $\alpha_2 = 2$. Notice that in this case the largest y value no longer occurs at $x = 1.5$. This is due to the two non-equal weights α_1, α_2.

Observe that by changing α_1, α_2, the model is capable to capture a variety of convex functions. In the third case $f_3(x)$, we take $f_2(x)$ and normalize it with the similarity sum $k(x_1, x) + k(x_2, x)$. This results in a linear function. Hence, if we desire to model a linear behavior between two samples, we can use the normalization method. Figure 11 illustrates that a simple two-SV learning model can implement a variety of interpolation functions between two samples x_1, x_2. We will use this observation to develop a notion of predictability in the context of Figure 4.

5.3 Constructing local predictors

Given a circuit, we partition the circuit into individual circuit elements (CEs). For example, partitioning can be based on design blocks or subjected to user choice. Partitioning allows the learning flow to be applied on individual CEs rather than on the entire circuit.

For learning a predictor for a CE, suppose a set of samples $(s_1, y_1), \ldots, (s_n, y_n)$ has been simulated and is available for the learning. For example, these samples are simulated inputs and outputs obtained during the circuit simulation from the previous iterations, in the iterative learning process of Figure 4.

With a set of the simulated samples, we can try to learn a single model $f(s) \rightarrow y$ for all samples, but this could be difficult if $f(s)$ is restricted to a two-sample model as shown in Figure 11. Hence, instead of learning a single model, we can try to learn a set of *local predictors*, each based on two input samples.

To construct a local predictor, we will first select two input samples s_a, s_b. Assume using the kernel $k() = k_x() + k_c()$ as discussed in Section 4.5 before. We first define a (potentially) predictable region as: $\forall s : k(s, s_a) \leq k(s_a, s_b) \wedge k(s, s_b) \leq k(s_a, s_b)$. Figure 12 illustrates how this region looks like in a 2-dimensional plane - it is simply the intersection of two circles (for $k()$ that is distance-based).

The next step is to extract a local dataset for the learning. Figure 13 illustrates the local dataset consisting of all the input samples $s_1, \ldots, s_i$ that fall inside the predictable region.

Then, the learning is to construct a two-sample model based on s_a and s_b to predict the outputs of $s_1, \ldots, s_i$ within a given accuracy, e.g. by finding the two α's coefficient values in the model. If this can be done, then a local predictor is found. In actual application, a new input sample s is first checked to see if it is inside a predictable region. If it is inside the region of a local predictor, then the output of s

is predicted by the local predictor. For a given CE, one can build many local predictors based on many input pairs.

In the proposed approach to apply the learning flow in Figure 4, predictability of an input sample is decided at two levels: (1) The first level is based on information and complexity measures. At this level a circuit element is decided if it is suitable to apply learning. If it is not, then no simulation cost saving is attempted on the circuit element. (2) The second level is based on the predictable region defined by two input samples associated with a local predictor. This region defines when the local predictor can be applied.

5.4 Experimental Result

The experiments were based on the setup discussed in Section 4.4. For the UWB-PLL, 16 circuit elements (CEs) were selected, each with one input and one output. The sizes of the CEs were from 10 to 20 transistors. As discussed in Section 4.4, 5000 waveforms were collected at each input point with corresponding 5000 waveforms collected at the output point. Hence, for each CE we had 5000 samples.

We took the first 1000 sample points as the *training dataset* and used the remaining 4000 sample points as the *validation dataset*. With a training dataset, we selected up to 6K pairs of input samples. For each pair we tried to learn a local predictor. If this succeeded, we counted it as a success. The success rates are reported in the row "Success %." For each CE, the collection of the local predictors were applied to the 4000 samples in the validation dataset to check how many of their outputs were predictable by at least one of the predictors. The percentages of the predictable outputs are reported in the row "Predictable %.'"

Results are shown in Table 2. The CEs are divided into two groups. The first group comprises CEs of various types. The second group comprises CEs of divider type. In the first group, CEs 6, 7 and 8 are less predictable, reflected in their low success % and low predictable %. Note that a low success % does not imply a low predictable % and vice versa. In the second group, the predictable % numbers are generally high. This shows that divider type of CEs are quite predictable. Note that in the table, the predictable % number could be thought of as a potential saving of the

	Group (1)								Group (2)							
CE index	1	2	3	4	5	6	7	8	9	10	11	12	13	14	15	16
Success %	54.7	11.7	12.2	55.1	25.8	8.51	9.49	10.9	27.3	32.1	39.5	28.5	24.6	39.1	19.3	17.6
Predictable %	96.3	77.2	75.7	74.2	62.3	26.7	33.5	43.3	95.5	94.5	94.3	93.6	91.9	90	79.4	82.2

Table 2: Summary of results for 16 circuit elements from UWB-PLL

simulation cost on the particular CE. This is because those outputs are predicted rather than simulated.

6. CONCLUSION

In this work, we present two learning flows to be applied in the context of simulation-based analysis. Both learning flows are designed to improve the efficiency of simulation analysis. In the first flow, the importance of input samples is predicted, and efficiency is improved by discarding unimportant input samples in the analysis. In the second flow, the outputs of selected inputs are predicted and simulation cost is saved by not simulating the selected inputs. We explain the machine learning concepts and methods needed to implement the two flows and present experimental results to demonstrate their feasibility. The proposed learning flows are generic and can be applied in different application contexts. Changing from one context to another requires implementation of specific kernel functions suitable for the respective application. The applicability of the proposed learning flows is not yet fully explored and is subjected to future research.

Acknowledgment: The authors thank Samantha Alt, Kou-Kai Hsieh, Sebastian Siatkowski, and Chia-Ling Chang from UCSB for their invaluable help on preparing the paper.

7. REFERENCES

[1] Li-C. Wang, Magdy Abadir. Data Mining In EDA - Basic Principles, Promises, and Constraints. in *ACM/IEEE Design Automation Conference*, 2014.

[2] C. Visweswariah, k. Ravindran, K. Kalafala, S.G. Walker, S. Narayan, D. K. Beece, J. Piaget, N. Venkateswaran, J. G. Hemmett. First-order incremental block-based statistical timing analysis. in *IEEE Trans. CAD*, v25, 10, 2006, pp. 2170 Ü- 2180.

[3] Xin Li, Jiayong Le, Lawrence T. Pileggi. Statistical Performance Modeling and Optimization. Now Publishers, 2007.

[4] A. Monti, F. Ponci, Member, T. Lovett. A polynomial chaos theory approach to uncertainty in electrical engineering. in International Conference on Intelligent Systems Application to Power Systems, 2005.

[5] F. Augustin, A. Gilg, M. Paffrath, P. Rentrop and U. Wever. Polynomial chaos for the approximation of uncertainties: Chances and limits. in *European Journal of Applied Mathematics*,v 19, 02, 2008, pp. 149-190.

[6] Amith Singhee, Rob A. Rutenbar. Statistical Blockade: A Novel Method for Very Fast Monte Carlo Simulation of Rare Circuit Events, and its Application. in *DATE* 2007, pp. 1-6.

[7] Xin Li, Wangyang Zhang and Fa Wang. Large-scale statistical performance modeling of analog and mixed-signal circuits. *IEEE Custom Integrated Circuits Conference* (CICC), 2012, pp. 1-8.

[8] Xin Li, Fa Wang, Shupeng Sun and Chenjie Gu. Bayesian model fusion: a statistical framework for efficient pre-silicon validation and post-silicon tuning of complex analog and mixed-signal circuits. *IEEE/ACM International Conference on Computer-Aided Design* (ICCAD), 2013, pp. 795-802.

[9] Onur Guzey, Li-C. Wang, Jeremy Levitt and Harry Foster. Functional Test Selection Based on Unsupervised Support Vector Analysis. in *Design Automation Conference*, 2008, pp. 262-267.

[10] Bernhard Schölkopf, John C. Platt, John Shawe-Taylor, Alex J. Smola, and Robert C. Williamson. Estimating the Support of a High-Dimensional Distribution. in *Journal Neural Computation*, v 13, 7, 2001, pp. 1443-1471.

[11] Po-Hsien Chang, Li-C. Wang, Jayanta Bhadra. A Kernel-Based Approach for Functional Test Program Generation. In *International Test Conference*, 2010, pp. 1-10.

[12] Wen Chen, Nik Sumikawa, Li-C Wang, Jayanta Bhadra, Shaun Feng, Magdy S. Abadir. Novel Test Detection to Improve Simulation Efficiency — A Commercial Experiment. *ACM/IEEE International Conference on Computer-Aided Design*, 2012, pp. 101-108.

[13] Li-C. Wang. Data Mining in Functional Test Content Optimization. in *Asian and South Pacific Design Automation Conference*, to appear, Jan 2015.

[14] Mango C.T. Chao, Li-C. Wang, and Kwang-Ting Cheng. Pattern selection for testing of deep sub-micron timing defects. in *Design Automation and Test in Europe*, 2004, pp. 1060-1065.

[15] Trevor Hastie, Robert Tibshirani, and Jerome Friedman. The Elements of Statistical Learning - Date Mining, Inference, and Prediction. *Springer Series in Statistics*, 2001.

[16] Olivier Chapelle, Bernhard Schölkopf and Alexander Zien. *Semi-Supervised Learning*. The MIT press, 2010.

[17] Bernhard Schölkopf, and Alexander J. Smola. Learning with Kernels: Support Vector Machines, Regularization, Optimization, and Beyond. The MIT Press, 2001.

[18] J. Shawe-Taylor, and N. Cristianini. Kernel Methods for Pattern Analysis. *Cambridge University Press* 2004.

[19] M. Elzeftawi, *Compact Low-Power Low-Noise Neural Recording Wireless Channel for High Density Neural Implants (HDNIs)*, Dissertation, University of California, Santa Barbara, December 2012.

[20] Vladimir Vapnik. The nature of Statistical Learning Theory. 2nd ed., *Springer*, 1999.

[21] Sayan Mukherjee and Vladimir Vapnik. Support Vector Method for Multivariate Density Estimation. A.I. Memo No. 1653, C.B.C.L. Paper No. 170, MIT 1999.

[22] http://scikit-learn.org/stable/user_guide.html#user-guide

Physical Layout Design of Directed Self-Assembly Guiding Alphabet for IC Contact Hole/via Patterning

H.-S. Philip Wong   He Yi   Maryann Tung   Kye Okabe

Stanford University
420 Via Ortega, Stanford, CA 94305
+1-650-725-0982
hspwong@stanford.edu

ABSTRACT

The continued scaling of feature size has brought increasingly significant challenges to conventional optical lithography.[1-3] The rising cost and limited resolution of current lithography technologies have opened up opportunities for alternative patterning approaches. Among the emerging patterning approaches, block copolymer self-assembly for device fabrication has been envisioned for over a decade. Block copolymer DSA is a result of spontaneous microphase separation of block copolymer films, forming periodic microdomains including cylinders, spheres, and lamellae, in the same way that snowflakes and clamshells are formed in nature – by self-assembly due to forces of nature (Fig. 1a). DSA can generate closely packed and well controlled sub-20 nm features with low cost and high throughput, therefore stands out among other emerging lithographic solutions, including extreme ultraviolet lithography (EUV), electron beam lithography (e-beam), and multiple patterning lithography (MPL).[2;6]

Previous research has shown a high degree of dimensional control of the self-assembled features over large areas with long range ordering and periodic structures.[5; 6] The exquisite dimensional control at nanometer-scale feature sizes is one of the most attractive properties of block copolymer self-assembly. At the same time, device and circuit fabrication for the semiconductor industry requires accurate placement of desired features at irregular positions on the chip. The need to coax the self-assembled features into circuit layout friendly location is a roadblock for introducing self-assembly into semiconductor manufacturing. Directed self-assembly (DSA) and the use of topography to direct the self-assembly (graphoepitaxy) have shown great potential in overcoming the current lithography limits.[4]

Recognizing that typical circuit layouts do _not_ require long range order, we adopt a lithography sub-division approach akin to double-patterning and spacer patterning, using small guiding topographical templates. Guiding topographical templates with sizes of the order of the natural pitch of the block copolymer can effectively guide the self-assembly of block polymer (Fig. 1b-c). Therefore, circuit contact hole patterns can be placed at arbitrary

location by first patterning a coarse guiding template using conventional lithography.[7; 8] This procedure enables generating a higher resolution feature at a location determined by the coarse lithographic pattern. The size and registration of the features are determined by parameters of the template as well as the block copolymer itself.

Using this technique, we have proposed a general template design strategy that relates the block copolymer material properties to the target technology node requirements, and demonstrated contact hole patterning at the technology node from 22 nm to 7 nm, for both memory circuits and random logic circuits.[11] The critical dimension of DSA patterns is highly uniform, with their position controlled precisely. As technology scales down, the contact/via density scales up, which simultaneously opens the possibility of using multiple-hole DSA patterns for contact hole patterning and brings in the challenge of printing guiding templates at a small pitch. Using DSA for patterning IC contacts requires further knowledge of the placement of contacts in an IC layout, as the placement of contacts in the IC layout determines the shape and size of the required templates.

We hypothesize that there exists a limited set of guiding templates analogous to the letters of an alphabet that can cover all the possible contact hole patterns of a full chip contact layer.[12] This alphabet approach would significantly simplify DSA contact hole patterning when the total number of letters of the alphabet is small and would allow us to focus on fully characterizing only the design spaces for the letters of the alphabet. By positioning these letters in various locations we would be able to pattern the full chip contact layer in the same way that the 26 letters of the English alphabet is sufficient to compose an English newspaper. Some of the most basic letters, such as circular templates for 1-hole DSA patterns and elliptical templates for 2- and 3-hole DSA patterns, have been studied extensively.[12] To establish a complete alphabet, though, requires the examination of the entire standard cell library, as well as the optimization of the layout to further reduce the number of letters in the alphabet.[5]

The broad community of DSA researchers has made tremendous progress in the past few years. However to make DSA fully qualified for large-scale semiconductor manufacturing, technical issues such as defectivity reduction and overlay optimization must be solved. While many researchers are developing new block copolymer materials for better chemical properties, there remains more works to be accomplished from the circuit and system design level, including IC layouts optimization for the improvement of DSA process yield and DSA full-chip hotspot detection. Challenges such as optimizing and tuning the template design based on overlay, defectivity, and lithography

ISPD'15, Mar 29 - Apr 01, 2015, Monterey, CA, USA
ACM 978-1-4503-3399-3/15/03.
http://dx.doi.org/10.1145/2717764.2723574

requirements will need to be further investigated in order for practical implementation in industry.

Keywords

Directed self-assembly, block copolymer, layout design, contact hole, lithography

Figures

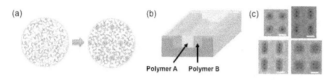

Figure 1. (a) The process of block copolymer self-assembly. The heat causes microphase separation in block copolymer films. (b) Topographical templates bring strong physical confinements so that DSA only happens inside the templates. (c) Top-down Scanning Electron Microscope (SEM) images of DSA patterns. The black spots are polymer A as shown in (b), while the dark grey parts are polymer B as shown in (b). The bright part is the top surface of the templates.

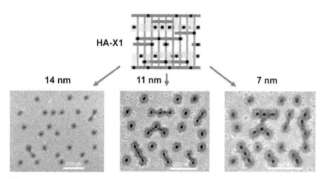

Figure 2. Top: 1-bit half adder layout based on gridded design rule. Bottom: Contact hole patterned by DSA at different technology nodes. As technology node scales down, the multiple-hole templates become increasingly important.

ACKNOWLEDGMENTS

This work was supported in part by US NSF (CMMI, No.1029452), the Global Research Collaboration (GRC) of the Semiconductor Research Corporation (SRC), the W. M. Keck Foundation through the W.M. Keck Foundation Faculty Scholar Award, and the Willard R. and Inez Kerr Bell Professorship endowment. Discussions with Y. Du, Z. Xiao, and Prof. Martin Wong (University of Illinois, Urbana-Champaign), Bart Laenens (ASML), James Conway (Stanford) are much appreciated.

REFERENCES

[1] Bates, F. S.; Fredrickson, G. H., Block copolymers—designer soft materials. *Physics today* **2008,** *52* (2), 32-38.

[2] Bencher, C.; Dai, H.; Chen, Y. In *Gridded design rule scaling: taking the CPU toward the 16nm node*, SPIE Advanced Lithography, International Society for Optics and Photonics: 2009; pp 72740G-72740G-10.

[3] Bita, I.; Yang, J. K.; Jung, Y. S.; Ross, C. A.; Thomas, E. L.; Berggren, K. K., Graphoepitaxy of self-assembled block copolymers on two-dimensional periodic patterned templates. *Science* **2008,** *321* (5891), 939-943.

[4] Black, C. T.; Ruiz, R.; Breyta, G.; Cheng, J. Y.; Colburn, M. E.; Guarini, K. W.; Kim, H.-C.; Zhang, Y., Polymer self assembly in semiconductor microelectronics. *IBM J. Res. Dev.* **2007,** *51* (5), 605-633.

[5] Du, Y.; Guo, D.; Wong, M. D.; Yi, H.; Wong, H.-S. P.; Zhang, H.; Ma, Q. In *Block copolymer directed self-assembly (DSA) aware contact layer optimization for 10 nm 1D standard cell library*, Computer-Aided Design (ICCAD), 2013 IEEE/ACM International Conference on, IEEE: 2013; pp 186-193.

[6] Koay, C.-s.; Halle, S.; Holmes, S.; Petrillo, K.; Colburn, M.; Van Dommelen, Y.; Jiang, A.; Crouse, M.; Dunn, S.; Hetzer, D. In *Towards manufacturing of advanced logic devices by double-patterning*, SPIE Advanced Lithography, International Society for Optics and Photonics: 2011; pp 79730F-79730F-18.

[7] Segalman, R. A.; Yokoyama, H.; Kramer, E. J., Graphoepitaxy of spherical domain block copolymer films. *Adv. Mater.* **2001,** *13* (15), 1152-1155.

[8] Stoykovich, M. P.; Müller, M.; Kim, S. O.; Solak, H. H.; Edwards, E. W.; De Pablo, J. J.; Nealey, P. F., Directed assembly of block copolymer blends into nonregular device-oriented structures. *Science* **2005,** *308* (5727), 1442-1446.

[9] Tang, C.; Lennon, E. M.; Fredrickson, G. H.; Kramer, E. J.; Hawker, C. J., Evolution of block copolymer lithography to highly ordered square arrays. *Science* **2008,** *322* (5900), 429-432.

[10] Yi, H.; Bao, X.-Y.; Zhang, J.; Tiberio, R.; Conway, J.; Chang, L.-W.; Mitra, S.; Wong, H.-S. P. In *Contact-hole patterning for random logic circuits using block copolymer directed self-assembly*, SPIE Advanced Lithography, International Society for Optics and Photonics: 2012; pp 83230W-83230W-6.

[11] Yi, H.; Bao, X. Y.; Zhang, J.; Bencher, C.; Chang, L. W.; Chen, X.; Tiberio, R.; Conway, J.; Dai, H.; Chen, Y., Flexible Control of Block Copolymer Directed Self☐Assembly using Small, Topographical Templates: Potential Lithography Solution for Integrated Circuit Contact Hole Patterning. *Adv. Mater.* **2012,** *24* (23), 3107-3114.

[12] Yi, H.; Bao, X.-Y.; Tiberio, R.; Wong, H. S. P., A General Design Strategy for Block Copolymer Directed Self-Assembly Patterning of Integrated Circuits Contact Holes using an Alphabet Approach. *Nano Letters* **2014.**

A Cell-Based Row-Structure Layout Decomposer for Triple Patterning Lithography

Hsi-An Chien, Szu-Yuan Han, Ye-Hong Chen, and Ting-Chi Wang
Department of Computer Science
National Tsing Hua University, Hsinchu 300, Taiwan
{hsianchien, y2k20096, ckbh1621}@gmail.com, tcwang@cs.nthu.edu.tw

ABSTRACT

In this paper, we study a cell-based row-structure layout decomposition problem for triple patterning lithography (TPL) which asks to minimize a weighted sum of coloring conflicts and stitches. We show how to extend a prior graph-based approach to solve the problem optimally under certain assumptions. Furthermore, several methods to substantially reduce the graph size and hence to accelerate the extended approach are presented. Experimental results show that our decomposer can significantly outperform a state-of-the-art work in terms of both solution quality and run time.

Categories and Subject Descriptors

B.7.2 [**Integrated Circuits**]: Design Aids

General Terms

Algorithms, Design

Keywords

Cell-Based Row-Structure Layout, Triple Patterning Lithography (TPL), TPL Layout Decomposition

1. INTRODUCTION

While double patterning lithography (DPL) [9] has been successfully applied in mass production of 20nm technology node, however, it will not be able to completely resolve conflicting features for layers with much denser and finer features, e.g., the first metal layer (M1 layer) in sub-20nm technology node. In addition, the next-generation lithography technologies (e.g., extreme ultraviolet lithography and electron-beam lithography) are still not ready. Accordingly, triple patterning lithography (TPL) is regarded as one of the most promising solutions for 14/10nm because it could be more flexible in mask assignment and introduce less coloring conflicts than DPL .

ISPD'15, March 29–April 1, 2015, Monterey, CA, USA.
Copyright © 2015 ACM 978-1-4503-3399-3/15/03 ...$15.00.
http://dx.doi.org/10.1145/2717764.2717768 .

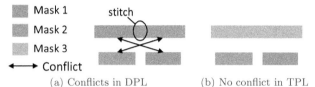

(a) Conflicts in DPL	(b) No conflict in TPL

Figure 1: DPL vs. TPL Decompositions.

If the distance between two polygons on a layer is less than the minimum coloring distance d_{min} in multiple patterning lithography, the polygons must be assigned to different masks (i.e., different colors) to prevent a *coloring conflict*. Besides, a polygon can be split into two sub-polygons by inserting a stitch to further resolve conflicts. However, [1, 12] pointed out that even stitch insertion can not avoid coloring conflict in DPL. Fig. 1(a) gives an example where the distance between any two of the polygons is less than d_{min} so that there still exist two conflicts by using DPL with stitch insertion. Nonetheless, a conflict-free decomposition can be easily found by dividing the layout into three masks (i.e., TPL) as shown in Fig. 1(b).

Recently, several relevant problems in TPL such as layout decomposition [2, 4, 10, 12], TPL-aware routing [5, 6] and TPL-aware placement [3, 7, 11] have been explored and studied. Although the TPL layout decomposition problem is NP-hard for general layouts [12], it has been shown that for any cell-based row-structure layout, whether a TPL decomposition solution that has no coloring conflict and no stitch insertion exists for the M1 layer can be exactly determined in polynomial time [8]. However, the algorithm in [8] will return nothing for an indecomposable layout (i.e., there is no conflict-free solution for the layout) to help designers further resolve the conflicts in the layout. Instead, if there is a decomposition solution with the minimal total cost in terms of conflicts and stitches, it will be more helpful to designers for subsequent layout modifications.

In this paper, we study a cell-based row-structure TPL layout decomposition problem which asks to minimize a weighted sum of coloring conflicts and stitches. Different from [8], our algorithm can always find a decomposition with a minimal cost even though the given layout is indecomposable. Our contributions are summarized as follows:

- We extend an existing graph-based approach [8] to solve the cell-based row-structure TPL layout decomposition problem.

- We present several methods to substantially reduce the graph size and hence to accelerate the extended approach.

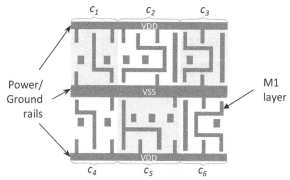

Figure 2: A sample cell-based row-structure layout.

- We parallelize our proposed approach to tackle a layout with multiple rows simultaneously.

- The superiority of our approach over prior works is demonstrated through extensive experiments.

The rest of this paper is organized as follows. Section 2 formulates a cell-based row-structure TPL layout decomposition problem for M1 layer. Section 3 describes our algorithm by extending the approach in [8] as well as explains how to parallelize the algorithm to simultaneously handle multiple rows. Section 4 presents and details several acceleration methods. Experimental results are reported in Section 5, and the conclusion is drawn in Section 6.

2. PROBLEM FORMULATION

Problem 1 (TPL Layout Decomposition). *Given a cell-based row-structure M1 layout (see an example shown in Fig. 2) and a minimum coloring spacing d_{min}, the TPL layout decomposition problem asks to find a TPL layout decomposition with a minimal weighted sum of coloring conflicts and stitches. The weighted sum is defined by Eq. (1), where α and β are user-defined parameters. #conflicts and #stitches denote the number of coloring conflicts and the number of stitches, respectively.*

$$Cost = \alpha \#conflicts + \beta \#stitches. \quad (1)$$

Because there is no coloring conflict between the polygons in different rows [8, 11], the TPL layout decomposition problem for each row can be individually solved. In other words, the TPL layout decomposition problem can be considered as a set of single-row decomposition problems. For an unrouted design, there is also no conflict between two polygons respectively in two non-adjacent cells in a row.

3. LAYOUT DECOMPOSITION APPROACH

3.1 Graph Model

Since our layout decomposition approach is inspired from the algorithm in [8], we will review some basic definitions presented in [8] (see Definitions 1, 2, 3, and 4) and then elaborate our approach. Let P be the set of polygons in the M1 layer of a cell row and $X = \{x_1, x_2, ..., x_m\}$ be the set of m distinct x-coordinates of the left boundaries of all polygons in P, where x_i is to the left of x_j if $i < j$.

Definition 1 (Conflict Graph). *The conflict graph CG of P is an undirected graph. Each node in CG is associated with a polygon in P, and an edge between two nodes*

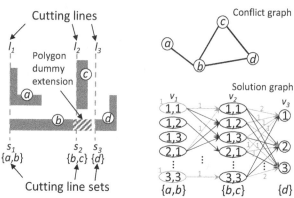

(a) Polygon dummy extension, cutting lines, and cutting line sets

(b) Conflict graph and solution graph

Figure 3: Illustration of Definitions 1 to 5.

means that the distance between the two corresponding polygons is less than d_{min}.

In TPL layout decomposition, two polygons connected by an edge in CG should be assigned to different masks (i.e., different colors); otherwise, they will cause a coloring conflict. In the rest of this paper, two polygons are said to have a *potential conflict* when they are connected by an edge in CG.

Definition 2 (Polygon Dummy Extension). *The polygon dummy extension for a polygon p in P is to extend the right boundary of p to a location x such that $x_{j-1} \leq x < x_j$, where $x_{j-1}, x_j \in X$ and x_j is the the largest coordinate among the left boundaries of the set of polygons each of which has an edge connecting p in CG. Note that when the left boundary of p is located at x_{j-1}, the right boundary of p remains intact after polygon dummy extension.*

Definition 3 (Cutting Line). *For each $x_i \in X$, the cutting line l_i is a vertical line from the top to the bottom of the cell row and is located at x_i.*

Definition 4 (Cutting Line Set). *After performing polygon dummy extension for each polygon in P, the cutting line set s_i of a cutting line l_i is the set of polygons intersecting with l_i.*

According to Definitions $1 \sim 4$, we have the set $L = \{l_1, l_2, ..., l_m\}$ of cutting lines derived from X and the set $S = \{s_1, s_2, ..., s_m\}$ of the corresponding cutting line sets. For a polygon p in P, if a cutting line l_i is located at the left boundary of p, we say p creates l_i. Clearly, each cutting line is *created* by at least one polygon.

Definition 5 (Solution Graph). *The solution graph SG of P is a directed graph, where each node in SG records a coloring solution of a cutting line set, and an edge connecting from a node v_i^j of s_i in S to a node v_{i+1}^k of s_{i+1} in S indicates the coloring solutions of v_i^j and v_{i+1}^k are compatible[1]. Note that all the possible coloring solutions of a cutting line set are enumerated no matter whether each of them is legal or not. Each node (each edge, respectively) in*

---

[1]If a polygon is in both s_i and s_{i+1}, its color in v_i^j and its color in v_{i+1}^k should be the same.

SG is assigned a weight indicating the amount of conflicts in the corresponding coloring solution (the corresponding coloring solutions of the two nodes connected by the edge, respectively). The computation of the weights on a node and an edge will be explicitly described later.

For the layout in Fig. 3(a) and the conflict graph in the top of Fig. 3(b), there are three cutting lines, l_1, l_2, and l_3, and three corresponding cutting line sets, s_1, s_2, and s_3. The right boundary of polygon b is virtually extended by polygon dummy extension such that b is cut by l_2 and hence appears in s_2. Note that the solution graph is partly illustrated in Fig. 3(b) to save space since the entire graph is a bit large; the numbers inside each node represent the coloring solution associated with the node, and the numbers 1, 2, 3 indicate three different colors. The amounts of nodes with respect to cutting line sets $\{a, b\}$ and $\{b, c\}$ are both $3^2 = 9$, as the number of polygons in each of the two sets is 2 and each polygon has three colors to choose. The numbers of edges between adjacent cutting line set pairs ($\{a, b\}$, $\{b, c\}$) and ($\{b, c\}$, $\{d\}$) are 27 and 27 individually.

A *path* in SG goes from a node of the first cutting set (i.e., s_1 in S) to a node of the last cutting set (i.e., s_m in S), and it corresponds to a decomposition of P without stitch insertion. To correctly capture the number of conflicts when finding a decomposition (i.e., a path in the graph), we now describe how to formulate the conflict weights in a node and an edge, respectively. For each cutting line set s_i, there must exist a subset s_i^* of s_i such that s_i^* is the set of polygons creating the cutting line of s_i. We assign a weight of w to a node v_i^j of s_i when the coloring solution of v_i^j induces w conflicts for the polygons in s_i^*. Since all the polygons that have potential conflicts with s_i^* will be in the cutting line set s_{i-1} due to polygon dummy extension, we assign a weight of w to an edge connecting from a node v_{i-1}^k of s_{i-1} to a node v_i^j of s_i when the coloring solutions of v_{i-1}^k and v_i^j induce w conflicts for all pairs of polygons (p, q) with $p \in s_{i-1}$ and $q \in s_i^*$. The reason why we are only concerned with the conflicts for the polygons creating a cutting line is because a polygon could be cut by multiple cutting lines but it creates exactly one cutting line. Therefore, the conflict cost of a path in the graph will not be over-counted and remain correct. Let us see an example in the solution graph of Fig. 3(b). The weight of node v_1 is 1 because there is a potential conflict between two polygons, a and b, the colors of a and b are the same (i.e., color 1), and a and b create the cutting line of $\{a, b\}$. Although polygons b and c have a potential conflict and their colors are also the same in v_2, the weight of v_2 is 0 because c is the only polygon creating the cutting line of $\{b, c\}$. The weight of edge (v_1, v_2) is 1 since there is a coloring conflict between b and c. The weight of edge (v_2, v_3) is 2 since there are a coloring conflict between b and d and a coloring conflict between c and d, respectively. Note that if there is no weight on a node or an edge in Fig. 3, Fig. 4, and Fig. 5, it means the weight of the node or edge is 0.

Basically, SG is almost the same as the one defined in [8] except that it allows (1) the coloring solution of a node to have conflict(s), (2) two nodes to be connecting by an edge when the colors of two different polygons respectively in the nodes cause a coloring conflict, and (3) a node (an edge, respectively) to have a weight. Apparently, the following lemma, i.e., Lemma 1, holds for SG.

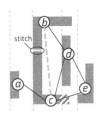
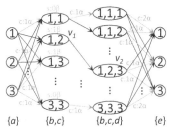

| $\{a\}$ | $\{b,c\}$ | $\{b,c,d\}$ | $\{e\}$ |

(a) Cutting lines, cutting line sets, and conflict graph

(b) Solution graph, where two tags, c and s, indicate conflict weight and stitch weight, respectively

Figure 4: Stitch insertion: α and β in (b) are user-defined parameters in Eq. (1).

Lemma 1. *Each possible decomposition of P without stitch insertion corresponds to a path in SG.*

Lemma 2. *The TPL layout decomposition problem without stitch insertion for P can be optimally solved by finding a least-cost path in the solution graph SG of P, where the cost of a path in SG is the accumulated cost of nodes and edges along the path.*

PROOF. Suppose that a valid decomposition which has no stitch insertion and no coloring conflicts exists in P. [8] has proved that they can get a valid decomposition by finding a path in their proposed solution graph for P. By the definition of our solution graph SG for P, such a valid decomposition can be also found from a path with cost of 0 in SG. When there is no conflict-free decomposition in P, the optimal decomposition is the one with minimum conflicts. According to Lemma 1, the optimal decomposition must exist in SG. Besides, the cost of a path in SG exactly indicates the amount of coloring conflicts of the decomposition associated with the path. Thus, the corresponding decomposition of a shortest (i.e., least-cost) path in SG is an optimal TPL layout decomposition. □

3.2 Stitch Insertion

Given a layout with a set of stitch candidates, the polygons are fractured based on the stitch candidates, and the conflict graph is constructed for the fractured polygons. If a stitch candidate is between two polygons, the stitch edge connecting two nodes corresponding to the polygons in the conflict graph denotes that a *stitch* occurs when the polygons are assigned to different masks. Fig. 4 gives an example to describe how to formulate the stitch weights in a solution graph. As can be seen in Fig. 4(a), there is one stitch edge shown in green dashed line connecting two polygons b and c in the conflict graph, and the solution graph with conflict weights and stitch weights is shown in Fig. 4(b). Conflict weight is represented in red color with a tag c, and stitch weight is represented in green color with a tag s. Similar to the computation for conflict weight, for each cutting line set s, there must exist a subset s^* of s such that s^* is the set of polygons creating the cutting line of s. We assign a weight of w to a node v of s when the coloring solution of v induces w stitches for the polygons in s^*. For example, there is a stitch weight of 1β on the node v_1 of cutting line set $\{b, c\}$, since b and c are the polygons creating the cutting line of $\{b, c\}$ and their colors in the coloring solution (i.e., (1, 2)) are different. Although the colors of b and c are also different in the coloring solution of the node v_2 of cutting line set $\{b, c, d\}$, the stitch weight on v_2 is 0 because b and c are not the polygons creating the cutting line of $\{b, c, d\}$ but d is. In this way, the stitch cost of a path in the graph will not be over-counted and remain correct.

Lemma 3. *The TPL layout decomposition problem for P with a given set of stitch candidates can be optimally solved by finding a shortest path in the solution graph of the fractured polygons of P.*

PROOF. With the given stitch candidates, the polygons of P are fractured into more polygons. According to Lemma 1, the optimal decomposition of the fractured polygons still exists in the corresponding solution graph. Similar to the proof of Lemma 2, we can find a shortest path (i.e., a decomposition with a minimum weighted sum of Eq. (1)) in the solution graph to optimally solve the layout decomposition problem. $\square$

3.3 Hierarchical Method

Since the concepts of conflict graph, polygon dummy extension, cutting line, cutting line set, and solution graph are all applicable to a standard cell as well, we also adopt a speedup method in a similar way as [8]. The solution graph for each cell in the cell library is first built and stored in a table. For a set of cells placed in a row, the solution graph of the layout in the row can be first constructed by sequentially copying the solution graph of each cell in the row directly from the one stored in the table according to the cell order from left to right. But there might be some additional potential conflicts introduced between two adjacent cells. In order to capture the additional potential conflicts, the *boundary conflicting polygon set* of two adjacent cells is introduced and defined as follows.

Definition 6 (Boundary Conflicting Polygon Set).

The boundary conflicting polygon set (BCP) for two adjacent cells c_i and c_j is a subset of polygons in c_i and c_j, where c_i is to the left of c_j. A polygon p in c_i (c_j, respectively) will be in the BCP when p is within a distance of d_{min} from the right boundary of c_i (the left boundary of c_j, respectively).

Similarly, conflict graph, polygon dummy extension, cutting line, cutting line set, and solution graph are also applicable to a BCP. Therefore, we then combine the solution graphs of two adjacent cells with the solution graph of the corresponding BCP to capture the potential conflicts between the cells. Fig. 5 gives an example to show how to construct the solution graph for two adjacent cells. We first construct the conflict graph for the BCP of two adjacent cells c_1 and c_2 (see Fig. 5(a)). Based on the conflict graph, we then construct the solution graph for the BCP in Fig. 5(b). Finally, by combining the three solution graphs of c_1, c_2, and the BCP, the final solution graph (see Fig. 5(c)) is done. Note that the solution graph of the BCP for each pair of adjacent cells with a fixed distance between them can be also built and stored in the table in advance for speedup.

For a routed design, there might be some M1 wire connections overlapping with a set of cells in a row so that the solution graphs, which are associated with the cells in the set and are stored in the table, can not be directly used. The cells covered by the wire connections can be divided into disjoint sets of consecutive cells, where two cells covered by

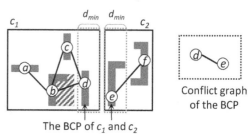

(a) Two cells, c_1 and c_2, placed in a row, and the conflict graph of the BCP, $BCP_{c_1,c_2} = \{d, e\}$, of c_1 and c_2

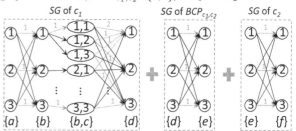

(b) Three solution graphs (SGs) of c_1, c_2, and BCP_{c_1,c_2}, where the solution graph of c_1 is partly shown

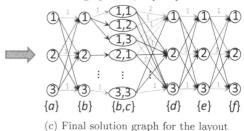

(c) Final solution graph for the layout

Figure 5: Illustration of constructing the solution graph for a layout of two adjacent cells.

a wire connection must be in the same set. Similar to the algorithm in [8], each set can be considered as one large cell when constructing the solution graph by our approach.

3.4 Power/Ground Rail

Though all the cutting lines must cut the power (VDD) and the ground (VSS) rails in a row, it is not necessary to add both VDD and VSS into each cutting line set. We can pre-assign colors to VDD and VSS (the colors are either the same or different) before constructing the solution graph SG. The coloring conflict between VDD/VSS and one polygon p is captured in SG by increasing the weight by 1 for each node v of the cutting line set s, where the cutting line of s is created by p and p's color specified by the coloring solution of v causes a coloring conflict with VDD/VSS. In addition, we only need to try one color combination for each pre-coloring case of VDD and VSS when constructing SG, because the colors of SG can be rotated to get another solution graph for a different color combination. Finally, the best decomposition result of the row can be chosen from the two pre-coloring cases for VDD and VSS. For the hierarchical method (mentioned in Section 3.3), we therefore need to build a table for one pre-coloring case and another table for the other pre-coloring case.

3.5 Parallelism for Multiple Rows

Given a design with m rows, the TPL decomposition problem of each row can be independently and simultaneously

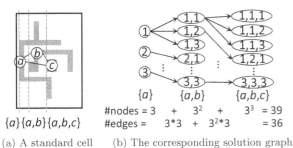

(a) A standard cell   (b) The corresponding solution graph

Figure 6: The solution graph of a standard cell.

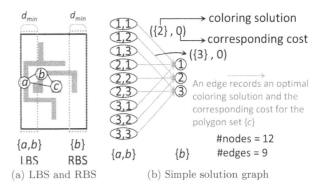

(a) LBS and RBS   (b) Simple solution graph

Figure 7: The simple solution graph of the cell in Fig. 6(a).

solved by our approach, because there is no coloring conflict between the polygons in different rows. Thus, we can directly parallelize our algorithm by assigning the TPL decomposition problem of each row to one thread. For each row, it will select a best decomposition solution from the two pre-coloring cases for VDD and VSS, and the result of each row is just combined together directly from the first row to the last row. If two adjacent rows have different colors for the sharing VDD or VSS connection, the colors of the second row need to be rotated to make the color of the sharing VDD or VSS connection the same.

4. GRAPH REDUCTION TECHNIQUES

In this section, we will present several techniques to reduce the size of solution graph so as to accelerate our approach without loss of decomposition quality. For easy understanding, there are no stitches in the layouts and no weights in the solution graphs of the remaining figures, and the solution graphs are partly presented. Besides, the discussions in Sections 4.1 ∼ 4.3 are for one pre-coloring case of VDD and VSS.

4.1 Simple Solution Graph

Fig. 6(b) shows the solution graph of a standard cell in Fig. 6(a), where the solution graph has totally 39 nodes and 36 edges. With a careful observation on the three cutting line sets $\{a\}$, $\{a,b\}$, and $\{a,b,c\}$, $\{a,b,c\}$ includes all the polygons in the cell so that there is no need to keep the other cutting line sets when constructing the solution graph. As a result, the numbers of nodes and edges in the graph are reduced to 27 and 0, respectively. Thus, we can find that the original construction method of solution graph is not clever and could create too many nodes and edges which can be abandoned to reduce the graph size. Hence, we devise a new graph model called *simple solution graph* to simplify the original solution graph. Let P_{c_i} be the set of polygons in the M1 layer of a cell c_i in the cell library. The *left boundary set* (LBS) (*right boundary set* (RBS), respectively) of c_i is a subset of P_{c_i} such that each polygon in the LBS (RBS, respectively) is within a distance of d_{min} from the left (right, respectively) boundary of c_i. Let LBS_{c_i} and RBS_{c_i} denote the LBS and the RBS of c_i, respectively. $OP_{c_i} = P_{c_i} \setminus (LBS_{c_i} \cup RBS_{c_i})$ is the set of the *other polygons* (OP) of c_i. Without loss of generality, we assume that LBS_{c_i} and RBS_{c_i} are not empty sets.

Definition 7 (Simple Solution Graph). *The simple solution graph of P_{c_i} is defined as a solution graph for $LBS_{c_i} \cup RBS_{c_i}$. Each edge e connecting from a node of LBS_{c_i} to a node of RBS_{c_i} records an optimal coloring solution of OP_{c_i} and a cost of w computed by Eq. (1) for the*

optimal coloring solution, given the two associated coloring solutions of the nodes of e.

It can be observed that LBS_{c_i} and RBS_{c_i} are basically the sets of boundary conflicting polygons close to c_i's left boundary and right boundary, respectively, but OP_{c_i} is not. Because OP_{c_i} does not cause any conflicts with the polygons in other cells, we can try to remove the coloring solutions of OP_{c_i} from the solution graph, which will not affect the decomposition quality. For the cell in Fig. 6(a), its simple solution graph (see Fig. 7(b)) is constructed based on its LBS and RBS (see Fig. 7(a)). Each edge between the nodes of the LBS and the RBS is associated with an optimal coloring solution and the corresponding cost for OP_{c_i}. The number of nodes enumerated by both the LBS and RBS is 12 and the number of edges between the nodes is 9. As compared with the solution graph in Fig. 6(b), we can see that the simple solution graph gets a significant reduction in both the numbers of nodes and edges.

To find the coloring solution of OP_{c_i} associated with each edge in the simple solution graph, we construct the solution graph SG for OP_{c_i} and copy the nodes of both LBS_{c_i} and LBS_{c_i} to SG. Besides, a node of LBS_{c_i} to a node of the first cutting line set of SG (a node of the last cutting line set of SG to a node of RBS_{c_i}, respectively) is connected by an edge when the two nodes are compatible. Then, we find the shortest path in SG from a node of LBS_{c_i} to a node of RBS_{c_i} to get an optimal coloring solution of OP_{c_i} when the colors of $LBS_{c_i} \cup RBS_{c_i}$ are specified by the coloring solutions of the two nodes. Actually, we can easily find the shortest paths from a node v of LBS_{c_i} to all nodes of RBS_{c_i} by running one breadth-first search starting from v till all nodes of RBS_{c_i} are visited, since SG is a directed acyclic graph.

Moreover, we find that some polygons in LBS_{c_i} (RBS_{c_i}, respectively) can be removed and added into OP_{c_i} to further reduce the size of the simple solution graph without loss of decomposition quality. To determine if a polygon p of c_i can be removed from LBS_{c_i} or RBS_{c_i}, we can check if there is no potential conflict between p and any polygon of each cell c_j in the library when c_i and c_j are abutted. For example, there are two cells c_1 and c_2 in Fig. 8(a), and polygon b in c_2 has no potential conflict with the polygons in c_1. Thus, b is removed from LBS_{c_2}, and the simple solution graph of c_2 as shown in Fig. 8(b) will be constructed based on the new LBS_{c_2} and the original RBS_{c_2}. Consequently, the graph is further simplified relative to the one in Fig. 7(b).

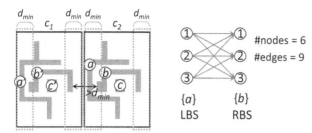

(a) Two abutted cells c_1 and c_2 (b) Simple solution graph of c_2

Figure 8: The simple solution graph of the cell in Fig. 6(a) with the reduced LBS.

4.2 Reduced Simple Solution Graph

Since the simple solution graph of a cell is constructed based on the LBS and the RBS, the amount of edges of the graph could dramatically increase as the number of polygons in both the LBS and the RBS increases. If the LBS has n polygons and the RBS has m polygons, the number of the edges between the nodes in the graph could be up to 3^{m+n}. Fig. 9(a) and Fig. 9(b) give an example showing the total number of polygons in both the LBS and the RBS is 5 and the number of edges is $3^5 = 243$. To reduce the number of edges, we create the *dummy LBS* (abbreviated as DLBS) and the *dummy RBS* (abbreviated as DRBS) for a LBS and a RBS, respectively. The DLBS (DRBS, respectively) of c_i is a subset of LBS_{c_i} (RBS_{c_i}, respectively) in which each polygon in the DLBS (DRBS, respectively) has a potential conflict with at least a polygon in RBS_{c_i} (LBS_{c_i}, respectively) or OP_{c_i}. Besides, if a polygon is in both LBS_{c_i} and RBS_{c_i}, it will be also added to the DLBS and DRBS of c_i. Let $DLBS_{c_i}$ and $DRBS_{c_i}$ denote the DLBS and DRBS of c_i, respectively. Now, the *reduced simple solution graph* of c_i is constructed based on the four polygon sets LBS_{c_i}, $DLBS_{c_i}$, $DRBS_{c_i}$, and RBS_{c_i} in the order of LBS_{c_i}, $DLBS_{c_i}$, $DRBS_{c_i}$, RBS_{c_i}. Different from a simple solution graph, the optimal coloring solution and the cost of OP_{c_i} are recorded on each edge between the nodes of $DLBS_{c_i}$ and $DRBS_{c_i}$. Note that we assign weights 0 to the nodes of both $DLBS_{c_i}$ and $DRBS_{c_i}$ and to the edges between the nodes of LBS_{c_i} and $DLBS_{c_i}$ ($DRBS_{c_i}$ and RBS_{c_i}, respectively).

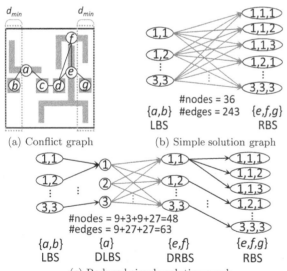

(a) Conflict graph   (b) Simple solution graph

(c) Reduced simple solution graph

Figure 9: The reduced simple solution graph of a cell.

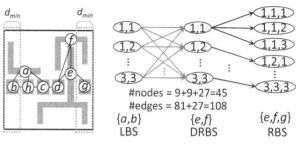

(a) Conflict graph   (b) Reduced simple solution graph

Figure 10: The reduced simple solution graph of a cell.

The reason why adding two dummy sets $DLBS_{c_i}$ and $DRBS_{c_i}$ is because the amount of the coloring solutions of OP_{c_i} (i.e., the edges between LBS_{c_i} and RBS_{c_i} in the simple solution graph) can be further reduced when $DLBS_{c_i} \subset LBS_{c_i}$ or $DRBS_{c_i} \subset RBS_{c_i}$. Besides, the decomposition quality for c_i still remains unaffected since there is no potential conflict between a polygon in $LBS_{c_i} \setminus DLBS_{c_i}$ ($RBS_{c_i} \setminus DRBS_{c_i}$, respectively) and a polygon in OP_{c_i}. Fig. 9(c) demonstrates the reduced simple solution graph for the simple solution graph in Fig. 9(b). Apparently, the total graph size is reduced after adding the DLBS and the DRBS though the number of nodes is more than before.

There are three scenarios for the construction of a reduced simple solution graph, where both the DLBS and DRBS are not empty sets for the scenarios 1 and 2:

1. DLBS is not equal to LBS and DRBS is not equal to RBS:
   As the aforementioned description for Fig. 9(c), both the DLBS and the DRBS are added into the graph for reducing the graph size.

2. DLBS is equal to LBS or DRBS is equal to RBS:
   When the DLBS (DRBS, respectively) is equal to the LBS (RBS, respectively) for a cell, we do not create the DLBS(DRBS, respectively) to avoid enlarging the graph size instead. Fig. 10 shows an example in which the DLBS is equal to the LBS for the cell so that the DLBS is excluded from the reduced simple solution graph.

3. DLBS and/or DRBS is an empty set:
   If the DLBS (DRBS, respectively) for a cell is an empty set, a pseudo node with weight of 0 is created for the DLBS (DRBS, respectively). As can be seen from Fig. 11, the DLBS of the cell is empty since there is no conflict between the polygons of the LBS and the others. Accordingly, we build the reduced solution graph with the pseudo node of the DLBS for the cell as shown

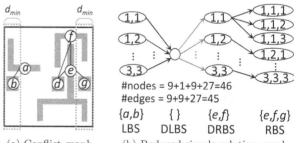

(a) Conflict graph   (b) Reduced simple solution graph

Figure 11: The reduced simple solution graph of a cell.

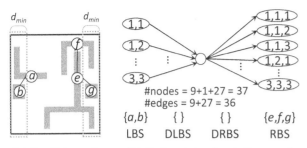

(a) Conflict graph   (b) Reduced simple solution graph

Figure 12: The reduced simple solution graph of a cell.

in Fig. 11(b). Moreover, if both the DLBS and the DRBS are empty, we can merge their pseudo nodes into one, and there will be only one coloring solution of the OP recorded on the merged pseudo node (see the example in Fig. 12).

4.3 Reduced Simple Solution Graph for BCP

As we redesign the solution graph to be the simple solution graph for a cell, the solution graph for a BCP cannot be directly used to combine with a simple solution graph. Thus, we also devise a reduced simple solution graph for the BCP of two adjacent cells c_i and c_j. RBS_{c_i} of the left cell c_i and LBS_{c_j} of the right cell c_j, respectively, can be considered as the LBS and the RBS of the BCP, while the OP of the BCP is an empty set. As a result, the reduced simple solution graph of the BCP can be easily constructed in the same way as before. Fig. 13 gives an example. The simple solution graph for the BCP of c_1 and c_2 is shown on the left side of Fig. 13(b). Obviously, there is no potential conflict between RBS_{c_1} and LBS_{c_2}, and hence we can create two empty sets, $DRBS_{c_1}$ and $DLBS_{c_2}$, to reduce the graph size (i.e., the third scenario in Section 4.3.2). Finally, the reduced simple solution graph for the BCP of c_1 and c_2 is shown on the right side of Fig. 13(b).

4.4 Overall Approach

Given a cell library and a set of stitch candidates for each cell, we first off-line build a look-up table in each pre-coloring case for VDD and VSS, where the table contains the reduced simple solution graph for each single cell and the set of reduced simple solution graphs for the BCPs of each cell pair.[2] For a row r of n cells, we can construct a solution graph for r under each pre-coloring case, by combining the reduced simple solution graphs stored in the corresponding table for each cell and each pair of adjacent cells in r. The shortest path in the solution graph corresponds to the best decomposition for a pre-coloring case, and therefore the decomposition of r is the one with less cost between the two pre-coloring cases.

5. EXPERIMENTAL RESULTS

The proposed algorithm has been implemented in C++ language, and all experiments were conducted on a Linux

---

[2]The number of reduced simple solution graphs in the set is $k + 1$ for the BCPs of two adjacent cells, where k is the minimum number of sites (white space) between the cells such that there is no potential conflict between the cells. The reduced simple solution graph for the BCP of the cells with q sites between the cells is the same as the one with k sites if $q > k$.

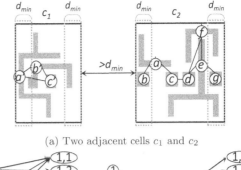

(a) Two adjacent cells c_1 and c_2

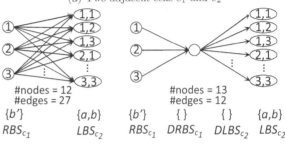

(b) Simple solution graph on the left side and reduced simple solution graph on the right side for the BCP of c_1 and c_2

Figure 13: The reduced simple solution graph of a BCP.

workstation with 2.0 GHz Intel Xeon CPU and 96 GB memory. Two benchmark suites provided by the authors of [11] and [10] are used. The first one is a set of placed circuits from the OpenSPARC T1 designs, and the other is the set of ISCAS-85&89 routed circuits. The parameter setting such as d_{min}, α, and β for each benchmark is the same as [11] and [10]. Finally, The stitch candidates of all test cases are generated by [4], which is the same as [10].

In Tables 1 ~ 3, we report the value of Eq. (1) (in the "Cost" column), the number of conflicts (in the "#C" column), the number of stitches (in the "#S" column), and the runtime measured in second on t threads (in #T-t). "Ours" and "Ours-GR" represent our algorithms with and without graph reduction, respectively.

To the best of our knowledge, the algorithm in [10] is the current state-of-the-art TPL decomposer. For making fair comparisons, we ran the decomposer provided by [10] on our machine.[3] Note that the released TPL decomposer does not consider the layout density issue. First, we compare our algorithm with the TPL decomposer [10] on the OpenSPARC T1 designs whose layouts are much denser than the ISCAS-85&89 circuits. As can be seen from Table 1, our decomposer with graph reduction successfully obtained the decomposition for each test case in a few seconds; however, the one in [10] could not complete in the time limit (i.e., five hours) for almost half of the test cases. In addition, our approach produced much better decomposition quality and ran much faster for every test case that [10] could also complete in the time limit; though we used more stitches, the total cost is still less than that produced by [10].

We also make an analysis for the graph reduction methods proposed in this paper. The comparisons between our approaches with and without graph reduction are shown in Table 2. We can find that the amount of nodes and the amount of edges are averagely reduced by 94% and 77%, respectively. Consequently, there are 76% ~ 80% runtime

---

[3]Since the algorithm in [10] cannot be executed in a multi-threaded mode, we ran it on a single thread.

improvements on average in the multi-threaded modes with 4, 2, and 1 threads.

To further observe the decomposition quality that our decomposer can achieve, we compare with the algorithms in [8] and [10] on the frequently used benchmarks ISCAS-85&89 circuits in Table 3. Note that in Table 3, the results of [10] are obtained by executing the decomposer of [10] on our machine and are slightly different from those reported in [10], while the results of [8] are directly quoted from [8]. Apparently, it supports again that our approach can find the decomposition without any conflict for a layout if the layout is decomposable (i.e., conflict-free), when compared with [8]. Moreover, as compared with [10], our approach also produced better or same results in terms of the amount of conflicts, the amount of stitches, and, consequently, the total cost.

6. CONCLUSIONS

In this work, we extend an existing approach to solve a row-structure TPL layout decomposition problem. Several methods to substantially reduce the graph size and hence to accelerate the extended approach are also presented. The experimental results show that our algorithm is not only effective but also efficient.

7. REFERENCES

[1] V. O. Anton, N. Peter, H. Judy, G. Ronald, and N. Robert. Pattern split rules! a feasibility study of rule based pitch decomposition for double patterning. In *Proc. of SPIE*, volume 6730, 2007.

[2] S.-Y. Fang, Y.-W. Chang, and W.-Y. Chen. A novel layout decomposition algorithm for triple patterning lithography. In *Proc. of DAC*, pages 1185–1190, 2012.

[3] J. Kuang, W.-K. Chow, and E. F. Y. Young. Triple patterning lithography aware optimization for standard cell based design. In *Proc. of ICCAD*, pages 108–115, 2014.

[4] J. Kuang and E. F. Y. Young. An efficient layout decomposition approach for triple patterning lithography. In *Proc. of DAC*, pages 1–6, 2013.

[5] Y.-H. Lin, B. Yu, D. Z. Pan, and Y.-L. Li. Triad: A triple patterning lithography aware detailed router. In *Proc. of ICCAD*, pages 123–129, 2012.

[6] H. Z. Q. Ma and M. D. F. Wong. Triple patterning aware routing and its comparison with double patterning aware routing in 14nm technology. In *Proc. of DAC*, pages 591–596, 2012.

[7] H. Tian, Y. Du, H. Zhang, Z. Xiao, and M. D. F. Wong. Triple patterning aware detailed placement with constrained pattern assignment. In *Proc. of ICCAD*, pages 116–123, 2014.

[8] H. Tian, H. Zhang, Q. Ma, Z. Xiao, and M. D. F. Wong. A polynomial time triple patterning algorithm for cell based row-structure layout. In *Proc. of ICCAD*, pages 57–64, 2012.

[9] Y. Xu and C. Chu. A matching based decomposer for double patterning lithography. In *Proc. of ISPD*, pages 121–126, 2010.

[10] B. Yu, Y.-H. Lin, G. Luk-Pat, D. Ding, K. Lucas, and D. Z. Pan. A high-performance triple patterning layout decomposer with balanced density. In *Proc. of ICCAD*, pages 163–169, 2013.

[11] B. Yu, X. Xu, J.-R. Gao, and D. Z. Pan. Methodology for standard cell compliance and detailed placement for triple patterning lithography. In *Proc. of ICCAD*, pages 349–356, 2013.

[12] B. Yu, B. Zhang, D. Ding, and D. Z. Pan. Layout decomposition for triple patterning lithography. In *Proc. of ICCAD*, pages 1–8, 2011.

Table 1: Comparisons with a state-of-the-art TPL decomposer [10] on the OpenSPARC T1 designs

Test Case	[10]				Ours-GR			
	Cost	#C	#S	T-1	Cost	#C	#S	T-4
alu-70	408.1	336	721	213	286.5	185	1015	4
alu-80	N/A	N/A	N/A	>18000	474.4	353	1214	8
alu-90	N/A	N/A	N/A	>18000	520.6	398	1226	5
byp-70	656.9	502	1549	830	636.0	437	1990	10
byp-80	1076.5	897	1795	2544	831.2	612	2192	14
byp-90	N/A	N/A	N/A	>18000	1012.4	780	2324	22
div-70	726.2	568	1582	913	620.7	424	1967	12
div-80	703.7	545	1587	1182	578.4	383	1954	11
div-90	656.9	502	1549	830	528.9	338	1909	11
ecc-70	N/A	N/A	N/A	>18000	134.6	89	456	3
ecc-80	207.3	159	483	485	197.5	140	575	4
ecc-90	N/A	N/A	N/A	>18000	275.4	214	614	6
efc-70	N/A	N/A	N/A	>18000	218.4	143	754	5
efc-80	N/A	N/A	N/A	>18000	247.1	172	751	4
efc-90	302.8	241	618	202	209.0	134	750	3
ctl-70	248.5	215	335	970	209.3	170	393	4
ctl-80	N/A	N/A	N/A	>18000	212.6	167	456	4
ctl-90	187.5	150	375	537	152.4	111	414	4
top-70	N/A	N/A	N/A	>18000	2320.3	1754	5663	15
top-80	3221.1	2774	4471	3807	2702.0	2118	5840	31
top-90	3506.0	3002	5040	9305	3233.9	2618	6159	36

Table 2: Comparisons of our approaches on the OpenSPARC T1 designs

Test Case	Ours					Ours-GR				
	#V	#E	T-1	T-2	T-4	#V	#E	T-1	T-2	T-4
alu-70	7.67e+06	5.45e+07	29	16	11	5.28e+05	1.55e+07	8	4	4
alu-80	7.91e+06	5.82e+07	34	18	20	5.37e+05	2.44e+07	13	7	8
alu-90	7.90e+06	5.66e+07	32	20	19	5.41e+05	2.49e+07	13	7	5
byp-70	2.75e+07	2.16e+08	114	75	43	1.75e+06	4.42e+07	23	13	10
byp-80	2.78e+07	2.19e+08	121	76	64	1.76e+06	5.56e+07	30	17	14
byp-90	2.81e+07	2.22e+08	120	75	69	1.77e+06	7.18e+07	38	22	22
div-70	2.02e+07	1.60e+08	90	50	39	1.20e+06	3.70e+07	19	11	12
div-80	2.02e+07	1.62e+08	94	51	60	1.20e+06	4.39e+07	24	14	11
div-90	2.01e+07	1.60e+08	88	55	26	1.20e+06	3.74e+07	20	11	11
ecc-70	1.02e+07	8.93e+07	51	28	25	5.06e+05	1.12e+07	5	3	3
ecc-80	1.03e+07	8.99e+07	53	29	27	5.07e+05	1.47e+07	7	4	4
ecc-90	1.04e+07	8.96e+07	55	30	22	5.11e+05	1.83e+07	9	5	6
efc-70	9.80e+06	6.08e+07	33	19	19	3.27e+05	1.13e+07	5	3	3
efc-80	9.80e+06	6.15e+07	34	18	15	3.29e+05	1.27e+07	6	4	4
efc-90	9.84e+06	6.13e+07	33	18	19	3.27e+05	1.20e+07	6	3	3
ctl-70	1.26e+07	1.03e+08	57	39	20	5.83e+05	1.57e+07	7	4	3
ctl-80	1.25e+07	1.02e+08	58	33	35	5.81e+05	1.47e+07	7	4	4
ctl-90	1.25e+07	1.01e+08	57	32	22	5.79e+05	1.46e+07	7	4	4
top-70	6.73e+07	4.87e+08	155	105	105	3.72e+06	9.67e+07	48	26	15
top-80	6.76e+07	4.92e+08	291	154	152	3.74e+06	1.08e+08	54	30	31
top-90	6.79e+07	4.97e+08	292	156	89	3.77e+06	1.20e+08	63	34	36
Ratio	1	1	1	1	1	0.06	0.23	0.20	0.20	0.24

Table 3: Comparisons with two previous works [8] and [10] on the ISCAS85&89 circuits

Test Case	[8]			[10]			Ours		
	Cost	#C	#S	Cost	#C	#S	Cost	#C	#S
C432	N/A	N/A	N/A	0.4	0	4	0.4	0	4
C499	0	0	0	0	0	0	0	0	0
C880	0.7	0	7	0.7	0	7	0.7	0	7
C1355	0.3	0	3	0.3	0	3	0.3	0	3
C1908	0.1	0	1	0.1	0	1	0.1	0	1
C2670	0.6	0	6	0.6	0	6	0.6	0	6
C3540	N/A	N/A	N/A	1.9	1	9	1.8	1	8
C5315	N/A	N/A	N/A	0.9	0	9	0.9	0	9
C6288	N/A	N/A	N/A	22.2	1	212	20.5	0	206
C7552	N/A	N/A	N/A	2.6	0	26	2.3	0	22
S1488	0.2	0	2	0.3	0	3	0.2	0	2
S38417	N/A	N/A	N/A	25.7	20	57	24.4	19	54
S35932	N/A	N/A	N/A	52	46	60	48	44	40
S38584	N/A	N/A	N/A	49.1	36	131	47.6	36	116
S15850	N/A	N/A	N/A	45.9	34	119	44.1	34	98
Ratio				1.06	1.03	1.12	1	1	1

TPL-Aware Displacement-driven Detailed Placement Refinement with Coloring Constraints

Tao Lin
Iowa State University
tlin@iastate.edu

Chris Chu
Iowa State University
cnchu@iastate.edu

ABSTRACT

To minimize the effect of process variation for a design in triple patterning lithography (TPL), it is beneficial for all standard cells of the same type to share a single coloring solution. In this paper, we investigate the TPL-aware detailed placement refinement problem under these coloring constraints. Given an initial detailed placement, the positions of standard cells are perturbed and a TPL solution complying with the coloring constraints is derived while minimizing cell displacement, lithography conflicts and stitches. We prove that this problem is NP-complete and show that it can be formulated as a mixed integer linear program. Since mixed integer linear programming is very time consuming, we propose an effective heuristic algorithm. In our approach, important adjacent pairs of standard cells are recognized firstly, since they have significant impact on cell displacement. Then a tree-based heuristic is applied to generate a good initial solution for our linear programming-based refinement. Experimental results show that compared with mixed integer linear programming, our heuristic approach is comparable in solution quality while using very short CPU runtime.

1. INTRODUCTION

With the technology node scaling to sub-16nm, electron beam (E-beam), extreme ultraviolet lithography (EUVL) and TPL are considered the most promising lithography technologies. In this paper, we are focusing on TPL.

There are many previous works on TPL optimization. The fundamental problem of TPL is to eliminate lithography conflicts while minimizing stitch count. [1–8] are related to TPL layout decomposition. [1–4] focus on 2-Dimension layout decomposition. [5, 6] focus on row-based 1-Dimension layout decomposition. [9, 10] consider TPL during detailed routing stage.

Recently, [11] presents a TPL aware detailed placement approach in which layout decomposition and placement are resolved simultaneously. The approach is effective in resolv-

ing lithography conflicts. However, the approach only considers the optimization of wirelength together with lithography conflicts and stitch number. It is not clear how to incorporate other placement objectives like timing and routability.

Besides, [6] points out the advantage of assigning the same lithography pattern for the same standard cell type during TPL layout decomposition. This would minimize the effect of process variation and best guarantee that those standard cells of the same type eventually have similar physical and electrical characteristics. However, [6] only considers the decomposition of a fixed layout, and hence often cannot completely satisfy these constraints.

In this paper, we investigate the TPL-aware detailed placement refinement problem under the coloring constraints that all standard cells of the same type should share the same TPL coloring solution. Given an initial detailed placement, the positions of standard cells are perturbed and a TPL solution complying with the coloring constraints is derived while minimizing total cell displacement, lithography conflicts and stitches simultaneously.

Different from [11], our approach is applied to an optimized detailed placement under any conventional placement metrics. By refining it with minimal perturbation, the quality of the detailed placement can be preserved. In addition, we consider the coloring constraints. Compared with [6], as placement perturbation is allowed, the coloring constraints are always satisfied in our approach. We prove that this problem is NP-complete and show that it can be formulated as a mixed integer linear program (MILP). Since the MILP is time consuming to solve, we propose an effective heuristic algorithm to solve it. In our algorithm, important adjacent pairs of standard cells are recognized firstly, since they have significant impact on cell displacement. Then a tree-based heuristic is applied to generate a good initial solution which is then refined by a linear programming (LP)-based technique. Experimental results show that compared with MILP solution, the heuristic method is comparable in solution quality while using very limited CPU runtime. The contributions of this paper are summarized as follows.

- We formulate a new TPL optimization problem considering TPL coloring constraints for standard cells during detailed placement.

- We prove that this new problem is NP-complete.

- We propose a MILP formulation for this new problem.

- Since MILP is very time consuming to solve, we propose an effective heuristic algorithm.

ISPD'15, March 29–April 1, 2015, Monterey, CA, USA.
Copyright © 2015 ACM 978-1-4503-3399-3/15/04 ...$15.00.
http://dx.doi.org/10.1145/2717764.2717770.

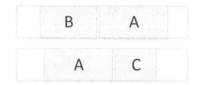

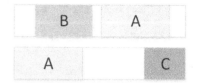

(a) Given initial detailed placement.

(b) One solution: try to optimize the displacement of the second row.

(c) Another solution: try to optimize the displacement of the first row.

Figure 1: An instance of problem: choosing different coloring solutions for types A, B and C plus cell shifting.

The rest of paper is organized as follows. In Section 2, we gives the formal problem definition and its MILP formulation. In Section 3, we prove that this problem is NP-complete. In Section 4, we illustrate the heuristic algorithm. In Section 5, we present the experimental results. Finally, we make our conclusions in Section 6.

2. PROBLEM DEFINITION

Given a standard cell library, all feasible coloring solutions for each cell type are found out firstly. Since each cell contains only a small number of layout features, the enumerative approach proposed in [11] works well. Besides, this step is performed once per library. For the i-th type of cell denoted by t_i, there are n_i feasible coloring solutions $p_i^1, p_i^2, \cdots, p_i^{n_i}$. The corresponding stitch counts are $s_i^1, s_i^2, \ldots, s_i^{n_i}$. The width of t_i is w_i. There are k types of standard cells in the library. Given a detailed placement, which has n rows. For the j-th row, the types of standard cells ordered from left to right are $c_j^1, c_j^2, \cdots, c_j^{r_j}$, where r_j is the number of cells in the j-th row.

The TPL-aware displacement-driven detailed placement with coloring constraints is defined as follows.

Given a standard cell library with a set of feasible coloring solutions for each standard cell type, and an initial detailed placement, eliminate all lithography conflicts by choosing one coloring solution for each type of standard cell and shifting the standard cells without changing the cell ordering in each row. The objective is to minimize the total cell displacement and the number of stitches.

Fig. 1 gives an instance of this problem. By choosing coloring solutions for types A, B and C and shifting cells, conflicts are eliminated. In Fig. 1(a), an initial detailed placement with two rows is given. In Fig. 1(b), cell displacement of the second row is optimized well while that of the first row is not. On the contrary, in Fig. 1(c), cell displacement of the first row is optimized well while that of the second row is not. It shows that different TPL solutions may lead to significantly different cell distribution in each row.

2.1 MILP formulation

The above problem can be formulated as a MILP. We use a binary variable b_i^j to denote whether the coloring solution p_i^j is assigned to standard cell type t_i. In the i-th row, the original central x-coordinates of cells ordered from left to right are $o_i^1, o_i^2, \cdots, o_i^{r_i}$, their new central x-coordinates are $x_i^1, x_i^2, \cdots, x_i^{r_i}$, their displacement are $q_i^1, q_i^2, \cdots, q_i^{r_i}$. For any two adjacent cells, the type of left one is t_i and its

coloring solution is p_i^u, the type of right one is t_j and its coloring solution is p_j^v. To avoid lithography conflict, the minimal distance between these two cells is a constant denoted by $d_{i,j}^{u,v}$. For any two adjacent cells in the row i, let x_i^{j-1} and x_i^j be their central x-coordinates, their actual distance is denoted by z_i^j. Besides, the width W of placement region is also given. The problem can be formulated into the following mathematical programming. Note that in this paper, for any pair of adjacent cells, the distance is from the center of the left one to the center of the right one.

$$\text{Minimize: } \alpha \sum_{i=1}^{n} \sum_{j=1}^{r_i} \sum_{k=1}^{n_{c_i^j}} b_{c_i^j}^k \times s_{c_i^j}^k + \beta \sum_{i=1}^{n} \sum_{j=1}^{r_i} q_i^j$$

Subject to:

$$\sum_{j=1}^{n_i} b_i^j = 1, \forall 1 \leq i \leq k$$

$$x_i^j - x_i^{j-1} = z_i^j, \forall 1 \leq i \leq n \wedge 2 \leq j \leq r_i$$

$$z_i^j \geq \sum_{u=1}^{n_{c_i^{j-1}}} \sum_{v=1}^{n_{c_i^j}} b_{c_i^{j-1}}^u \times b_{c_i^j}^v \times d_{c_i^{j-1},c_i^j}^{u,v}, \forall 1 \leq i \leq n \wedge 2 \leq j \leq r_i$$

$$x_i^j - o_i^j \leq q_i^j, \forall 1 \leq i \leq n \wedge 1 \leq j \leq r_i$$

$$o_i^j - x_i^j \leq q_i^j, \forall 1 \leq i \leq n \wedge 1 \leq j \leq r_i$$

$$x_i^j \geq \frac{w_{c_i^j}}{2}, \forall 1 \leq i \leq n \wedge 1 \leq j \leq r_i$$

$$x_i^j \leq W - \frac{w_{c_i^j}}{2}, \forall 1 \leq i \leq n \wedge 1 \leq j \leq r_i$$

$$b_i^j = 0 \ \ or \ \ 1, \forall 1 \leq i \leq k \wedge 1 \leq j \leq n_i$$

The objective is a weighted sum of total cell displacement and stitch count. The first constraint represents that standard cells of the same type should have the same coloring solution. The second and third constraints represent that for any two adjacent cells, there is enough distance to avoid lithography conflict. The fourth and fifth constraints represent cell displacement. Finally, the last two constraints mean that cells should be put inside of placement region. The product of two binary variables in the third constraint can be transformed into linear constraints as follows: $c = a * b \Leftrightarrow a + b - c \leq 1 \wedge a - c \geq 0 \wedge b - c \geq 0$, where a, b, c are all binary variables. Therefore, the problem can be formulated as a MILP.

3. COMPLEXITY OF PROBLEM

To see the complexity of this problem, let us look at a special version of its decision problem firstly.

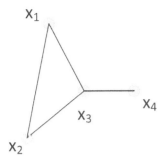

(a) An instance of 3-coloring problem. The three colors are RED, BLUE and GREEN.

t_1	t_2	t_0	t_1	t_3	t_0	t_2	t_3	t_0	t_3	t_4

(b) An instance of single-row version. The widths of cells are 1. The width of row is 11. For any type of standard cell t_i, it has three feasible coloring solutions (p_i^1, p_i^2, p_i^3). p_i^1, p_i^2 and p_i^3 are respectively corresponding to RED, BLUE and GREEN.

Figure 2: The reduction from 3-coloring problem to single-row version.

DEFINITION 1 (SINGLE-ROW VERSION). *The given initial detailed placement has only one row. The problem is to decide whether there is a feasible solution to accommodate all cells without conflicts.*

THEOREM 1. *The single-row version is NP-complete.*

PROOF. It is easy to see that the single-row version is NP. We show that the 3-coloring problem can be reduced to single-row version. Since the 3-coloring is NP-complete [12], the single-row version is NP-complete.

Suppose in a 3-coloring problem instance, there are n nodes denoted by $x_1, x_2, \cdots, x_n$. There are m edges denoted by $e_1, e_2, \cdots, e_m$. We can construct the following single-row version instance.

Each node x_i is corresponding to one type of standard cell t_i, which has three feasible coloring solutions p_i^1, p_i^2, p_i^3. p_i^1, p_i^2 and p_i^3 are corresponding to RED, BLUE and GREEN respectively. There is a special type of standard cell t_0. The width of standard cells are all 1.

We define the minimal distance between t_i and t_j to eliminate conflict as follows.

$$d_{i,j}^{u,v} = \begin{cases} 1 & \text{if } u \neq v \text{ and } i \neq 0 \text{ and } j \neq 0 \\ 2 & \text{if } u = v \text{ and } i \neq 0 \text{ and } j \neq 0 \\ 1 & \text{if } i = 0 \text{ or } j = 0 \end{cases}$$

It means that for any pair of adjacent cells, if the type of either one is t_0, the minimal distance between these two

cells to avoid conflict is 1 no matter what the final coloring solutions are. Otherwise, if the left one is assigned the coloring solution which is corresponding to p_i^k ($1 \leq k \leq 3$) and the right one is assigned the coloring solution which is corresponding to p_j^k, the minimal distance between these two cells to avoid lithography conflict is 2. Otherwise the minimal distance is 1.

For any two nodes x_i and x_j, suppose $i < j$ without loss of generality. If there is an edge $e = (x_i, x_j)$, then we construct a pair of adjacent cells (t_i, t_j). Besides, we add a standard cell of type t_0 between any two pairs of constructed adjacent cells. And the width of row is defined as the number of constructed standard cells, i.e., 3m-1. Fig.2 (b) shows the corresponding single-row version instance of the 3-coloring problem instance in Fig.2 (a).

If the above 3-coloring problem instance is true, then in the constructed single-row version instance, for any two adjacent cells t_i and t_j ($i < j$), we can choose the coloring solutions so that the minimal distance between these two cells to avoid lithography conflict is 1. Therefore, all the constructed standard cells can be put inside of the row. Similarly, if single-row version instance is true, then we can find a solution that satisfies the corresponding 3 coloring problem instance.

□

The displacement-driven TPL-aware detailed placement with ordering and coloring constraints is a generalization of the single-row version, so it is also NP-complete [12].

4. METHODOLOGY

Since the problem is NP-complete and MILP is very time consuming, we propose an effective heuristic algorithm to solve this problem. In this section, we firstly show the motivation of our approach. Next, we present its overview which is composed of three stages. Finally, we illustrate these three stages respectively.

4.1 Motivation

Since standard cells of the same type should have the same coloring solution, we define adjacent pair as follows.

DEFINITION 2. *An adjacent pair is a pair of types of two adjacent standard cells.*

For example, if the type of left cell is t_i and the type of right one is t_j, the corresponding adjacent pair is (t_i, t_j). The minimal distances of adjacent pairs to avoid lithography conflicts have significant impact on solution quality of this problem. There are two reasons. Firstly, if these minimal distances are not optimized well, then it would be difficult to put all cells inside of the row region, as shown in Fig. 3(a). Secondly, different adjacent pairs have different impact on total cell displacement, as shown in Fig. 3(b). Therefore, our method tries to focus on the minimal distances of important adjacent pairs.

4.2 Overview

Our approach is composed of three stages. In the first stage, we propose a method to recognize the important adjacent pairs. In the second stage, we try to optimize minimal distances of important adjacent pairs and a tree-based

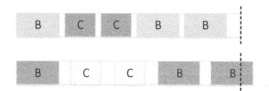

(a) The upper figure represents that all the cells are put inside of row if the minimal distances (to eliminate lithography conflicts) of adjacent pairs are optimized well. On the contrary, in the lower figure, the right most cell B is outside of row if those minimal distances of adjacent pairs are not optimized well.

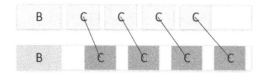

(b) In the upper figure which represents the original placement, the left-most adjacent pair (cell B and cell C) is the most important one to optimize cell displacement. If the minimal distance of this pair to eliminate conflict is not optimized well, all the other cells on the right hand side would be shifted right as shown in lower figure.

Figure 3: The two examples reveal the motivation of our heuristic approach.

heuristic is applied to get a good initial solution. In the last stage, we apply LP-based method to refine the solution. The overview is presented in Fig. 4.

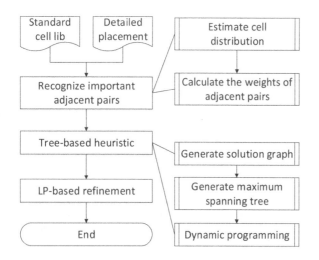

Figure 4: The overview of our heuristic approach.

4.3 Important adjacent pair recognition

We use a positive integer to represent how important an adjacent pair is. We call this integer the weight of adjacent pair. Higher weight means more important. For example,

as shown in Fig. 3(b), apparently, the adjacent pair (B, C) should have the highest weight. We use $weight[i][j]$ to denote the weight of adjacent pair (t_i, t_j).

At this stage, we do not know what the final coloring is. Therefore, we propose a simple method to estimate the new cell distribution. For any adjacent pair (t_i, t_j), we calculate the average minimal distance $d_{i,j}^{ave}$ to avoid lithography conflict. This value is given by the following formula.

$$d_{i,j}^{ave} = \frac{\sum_{u=1}^{n_i} \sum_{v=1}^{n_j} d_{i,j}^{u,v}}{n_i * n_j}$$

The minimal total cell displacement can be achieved by LP as follows.

Minimize: $\sum_{i=1}^{n} \sum_{j=1}^{r_i} q_i^j$

Subject to:

$$x_i^j - x_i^{j-1} \geq d_{c_i^{j-1}, c_i^j}^{ave}, \forall 1 \leq i \leq n \wedge 2 \leq j \leq r_i$$
$$x_i^j - o_i^j \leq q_i^j, \forall 1 \leq i \leq n \wedge 1 \leq j \leq r_i$$
$$o_i^j - x_i^j \geq q_i^j, \forall 1 \leq i \leq n \wedge 1 \leq j \leq r_i$$
$$x_i^j \geq \frac{w_{c_i^j}}{2}, \forall 1 \leq i \leq n \wedge 1 \leq j \leq r_i$$
$$x_i^j \leq W - \frac{w_{c_i^j}}{2}, \forall 1 \leq i \leq n \wedge 1 \leq j \leq r_i$$

Then we define shifting direction of standard cell below.

DEFINITION 3. *For the j-th standard cell in row r_i, its shifting direction is left if $x_i^j < o_i^j$, and right if $x_i^j > o_i^j$, otherwise no shifting. We use ↰ to denote left shifting, ↱ for right shifting, and = for no shifting.*

Algorithm 1 gives the method to calculate the weights of adjacent pairs. The idea is that for a pair of adjacent cells, if their minimal distance to eliminate conflict is increased, the weight of this pair would roughly reflect the increment of total cell displacement. Let us look at an example. A placement row contains six cells and five adjacent pairs. The shifting directions of these six cells are ↱, ↱, ↱, ↱, ↱, ↱. The five adjacent pairs' weights ordered from left to right are respectively 5, 4, 3, 2 and 1. The weight of the left-most one is 5, because if its minimal distance is increased by 1 unit, the total cell displacement would be increased by 5 units roughly.

4.4 Tree-based heuristic

After the weights of all adjacent pairs are computed, a solution graph can be constructed as follows. In the solution graph, each node represents a standard cell type. The edge between two nodes represents an adjacent pair.

Let f_i be the coloring solution that standard cell type t_i uses. The cost $cost_i$ of node t_i and the cost $cost_{i,j}$ of edge connecting t_i and t_j in the solution graph are defined as follows.

$$cost_i[f_i] = \beta * weight[i][i] * d_{i,i}^{f_i,f_i} + \alpha * s_i^{f_i}$$
$$cost_{i,j}[f_i, f_j] = \beta * [weight[i][j] * d_{i,j}^{f_i,f_j} + weight[j][i] * d_{j,i}^{f_j,f_i}]$$

The purpose of our tree-based heuristic is to find the coloring solution for each standard cell type, so that the total cost including cost of nodes and edges in the solution graph is minimized. It is not hard to see that if solution graph is

Algorithm 1 Method to calculate the weights of adjacent pairs

---

1: Calculate $d_{i,j}^{ave}$ for each pair of adjacent pair (t_i, t_j);
2: Solve the LP to get the shifting direction of each standard cell;
3: **for** each placement row **do**
4:     [start, end] is the index range of cells (in ascending order of their x-coordinate) in this row;
5:     **for** any adjacent pair $P = (t_i, t_j)$ in the row **do**
6:         ll and rr are the indexes of t_i and t_j in the row;
7:         **if** the left cell is ⌐ **then**
8:             **for** k from ll to $start$ **do**
9:                 **if** the cell whose order is k is ⌐ or $=$ **then**
10:                     $weight[i][j]+=1$;
11:                 **else**
12:                     break;
13:                 **end if**
14:             **end for**
15:         **end if**
16:         **if** the right cell is ⌐ **then**
17:             **for** k from $ll + 1$ to end **do**
18:                 **if** the cell whose order is k is ⌐ or $=$ **then**
19:                     $weight[i][j]+=1$;
20:                 **else**
21:                     break;
22:                 **end if**
23:             **end for**
24:         **end if**
25:     **end for**
26: **end for**

---

of a tree structure, then dynamic programming can be applied to get the optimal coloring solution. Fortunately, it is observed that solution graphs for industrial benchmarks are sparse graphs. Next, we propose a method to leverage this observation.

4.4.1 *Maximum spanning tree generation*

The basic idea to leverage the observation is to ignore some relatively less important adjacent pairs and turn the solution graph into a tree. The cost of each edge connecting t_i and t_j in solution graph is replaced by $cost'_{i,j} = \alpha * [weight[i][j] * (d_{i,j}^{max} - d_{i,j}^{min}) + weight[j][i] * (d_{j,i}^{max} - d_{j,i}^{min})]$, where $d_{i,j}^{max}$ and $d_{i,j}^{min}$ are defined as follows.

$$d_{i,j}^{max} = \max_{1 \le u \le n_i} \max_{1 \le v \le n_j} d_{i,j}^{u,v}$$
$$d_{i,j}^{min} = \min_{1 \le u \le n_i} \min_{1 \le v \le n_j} d_{i,j}^{u,v}$$

It is easy to see that for any edge connecting t_i and t_j, if $cost'_{i,j}$ is small, then no matter what the final coloring solutions for t_i and t_j are, the cost of this edge in the solution graph is similar. Therefore, we use maximum spanning tree to replace the original solution graph. Note that, $cost'_{i,j}$ is only used during generating maximum spanning tree rather than the following dynamic programming.

4.4.2 *Dynamic programming solution*

After maximum spanning tree is generated, dynamic programming could be applied to find an initial coloring solution. We use the node which has maximal out-degree as the root to generate the tree topology. Then bottom-up method is adopted to construct optimal solutions in the tree. For any node t_i, we maintain a vector $Best[i]$. The entry $Best[i][j]$ stores the best cost over all possible coloring solutions for the sub-tree rooted at node t_i if t_i is choosing coloring solution p_i^j. Suppose it has m children $(x_1, x_2, \cdots, x_m)$, and the

vectors for these m children have already been constructed. The vector for t_i can be constructed by the following formula. The final total cost is the minimal element of $Best[i]$ if t_i is the root of the tree.

$$Best[i][j] = cost_i[p_i^j] + \sum_{1 \le p \le m} \min_{1 \le z \le n_{x_p}} \left(Best[x_p][z] + cost_{i,x_p}[p_i^j, p_{x_p}^z] \right)$$

4.5 LP-based refinement

The LP-based refinement technique is presented in Algorithm 2. The idea is that we enumerate all the coloring solutions for one standard cell type while others are fixated. The node whose associated edges' costs are larger is given a higher priority. In Line 4 of Algorithm 2, once the coloring solutions for all the cells are fixed, it is easy to see that minimal cell displacement can be achieved by solving the following LP, where $d_{c_i^{j-1}, c_i^j}$ is the minimal distance to eliminate conflict for adjacent cells c_i^{j-1} and c_i^j in the i-th row.

Minimize: $\sum_{i=1}^{n} \sum_{j=1}^{r_i} q_i^j$

Subject to:

$$x_i^j - x_i^{j-1} \ge d_{c_i^{j-1}, c_i^j}, \forall 1 \le i \le n \wedge 2 \le j \le r_i$$
$$x_i^j - o_i^j \le q_i^j, \forall 1 \le i \le n \wedge 1 \le j \le r_i$$
$$o_i^j - x_i^j \ge q_i^j, \forall 1 \le i \le n \wedge 1 \le j \le r_i$$
$$x_i^j \ge \frac{w_{c_i^j}}{2}, \forall 1 \le i \le n \wedge 1 \le j \le r_i$$
$$x_i^j \le W - \frac{w_{c_i^j}}{2}, \forall 1 \le i \le n \wedge 1 \le j \le r_i$$

Algorithm 2 LP-based refinement

1: Calculate the associated edges' costs of each node;
2: **for** each node in descending order of associated edges' costs **do**
3:     **for** each coloring solution for this node **do**
4:         Minimize the total cell displacement by solving the LP in Section 4.5;
5:         **if** the value of cost function is better than the current best **then**
6:             Update the current best;
7:             Update the coloring solution for this node.
8:         **end if**
9:     **end for**
10: **end for**

---

5. EXPERIMENTAL RESULTS

Our approach is implemented in C++ on a Linux server with Intel Xeon X5550 2.67GHz CPU, 94GB main memory. The benchmarks are derived from [11]'s. Gurobi [13] is used to solve MILP and LP. Since the problem is NP-complete and it cannot be expected to get the optimal solutions for some benchmarks within limited CPU runtime. We limit the MILP solver to run 7200s and report the best solutions within the time limit of MILP solver.

The experimental results are shown in Table I. Compare with MILP solutions, our heuristic approach achieves the same number of stitches. For total cell displacement, the heuristic method is only 2.9% worse than that of MILP solutions on average. However, the heuristic method gets 207× speed up on average. Besides, our method only increases wirelength by less 1% over the initial detailed placement.

Table 1: Experiment results: MILP V.S. Heuristic.

benchmark	MILP				Heuristic				
	displacement	# of conflicts	# of stitches	runtime(s)	displacement	# of conflicts	# of stitches	WL increase	runtime(s)
alu-70	2.88E+05	0	610	1245	2.94E+05	0	610	0.6%	12
alu-80	6.76E+05	0	610	7200	6.87E+05	0	610	1.4%	14
alu-90	1.94E+06	0	610	7200	1.97E+06	0	610	4.0%	15
byp-70	1.04E+05	0	1134	739	1.04E+05	0	1134	0.0%	21
byp-80	3.85E+05	0	1134	7200	3.68E+05	0	1134	0.1%	28
byp-90	1.54E+06	0	1134	7200	1.60E+06	0	1134	0.7%	31
div-70	1.60E+05	0	1316	3042	1.60E+05	0	1316	0.1%	28
div-80	3.53E+05	0	1316	7200	3.64E+05	0	1316	1.7%	35
div-90	3.62E+06	0	1316	7200	3.61E+06	0	1316	3.8%	32
ecc-70	2.76E+04	0	258	13	2.90E+04	0	258	0.0%	4
ecc-80	8.91E+04	0	258	11	1.09E+05	0	258	0.1%	5
ecc-90	3.55E+05	0	258	23	3.55E+05	0	258	0.9%	6
efc-70	2.84E+04	0	671	420	3.15E+04	0	671	0.0%	6
efc-80	1.14E+05	0	671	4127	1.16E+05	0	671	0.3%	8
efc-90	5.95E+05	0	671	4800	6.00E+05	0	671	2.4%	8
ctl-70	4.55E+04	0	275	351	4.89E+04	0	275	0.0%	10
ctl-80	1.38E+05	0	275	4345	1.40E+05	0	275	0.0%	12
ctl-90	3.49E+05	0	275	7200	3.50E+05	0	275	0.6%	13
top-70	4.95E+05	0	4731	3165	5.12E+05	0	4731	0.0%	326
top-80	1.48E+06	0	4731	7200	1.51E+06	0	4731	0.2%	391
top-90	7.36E+05	0	4731	7200	7.19E+05	0	4731	0.1%	482
Norm.	0.971	1	1	207	1.000	1	1	0.8%	1

6. CONCLUSIONS

In this paper, we are focusing on displacement-driven TPL optimization in detailed placement stage under coloring constraints. We recognize this problem as NP-complete, then propose two solutions. The first one is MILP, the other is heuristic approach. We show that the heuristic approach is very efficient compared with MILP by experiment. The proposed heuristic method can produce competitive solution quality within very limited CPU runtime.

References

[1] B. Yu, K. Yuan, B. Zhang, D. Ding, and D. Z. Pan, "Layout decomposition for triple patterning lithography," in *Proceedings of the International Conference on Computer-Aided Design*, pp. 1–8, 2011.

[2] S.-Y. Fang, Y.-W. Chang, and W.-Y. Chen, "A novel layout decomposition algorithm for triple patterning lithography," in *Proceedings of the 49th Annual Design Automation Conference*, pp. 1185–1190, 2012.

[3] J. Kuang and E. F. Y. Young, "An efficient layout decomposition approach for triple patterning lithography," in *Proceedings of the 50th Annual Design Automation Conference*, pp. 69–75, 2013.

[4] Y. Zhang, W.-S. Luk, H. Zhou, C. Yan, and X. Zeng, "Layout decomposition with pairwise coloring for multiple patterning lithography," in *Proceedings of the International Conference on Computer-Aided Design*, pp. 170–177, 2013.

[5] H. Tian, H. Zhang, Q. Ma, Z. Xiao, and M. D. F. Wong, "A polynomial time triple patterning algorithm for cell based row-structure layout," in *Proceedings of the International Conference on Computer-Aided Design*, pp. 57–64, 2012.

[6] H. Tian, Y. Du, H. Zhang, Z. Xiao, and M. D. F. Wong, "Constrained pattern assignment for standard cell based triple patterning lithography," in *Proceedings of the International Conference on Computer-Aided Design*, pp. 178–185, 2013.

[7] B. Yu, Y.-H. Lin, G. Luk-Pat, D. Ding, K. Lucas, and D. Z. Pan, "A high-performance triple patterning layout decomposer with balanced density," in *Proceedings of the International Conference on Computer-Aided Design*, pp. 163–169, 2013.

[8] Z. Chen, H. Yao, and Y. Cai, "Suald: Spacing uniformity-aware layout decomposition in triple patterning lithography.," in *ISQED*, pp. 566–571, 2013.

[9] Q. Ma, H. Zhang, and M. D. F. Wong, "Triple patterning aware routing and its comparison with double patterning aware routing in 14nm technology," in *Proceedings of the 49th Annual Design Automation Conference*, pp. 591–596, 2012.

[10] Y.-H. Lin, B. Yu, D. Z. Pan, and Y.-L. Li, "Triad: A triple patterning lithography aware detailed router," in *Proceedings of the International Conference on Computer-Aided Design*, pp. 123–129, 2012.

[11] B. Yu, X. Xu, J.-R. Gao, and D. Z. Pan, "Methodology for standard cell compliance and detailed placement for triple patterning lithography," in *Proceedings of the International Conference on Computer-Aided Design*, pp. 349–356, 2013.

[12] M. R. Garey and D. S. Johnson, *A Guide to the Theory of NP-Completeness*. Macmillan Higher Education, 1979.

[13] "Gurobi." http://www.gurobi.com.

Concept & Research to Revenue:
An Entrepreneurial Story

Dean Drako
President & CEO, IC Manage. Founder & former CEO
Barracuda Networks

Abstract

Speaker Dean Drako will draw from his experience in founding
and building 6 technology start-up companies - sometimes two at
a time, including his recent companies: Barracuda Networks -
November 2013 IPO, and IC Manage - a Deloitte Fast500
company.

Many great technology success stories begin with, or depend upon
research. Whether it's for a startup or a large public company, the
same concept applies: Research drives innovation to solve hard
problems.

Drako will share some of his techniques to help turn technology
innovation into successful products and companies using
entrepreneurial skills.

ACM Classification:
D.0 General

Author Keywords:
Dean Drako; Distinguished Entrepreneur; ISPD; IC Manage;
Barracuda Networks

Short Bio

Dean founded IC Manage in 2003, a company that he has helped
expand to become the IC/SoC design and IP management
technology leader. Dean was also founder, President and CEO of
Barracuda Networks from 2003 to 2012, where he built and
expanded Barracuda from a spam and virus firewall provider to a
broad line enterprise technology company with more than 150,000
customers.

Previously, Dean was founder of Boldfish, a leading provider of
enterprise messaging solutions that was acquired by Siebel
Systems in 2003. Dean was also founder, President and CEO of
Design Acceleration, Inc. (DAI), a maker of superior design
analysis and verification tools. Cadence Design Systems acquired
DAI in 1998. Prior to DAI, he was VP of Product Engineering at
the 3DO Company and was instrumental in the development of
the PowerPC architecture at Apple Computer.

Dean received his BSEE from the University of Michigan, Ann
Arbor and MSEE from the University of California, Berkeley. In
2007, Ernst & Young named Dean "Entrepreneur of the Year" in
Northern California for Networking and Communications.
Goldman Sachs named Dean as one of the "100 Most Intriguing
Entrepreneurs of 2014."

ISPD '15, March 29–April 1, 2015, Monterey, California, USA.
ACM 978-1-4503-3399-3/15/03.
http://dx.doi.org/10.1145/2717764.2724579

Analog Circuit and Layout Synthesis Revisited

Rob A. Rutenbar
Department of Computer Science
University of Illinois at Urbana-Champaign
Urbana, Illinois 61801, USA
+1 217-333-3373
rutenbar@illinois.edu

ABSTRACT

In the first decade of the twenty first century, the first generation of analog synthesis tools--for circuit sizing and optimization and for physical design-- moved from academic research projects, to startups, to integration on various standard platforms. In addition, we began to see some concerted efforts to formulate the verification problem in formal terms, albeit on rather simplified version of designs. In this invited talk I will try to summarize what we got right in that first generation effort, but also, what we got wrong. The "right" part is the idea that all design is optimization: continuous, combinatorial, geometric, etc. Formulating tough analog circuit and layout problems as the "right" optimization problem(s) got us the first generation of tools that did anything right. The "wrong" part was an incomplete appreciation of the importance of designer use models--how real people do real designs in this business. Closing that gap is one remaining challenge. Another is the leap to non-planar end-of-roadmap CMOS technologies, where lithographic and manufacturability concerns combine to create some difficult problems, and new opportunities for tool innovation.

This talk will revisit and extend some elements of an earlier ISPD invited talk [1], and a recent talk at the 2011 CAV Frontiers in Analog Circuit(s) (FAC) workshop [2], and also introduce some new problems related to end-of-roadmap analog.

Categories and Subject Descriptors

B.7.1 [**Integrated Circuits**]: Types and Design Styles – *VLSI (very large scale integration).*
B.7.2 [**Integrated Circuits**]: Design Aids – *layout.*

General Terms

Algorithms, Performance, Design, Verification.

Keywords

Analog, Mixed-Signal, Electronic Design Automation (EDA).

1. REFERENCES

[1] Rutenbar, R.A., Analog Layout Synthesis: What's Missing? Invited Talk, at *ACM Int'l. Symposium on Physical Design.* (March 2010). http://www.ispd.cc/slides/slides10/3_01.pdf

[2] Rutenbar, R.A., Analog Synthesis (and Verification) Revisited: What's Missing? Invited Talk, at *Computer Aided Verification (CAV) Frontiers in Analog Circuit (FAC) Synthesis and Verification Workshop* . (July 2011). http://www.async.ece.utah.edu/FAC2011/abstracts/RutenbarSlides.pdf

A Useful Skew Tree Framework for Inserting Large Safety Margins

Rickard Ewetz and Cheng-Kok Koh
School of Electrical and Computer Engineering
Purdue University
West Lafayette, IN 47907-2035
rewetz,chengkok@purdue.edu

ABSTRACT

The construction of clock trees for modern designs is challenging because the clock trees need to be constructed with adequate safety margins such that the skew constraints are satisfied even under variations. The amount of safety margin required in a skew constraint is dependent on the distance of the corresponding sequential elements in the tree topology. In certain cases, the amount of safety margin that can be inserted may be limited. Consequently, the corresponding sequential elements should be placed close in the topology, i.e., the point of divergence to these elements is low in the clock tree, in order to reduce the influence of variations. By using safety margins and lowering the point of divergence, we present a framework for the construction of useful skew trees with large safety margins inserted in the skew constraints. The framework, called UST-LSM, first identifies tight skew constraints by the detection of negative cycles in a weighted skew constraint graph. Next, the corresponding sequential elements of these skew constraints are clustered early in tree topology. Compared to earlier studies, we can allow larger safety margins in skew constraints spanning between sequential elements within a subtree. This translates into an improvement of yield from 46.8% to 98.8% on a synthesized benchmark with 7,674 sequential elements and 63,440 skew constraints.

Categories and Subject Descriptors

B.7.2 [**Hardware, Integrated Circuits**]: Design Aids

General Terms

Algorithms, Design, Performance, Reliability

Keywords

VLSI CAD, Useful skew, Clock skew scheduling

1. INTRODUCTION

In modern designs, process, voltage, and temperature (PVT) variations continue to cause the available safety margins in various timing constraints to dwindle. Skew is the difference of the arrival times of the clock signal at a pair of sequential elements. The clock network of each VLSI circuit must satisfy a set of skew constraints, commonly known as the setup and hold time constraints. The International Symposium on Physical Design hosted two clock contest in 2009[16] and 2010 [15] to emphasize the importance of constructing low power clock networks that can meet skew constraints even under PVT variations. However, the two contest considered uniform and regular skew constraints. In reality, data and control paths may be irregular, which give rise to non-regular skew constraints, requiring the clock network to be constructed with useful skew [9] to satisfy the skew constraints and to provide the required safety margins.

Clock networks considering arbitrary skew constraints can be constructed using static [9, 10, 12, 14] or dynamic [17] clock scheduling. Clock scheduling is the process of specifying the relative arrival times to the sequential elements (or clock sinks). In static clock scheduling, the relative arrival times are determined before the construction of a useful skew tree (UST). In dynamic clock scheduling, the determination of the relative arrival times are integrated into the construction of USTs.

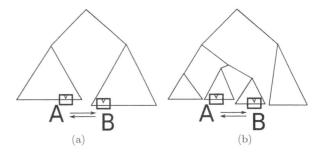

Figure 1: Sequential elements A and B have tight skew constraints. If A and B are distant in the topology, as in (a), the safety margin may be inadequate. The two elements should be placed closer, as in (b), in the topology.

In [18], a clock tree is modified using simulated annealing to improve its performance by exploiting useful skew. In [17], the Greedy-UST/DME method was presented to construct USTs based on dynamic clock scheduling and deferred merge embedding [6]. In [9], it was shown that there exists a maximum uniform safety margin M that could be inserted in all skew constraints. In [11], it was concluded that a user-specified safety margin M_{user} greater than M may be required in certain skew constraints. To insert safety margins larger than M, the skew constraints were tightened dynamically during the tree construction. Smaller safety margins were inserted at the bottom of the clock tree and larger safety margins (if available) were inserted higher up in the tree topology, which could be greater than M. The limitation of the approach in [11] is that the safety margin required at the top of the tree may have been utilized at the bottom of the tree (see Figure 1(a)). Moreover, for certain tree topologies, a safety margin greater than M can never be provided at the root of the tree regardless of how the safety margins are budgeted.

We propose a framework for constructing useful skew trees with large safety margins, called (UST-LSM), in order to meet arbitrary skew constraints even under the influence of variations. The UST-LSM framework ensures that there is a user specified safety margin of M_{user} in a majority of the skew constraints. For skew constraints where it is impossible to insert a safety margin of M_{user}, we instead insert at least the maximum uniform safety margin M [9]. Moreover, the corresponding clock sink pairs are placed close in the clock tree topology, as shown in Figure 1(b), so that the point of divergence is lower (closer to the sinks) to ensure that M is adequate to account for the influence of variations. The point of divergence with respect to a pair of sinks is the lowest common ancestor of the pair in the clock tree.

The UST-LSM framework is driven by intentionally creating, detecting, and removing negative cycles from the skew constraint graph (SCG) defined by the set of skew constraints with a safety margin of M_{user} inserted. The negative cycles correspond to clusters of sinks that could not have a safety margin of M_{users} inserted in their skew constraints. These clusters of sinks are joined early in the topology.

For safety margins of $M_{user} \leq M$, the UST-LSM framework is equivalent to the approach in [17] (except that our USTs are constructed with buffers to meet transition constraints). Moreover, the UST-LSM framework overcomes the limitation of $M_{user} \leq M$ in [17] and is capable of handling safety margins $M_{user} > M$ by lowering the point of divergence with respect to certain sequential elements. We view the proposed framework to be orthogonal to [11]. The main difference is that by identifying the clusters of sinks that should be joined first, we avoid the construction of certain tree topologies that would not have M_{user} available at the top of the tree.

The experimental results show that the UST-LSM framework can increase the yield on benchmarks with tight skew constraints. On a synthesized benchmark with 7,674 sequential elements and 63,440 skew constraints, we show that we have a smooth trade-off between safety margin and yield and that our methodology can improve the yield from 46.8% to 98.8%.

2. SKEW CONSTRAINTS AND SAFETY MARGINS

A pair of flip flops (FF) i and j separated by only combinational logic must meet setup and hold time constraints,

which are specified as follows:

$$t_i + t_{CQ} + t_{max}^{ij} + t_S \leq t_j + T, \qquad (1)$$
$$t_i + t_{min}^{ij} + t_{CQ} \geq t_j + t_H.$$

The arrival times of the clock signal to the launching FF_i and capturing flip flop FF_j are denoted as t_i and t_j, respectively. T is the clock period, t_{CQ} is the clock to output delay, t_S is the setup time of flip flop j, and t_H is the hold time of flip flop j. The maximum and minimum propagation delay through the combinational logic are respectively denoted as t_{max}^{ij} and t_{min}^{ij}. Let the skew $t_i - t_j$ be denoted $skew_{ij}$. Let $l_{ij} = t_H - t_{CQ} - t_{min}^{ij}$ and $u_{ij} = T - t_{CQ} - t_{max}^{ij} - t_S$. We re-write the timing constraints in Eq. (1) as follows:

$$l_{ij} \leq skew_{ij} \leq u_{ij}. \qquad (2)$$

All the skew constraints in Eq. (2) can be captured in a skew constraint graph (SCG). In an SCG $G(V, E)$, the vertices V represent the sequential elements and the edges E represent the skew constraints. A directed edge e_{ij} with a weight w_{ij} of $-l_{ij}$ is added from i to j and a directed edge e_{ji} with a weight w_{ji} of u_{ij} is added from j to i. A set of feasible arrival times can be determined using the Bellman-Ford algorithm [5]. Such a set of feasible arrival times exists if and only if the SCG does not contain any negative cycles.

Note that for each SCG there exists a maximum uniform safety margin M that can be added to all of the skew constraints [9]. To add non-uniform safety margins in the constraints, we tighten the setup and hold time constraints by non-negative safety margins m_{ij} and m_{ji}, respectively, as follows:

$$l_{ij} + m_{ji} \leq skew_{ij} \leq u_{ij} - m_{ij}. \qquad (3)$$

When safety margins greater than M are added to all the constraints, a negative cycle is created in the SCG constructed for Eq. (3).

2.1 Cycles of skew constraint

It is important to understand that a single skew constraint by itself does not limit the amount of safety margin that can be inserted in the constraint. The arrival time between the two sinks of a constraint can be skewed arbitrarily to create an arbitrarily large safety margin. It is the total amount of safety margin that can be inserted in every cycle of skew constraints that is limited, as explained below.

Consider an arbitrary cycle $C = (v_1, v_2), (v_2, v_3), \ldots, (v_{n-1}, v_n), (v_n, v_1)$, where v_i, $1 \leq i \leq n$, are vertices in the SCG for Eq. (3). Each edge in the SCG represents an inequality constraint $t_i - t_j \leq w_{ji} - m_{ij}$. Let $|C| = n$ be the number of edges in the cycle C and $W_C = \sum_{(i,j) \in C} w_{ji}$. By summing the inequality constraints corresponding to a cycle C, we obtain the following equations:

$$\sum_{(i,j) \in C} (t_i - t_j) \leq \sum_{(i,j) \in C} w_{ji} - m_{ij}, \qquad (4)$$

$$\sum_{(i,j) \in C} m_{ij} \leq W_C. \qquad (5)$$

Eq. (5) specifies that the maximum safety margin that can be allocated across a cycle in total is at most W_C. The ratio $W_C/|C|$ is defined to the the *average margin* of a cycle. We also define the *maximum margin* of an edge as follows: Consider all cycles that the edge participates in. The *maximum margin* of the edge is the minimum of the average margin of all these cycles. Note that the minimum of the maximum margins of all edges is the maximum uniform safety margin M in [9].

2.2 Previous work on improving robustness using safety margins

In [17], a user specified safety margin M_{user} is imposed on all the skew constraints. A smooth trade-off between cost and robustness is obtained for different values of the safety margin M_{user}. A limitation is that the user specified safety margin M_{user} is required to be no greater than the maximum uniform safety margin M in [9].

The case of $M_{user} > M$ is of particular interest for modern designs with tight skew constraints. In [11], this problem of large required safety margins was partly addressed. In that work, the safety margins were dynamically added during the bottom-up process of constructing a clock tree. In the synthesis process, which consists of iterative merging of subtrees, the required safety margin between two subtrees is computed and inserted when two subtrees are joined to form larger subtree. Effectively, the approach inserts small safety margins at the bottom of the topology and large safety margins near the root node. In a sense, the algorithm non-uniformly distributes the total available margin in each cycle in the SCG such that smaller safety margins are inserted at the bottom of the tree topology, potentially leaving larger margins for the top of the topology.

The first drawback of the approach is that all the safety margins may be completely utilized at the bottom of the clock tree, leaving none at the top. Sink pairs residing in different subtrees that are joined close to the top of the eventual tree topology have the most need for safety margins, but would have none available. The second drawback is that for some pair of sinks, it may not be possible to insert a safety margin greater than M. Consider a cycle C with an average margin of M and $|C| = 2$. As the cycle is of length 2, it is not possible to skew the margin in the cycle. Therefore, the maximum safety margin between the pair of sinks will be M no matter how the other safety margins are inserted in the tree. The algorithm in [11] did not consider this aspect of the problem and could therefore not guarantee that such sink pairs be joined with adequate safety margins. In particular, if the sink pair are joined at the root, as shown in Figure 1(a), the available safety margin may be inadequate.

Based on this argument we conclude that to ensure safety margins $M_{user} > M$ at the root of the tree topology the problem of inserting safety margins is not separable from the choice of the tree topology.

2.3 Insertion of large safety margins

We propose a framework that can handle large user-specified safety margins M_{user}, i.e., the case when $M_{user} > M$. The main idea is to insert a safety margin of M_{user} where it is possible. Sink pairs whose skew constraints with a safety margin less than M_{user} are placed close in the tree topology, and a safety margin at least M is ensured. Note that the framework is equivalent to the approach in [17] for $M_{user} \leq M$.

By definition, there exist at least one cycle with an average margin of $W_C/|C| = M < M_{user}$. However, the number of such cycles and edges with a maximum margin of less than M_{user} may be limited. (We confirm this assumption empirically in Section 5). We refer to edges with a maximum margin of $W_C/|C| = M < M_{user}$ as *tight* edges or tight skew constraints.

We propose to insert a safety margin in each edge, or skew constraint, equal to the maximum margin of the edge (as defined in Section 2.1), with an upper limit of M_{user}. In other words, only edges on the cycle with an average margin of M will have a safety margin of M. All other edges have safety margins strictly greater than M.

All skew constraints corresponding to non-tight edges have a safety margin of M_{user} and do not require further consideration. It remains to ensure that all the skew constraints corresponding to tight edges will be met under variations. We propose to do this by placing the corresponding sinks close in the topology. It is well known that the variations-induced skew between sinks that are close in the topology is less than for sinks that are distant in the tree because of a lower point of divergence. Therefore, we propose to place the sinks corresponding to tight edges close in the topology, as shown in Figure 1(b).

In Section 3, we present the UST-LSM framework in detail. Computing the maximum margin of each edge in the SCG is computationally expensive. However, for a specific safety margin M_{user}, it is not too difficult to find the corresponding tight edges. The tight edges are found by inserting a safety margin of M_{user} in every edge. Next, by detecting negative cycles in the SCG, all the tight edges can be determined. Lastly, the sinks corresponding to tight edges are clustered, so that they are placed close in the tree topology.

3. THE UST-LSM FRAMEWORK

The flow of the proposed UST-LSM framework is shown in Figure 2 and illustrated with an example in Figure 3. The UST-LSM framework takes an input design with skew constraints and a user specified safety margin M_{user}, and constructs a useful skew clock tree using either the Greedy-UST/DME algorithm [17] or our buffered Greedy-UST/DME algorithm, briefly described in Section 4.

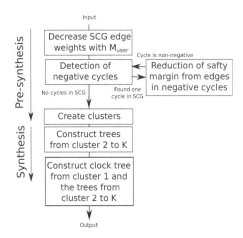

Figure 2: The flow for the proposed UST-LSM framework.

A user specified safety margin M_{user} is introduced to all the skew constraints in the SCG constructed from Eq. (2) (note that this is the set of constraints without safety margins). Inserting a safety margin is equivalent to decreasing

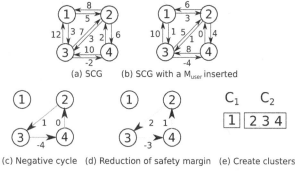

(a) SCG   (b) SCG with a M_{user} inserted

(c) Negative cycle   (d) Reduction of safety margin   (e) Create clusters

(f) Tree from C_2 (g) Tree from C_1 and tree of C_2

Figure 3: Illustration of the proposed UST-LSM framework.

the weight of the corresponding edge in the SCG. In the example in Figure 3, a safety margin $M_{user} = 2$ is inserted to the skew constraints in the SCG in (a) to form the updated SCG in (b). Note that the original SCG in Figure 3(a) has a maximum uniform safety margin $M = 1$. Recall that a feasible clock schedule exists if the SCG does not contain any negative cycles. All cycles with an average margin of less than M_{user} will now become negative. As $M_{user} > M$, at least one negative cycle will be created, i.e., no feasible clock schedule exists.

To recover a feasible clock schedule, all the created negative cycles must be removed by increasing the weights of the edges in the cycle, i.e., reducing the safety margins. A feasible clock schedule is recovered when we reduce the safety margin of each edge to its respective maximum margin, as defined in Section 2.1. In Figure 3(c), a negative cycle is illustrated and after the safety margins on the edges have been reduced, the non-negative cycle in Figure 3(d) is obtained. The negative cycle detection is detailed in Section 3.1 and reduction of safety margin is explained in Section 3.2.

After all the negative cycles have been removed, all the non-tight edges have a safety margin of M_{user} and all the tight edges have safety margins less than M_{user}, but at least M. As the safety margins have been reduced for tight edges, the corresponding sinks to these skew constraints should be placed close in the topology to lower the point of divergence. We join such pairs of sinks before we construct the remainder of the clock tree to ensure a low point of divergence in the tree topology. To facilitate that, we cluster all sinks in a cycle of tight edges together. If two clusters share some common sinks, the two clusters are grouped together to form a larger cluster. All other sinks not in any negative cycles are grouped together to form another cluster C_1.

In Figure 3(e), we show two clusters: C_2 is formed by the three sinks in the cycle of tight edges, and C_1 contains a singleton sink. In reality, we expect C_1 to be much larger.

Assume that K sink clusters $C_1, \ldots, C_K$ have been formed. Next, $K - 1$ clock trees are constructed, one for each of the clusters $C_2, \ldots, C_K$, using the sinks of the respective clusters, which is shown in Figure 3(f). Note that the constructed clock trees may contain buffers (as shown in Fig-

ure 3(f)). Next, a clock tree is constructed using the sinks of cluster C_1 and the $K - 1$ trees obtained for clusters $C_2, \ldots, C_K$, which is shown in Figure 3(g).

A limitation of this work is that for designs with extremely uniform and regular skew constraints, such an approach would not be particularly advantageous. For such designs, there is only one cluster, and the Greedy-UST/DME approach [17] would suffice. However, in the synthesized designs from [13], the timing constraints are rather irregular. The details of the synthesized designs are provided in Section 5.

3.1 Detection of Negative Cycles

The negative cycle detection (NCD) problem is that of determining if an SCG contains a negative cycle and if any such negative cycles exists, find one such cycle. The general NCD problem has been studied extensively and an excellent review of several efficient algorithms using different auxiliary data structures is provided in [4].

We use a practical approach based on the Bellman-Ford algorithm [5] to solve the NCD problem with a worst case run-time complexity of $O(VE)$. However, our algorithm performs much better than $O(VE)$ on the average because it contains two early termination features.

The Bellman-Ford solves the single source shortest path algorithm by performing $V - 1$ iterations of edge relaxations. The Bellman Ford algorithm can directly be adopted to solve the NCD problem in $O(VE)$. The shortest path to a vertex needs to be updated at most $V - 1$ times because the shortest path from the source can have at most $V - 1$ edges, if no negative cycles exist in the graph. Consequently, to check if a negative cycle exists, one additional iteration of edge relaxations is performed; if any shortest paths are updated, a negative cycle must exist. At least one negative cycle can be found by tracing the predecessors from any vertex v, which had the shortest path updated in the last iteration.

When no negative cycles exist, the Bellman-Ford algorithm can terminate early if no shortest paths are updated in successive iterations [5]. It is also known that if a graph contains a negative cycle, there is a chance that the cycle can be detected before V iterations, especially when the cycle size is small [4]. Therefore, the algorithm can again terminate early. The two early termination methods are incorporated into the Bellman-Ford algorithm.

3.2 Reduction of safety margin from edges in negative cycles

A negative cycle in the SCG indicates that no feasible clock schedule exists, i.e., some or all the edges in the cycle have been allocated infeasible safety margins higher than the maximum margin of each respective edge. Note that this situation was intentionally created by inserting too much safety margin on all the edges. To remove the negative cycle, safety margin equal to the magnitude of the total weight of the negative cycle must be reduced from the edges of the cycle. We propose two techniques to distribute the reduction of the safety margins across the edges of the cycle.

- Reduce the safety margin uniformly from all edges of the negative cycle.

- Reduce the safety margin non-uniformly from the edges in the negative cycle.

The first approach maximizes the minimum safety margin in the skew constraints of the cycle. Using the first method it is straightforward to reduce the amount of safety margin on the edges of the cycle. By definition, we can guarantee that all edges will have a safety margin m, with $M \leq m < M_{user}$.

The second method reduces the safety margin from fewer edges. In particular, the second method is suitable for adaptively determining the safety margin to be inserted as we construct a subtree for the sinks in the negative cycle. In other words, the method in [11] would be useful for the second method.

For the synthesized circuits in [13], the cycles typically contain only a few edges. Therefore, we used only the first approach. However, for circuits with large cycles, we believe that the second approach could be more flexible and effective.

4. CONSTRUCTION OF BUFFERED USTS

In this section, we give an outline how we construct our buffered useful-skew trees with consideration of transition time constraints. This is a minor adaptation of the Greedy-UST/DME algorithm in [17], incorporating the speed-up improvement in [7], and the use of stem wire and buffer insertion in [3, 2].

The Greedy-UST/DME algorithm in [17] is based on iteratively joining sinks and/or subtrees to form larger subtrees. Based on a nearest neighbour graph (NNG) where the distance between two subtrees is defined according to the wiring cost of merging the pair of subtrees, the two closest sinks and/or subtrees are selected for merging. It was shown that there exists a feasible skew range (FSR) between every pair of subtrees and if and only if the two subtrees are joined with a skew within the FSR, a feasible clock schedule exists.

Finding an FSR is equivalent to finding two corresponding shortest paths in the SCG. The shortest paths in the SCG are computed using the on-the-fly sparse-graph-based scheduler in [7], which is based on Dijkstra's shortest path algorithm with the same edge weight modification as in Johnson's algorithm (as negative edge weights may exist in the SCG).

In Algorithm 1, a brief overview of the Greedy-UST/DME algorithm is presented. Please refer to [17] for details. In Algorithm 1, T denotes a subtree, L are Manhattan segments, mr are collections of Manhattan segments or regions.

We directly extend the Greedy-UST/DME algorithm in Algorithm 1 to include stem wire insertion and buffer insertion, as in [3, 2]. After two subtrees T_u and T_w have been merged to form a single subtree T_v, the 10% to 90% transition time, is evaluated. If the transition time of T_v is greater than a transition time constraint S_{tran}, the two subtrees T_u and T_w are unmerged and locked from further merging. After all the subtrees have been locked, a piece of stem wire is extended from the root of every locked subtree. Next, a buffer is inserted to drive each subtree through the inserted stem wire. Iteratively, the merging in the NNG and buffer insertion is performed until a single clock tree is obtained.

The quality of our implementation of the Greedy-UST/DME is similar to in [14] and comparison can be found in [7].

Algorithm 1 Greedy-UST/DME algorithm [17]

Input: Clock pins S, skew constraints C
Output: Locked subtrees satisfying constraints C.
1: Construct SCG G=(V,E) from C.
2: **for** each merging of subtrees T_u and T_w to form T_v **do**
3:     /* Based on a nearest neighbour graph (NNG). */
4:     **if** T_u is not a clock sink, i.e. with children T_1 and T_2 **then**
5:         Compute the FSR of T_u
6:         Update $mr(u)$ based on the FSR of T_u
7:         Select $L_u \in mr(u)$ that is closest to mr(v)
8:         Pick clock pins $s_i \in T_i$ and $s_j \in T_2$
9:         Compute $skew_{i,j} = a$ when u is embedded in L_u
10:         Update the SCG with $skew_{i,j}$
11:     **if** T_w is not a clock sink **then**
12:         Perform steps 5 to 10 with u and w exchanged.
13:     Compute the FSR of T_v
14:     Update $mr(v)$ based on the FSR of T_v
15: **return:** T

---

5. EXPERIMENTAL RESULTS

The experimental results are obtained on a quad core 3.10 GHz Linux machine with 7.7 GB memory. The proposed algorithms are implemented in C++.

Two set of benchmarks are used to validate the proposed UST-LSM framework. A scaled version of the ISCAS89 benchmark suite [18], referred to as scaled_ISCAS89, and an synthesized Open Cores benchmark suite [8]. The scaled_ISCAS89 and the Open Cores benchmark suites (see Table 1) are created because there are no publicly available benchmarks with tight skew constraints representative of today's designs and the ISCAS89 benchmarks have very loose skew constraints.

The scaled_ISCAS benchmarks are obtained by scaling the ISCAS89 circuits in terms of physical locations of the sinks, the load capacitances, propagation delays, and operating frequency based on the ITRS road-map. The Open Cores benchmarks are obtained by synthesizing a set of Open Cores [13] with Synopsys DC and Synopsys ICC. We synthesize the verilog specifications three times and pick the one with the lowest operating frequency where the synthesis is successful up to the clock synthesis step.

To evaluate the ability of UST-LSM frameworks to improve the robustness to variations, we adopt a similar Monte Carlo simulation framework as in the ISPD 2010 contest [15]. In the Monte Carlo simulation framework, the clock network is affected by wire width variations (10%) and supply voltage variations (15%) as in the ISPD 2010 contest. In addition, we extend the variations model to also include temperature variations (30%), and channel length variations (10%). Moreover, all the variations are assumed to exhibit spatial correlation using a 5-level quad-tree model [1]. The variations are evenly assigned to the bottom three levels of the quad-tree. The variations in each level of the quad-tree are generated using a uniform distribution. This is an improvement over the ISPD 2010 contest variations model where the variations exhibited no spatial correlation. It is also an improvement over the variations model in [2] where devices placed at the same location experienced the same voltage variations. We assume the same technology parameters for the devices and wires in the ISPD 2010 contest [15]. Timing evaluation of the constructed clock trees is performed using a stage-by-stage SPICE simulation approach using transition time propagation [19].

Table 1: Properties of the scaled ISCAS89 and synthesized Open Cores benchmarks.

Name	Clock period (ns)	Number of nets	Number of cells	Number of sequential elements	Number of skew constraints
scaled_s1423	0.32	-	-	74	78
scaled_s5378	0.32	-	-	179	175
scaled_s15850	0.32	-	-	597	318
msp	12.30	5239	4787	683	44990
fpu	40.00	42104	41565	715	16263
ecg	1.00	62164	61491	7674	63440

The performance of each clock network is evaluated using its yield and timing slack. Given the actual timing obtained through simulation, we define the *slack* in the setup and hold time constraints in Eq. (2) to be $u_{ij} - skew_{ij}$ and $skew_{ij} - l_{ij}$, respectively. Positive slacks imply that the constraints are satisfied while negative slacks correspond to constraint violations. Each clock network is simulated with 500 Monte Carlo simulations, with the PVT variations applied as specified earlier. For each simulation, the worst slack, denoted as wSlack, in all the skew constraints is recorded. The 95%-slack is defined to be the 95%-tile of the 500 wSlacks (ordered in descending order). Moreover, at every point in the clock network the transition time of the clock signal must meet a 100 ps transition time constraint. We consider each simulation as a testing of a chip. If the wSlack is non-negative and the transition time constraint is satisfied, we classify the tested chip as a good chip. The yield is obtained by dividing the number of good chips with the total number of chips tested.

We also report the capacitive cost (Cap cost) as this correlates with the power consumption of the clock network. We believe this is acceptable as we are constructing clock trees and not non-tree structures. The run-times of the synthesis tool are given in the columns labeled "Run-time" in the tables.

5.1 Negative cycle detection and sink clustering

We assume that the user specified safety margin M_{user} will never be larger than $M_{user}^{max} = 100$ ps for designs with tight timing constraints. If a benchmark circuit has $M > M_{user}^{max}$, we say the circuit has loose skew constraints; otherwise, we say that the benchmark circuit has tight skew constraints. We find the benchmark circuits scaled_s1423, scaled_s5378, msp, and fpu have loose skew constraints and scaled_s15850 and ecg have tight skew constraints. The maximum uniform safety margins for scaled_s15850 and ecg are $M = 27$ ps and $M = 15$ ps, respectively. For benchmark circuits with loose skew constraints, our proposed UST-LSM framework is equivalent to the method in [17].

For the benchmarks circuits with tight skew constraints, the UST-LSM framework is different from [17]. Negative cycles will be found when $M_{user} > M$. In Table 2, we show the number of negative cycles found in the SCG for different values of M_{user}. In Figure 4, the negative cycles found for benchmark circuit ecg are shown. We find that our simple early termination procedure is sufficient to perform early termination in every case where a negative cycle exists in the SCG. On benchmark circuit scaled_s15850, there is only one negative cycle when M_{user} is set to anywhere in the range $M < M_{user} \leq M + 50$ ps. On benchmark circuit ecg,

the number of cycles varies for different settings of M_{user}, which is shown in Table 2.

Table 2: Negative cycles found for different settings of M_{user} on benchmark circuits scaled_s15850 and ecg.

BM	Safety margin (ps)	Negative cycles (num)	Early termination (num)
scaled_s15850	$M_{user} = M + 20 = 47$	1	1
scaled_s15850	$M_{user} = M + 50 = 77$	1	1
ecg	$M_{user} = M + 15 = 30$	5	5
ecg	$M_{user} = M + 25 = 40$	7	7

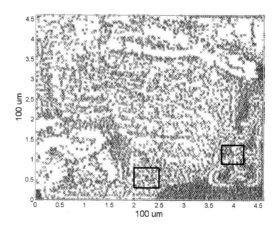

Figure 4: The plot shows the sinks of the circuit ecg from the Open Cores benchmark suite. The negative cycles obtained when M_{user} is set to $M + 15 = 30$ are shown with red edges enclosed in black boxes.

The sink clusters constructed based on the negative cycles are shown in Table 3. In addition to the trivial cluster C_1, one cluster C_2 is obtained for scaled_15850 and for ecg, we obtain two additional clusters when $M_{user} = M + 15$ ps and three additional clusters when $M_{user} = M + 25$ ps. On scaled_15850 the cluster C_2 contains 3 sinks and on ecg the clusters C_2 and C_3 contain a total of seven sinks when $M_{user} = M + 15$ ps. When $M_{user} = M + 25$ ps, the clusters C_2, C_3, and C_4 for ecg contain a total of nine sinks. That there are few clusters implies that there are few skew constraints that limit the maximum value of M; the UST-LSM framework was designed specifically to overcome such limitation.

In Table 3, we show the numbers of buffer stages of trees constructed for these clusters in the column labeled "Max stages". We observe that when clustering is applied, the maximum numbers of buffer stages of the clusters are reduced from 7 or 9 to 3 for scaled_s15850 and from 6, 8, and 6 to 3, 1, and 1, respectively, for ecg. The smaller the buffer stages, the closer are the sinks of the negative cycles in the clock trees. With the ensured lower point of divergence, variations will not affect these sinks too adversely. Moreover, buffer stages above these clusters would have the full safety margin of M_{user}.

Table 3: Clusters other than C_1 created for scaled_s15850 and ecg. The number of such clusters is dependent on M_{user}. The "Max stages" columns refer to the numbers of buffer stages of the trees constructed for the clusters.

	Safety margin M_{user} (ps)	Clustering	Max stages C_2 (num)	C_3 (num)	C_4 (num)
scaled_s15850	$M + 20 = 47$	yes	3	-	-
scaled_s15850	$M + 20 = 47$	no	7	-	-
scaled_s15850	$M + 50 = 77$	yes	3	-	-
scaled_s15850	$M + 50 = 77$	no	9	-	-
ecg	$M + 15 = 30$	yes	3	1	-
ecg	$M + 15 = 30$	no	6	8	-
ecg	$M + 25 = 40$	yes	3	1	1
ecg	$M + 25 = 40$	no	3	6	1

Table 4: Performance of the USTs constructed for benchmark circuits with loose skew constraints.

BM	Safety margin M_{user}	Yield (%)	95%-slack (ps)	Cap (fF)	Run-time (s)
scaled	ZST	100	140.00	4630	52
_s1423	No margin	100	140.00	3445	21
	50	100	140.00	3445	21
scaled	100	100	140.00	3445	21
_s5378	ZST	100	12.86	6764	38
	No margin	100	12.86	5703	40
	50	100	31.99	8780	139
	100	100	35.37	9251	150
msp	ZST	100	80.00	2473	209
	No margin	100	80.00	1872	193
	50	100	80.00	1872	200
	100	100	100.00	1977	184
fpu	ZST	100	49.11	3185	78
	No margin	100	50.00	2264	49
	50	100	50.00	2264	46
	100	100	87.36	4499	71

Table 5: Experimental results for scaled_s15850 and ecg. On these two benchmarks a $M_{user} > M$ is required to maximize the yield.

BM	Safety margin M_{user}	Yield (%)	95%-slack (ps)	Cap (fF)	Run-time (s)
scaled	ZST	0.0	-12.98	17383	136
_s15780	No margin=0	26.4	-14.54	14520	181
	M=27	96.6	3.26	20197	292
	M+10=37	99.6	11.25	25916	678
	M+20=47	99.8	17.40	30050	1092
	M+30=57	100.0	24.30	34890	1484
	M+40=67	100.0	24.74	40815	1763
	M+50=77	100.0	23.30	47177	3026
ecg	ZST	0.0	-30.53	25878	1771
	No margin	0.0	-19.55	22256	1118
	M=15	46.8	-9.04	44853	1827
	M+5=20	82.6	-5.34	47129	1761
	M+10=25	93.0	-1.13	56974	2127
	M+15=30	98.8	4.64	66829	2360
	M+20=35	95.4	0.15	89223	4011
	M+25=40	96.2	5.17	96845	6388

5.2 Designs with loose skew constraints

The UST-LSM framework is equivalent to the method in [17] for benchmarks with loose design constraints, i.e., $M_{user} \leq M$. The experimental results for the benchmark circuits with loose skew constraints are presented in Table 4.

On scaled_s1423, the skew constraints are so loose that for three different safety margins of $M_{user} = 0$ ps, 50 ps, or 100 ps, the same clock tree is obtained. When simulated with variations, the worst slack came from a particular pair of clock sinks that are really close in the topology. So, the worst slack is consistently 140 ps in every Monte Carlo simulation. We also construct a zero skew clock tree to show that the our buffered Greedy-UST/DME algorithm can take advantage of the loose skew constraints to reduce cost.

On scaled_s5378, different clock trees are obtained when different safety margins M_{user} are imposed. Three different capacitive costs are obtained. Moreover, the 95%-slack improves from 12.86 ps to 35.37 ps. It is expected that the 95%-slack is smaller that M_{user} because M_{user} is the safety margin in every skew constraint in the nominal case, i.e, when there are no variations. The variations-induced skew on scaled_s5378 is very large because when $M_{user} = 100$ ps, large useful skew is required. Typically, when large useful skew are required, the size of the clock tree grows because buffers may have to be inserted to provide useful skew. However, a skewed buffered tree may lead to an increase of variations induced skew. Nevertheless, the 95%-slack is effectively increased when the M_{user} is increased. The performances of msp and fpu are similar to scaled_s5378.

5.3 Designs with tight skew constraints

To obtain a high yield on scaled_1585 and ecg, the safety margin M_{user} is required to be greater than M. The experimental results of these two benchmarks are tabulated in Table 5.

On scaled_1585 we observe a 96.6% yield when the safety margin M_{user} is set to $M = 27$ ps. To increase the yield further, $M_{user} > M$ is required. When M_{user} is increased, the capacitive cost and the yield increased as expected. However, the 95%-slack saturates around 24 ps, which is shown in Figure 5. The reason for this is that the safety margin in the skew constraints of cluster C_2 is $M = 27$ ps. When M_{user} is increased beyond $M + 30$ ps the wSlacks of the 500 Monte Carlo simulations are obtained within the cluster C_2.

The yield curve for Open Cores benchmark circuit ecg is shown in Figure 6. A safety margin of $M_{user} = M = 15$ ps results in a yield of only 46.8%. To improve the yield further, $M_{user} > M$ is required as can be seen in Table 5 and in Figure 6.

Now, we analyze the results of ecg in Table 5. As expected, we find that the capacitive cost goes up when the safety margin is increased. The 95%-slack and the yield are monotonically increasing until M_{user} is set to $M + 20 = 35$ ps. A possible explanation for the slight decrease in 95%-slack and yield is that when the safety margin M_{user} is increased from $M + 15 = 30$ ps to $M + 20 = 35$ ps, the synthesis problem becomes significantly more difficult and the resulting clock tree becomes substantially larger, which can be confirmed with the increase in capacitive cost (see Table 5). A larger clock tree is more susceptible to variations. Here, it seems that the increase in variations may have been larger than the increase in the safety margin M_{user}.

In conclusion, we show that the UST-LSM framework extends the work in [17] to handle the case when M_{user} is required to be greater than M to increase 95%-slack and yield.

6. SUMMARY AND FUTURE WORK

By identifying and clustering critical sinks, the proposed UST-LSM framework allows such critical sinks to be joined

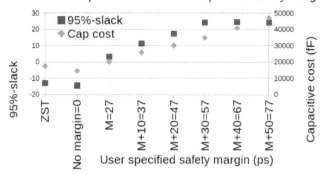

95%-slack and capacitive cost vs. user specified safety margin

Figure 5: Trade-off between the 95%-slack (left vertical axis) and the safety margin M_{user} (horizontal axis) for scaled_s15850. Trade-off between the capacitive cost (right vertical axis) and M_{user} is also shown. The 95%-slack saturates at 22 ps. The saturation of the 95%-slack is because of the skew constraints in cluster C_2 where the safety margin is $M = 27$ ps, which is further reduced to 22 ps under variations.

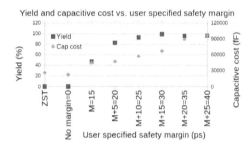

Yield and capacitive cost vs. user specified safety margin

Figure 6: Trade-off between yield, capacitive cost, and safety margin for ecg.

earlier in a buffered UST, allowing the skew constraints to have maximal safety margins. The framework allows large safety margins to be inserted so that the buffered USTs are robust enough to offset the impacts of variations.

The approach can be enhanced with the incorporation of the dynamic safety margin allocation method in [11], especially in the construction of buffered USTs for each of the identified clusters.

Acknowledgments

This work was supported in part by NSF award CCF-1065318 and SRC task 292-074. We are grateful to Timothy Trippel for his assistance in preparing the paper.

7. REFERENCES

[1] A. Agarwal, D. Blaauw, and V. Zolotov. Statistical timing analysis for intra-die process variations with spatial correlations. ICCAD'03, pages 900–907, 2003.

[2] S. Bujimalla and C.-K. Koh. Synthesis of low power clock trees for handling power-supply variations. ISPD '11, pages 37–44, 2011.

[3] Y. P. Chen and D. F. Wong. An algorithm for zero-skew clock tree routing with buffer insertion. EDTC'96, pages 230–237, 1996.

[4] B. V. Cherkassky and A. V. Goldberg. Negative-cycle detection algorithms. ESA'96, pages 349–363, 1996.

[5] T. H. Cormen, C. Stein, R. L. Rivest, and C. E. Leiserson. *Introduction to Algorithms*. McGraw-Hill Higher Education, 2001.

[6] M. Edahiro. Minimum skew and minimum path length routing in VLSI layout design. In *NEC Research and Development*, pages 569–575, 1991.

[7] R. Ewetz, S. Janarthanan, and C.-K. Koh. Fast clock skew scheduling based on sparse-graph algorithms. ASP-DAC '14, 2014.

[8] R. Ewetz and C.-K. Koh. Benchmark circuits for clock scheduling and synthesis. https://purr.purdue.edu/publications/1759, 2015.

[9] J. Fishburn. Clock skew optimization. *IEEE Transactions on Computers*, pages 945–951, 1990.

[10] I. Kourtev and E. Friedman. Clock skew scheduling for improved reliability via quadratic programming. ICCAD'99, pages 239–243, 1999.

[11] W.-C. D. Lam and C.-K. Koh. Process variation robust clock tree routing. ASP-DAC '05, pages 606–611, 2005.

[12] M. Ni and S. Memik. A revisit to the primal-dual based clock skew scheduling algorithm. ISQED'10, pages 755–764, 2010.

[13] OpenCores. http://opencores.net/.

[14] S. S. Sapatnekar and R. B. Deokar. Utilizing the retiming-skew equivalence in a practical algorithm for retiming large circuits. *IEEE Transactions on VLSI Systems*, pages 74–83, 1996.

[15] C. Sze. ISPD 2010 high performance clock network synthesis contest: Benchmark suite and results. ISPD'10, pages 143–143, 2010.

[16] C. N. Sze, P. Restle, G.-J. Nam, and C. J. Alpert. ISPD 2009 clock network synthesis contest. ISPD'09, pages 149–150, 2009.

[17] C.-W. A. Tsao and C.-K. Koh. UST/DME: a clock tree router for general skew constraints. *ACM Transactions on Design Automation of Electronic Systems (TODAES)*, pages 359–379, 2002.

[18] J. G. Xi and W. W.-M. Dai. Useful-skew clock routing with gate sizing for low power design. DAC '96, pages 383–388, 1996.

[19] M. Zhao, K. Gala, V. Zolotov, Y. Fu, R. Panda, R. Ramkumar, and B. Agrawal. Worst case clock skew under power supply variations. TAU '02, pages 22–28, 2002.

Analytical Clustering Score with Application to Post-Placement Multi-Bit Flip-Flop Merging

Chang Xu[1], Peixin Li[1], Guojie Luo[1,2], Yiyu Shi[3], and Iris Hui-Ru Jiang[4]
[1]Center for Energy-Efficient Computing and Applications, School of EECS,
Peking University, Beijing, 100871, China
[2]PKU-UCLA Joint Research Institute in Science and Engineering
[3]Dept. of ECE, Missouri University of Science and Technology, Rolla, MO 65409, USA
[4]Dept. of EE and Inst. of Electronics, National Chiao Tung University, Hsinchu 30010, Taiwan
{changxu, gluo}@pku.edu.cn, pageli328@gmail.com
yshi@mst.edu, huiru.jiang@gmail.com

ABSTRACT

Circuit clustering is usually done through discrete optimizations, with the purpose of circuit size reduction or design-specific cluster formation. Specifically, we are interested in the multi-bit flip-flop (MBFF) design technique for clock power reduction, where all previous works rely on discrete clustering optimizations. For example, INTEGRA was the only existing post-placement MBFF clustering optimizer with a sub-quadratic time complexity. However, it degrades the wirelength severely, especially for realistic designs, which may cancel out the benefits of MBFF clustering. In this paper we enable the formulation of an analytical clustering score in nonlinear programming, where the wirelength objective can be seamlessly integrated. It has sub-quadratic time complexity, reduces the clock power by about 20% as the state-of-the-art techniques, and further reduces the wirelength by about 25%. In addition, the proposed method is promising to be integrated in an in-placement MBFF clustering solver and be applied in other problems which require formulating the clustering score in the objective function.

Categories and Subject Descriptors

B.7 [Integrated circuits]: design aids placement and routing

Keywords

Multi-bit flip-flops, placement, clock power, timing

1. INTRODUCTION

Circuit clustering technique is a useful stage in electronic design automation. There are two categories of clustering problems: one is for circuit size reduction, where a short survey can be found in [20]; the other is for design-specific

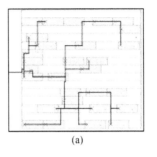 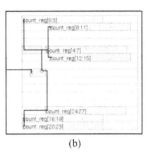

(a) (b)

Figure 1: Clock tree synthesis for (a) conventional flow (b) MBFF flow

Table 1: The power and area of our MBFF library

Bit number	Normalized power per bit	Normalized area per bit
1	1.00	1.00
2	0.86	0.96
4	0.78	0.71

cluster formation, such as voltage island grouping [19] and register grouping [5],[6].

In this paper we are interested in the multi-bit flip-flop (MBFF) clustering problem, which is a promising technique for clock power reduction, due to the power savings on clock nets and flip-flops (FFs) themselves. As shown in Figure 1, the basic idea of MBFF technique is to reduce the load capacitance on the clock network, including the reduction of metal wires in the last-level of the clock tree, as well as the reduction of clock pins. In addition, the normalized per-bit power and area of a MBFF are less than a single-bit FF. Specifically, for the MBFF library we used as shown in Table 1, 4-bit MBFF is the most power-efficient and area-efficient.

Existing works explore MBFF clustering in three design stages: pre-placement stage [1][10], in-placement stage [17] [7], and post-placement stage. Because of the adequate physical information, post-placement MBFF clustering has attracted a lot of attentions, such as [21][11][18][9]. Among all these works, INTEGRA[9] delivers the best performance in both power reduction and runtime consumption and is the only one with sub-quadratic complexity. However, almost all previous works pay little attention to the signal wirelength, either regarding it as secondary objective [21][11][18] or even ignoring it at all [9]. We demonstrate latter that for a series of realistic benchmarks, INTEGRA's clustering degenerates into a random clustering of MBFFs and induces huge degradation of signal wirelength, which might cancel out the power benefit of MBFFs.

In this paper we propose an analytical model for the clustering score. The basic idea is to first propose an exact formulation of the number of clusters based on the Dirac delta function, and smooth it using the Gaussian function to make it applicable in a nonlinear programming (NLP) framework with another objective in wirelength. With a well-designed NLP solver, the acceleration techniques such as customized fast Gauss transformation, and a further discrete refinement, our clustering flow delivers high-quality MBFF clustering results with short wirelength in sub-quadratic time. Taken IN-TEGRA as baseline, our method shows a comparable power reduction, reducing clock power by about 20%. Furthermore, our method optimizes signal wirelength by about 25%. What's more, the proposed method is promising to be integrated in an in-placement MBFF clustering solver, and be applied in other problems which require formulating the clustering score in the objective function.

The rest of this paper is organized as follows. Section 2 reviews the effectiveness and limitations of previous work. Section 3 introduces our optimization flow, including analytical clustering model and discrete refinement. Section 4 elaborates the details of NLP solver and the acceleration technique. Section 5 evaluates our method, and shows experimental data and comparisons. Finally, Section 6 concludes this work.

2. PRELIMINARY AND MOTIVATION

This section will focus on two concepts, the timing violation-free distance (TVFD) and the average distance between neighboring flip-flops (AFFD). The concept of TVFD will be described in Section 2.1, and the concept of AFFD and our motivations will be discussed in Section 2.2.

2.1 Post-placement MBFF Problem Formulation and Previous Solutions

Given the following inputs, **the post-placement MBFF clustering problem** will replace a few single-bit FFs with MBFF such that the power is minimized and the timing constraint and placement density constraint are satisfied.

- The number of N placed flip-flops (FFs), where each FF_i with coordinate (x_i, y_i) can either be single-bit or multi-bit.

- The upstream pin PI_i and downstream pin PO_i of FF_i, and corresponding timing slacks $T_s(PI_i, FF_i)$ and $T_s(PO_i, FF_i)$ between the pins and FF on the upstream and downstream timing paths, respectively.

- The MBFF library with information of power and area.

- The locations of placement blockages.

Timing constraint is proposed to prevent MBFF clustering from violating cycle delay. The basic idea is shown in Figure 2. With timing analysis, we could obtain timing slack between input (output) pins and FF. By transforming the timing slack into equivalent metal wirelength using Elmore

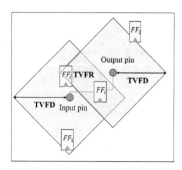

Figure 2: Concept of timing-violation-free distance (TVFD) and timing-violation-free region (TVFR)

delay model [4], we can find the timing-violation-free distance (**TVFD**) between FF and input (output) pins. Taken the input and output TVFDs into account, each FF can find a feasible region for movement without violating timing, which we label as timing-violation-free region (**TVFR**) in Figure 2. Consequently, clustering a few single-bit FFs with overlapped TVFRs can optimize power and area without violating timing constraint. Specifically, using the library in Table 1, the basic objective of MBFF clustering problem should merge FFs with overlapped TVFRs into 4-bit groups as many as possible.

Previous works certify the timing constraint with well-designed structures: intersection graph [21][11][18] or interval graph [9] and search the MBFF candidates on these graphs.

The MBFF clustering based on intersection graph has the following defects: 1) searching maximum clique is computational expensive with known best performance of $O(N^3)$. 2) The window-based optimization technique for problem size reduction limits the clustering ratio of MBFF due to the difficulty of manipulating the boundaries.

Unlike window-based technique, INTEGRA considers all FFs simultaneously, with a well designed structure: interval graph. Searching on the interval graph is more efficient, with sub-quadratic complexity. Moreover, the optimization with global information delivers better clustering ratio than the optimization with local information only. Thus, INTEGRA outperforms the previous work in terms of power reduction and runtime complexity.

However, the efficient runtime of INTEGRA partially benefits from the simple strategy of choosing MBFF candidates without measuring the impact to signal wirelength. Taking an extreme case as example, where the intervals of feasible region for each FF is as large as the placement region, INTE-GRA's solution degenerates to a random solution. Although the wirelength degradation on widely used benchmarks C1-C6 [11] is acceptable (around 3%), we analyze in the following subsection that for a series of realistic designs, wirelength degradation is quite huge. Such observation motivates us to propose a new solution with great power reduction, better signal wirelength and efficient time complexity.

2.2 Previous Solutions are Inappropriate for Realistic Designs

We demonstrate in this part that 1) the widely used benchmarks C1-C6 [11] can only represent a single kind of circuit; 2) realistic designs from IWLS[2] are quite different from C1-C6 in terms of TVFR. Specifically, for the realistic designs, MBFF clustering is quite easy if no signal wirelength is considered. Thus, what really matters is to find a solution with short signal wirelength while keeping the clustering ratio high.

Firstly, we define the average FF distance (AFFD) as $\sqrt{ChipArea/\#FF}$. It is obvious that the average distance between every pair of nearest FFs is approximately AFFD, assuming all the FFs are evenly placed. Then TVFD/AFFD is calculated for every FFs to roughly estimate how many FFs can be covered within the range of TVFD.

As is shown in Figure 3(a), the histogram of TVFD/AFFD for the benchmark C1 indicates that the range of TVFD is limited. The majority of FFs can only reach 3 other FFs on average within the range of TVFD.

Interestingly, all other benchmarks, C2-C6, follow exactly the same distributions as C1, even though the number of FFs is different. Moreover, if we look at the number of FFs and the placement region of these benchmarks, they scale in exactly the same ratio. These facts indicate that the benchmarks C1-C6 can only represent a single kind of circuit. They are not sufficient to evaluate the performance of MBFF clustering algorithms.

Similarly, we pick a realistic design, vga, from the IWLS benchmark suite, and synthesize it by Synopsys DC and Cadence SOC Encounter with a tight timing constraint. Specifically, the worst negative slack (WNS) reported after placement is 0.108 ns with clock cycle time of 3.5 ns and 2.5 ns for the two clock domains. The TVFD/AFFD distribution is revealed in Figure 3(b).

Comparing Figure 3(a) and Figure 3(b), we can easily find that TVFD in realistic designs is two orders of magnitude greater than TVFD in C1-C6. Thus, realistic designs have much greater freedom of choosing clustering candidates. However, INTEGRA almost has no evaluation on signal wirelength. With the analysis in Subsection 2.1 and statistics in Table 4, we see that the solution of INTEGRA damages the signal wirelength a lot for realistic designs. For example, the degradation of wirelength for ethernet is up to 20 times of original wirelength.

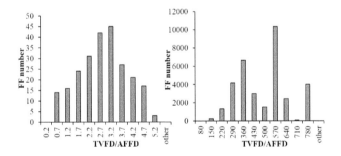

Figure 3: The histogram of TVFD/AFFD for benchmark (a) C1 (b) realistic design Vga

3. ANALYTICAL MODEL AND THE OPTIMIZATION FLOW

3.1 The Basic Idea

In this paper, we view the MBFF clustering problem as an optimization problem subject to timing constraint. The objective function optimize the number of MBFF clusters

as many as possible while taking the signal wirelength into account.

Our optimization includes two steps: the analytical optimization step and the discrete refinement step. In the analytical optimization, we carefully define the formulation with a continuous and differentiable objective function and exploit an effective non-linear programming (NLP) solver [12] to make our method practical. After the analytical optimization, we can get a rough clustering. Then we invoke the discrete optimization to discretize and further improve the clustering solution. The overall flow is shown in Figure 4 and details will be illustrate in the following part.

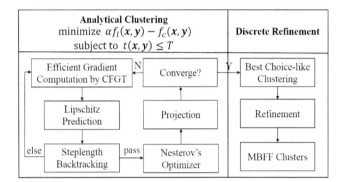

Figure 4: Optimization Flow

3.2 Analytical Optimization Step

3.2.1 Definition of Clustering Score

Our objective function trades off the signal wirelength $f_l(\boldsymbol{x}, \boldsymbol{y})$ and cluster number $f_c(\boldsymbol{x}, \boldsymbol{y})$ with parameter α, where $\boldsymbol{x} = (x_1, \ldots, x_N)^T$ and $\boldsymbol{y} = (y_1, \ldots, y_N)^T$ represent coordinates for N FFs. Because of the timing constraint, FFs' locations are bounded within their feasible regions. Thus, the problem is formulated as optimization problem under the timing constraint.

$$
\begin{aligned}
\text{minimize} \quad & \alpha \cdot f_l(\boldsymbol{x}, \boldsymbol{y}) - f_c(\boldsymbol{x}, \boldsymbol{y}) \\
\text{subject to} \quad & t(\boldsymbol{x}, \boldsymbol{y}) \leq T
\end{aligned} \tag{1}
$$

The signal wirelength $f_l(\boldsymbol{x}, \boldsymbol{y})$ is measured by the total half-perimeter wirelength (HPWL) between locations of FFs and their upstream and downstream pins. Since HPWL is non-differentiable, we use the weighted-average approximation in [8].

The cluster number $f_c(\boldsymbol{x}, \boldsymbol{y})$ is measured by the distance metric. If FF_i and FF_j are clustered eventually, their coordinates will be exactly the same. Analytically, we use the delta function to evaluate the relationship between two FFs. As shown in Equation 2 and Equation 3, the value of delta function becomes one if and only if two FFs are placed at the same location. The summation in Equation 3 calculates the total number of FFs that can be "clustered" with FF_i. For example, if $N_i(\boldsymbol{x}, \boldsymbol{y})$ equals to 3, we can see FF_i is placed at the same location as three other FFs. They form a 4-bit cluster together.

$$
\delta(\omega, z) = \begin{cases} 1 & (\omega = z) \\ 0 & (\omega \neq z) \end{cases} \tag{2}
$$

$$N_i(\boldsymbol{x}, \boldsymbol{y}) = \sum_{j \neq i} \delta(\| (x_i, y_i) - (x_j, y_j) \|, 0) \quad (3)$$

According to the library in Table 1, the 4-bit MBFF is the most efficient in power and area reduction. Thus, each FF is encouraged to cluster with three other FFs. As shown in Equation 4, minimizing the $-f_c$ term of the objective function encourages maximizing the number of FFs in 4-bit clusters. In the next subsection, we will demonstrate that our clustering function (f_c) is capable of generating attractive and repelling forces during the optimization so that it enables the formation of 4-bit clusters as many as possible.

$$\min -f_c = -\max f_c = -\max \sum_{i=1}^{N} \delta(N_i(\boldsymbol{x}, \boldsymbol{y}), 3) \quad (4)$$

The delta function is non-differentiable. In practice, we smooth it with Gaussian function. As Equation 5 shows, the Gaussian function can degenerate very quickly. The parameters ε and d_0^2 are used to control the degenerate speed, where ε ranges from 0 to 1 and d_0 is a distance metric. Equation 6 quantifies that the function value will decrease below ε when distance is greater than d_0. The effect of parameter d_0 will be discussed in the Subsection 4.3. With the smoothing technique, our constraint optimization problem can be solved by non-linear programming (NLP) solvers. In Subsection 4.1, we will systematically illustrate our efficient and effective NLP solver.

$$\delta(\omega, z) \approx D(\omega, z) = \exp((\omega - z)^2 \ln \varepsilon / d_0^2) \quad (5)$$

$$\begin{cases} D(\omega - z) = 1 & \text{when} \quad w = z \\ D(\omega - z) < \varepsilon & \text{when} \quad | \omega - z | > d_0 \end{cases} \quad (6)$$

3.2.2 Insights of the Clustering Function

PROPERTY 1. FF_i contributes a term $f_{c,i} = \delta(N_i(\boldsymbol{x}, \boldsymbol{y}), 3)$ to the clustering score f_c. When FF_i lies in an under-sized ($N_i < 3$) cluster, maximizing this term results in attractive forces for the neighboring FFs of FF_i; when FF_i lies in an over-sized ($N_i > 3$) cluster, maximizing this term results in repelling forces for the neighboring FFs of FF_i.

PROOF. The force direction of FF_j resulting from $f_{c,i}$ towards can be detected by checking the sign of Equation 7. Here we only consider the x-direction without loss of generality.

$$\begin{aligned} FF_i \text{ attracts } FF_j \text{ when } (x_i - x_j) \cdot \frac{\partial f_{c,i}}{\partial x_j} > 0 \\ FF_i \text{ repels } FF_j \text{ when } (x_i - x_j) \cdot \frac{\partial f_{c,i}}{\partial x_j} < 0 \end{aligned} \quad (7)$$

When smoothing with Gaussian function, the calculation of partial derivative is shown in Equation 8, 9, 10.

$$\frac{\partial f_{c,i}}{\partial N_i} = 2\lambda_1 (N_i - 3) \exp((N_i - 3)^2 \lambda_1) \quad (8)$$

$$\frac{\partial N_i}{\partial x_j} = 2\lambda_2 \exp(\lambda_2((x_i - x_j)^2 + (y_i - y_j)^2))(x_j - x_i) \quad (9)$$

$$\frac{\partial f_{c,i}}{\partial x_j} = \frac{\partial f_{c,i}}{\partial N_i} \cdot \frac{\partial N_i}{\partial x_j} \quad (10)$$

Please note that both λ_1 and λ_2 equal to $\ln \varepsilon / d_0^2$, which are negative when ε is less than 1. Thus, the force direction is

only related to N_i, which is shown in Equation 11

$$\begin{cases} (x_i - x_j) \cdot \frac{\partial f_{c,i}}{\partial x_j} > 0 & \text{when } N_i < 3 \\ (x_i - x_j) \cdot \frac{\partial f_{c,i}}{\partial x_j} < 0 & \text{when } N_i > 3 \end{cases} \quad (11)$$

$\square$

In Figure 5, we illustrate the force direction and strength from FF_i towards other FFs and the convexity of clustering function. As is shown in Figure 5(a), when FF_i is adjacent to less than 3 FFs, FF_i will attract more FFs to form a cluster of size 4; when there are more than 3 neighbors, FF_i will repel the extra FFs. Thus, it guarantees the maximization of 4-bit clusters' number. Since $f_{c,i}$ part contains Exp function, which degenerates quickly, FF_i will only affects other FFs within distance of r in Figure 5(a).

Here we take a specific case as an example to illustrate the force strength from FF_i, where FF_i locates at $(0,0)$ point, ε is set to 0.5, and d_0 is set to 100. In Figure 5(b), where the x-axis represents the change of x_j of another FF and y-axis indicates the value of $\partial f_{c,i}/\partial(x_j)$, we can see that FF_i only affects other FFs in the neighbourhood. We consider such feature to accelerate the gradient calculation with fast gauss transformation (FGT) in Subsection 4.2.

From the previous analysis, the f_l term of the objective function can pull FFs towards their "optimal locations" in terms of signal wirelength. While the f_c term of the objective function can effectively cluster FFs in the neighborhood into 4-bit groups as many as possible. Thus, our objective function achieves high-quality results in both signal wirelength and clustering ratio.

In fact, our clustering function is not convex. Supposing in the following circumstance, for FF_i, its' neighbouring FFs are FF_a and FF_b and they are aligned in horizontal. The value of $f_{c,i}$ term changes with different locations of FF_i, which has been illustrated in Figure 5(c). Although it is not convex, we will show its efficiency in Section 5.

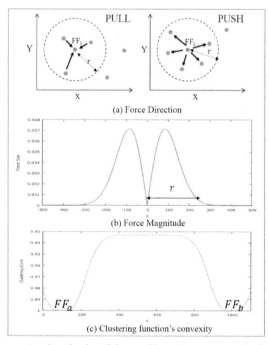

Figure 5: Analysis of force direction, magnitude and convexity of clustering function

3.3 Discrete Optimization Step

Since the analytical solution is an approximately continuous solution, additional steps are required to map the continuous solution to a final discrete solution.

We apply discrete optimization in Algorithm 1 to complete the conversion from a given analytical solution to the final solution. The discrete optimization flow looks like two-passes of best-choice clustering [3]. In the first pass (line 6-11), we extract partial clusters by bottom-up clustering based on the proximity relation after analytical solution. In this step the size of partial clusters will not exceed the maximum size (i.e. 4-bit in our library). Then we perform further refinement to improve the ratio of 4-bit clusters in the second pass (in line 12-20). It is necessary since there will be some 2-bit or 3-bit clusters after the first pass. In this step we temporally form clusters that exceed the maximum size and kick out the extra FFs immediately based on the heuristic score. Please note that we perform **timing constraint** check during cluster formation to guarantee that FFs in the same cluster have overlapped feasible regions.

Algorithm 1 Discrete Optimization
Require:
    1) The initial FFs' locations based on analytical solution
    2) The feasible region for each FF
    Preprocessing
1: Construct Bin-Structure for nearest neighbour searching

2: Search three nearest neighbours on Bin-Structure and Insert tuples into Priority Queue
    Clustering & Refinement
3: $Pass \leftarrow 1$
4: **while** $Pass <= 2$ **do**
5:     Pop top tuple(FF_i, FF_j, d) from PQ
6:     **if** $Pass == 1$ **then**
7:         **if** $|\text{Group}(FF_i) \bigcup \text{Group}(FF_j)| < 4$ **then**
8:           **if** satisfy timing constraint **then**
9:             Merge Group(FF_i) and Group(FF_j)
10:           **end if**
11:         **end if**
12:     **else**
13:         **if** $|\text{Group}(FF_i) \bigcup \text{Group}(FF_j)| < 4$ **then**
14:           **if** satisfy timing constraint **then**
15:             Merge Group(FF_i) and Group(FF_j)
16:           **end if**
17:         **else**
18:           Merge Group(FF_i) and Group(FF_j) and Kick out excess FFs
19:         **end if**
20:     **end if**
21:     **if** PQ.empty && Pass==1 **then**
22:         Remove the 4-bit groups and insert the tuples for nearest neighbors for the remaining FFs.
23:     **end if**
24:     $Pass++$
25: **end while**
26: **return** MBFF clustering result

Line 1-2 extracts the proximity relation based on the analytical solution. For each FF, we calculate distances with three nearest neighbors. For the purpose of maintaining

proximity relation, FF pair with small distance will be manipulated in high priority during the later cluster formation. In order to identify the globally nearest FF pair, we insert tuple(FF_i, FF_j, d) into a priority-queue (PQ) with the distance d between FF_i and FF_j as the sort key. Naive searching of three nearest neighbors requires $O(N^2)$ complexity for N FFs. In order to accelerate the $O(N^2)$ searching to $O(N)$, we design an efficient bin-structure, which will be explained in Section 4.2. With our bin-structure, we can efficiently search three nearest neighbors for N FFs in $O(N)$ time, assuming that FFs are well distributed.

Line 6-11 is the clustering step (first pass). Since 4-bit MBFF is the most power-efficient and area-efficient, the cluster's capacity is limited to 4, which we call **capacity constraint**. After the preprocessing stage, we pick up the top tuple(FF_i, FF_j, d) from PQ. If merging the groups that FF_i and FF_j belong to does not violate the capacity constraint and timing constraint, we commit the merge. Supposing the top two tuples are (A, B, d_1) and (A, C, d_2) (as in Figure 6(a)), after checking the capacity constraint, A and B will be firstly merged into a group of two. Then the group of AB and the group of CD will be clustered into a 4-bit group. However, group of HI and group of EFG can not be merged because of capacity constraint. The group information after clustering step is shown in Figure 6(b).

Line 12-20 is the refinement step (second pass). In this step, we allow the clustering of two groups, the sum of whose size exceeds 4, and then kick out the excess part by comparing heuristic score. The heuristic score will estimate the HPWL of signal nets if a FF candidate is stayed in the group, which is bounded by the locations of pins connected to all the FFs in the group. The less the score is, the more possibility of that FF will be stayed in the group. In Figure 6(c), we pick up the top tuple, namely (I, E, d_3), from PQ. Since merging the two groups results in a group size of 5, we kick out one FF with maximum heuristic score. The final FFs groups' formation is shown in Figure 6(d).

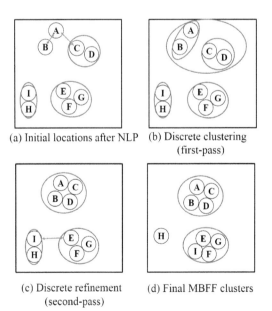

(a) Initial locations after NLP   (b) Discrete clustering (first-pass)

(c) Discrete refinement (second-pass)   (d) Final MBFF clusters

Figure 6: Discrete optimization

4. IMPLEMENTATION DETAILS

4.1 Nonlinear Programming Solver

As shown in Section 3.2, we formulate an analytical objective function in the constrained nonlinear programming model. Instead of the penalty methods, we apply a gradient projection method to handle the timing constraints.

In this work we use the Nesterov's method [12] to choose the step size to minimize the objective function efficiently. The key algorithm for the NLP solver is described in Algorithm 2.

Step size α_k is crucial to guarantee the convergence of Nesterov method. As [14] shows, $\alpha_k = L^{-1}$ satisfies steplength requirement, where L is the Lipschitz constant. Similar with [12], we approximate Lipschitz constant instead of precisely calculating. At line 1, we use backtrack method to further refine the step size.

The solution after one step of the Nesterov's method, at line 4, may violate the timing constraint. Therefore, we apply a projection step in line 5 to find a closest solution in the feasible space to replace the intermediate infeasible solution. Since the feasible solution space with respect to timing constraint is a convex space, the projection is straightforward to implement. The feasible region of a flip-flop is a circle with Manhattan distance, and it becomes a rectangle after rotating the coordinates by 45 degree. Thus, the projection can be done by rotating the coordinates by 45 degree first, and then project the location of a timing-infeasible flip-flop into its rotated rectangular timing-feasible region.

Algorithm 2 Projected Nesterov Method
Require:
$\quad \alpha_k, \mu_k, v_k, v_k - 1, \nabla f(v_k), \nabla f(v_{k-1})$
1: $\alpha_k = BackTrack(v_k, v_k - 1, \nabla f(v_k), \nabla f(v_{k-1}))$
2: $\mu_{k+1} = v_k - \alpha_k \nabla f(v_k)$
3: $\alpha_{k+1} = (1 + \sqrt{4\alpha_k^2 + 1}/2)$
4: $v_{k+1} = \mu k + 1 + (\alpha_k - 1)(\mu k + 1 - \mu k)/\alpha k + 1$
5: $v_{k+1} = \text{Project}(v_{k+1})$
6: **return** $\mu_{k+1}, v_{k+1}, \alpha k + 1$

4.2 Customized Fast Gauss Transformation

The computation of Equation 4, in the objective function is expensive. A direct computation requires $O(N^2)$ complexity for all the N flip-flops. We use the fast Gauss transformation (FGT)[15] method to reduce the computation complexity to $O(N)$.

The basic idea of the FGT is demonstrated in Figure 7, where the evaluation of the exponential function is only needed for the neighbourhood flip-flops. Supposing FF_i is located in a square with side length $\sqrt{H}$, which equals to $\sqrt{-d_0^2/\ln(\varepsilon)}$ in our problem, as demonstrated in [15], the searching within side length of $4\sqrt{H}$ is satisfied with four digits of accuracy.

However, even using the stage-of-the-art FGT library Figtree [13], the runtime is still too slow due to the overhead of maintaining essential data structure KD-Tree, which is more suitable for high-dimensional data. Thus, we implemented a customized multithreaded FGT solver with an efficient bin structure instead of the KD-Tree structure for our two-dimensional data.

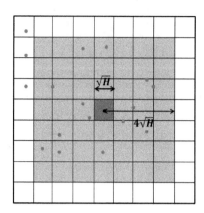

Figure 7: Explanation to fast Gauss transformation (FGT)

Table 2: Comparison of Figtree and our customized FGT

#FF	NLP solver with Figtree for FGT(s)	NLP solver with customized FGT(s)	SpeedUp
120	1.25	0.72	1.74
480	5.80	0.52	11.15
1920	31.43	1.59	19.76
5880	143.33	4.20	34.13
12000	413.45	7.92	52.20
192000	7817.23	207.68	34.64
Avg.	-	-	**25.60**

In our bin-structure, the whole chip is partitioned into a mesh of bins. And we record the amount of FFs that each bin holds. By querying adjacent bins, we can quickly obtain FFs in the neighbourhood. Time complexity is linear and the practical runtime is fast. Compared with Figtree-based implementation, our bin-structure based implementation can achieve **25.6X** speed up on average for different amount of FFs in benchmark C1-C6. Please refer to Table 2 for detailed statistics.

4.3 Parameters Tunning

The value of α (in Equation 1) is set to balance the magnitude of f_l part and f_c part. In fact, the magnitudes of f_l and f_c are positively related to $\text{Chip}_{\text{width}}$ and the total number of FFs (N), respectively. Thus, α is set as Equation 12.

$$\alpha = \frac{N}{\text{Chip}_{\text{width}}} \quad (12)$$

The value of ε and d_0 (in Equation 5) are critical for the performance. If d_0 is too small, FFs do not have enough force to affect others. However, if d_0 is too big, each FF can "see" too many FFs. Finally, FFs will reach their "balanced" states under the effects of many forces. In practice, we observe the best performance when d_0 is set as the average distance between every second nearest FF pairs in Equation 13.

$$d_0 = \frac{1}{N} \sum_i^N \| \text{FF}_i - \text{FF}_{\text{second\_nearest\_to\_FF}_i} \| \quad (13)$$

In our implementation, ε is set to 0.5, meaning that clustering score between two FFs is less than 0.5 when their distance exceeds d_0.

Table 3: Comparisons between INTEGRA and our method on C1-C6

Circuit	INTEGRA			Ours				
	PWR	WLR	RT-all (s)	PWR	WLR	#iter-NLP	RT-NLP(s)	RT-all (s)
C1	82.8	96	0.01	83.5	77.4	151	0.42	0.42
C2	80.9	102	0.01	82.3	76.4	208	0.96	0.96
C3	80.8	104	0.01	82.3	74.9	300	3.11	3.14
C4	81.0	104	0.02	82.4	75.6	423	10.45	10.59
C5	80.7	105	0.05	82.1	76.4	421	15.98	16.66
C6	80.7	105	1.11	82.3	82	351	197.91	217.41
Avg.	1	1.33	1	1.02	1	-	244.88	251.83

Table 4: Comparisons between INTEGRA and our method on realistic designs

Circuit	INTEGRA			Bound-INTEGRA				Ours				
	PWR	WLR	RT(s)	factor	PWR	WLR	RT(s)	PWR	WLR	#iter-NLP	RT-NLP	RT-all(s)
tv80	78.11	350.46	0.01	0.05	78.11	109.20	0.01	78.10	95.71	212	0.93	0.94
wbconmax	78.02	540.81	0.02	0.05	78.26	128	0.03	78.02	105	449	2.29	2.30
pairing	78.00	931.45	0.05	0.05	78.00	132.17	0.03	78.00	109	501	6.51	6.61
dma	78.03	798.29	0.06	0.05	78.04	124.71	0.05	78.02	96	501	5.39	5.43
ac97	78.02	673.28	0.09	0.05	78.02	120	0.02	78.02	95.71	351	4.74	4.88
ethernet	78.00	2038.71	1.61	0.05	78.00	216.51	0.63	78.00	87.92	501	20.81	24.51
Avg.	1	9.32	1	-	1	1.43	0.76	0.99	1	-	82.19	83.52

5. EXPERIMENTAL RESULTS

5.1 Performance Comparison

We implement our two-steps post-placement clustering method in C++, and evaluate it on an Intel Xeon machine with 16 logical threads. The MBFF clustering benchmarks include widely used C1-C6 [11] and realistic designs from IWLS-2005 suite.[2]

5.1.1 Results on the Widely Used C1-C6

We compare our results with the state-of-the-art post-placement MBFF clustering method INTEGRA in Table 3. Notations like "PWR", "WLR", "#iter-NLP", "RT-NLP" and "RT-all" represent power reduction, wirelength reduction, iterations in NLP, the runtime of NLP, and total runtime respectively. Table 3 shown that our method achieves almost the same power reduction, and further reduces the wirelength by about **33%** compared with INTEGRA. The only drawback is runtime. However, the runtime is practical for realistic circuits, and we can show that its time complexity is sub-quadratic in the next subsection.

5.1.2 Results on the Realistic Designs

We use Synopsys DC and Cadence Encounter SOC to synthesize realistic designs with tight timing constraint. Properties of these benchmarks can be found in Table 5, in which "#FF" represents the number of FFs in the circuit, "WNS" denotes worst negative timing slack after placement. Then the FFs and slacks information will feed in INTEGRA to do MBFF clustering.

Table 5: Realistic Design Property

Circuit	#FF	WNS
tv80	359	0.015
wbconmax	770	0.038
paring	1338	0.094
dma	1816	0.109
ac97	2191	0.078
ethernet	10443	0.046

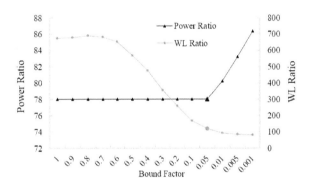

Figure 8: Effect of different bound factors to power ratio and WL ratio.

From the statistics in Table 4, we can find INTEGRA damages the wirelength about **932%** on average. According to our previous analysis, the damage of signal wirelength mainly due to the large timing-feasible region. In order to relieve this defect, we shrink the TVFD with bound factor to limit the movement of FFs for INTEGRA, which we call Bound-INTEGRA. Figure 8 compares the impacts of different bound factors to power ratio and WL ratio. We choose the one that can achieve best WL ratio when guarantee the best power reduction in our implementation. For example, in Figure 8, the best bound factor is 0.05.

As shown in Table 4, Bound-INTEGRA can achieve much better signal wirelength. Even compared with Bounded-INTEGRA, we can still obtain **43%** wirelength improvement on average. Besides, our power reduction is comparable with INTEGRA. Although our runtime is longer than INTEGRA, it is acceptable in practice.

5.2 Time Complexity Analysis

Our method consists of two steps, the analytical optimization step and the discrete optimization step.

For the analytical optimization, it requires evaluating the derivative of objective function. The derivative evaluation of wirelength part is $O(N)$, and the derivative evaluation of clustering score is $O(N)$ with the customized FGT accelerating technique. Though it is difficult to analyze how many iterations it takes for the NLP solver, the practice in placement shows that empirical number of iterations of the placement-like NLP problem is $O(N^{1.18})$ [16]. Thus, the overall runtime for the analytical optimization is $O(N^{\alpha})$ with $\alpha < 2$.

For the discrete optimization, the most time consuming part is on the pair-wise distance calculation at line 2 and 22 in Algorithm 1. With our efficient bin-structure, the searching process can be done in $O(N)$ time.

Therefore, the empirical time complexity for the overall algorithm is sub-quadratic.

6. CONCLUSION

In this paper we propose an analytical model for the clustering objective. The basic idea of this model is to first propose a function that computes the number of clusters given a final clustering solution. The definition of such function relates to the non-differentiable Dirac delta function. In order to make it compatible with nonlinear program method, we smooth it using Gaussian function. The naive quadratic-time evaluation of the Gauss summation can be computed by the Figtree library for fast gauss transformation. However, this general implementation still does not meet the requirement of massive evaluations in an NLP solver. Thus, we implement a customized fast Gauss transformation using multithreading. The final runtime of this approach is practical, and the overall runtime is sub-quadratic. Compare to other post-placement MBFF clustering methods, our method achieves the same power reduction of about 20%, and also reduces the wirelength by 25%.

The proposed method is promising to be integrated in an in-placement MBFF clustering solver, and be applied in other problems which require formulating the clustering score in the objective function.

7. ACKNOWLEDGEMENT

The author would like to thank Tao Wang from MST and Chih-Long Chang from NCTU for their help with using Cadence and INTEGRA respectively.

This work is partly supported by National Natural Science Foundation of China (NSFC) Grant 61202073, Research Fund for the Doctoral Program of Higher Education of China (MoE/RFDP) Grant 20120001120124, and Beijing Natural Science Foundation (BJNSF) Grant 4142022.

8. REFERENCES

[1] Encounter rtl compiler advanced physical option datasheet, 2014. http://www.cadence.com/rl/resources/datasheets/rtl_physical_ds.pdf.

[2] Iwls 2005 benchmarks. http://iwls.org/iwls2005/benchmarks.html.

[3] C. Alpert, A. Kahng, G.-J. Nam, S. Reda, and P. Villarrubia. A semi-persistent clustering technique for vlsi circuit placement. In *Proceedings of the 2005 International Symposium on Physical Design*, ISPD '05, pages 200–207, New York, NY, USA, 2005. ACM.

[4] Z.-W. Chen and J.-T. Yan. Routability-driven flip-flop merging process for clock power reduction. In *Computer Design (ICCD), 2010 IEEE International Conference on*, pages 203–208, Oct 2010.

[5] Y. Cheon, P.-H. Ho, A. B. Kahng, S. Reda, and Q. Wang. Power-aware placement. In *Proceedings of the 42Nd Annual Design Automation Conference*, DAC '05, pages 795–800, New York, NY, USA, 2005. ACM.

[6] W. Hou, D. Liu, and P.-H. Ho. Automatic register banking for low-power clock trees. In *Quality of Electronic Design, 2009. ISQED 2009. Quality Electronic Design*, pages 647–652, March 2009.

[7] C.-C. Hsu, Y.-C. Chen, and M.-H. Lin. In-placement clock-tree aware multi-bit flip-flop generation for power optimization. In *Computer-Aided Design (ICCAD), 2013 IEEE/ACM International Conference on*, pages 592–598, Nov 2013.

[8] M.-K. Hsu, Y.-W. Chang, and V. Balabanov. Tsv-aware analytical placement for 3d ic designs. In *Design Automation Conference (DAC), 2011 48th ACM/EDAC/IEEE*, pages 664–669, June 2011.

[9] I. H.-R. Jiang, C.-L. Chang, Y.-M. Yang, E. Y.-W. Tsai, and L. S.-F. Chen. Integra: Fast multi-bit flip-flop clustering for clock power saving based on interval graphs. In *Proceedings of the 2011 International Symposium on Physical Design*, ISPD '11, pages 115–122, New York, NY, USA, 2011. ACM.

[10] Y. Kretchmer and L. Logic. Using multi-bit register inference to save area and power: the good, the bad, and the ugly. *EE Times Asia*, 2001.

[11] M.-H. Lin, C.-C. Hsu, and Y.-T. Chang. Post-placement power optimization with multi-bit flip-flops. *Computer-Aided Design of Integrated Circuits and Systems, IEEE Transactions on*, 30(12):1870–1882, Dec 2011.

[12] J. Lu, P. Chen, C.-C. Chang, L. Sha, D. J.-H. Huang, C.-C. Teng, and C.-K. Cheng. eplace: Electrostatics based placement using nesterov's method. In *Proceedings of the The 51st Annual Design Automation Conference on Design Automation Conference*, DAC '14, pages 121:1–121:6, New York, NY, USA, 2014. ACM.

[13] V. I. Morariu, B. V. Srinivasan, V. C. Raykar, R. Duraiswami, and L. S. Davis. Automatic online tuning for fast gaussian summation. In D. Koller, D. Schuurmans, Y. Bengio, and L. Bottou, editors, *Advances in Neural Information Processing Systems 21*, pages 1113–1120. Curran Associates, Inc., 2009.

[14] Y. Nesterov. A method of solving a convex programming problem with convergence rate o (1/k2). In *Soviet Mathematics Doklady*, volume 27, pages 372–376, 1983.

[15] A. M. Odlyzko and A. Schönhage. Fast algorithms for multiple evaluations of the riemann zeta function. *Transactions of the American Mathematical Society*, 309(2):797–809, 1988.

[16] P. Spindler, U. Schlichtmann, and F. Johannes. Kraftwerk2 2014;a fast force-directed quadratic placement approach using an accurate net model. *Computer-Aided Design of Integrated Circuits and Systems, IEEE Transactions on*, 27(8):1398–1411, Aug 2008.

[17] C.-C. Tsai, Y. Shi, G. Luo, and I. H.-R. Jiang. Ff-bond: Multi-bit flip-flop bonding at placement. In *Proceedings of the 2013 ACM International Symposium on International Symposium on Physical Design*, ISPD '13, pages 147–153, New York, NY, USA, 2013. ACM.

[18] S.-H. Wang, Y.-Y. Liang, T.-Y. Kuo, and W.-K. Mak. Power-driven flip-flop merging and relocation. *Computer-Aided Design of Integrated Circuits and Systems, IEEE Transactions on*, 31(2):180–191, Feb 2012.

[19] H. Wu, M. Wong, I.-M. Liu, and Y. Wang. Placement-proximity-based voltage island grouping under performance requirement. *Computer-Aided Design of Integrated Circuits and Systems, IEEE Transactions on*, 26(7):1256–1269, July 2007.

[20] J. Yan, C. Chu, and W.-K. Mak. Safechoice: A novel approach to hypergraph clustering for wirelength-driven placement. *Computer-Aided Design of Integrated Circuits and Systems, IEEE Transactions on*, 30(7):1020–1033, July 2011.

[21] J.-T. Yan and Z.-W. Chen. Construction of constrained multi-bit flip-flops for clock power reduction. In *Green Circuits and Systems (ICGCS), 2010 International Conference on*, pages 675–678, June 2010.

Physical Design Challenges in the Chip Power Distribution Network

[Extended Abstract]

Farid N. Najm
ECE Department
University of Toronto
Toronto, Ontario, Canada
f.najm@utoronto.ca

ABSTRACT

The power supply and ground networks in large integrated circuits or, simply, the power grids, have become very large billion-node metal interconnect structures that often span all levels of the metal stack. The grid may be connected to about 2,000 C4 pads at the top layers and to hundreds of millions of gates and other circuitry at the bottom. It is not uncommon to reserve the top metal layers exclusively for the power grid. However, the extensive use of metal resources on lower metal layers for the grid has become a real bottleneck for signal routing. This adds time and cost to the overall chip design project and represents a problem for physical design. Yet there are reasons to believe that allocation of so much metal resources to the grid is "overkill" and that there is much room for improvement. The grid is over-designed because of lack of certainty about its safety from various concerns, like electromigration, IR drop, and inductive drop. There are also open problems in the grid design problem itself, which may be viewed as an optimization problem, albeit a very difficult one. In this talk, I will review developments in the verification of power grids that aim to provide certainty that the grid is safe, and indicate directions for possible ways that the grid may be automatically generated to suit various objectives.

Categories and Subject Descriptors

B.7 [**Integrated Circuits**]: VLSI

General Terms

Algorithms, Verification

Keywords

Power grid, physical design, verification

ISPD'15, March 29–April 01, 2015, Monterey, CA, USA
ACM 978-1-4503-3399-3/15/03.
http://dx.doi.org/10.1145/2717764.2724580.

BIOGRAPHY

Farid N. Najm is a Professor in the Edward S. Rogers Sr. Department of Electrical and Computer Engineering (ECE) at the University of Toronto. He received the B.E. degree in electrical engineering from the American University of Beirut in 1983 and the Ph.D. degree in ECE from the University of Illinois at Urbana-Champaign (UIUC) in 1989. From 1989 to 1992, he worked with Texas Instruments, Dallas, Texas. He then joined the ECE department at UIUC as an Assistant Professor and became Associate Professor in 1997. In 1999, he joined the ECE department at the University of Toronto, where he is now Professor and Chair.

Dr. Najm is a Fellow of the IEEE and a Fellow of the Canadian Academy of Engineering (CAE). He served as Associate Editor for the IEEE Transactions on Computer-Aided Design (CAD) of Integrated Circuits and Systems from 2001 to 2009, and for the IEEE Transactions on Very Large Scale Integration (VLSI) Systems from 1997 to 2002. He has received an IEEE Transactions on CAD Best Paper Award, an NSF Research Initiation Award, the NSF CAREER Award, and the Design Automation Conference (DAC) Prolific Author Award in 2013. He served on the executive committee of the International Symposium on Low-Power Electronics and Design (ISLPED) 1999-2013, and has served on the technical committees of various conferences, including ICCAD, DAC, CICC, ISQED, and ISLPED. In 2010, Dr. Najm authored the book *Circuit Simulation* (John Wiley and Sons, New York). His research is on CAD for VLSI, with emphasis on circuit level issues related to power, the chip power grid, circuit timing, variability, and reliability.

Accelerated Path-Based Timing Analysis with MapReduce

Tsung-Wei Huang
Dept. of Electrical and Computer Engineering
University of Illinois Urbana-Champaign
IL, USA
twh760812@gmail.com

Martin D. F. Wong
Dept. of Electrical and Computer Engineering
University of Illinois Urbana-Champaign
IL, USA
mdfwong@illinois.edu

ABSTRACT

Path-based timing analysis (PBA) is a pivotal step to achieve accurate timing signoff. A core primitive extracts a large set of paths subject to path-specific or less-pessimistic timing update. However, this process in nature demands a very high computational complexity and thus has been a major bottleneck in accelerating timing closure. Therefore, we introduce in this paper a fast and scalable PBA framework with *MapReduce* – a recent programming paradigm invented by Google for big-data processing. Inspired by the spirit of MapReduce, we formulate our problem into tasks that are associated with keys and values and perform massively-parallel map and reduce operations on a distributed system. Experimental results demonstrated that our approach can easily analyze million nodes in a single minute.

Categories and Subject Descriptors

J.6 [**Computer-aided design (CAD)**]: Timing analysis;
D.1.3 [**Parallel programming**]: Distributed computing

Keywords

Path-based static timing analysis, MapReduce

1. INTRODUCTION

Static-timing-analysis (STA) is a crucial step in verifying the expected timing behaviors of an integrated circuit [6]. During the STA, both graph-based timing analysis (GBA) and path-based timing analysis (PBA) are used. GBA performs linear scan on the circuit graph and estimates the worst timing quantities at each endpoint. GBA is very fast but the results are pessimistic. Hence, PBA is often performed after GBA to remove unwanted pessimism. Starting from a negative endpoint, a core PBA procedure peels a set of paths in non-increasing order of criticality and applies path-specific timing update to each of these paths [7]. However, path peeling is a computationally expensive process.

ISPD'15, March 29–April 1, 2015, Monterey, CA, USA.
Copyright © 2015 ACM 978-1-4503-3399-3/15/04 ...$15.00.
http://dx.doi.org/10.1145/2717764.2717771.

The high runtime demand severely restrains the capability of PBA during timing signoff.

Unfortunately, current literature still lacks for novel ideas of fast PBA [12]. As pointed out by 2014 TAU timing analysis contest, algorithms featuring multi-threaded or massively-parallel accelerations are eagerly in demand [9]. Howbeit, parallel PBA has been reported as a tough challenge primarily because a path can be prototypically various. For instance, a path can exhibit arbitrary lengths and span different logical cones and physical boundaries. Computations in this way are typically hard to be issued in parallel. Although a few prior works claimed to have a solution, the results are usually compromised with accuracy [5, 11].

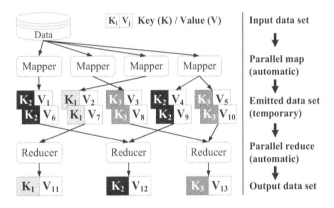

Figure 1: The execution flow of a MapReduce job.

As a consequence, we introduce in this paper an ultra-fast PBA framework with MapReduce. The concept of MapReduce is shown in Figure 1. A MapReduce program applies parallel map operations to input tasks and generates a set of temporary key/value pairs. Then parallel reduce operations are applied to all values that are associated with the same key in order to collate the derived data properly [8]. Users only need to provide desired map/reduce functions while parallelization details are encapsulated in a MapReduce library [1, 2]. This programming paradigm inspires us to rethink the PBA problem as "map" operations followed by "reduces". Specifically, we cast the PBA problem into tasks with keys and values that are sandwiched around massively-parallel map and reduce operations.

Our contributions are summarized as follows. 1) We successfully investigated the applicability of MapReduce to accelerate PBA. Our framework is very general in gaining massively-parallel computations, imposing no physical and logic constraints. 2) Our framework increases the productivity as designers can focus on timing-oriented turnaround, leaving all hassle of parallelization details to the MapReduce library. 3) We have seen a substantial speedup from the experimental results. On a large distributed system, millions of cells can be easily analyzed in a few minutes. These features all add up to faster design cycle. Our work can be beneficial for the speedup of the signoff timing closure, on which up to 40% of the design flow are typically spent.

2. PATH-BASED TIMING ANALYSIS

PBA has gained much attention in deep submicron era due to its capability of configuring features such as clock-reconvergence-pessimism removal (CRPR) and advanced-on-chip-variation (AOCV) derating for less-pessimistic timing reports [9, 10]. Since most of these features are path-specific, a core yet computationally expensive building block of PBA is to peel a path set from each endpoint and recompute the timings path-by-path. By analyzing the path with reduced pessimism, many timing violations can be waived which in turn tells better timing signoff. Because of this crucial benefit, studies in accelerating PBA are in demand especially when we move to many-core era. Simply put, the following aspects are in particular of interests.

- Performance is the top concern. A substantial runtime saving will make a breakthrough in timing signoff.

- Modern circuits are complex. Practical parallelization must scale up with the growth of the circuit size.

- The framework needs to be general and flexible, imposing least constraints and complexity.

- Adequate granularity control is necessary in order to effectively organize computations at a massive scale.

- Orthogonality should be featured. Compromised solutions to the design methodology are discouraged.

The above issues all combine to challenges in the development of parallel PBA algorithms. If the PBA runtime can be significantly improved, designers are able to utilize PBA on a larger set of paths and perform their analyses earlier in the design closure flow. As a result, researchers must continue to provide viable parallel solutions along with the rapid evolution of the computational power.

3. PROBLEM FORMULATION

The circuit network is input as a directed-acyclic graph $G = \{V, E\}$, where V is the pin set of circuit elements and E is the edge set specifying pin-to-pin connections. Each edge e is associated with a tuple of earliest and latest delays. A path is an ordered sequence of nodes or edges and the path delay is the sum of delays through all edges. In this paper, we are in particular emphasizing on the *data path*, which is defined as a path from either the primary input pin or the clock pin of a launching flip-flop (FF) to the data pin of a capturing FF. A test is defined w.r.t. an FF as hold or setup check on any data paths captured by this FF. Considering a test set T as well as a positive integer k, the following two tasks are essential for PBA [7, 9].

Task 1 – Sweep report: *The program is asked to sweep all tests and output the top k critical paths for each test.*

Task 2 – Block report: *The program is asked to report the top k critical paths across all tests.*

4. MAPREDUCE FRAMEWORK

In this section we discuss our PBA framework with MapReduce. We first brief the MapReduce programming paradigm and then detail each step of our framework.

4.1 MapReduce Programming Paradigm

Since being first introduced by Google in 2004, the MapReduce programming paradigm has been widely applied to many domains such as data mining, database system, and high-performance computing [8]. The spirit of a MapReduce program lies in *"keys"* and *"values"* which are generated and manipulated by user-defined functions *"mapper"* and *"reducer"*. A key and a value are simply bytes of strings of arbitrary length which are logically associated with each other and thus can represent generic data types. The MapReduce library automatically schedules parallel map and reduce operations linking mapper and reducer to handle the input data on a distributed system. State-of-the-art libraries for this purpose such as Apache Hadoop and MR-MPI from Sandia National Lab. are readily available [1, 2].

Algorithm 1: CanonicalForm(D, mapper, reducer)

Input: input data D, user-defined mapper and reducer

1 $\{M \mid <tmp\_key : tmp\_value>\} \leftarrow \text{Map}(D, \text{mapper})$;
2 $\{C \mid <unique\_key : value\_list>\} \leftarrow \text{Collate}(M)$;
3 $\{R \mid <key : value>\} \leftarrow \text{Reduce}(C, \text{reducer})$;
4 **return** R

A canonical MapReduce program is presented in Algorithm 1. The first is the map step, which takes a set of data and converts it into another set of data produced by the function mapper, where individual elements are represented as temporary key/value pairs. The collate step aggregates across temporary key/value pairs where each unique key appears exactly once and the corresponding value is a concatenated list of all the values associated with the same key [1]. The reduce step then takes a single entry from the aggregated key/value pairs and creates a new key/value pair which stores the output generated by the function reducer. Parallelism is evident since function calls by map and reduce are independent to each other and can be executed on different processors simultaneously. In general, map and reduce are intra-process operations while collate involves inter-process communication because of aggregation.

4.2 Formulation of Task Graphs

In order to develop a MapReduce program, computations that can be issued to parallel map and reduce operations must be exploited from our problem. Considering a test t, we observe: 1) every data path captured by this testing FF reaches the same endpoint; 2) the *source pins* from where a path originates is prototypically consistent, being either the primary input pins or the clock pin of a launching FF. The first feature implies that paths feeding the same endpoint belong to the same test. By tagging each path with a key indicating the corresponding test index, the program can keep track of the test to which a path belongs. The second

---

[1]In some articles the collate is absorbed into the reduce step.

feature implies that paths are wrapped in a multi-source single-target graph. This motivates us to decompose a test into several task graphs with regard to different and smaller groups of source pins.

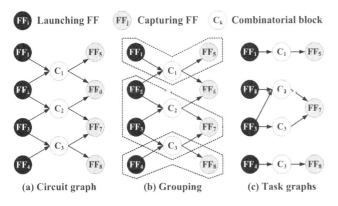

Figure 2: An example formulation of the task graphs.

We define g_t for each test t as a set of task graphs $g_t = \{g_t^1, g_t^2, ..., g_t^i\}$ and G_T as a union set of all task graphs. Deriving from a test t, a task graph g_t^i is a subgraph spanning all connectivities from a subset of source pins to the data pin of this test. Under the same test, the source pins corresponding to different task graph are mutually disjointed. We associate each task graph with a key indicating the test index to which this task graph belongs. An example is illustrated in Figure 2. We can see three task graphs are derived from the tests on capturing FFs 5, 7, and 8, respectively. Notice that a task graph is indeed a portion of the original circuit graph. Every edge of the task graph comes with the same delay values as the original circuit graph.

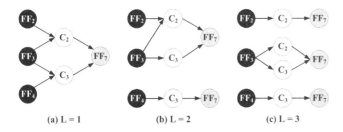

Figure 3: Granularity control of the task graph.

The granularity control of the task graphs is an important factor as it arises performance concern such as process communication and computation load. We define L-way partition as a partition of each test into L task graphs such that each task graph has roughly even size on the corresponding set of source pins. Figure 3 shows an example of 1-way, 2-way, and 3-way partitions of the test on FF 7 from Figure 2. While discovering a suitable granularity level tends to be case-dependent, we consider in this paper only the case where the number of tests is less than the number of available computing cores. Assuming P cores are available in such the case, up to P task graphs are generated from each test in order to balance the computation load. We should be mindful that dividing a test into multiple task graphs facilitates the parallelism but also gives rise to process communication because of data merging afterwards.

The generation of task graphs is presented in Algorithm 2. We first identify all source pins of a given test t through a backtrace starting at the data pin d of this test (line 1:2). The number of task graphs being generated is determined by a comparison between the number of input tests and the number of available computing cores (line 3:8). Then we iteratively group a set of source pins S_d^k in accordance to the specified number of task graphs and perform depth-first-search (DFS) to induce the corresponding task graph (line 9:15). Each induced task graph is assigned a key indicating its test index and is emitted as a key/value object in the end of each iteration (line 14).

Algorithm 2: Generator(t)

Input: a test t
Output: a set of task graphs $g_t = \{g_t^1, g_t^2, ..., g_t^i\}$

1 $d \leftarrow$ data pin of the test t;
2 $S_d \leftarrow$ source pins obtained through a back traversal at d;
3 $P \leftarrow$ number of available computing cores;
4 $L \leftarrow 1$;
5 **if** $|T| < P$ **then**
6 $\quad |\quad L = P$;
7 **end**
8 $num\_src \leftarrow \lceil |S_d|/L \rceil$;
9 **for** $i \leftarrow 1$ **to** L **do**
10 $\quad | \quad S_d^i \leftarrow \{num\_src$ frontmost elements in $S_d\}$;
11 $\quad | \quad S_d \leftarrow S_d \setminus S_d^i$;
12 $\quad | \quad g_t^i \leftarrow$ subgraph induced from S_d^i to d;
13 $\quad | \quad key[g_t^i] \leftarrow t$;
14 $\quad | \quad$ Emit make_pair(t, g_t^i);
15 **end**

Based on the knowledge constructed so far, we deliver a high-level sketch of our MapReduce-based PBA framework. The map operation is responsible for 1) the generation of task graphs from each test and 2) the path extraction from each task graph. Because of the granularity control, a test might be broken into several task graphs that are distributed to different processors during the map operations. Collate method is required in order to reorganize paths to their right places. Eventually, the reduce operation peels out a desired path set and emits it as the final solution. We conclude this section by the following lemma.

LEMMA 1. *Every path exactly and uniquely exists in one task graph.*

4.3 Mapper and Reducer Functions

Based on the definition of task graphs, we develop the function calls for map and reduce operations. As presented in Algorithm 3, our mapper function takes an arbitrary task graph and extracts the top-k critical paths (line 1). We leave this extraction process as a black box for user preferences. In this paper, the optimal path ranking algorithm by [10] is used as our default engine. Then it iterates through each path and performs path-specific update according to user-configured features such as CRPR and AOCV (line 3). Each iteration ends with an emission of a key/value pair where the value is a path string and the key is being either 1) the key of the input task graph if sweep is the task objective (line 5:6) or 2) a nominal number instead (line 7:9).

Any key/value pair emitted by our mapper is in fact a solution fragment, where the key indicates the test index to which the value of a path string belongs. It can be inferred

Algorithm 3: Extracter(g_t^i)

Input: an arbitrary task graph g_t^i
Output: an emitted set of key/value pairs

1   $P \leftarrow$ top k critical paths extracted from g_t^i;
2   **foreach** *path* $p_i \in P$ **do**
3      $p_i' \leftarrow$ update p_i according to user-configured features;
4      $value \leftarrow$ make_string(p_i');
5   **if** *sweep is the task objective* **then**
6         $key \leftarrow key[g_t^i]$;
7   **else**
8         $key \leftarrow -1$;
9   **end**
10   Emit make_pair(key, $value$);
11 **end**

that after calling the collate method, there are two possible outcomes: either paths that belongs to the same task graph are aggregated together or all paths are put in a single group, depending on the task objective. Eventually, our reducer takes each unique key/value pair and peels out the final top-k critical paths from the path set stored in each value list. This implementation is given in Algorithm 4.

Algorithm 4: Peeler(r)

Input: an unique key/value pair r
Output: an emitted key/value pair

1   $key \leftarrow r.key$;
2   $P \leftarrow$ paths parsed from $r.value$;
3   sort P in non-increasing order of criticality;
4   $P' \leftarrow \{k$ frontmost elements in $P\}$;
5   $value \leftarrow$ make_string(P');
6   Emit make_pair(key, $value$);

LEMMA 2. *There are either $|T|$ or $O(P|T|)$ mapper calls on a distributed cluster with P computing processors.*

PROOF. The execution of each benchmark has two possible conditions, either the number of tests is greater the number of computing processors or the number of tests is less than the computing resources. For the former case, each test is processed by an independent mapper function and thus there are totally $|T|$ mapper calls. For the later case where the number of tests is less than the available core count, each test is decomposed into $O(P)$ task graphs. Hence, there are totally $O(P|T|)$ mapper calls. □

LEMMA 3. *There is only one reducer call for block report while there are $|T|$ reducer calls for sweep report.*

PROOF. For block report, the key/value pairs emitted by the extractor all have the same key value (i.e., -1). Therefore, the collate operation produces only one key/value pair for the following reduce operation. On the other hand, the intermediate key values for sweep report adhere to the test indices of the task graphs. Therefore, the collate operation produces a total of $|T|$ distinct key/value pairs for the following reduce operation. □

4.4 Main Program

The main program of our PBA framework is shown in Algorithm 5. The first two lines perform map operations that call Algorithm 2 to generate a set of task graphs. Using the task graphs as input, the next three lines follow the

canonical form of a MapReduce program, where map operations call Algorithm 3 to perform path extraction on each task graph, and reduce operations call Algorithm 4 to peel out the final solution. Prior to the function return, paths are parsed from the output values of our reducer (line 6:15). Each path is conventionally tagged with the corresponding test index which can be retrieved from the key value (line 10).

Algorithm 5: MapReducePBA(G)

Input: a circuit graph G, a test set T
Output: an analyzed path set

1   $D \leftarrow$ Map(T, Generator) ;
2   $G_T \leftarrow$ task graphs parsed/read from D;
3   $M \leftarrow$ Map(G_T, Extracter) ;
4   $C \leftarrow$ Collate(M);
5   $R \leftarrow$ Reduce(C, Peeler);
6   **if** *sweep is the task objective* **then**
7      $P \leftarrow \phi$;
8   **foreach** *pair* r *in* R **do**
9         $P_r \leftarrow$ paths parsed from $r.value$;
10   Tag P_r with the test index t retrieved from $r.key$;
11        $P \leftarrow P \cup P_r$;
12   **end**
13   **return** P
14 **end**
15 $P \leftarrow$ paths parsed from the value in R;
16 **return** P

THEOREM 1. *The proposed framework is correct.*

PROOF. Lemma 1 has shown the exactness and uniqueness of every path. Proving the correctness of our framework is equivalent to showing that the path set from the input of a reducer contains the top-k critical paths for the corresponding test. Recalling that the input of our reducer is an unique key/value pair. The key indicates the test index and the value is a concatenated list of values with each value storing the top-k critical paths of a task graph generated from this test. It is obvious by set properties that the top-k critical paths for this test must be a subset of the path set stored in the value list. Since our reducer is in fact a sorting process, the output is the value that stores the final top-k critical paths for this test. Notice that for block report the test index is nominal while this fact has no impact on the truth of this proof. □

5. DATA MANAGEMENT

Efficient data management is crucial to a MapReduce program. We discuss in this section some technical details and data management through our implementations.

5.1 Data Locality

Exploiting the data locality is an important principle to efficient MapReduce programs. Improving the data locality can reduce the network overhead during the execution, which in turn tells better runtime performance. In order to improve the data locality, each processor stores a replicate of the circuit graph in its own local memory. Despite higher memory demand, accesses to the circuit graph such as generation of task graphs and extraction of critical paths are reached in hand without extra data passing which is normally time-consuming.

5.2 Storage Efficiency

The communication load is a non-negligible cost for a MapReduce program in particular during the collate operation. Passing long values of paths gives rise to the problem of frequent memory allocation which is typically time consuming. In order to minimize the communication load, explicit path traces are stored in the memory of each individual machine. Each path is tagged with an unique index which is used to represent the storage address and machine number or the temporary file name. Paths are passing through these indices during collate operation and the final recovery of path traces is done by indexing back to these tags.

5.3 Hidden Reduce

Another way to alleviate the communication overhead is to avoid unnecessary data passing during the collate operation. Within a same processor, a reduce operation before the collate call is pre-applied to those path sets having the same key label. We term this reduce operation as "hidden reduce" because it is implicitly processed after each mapper call of path extraction. In other words, multiple data with the same key label in a each processor are merged first so as to reduce the amount of data passing. It is obvious by Theorem 1 the optimality of the final solution is not affected by this hidden reduce operation.

6. EXPERIMENTAL RESULTS

Our program is implemented in C++ language on a 64-bit linux operating system. The C++ based MR-MPI API is used as our MapReduce library [2]. Evaluation is taken on an academic computer cluster which has over 500 compute nodes. Each compute node is configured with 16 Intel 2.60GHz cores and 128GB RAM. The network infrastructure uses 384-port Mellanox MSX6518-NR FDR InfiniBand in order to offer high speed interconnect between clusters. Access to the compute nodes for running a program is done via a script submission specifying the number of process cores or threads to be used.

Table 1: Statistics of the benchmarks from 2014 TAU timing analysis contest [9].

Circuit	$|V|$	$|E|$	$|I|$	$|O|$	# Tests	# Paths
combo5	2051804	2228611	432	164	79050	19227963
combo6	3577926	3843033	486	174	128266	19227963
combo7	2817561	3011233	459	148	109568	19227963

$|V|$: # of pins. $|E|$: # of edges. $|I|$: # of primary inputs.
$|O|$: # of primary outputs. # Tests: # of setup/hold tests.
Paths: maximum # of data paths per test.

Experiments are undertaken on the three largest benchmarks, combo5, combo6, and combo7 from 2014 TAU timing analysis contest [9]. Each of the three testcases is created by combining a set of industrial circuits (e.g., vga_lcd, systemcde2, aes_core, des_perf, usb_funct, wb_dmav, systemcaes, and tv80) that were already open-source to academia. combo5 is the combination of circuits vga_lcd, usb_funct, des_perf, tv80, wb_dmav, and systemcaes. combo6 is the combination of circuits vga_lcd, aes_core, des_perf, usb_funct, systemcde2, and tv80. combo7 is the combination of circuits vga_lcd, tv80, aes_core, systemcaes, and vga_lcd. Statistics of these testcases are summarized in Table 1. All testcases are million-scale circuit graphs and the number of tests could reach up to 128266 in combo6.

6.1 Baseline Setting

We configure CRPR as the baseline application in our PBA framework. CRPR is an important step during the signoff timing cycle. Without CRPR, signoff timing analyzer reports worse violation than the true timing properties owned by the physical circuits. The 2014 TAU timing analysis contest has addressed this issue in order to motivate novel ideas for fast and accurate path-based CRPR [9]. The optimal path ranking algorithm proposed by the first-place winner, UI-Timer, is applied to our path extractor [10]. In order to enable CRPR, the third line of Algorithm 3 is implemented as follows: For each path being iterated, the common clock segment is found by a simple walk through the corresponding launching clock path and the capturing clock path. The path slack is then adjusted by the amount of pessimism on the common segment.

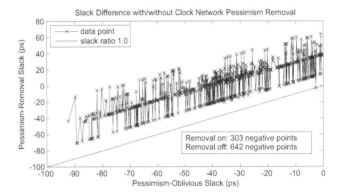

Figure 4: Impact of CRPR on path slacks.

Figure 4 illustrates the impact of CRPR on path slacks of the hold test from a subcircuit block of the testcase combo6. It can be observed that the values of path slacks are in general increased after the clock network pessimism was removed. The number of failing tests was able to be reduced from 642 to less than half [10]. Another evidence which can be discovered from Figure 4 is the path-specific property of the clock network pessimism. The most critical path prior to CRPR is not necessarily reflective of the true counterpart after CRPR. Such a fact reveals the necessity of PBA in order to peel out the true critical path. More knowledge about CRPR can be referred to [9].

6.2 Performance Characterization

We begin by discussing the generic performance of our MapReduce-based PBA. Evaluation is undertaken through cross combinations of path count (i.e., k) and core count in running our program. We request 1 to 10 compute nodes with each configured by 10 cores. That is, the core count varies from 10 to 100 using 10 as the scaling interval. A special case with only 1 core is also evaluated in order to demonstrate the baseline without any parallelism. The path count starts at 1 and varies from 10 to 100 using 10 as the scaling interval. A total of 121 combinations of path count and core counts are executed for each benchmark.

The number of key/value pairs processed on each circuit benchmark is illustrated in Figure 5. It can be observed that for each circuit graph the number of key/value pairs processed by map and reduce operations grows as the path count increases. Notice that the path count is the only factor

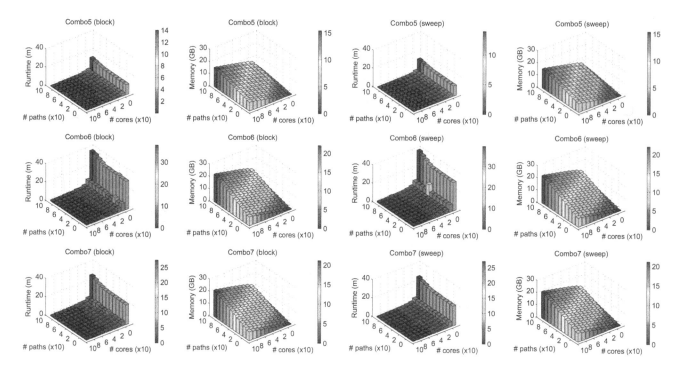

Figure 6: Performance characterization of our MapReduce-based PBA on circuit benchmarks combo5, combo6, and combo7 under block report and sweep report. Within a single minute, all tests can be accomplished using approximately 40 cores, 100 cores, and 80 cores, for combo5, combo6, and combo7, respectively.

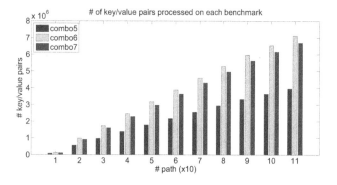

Figure 5: Bar chart of the number of key/value pairs processed on each circuit benchmark.

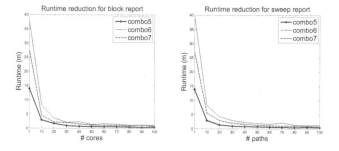

Figure 7: Runtime reduction versus core count.

that contributes to the growth of the number of key/value pairs since the construction of key/value pairs is dedicated to paths. The largest number appears in the report of 100 paths path, in which the program generated 3953344 key/value pairs for combo5, 7114972 key/value pairs for combo6, and 6696880 key/value pairs for combo7. In general, the more the number of key/value pairs is, the higher the runtime and memory storage the program demands.

The overall performance of our MapReduce-based PBA is shown in Figure 6. The left two columns of plots show the runtime value and memory usage of our program under block report, while the right two columns show the plots under sweep report. We first discuss the runtime performance of our program. In a rough view, the runtime scales down drastically as the core count increases. Using only a single core without any parallelism, the program

took up to (i.e., among all path settings) 14.03 (13.92) minutes, 37.76 (39.53) minutes, and 27.41 (27.07) minutes to accomplish block (sweep) reports for combo5, combo6, and combo7, respectively. It can be seen that the runtime significantly goes down when MapReduce begins distributing works across processors. Even using only 10 processors, the runtime values can be significantly reduced to 2.92 (2.91) minutes, 8.22 (8.24) minutes, and 4.63 (5.55) minutes under block (sweep) reports of combo5, combo6, and combo7, respectively. The slope of the runtime reduction can be clearly seen in the sliced 2D plot fixing path count to 100 in Figure 7. Within a single minute, all tests can be accomplished using approximately 40 cores, 100 cores, and 80 cores, for combo5, combo6, and combo7, respectively.

Figure 8 discovers the runtime portions taken by map operations, collate operations (i.e., process communication or "Comm" for short), and reduce operations. We measure the runtime portion as an average value across all different settings of path counts and core counts. We have observed that

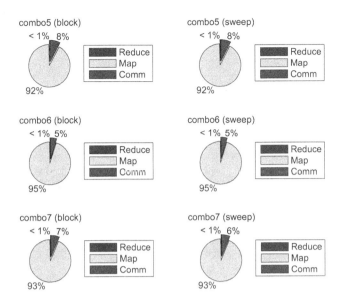

Figure 8: Runtime portion of map operations, reduce operations, and process communication.

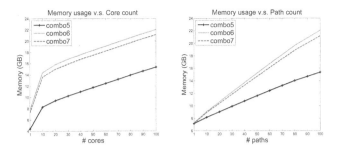

Figure 9: Memory usage in terms of path count and core count.

reduce operations spend the least amount of time ($< 1\%$) comparing to the others since it involves only string parsing and value sorting. On the other hand, the time spent on map operations occupies the majority of the entire runtime. This is because map operations are responsible for the generation of task graphs and the extraction of critical paths, which are relatively expensive computations. For all benchmarks, more than 90% of the entire runtime is taken by map operations. The rest portion of the runtime is occupied by the collate operation, from which we can see about 4–5% of the entire runtime is spent on the process communication. In fact, without applying the trick mentioned in Section 5.2, the process communication burdens the entire runtime by over 20%.

Next we discuss the memory cost of our program. The amount of memory usage is measured by the peak moment during the execution across all processors (i.e., including the master processor). Generally speaking, the amount of memory usage grows as the increase of either path count or core count, which can be seen in Figure 6. The peak memory usage we observed are approximately 15GB, 22GB, and 21GB for combo5, combo6, and combo7, all under sweep report with 100 cores and 100 paths, respectively. We provide two extra sliced plots from the sweep report in Figure 9 to show clearer memory cost in terms of the growth of 1) core count with path count fixing to 100 and 2) path count with core count fixing to 100. As the path count or the core count increases, the amount of memory usage grows gradually except for the sharp spot at 10-core level where the distributed MapReduce begins taking effect.

To sum up, the experimental results have demonstrated the performance of our PBA framework with MapReduce. It is highly scalable as we have seen a significant runtime reduction as the core count grows. Even in the first level at which only 10 cores are involved in parallelism, the runtime is decreased by 75–86% across all runs. From the storage point of view, the memory consumption of our approach is fairly reasonable. At the highest peak we have observed in running combo6 with 100 cores and 100 paths, the to-

tal amount of memory demanded by our program is about 22GB. In other words, the average amount of memory usage per processor is less than 1GB. These evidences have justified the practical viability of our approach. The substantial speedup we have obtained is beneficial for the discovery of a way to fast timing closure.

6.3 Competence over Multi-Threading

We evaluated in this section the competence of our approach over the implementation using multi-threading, another popular type of parallel programming with shared-memory model. The inherent architecture of a multi-threaded program is distinct from that of distributed computation such as the MapReduce programming environment we discussed in this paper. In multi-threaded programming, multiple threads or processors can operate independently on a stand-alone machine but share the same memory resources. The memory bandwidth of the machine typically dominates the entire runtime performance. As a result, the scalability of multi-threaded computation is typically not as decent as the one of distributed computation. Several libraries for using shared memory such as OpenMP and POSIX are reachable in the public domain [3, 4].

We refit our MapReduce program to the multi-threaded version by replacing the mapper calls and reducer calls with parallel for loop (e.g., #pragma omp statement) using the API from OpenMP 3.0 [3]. In our cluster each compute node is configured with 16 Intel 2.60GHz cores and 128GB RAM in a stand-alone machine. Up to 16 threads or 16 processors can be concurrently executed using either multi-threaded computation or distributed MapReduce operations. Due to the architectural limitation of multi-threading, evaluations are undertaken in a single compute node using different core counts from 1 to 16. The performance differences between multi-threading and MapReduce are interpreted in terms of runtime values and memory usage, as illustrated in Figure 10. For page efficiency, we discuss only the experiment of block report with the single-most critical path.

The competence of MapReduce over multi-threading is clearly demonstrated by the runtime plot in Figure 10. In comparison to multi-threading, our MapReduce program obtains higher runtime speedup (i.e., over multi-threading) and better scalability as core count grows up. The largest difference we observed was in combo6 with 2 cores, where our MapReduce program accomplished all tests by 32 minutes faster than the multi-threaded implementation. Similar trends can also be discovered in other two cases. The reason for having our MapReduce program perform worse at the level of 1 core comes from the redundant overhead of

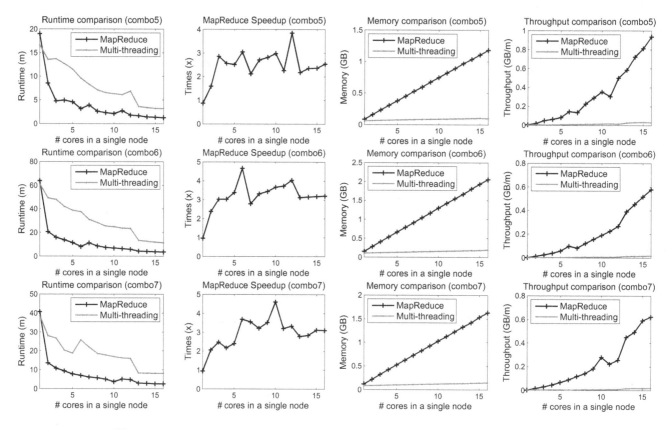

Figure 10: Performance comparison between MapReduce and multi-threading.

key/value processing because of the null parallelism. Nevertheless, such negative margins are solely less than 3 minutes.

It is expected that our MapReduce program consumes higher memory requirements than the multi-threaded implementation. The distributed computation of MapReduce requires an individual block of memory to be allocated for each processor. As shown in the memory comparison in Figure 10, the memory cost of our MapReduce program is linearly proportional to the growth rate of the core count. On the other hand, the amount of memory usage in multi-threading is relatively constant regardless of the increase of core count. Despite less memory cost by multi-threading, the performance of concurrent access to the same global memory block is limited by the memory bandwidth. It can be clearly seen in Figure 10 the process throughput grows poorly compared to the curve achieved by distributed MapReduce. As a consequence, the runtime performance of multi-threading is not as promising as distributed MapReduce even in a stand-alone machine.

7. ACKNOWLEDGEMENT

This work was partially supported by the National Science Foundation under Grant CCF-1320585.

8. CONCLUSION

In this paper we have presented a fast PBA framework with MapReduce. We have achieved a success in accelerating PBA by a substantial order of magnitude in comparison to non-MapReduce implementations such as single core and multi-threading. The experimental results have demonstrated the pronounced performance of our approach whereby million-scale circuit graphs can be quickly and correctly analyzed within a few minutes on a distributed computer cluster.

9. REFERENCES

[1] Apache Hadoop: http://hadoop.apache.org/
[2] MapReduce MPI Library: http://mapreduce.sandia.gov/
[3] OpenMP: http://openmp.org/wp/
[4] POSIX: https://computing.llnl.gov/
[5] S. Bhardwaj, K. Rahmat, and K. Kucukcakar, "Clock-Reconvergence Pessimism Removal in Hierarchical Static Timing Analysis," US patent 8434040, 2013.
[6] J. Bhasker and R. Chadha, "Static Timing Analysis for Nanometer Designs: A Practical Approach," *Springer*, 2009.
[7] S. Cristian, N. H. Rachid, and R. Khalid, "Efficient exhaustive path-based static timing analysis using a fast estimation technique," US patent 8079004, 2009
[8] J. Dean and S. Ghemawat, "MapReduce: Simplified Data Processing on Large Clusters," *CACM*, vol. 51, no. 1, 107–113, 2008
[9] J. Hu, D. Sinha, and I. Keller, "TAU 2014 Contest on Removing Common Path Pessimism during Timing Analysis," *Proc. ACM ISPD*, pp. 153–160, 2014.
[10] T.-W. Huang, P.-C. Wu, and M. D. F. Wong, "UI-Timer: An Ultra-Fast Clock Network Pessimism Removal Algorithm," *Proc. IEEE/ACM ICCAD*, 2014.
[11] O. Levitsky, "Sign Off Quality Hierarchical Timing Constraints: Wishful Thinking or Reality?" *TAU workshop*, 2014.
[12] R. Molina, "EDA Vendors should Improve the Runtime Performance of Path-Based Timing Analysis," *Electronic Design*, 2013

Blech Effect in Interconnects:
Applications and Design Guidelines

Ali Abbasinasab
University of California, Santa Barbara
Santa Barbara, CA, 93106
ali@ece.ucsb.edu

Malgorzata Marek-Sadowska
University of California, Santa Barbara
Santa Barbara, CA, 93106
mms@ece.ucsb.edu

ABSTRACT

The majority of the existing experimental, theoretical and modeling works on electromigration (EM) are focused on simple, via-to-via structures, but complex interconnect structures have not been studied well. The lack of correct models for such interconnects may result in either conservative or weak design decisions which may result in catastrophic reliability failures. This paper proposes a physical model which holds for material migration as well as for lattice vacancy generation/annihilation. Using the developed model, well known circuit level EM assessment methods are examined by finite element modeling and simulation. The paper provides a compact model for EM analysis which can be easily implemented in CAD tools. We also explain some recent experimental results and empirical models published by other researchers.

Categories and Subject Descriptors

B.8.1 [**Hardware**]: Performance and Reliability - Reliability, Testing, and Fault-Tolerance.

General Terms

Physics, Algorithms, Design.

Keywords

Electromigration, Blech Effect, Interconnects, Reliability.

1. INTRODUCTION

Electromigration (EM) is a phenomenon of mass transport in metal wires stressed with high electrical current density. In modern IC chips, due to the small cross sectional area of the conductor lines, current density in wires is very high. The effect of EM in interconnect lines usually manifests itself as resistance change and over time may result in shorts or opens.

EM has been one of the critical reliability concerns for semiconductor industry over a long time. Recently, due to aggressive wire scaling and increasing number of interconnects on chips, EM has become an underlying cause of many IC chip failures. Based on International Technology Roadmap for Semiconductors (ITRS) report [1], the total wire length and the max current density exponentially increase. The trends clearly point to the increasing importance of EM modeling and prevention.

EM in IC chip interconnects, especially in power delivery network has been investigated for a long time. Many experiments have been carried out to help finding more EM resilient materials [2-3]. Several physics-based and TCAD models have been developed to capture the EM phenomenon including material and topology effects [4-5]. On the other hand, circuit level EM assessment and validation techniques have not advanced at the same rate. Pioneering research conducted by Blech resulted in a compact EM validation criterion which determines the critical current density – wire length (jL) product for void nucleation [6]. This study was performed for simple via-to-via interconnects. However, extending of Blech criterion to complex structures is still an active research. Foundries usually provide EM rules based on the interconnect geometry and current density for a specific technology. Industry standard CAD tools still use end-to-end Blech-effect-based techniques to determine mortality and immortality of net segments [7]. Recently some EM assessment techniques and validation methods have been developed [8-10] to address EM in complex structures.

Establishing an EM assessment method is difficult because modeling of EM involves many underlying physical phenomena – those are difficult to observe, perceive and therefore model. Moreover, solving multi-physics equations of electromigration requires computationally complex numerical methods and capturing the results as a descriptive, comprehensive, scalable and accurate model is challenging.

Most of the circuit-level EM studies have been performed for simple interconnect segments with blocking boundary conditions at both ends. Authors in [10] developed a methodology for circuit level EM assessment based on the findings in [8]. This method extends the Blech criterion (jL_{crit}) from one segment to a multi-segment tree. They showed that the maximum stress difference in an interconnect tree $\Delta\sigma_{max}$ is given by the path with the greatest sum of segment jL products. The effective jL product (jL_{eff}) is then calculated and compared to the jL_{crit_nuc}. In this method, $\Delta\sigma_{max}$ was assumed to be equal to $2\sigma_{crit\_nuc}$ where σ_{crit_nuc} is the critical tensile stress for a void to nucleate. This assumption can be valid for symmetric structures. However, in multi-branch nets with arbitrary topology, jL_{eff} may reach $\Delta\sigma_{max}$ but void nucleation may not occur since the stress in cathode is less than σ_{crit_nuc}. Such situations occur for critical compressive stress for low-k dielectric breakage or extrusion. Immortality of a wire should be studied jointly with other wires connected within the same net. The amount of hydrostatic stress experienced by a wire depends on the stress in other segments. Therefore, a true EM validation can be achieved by obtaining stress distribution in the entire net. To include the effect of other connected segments, authors of [9] proposed a method to calculate effective current density based on atomic flux divergence at via nodes. This method only explains the effect of immediately adjacent segments and does not include the effect of other segments in the net, passive extensions or their material properties. It is known that Blech criterion for the end-to-end connection cannot be directly applied to multi-branch nets as it does not explain how connected segments affect each other.

In this paper we present a detailed, systematic study of Blech effect-based model for EM in complex structures including the effect of adjacent segments and take into account current density, geometry, topology and material properties of interconnect. The presented model applies to passive and active elements.

The model is justified not only by FEM simulations but is also matched to experimental observations. Finally, the paper provides insights for designers to take advantage of some structures and adopt them to make the design more robust to EM. The presented model can easily replace the limited solutions in CAD tools which are mainly based on Blech analysis of straight end-to-end wires.

2. BACKGROUND

Electromigration has been studied extensively for simple interconnect segments with blocking boundary conditions at both ends. Stress evolution, void nucleation and failure conditions are well established for such structures. The compact model for simple structures is known as *Blech length* or *Blech effect* [6]. In this paper we consider copper (Cu) interconnects manufactured in dual damascene technology. We say that a connection is simple if it consists of a straight segment of Cu wire terminating at both ends at a via or a contact. An interconnect tree, also referred to as a net or a complex interconnect, consists of a Cu structure within one layer of metallization which terminates at diffusion barriers such as vias or contacts. The diffusion barriers allow electrons to pass through but block the movement of atoms. In this section we briefly revisit EM underlying physics which is required for extending Blech effect to complex structures. The finite element simulations are performed for direct current (DC) in bamboo-like dual damascene copper interconnects with Ta liner, and SiN_x capping layer embedded in SiO_2.

2.1 Physics

A metallic interconnection is considered reliable if it has an almost constant material concentration across the entire wire within a specific period of time (i.e. several years). A change in atom concentration (or similarly vacancy concentration) can be caused by various factors ranging from electrical, mechanical, and thermal and can be affected by material chemical properties. Each factor contributes to a force causing the atomic flux. The overall flux can be expressed as:

$$J = -D(\frac{c_v}{kT}eZ^*\rho j + \frac{c_v}{kT}f\Omega\nabla\sigma + \nabla c_v + \frac{c_v}{kT}\frac{Q^*}{T}\nabla T) \quad (1)$$

Where D is the temperature dependent effective diffusion coefficient, c_v is the vacancy concentration, k is the Boltzmann constant, T is the temperature.

The first term (J_{em}) models the effect of collisions between electrons and ionized atoms caused by electric field. In this term, e is the fundamental electron charge, Z^* is the effective atomic charge number, ρ is the electrical resistivity of the metal, and j is the current density [11].

The second term (J_{sm}) which opposes the first term, arises due to the mechanical stress gradient created at diffusion barriers caused by atom depletion at cathode end and accumulation at the anode end. Here Ω is the atomic volume and f is the contraction ratio

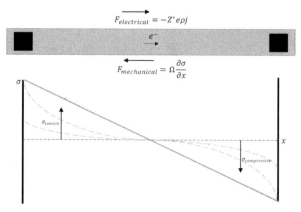

Figure 1. Stress evolution as a result of electron wind force and back stress force.

describing the relaxation of the atoms when an atom leaves its original neighborhood.

The third term (J_{mm}) describes the local variation in the atomic concentration mostly caused by the grain boundary regions during the crystal growth.

In addition, a metal structure under high current density induces an inhomogeneous temperature distribution and thus an appearance of temperature gradients. These temperature gradients also contribute to the EM process through the fourth term, J_{tm}, where Q^* represents the specific heat of transport of the metallic material.

2.2 Blech Effect

Effects of these four different driving forces which contribute to the EM process are not equal. Their typical contributions in terms of atomic flux are $|J_{tm}| \ll |J_{mm}| < |J_{sm}| \approx |J_{em}|$. The author in [6] studied EM in simple end-to-end interconnects (Fig 1) and observed that there is no mass transport when current density is less than a certain threshold value for a given wire length. He suggested that the presence of a back flow of atoms due to the back stress at the anode end opposes the electron wind. If the stress difference between the cathode and anode ends is less than that needed for void nucleation, the stress profile will evolve towards a steady state at which point the net atomic flux becomes zero and the wire is considered immortal. The condition of J_{sm} and J_{em} being equal is mathematically expressed as:

$$\frac{\partial\sigma}{\partial x} = \frac{e|Z^*|\rho j}{\Omega} \quad (2)$$

Integrating along the interconnect line, the solution for 1D model is expressed as:

$$\sigma(x) = \sigma_0 + \frac{e|Z^*|\rho j}{\Omega}x \quad (3)$$

where σ_0 is the stress at $x = 0$. Assuming $\Delta\sigma_{max}$ is the maximum stress between cathode and anode for void nucleation, *Blech product* can be expressed as

$$(jL)_{crit} = \frac{\Omega\Delta\sigma_{max}}{e|Z^*|\rho} \quad (4)$$

$(jL)_{crit}$ is experimentally reported as a value between 1500 A/cm to 3700 A/cm depending on materials (inter layer dielectric/liner/cap) and interconnect configuration [12-13].

2.3 Nucleation and Saturation

Based on Blech effect the condition for a void to nucleate can be stated as follows:

$$jL > jL_{crit\_nuc} = \frac{\Omega \Delta \sigma_{critical}}{e|Z^*|\rho} \qquad (5)$$

However, if the void forms in an area that does not completely block the current flow the wire may still conduct current. A void may continue to grow as the current is shunted around it until the electron wind force and the back stress force balance each other. In this situation, the interconnect line is considered immortal if the resistance decrease is less than the $\Delta R_{threshold}$. In this case immortality is based in the saturation and expressed by:

$$(jL)_{crit\_sat} = \frac{\rho/_A}{\rho_1/_{A_1}} \frac{\Delta R_{th}}{R} \frac{2\,\Omega\,B}{Z^* e\rho} \qquad (6)$$

here ρ and ρ_1 are the resistivity of conductor and shunt layers, respectively; and A and A_1 are the cross sectional areas of metal and shunt layer; and R is the initial resistance of the interconnect line.

In mature dual damascene technology, $(jL)_{crit}$ depends on the via configuration at the end of interconnect line. For a via-above structure (i.e. via to the upper level metallization), a tiny void under a via may result in a complete blockage of the current path. In this case, $(jL)_{nuc,crit}$ value is of about 1500 A/cm. On the other hand, for via-below (i.e. via to the lower metallization level) current path is more resilient to EM, the void needs to grow and span across the width and height of the line. In this case, $(jL)_{sat,crit}$ is reported to be of about 3700 A/cm. While the extrusion is not the primary failure mode, similar studies and experiments were carried out to obtain the critical compressive stress and jL product for extrusion and dielectric breakage [14].

2.4 Growth

A void formed in a wire increases the resistance and may finally result in fatal failure. Einstein's equation relating the drift velocity of the void surface can be expressed using the atomic flux as [15]:

$$v = \frac{D}{kT} e Z^* \rho j \qquad (7)$$

This relationship can be used to extract the wire resistance change. Yet, the complete analysis of growth phase is complicated and can be captured by morphological void evolution models based on phase field model techniques [16].

2.5 Multi-Segment Structures

Authors in [8] extend the Blech criterion (jL_{crit}) from one segment to a multi-segment tree. They showed that the maximum stress difference in an interconnect tree, $\Delta\sigma_{max}$, is given by the path with the greatest sum of segment jL products:

$$\Delta\sigma_{max} = \frac{\rho e Z^*}{\Omega} (jL)_{eff} \qquad (8)$$

where

$$(jL)_{eff} = \max_{\substack{all\ junction \\ pairs\ i,j}} \sum_k j_k L_k \qquad (9)$$

The effective jL product (jL_{eff}) is then calculated and compared to the jL_{crit_nuc}. Using their method the failure due to the void saturation can be checked by comparing jL_{eff} to jL_{crit_sat}. In this method, $\Delta\sigma_{max}$ was assumed to be equal to $2\sigma_{crit\_nuc}$ where

σ_{crit_nuc} is the critical tensile stress for a void to nucleate. This assumption can be valid for symmetric structures. However, in multi-branch nets with arbitrary topology, jL_{eff} may reach $\Delta\sigma_{max}$ but void nucleation may not occur because the stress at the cathode may be less than σ_{crit_nuc}. Such situations occur for critical compressive stress for low-k dielectric breakage or extrusion. Although this model is very powerful, it does not capture the effect of segments adjacent to the path with the highest sum of the jL products, yet not belonging to it. In other words, while the max jL product remains the same, the entire stress distribution might be affected by the segments not on the path with the maximum sum of the jL products. For instance, consider two nets shown in Fig 2; the only difference between these nets is the connectivity at node b_1

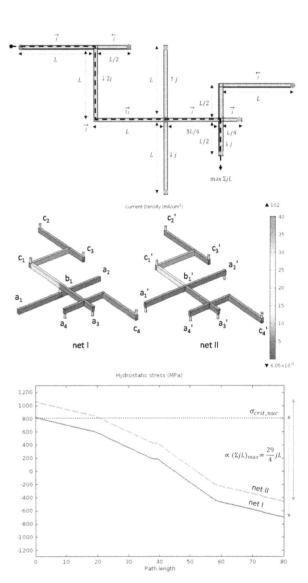

Figure 2. A multi-segment net. $jL_{eff} = max\Sigma jL$ is the same when segment $a_1'a_2'$ is connected to b_1' as a side branch directly in the same layer or when a_1a_2 is connected through a via to the lower layer. Red and green dots indicate a via above and via below, respectively. Hydrostatic stress along the broken line near the interface is shown at the bottom (in all figures arrows show electron flow $j= 10mA/um^2$).

113

(or b_1'). Net I has a branch a_1a_2 which is connected to the net on the same layer. On the other hand, net II has an alternative configuration in which the segment $a_1'a_2'$ is connected through a via below at b_1'. Based on the method developed in [8] and continued in [10], both configurations, have the same $jL_{eff} = \frac{29}{4}jL$ (the path with greatest summation of jL is marked by the broken line arrow). This is, both structures should experience the same EM conditions. But the stress distributions on net I and net II are different. In other words, even though $(jL)_{eff}$ are the same in these structures, due to the other segments configuration (i.e. a_1a_2 in net I and $a_1'a_2'$ in net II), the overall stress distribution is different.

Fig 2 shows the hydrostatic stress along the broken line (i.e. the path with greatest ΣjL). In this particular example, analyzing stresses in different nodes and juxtaposing them with the corresponding nodes in the other structure demonstrates this disparity. The number of atoms accumulated in the anodes a_3 and a_4 of net I is greater than in the anodes a_3' and a_4' of net II, since the only places for accumulation of atoms migrating from the cathodes end are a_3 and a_4. On the other hand, in net II, atoms can be accumulated in a_1', a_2', a_3' and a_4'. Therefore, the compressive stresses in nodes a_3 and a_4 are less than those of node a_3' and a_4'. Similarly, node b_1 is experiencing a large atom flux divergence since the segment b_1c_1 supplies more atoms than what is taken by segments b_1a_3 and b_1a_4. However, in net II, b_1' is experiencing less atomic flux divergence since $b_1'a_1'$ and $b_1'a_2'$ also contribute in atom accumulation (i.e. atom suction). This disparity in stress is caused by the fact that the via located in b_1 in net I only supplies electrons but no atoms. Yet, node b_1' is supplied with atoms by the wire segments $b_1'a_1'$ and $b_1'a_2'$. Likewise, cathode c_2' of net II experiences less back stress (since atoms can distribute among more branches) and therefore supplies more atoms (i.e. more atoms are depleted) compared to cathode c_2 in net I. Thus, the tensile stress in cathode c_2 is less than that of cathode c_2'. These differences may result in different failure mechanisms. One structure may even be immortal and the other one may be mortal.

Another effort to model immortality in complex interconnect is presented in [9]. The authors propose a method to calculate effective current density based on atomic flux divergence at each via node. This method states that the effective atomic flux can be expressed as $j_{eff} = (F_L F_W F_B)j$ where F_L, F_W and F_B model the non-electrical effects such as length, width and wire segment interaction on the atomic flux of a lead. Then, effective current density divergence at each node is calculated by $j_{eff.div} = \Sigma j_{eff}$. The limitation of this model is that it only explains the effect of the immediately adjacent segments and does not include the effect of other segments in the net, passive extensions or their material properties.

We believe that the method presented in this paper has broader and more accurate application. It not only includes the non-electrical and interaction effects of adjacent segments but also explains the non-electrical effects of all connected segments as well as the effects of passive wire extensions.

3. CAD MODEL

3.1 Immortality

In the previous section, using a complex structures (Fig 2), it was shown that the sole usage of jL_{eff} does not capture the effect of connected segments. In this section, we present a model that together with (2) can capture the effect of all connected segments. This model offers a systematic way of determining the actual $(jL)_{eff}$ and the actual stress distribution based on the atom conservation principle:

$$\iiint_{net} c\, dV = N_0 \qquad (10)$$

where c is the concentration of atoms along the net and N_0 is the total number of atoms. The total number of atoms must be equal in the initial state and in the steady state. In other words, the number of atoms accumulated and depleted in different segments of the net is zero:

$$\iiint_{net} \Delta c\, dV = 0 \qquad (11)$$

From Blech's equation (2), the stress within a segment $\alpha\beta$ in 1D model is given by (3) and the maximum stress difference ($\Delta\sigma$) is proportional to jL. A first order approximation of σ depends linearly on the concentration of atomic lattice sites C by

$$c = c_0 \exp\left(-\frac{\sigma}{B}\right) \approx c_0\left(1 - \frac{\sigma}{B}\right) \qquad (12)$$

where c_0 is the initial concentration, B is the effective bulk modulus. At the steady state Δc is equal to $c_0\frac{\sigma}{B}$. Thus, the total number of added/removed atoms in a segment (or branch):

$$\int_{segment} \Delta c\, dV = \int_{segment} c_0 \frac{\sigma}{B}\, dV = \left(c_0 \frac{\sigma_{anode}}{B} - c_0 \frac{Z^*e\rho}{2B\Omega} jL\right) V$$

thus

$$\int_{segment} \Delta c\, dV = \left(c_0 \frac{\sigma_{anode}}{B} - c_0 \frac{\Delta\sigma}{2B}\right) V = \frac{\sigma_{anode} + \sigma_{cathode}}{2B} V. \quad (13)$$

Therefore the original integral of atom concentration change is written as follows:

$$\int_{net} \Delta c\, dV = \sum_{net} \int_{segment} \Delta c\, dV.$$

Thus,

$$\Sigma_{segments\,k} \frac{\sigma_{k-anode} + \sigma_{k-cathode}}{2B_k} V_k = 0 \qquad (14)$$

where V_k is the volume of segment-k.

If the cross sectional area of the net is assumed to be constant everywhere as well as the effective bulk modulus, the model can be compacted to:

$$\Sigma_{segments\,k}(\sigma_{a_k} + \sigma_{c_k}) L_k = 0 \qquad (15)$$

where σ_{a_k}, σ_{c_k} and L_k are the hydrostatic stress in anode and cathode ends and the length of segment-k, respectively.

The presented model constitutes of equation (14) together with Blech's original equation (2) and the maximum summation of the jL products (9). This model holds true for any multi-segment complex structure.

As an example, the stress distribution is calculated for the nets shown in Fig 3. It is assumed that the cross sectional area of the net is constant everywhere as well as is the effective bulk modulus. For net I:

$$\sigma_b - \sigma_a = -\frac{Z^*e\rho}{\Omega} jL$$

$$\sigma_c - \sigma_b = -\frac{Z^*e\rho}{\Omega} 2jL$$

and using (14):

$$\frac{\sigma_b + \sigma_a}{2B_{ab}}V_{ab} + \frac{\sigma_c + \sigma_b}{2B_{bc}}V_{bc} = 0$$

$$\frac{\sigma_b + \sigma_a}{2B_{ab}}A_{ab}L_{ab} + \frac{\sigma_c + \sigma_b}{2B_{bc}}A_{bc}L_{bc} = 0$$

therefore,

$$\sigma_a = \frac{5Z^*e\rho}{4\Omega}jL, \sigma_b = \frac{Z^*e\rho}{4\Omega}jL, \sigma_c = -\frac{7Z^*e\rho}{4\Omega}jL.$$

Similarly for net *II*,

$$\sigma_{b\prime} - \sigma_{a\prime} = -\frac{Z^*e\rho}{\Omega}jL$$

$$\sigma_{c\prime} - \sigma_{b\prime} = -\frac{Z^*e\rho}{\Omega}2jL$$

$$\sigma_{b\prime} - \sigma_{d\prime} = -\frac{Z^*e\rho}{\Omega}jL$$

and

$$\frac{\sigma_{b\prime} + \sigma_{a\prime}}{2B_{a\prime b\prime}}V_{a\prime b\prime} += \frac{\sigma_{b\prime} + \sigma_{d\prime}}{2B_{d\prime b\prime}}V_{d\prime b\prime} + \frac{\sigma_{c\prime} + \sigma_{b\prime}}{2B_{b\prime c\prime}}V_{b\prime c\prime} = 0$$

accordingly,

$$\frac{\sigma_{b\prime} + \sigma_{a\prime}}{2B_{a\prime b\prime}}A_{a\prime b\prime}L_{a\prime b\prime} + \frac{\sigma_{b\prime} + \sigma_{d\prime}}{2B_{d\prime b\prime}}A_{d\prime b\prime}L_{d\prime b\prime} + \frac{\sigma_{c\prime} + \sigma_{b\prime}}{2B_{b\prime c\prime}}A_{b\prime c\prime}L_{b\prime c\prime} = 0$$

therefore,

$$\sigma_{a\prime} = \frac{Z^*e\rho}{\Omega}jL, \sigma_{d\prime} = \frac{Z^*e\rho}{\Omega}jL, \sigma_{b\prime} = 0, \sigma_{c\prime} = -\frac{2Z^*e\rho}{\Omega}jL.$$

Fig 3 illustrates these computations, where $\frac{\sigma_b + \sigma_a}{2}L_{ab}$ and $\frac{\sigma_c + \sigma_b}{2}L_{bc}$ are the marked areas of rectangles S_{ab} and S_{bc}. Based on the atomic

conservation, the absolute values of these areas must be equal. On the other hand, for net *II*, $\frac{\sigma_{b\prime} + \sigma_{a\prime}}{2}L_{a\prime b\prime}$ and $\frac{\sigma_{b\prime} + \sigma_{d\prime}}{2}L_{d\prime b\prime}$ represent the areas of rectangles $S_{a\prime b\prime}$ and $S_{d\prime b\prime}$ which correspond to the segments $a\prime b\prime$ and $d\prime b\prime$ respectively. According to the atomic conservation, the summation of these areas must be equal to the area of $S_{b\prime c\prime}$ which is calculated as $\frac{\sigma_{c\prime} + \sigma_{b\prime}}{2}L_{b\prime c\prime}$. Comparing hydrostatic stress of corresponding nodes in net *I* and *II* shows that having segment $d\prime b\prime$ affects the stress distribution by $-\frac{Z^*e\rho}{4\Omega}jL$ tensile stress. Note that, node b is experiencing an atom flux divergence since the segment bc supplies more atoms than what is taken by segment ba. This atomic flux divergence results in stress. However, in net *II*, $b\prime$ is not experiencing atomic flux divergence since $b\prime a\prime$ and $b\prime d\prime$ together take same amount of atoms depleted from segment $c\prime b\prime$. Therefore, $b\prime$ experience zero stress.

This model provides an accurate systematic way to find EM prone sections of any multi-segment interconnect structure by calculating the hydrostatic stress distribution over the entire net using (14) together with Blech's original equation (2) and the maximum summation of the jL products (9).

3.2 Geometry

In addition to current density, the stress growth in an interconnect depends not only on its geometry but also on the geometry of other segments of the same net. The effect of geometry, including length, width and thickness are all captured by (9) and (14).

Fig 4 shows the effect of length of adjacent segments. In both nets, all segments carry the same current density J, flowing into the middle via. This can also be explained by the back stress built up

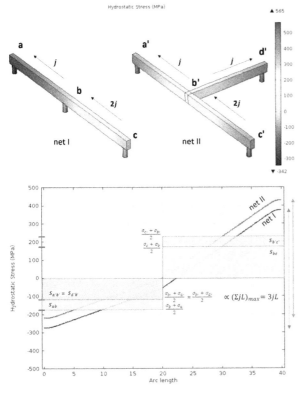

Figure 3. Graphical proof of atoms conservation based the hydrostatic distribution (j= $10mA/um^2$). (Equ 14).

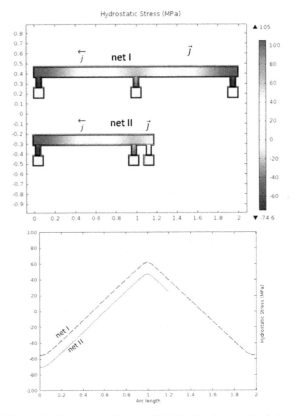

Figure 4. Current and stress distribution in two back-to-back connected segments with different lengths. The graph shows the effect of length on immortality (j= $10mA/um^2$).

in a shorter segment. In net *II*, the shorter segment sucks fewer atoms from the middle via compared to symmetric situation in net *I*. Such effects have been explained in [9] based on atomic divergence. However, we show that the model consisting of jL_{eff} and (14) is also able to explain the effect of geometry with no new conventions and holds for segment interactions as those discussed in [9]. The effect of width and thickness are also captured similarly using the proposed compact model.

3.3 Passive Elements

The effects of passive elements (i.e. metal extensions with zero current) such as those added at cathode (reservoir), or anode (sink), or dummy vias have been investigated in many works [17]. However, a compact model suitable for CAD tools that can explain and model the underlying physics has not been proposed.

Figure 5. An arbitrary active segments, attached to two inactive segments (sink and reservoir with the length of L_s and L_r respectively).

Our method not only explains the active segments but also offers a general model for reservoir and sink extension. Fig 5 shows interconnect of a length L. This segment is connected to a reservoir of lengths L_r and sink of length L_s. Solving equations (2) and (14) for the net shown in Fig 5 is as follows:

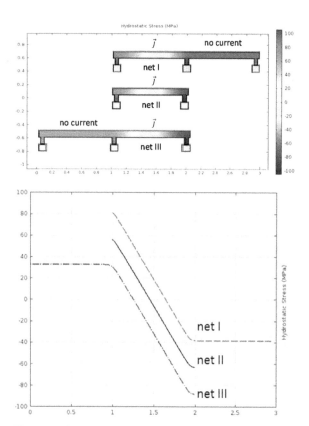

Figure 6. Current and stress distribution in 3 nets, with different configurations. The graph at the bottom shows the effect of the same length sink and reservoir on an active segment mortality (j= $10mA/um^2$).

$$\sigma_c - \sigma_a = -\frac{Z^*e\rho}{\Omega}jL$$

$$\sigma_r - \sigma_c = -\frac{Z^*e\rho}{\Omega}0L \rightarrow \sigma_r = \sigma_c$$

$$\sigma_a - \sigma_s = -\frac{Z^*e\rho}{\Omega}0L \rightarrow \sigma_s = \sigma_a$$

$$\frac{\sigma_r + \sigma_c}{2B_{rc}}V_{sc} + \frac{\sigma_c + \sigma_a}{2B_{ca}}V_{ca} + \frac{\sigma_a + \sigma s_r}{2B_{as}}V_{as} = 0$$

We assume that the cross sectional area of the net is constant everywhere as well as is the effective bulk modulus. Thus, the stresses at the cathode and anode ends of the active segment in presence of the extensions are:

$$\sigma_a = \frac{L+2L_r}{2(L_s+L+L_r)}jL \tag{16}$$

$$\sigma_c = -\frac{L+2L_s}{2(L_s+L+L_r)}jL \tag{17}$$

Therefore, the critical current density for interconnect void nucleation in a wire connected to a passive reservoir and a sink is:

$$j_{extension-critical} = \frac{L_s+L+L_r}{L+2L_s}j_{critical} \tag{18}$$

The critical current density for extrusion can be similarly obtained.

Fig 6 shows the effect of extension on the active segment. Reservoirs in general improve EM performance as they provide extra atoms to the cathode and decrease the tensile stress. On the other hand, sinks in general degrade EM performance by reducing the back stress built up at anode. The simulations results explain experimental results reported in [23].

3.4 Material Effects on Lifetime: Microstructures, Grain Boundaries, Capping and Liner Interfaces, impurity

The rate of mass transport and void growth in dual damascene process largely depends on grain boundaries and interfaces. The fastest path for atoms to migrate is at the capping layer interface. The effective diffusivity in copper interconnects can be written in terms of diffusions and dimensions of bulk, grain boundaries, liner interface and capping surface.

In addition, impurity or bulk imperfection which usually appear in a form of pre-existing voids in capping interface or dislocations, can be included similarly. These embryo voids are mainly produced by the thermal mismatch between copper and the surrounding dielectric and can signifacntly affect the electromigration lifetime [18].

While the effects of microstructure and interfaces are affecting EM lifetime, their influence in general is not visible in the steady state. In other words, although Blech effect-based method provides critical information about mortality or immortality of interconnects, it does not offer temporal information of failure. The applicability of Blech criterion is limited to predicting void nucleation, extrusion and saturation. Temporal information cannot be inferred from the steady state of the system. A comprehensive knowledge of failure mechanism (i.e. temporal and spatial) can be obtained by concurrent study of electrical, mechanical, thermal effects, materials properties, geometry and topology of the whole net.

The model discussed here has the capability of describing interconnect interactions; however, it does not explain the local effects of microstructure. This limitation is caused by the fact that this model is based on the steady state of the system. Such models do not distinguish between the structures shown in Fig 7. The

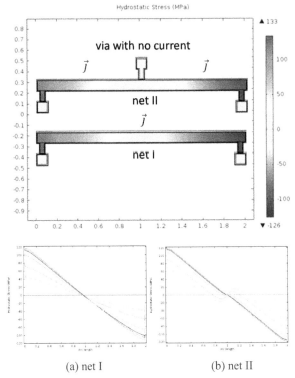

Hydrostatic Stress (MPa)

(a) net I   (b) net II

Figure 7. Current and stress distribution in two segments. (a) a simple interconnect (b) the same interconnect segment with a dead via in the middle. The via does not carry current but changes the bulk effective diffusion which prolongs the time to reach steady state. Yet, the effect is not visible in steady state. (J=1mA/um^2) [20].

structure shown in Fig 7 (b) differs from that in Fig 7 (a) in that it has one dummy via above the active wire. Even though it does not carry current, it affects the EM process by slowing down the atom and vacancy fast track at the interface of the copper and capping layers. Note that the effective diffusivity of interconnect is affected and can be modeled using (14). However, the steady state does not depend on the microstructure. A huge slack in the interface by introducing more dummy vias can lead to a very long time to failure and therefore the wire might practically be considered immortal [21]. This is observed in finite element simulation [20] as the steady state for net *I* is reached 5 times earlier than that for net *II* (Fig 7).

While the steady state analysis provides information about the mortality and immortality of wires, a comprehensive EM performance analysis tool, in addition to steady state analysis, must also consider lifetime by modeling some dynamic processes occurring in wires.

The lifetime of conductor interconnects evaluates their resistance to EM. It is usually presented in terms of median time to failure (MTTF) which is in fact the time when half of a number of identical interconnects fail. MTTF is described as a log normal distribution. The lifetime of interconnect was formulated originally in [19] using an Arrhenius-like empirical equation:

$$MTTF = Aj^{-n}\exp(E_a/kT)$$

where A is a constant which depends on mechanical and electrical properties of a thin film conductor, E_a is the activation energy for EM-induced failure, k is the Boltzmann constant, T is operating temperature, j is the current density, n is a constant with typical

value between 1 and 2 depending on failure mechanisms. The values of n greater than 2 are most likely due to Joule heating [11].

More recent models for predicting the lifetime of interconnects rely on the nucleation of void as well as its growth. In other words, failure mechanism may vary depending on the interconnect configuration and the properties of materials used in the system (including the conductor, diffusion barriers, capping layer and low-k ILD). The common logic among the other lifetime models is that the MTTF can be obtained based on the void nucleation time, void growth time and extrusion time. All predicting lifetime models (including analytical ones) can be summarized into a general model which describes the effects of nucleation, growth and extrusion.

$$TTF = \min_{all\ segments}(t_{nuc} + t_{growth}, t_{ext})$$

where t_{nuc}, t_{nuc} and t_{nuc} are the nucleation time, void growth time and time to extrusion, respectively. In some interconnect configurations (e.g. via-above) void nucleation solely is considered as the condition for the failure. These times to failure terms are computed differently in various papers [9, 22].

While the steady state of the system does not rely on microstructures property, these timing terms do. Therefore, to have a complete study of failure, CAD tools may need to implement TTF models too.

4. Conclusions

The steady state solution for vacancy/atom continuity equation was studied by Blech. The result for in a compact EM validation criterion which determines the critical product of current density and wire length *(jL)* for void nucleation was proposed in [6]. However, these studies were performed for simple via-to-via interconnects and could not be used for multi-segment structures. While extending Blech criterion to complex structures was studied in some papers [8-9], they have limitation in terms of either capturing all effects or in accuracy. The model proposed in this paper computes the stress distribution and captures the electrical and non-electrical effects of all segments connected in a net. The presented compact model can be easily used in CAD tools to replace inaccurate EM failure prediction. This model is also capable of capturing the effect of passive extensions. Application of this model offers design guidance. This model is justified by finite element implementation of vacancy continuity equation and matched with similar experimental results.

5. ACKNOWLEDGMENTS

This work was supported by NSF grant CCF-1115663.

6. REFERENCES

[1] The International Technology Roadmap for Semiconductors (ITRS) [online]. available: http://www.itrs.net/

[2] J.P. Gambino, "Improved reliability of copper interconnects using alloying." *17th IEEE International Symposium on the Physical and Failure Analysis of Integrated Circuits (IPFA)*, pp. 1-7, 2010.

[3] C. Christiansen *et al.* "Electromigration-resistance enhancement with CoWP or CuMn for advanced Cu interconnects." *IEEE International Reliability Physics Symposium (IRPS)*, 2011.

[4] R. Kirchheim, "Stress and electromigration in Al-lines of integrated circuits," *Acta Metallurgica et Materialia*, Volu. 40, no. 2, February 1992, Pages 309-323.

[5] V. Sukharev, E. Zschech, and W.D. Nix, "A model for electromigration-induced degradation mechanisms in dual-

inlaid copper interconnects: Effect of microstructure,", *Journal of Applied Physics,* 102, 053505 (2007).

[6] I.A. Blech, *J. Appl. Phys.* 47, 1203 (1976).

[7] Ansys (Apache) RedHawk https://www.apache-da.com/products/redhawk Apache Design, Inc., a subsidiary of ANSYS, Inc.

[8] S.P. Hau-Riege, " New methodologies for interconnect reliability assessments of integrated circuits," PhD thesis, Massachusetts Institute of Technology, 2000

[9] Y.J. Park, P. Jain, and s. Krishnan, "New electromigration validation: Via Node Vector Method," *Reliability Physics Symposium (IRPS)*, 2010 IEEE International (pp. 698-704).

[10] S.M. Alam *et al.* "Circuit-level reliability requirements for Cu metallization." *IEEE Transactions on Device and Materials Reliability,* 5.3 (2005): 522-531.

[11] J. R. Lloyd, "Black's law revisited - Nucleation and growth in electromigration failure," *Microelectronics Reliability* 47(9-11): 1468-1472 (2007).

[12] K.D. Lee, E.T. Ogawa, H. Matsuhashi, P.R. Justison, K.S. Ko, P.S. Ho, and V.A. Blaschke, "Electromigration critical length effect in Cu/oxide dual-damascene interconnects," *Applied Physics Letters*, 79, 3236-3238 (2001).

[13] C. S. Hau-Riege, A. P. Marathe, and V. Pham, "The effect of line length on the electromigration reliability of Cu interconnects", *Proc. Advanced Metallization Conf.*, pp.169 2002.

[14] F.L. Wei, *et al.* "Electromigration-induced extrusion failures in Cu/low-k interconnects." *Journal of Applied Physics* 104.2 (2008): 023529.

[15] Z. Suo, "Reliability of Interconnect Structures, ser. Comprehensive Structural Integrity" *Amsterdam: Elsevier*, 2003, vol. 8.

[16] D. N. Bhate, A. F. Bower, A. Kumar, "A phase field model for failure in interconnect lines due to coupled diffusion mechanisms," *Journal of the Mechanics and Physics of Solids*, Volume 50, Issue 10, October 2002, Pages 2057-2083.

[17] F.L. Wei, C. Hau-Riege, A.P. Marathe, and C.V. Thompson, " Effects of active atomic sinks and reservoirs on the reliability of Cu/low-k interconnects," *Journal of Applied Physics*, 103, 084513 (2008).

[18] B.M. Clemens, W. D. Nix, and R. J. Gleixner. "Void nucleation on a contaminated patch," *Journal of Materials Research* 12.08 (1997): 2038-2042.

[19] J.R. Black, *IEEE Trans. Electron Devices*, 16 (1969), pp. 338–347.

[20] Comsol multiphysics, http://www.comsol.com COMSOL, Inc., 8 New England Executive Park, Burlington, MA 01803

[21] B. Li, *et al.* "Short line electromigration characteristics and their applications for circuit design." *IEEE International Reliability Physics Symposium (IRPS)*, 2013.

[22] C. M. Tan, A. Roy, "Electromigration in ULSI interconnects," *Materials Science and Engineering: R: Reports*, Volume 58, Issues 1–2, 1 Oct. 2007, Pages 1-75.

[23] I. Jeon, Y.-B. Park," Analysis of the reservoir effect on electromigration reliability, *Microelectronics Reliability*," Volume 44, Issue 6, June 2004, Pages 917-928.

On Resilient System Performance Binning

Qiang Han, Jianghao Guo, Qiang Xu*, Wen-Ben Jone
University of Cincinnati, *The Chinese University of Hong Kong
{hanqg, guojh}@mail.uc.edu, *qxu@cse.cuhk.edu.hk, jonewb@ucmail.uc.edu

ABSTRACT

By allowing timing errors to occur and recovering them online, resilient systems can be used to eliminate the voltage/frequency guardband to improve energy efficiency/throughput. Due to the nature of fault tolerance computing, resilient systems have a different binning strategy from traditional circuits. In this paper, we study, for the first time, the binning metrics of resilient systems. We propose a solution for resilient system binning based on structural at-speed delay testing. Then an adaptive clock configuration technique is proposed for yield improvement. Experimental results demonstrate the effectiveness of our proposed binning method, and significant yield improvement accomplished by the adaptive clock configuration technique.

Categories and Subject Descriptors

B.8.0 [**Hardware**]: Performance and Reliability—*General*

General Terms

Reliability, Verification

Keywords

Resilient System; Performance Binning; Yield Improvement

1. INTRODUCTION

As technology scales down, variability in device and circuit parameters has more and more critical impacts on the circuit performance. These uncertainties of a circuit can be attributed to supply voltage fluctuations, temperature hotspots, inter- and intra-die process variations, signal integrity concerns, aging effects and so on [4]. To guarantee fault-free computation, conventional design methods resolve those uncertainties by driving the circuit working at the clock frequency with a safe guardband [3]. However, such designs are too pessimistic because the worst case failure occurs infrequently.

To eliminate these design margins, several works were proposed in [10, 6, 5] known as *resilient computing*. All these works share a similar idea of further lowering the supply voltage or increasing the clock frequency to reduce power consumption or enhance circuit performance by allowing the occurrence of system failures at a low rate and recovering them online. To protect the circuit from failure, flip-flops (FFs) on critical paths are converted into the *error detection circuits* circuits to detect timing errors. When a late arrival signal arrives within the its error detection window, the online error detector will report an ERROR signal and the system will roll back to a known good state, and reoperate the erroneous instruction with the guaranteed-safe guardband.

Speed binning is an industry term that refers to the test procedures used to determine the maximum functional operating frequency of a chip, so that it can be offered to customers at an appropriate speed-grade [2]. By inserting on-chip timing monitor, the study in [15] used an intrusive method to measure the performance of circuits. In [8, 22], the authors tested and verified the correlation between structural at-speed test approach and functional performance testing for binning. The work in [16] proposed a speed binning methodology for multi-core processors. [9] presented a statistical design method to improve profit of a design considering frequency binning and product price profile. The problem of computing optimal supply voltages for a given binning scheme was solved in [23]. All the above works follow the same principle that the traditional circuits are binned according to their frequencies, because the performance of a traditional circuit is only determined by its working frequency.

Differently, due to the existence of timing errors and online recovery circuits, the metrics of resilient system binning do not refer to the system clock frequency alone. For example, two resilient processors can work at the same frequency, however due to process variation, one may have more timing errors than the other when running the same benchmark program. Therefore, the metrics of resilient system binning are more complicated than traditional binning. Working frequency, error rate and error recovery time must all be taken into consideration for binning, because they determine the performance of a resilient circuit jointly. Consequentially, the binning method of a resilient system needs to be researched.

To the best of our knowledge, this is the first work on performance binning for resilient circuits, and we make the following contributions in this paper:

- The metrics of resilient circuit performance binning are explored for the first time.

- We propose the idea of structural at-speed testing based resilient circuit binning method, which takes advantage of the timing error count obtained from the built-in error detection circuits to evaluate the circuit quality.

- An adaptive clock tuning technique for binning is proposed for yield improvement.

In the following, Section 2 reviews a resilient system design [6, 5] and the corresponding timing analysis. Section 3 discusses a proposed design for testability (DFT) method, which is used for the resilient circuit binning in this work. In Section 4, the resilient circuit performance binning methodology is proposed and explained in detail. Section 5 discusses our adaptive clock tuning method for yield improvement. Experimental results are shown in Section 6, and Section 7 concludes this paper.

2. RESILIENT SYSTEM OVERVIEW AND TIMING ANALYSIS

2.1 Error Detection Sequential Circuit

The error detection sequential (EDS) in an Intel resilient microprocessor core [6, 5] is illustrated in Fig. 1(a). In an EDS, a latch is used on the data-path instead of a FF. A shadow FF samples the same input signal to the latch at the rising edge of the clock. Outputs of the FF and latch come to a 2-input XOR-gate to generate the ERROR signal. As illustrated in Fig. 1(b), the latch is transparent during the clock's high level but the shadow FF captures data at the clock's rising edge and holds this logic value. The error-detection window (T_w) of an EDS is the period of its clock's high level. If a delayed transition on the critical path occurs during T_w, an ERROR signal is generated by the XOR-gate as shown in Fig. 1(b).

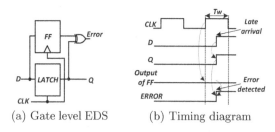

(a) Gate level EDS   (b) Timing diagram

Figure 1: Intel EDS design [6]

Since the error detection window adds more time slack on the EDS paths, the maximum EDS path delay (EDS max-delay) constraint is determined in Eq. (1)

$$T_{EDS,max} < T_{cycle} + T_w - T_{setup,clk} \qquad (1)$$

where $T_{EDS,max}$ is the maximum delay allowed on the propagation paths to the EDS, T_{cycle} is the system clock cycle time, and $T_{setup,clk}$ is the setup time of FFs. Similar to the hold time constraint, the short path to an EDS cannot be less than the error detection window, so the minimum path delay (EDS min-delay) constraint is defined in Eq. (2)

$$T_{EDS,min} > T_w + T_{hold,clk} \qquad (2)$$

where $T_{EDS,min}$ is the minimum delay allowed on the propagation paths to each EDS, and $T_{hold,clk}$ is the hold time of FFs. With the traditional FF max-delay constraint in Eq. (3) for FFs without timing error detectors, we have totally three timing constraints for the resilient system data-path.

$$T_{FF,max} < T_{cycle} - T_{setup,clk} \qquad (3)$$

2.2 Error-Recovery Design

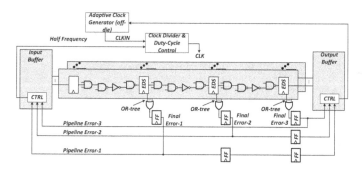

Figure 2: Schematic view of Intel resilient processor design [6].

Fig. 2 shows a 3-stage pipeline resilient circuit block [6]. Error signals from all EDS circuits per pipeline stage are merged via an OR-tree to propagate to a single final-error-FF. The three pipeline errors are connected to the input buffer to replay the failed instruction, and are also routed to the output buffer to invalidate the erroneous data. When the input buffer receives an error indication, it signals the clock divider to halve F_{CLK} to recover the erroneous instruction, while maintaining a constant high clock phase delay due to the EDS min-delay constraint. After the recovery finishes, the system clock returns to the normal frequency.

3. RESILIENT SYSTEM DESIGN FOR TESTABILITY

In this section, we study the resilient system DFT method and illustrate its capability of supporting our proposed binning method.

3.1 Scannable EDS (SEDS) Design

In EDS circuits, latches are unable to perform shift operations by themselves in the scan chain. In order to make EDS circuits scannable, edge-triggered FF [21] and LSSD-style [13] scannable EDS (SEDS) have been proposed. This work uses the LSSD style shown in Fig. 3(a). A tail latch ($L2$) is attached to the EDS latch ($L1$) and an inverter is added before $L2$'s T_CLK to form the basic scan cell in SEDS. SEDS uses two independent clocks, the system clock (CLK) and scan clock (T_CLK), to switch between functional and shift modes.

When the system works in functional mode, T_CLK is set to logic-low, the system clock CLK is at the functional clock rate, and thus $L1$, FF and XOR-gate work together as a normal EDS. When it works in shift mode, CLK is set to logic-low and T_CLK is working at the shift frequency. When T_CLK is at logic-high in shift mode, $L1$ is transparent to S_i and at the same time $L2$ hold its previous value; when T_CLK becomes logic-low, $L1$ is locked up and $L2$ fetches data from $L1$. Therefore, SEDS can be treated as

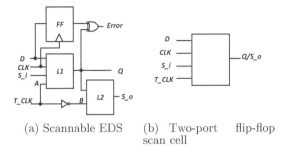

(a) Scannable EDS   (b) Two-port   flip-flop
                        scan cell

Figure 3: Scan cell circuits in resilient system.

a black box – in functional mode ($T\_CLK = 0$), D, CLK
and Q work together as a high level sensitive latch with error detection function, and in shift mode ($CLK = 0$), S_i,
T_CLK and S_o form a negative-edge triggered FF.

3.2   Scan Path in Resilient System

In a resilient system, scannable normal FFs, which are not
converted to EDSs, need to be reconsidered. Muxed-FF scan
cell design has been widely used in modern circuits; however
the inputs and timing scheme of muxed-FF and SEDS are
not compatible. Therefore, the two-port flip-flop scan cell
[20] can be used to replace normal FFs as shown in Fig.
3(b). Compared to the traditional muxed-FF design, the
two-port flip-flop scan cell has the same inputs and timing
behavior as SEDS. Therefore they are capable of working
together to form a scan chain seamlessly.

Similar to SEDS, in the two-port flip-flop scan cell in [20],
D and S_i are selected using two independent clocks, CLK
and T_CLK, while Q and S_o share the same output. When
performing launch-on-capture operation, the two-port flip-
flop scan cell has the same timing diagram as SEDS, but
it captures data at the second rising of CLK in Fig. 4,
the same capture time as the traditional muxed-FF. Notice
that in shift mode, the clocked-scan cell normally operates
as a positive-edge triggered FF, which shifts the data at the
rising edge of T_CLK, while SEDS captures data at the
falling edge. This problem is called mixed negative- and
positive-edge triggered FF scan chain, and it can be solved
by lockup latch insertion [17]. In fact, it does not affect the
functional mode.

3.3   Resilient System Delay Fault Testing

Fig. 4 shows the scan chain launch-on-capture operation
timing diagram along with the corresponding faults occurring and detection events. Test vectors $V1$ and $V2$ are
scanned through the scan chain in shift mode. After vectors
arrive at the corresponding scan cells, the $V1$ test vector is
automatically loaded on the combinational circuit under test
(CUT). Next, T_CLK becomes logic-low to set up the functional mode, and then a pulse is applied on CLK to launch
$V2$. If an EDS min-delay fault occurs, within T_w of the
first cycle, the EDS sends an ERROR to its final-error-FF
as shown in Fig. 4. At the rising edge of the second CLK
cycle, the final-error-FF captures the ERROR signal, and
meantime the normal scan FFs also capture their data. For
EDS max-delay testing, the latch $L1$ captures data exactly
at ($T_{cycle} + T_w - T_{setup,clk}$) of CLK, and then $L2$ fetches the
value from $L1$ ready for the data scan-out. It is a significant
benefit because, by Eq. (1), we need to compare the value

at ($T_{cycle} + T_w - T_{setup,clk}$) with the golden value to verify
the EDS max-delay constraint. Finally, the scan chain shifts
out all the captured data for test response analysis.

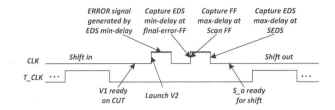

Figure 4: Scan chain launch-on-capture timing diagram.

4.   RESILIENT SYSTEM PERFORMANCE BINNING

4.1   Metrics of Resilient System Binning

Traditionally, speed binning focuses on how fast a circuit
can perform its desired function, and this maximum operating frequency determines the quality at which the chip will
be offered to the market [8, 22]. The most general form of
speed binning starts from the highest rated speed for circuits
of high performance. The passed circuits are selected into
the current bin, while the failed will be tested at a lower
speed. This procedure continues until all the circuits are
selected into their appropriate bins. In essence, traditional
binning procedures sieve circuits only by their maximal operating frequencies.

However, traditional binning methods discussed above are
not suitable for resilient circuits. With significant process
variations, a resilient circuit can have higher or lower error
rate than expected, but it may still pass the structural at-
speed delay testing. This observation leads us to rethink
what metrics must be included for error resilient circuit binning.

The performance of a resilient system is determined by the
clock cycle (T), resilient system error rate (P) and recovery
penalty (r), and it can be estimated in Eq. (4) similar to
[19, 12].

$$Perf = \frac{1}{T \times (1 - P + P \times r)} \qquad (4)$$

Here, P represents the probability that one or multiple timing errors occur and are captured by EDS(s) in the resilient
system at clock cycle T. When a timing error occurs, the recovery period is the penalty to rerun it for the correct result,
and thus r is decided by the system architecture. Therefore,
at a fixed T, the resilient system performance is only determined by P, and it is monotonic to P. Due to the above
facts, with a given clock, the error rate stands for the system performance, and thus resilient circuits can be binned
by their error rates.

4.2   Performance Binning Flow

As discussed, binning resilient systems using traditional
frequency binning is not sufficient, since circuits that pass
structural at-speed test can have different error rates (performance) and some of them may have unacceptable performance. The basic idea of our proposed method is using the

error count information from structural at-speed testing to bin resilient circuits. As discussed in the previous section, there are three types of structural tests on a resilient circuit data path – EDS min-delay, EDS max-delay, and FF max-delay. We use the EDS max-delay and FF max-delay fault testing to count the number of timing errors, because test vectors for these two kinds of faults essentially have high correlation to trigger long path delay; EDS min-delay test vectors focus on short paths, and thus they inadequately trigger timing errors. Therefore, when test vectors for EDS max-delay and FF max-delay fault testing are applied, the number of timing errors (at final-error-FFs in Fig. 2) is counted. The higher number is counted from test vectors of these two kinds, the worse the circuit performance is.

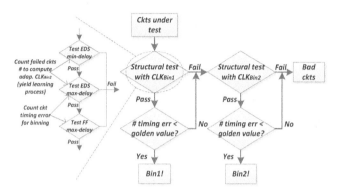

Figure 5: Resilient system performance binning flow.

Now we know the timing error count from structural at-speed testing represents the performance of a circuit; however, we need to have a golden number as the bin boundary. In this study, **two bins** are assumed. The timing error count of the golden design (which does not have variations) on EDS max-delay and FF max-delay testing is used as **the pivot** for bin selection, and this golden number can be obtained by fault simulation prior to the actual binning procedure. Fig. 5 shows the proposed resilient system performance binning flow. It starts with the structural at-speed testing with the Bin1 clock configuration. Circuits failed from Bin1 testing are further tested by structural at-speed testing with CLK_{Bin2}. However, as discussed, not all circuits that pass Bin1 structural at-speed testing will be qualified in Bin1 due to variations. So the timing error count from EDS max-delay and FF max-delay testing needs to be compared with the pivot (the count from the golden design). Circuits with less error counts than the pivot are selected into Bin1, while others will go with the failed circuits (by delay testing) to the Bin2 testing.

Bin2 testing is similar to Bin1 – it also tests the three timing constraints in structural at-speed delay testing with CLK_{Bin2}, but the failed circuits are abandoned. We will explain how to determine CLK_{Bin2} with our adaptive clock configuration technique in the next section. The timing error counts of passed circuits need to be compared with the pivot. Circuits with less timing errors are selected into Bin2, and the others are abandoned. Notice that the pivot in Bin2 testing is the same as Bin1's, because it reflects the expected error rate decided in the design phase.

Our proposed performance binning method takes advantage of the presence of error detection circuits, and uses

them to evaluate the quality of circuits. However, timing error counters are needed to count the number of ERROR signals from the OR-tree output of each pipeline stage in Fig. 2. In modern processor designs, on-chip performance counters might already be available as part of the normal operation [18]. Therefore these counters can be reused in the test mode to count the number of timing errors, and the hardware overhead can be small. The numbers in the counters will be shifted out for binning analysis. We emphasize that structural at-speed delay testing shown in 5 is the traditional delay testing, and the error count can be obtained by scanning out the final-error-FFs or by scanning out the embedded counters if they exist.

4.3 Evaluation Method

Error rate determines the performance of a resilient system for a specific clock frequency. When we estimate the error rate (P), it is the probability that there exists at least one path to the EDS(s) with delay (T_{EDS}) longer than the system clock cycle (T), which is simply represented by

$$P = Pr(T_{EDS}(x) > T | x \in \text{input vectors}) \qquad (5)$$

To calculate error rate P, we need to derive the sensitization probability of every path in the circuit, which is an NP-hard problem for general circuits [7]. Another way to calculate error rate is to use timing simulation in Eq. 6 shown below.

$$P = \frac{\text{timing errors \# on EDS}}{\text{test vectors \# simulated}} \qquad (6)$$

However, to calculate the exact P requires an exhaustive simulation, which needs to simulate all possible input combinations. To reduce time complexity, in our experiments we use a Monte Carlo simulation method to apply random test vectors to approximate the real error rate for each circuit, and we developed a timing simulator based on [11].

Fig. 6 shows plot of the circuit error rate obtained from the random test vector simulation versus the timing error count from structural at-speed delay testing on benchmark circuit C5315. We made 1,000 circuits with process variations injected into each chip, described in the following section, and each node in the figure represents a circuit. The X axis stands for the timing error number counted in the structural at-speed delay testing, and the structural testing is simulated with the delay fault test vectors, particularly the test vectors of EDS-max and FF-max delay testing. The Y axis is the error rate from random test vector simulation.

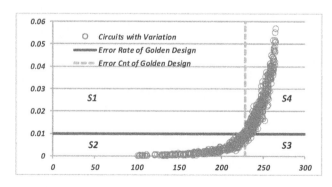

Figure 6: Plot of timing error count in structural at-speed testing (x-axis) and error rate (y-axis) for benchmark circuit C5315.

Ideally, error rate of the golden design (without process variation), the solid line in Fig. 6, determines the boundary of two bins – circuits with lower error rate are in $Bin1$, while others will be further tested for $Bin2$. By using structural delay testing for binning, the golden timing error count, the dotted line in Fig. 6, is the pivot for bin selection. This count is obtained by fault simulation on the golden design with the same delay test patterns that are used to test fabricated circuits. After a circuit finishes and passes its structural testing, its timing error count is compared with the pivot to determine its bin. For example, in Fig. 6, the passed C5315 circuits are selected into $Bin1$ in $S1 + S2$, while circuits in $S3 + S4$ need to be tested for $Bin2$ later. However, by the golden error rate value, the circuits should be binned into $S1 + S4$ and $S2 + S3$. Therefore, circuits in $S1 + S3$ are wrongly binned, and the number of chips in $S1 + S3$ represents the accuracy of our method. Notice that circuits in $S1$ will be sold at a high price, but in fact they are not of high performance, which is not tolerable. Contrarily, the fast circuits in $S3$ will be sold as low-price products. This inaccuracy is tolerable, but it leads to loss of profits.

5. ADAPTIVE CLOCK CONFIGURATION FOR YIELD

5.1 Clock Duty Tuning Method

For the Bin2 clock, it has larger time slack than the Bin1 clock to rescue a number of failed circuits. However, different from traditional circuits, resilient system has more timing constraints. Our proposed method tries to find an optimal proportion of the time slack to the different timing constraints to save more failed circuits. In Fig. 7, three types of faults discussed above are attached on CLK_{Bin1} at their individual timing periods of occurrences, represented by dotted arrows. CLK_{Bin1} is determined in the design phase, and CLK_{Bin2} has a longer period which is set as $1.1 \times CLK_{Bin1}$ in this study. However, due to the EDS min-delay constraint in Eq. (2), T_w cannot be increased when the clock period is increased. For CLK_{Bin2} in Fig. 7, $\delta_{FFmax,ori.}$ and $\delta_{EDSmax,ori.}$(both $= 0.1 \times CLK_{Bin1}$) add time slacks for the FF and EDS max-delay constraints, and thus save the failed circuits by these two fault types respectively. However, because Ori. CLK_{Bin2} does not change T_w, this method cannot save any failed circuit due to EDS min-delay faults.

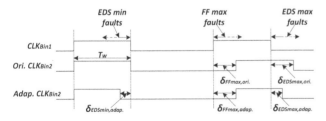

Figure 7: Resilient system performance binning timing diagram.

To improve the yield in $Bin2$, an adaptive clock configuration method is proposed for CLK_{Bin2}. By keeping $CLK_{Bin2} = 1.1 \times CLK_{Bin1}$, $\delta_{FFmax,adap.}$ has to be fixed as $0.1 \times CLK_{Bin1}$. Therefore only $\delta_{EDSmin,adap.}$ and $\delta_{EDSmax,adap.}$ are tunable. Intuitively, a certain amount of time slack can

be borrowed from the EDS max-delay constraint relaxation to save EDS min-delay faults, and thus the relaxation time can be used more effectively to save more failed circuits in total. As shown in Fig. 7, the adaptive $Bin2$ clock adds the time slack ($\delta_{EDSmin,adap.}$) on the EDS min-delay faults, but it shortens the EDS max-delay slack ($\delta_{EDSmax,adap.}$). To be specific, the ratio of $\delta_{EDSmin,adap.}$ to $\delta_{EDSmax,adap.}$ should be equal to the number of the failed circuits caused by EDS min-delay faults over the number by the EDS max-delay faults, expressed in Eq. (7). The sum of these two relaxation timing values has to be $0.1 \times CLK_{Bin1}$ in Eq. (8). By these two equations, an optimal adaptive CLK_{Bin2} configuration can be calculated. It is important to emphasize that, the proposed binning clock configuration method may cause more circuits failed by EDS max faults, but for the circuits that qualify both original and adaptive $Bin2$ clock, their performances (error rates) do not change. What is more, our method does not hurt the OR-tree timing constraint, and in fact it makes the constraint in [13] even more relaxed.

$$\frac{\delta_{EDSmin,adap.}}{\delta_{EDSmax,adap.}} = \frac{failed\ ckt.\ \#\ by\ EDS\ min\text{-}delay\ fault}{failed\ ckt.\ \#\ by\ EDS\ max\text{-}delay\ fault} \quad (7)$$

$$\delta_{EDSmin,adap.} + \delta_{EDSmax,adap.} = \delta_{EDSmax,ori.}$$
$$= 0.1 \times CLK_{Bin1} \quad (8)$$

5.2 Binning With Adaptive Clock Configuration

From the resilient system performance binning method presented in Fig. 5, the failed circuit numbers by EDS min-delay and EDS max-delay faults are counted to compute the adaptive $Bin2$ clock in Eq. (7). In practice, these two numbers are only counted on a sufficient number of fabricated circuits and it is a one time process. We call it *yield learning process*. In the yield learning process, if a circuit has a fault in the EDS min-delay test, it still needs to go through the EDS max-delay test to count the failed chip number for Eq. 7. However if a circuit that is not in the yield learning process has a fault, it goes to the $Bin2$ test immediately. It is worthwhile to note that when a circuit passes $Bin1$ delay testing but not its timing error count is smaller than the pivot, this circuit goes to the $Bin2$ testing. However, it only needs to precess the EDS max-delay and FF max-delay testing for the count of timing errors, but not EDS min-delay testing, because our adaptive clock configuration relaxes min-delay constraint.

6. EXPERIMENTS AND RESULTS

6.1 Evaluation on Delay Testing Based Performance Binning

The performance binning method is simulated on ISCAS85 benchmark circuits for 1,000 chips for each circuit with different intra- and inter-die variations on gate and wire delays. Synopsys Design Compiler and Primetime are used for logic synthesis and timing analysis using a 45nm technology [1]. About top 10% critical FFs are converted to EDSs manually, and then buffers are inserted as engineering change order (ECO) fixing to meet the EDS min-delay constraint. Using the similar experimental setup in [14], we choose K longest testable EDS paths, K longest testable normal FF paths, and K shortest testable EDS paths respectively to generate test patterns by TetraMax, where K is approximately equal to the number of gates in the circuit. The numbers of examined (tested) paths, testable paths, and test vectors for each of the three timing constraints are listed in Tab. 1. The number of test vectors is less than that of testable paths in each item, because TetraMax performs test pattern compression.

Table 1: Benchmark circuits examined paths #/ testable paths #/ test vectors # for the three timing constraint testing.

Ckt.	EDS max-delay	EDS min-delay	FF max-delay
C880	240/240/55	240/240/92	245/242/87
C2670	860/385/248	425/385/102	387/385/37
C3540	2671/430/168	656/430/224	2387/430/122
C5315	1877/925/187	926/916/123	1144/916/85
C7552	2276/1029/216	1242/1025/139	1359/1028/232

As mentioned in Section 4, the proposed performance binning method uses timing error counts during structural testing to determine the bin selection. Tab. 2 shows the accuracy of our proposed method by error count vs. the golden binning method by error rate estimation method. The error rate of each circuit is calculated using a Monte Carlo simulation discussed in Subsection 4.3 implemented by using a timing simulator similar to [11]. In this table, columns two and three correspond to the numbers of circuits falling into regions S1 and S3 in Fig. 6. Column four is the ratio of the number of wrongly binned circuits (i.e. in S1 + S3) to the total number of circuits selected into Bin1 and Bin2 by our adaptive clock configuration method. The worst case occurs at C2670 where 11.0% of passed circuits are wrongly binned, while all other circuits have low rates and the average wrongly binned rate is 6.99%.

Table 2: The number of circuits wrongly binned by structural testing.

Ckt.	# in S1	# in S3	Wrongly Binned % (S1+S3)
C880	9	44	7.60%
C2670	93	14	12.13%
C3540	4	30	3.92%
C5315	2	42	5.28%
C7552	28	26	6.04%
Avg.			6.99%

6.2 Yield Improvement by Adaptive Clock Configuration

Yield improvement for both the original and adaptive clock configuration methods are compared in this experiment. Tab. 3 shows the results where columns two, three and five are the numbers of circuits in *Bin1*, and *Bin2* of the original and the adaptive methods. $Y_{Ori.}$ and $Y_{Adap.}$ stand for the yields by the original and adaptive methods, while Y Imp. is the yield improvement of our adaptive method over the original method. Our adaptive binning method improves yield by 11.9% on average. C880 has the largest yield improvement, because in C880 delay testing there exists a large proportion of EDS min-delay faults. Our method adaptively assigns more time slack on EDS min-delay faults to

fix them, which gives a better yield improvement. However the improvement on C7552 is minor, because few circuits are failed by EDS min-delay faults, and thus our adaptive method assigns the majority of time slack to EDS max-delay faults, which is the same as the original method. It is demonstrated that even in this extreme case, the adaptive method has the result as good as the orignal method.

Table 3: Adaptive clock configuration results.

Ckt.	Bin1	Bin2				Y Imp.
		Ori.	$Y_{Ori.}$	Adap.	$Y_{Adap.}$	
C880	233	458	69.1%	704	93.7%	35.6%
C2670	538	378	91.6%	448	98.6%	7.64%
C3540	403	463	86.6%	510	91.3%	5.43%
C5315	363	475	83.8%	566	92.9%	10.86%
C7552	468	435	90.3%	436	90.4%	0.11%
Avg.						11.9%

7. CONCLUSION

This paper is focused on performance binning for resilient systems and attempts to push forward the pace of resilient system commercialization. In this paper, we have studied performance binning for resilient systems for the first time. The performance binning method using timing error counts obtained during structural at-speed delay testing is proposed and evaluated for resilient systems. The wrongly binned percentage by our method is 6.99% on average. An adaptive clock configuration method has been proposed and experimental results showed it improves yield by 11.9% on average over the original method. Future works include: (1) developing an efficient hybrid solution combining our error count based method and functional binning method to reduce wrongly binned percentage, and (2) extending our binning method to multi-stage pipeline circuits.

8. REFERENCES

[1] Nangate open cell library. http://www.si2.org/openeda.si2.org/projects/nangatelib.

[2] D. Belete, A. Razdan, W. Schwarz, R. Raina, C. Hawkins, and J. Morehead. Use of dft techniques in speed grading a 1 ghz+ microprocessor. In *Proceedings of IEEE International Test Conference (ITC)*, pages 1111–1119, 2002.

[3] S. Borkar. Designing reliable systems from unreliable components: the challenges of transistor variability and degradation. *Proceedings of IEEE/ACM International Symposium on Microarchitecture (MICRO)*, 25(6):10–16, Nov.–Dec. 2005.

[4] S. Borkar, T. Karnik, S. Narendra, J. Tschanz, A. Keshavarzi, and V. De. Parameter variations and impact on circuits and microarchitecture. In *Proceedings of ACM/IEEE Design Automation Conference (DAC)*, pages 338–342, 2003.

[5] K. A. Bowman, J. Tschanz, S. Lu, P. Aseron, M. Khellah, A. Raychowdhury, B. Geuskens, C. Tokunaga, C. Wilkerson, T. Karnik, et al. A 45 nm resilient microprocessor core for dynamic variation tolerance. *IEEE Journal of Solid-State Circuits*, 46(1):194–208, Jan. 2011.

[6] K. A. Bowman, J. W. Tschanz, N. S. Kim, J. C. Lee, C. B. Wilkerson, S.-L. Lu, T. Karnik, and V. K. De. Energy-efficient and metastability-immune resilient circuits for dynamic variation tolerance. *IEEE Journal of Solid-State Circuits*, 44(1):49–63, Jan. 2009.

[7] J. Cong and K. Minkovich. Logic synthesis for better than worst-case designs. In *Proceedings of International Symposium on VLSI Design Automation and Test*, pages 166–169, 2009.

[8] B. D. Cory, R. Kapur, and B. Underwood. Speed binning with path delay test in 150-nm technology. *Proceedings of IEEE Design & Test of Computers*, 20(5):41–45, Sep.–Oct. 2003.

[9] A. Datta, S. Bhunia, J. H. Choi, S. Mukhopadhyay, and K. Roy. Speed binning aware design methodology to improve profit under parameter variations. In *Proceedings of IEEE/ACM Asia and South Pacific Design Automation Conference (ASP-DAC)*, pages 712–717, 2006.

[10] D. Ernst, N. Kim, S. Das, S. Pant, R. Rao, T. Pham, C. Ziesler, D. Blaauw, T. Austin, K. Flautner, et al. Razor: A low-power pipeline based on circuit-level timing speculation. In *Proceedings of IEEE/ACM International Symposium on Microarchitecture (MICRO)*, pages 7–18, 2003.

[11] P. Girard, C. Landrault, and S. Pravossoudovitch. A novel approach to delay-fault diagnosis. In *Proceedings ACM/IEEE Design Automation Conference (DAC)*, pages 357–360, 1992.

[12] B. Greskamp, L. Wan, U. R. Karpuzcu, J. J. Cook, J. Torrellas, D. Chen, and C. Zilles. Blueshift: Designing processors for timing speculation from the ground up. In *Proceedings of IEEE International Symposium on High Performance Computer Architecture (HPCA)*, pages 213–224, 2009.

[13] Q. Han, J. Guo, W.-B. Jone, and Q. Xu. Path delay testing in resilient system. In *IEEE International Midwest Symposium on Circuits and Systems (MWSCAS)*, pages 645–648, 2013.

[14] W. Qiu, X. Lu, J. Wang, Z. Li, D. Walker, and W. Shi. A statistical fault coverage metric for realistic path delay faults. In *Proceedings of IEEE VLSI Test Symposium (VTS)*, pages 37–42, 2004.

[15] A. Raychowdhury, S. Ghosh, and K. Roy. A novel on-chip delay measurement hardware for efficient speed-binning. In *Proceedings of IEEE International On-Line Testing Symposium (IOLTS)*, pages 287–292, 2005.

[16] J. Sartori, A. Pant, R. Kumar, and P. Gupta. Variation-aware speed binning of multi-core processors. In *IEEE International Symposium on Quality Electronic Design (ISQED)*, pages 307–314, 2010.

[17] J. Saxena, K. M. Butler, J. Gatt, R. Raghuraman, S. P. Kumar, S. Basu, D. J. Campbell, and J. Berech. Scan-based transition fault testing-implementation and low cost test challenges. In *Proceedings of IEEE International Test Conference (ITC)*, pages 1120–1129, 2002.

[18] B. Sprunt. Pentium 4 performance-monitoring features. *Proceedings of IEEE/ACM International Symposium on Microarchitecture (MICRO)*, 22(4):72–82, Jul.–Aug. 2002.

[19] L. Wan and D. Chen. Dynatune: circuit-level optimization for timing speculation considering dynamic path behavior. In *Proceedings of IEEE/ACM International Conference on Computer-Aided Design (ICCAD)*, pages 172–179, 2009.

[20] L.-T. Wang, C.-W. Wu, and X. Wen. *VLSI test principles and architectures: design for testability*. Morgan Kaufmann, 2006.

[21] F. Yuan, Y. Liu, W.-B. Jone, and Q. Xu. On testing timing-speculative circuits. In *Proceedings of ACM/IEEE Design Automation Conference (DAC)*, pages 1–6, 2013.

[22] J. Zeng, M. Abadir, G. Vandling, L. Wang, A. Kolhatkar, and J. Abraham. On correlating structural tests with functional tests for speed binning of high performance design. In *Proceedings of IEEE International Test Conference (ITC)*, pages 31–37, 2004.

[23] V. Zolotov, C. Visweswariah, and J. Xiong. Voltage binning under process variation. In *Proceedings of IEEE/ACM International Conference on Computer-Aided Design (ICCAD)*, pages 425–432, 2009.

From 2D to Monolithic 3D:
Design Possibilities, Expectations and Challenges

Olivier Billoint[1], Hossam Sarhan[1], Iyad Rayane[2], Maud Vinet[1], Perrine Batude[1],
Claire Fenouillet-Beranger[1], Olivier Rozeau[1], Gerald Cibrario[1], Fabien Deprat[1],
Ogun Turkyilmaz[1], Sebastien Thuries[1], Fabien Clermidy[1]

[1]Univ. Grenoble Alpes, F-38000 Grenoble, France
CEA, LETI, MINATEC Campus, F-38054 Grenoble, France
[2]Mentor Graphics, 110 rue Blaise Pascal, 38330 Montbonnot-Saint-Martin, France
olivier.billoint@cea.fr

ABSTRACT

Design of conventional 2D integrated circuits is becoming more and more challenging as we strive to keep on following Moore's law. Cost, thermal behavior, multiple patterning, increasing number of design rules, transistor characteristics, variability and back end properties coupled with a constant need for a higher integration of functions / peripherals are creating an increasingly complex equation to solve for designers. Moving to the next node and taking advantage of the technology are now far from being straightforward as time to market has never been so short for industry. In order to overcome or at least postpone the time when we'll have to face the "next node migration constraints", a possible solution could be staying at the same node and go 3D with possible benefits such as wire length reduction, power savings and increased operating frequency. Since more than ten years now, interconnect technologies like Through Silicon Via (TSV), High Density (HD)-TSV and Copper to Copper (Cu-Cu) have arisen to take advantage of this possible 3-dimensional physical implementation with proofs of concept [1] or more recently industrial products [2]. Main drawback of these technologies is that they are not shrinking at the same speed as transistors are, making them somehow power hungry; moreover the more they will shrink, the more precision will be needed for chip to chip alignment. To reach the highest possible standard cell and tier to tier interconnect densities required for cost-effective chips, 3D sequential integration process [3][4][5] (also known as Monolithic 3D or CoolCube™) is currently developed with main features being sequential fabrication of MOS layers and correlation of tier to tier interconnect size with process node allowing fine-grain 3D partitioning of designs. These particularities make it a durable opportunity to slow down next node design migration while still improving integration. To fully benefit from CoolCube™ technology, a whole new way of designing circuits, from synthesis to place and route, will be required as some new challenges will arise. The point of this presentation is to show the possible use and limitations of the aforementioned technologies with a focus on Monolithic 3D and to give some insights about market expectations, challenges and available design techniques.

ISPD'15, March 29 - April 1, 2015, Monterey, CA, USA.
ACM 978-1-4503-3399-3/15/03.
http://dx.doi.org/10.1145/2717764.2723573

Categories and Subject Descriptors

B.7.1 [**Integrated Circuits**]: Types and Design Styles – *Advanced Technologies, VLSI (very large scale integration)*.

General Terms

Performance, Design, Reliability.

Keywords

CoolCube™; Monolithic 3D; TSV; Cu-Cu; Design; Place&Route.

Short Biography

Olivier Billoint received the M.S degree in electrical engineering from ISEN (Institut Supérieur de l'Electronique et du Numérique), France, in 2002. In 2003, he joined CEA-LETI IC Design Department where he has been working on analog and mixed-signal circuits for imagers and displays until 2010. Since 2011 he is working on monolithic 3D digital design and benchmark. He has 20 publications and 6 patents.

REFERENCES

[1] B. Black, D.W. Nelson, C. Webb and N. Samra, 3D processing technology and its impact on iA32 microprocessors. In proceedings of the 2004 IEEE International Conference on Computer Design (ICCD). DOI: 10.1109/ICCD.2004.1347939

[2] Samsung Starts Mass Producing Industry's First 3D TSV Technology Based DDR4 Modules for Enterprise Servers, Seoul, Korea on August 28th 2014, http://www.samsung.com/global/business/semiconductor/news-events/press-releases/printer?newsId=13602

[3] P. Batude, B. Sklenard, C. Fenouillet-Beranger, B. Previtali, C. Tabone, O. Rozeau, O. Billoint, O. Turkyilmaz, H. Sarhan, S. Thuries, G. Cibrario, L. Brunet, F. Deprat, J.-E. Michallet, F. Clermidy, M. Vinet. 3D sequential integration opportunities and technology optimization. In proceedings of the 2014 IEEE Interconnect Technology Conference / Advanced Metallization Conference (IITC/AMC). DOI: 10.1109/IITC.2014.6831837

[4] M. Shulaker, T. Wu, A. Pal, K. Saraswat, H.-S.P. Wong, S. Mitra, Monolithic 3D Integration of Logic and Memory: Carbon Nanotube FETs, Resistive RAM, and Silicon FETs. In Proceedings of the 2014 IEEE International Electron Devices Meeting (IEDM).

[5] Z. Or-Bach. The monolithic 3D advantage: Monolithic 3D is far more than just an alternative to 0.7x scaling. In proceedings of the 2013 IEEE 3D Systems Integration Conference (3DIC). DOI: 10.1109/3DIC.2013.6702316

Early Days of Circuit Placement

Martin D. F. Wong
Department of Electrical and Computer Engineering
University of Illinois at Urbana-Champaign

Abstract

In this talk, we will give a brief survey of circuit placement techniques in the early days of EDA. We will present the main contributions by Prof. Kurt Antreich on circuit placement, focusing on the classical works GORDIAN and DOMINO.

Categories and Subject Descriptors

B7.2 **[Integrated Circuits]:** Design Aids - *Placement and routing*

Keywords

circuit placement

Speaker Bio

Martin D. F. Wong received his Ph.D. in CS from the University of Illinois at Urbana-Champaign (UIUC) in 1987. From 1987-2002, he was a faculty member at UT-Austin. He is currently the Executive Associate Dean in the College of Engineering and the Edward C. Jordan Professor in Electrical and Computer Engineering at UIUC. His primary research area is EDA focusing on physical design. He has published over 400 papers and graduated more than 40 Ph.D. students in EDA. He is a Fellow of IEEE.

ISPD '15, March 29–April 1, 2015, Monterey, California, USA.
ACM 978-1-4503-3399-3/15/03.
http://dx.doi.org/10.1145/2717764.2717788

Force-Directed Placement of VLSI Circuits

Hans Eisenmann
PDF Solutions
hans.eisenmann@pdf.com

ABSTRACT

The placement significantly influences the quality of a circuit. In the past decades a lot of placement algorithms were presented. The most popular ones are summarized here. Force-directed placers are able to place VLSI circuits with low wirelength within a suitable time. Examples for force-directed placers are Kraftwerk and Kraftwerk2, which start with an initial placement and use forces to evenly distribute the modules inside the placement area.

Categories and Subject Descriptors

B.7.2 [**Integrated Circuits**]: Design Aids—*Layout, Placement and Routing*

Keywords

force-directed placement; Kraftwerk; Kraftwerk2

1. INTRODUCTION

The placement of an integrated circuit (IC) strongly influences the quality of the IC. A good placement algorithm at least minimizes the wirelength and matches timing constraints at the same time. Additional objective functions like the minimization of the highest local temperature on the chip can be interesting as well. Commonly, the placement task is formulated as the minimization of the wirelength while placing all components overlap-free inside the chip area. The minimization of the wirelength indirectly improves the timing and power consumption of the IC. Due to the increasing complexity of today's circuits fast and efficient algorithms are needed for the automatic placement. Common placement algorithms can be divided into different groups, one of which are the force-directed placement algorithms. These view the placement problem as determining the equilibrium state of a spring system. Force-directed placers are able to determine a layout with low wirelength with reasonable computational effort.

The rest of this paper is structured as follows: In Section 2 we present a classification of placement algorithms. In Section 3 and 4 we give an overview about Kraftwerk and Kraftwerk2 respectively. We conclude in Section 5.

2. CLASSIFICATION OF PLACEMENT ALGORITHMS

Within the last decades a lot of different global placement algorithms were proposed. Stochastic placers often use the principles of Simulated Annealing (e.g. Timberwolf [14]) or of Genetic Algorithms. Another class of placement algorithms use greedy approaches or the principle of cluster growth. More popular is the idea of MinCut-based placers like Capo [11] and Dragon [15]. Analytical placers formulate the placement problem as a linear, quadratic or nonlinear function. The placers mPL [4], APlace [8], NTU-Place [5] and Vaastu [1] use a nonlinear function. Analytical quadratic placers can be based on Eigenvalues, partitioning or force-directed approaches. Partitioning algorithms such as Gordian [9] and BonnPlace [3] iteratively divide the placement area and the net list. Force-directed placers use forces to distribute the modules iteratively and equally on the placement area. Examples of force-directed placers are mFAR [7], FastPlace [16], Kraftwerk [6] and Kraftwerk2 [13]. In the following Kraftwerk and Kraftwerk2 are presented in more detail.

3. KRAFTWERK

Kraftwerk follows the basic approach of formulating the optimization objective as weighted sum of the quadratic distances between the modules, i.e.,

$$\sum_{i,j} \frac{1}{2} \left(\omega_{ij,x}(x_i - x_j)^2 + \omega_{ij,y}(y_i - y_j)^2 \right) \qquad (1)$$

Here, x_i and y_i denote the x- and y-coordinate of module i. The weights w_{ij} result from a clique model for nets: Each net connecting k modules is transformed into a clique of two-pin connections among the k modules with a weight of $\frac{2}{k}$ for each two-pin connection. The netlist is then modeled as a graph with modules as vertices and with edges between the modules with a weight that is the sum of weights of all two-pin connections from the clique transformation. A number of modules are fixed with predefined positions. If a movable module (i.e., one to be placed) is connected to such a fixed module, the corresponding term in Eq. (1) will yield a linear and a constant component. If the coordinates for movable modules are collected in a vector $\mathbf{p} = (x_1, \ldots, x_n, y_1, \ldots, y_n)$, the optimization objective can therefore be written in the following form:

$$\frac{1}{2}\mathbf{p}^T\mathbf{Cp} + \mathbf{d}^T\mathbf{p} + const \qquad (2)$$

ISPD'15, March 29–April 1, 2015, Monterey, CA, USA.
ACM 978-1-4503-3399-3/15/04.
http://dx.doi.org/10.1145/2717764.2717787

The minimization of (2) is realized by setting the derivative to 0:

$$\mathbf{Cp} + \mathbf{d} = \mathbf{0} \qquad (3)$$

This equation can be interpreted as modeling the nets as springs and calculating the state of equilibrium. A solution of this equation will result in a placement with minimal wirelength but a lot of module overlap and some modules might not be placed inside the chip area. In Kraftwerk an additional force $\mathbf{e}$ is added to equation (3) to remove cell overlap and to consider the chip area.

$$\mathbf{Cp} + \mathbf{d} + \mathbf{e} = \mathbf{0} \qquad (4)$$

The additional force $\mathbf{e}$ working on a given module only depends on the current center position of this module. The forces attract the modules to regions with lower density. No circular forces are allowed and the forces should be zero in infinity. Choosing the forces corresponding to these requirements results in a Poisson's equation, whose solution is used to determine the additional forces. Kraftwerk is an iterative approach. Initially, all modules are placed at the center of the chip area and the additional forces $\mathbf{e}$ are set to zero. Then, the module overlap is removed iteratively. In each iteration Poisson's equation is solved, the additional forces are determined and equation (4) is solved. The iteration is stopped, if no empty square with the size of four times of the average module area exists on the chip area. Kraftwerk can also be adapted for timing, congestion or heat driven placement [10]. Compared to state-of-the-art placers of the time period when Kraftwerk was introduced to the scientific community, Kraftwerk reduced the wirelength by 6 to 8% using the same CPU time.

4. KRAFTWERK2: A NEW NETMODEL

The placer Kraftwerk2 is an improved and accelerated version of Kraftwerk. Because there is a significant difference between the clique net model and the half-perimeter wirelength (HPWL), Kraftwerk2 uses the Bound2Bound net model, which has a lower number of two-pin connections than the clique net model. All nets are split into their two-pin connections. Since inner two-pin connections do not have any influence on the HPWL of the net, they are neglected, which results in lower computation costs. The weights for the nets which are connected to the boundary pins are chosen corresponding to the HPWL. Furthermore, the additional force is separated into two forces: The move force and the hold force. For the first time the move force is modeled with the help of target points. These are directly given by the Poisson potential, which is given by a demand and supply system. The move force attracts the modules to less congested regions. The hold force is a constant force, which does not depend on any fixed points. The hold force compensates the net force in each iteration to ensure that the modules are not collapsed back to the center of the chip. Kraftwerk2 is an iterative approach. First, all modules are placed initially with minimal net length. Then, iteratively, the net force, hold force and move force are calculated, where the move force is obtained with the help of a demand and supply system and the solution of Poisson's equation. The sum of all three forces is set to 0:

$$\mathbf{F_{net}} + \mathbf{F_{move}} + \mathbf{F_{hold}} = \mathbf{0}, \qquad (5)$$

which corresponds to the solution of a linear equation system. A quality control at the end of each iteration either ensures fast convergence or can be used to improve the quality of the placement. This iteration is repeated until the module overlap is less than 20%. The remaining overlap of macro modules is removed with the help of a quadratic program solver. The standard cells are shifted to the standard cell rows by Abacus [12]. The module density can be controlled with the help of an advanced approach for the module supply. In addition, halos around large modules can be prevented by the advanced module demand.

In the ISPD 2006 contest the quality of the layouts was measured by a scoring function, which contains the HPWL, CPU time and an overflow factor. Kraftwerk2 won this contest.

5. CONCLUSION

Force-directed placers are able to create layouts of VLSI circuits with low wirelength and a low runtime. We presented Kraftwerk and Kraftwerk2, which outperformed most state-of-the-art placers of the time they were published. In future research, the basics of Kraftwerk and Kraftwerk2 can be used for the placement of new technologies such as 3D integrated circuits. Kraftwerk also paved the foundation for placement and routing research in emerging technologies such as ONoCs [2].

6. REFERENCES

[1] A. R. Agnihotri et al. Fast analytic placement using minimum cost flow. In *ASPDAC*, 2007.

[2] A. Boos et al. Proton: An automatic place-and-route tool for optical networks-on-chip. In *ICCAD*, 2013.

[3] U. Brenner et al. Faster and better global placement by a new transportation algorithm. In *DAC*, 2005.

[4] T. F. Chan et al. mpl6: Enhanced multilevel mixed-size placement. In *ISPD*, 2006.

[5] T.-C. Chen et al. Ntuplace3: An analytical placer for large-scale mixed-size designs with preplaced blocks and density constraints. *TCAD*, 27:1228–1240, 2008.

[6] H. Eisenmann et al. Generic global placement and floorplanning. In *DAC*, 1998.

[7] B. Hu et al. Multilevel fixed-point-addition-based vlsi placement. *TCAD*, 24:1188–1203, 2005.

[8] A. B. Kahng et al. Implementation and extensibility of an analytic placer. *TCAD*, 24:734–747, 2005.

[9] J. M. Kleinhans et al. Gordian: a new global optimization/rectangle dissection method for cell placement. In *ICCAD*, 1988.

[10] B. Obermeier et al. Temperature-aware global placement. In *ASPDAC*, 2004.

[11] J. A. Roy et al. Capo: Robust and scalable open-source min-cut floorplacer. In *ISPD*, 2005.

[12] P. Spindler et al. Abacus: Fast legalization of standard cell circuits with minimal movement. In *ISPD*, 2008.

[13] P. Spindler et al. Kraftwerk2: A fast force-directed quadratic placement approach using an accurate net model. *TCAD*, pages 1398–1411, Aug 2008.

[14] S. Sutanthavibul et al. An adaptive timing-driven placement for high performance vlsis. *TCAD*, 12:1488–1498, 1993.

[15] T. Taghavi et al. Dragon2005: Large-scale mixed-size placement tool. In *ISPD*, 2005.

[16] N. Viswanathan et al. Fastplace: efficient analytical placement using cell shifting, iterative local refinement,and a hybrid net model. *TCAD*, 24:722–733, 2005.

Beyond GORDIAN and Kraftwerk: EDA Research at TUM

Ulf Schlichtmann
Institute for Electronic Design Automation
Technische Universität München
ulf.schlichtmann@tum.de

ABSTRACT

At the Institute for Electronic Design Automation of Technische Universität München (TUM), founded in 1975 by Prof. Kurt Antreich as Germany's first university institute dedicated to EDA, a broad range of research has been performed in the past 40 years. We describe here the research activities that Prof. Antreich undertook in addition to his research on physical design, as well as the physical design research undertaken in the past decade after his official retirement.

Categories and Subject Descriptors

B.7.2 [**Integrated Circuits**]: Design Aids—*Simulation, Placement and Routing*

Keywords

ATPG, logic simulation, logic synthesis, analog design centering, PCB routing, analog placement, optical network-on-chip layout

1. INTRODUCTION

Kurt Antreich founded TUM's Institute for Electronic Design Automation in 1975. At the time, it was still called Institute for Computer-Aided Design. It was the first institute dedicated to EDA research in Germany. Under the three decade-long guidance of Prof. Antreich, it became a widely recognized force in EDA research, and continues to thrive today.

The research on physical design, which Kurt Antreich initiated and then built up over many years, later joined by Frank Johannes, is well covered by other papers in this session. Here, we will describe two additional aspects of the research undertaken at his institute. First, we will report in Section 2 on research activities besides physical design which Kurt Antreich undertook during his tenure of almost three decades. Section 3 then describes current research activi-

ties at the institute which address diverse topics in physical design, building on Kurt Antreich's legacy.

2. RESEARCH BEYOND PHYSICAL DESIGN

Kurt Antreich's EDA research has always been characterized not only by the scientific rigor with which he attacked problems, but also by the fact that he focused on a small number of research areas, which he then worked on for decades, making groundbreaking contributions.

2.1 Analog Design Centering

When Prof. Antreich joined TUM in 1975, after an illustrious career of more than 15 years in industry, his initial focus was EDA (still called CAD at the time) for analog circuits - which even today still is a hallmark of the chair. Specifically, he attacked the problem of design centering. In the 1970s and early 80s, many researchers approached the yield optimization problem with a geometric approach of inscribing maximum ellipsoids in approximations of the tolerance region, e.g., the group around Steve Director at Carnegie Mellon University [1,2]. Kurt Antreich focused instead on a statistical approach based on Monte-Carlo analysis. In [3,4], he presented a complete derivation of first- and second-order yield derivatives and a quadratic programming approach. In addition, the step length procedure was supported by a yield variance prediction formula that considers the accuracy of the yield estimation. This approach gained a lot of international attention and established Kurt Antreich's reputation as one of those who "mathematically beat a technical problem to death".

Another important contribution of Kurt Antreich was in nominal sizing of analog circuits. In the 1980s, automatic optimization was possible mathematically, yet, analog circuit sizing required a lot of design knowledge which was not formulated as constraints to the optimization problem. A mathematical optimization tool, not given the technical constraints, then tuned the circuit in the wrong way, which only became visible when looking at properties a-posteriori. Against this background, Kurt Antreich proposed an interactive optimization process [5]. The crux of his approach was the so-called characteristic boundary curve, which illustrates the progress towards given targets over the change in design parameters, based on a Gauss-Newton approach augmented by a trust-region support. He derived that technical problems, with typically lots of degrees of freedom resulting in ill-conditioned optimization problems, lead to sharp bends in the characteristic boundary curve. This allowed for interactively determining good optimization steps, which are short but provide significant improvement.

Later on, an interesting swap in approaching design centering between Antreich and the CMU group of Director happened. While Director moved to yield optimization with statistical methods [6], Antreich took the geometric approach [7, 8]. He approached by defining the statistical parameter set with largest probability of violating a spec. This general definition of worst-case has been used very early in civil engineering and implicitly applied in circuit design [9]. But Antreich developed the mathematical foundation for generally computing worst-case points and formulating design centering as a deterministic multi-objective optimization problem. A tool called WiCkeD was created, whose name refers to the Worst-Case Distance as a user-friendly metric of each performance's robustness in x-sigma [10].

Together with the first systematic and automatic approach to construct sizing constraints [11], the way for automatic sizing and design centering of analog integrated circuits in industry was now paved. While the corresponding tools of CMU's Rob Rutenbar [12, 13] found their way to Cadence, the TUM spin-off MunEDA with its tool suite for nanometer design today is an independent EDA vendor [http://www.muneda.com].

2.2 ATPG and Logic Simulation

In the mid-1980s, EDA for IC testing followed as the next major focus area of the institute. Initially, Kurt Antreich tackled the task of Automatic Test Pattern Generation (ATPG) for combinational circuits. Building on Fujiwara's FAN algorithm [14], SOCRATES was developed [15, 16]. The tool combined improvements in fault simulation with significant enhancements of the test pattern generation itself. Key were techniques to reduce the search space. Most important was the concept of global implications in addition to local implications, which previously had been considered only. Global implications could be determined in a preprocessing step. Also, sensitization and multiple backtrack procedures were optimized. These enhancements dramatically improved the efficiency of ATPG. Enhanced techniques for redundancy identification then further improved the performance of SOCRATES [17]. For many years, SOCRATES clearly marked the state of the art in ATPG. It was the first ATPG tool which managed to identify all non-testable faults in a common suite of 10 benchmark circuits. SOCRATES was used in industry, it actually became part of the CAD system that Siemens was building at the time. With the task of ATPG for combinational circuits essentially solved, sequential circuits were then tackled by the tool ESSENTIAL [18].

Next, testing for delay faults was addressed. Both simulation and ATPG for delay faults were considered, using the path delay model. For the resulting ATPG tool DYNAMITE [19] again, a powerful implication procedure was key, as well as a stepwise sensitization procedure. Further optimization was obtained through a new path selection procedure which eliminated unsensitizable paths. The techniques were built on both a 10-valued and a 3-valued logic. This research was later extended [20, 21].

Related to ATPG was research on improved logic simulation techniques for digital circuits which was initiated in the late 1980s. Much of this research was part of a large German research effort on parallel computing. Therefore, a major focus of the simulation research was on how large circuits could be partitioned such that their simulation could be distributed over many compute engines. The concept of corrola partitioning proved to be very useful in this context [22], as did the application of the Time-Warp concept to logic simulation [23]. Dynamic Load Balancing further improved the simulation efficiency [24].

2.3 Logic Synthesis

Finally, in the late 1980s, logic synthesis was tackled. At the time, FPGAs were just starting to make their first serious appearances in industry. However, little research effort had been devoted to supporting their specific architectures in the design flow. This became the initial target of the logic synthesis research of Kurt Antreich. Both architectures based on Lookup-Tables (LUTs, e.g. Altera, Xilinx) as well as based on multiplexers (e.g. Actel) were addressed. For LUT architectures, the focus was on efficient techniques for Boolean function decomposition using BDDs [25]. For multiplexer-based architectures, Boolean Matching algorithms based on signatures of Boolean functions [26, 27] as well as algorithms for efficient mapping on BDDs were proposed [28]. The algorithms were implemented into a tool called TOS (Technology Oriented Synthesis), which was used at industrial partners such as Siemens, and also commercially distributed by German EDA companies at the time. As TOS contained a large library of fundamental algorithms for logic synthesis and technology mapping, it proved to be a useful foundation for further synthesis research. Of course, this research and the tool TOS also built on the groundbreaking work done e.g. at UC Berkeley and CMU [29, 30]. Later, the work on decomposition of Boolean functions was extended to multiple-output functions, utilizing implicit algorithms and relational representations [31–34].

Thereafter the focus of logic synthesis research widened further. As power consumption became a more important consideration in design optimization, a fast technique for computing the power consumption in digital circuits was developed [35]. In the mid-90s, leakage power was not a concern yet, so dynamic power clearly dominated, which in turn depends on how often a gate switches. Thus the key for power estimation on logic level was to compute the switching probabilities of all logic gates in the circuit. An efficient method to compute the switching probabilities with consideration of correlations was proposed. It is based on analysis of the circuit structure to identify re-convergence regions, and on decomposition of Boolean functions into statistically independent components to allow an efficient, BDD-based computation of switching probabilities [36, 37].

Then, Retiming was considered. Specifically, its application to FPGA architectures was optimized [38]. In a next step, the competencies of the physical design and the synthesis groups were combined and layout information was considered during retiming [39].

3. BRANCHING OUT IN PHYSICAL DESIGN

After Prof. Antreich's and Prof. Johannes' retirement, research on physical design was continued at TUM's EDA institute. The addressed topics started to become more diverse, however. The guiding principles advocated by Kurt Antreich still form the foundation of the research: the desire to obtain a very thorough and deep understanding of a problem before a solution is attempted; a strong focus on mathematically sound deterministic solution approaches; implementation of developed algorithms into prototype tools capable of solving real-life industry problems as a proof of concept.

Initially, the institute's long-standing competencies in both physical design and analog EDA were combined to reignite research on physical design for analog circuits (Section 3.1). Then, the research on timing analysis which had been undertaken in the logic synthesis group in the meantime (e.g. [40, 41]) was considered in a topic dedicated to improving the timing of PCB routing (Section 3.2). The most recent activity is physical design for optical networks on chip (ONoCs), described in Section 3.3.

3.1 Plantage: Analog Layout

For analog circuits, a multitude of constraints must be considered during physical design to ensure correct functionality of the resulting circuit. The purpose of these constraints is to minimize the impact of process variations, parasitics and different operating conditions on circuit performance. Constraints to be taken into account are: matching, proximity, symmetry, common centroid, minimum distance, variants. Variant constraints recognize that while there may be different options to implement a certain device (e.g. number of fingers of a transistor, or aspect ratios of capacitors), for devices that need to be matched, identical choices should be taken.

Physical Design for analog and mixed-signal circuits had been on the minds of Kurt Antreich and Frank Johannes already in the early 1990s. First research activities were initiated together with TEMIC, resulting in TINA [42]. TINA is based on GORDIAN [43] and proceeds in two steps. GORDIAN computes an initial placement. The resulting global placement is then legalized by eliminating overlap and optimized. A recursive slicing tree is utilized. Shape functions are computed on every level of the slicing tree, starting from the leaf nodes. Net length can be minimized using modified shape functions. Only symmetry constraints could be considered, however.

In retrospective, the research was too early at the time. The complex boundary conditions of analog placements could not yet sufficiently be taken into account. Attitude in industry was split: while CAD departments saw an interesting opportunity for productivity improvement now that physical design for digital circuits had been widely automated, analog designers were certainly not receptive to the idea that their tasks could benefit from any EDA beyond SPICE simulators.

The topic was taken up again about a decade later. Again, the research was supported by interest of industrial partners, Infineon and TI. As more and more design tasks had been automated for the design of digital circuits, it was becoming ever more obvious to some design managers that analog design was emerging as a key bottleneck for productivity and correctness of design - both for purely analog ICs, and especially for the (small) analog parts of essentially digital ICs. Physical design of analog circuits stood out as a stage of the design flow that had not benefited from any automation yet (besides using P-cells). Martin Strasser's research, resulting in the tool Plantage [44], originated from this situation. Plantage focuses on placement of analog circuits, routing is not yet addressed.

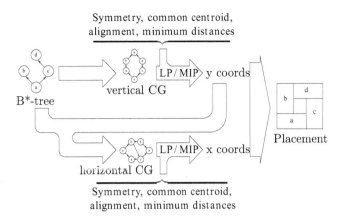

Figure 1: Placement generation from a B*-tree considering constraints.

While initial research into analog placement used absolute coordinates, topological representations have the advantage of a much smaller solution space and thus exhibit superior computational complexity. Still, all admissible placements [45] can be encoded. Topological representations include Sequence Pair [46], Bounded Sliceline Grid [47], O-Tree [45, 48], Corner Block List [49, 50], TCG-S [51], and B*-tree [52, 53]. Plantage is based on B*-trees, as this representation exhibits the lowest redundancy in the solution space.

While previous approaches to physical design of analog circuits [48, 50, 53–59] were based on stochastic approaches (primarily Simulated Annealing), Plantage took a deterministic approach - in line with the strong conviction of Kurt Antreich that while deterministic approaches are more difficult to implement as they require a significantly deeper understanding of the problem to be solved, they will reward the researcher with superior results and computational efficiency. Plantage could also consider more different types of constraints than any previous approach.

Plantage employs relations to represent constraints. Especially symmetry constraints can be represented very elegantly. From this relational representation the required inorder or preorder traversals of the B*-trees are derived which ensure that constraints are obeyed. Then horizontal and vertical constraint graphs are derived from the B*-trees. Using graph-theory concepts, these can be converted into a linear program which also takes the constraints into account. Minimum distance constraints can be considered very efficiently. For piecewise linear constraints (e.g. minimum distances for deep trench isolation transistors) a mixed-integer optimization problem is formulated. Enhanced shape functions are proposed which represent not only the aspect ratios of all possible Pareto-optimal placement options, but also the respective B*-trees. This allows to combine subcircuits represented by B*-trees on higher levels.

Ideally, all possible B*-trees of a given circuit would be enumerated, since they can generate all admissible placements. This is computationally infeasible for circuits of industrially relevant size, since the number of B*-trees grows more than exponentially in the number of modules that are to be placed. Thus Plantage chooses a mixed approach, using the hierarchy to bound enumeration. For basic module sets, consisting of a few devices, exhaustive enumeration

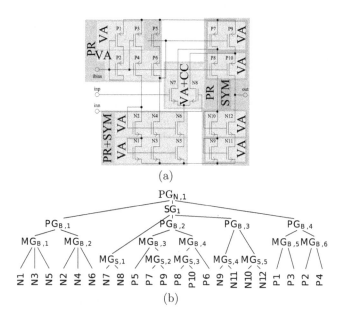

(a)

(b)

Figure 2: Example of a Folded Cascode op amp ([44], © IEEE 2008): Schematic (a) and hierarchy tree (b).

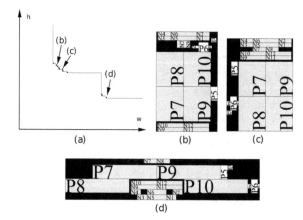

(a)   (b)   (c)

(d)

Figure 3: Example ([44], © IEEE 2008): Placements (b)-(d) and the corresponding shape function (a).

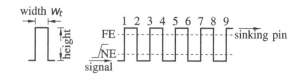

Figure 4: (a) Meander segment (b) A wire with concatenated meander segments (© IEEE 2013).

is performed. The results - all possible aspect ratios for the basic module set - are represented by enhanced shape functions. For identification of the basic module sets, the natural hierarchy of analog circuits is used. It is identified using structure recognition [60–63] and represented as a hierarchy tree. The creation of the hierarchy tree is guided by the relevant placement constraints, which help to speed up the enumeration significantly (Figure 1). The constraints are generated automatically. They are modeled in a placement requirement graph. For higher levels of the hierarchy tree, possible combinations of their child nodes are enumerated. In order to avoid white space, the combinations are not based on the bounding boxes of their components, but instead an approach is used which derives a combined placement from the B*-trees of the components.

Results on standard benchmark circuits demonstrate that Plantage beats most previous approaches in terms of the resulting circuit area and is on par with the best previous work, while being more industrially applicable due to its ability to consider more types of constraints than previous approaches. Figure 2 shows the schematic and the resulting hierarchy tree of a folded cascode op amp. Figure 3 shows the shape function generated by Plantage in less than a minute. It consists of 12 possible aspect ratios, three of which are shown in the figure.

Also, Plantage is the first deterministic approach, thus giving repeatable results.

3.2 PCB Routing

In high-performance printed circuit boards (PCBs), delay matching between bus signals has become a mainstream problem, and several modern PCB routers [64,65] have proposed solutions based on length matching. In these methods, wires that do not have sufficient lengths are extended by creating snaking patterns in the routing, based on the assumption that signals across wires with the same length have the same delay. Since these patterns have a high rout-

ing density and can be relatively easily modeled, they have gained a wide acceptance. Figure 4 illustrates such a snaking pattern, which is called *meander segment* henceforth, and a wire with concatenated meander segments. NE and FE in Figure 4 are abbreviations of near end and far end, respectively.

All the methods above, however, do not consider the even distribution of meander segments. According to [66, 67], when a signal travels across meander segments, the crosstalks between the segments of the same wire accumulate gradually. Therefore, the signal may reach the sinking pin earlier than predicted. Consider the pattern in Figure 4. At time zero, the main signal switches at the near end of wire segment 1 and propagates from bottom to top. This signal stimulates crosstalk signals at the near ends of the other wire segments. Assume that the total propagation time of the signal from the near end of one wire segment to the far end of the next wire segment, or from the far end to the other near end, is t_d. At time t_d, the main signal reaches the far end of wire segment 2 and stimulates a new crosstalk voltage. This new voltage superposes on the crosstalk signal triggered by the main signal at time zero which reaches the far end of wire 3 also at t_d. This superposition process continues as the main signal propagates across each wire segment, and finally the crosstalk voltage may surpass the threshold of logic switching before the main signal, thus leading to a speedup effect on the wire.

If the crosstalk discussed above generates different speedup effects on different wires, the assumption of matching delays through matching wire lengths becomes invalid. To solve this problem, either the speedup effect on a wire should be modeled directly and compensated during length-matching, or the speedup effects on all wires should be reduced at the same time by extending the width of meander segments illustrated in Figure 4. The former method requires that wire

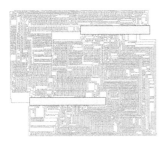

Figure 5: Routing result from [64] (© IEEE 2013).

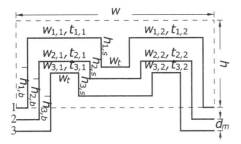

Figure 6: Model of meander segments for a wire group (© IEEE 2013).

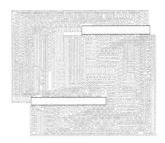

Figure 7: Refined routing by distributing wire patterns evenly in the routing area (© IEEE 2013).

delays can be evaluated accurately. But this is difficult in view of different numbers and varying shapes of meander segments. In addition, this method needs a close look on the signal propagation and is very sensitive to post-routing changes. On the contrary, the latter method tries to enlarge the widths of all meander segments at the same time so that crosstalks on all wires can be reduced. If the meander segments on all wires are expanded together in this way, they should be distributed evenly in the final routing without obvious dense wire patterns and unused routing area. Modern PCB routers, however, have not considered this unbalanced routing problem and may produce an uneven routing distribution. For example, the result of the highly efficient BSG-router is illustrated in Figure 5, where free spaces can be clearly observed.

To solve the uneven wire distribution problem, two methods have been proposed by TUM's EDA institute recently. The method in [68] takes an existing routing as input, and shifts meander segments along wires heuristically. If a meander segment can be moved to a free space, wire density is reduced. However, this method cannot produce a globally even distribution, because its iterative characteristic might lead to a local optimal result. The second method proposed in [69] first removes all dense meander patterns from a given routing. Thereafter, the wire group patterns are modeled mathematically, as shown in Figure 6. In this model, all the variables modeling the dimensions of these patterns are variables, from which the length of each wire in this pattern can be expressed directly. For example, the length of the first wire in this pattern can be calculated as $h_{1,b} + t_{1,1}w_{1,1} + h_{1,s} + w_t + t_{1,2}w_{1,2} + h_{1,b}$. Here the 0-1 variables $t_{1,1}$ and $t_{1,2}$ model whether upward patterns with the height $h_{1,s}$ appear in the patterns, respectively. While maintaining the original wire lengths from the given routing, the method in [69] maximizes the distance w_t between any segments in these dense patterns by solving an ILP problem transformed from the constraints with 0-1 variables.

Since the pattern generation in this method is performed by modeling the patterns in all free spaces at the same time, the dense wire patterns are pushed as far as possible from each other, so that the resulting routing is more evenly distributed. The routing shown in Figure 5 is improved by the method in [69] with a further segment shifting mechanism and the result is shown in Figure 7.

After enlarging the distance between any dense wire patterns, wire delays can be estimated by lengths more accurately because crosstalk on the same wire and thus the speedup effect are reduced significantly. In addition, the proposed method adjusts routing results from other routers, so that it can be integrated into an existing PCB design flow seamlessly.

3.3 PROTON: Physical Design of Optical NoCs

Optical Networks-on-Chip (ONoCs) are a promising technology to overcome bandwidth problems and improve the power consumption of multicore integrated systems. The physical design of an ONoC strongly influences the quality of the system [70]. Traditional place and route techniques developed for electronics cannot be utilized due to some key differences of ONoCs: only one layer is available for placing and routing the optical components; crossings of waveguides are permitted but should be minimized as they cause an increase of the required laser power. Previous work [71, 72] considered primarily routing only. PROTON [73] is the first algorithm to address both placement and routing for 3D ONoCs with the goal of minimizing the required laser power. As can be seen in Figure 8, PROTON assumes a 3D system consisting of a photonic layer, which is stacked on an electronic layer. On the electronic layer a grid of cores grouped into clusters is located. Each cluster is connected to a hub on the photonic layer via a Through-silicon-via (TSV). In addition, memory controllers are located on the photonic layer, which are connected to off-chip memory. Three different kinds of communication on the photonic layer have to be enabled: (a) between two hubs, (b) between a hub and a memory controller and (c) between a memory controller and a hub. Hubs and memory controllers are fixed and connected via waveguides and photonics switching elements (PSEs). Let a path be the connection between a hub and a memory controller or between two hubs. Then, the placement problem can be formulated as follows: Place all PSEs overlap-free inside the placement area on the photonic layer and route all waveguides on the same layer while minimizing the required laser power of the system. The system's laser power can be measured by the maximum insertion loss, which mainly depends on the waveguide length

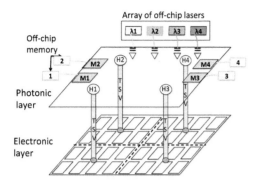

Figure 8: 3D Optical NoC (© IEEE 2013)

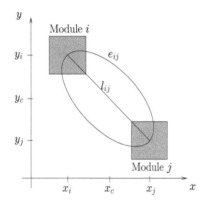

Figure 9: Net n_{ij} between module i and module j is approximated by line l_{ij}. Around l_{ij} the ellipse e_{ij} is defined (© IEEE 2013).

and the number of waveguide crossings of the path with highest insertion loss. Because placement and routing are NP-hard problems, they are performed sequentially. During placement, no waveguide positions are available. Thus, the waveguide length and the number of waveguide crossings have to be approximated for each path. The waveguide length $\widetilde{WL}_p(\mathbf{x})$ is approximated as the Euclidean distance:

$$\widetilde{WL}_p(\mathbf{x}) = \sum_{n_{ij}=(i,j)\in N_p} \sqrt{(x_i - x_j)^2 + (y_i - y_j)^2} \quad (1)$$

where N_p is the set of all two-pin connections n_{ij} contained in path p and (x_i, y_i) describes the center point of module i. A module can be a PSE, hub or memory controller. The number of crossings is approximated by a heuristic: For each two-pin connection we consider the straight line connecting the two modules. If two straight lines are located close to each other, the probability of a waveguide crossing is high. If they are located far away from each other, the probability of a waveguide crossing is low. To obtain a smooth function, which mathematically describes this behavior we use a Gaussian function. We define an ellipse around each straight line connecting two modules as illustrated in Figure 9. This ellipse is the level curve of a Gaussian function. The function values of the end points and of the center points of another straight line determines the crossing probability of

waveguides of these two-pin connections. To calculate the probability of a crossing of the waveguides approximated by this straight line l_{ij} and any other straight line l_{rs} connecting the two modules r and s, a weighted sum of the function values of the center point and the end points of line l_{rs} is used. After the waveguide length and the waveguide crossings are approximated, a minimization problem can be formulated. The objective function of the minimization problem considers the waveguide length and the number of waveguide crossings, where the constraints ensure that all modules are placed overlap-free inside the placement area. The problem is solved by an interior point method.

After the placement, the waveguides have to be routed. We use a maze router, which enables but penalizes waveguide crossings. All two-pin connections are routed sequentially. A grid overlays the chip area and all bins containing obstacles, e.g. PSEs, are blocked. For the first net, the shortest connection is determined. All bins used by previous nets are marked. They can be used by other nets but a usage is penalized. The penalizing term can be used to find a good trade-off between the waveguide length minimization and the minimization of the number of waveguide crossings. PROTON is the only placement and routing algorithm for 3D ONoCs, which considers waveguide crossings. In experiments we were able to reduce the required laser power up to 99.3% compared to a state-of-the-art hand layout. The 8x8 standard wavelength-routed optical NoCs could be placed in less than 7 minutes.

4. CONCLUSION

The research at TUM's Institute for Electronic Design Automation has addressed essential topics in its first 40 years of existence. Seminal contributions have been made under the leadership of Kurt Antreich. The spirit that he instilled is alive and well today, and the institute continues to approach key EDA problems for the design of electronic circuits and systems in a methodical and thorough manner.

5. REFERENCES

[1] S. Director, G. Hachtel, and L. Vidigal, "Computationally efficient yield estimation procedures based on simplicial approximation," *IEEE Transactions on Circuits and Systems CAS*, vol. 25, pp. 121–130, 1978.

[2] R. Brayton, S. Director, and G. Hachtel, "Yield maximization and worst-case design with arbitrary statistical distributions," *IEEE Transactions on Circuits and Systems CAS*, vol. 27, pp. 756–764, 1980.

[3] K. Antreich and R. Koblitz, "Design Centering by Yield Prediction," *IEEE Transactions on Circuits and Systems CAS*, vol. 29, pp. 88–95, 1982.

[4] K. J. Antreich, H. Graeb, and R. K. Koblitz, "Advanced Yield Optimization Techniques," *Advances in CAD for VLSI*, vol. 8, pp. 163–195, 1994.

[5] K. Antreich and S. Huss, "An Interactive Optimization Technique for the Nominal Design of Integrated Circuits," *IEEE Transactions on Circuits and Systems CAS*, vol. 31, pp. 203–212, 1984.

[6] P. Feldmann and S. Director, "Integrated Circuit Quality Optimization using Surface Integrals," *IEEE Transactions on Computer-Aided Design of Integrated Circuits and Systems*, vol. 12, pp. 1868–1879, 1993.

[7] K. Antreich and H. Graeb, "Circuit optimization driven by worst-case distances," in *IEEE/ACM International Conference on Computer-Aided Design (ICCAD)*, pp. 166–169, 1991.

[8] K. Antreich, H. Graeb, and C. Wieser, "Circuit analysis and optimization driven by worst-case distances," *IEEE Transactions on Computer-Aided Design of Integrated Circuits and Systems*, vol. 13, pp. 57–71, Jan. 1994.

[9] S. R. Nassif, A. Strojwas, and S. Director, "A methodology for worst-case analysis of integrated circuits," *IEEE Transactions on Computer-Aided Design of Integrated Circuits and Systems*, vol. 5, pp. 104–113, 1986.

[10] K. Antreich, J. Eckmueller, H. Graeb, M. Pronath, F. Schenkel, R. Schwencker, and S. Zizala, "WiCkeD: Analog Circuit Synthesis Incorporating Mismatch," in *IEEE Custom Integrated Circuits Conference (CICC)*, pp. 511–514, May 2000.

[11] H. Graeb, S. Zizala, J. Eckmueller, and K. Antreich, "The Sizing Rules Method for Analog Integrated Circuit Design," in *IEEE/ACM International Conference on Computer-Aided Design (ICCAD)*, pp. 343–349, 2001.

[12] E. S. Ochotta, R. A. Rutenbar, and L. R. Carley, "Synthesis of High-Performance Analog Circuits in ASTRX/OBLX," *IEEE Transactions on Computer-Aided Design of Integrated Circuits and Systems*, vol. 15, pp. 273–294, Mar. 1996.

[13] R. Phelps, M. Krasnicki, R. A. Rutenbar, L. R. Carley, and J. R. Hellums, "Anaconda: Simulation-Based Synthesis of Analog Circuits Via Stochastic Pattern Search," *IEEE Transactions on Computer-Aided Design of Integrated Circuits and Systems*, vol. 19, pp. 703–717, June 2000.

[14] H. Fujiwara and T. Shimono, "On the Acceleration of Test Generation Algorithms," *IEEE Transactions on Computers*, vol. 32, pp. 1137–1144, Dec. 1983.

[15] M. H. Schulz, E. Trischler, and T. M. Sarfert, "SOCRATES: A Highly Efficient Automatic Test Pattern Generation System," in *IEEE International Test Conference (ITC)*, pp. 1016–1026, Sept. 1987.

[16] M. H. Schulz, E. Trischler, and T. M. Sarfert, "SOCRATES: A Highly Efficient Automatic Test Pattern Generation System," *IEEE Transactions on Computer-Aided Design of Integrated Circuits and Systems*, vol. 7, pp. 126–137, Jan. 1988.

[17] M. H. Schulz and E. Auth, "Improved Deterministic Test Pattern Generation with Applications to Redundancy Identification," *IEEE Transactions on Computer-Aided Design of Integrated Circuits and Systems*, vol. 8, pp. 811–816, July 1989.

[18] M. H. Schulz and E. Auth, "ESSENTIAL: An Efficient Self–Learning Test Pattern Generation Algorithm for Sequential Circuits," *12th Annual IEEE Workshop on Design for Testability*, Apr. 1989.

[19] K. Fuchs, F. Fink, and M. H. Schulz, "DYNAMITE: An Efficient Automatic Test Pattern Generation System for Path Delay Faults," *IEEE Transactions on Computer-Aided Design of Integrated Circuits and Systems*, vol. 10, pp. 1323–1335, Oct. 1991.

[20] H. Wittmann and M. Henftling, "Path Delay ATPG for Standard Scan Designs," in *European Design Automation Conference with EURO-VHDL*, pp. 202–207, Sept. 1995.

[21] M. Henftling, H. C. Wittmann, and K. J. Antreich, "A Single-Path-Oriented Fault-Effect Propagation in Digital Circuits Considering Multiple-Path Sensitization," in *IEEE/ACM International Conference on Computer-Aided Design (ICCAD)*, pp. 304–309, Nov. 1995.

[22] C. Sporrer and H. Bauer, "Corolla Partitioning for Distributed Logic Simulation of VLSI-Circuits," in *ACM/SCS/IEEE Workshop on Parallel and Distributed Simulation (PADS)*, pp. 85–92, 1993.

[23] H. Bauer and C. Sporrer, "Reducing Rollback Overhead in Time-Warp Based Distributed Simulation with Optimized Incremental State Saving," in *SCS/IEEE Annual Simulation Symp. (ASS)*, 1993.

[24] R. Schlagenhaft, M. K. Ruhwandl, C. Sporrer, and H. Bauer, "Dynamic Load Balancing of a Multi-Cluster Simulator on a Network of Workstations," in *ACM/SCS/IEEE Workshop on Parallel and Distributed Simulation (PADS)*, pp. 175–180, June 1995.

[25] U. Schlichtmann, "Boolean Matching and Disjoint Decomposition for FPGA Technology Mapping," in *Proceedings of the IFIP Workshop on Logic and Architecture Synthesis*, pp. 83–102, Nov. 1993.

[26] U. Schlichtmann, F. Brglez, and M. Hermann, "Characterization of Boolean Functions for Rapid Matching in EPGA Technology Mapping," in *ACM/IEEE Design Automation Conference (DAC)*, pp. 374–379, June 1992.

[27] U. Schlichtmann, F. Brglez, and P. Schneider, "Efficient Boolean Matching Based on Unique Variable Ordering," in *International Workshop on Logic Synthesis (IWLS)*, pp. 3b–1–3b–13, May 1993.

[28] M. Hermann, U. Schlichtmann, and K. J. Antreich, "Fast Technology Mapping for Multiplexor-based Architectures with Area/Delay Tradeoff," in *European Conference on Design Automation (EDAC)*, pp. 300–304, Feb. 1993.

[29] R. K. Brayton, G. D. Hachtel, and A. L. Sangiovanni-Vincentelli, "Multilevel Logic Synthesis," *Proceedings of the IEEE*, vol. 78, pp. 264–300, Feb. 1990.

[30] K. S. Brace, R. L. Rudell, and R. E. Bryant, "Efficient Implementation of a BDD Package," in *ACM/IEEE Design Automation Conference (DAC)*, pp. 40–45, June 1990.

[31] B. Wurth, K. Eckl, and K. Antreich, "Functional Multiple-Output Decomposition: Theory and an Implicit Algorithm," in *ACM/IEEE Design Automation Conference (DAC)*, pp. 54–59, June 1995.

[32] B. Wurth, U. Schlichtmann, K. Eckl, and K. J. Antreich, "Functional multiple-output decomposition with application to technology mapping for lookup table-based fpgas," *ACM Trans. Des. Autom. Electron. Syst.*, vol. 4, pp. 313–350, July 1999.

[33] C. Legl, B. Wurth, and K. Eckl, "An Implicit Algorithm For Support Minimization During Functional Decomposition," in *European Design and Test Conference (EDTC)*, pp. 412–417, Mar. 1996.

[34] C. Legl, B. Wurth, and K. Eckl, "A boolean approach to performance-directed technology mapping for lut-based fpga designs," in *DAC'96*, pp. 730–733, 1996.

[35] P. H. Schneider, U. Schlichtmann, and B. Wurth, "Fast Power Estimation of Large Circuits," *IEEE Design and Test*, vol. 13, no. 1, pp. 70–78, 1996.

[36] P. H. Schneider and U. Schlichtmann, "Decomposition of Boolean Function for Low Power Based on a New Power Estimation Technique," in *ACM/IEEE International Workshop on Low Power Design*, pp. 123 – 128, Apr. 1994.

[37] P. H. Schneider, U. Schlichtmann, and K. J. Antreich, "A New Power Estimation Technique with Application to Decomposition of Boolean Functions for Low Power," in *European Design Automation Conference with EURO-VHDL*, pp. 112–117, Sept. 1994.

[38] K. Eckl, J. C. Madre, P. Zepter, and C. Legl, "A Practical Approach to Multiple-Class Retiming," in *ACM/IEEE Design Automation Conference (DAC)*, pp. 237–242, June 1999.

[39] U. Seidl, K. Eckl, and F. Johannes, "Performance-directed Retiming for FPGAs using Post-placement Delay Information," in *Design, Automation and Test in Europe (DATE)*, 2003.

[40] B. Li, N. Chen, M. Schmidt, W. Schneider, and U. Schlichtmann, "On Hierarchical Statistical Static Timing Analysis," in *Design, Automation and Test in Europe (DATE)*, Apr. 2009.

[41] D. Lorenz, M. Barke, and U. Schlichtmann, "Efficiently Analyzing the Impact of Aging Effects on Large Integrated Circuits," *Microelectronics Reliability*, vol. 52, pp. 1546–1552, Aug. 2012.

[42] T. H. Abthoff and F. M. Johannes, "TINA: Analog Placement using Enumerative Techniques Capable of Optimizing both Area and Net Length," in *European*

Design Automation Conference with EURO-VHDL, pp. 398–403, Sept. 1996.

[43] J. M. Kleinhans, G. Sigl, F. M. Johannes, and K. J. Antreich, "GORDIAN: VLSI Placement by Quadratic Programming and Slicing Optimization," *IEEE Transactions on Computer-Aided Design of Integrated Circuits and Systems*, vol. 10, pp. 356–365, Mar. 1991.

[44] M. Strasser, M. Eick, H. Graeb, U. Schlichtmann, and F. M. Johannes, "Deterministic Analog Circuit Placement using Hierarchically Bounded Enumeration and Enhanced Shape Functions," in *IEEE/ACM International Conference on Computer-Aided Design (ICCAD)*, pp. 306–313, Nov. 2008.

[45] P.-N. Guo, C.-K. Cheng, and T. Yoshimura, "An O-Tree Representation of Non-Slicing Floorplan and Its Applications," in *ACM/IEEE Design Automation Conference (DAC)*, vol. 36, pp. 268–273, June 1999.

[46] H. Murata, K. Fujiyoshi, S. Nakatake, and Y. Kajitani, "VLSI Module Placement Based on Rectangle-Packing by the Sequence-Pair," *IEEE Transactions on Computer-Aided Design of Integrated Circuits and Systems*, vol. 15, no. 12, pp. 1518–1524, 1996.

[47] S. Nakatake, K. Fujiyoshi, H. Murata, and Y. Kajitani, "Module placement on bsg-structure and ic layout applications," in *IEEE/ACM International Conference on Computer-aided Design*, ICCAD, pp. 484–491, 1996.

[48] Y. Pang, F. Balasa, K. Lampaert, and C.-K. Cheng, "Block Placement with Symmetry Constraints based on the O-tree Non-Slicing Representation," in *ACM/IEEE Design Automation Conference (DAC)*, pp. 464–468, June 2000.

[49] X. Hong, G. Huang, Y. Cai, J. Gu, S. Dong, C.-K. Cheng, and J. Gu, "Corner Block List: An Effective and Efficient Topological Representation of Non-Slicing Floorplan," in *IEEE/ACM International Conference on Computer-Aided Design (ICCAD)*, Nov. 2000.

[50] Q. Ma, E. F. Y. Yong, and K. P. Pun, "Analog Placement with Common Centroid Constraints," in *IEEE/ACM International Conference on Computer-Aided Design (ICCAD)*, Nov. 2007.

[51] J.-M. Lin and Y.-W. Chang, "TCG-S: orthogonal coupling of P*-admissible representations for general floorplans," *IEEE Transactions on Computer-Aided Design of Integrated Circuits and Systems*, vol. 23, pp. 968–980, June 2004.

[52] Y.-C. Chang, Y.-W. Chang, G.-M. Wu, and S.-W. Wu, "B*-Trees: A New Representation for Non-Slicing Floorplans," in *ACM/IEEE Design Automation Conference (DAC)*, vol. 37, pp. 458–463, 2000.

[53] F. Balasa, S. C. Maruvada, and K. Krishnamoorthy, "On the Exploration of the Solution Space in Analog Placement With Symmetry Constraints," *IEEE Transactions on Computer-Aided Design of Integrated Circuits and Systems*, vol. 23, pp. 177–191, Feb. 2004.

[54] A. Nassaj, J. Lienig, and G. Jerke, "A Constraint-driven Methodology for Placement of Analog and Mixed-signal Integrated Circuits," in *IEEE International Conference on Electronics, Circuits and Systems (ICECS)*, 2008.

[55] F. Balasa and K. Lampaert, "Symmetry Within the Sequence-Pair Representation in the Context of Placement for Analog Design," *IEEE Transactions on Computer-Aided Design of Integrated Circuits and Systems*, vol. 19, pp. 721–731, July 2000.

[56] K. Krishnamoorthy, S. C. Maruvada, and F. Balasa, "Fast Evaluation of Symmetric-Feasible Sequence-Pairs for Analog Topological Placement," in *5th IEEE Int. Conf. on ASIC (ASICON)*, pp. 71–74, 2003.

[57] K. Krishnamoorthy, S. C. Maruvada, and F. Balasa, "Topological Placement with Multiple Symmetry Groups of Devices for Analog Layout Design," in *IEEE International Symposium on Circuits and Systems (ISCAS)*, pp. 2032–2035, May 2007.

[58] P.-H. Lin and S.-C. Lin, "Analog Placement Based on Novel Symmetry-Island Formulation," in *ACM/IEEE Design Automation Conference (DAC)*, pp. 465–470, June 2007.

[59] Y.-C. Tam, E. F. Y. Young, and C. Chu, "Analog Placement with Symmetry and Other Placement Constraints," in *IEEE/ACM International Conference on Computer-Aided Design (ICCAD)*, Nov. 2006.

[60] T. Massier, H. Graeb, and U. Schlichtmann, "Sizing Rules for Bipolar Analog Circuit Design," in *Design, Automation and Test in Europe (DATE)*, pp. 140–145, Mar. 2008.

[61] T. Massier, H. Graeb, and U. Schlichtmann, "The Sizing Rules Method for CMOS and Bipolar Analog Integrated Circuit Synthesis," *IEEE Transactions on Computer-Aided Design of Integrated Circuits and Systems*, vol. 27, pp. 2209–2222, Dec. 2008.

[62] M. Eick, M. Strasser, H. Graeb, and U. Schlichtmann, "Automatic Generation of Hierarchical Placement Rules for Analog Integrated Circuits," in *ACM/SIGDA International Symposium on Physical Design (ISPD)*, pp. 47–54, Mar. 2010.

[63] M. Eick, M. Strasser, K. Lu, U. Schlichtmann, and H. Graeb, "ISPD10: Comprehensive Generation of Hierarchical Placement Rules for Analog Integrated Circuits," *IEEE Transactions on Computer-Aided Design of Integrated Circuits and Systems*, Feb. 2011.

[64] T. Yan and M. D. F. Wong, "BSG-Route: A Length-Constrained Routing Scheme for General Planar Topology," *IEEE Trans. Comput.-Aided Design Integr. Circuits Syst.*, vol. 28, no. 11, pp. 1679–1690, 2009.

[65] T.-Y. Tsai, R.-J. Lee, C.-Y. Chin, C.-Y. Kuan, H.-M. Chen, and Y. Kajitani, "On Routing Fixed Escaped Boundary Pins for High Speed Boards," in *Design, Autom., and Test Europe Conf.*, pp. 1–6, 2011.

[66] R.-B. Wu and F.-L. Chao, "Laddering Wave in Serpentine Delay Line," *IEEE Trans. Compon., Packag., Manuf. Technol. B*, vol. 18, no. 4, pp. 644–650, 1995.

[67] B. Rubin and B. Singh, "Study of Meander Line Delay in Circuit Boards," *IEEE Trans. Microw. Theory Tech.*, vol. 48, no. 9, pp. 1452–1460, 2000.

[68] T.-M. Tseng, B. Li, T.-Y. Ho, and U. Schlichtmann, "Post-route Refinement for High-frequency PCBs Considering Meander Segment Alleviation," in *Proc. Great Lakes Symp. VLSI*, pp. 323–324, 2013.

[69] T.-M. Tseng, B. Li, T.-Y. Ho, and U. Schlichtmann, "Post-route Alleviation of Dense Meander Segments in High-performance Printed Circuit Boards," in *Proc. Int. Conf. Comput.-Aided Des.*, pp. 713–720, 2013.

[70] L. Ramini, D. Bertozzi, and L. Carloni, "Engineering a Bandwidth-Scalable Optical Layer for a 3D Multi-core Processor with Awareness of Layout Constraints," in *Networks on Chip (NoCS), 2012 Sixth IEEE/ACM International Symposium on*, pp. 185–192, May 2012.

[71] C. Condrat, P. Kalla, and S. Blair, "Crossing-Aware Channel Routing for Integrated Optics.," *IEEE Trans. on CAD of Integrated Circuits and Systems*, vol. 33, no. 6, pp. 814–825, 2014.

[72] D. Ding, Y. Zhang, H. Huang, R. T. Chen, and D. Z. Pan, "O-Router: An Optical Routing Framework for Low Power On-chip Silicon Nano-photonic Integration," in *DAC*, pp. 264–269, ACM, 2009.

[73] A. Boos, L. Ramini, U. Schlichtmann, and D. Bertozzi, "PROTON: An Automatic Place-and-Route Tool for Optical Networks-on-Chip," in *Computer-Aided Design (ICCAD), 2013 IEEE/ACM International Conference on*, pp. 138–145, Nov 2013.

Timing-Driven Placement Based on Dynamic Net-Weighting for Efficient Slack Histogram Compression

Chrystian Guth[1], Vinicius Livramento[2], Renan Netto[1], Renan Fonseca[1],
José Luís Güntzel[1] and Luiz Santos[1,2]
[1]Dept. of Computer Science, Federal University of Santa Catarina, Brazil
[2]Dept. of Automation and Systems Engineering, Federal University of Santa Catarina, Brazil
{chrystian.guth, vinicius.livramento}@posgrad.ufsc.br

ABSTRACT

Timing-driven placement (TDP) finds new legal locations for standard cells so as to minimize timing violations while preserving placement quality. Although violations may arise from unmet setup or hold constraints, most TDP approaches ignore the latter. Besides, most techniques focus on reducing the worst negative slack and let the improvements on total negative slack as a secondary goal. However, to successfully achieve timing closure, techniques must also reduce the total negative slack, which is known as slack histogram compression. This paper proposes a new Lagrangian Relaxation formulation for TDP to compress both late and early slack histograms. To solve the problem, we employ a discrete local search technique that uses the Lagrange multipliers as net-weights, which are dynamically updated using an accurate timing analyzer. To preserve placement quality, our technique uses a small fixed-size window that is anchored in the initial location of a cell. For the experimental evaluation of the proposed technique, we relied on the ICCAD 2014 TDP contest infrastructure. The results show that our technique significantly reduces the timing violations from an initial global placement. On average, late and early total negative slacks are improved by 85.03% and 42.72%, respectively, while the worst slacks are reduced by 71.55% and 34.40%. The overhead in wirelength is less than 0.1%.

Categories and Subject Descriptors

B.7.2 [**Integrated Circuits**]: Design Aids – Placement and routing

Keywords

Physical Synthesis; Timing Closure; Timing-Driven Placement; Lagrangian Relaxation

1. INTRODUCTION

Timing closure is a challenging task of physical synthesis for high performance integrated circuits. To successfully meet the timing constraints and achieve the specified clock frequency, several techniques are used within the design flow such as gate sizing, buffer insertion, timing-driven routing and timing-driven placement [9].

Timing-driven placement (TDP) finds new legal locations for standard cells so as to minimize timing violations (or even satisfy the constraints) [9]. Although the quality of global placement has significantly advanced in the last years, there is a lack of efficient techniques to address the TDP problem, as recently pointed out by position papers from industry and academia [1] [15] [13]. Among the main requirements for an efficient timing-driven placer, one can highlight:

- Techniques must effectively compress the slack histogram to improve the timing of a large number of paths with negative slack. Focusing only on few critical paths may result in marginal improvements [1].

- Timing optimization must preserve the global placement quality in terms of wirelength and congestion. An increase by 10% in wirelength can lead to a severe routability penalty [26].

- There is a need for easier integration with other techniques like gate sizing and threshold voltage assignment, which is essential to achieve timing closure [26].

This work proposes a novel timing-driven placement technique that takes into account the abovementioned requirements. Our technique, based on Lagrangian Relaxation, improves the circuit timing while maintaining the overall global placement quality. Our specific contributions are as follows:

- A complete Lagrangian relaxation formulation for TDP to improve the slack histogram of sequential circuits, including setup and hold timing constraints.

- A net-based technique that uses Lagrange multipliers as net-weights, which are dynamically updated using an accurate timing analyzer. The use of a small fixed-size search window, which is anchored in the initial location of a cell, not only ensures the accuracy of delay estimates, but also preserves the placement quality.

- Experimental results, using the ICCAD 2014 incremental TDP contest infrastructure [11], show that our technique effectively compresses the slack histogram of a solution from a global placer. An average reduction of 85.03% in the late total negative slack was obtained with an overhead less than 0.1% in wirelength.

The rest of this paper is organized as follows. Section 2 reviews related work while Section 3 presents the timing modeling and the problem formulation. Section 4 describes our timing-driven placer. Experimental results and comparisons are given in Section 5 and conclusions are drawn in Section 6.

2. RELATED WORK

Net-based TDP techniques convert timing information into net-weights or net constraints, thereby minimizing a weighted wirelength objective. **Static** approaches generate net-weights before placement. To take the path sharing effect into account [12] assigns net-weights based on negative slack using a path counting scheme. To minimize the total negative slack based on slack sensitivities [19] proposes a net-weighting technique, showing experimentally that minimizing the total negative slack during TDP is essential to achieve timing closure. **Dynamic** approaches update net-weights during iterations, trying to keep an up-to-date timing profile. To minimize the weighted wirelength [5] employs a force-directed method that relies on iterative net-weighting. [21] proposes the use of a star interconnection model to accurately compute the net delay using Elmore and minimizes a weighted quadratic objective function. [8] uses an iterative conjugate gradient method in which the weights of critical nets are incremented during iterations. [6] presents an iterative bi-section method where the slacks are used to slowly tighten the length of critical nets. [18] employs analytical placement modifying forces to meet the wirelength constraints on critical nets in terms of HPWL.

Path-based TDP techniques minimize timing violations through accurate modeling of a few critical paths, generally using linear programming (LP). Both [23, 7] propose the use of primal-dual approaches based on Lagrangian Relaxation to iteratively minimize the delay of critical paths. [24] uses simulated annealing to improve the timing of critical paths. [3] proposes an LP formulation that models the circuit timing through the variation of delay and slew w.r.t. an accurate timing analyzer, called differential timing analysis. [20] improves the differential timing model from [3] using a pin-based timing LP formulation to reduce wirelength without timing degradation. [16] presents a discretized approach that uses branch-and-bound to choose the location of cells.

Recent **Hybrid** TDP techniques [14, 26] combine features of net and path-based approaches. [14] proposes a path delay sensitivity function to generate net weights and then minimizes critical nets' wirelength using LP. The technique is mainly net-based but takes advantage of the path delay sensitivity to simultaneously optimize the critical path and a few logically adjacent paths, called criticality adjacency network. [26] presents an iterative approach that relies on an accurate timer to smooth the circuit critical paths without disrupting the wirelength. Its framework periodically perform slack histogram compression using additional techniques, as buffering and gate sizing, to recover the timing of non-critical paths which, according to the authors, improves the convergence of the overall algorithm

Most TDP techniques focus on minimizing only the worst negative slack. Although [19] proposes a net-weighting scheme to minimize a total negative slack function, the net-weights are generated *a priori* and remain constant during optimization, which can undermine timing optimization [15]. [26] mainly focuses on minimizing the worst negative slack while the total negative slack is minimized in a few iterations. Besides, none of the previous works tackled hold violations of sequential elements. That is why this paper proposes a dynamic net-weighting technique to minimize **total** negative slack of **both** setup and hold timing violations.

3. TIMING-DRIVEN PLACEMENT

In our TDP formulation we consider setup and hold timing constraints. This requires proper modeling of delays and timing constraints as well as adequate tracking of viola-

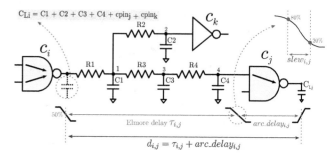

Figure 1: Gate and interconnect delay modeling.

tions. Section 3.1 details our timing modeling, then Section 3.2 presents our formulation for TDP as an optimization problem. Finally, Section 3.3 presents our casting of that problem into a Lagrangian Relaxation formulation.

3.1 Timing Modeling and Notation

A sequential circuit can be represented by a set $\mathcal{C}$ of standard cells, a set $\mathcal{PI}$ of primary inputs (circuit inputs or outputs of sequential elements) and a set $\mathcal{PO}$ of primary outputs (circuit outputs or inputs of sequential elements). There is also a set of nets representing the interconnections between these elements. Timing constraints are applied to sections of the circuit delimiting the combinational components between primary inputs and primary outputs.

Arrival times are measured at the output pin of each $c_j \in \mathcal{C}$ and at each $c_j \in (\mathcal{PI} \cup \mathcal{PO})$. To capture the impact of setup and hold times on circuit paths, *late* and *early* values [9] are defined. The late (early) arrival time corresponds to the latest (earliest) time when the signal transition reaches a given timing point. Let $\mathcal{F}_j$ be the set of cells connected to the input of $c_j \in \mathcal{C}$, i.e. its fanins. Let $d_{i,j}^L$ and $d_{i,j}^E$ denote the late and early values for the delay measured between c_i's output and c_j's output. Late and early arrival times of each cell c_j, denoted as a_j^L and a_j^E, can be recursively defined from primary inputs towards primary outputs, as below:

$$a_j^L = \max_{c_i \in \mathcal{F}_j}(a_i^L + d_{i,j}^L) \qquad a_j^E = \min_{c_i \in \mathcal{F}_j}(a_i^E + d_{i,j}^E) \quad (1)$$

The late (early) required time, denoted as r_j^L (r_j^E), corresponds to the latest (earliest) time when the signal transition must reach each $c_j \in \mathcal{PO}$ to ensure the clock frequency. To evaluate how far a design is from time closure, late and early slacks are tracked at primary outputs [22], as below:

$$s_j^L = r_j^L - a_j^L \qquad s_j^E = a_j^E - r_j^E, \; \forall j \in \mathcal{PO} \quad (2)$$

In the following, we explain our delay model, which is illustrated in Figure 1. We model the delay between c_i's output and c_j's output by adding the interconnection delay, denoted as $\tau_{i,j}$, to the arc delay from input to output of c_j, denoted as $arc\_delay_{i,j}$. The late and early values for the delays are defined as follows:

$$d_{i,j}^L = \tau_{i,j} + arc\_delay_{i,j}^L \quad (3)$$
$$d_{i,j}^E = \tau_{i,j} + arc\_delay_{i,j}^E \quad (4)$$

Interconnections are modeled as RC tree networks containing M nodes. Each capacitance C_k and resistance R_k is associated with a node k such that $1 \le k \le M$. The interconnection delay from the output of driver c_i to the input of receiver c_j is estimated using the Elmore delay: $\tau_{i,j} = \sum_{k \in M} C_k R_{kj}$, where R_{kj} is the shared resistance among the paths from driver c_i to nodes k and j.

Let C_{Lj} be the lumped downstream capacitance at the output of c_j and let $slew_{i,j}$ denote the wire slew from the output pin of driver c_i to the input pin of receiver c_j. We compute the wire slew using the PERI model, which uses the arc slew of driver c_i and the slew of the impulse response on receiver c_j, as detailed in [11]. Late and early values for arc delays can be precisely modeled as a linear combination of lumped capacitance and input slew [3], as follows:

$$arc\_delay_{i,j}^L = A_0 + A_1 C_{Lj} + A_2 slew_{i,j}^L \quad (5)$$

$$arc\_delay_{i,j}^E = A_0 + A_1 C_{Lj} + A_2 slew_{i,j}^E \quad (6)$$

Late and early arc slews are modeled similarly to delay, as shown in (7) and (8).

$$arc\_slew_{i,j}^L = B_0 + B_1 C_{Lj} + B_2 slew_{i,j}^L \quad (7)$$

$$arc\_slew_{i,j}^E = B_0 + B_1 C_{Lj} + B_2 slew_{i,j}^E \quad (8)$$

The coefficients A_0, A_1, A_2, B_0, B_1 and B_2 are constants determined during the standard cell library characterization.

3.2 Problem Formulation

Given the initial location (x_j^0, y_j^0) determined by global placement for each $c_j \in \mathcal{C}$, TDP finds a new location (x_j, y_j) for each movable cell so as to minimize the timing violations (or even satisfy the timing constraints) [9]. To quantify the amount of violation, we employ the *total negative slack* (tns), which is the sum of the negative slacks observed at the primary outputs of the circuit. We employ two values for the total negative slack (denoted as tns^L and tns^E), one obtained from late slacks and another from early slacks. To make sure that new locations are legal, chip physical dimensions (denoted as X_{left}, X_{right}, Y_{bottom}, Y_{top}, W_{site}, and H_{row}) and standard cell layout dimensions (denoted as W_j and H_j) are encoded within the constraints. There is also a bound constraint to ensure a maximum cell displacement from the initial location. As a result, we formulate TDP as the following optimization problem:

$$\textbf{Max} : tns_j^L + tns^E \quad (9)$$

$$\textbf{S.t.} : X_{left} \leq x_j \leq X_{right} - W_j \quad (10)$$

$$: Y_{bottom} \leq y_j \leq Y_{top} - H_j \quad (11)$$

$$: x_j = \left\lfloor \frac{x_j}{W_{site}} \right\rfloor \times W_{site} \quad (12)$$

$$: y_j = \left\lfloor \frac{y_j}{H_{row}} \right\rfloor \times H_{row} \quad (13)$$

$$: x_j + W_j \leq x_{j+1} \quad (14)$$

$$: y_j + H_j \leq y_{j+1} \quad (15)$$

$$: \max_{j \in \mathcal{C}}(|x_j - x_j^0| + |y_j - y_j^0|) \leq D_{max} \quad (16)$$

Although our formulation accounts for separate rise and fall signal transitions, we omitted such timing details for clarity. The objective (9) is to compress the slack histogram by maximizing the total negative slack. Note that, when the sum of the late and early values for tns is zero, all constraints are satisfied for the specified setup and hold times. Equations (10) to (15) encode constraints ensuring that the placement is legal. Equations (10) and (11) ensure that the chosen location (x_j, y_j) for the cell c_j is within chip boundaries, whereas (12) guarantees that c_j is aligned to the standard cell site and (13) ensures that the cell is aligned to a standard cell row. Equations (14) and (15) make sure that cells do not overlap. Finally, Equation (16) specifies an upper bound D_{max} for the displacement of a cell from its original location (x_j^0, y_j^0). This constraint ensures that TDP maintains a cell distribution similar to the one obtained by global placement, which is a desirable feature [26] [11].

3.3 Lagrangian Relaxation Formulation

Lagrangian Relaxation (LR) is an effective technique to tackle problems with hard constraints. The idea is to remove such hard constraints and incorporate them into the objective function, each one multiplied by a penalty term called Lagrange multiplier (LM) [17]. The LR problem is addressed by iteratively solving two subproblems: 1) Lagrangian relaxation subproblem (LRS) minimizes the new objective function, also known as Lagrangian function, for a set of fixed LMs. 2) Lagrangian dual problem (LDP) updates the LMs to maximize the solution from LRS.

First, to ensure that only non-positive values are accounted for in the objective function, let us define late negative slack as $\hat{s}_j^L = \min(0, s_j^L)$, and early negative slack as $\hat{s}_j^E = \min(0, s_j^E)$. Therefore, the TDP formulation can be rewritten as the minimization problem (17). We introduce the set of inequality constraints (18) to (20) in order to model the timing information in the circuit.

$$\textbf{Min} : -\sum_{j \in \mathcal{PO}} \hat{s}_j^L - \sum_{j \in \mathcal{PO}} \hat{s}_j^E \quad (17)$$

$$\textbf{S.t.} : \hat{s}_j^L \leq 0 \text{ and } \hat{s}_j^E \leq 0, \forall j \in \mathcal{PO} \quad (18)$$

$$: r_j^L - a_j^L \geq \hat{s}_j^L \text{ and } a_j^E - r_j^E \geq \hat{s}_j^E, \forall j \in \mathcal{PO} \quad (19)$$

$$: a_i^L + d_{i,j}^L \leq a_j^L \text{ and } a_i^E + d_{i,j}^E \geq a_j^E, \forall j \in \mathcal{C} \quad (20)$$

$$: (10) \text{ to } (16) \quad (21)$$

Equation (18) ensures that $\hat{s}_j^L$ and $\hat{s}_j^E$ only assume negative values, since we do not want to account for positive slack in the objective function. Equation (19) states that late/early slacks must be greater than or equal to late/early negative slacks. Finally, (20) defines late and early arrival times for each cell, as already presented in Section 3.1. The objective function (17) is also subject to legality and maximum displacement constraints (10) to (16).

Our idea is to relax the late and early timing constraints and incorporate them into the objective function, similarly to what has been proposed for gate sizing [17]. As consequence, each late and early timing constraint is accompanied by a non-negative Lagrange multiplier λ^L and λ^E, respectively. Therefore, each LM represents a net-weight indicating the criticality of the net i, j from the output of c_i to the output c_j. This leads to the following Lagrangian function, which incorporates the relaxed timing constraints as below:

$$L_\lambda : -\sum_{j \in \mathcal{PO}} \hat{s}_j^L - \sum_{j \in \mathcal{PO}} \hat{s}_j^E + \sum_{j \in \mathcal{PO}} \hat{\lambda}_j^L \hat{s}_j^L + \sum_{j \in \mathcal{PO}} \hat{\lambda}_j^E \hat{s}_j^E \quad (22)$$

$$+ \sum_{j \in \mathcal{PO}} \lambda_j^L (\hat{s}_j^L - r_j^L + a_j^L) + \sum_{j \in \mathcal{PO}} \lambda_j^E (\hat{s}_j^E - a_j^E + r_j^E)$$

$$+ \sum_{j \in \mathcal{C}} (\sum_{i \in \mathcal{F}_j} \lambda_{i,j}^L (a_i^L + d_{i,j}^L - a_j^L) + \sum_{i \in \mathcal{F}_j} \lambda_{i,j}^E (a_j^E - a_i^E - d_{i,j}^E))$$

The associated LRS minimizes the Lagrangian function L_λ by finding the location of each movable $c_j \in C$, assuming a set of fixed net-weights, as presented in (23). Then the LDP updates the net-weights to maximize the solution from LRS (Q_λ), as shown in (24).

$$\textbf{LRS} : Q_\lambda = \min_{(x_j, y_j) \forall j \in \mathcal{C}} L_\lambda \quad (23)$$

$$\textbf{LDP} : \max_{\lambda \geq 0} Q_\lambda \quad (24)$$

Some gate sizing techniques simplified the Lagrangian function using some flow conservation constraints resulting from applying the Karush-Kuhn-Tucker (KKT) conditions [17]. We apply similar flow conservation to simplify L_λ. First, the late negative slack variables $\hat{s}_j^L$ cancel out if $\forall j \in \mathcal{PO}$, $\hat{\lambda}_j^L +$

143

$\lambda_j^L = 1$. Early negative slack variables $\hat{s}_j^E$ also cancel out if $\forall j \in \mathcal{PO}$, $\hat{\lambda}_j^E + \lambda_j^E = 1$. From such simplification, we obtain the following Lagrangian function:

$$L_\lambda : \sum_{j \in \mathcal{PO}} \lambda_j^L(-r_j^L + a_j^L) + \sum_{j \in \mathcal{PO}} \lambda_j^E(-a_j^E + r_j^E) \quad (25)$$

$$+ \sum_{j \in \mathcal{C}}(\sum_{i \in \mathcal{F}_j} \lambda_{i,j}^L(a_i^L + d_{i,j}^L - a_j^L) + \sum_{i \in \mathcal{F}_j} \lambda_{i,j}^E(a_j^E - a_i^E - d_{i,j}^E))$$

We can further simplify that function by applying the KKT conditions for intermediate nodes. Flow conservation implies that the sum of input LMs must be equal to the sum of output LMs. Therefore, for late constraints, we get $\sum_{i \in \mathcal{F}_j} \lambda_{i,j}^L = \sum_{j \in \mathcal{F}_k} \lambda_{j,k}^L$, and for early constraints we get $\sum_{i \in \mathcal{F}_j} \lambda_{i,j}^E = \sum_{j \in \mathcal{F}_k} \lambda_{j,k}^E$. Besides, late and early required times can be assumed as constants during optimization. This leads to the final Lagrangian function minimized by our technique.

$$L_\lambda : \sum_{j \in \mathcal{C}}(\sum_{i \in \mathcal{F}_j} \lambda_{i,j}^L(d_{i,j}^L) + \sum_{i \in \mathcal{F}_j} \lambda_{i,j}^E(-d_{i,j}^E)) \quad (26)$$

From such simplified function (26), we can conclude that by minimizing the weighted summation of late (early) delay and late (early) net-weights, also minimizes tns^L and tns^E. To iteratively solve LRS and LDP, we employ the algorithms described in the next section.

4. PROPOSED TECHNIQUE

Figure 2 gives an overview of our iterative technique, comprising two major steps. **Solve LRS** minimizes L_λ (26) assuming a set of fixed net-weights, as detailed in Section 4.1. **Solve LDP** updates the net-weights relying on accurate timing analysis, as described in Section 4.2. The algorithm solves these two steps for a fixed number of 20 iterations and returns a legalized and timing optimized circuit.

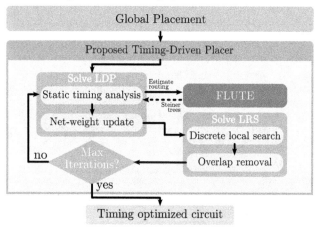

Figure 2: Overview of the proposed timing-driven placer.

4.1 Solve LRS

Our technique solves LRS in two steps. First, it performs **discrete local search** on every movable cell to minimize L_λ, but allowing overlaps between cells. Then a second step for **overlap removal** tries to keep the cells as close as possible from their locations found in the first step.

4.1.1 Discrete local search

First, we explain the general idea with the aid of Figure 3. Then we present Algorithm 1 and justify the decisions and impacts on the quality of solution. The initial location of a given cell, as determined by the global placer, is referred to

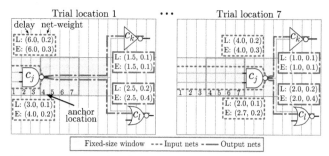

Figure 3: Example of discrete local search on nand cell within the fixed-size window of 7 candidate locations.

as its anchor location. Figure 3 shows the anchor location (rectangle in red solid line) and the search window (rectangle in light blue) of c_j, a nand cell that occupies 4 sites. The search window remains the same during the whole optimization. It is centered in the anchor location and covers 7 candidate locations for c_j, including the anchor location itself. The idea is to find the location with the lowest cost, since minimizing the cost of each cell individually also minimizes L_λ (26). Changing the location of c_j impacts on the size of its input and output interconnections, which affects the delay and slew of the subcircuit around c_j. We restrict the impact to the output interconnection of c_j (as will be justified later), which affects the arc delays of c_j, the interconnection delay and slew from c_j to each fanout and the arc delay of each fanout. Considering the late and early delays and net-weights from Figure 3, the cost of trial location 1 is: $L_\lambda = (6 \times 0.2) + (3 \times 0.1) + (1.5 \times 0.1) + (2.5 \times 0.2) + (-6 \times 0.3) + (-4 \times 0.2) + (-1.5 \times 0.1) + (-2.5 \times 0.4) = -1.60$. The cost of trial location 7 is: $L_\lambda = -1.14$. Comparing the trial locations 1 and 7, the former gives the lowest cost.

Algorithm 1 visits each movable cell in reverse topological order and performs discrete local search. For a $c_j \in \mathcal{C}$ in a given iteration, the locations of its fanouts have been previously defined, which allows to accurately estimate its lumped capacitance. Some recent work highlighted that cell delay is much more sensitive to lumped capacitance than to input slew [14, 20]. We observed similar behavior in the library adopted in our experiments [11]. Moreover, the slew propagation beyond the immediate fanout is time consuming [20]. That is why we limit the slew propagation when evaluating a candidate location. Therefore, the cost of a candidate location ρ measures the impact on delay of the subcircuit rooted in c_j, due to the variation on the output interconnection wirelength. The accuracy of the estimated costs is crucial to correctly decide the movements in a given iteration. Recomputing the Steiner trees for each candidate location is computationally expensive. Thus, we estimate the costs using the concept of differential timing model from [3]. The idea is to compute the cost based on the delay variation w.r.t. an accurate value updated at each iteration by the timing analyzer, which recomputes the Steiner trees.

In Algorithm 1, lines 4 to 14 estimate the cost of a candidate location based on the differential timing model. The hat symbol denotes a reference value computed during static timing analysis. Line 5 estimates the lumped capacitance variation ΔC_{Lj} of placing c_j on ρ, where L_j is the HPWL of the output interconnection. Lines 6 and 7 account for the impact of ΔC_{Lj} on each late and early arc delay of c_j, where A_1 corresponds to the characterization coefficient. Lines 8 to 14 estimate the cost related to the impact of delay and slew variations of each fanout. The interconnection delay of each segment from c_j to a fanout is computed using lumped Elmore: $\tau_{j,k} = K_D \cdot r \cdot l_{j,k}(\frac{c \cdot L_j}{2} + cpin_k)$. The constant K_D

ALGORITHM 1: Discrete Local Search

Input : Placed circuit with timing violations, $\vec{\lambda}^E$, $\vec{\lambda}^L$
Output: Timing optimized circuit

1 **for** *each movable $c_j \in \mathcal{C}$ in reverse topological order* **do**
2     $best\_cost \leftarrow \infty$
3   **for** *each candidate location ρ within the fixed-size window* **do**
4   place c_j in the coordinate of location ρ
5        $\Delta C_{Lj} \leftarrow (L_j - \hat{L}_j)c$
6        $cost^L \leftarrow \sum_{i \in \mathcal{F}_j}(\hat{d}_{i,j}^L + A_1 \Delta C_{Lj})\lambda_{i,j}^L$
7        $cost^E \leftarrow \sum_{i \in \mathcal{F}_j}(\hat{d}_{i,j}^E + A_1 \Delta C_{Lj})\lambda_{i,j}^E$
8   **for** *each fanout c_k* **do**
9           $\Delta\tau_{j,k} \leftarrow \left(K_D \cdot r \cdot l_{j,k}\left(\frac{c \cdot L_j}{2} + cpin_h\right)\right) - \hat{\tau}_{j,h}$
10           $\Delta slew_{j,k}^L \leftarrow (\sqrt{(arc\_slew_j^L)^2 + (2\beta_{j,k} - \tau_{j,k})} - s\hat{l}ew_{j,k}^L)$
11           $\Delta slew_{j,k}^E \leftarrow (\sqrt{(arc\_slew_j^E)^2 + (2\beta_{j,k} - \tau_{j,k})} - s\hat{l}ew_{j,k}^E)$
12           $cost^L \leftarrow cost^L + (\hat{d}_{j,k}^L + A_2 \Delta slew_{j,k}^L + \Delta\tau_{j,k})\lambda_{j,k}^L$
13           $cost^E \leftarrow cost^E + (\hat{d}_{j,k}^E + A_2 \Delta slew_{j,k}^E + \Delta\tau_{j,k})\lambda_{j,k}^E$
14   **end**
15        $cost_\rho \leftarrow \alpha cost^L + \omega cost^E$
16   **if** $cost_\rho < best\_cost$ **then**
17           $(best\_\rho, best\_cost) \leftarrow (\rho, cost_\rho)$
18   **end**
19   **end**
20   place c_j in the coordinate of $best\_\rho$
21 **end**

ALGORITHM 2: Overlap Removal

Input : Circuit with overlaps
Output: Circuit without overlaps

1 **for** *each standard cell row r* **do**
2     $\mathcal{RS}_r \leftarrow$ initialize a row structure and insert all macros $\in r$
3 **end**
4 Sort cells according to center x coordinates
5 **for** *each movable $c_j \in \mathcal{C}$* **do**
6     $q \leftarrow$ initialize a min-priority-queue with (x_j, y_j)
7   **while** *q is not empty* **do**
8        $(x_{trial}, y_{trial}) \leftarrow$ extract_min(q)
9        $k \leftarrow (x_{trial}, y_{trial})$ row
10   **if** *range $[x_{trial}, x_{trial} + W_j]$ is free at $\mathcal{RS}_k$* **then**
11   place c_j at (x_{trial}, y_{trial})
12   insert $[x_{trial}, x_{trial} + W_j]$ in $\mathcal{RS}_k$ and clear q
13   **else**
14   insert next free site at right of (x_{trial}, y_{trial}) in q
15   insert sites above and below (x_{trial}, y_{trial}) in q
16   **end**
17   **end**
18 **end**

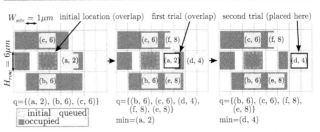

Figure 4: Example of overlap removal on the red cell.

is 0.69, whereas c, r are capacitance and resistance per micron and $l_{j,k}$ corresponds to the Manhattan distance from c_j to c_k. The interconnection delay variation is computed (line 9) as the difference between current lumped Elmore and reference value $\hat{\tau}_{j,k}$. The wire slew variation is computed (lines 10 and 11) as the difference between current wire slew and reference value $s\hat{l}ew_{j,k}$. Current wire slew is estimated through PERI model using the arc slew of driver c_j, second moment of impulse response on receiver c_k ($\beta_{j,k}$) and Elmore [11]. Lines 12 and 13 compute the partial cost associated to each fanout, where A_2 corresponds to the slew characterization coefficient. Note that such strategy allows for estimating the costs relying on accurate values computed using the Steiner trees. Line 15 uses the constants α and ω to account for different importances when minimizing late and early violations. Finally, line 20 places c_j in the candidate location with the lowest cost. Note that Algorithm 1 has a linear time complexity w.r.t. the number of movable cells, since the number of candidate locations ρ and number of fanouts are bounded and can be considered as constants.

We evaluated the accuracy of the differential delay model using different fixed-size windows: 7, 32 and 64 locations. The windows of sizes 7 and 32 allow for considering candidates within the same row, whereas the window of size 64 includes candidate locations in the rows above and below the anchor location. We randomly took a c_j placed on a benchmark circuit from [11] and evaluated, for each considered window, the cost of the farthest location from the anchor. To obtain the reference values to compare with the differential delay used in Algorithm 1, we recomputed the local Steiner tree using the timing analyzer. The average errors were 2.1%, 10,95% and 154,18% when the search uses windows of 7, 32 and 64 locations, respectively. The significant error produced by using a window of 64 locations comes from placing c_j in a different row. Due to the need for accurate delay estimates to choose the new location, we decided to use a search window of 7 locations. We also observed through experiments that the use of a small fixed-size window allows to change a large number of cells, which significantly reduces total negative slack with negligible overhead in wirelength, as detailed in Section 5.2.

4.1.2 Overlap removal

Typically, net-based approaches place the entire circuit (e.g., [6, 8]), thus requiring a final legalization step to align standard cells to rows and sites, and also to remove overlaps. However, such legalization can undermine the timing optimization [26]. Unlike, our discrete local search has the advantage of finding locations that are aligned to rows and sites, allowing overlaps between cells only, since candidate locations that overlap with macros are disregarded. Therefore, we developed a fast procedure to remove such overlaps (Algorithm 2), while keeping the cells as close as possible from their previously found locations to preserve timing improvements. We emphasize that iterative overlap removal helps preserving the timing, differently from a unique legalization step used in related techniques [3, 14]. Another strategy would be to perform instant legalization after each movement, as proposed in a recent work that reduces congestion through detailed placement [2]. However, if discrete local search and instant legalization are performed in reverse topological order, the displacement w.r.t. the location found may be very high. On the other hand, if they are performed sorting cells by their center coordinates, it may drastically impact on the accuracy of delay estimates due to inaccurate output capacitance values. That is why we propose to iteratively choose the locations and then remove overlaps (sorting cell by center coordinate x) keeping the cells as close as possible from their chosen locations.

Figure 4 presents an example of the overlap removal technique. Initially, the cell highlighted in red overlaps with an already placed cell or macro. The idea is to search for the nearest free location to remove such overlap with the shortest displacement, using Manhattan distance (a, distance of $2\mu m$; b and c, distance of $6\mu m$). To find the nearest free location, we iteratively increase the search area using a min-priority-queue to order the adjacent locations. The priority of a location corresponds to its distance to the location assigned by Algorithm 1. In the first part of Figure 4, three adjacent candidate locations are inserted in q. Then $(a, 2)$ is tried, but as it overlaps with an already placed cell, the next adjacent locations are inserted in q. Finally, the cell is placed in the free location with lowest cost $(d, 4)$.

Algorithm 2 details the proposed procedure to remove overlaps. The key feature is the use of a fast data structure to check if a cell can be inserted in a given location in a row. The row structure (line 2) is a self-balancing binary tree where each node represents an occupied range $[x, x+W]$ in a row, such that two overlapping ranges cannot be kept in the same row structure. Since the binary tree is always sorted and balanced, any operation of insert or find is performed in $O(log \; n)$. We emphasize that the adopted queue takes $O(1)$ time to insert a candidate location, since the algorithm only needs a minimum element when extracting a trial location, which takes $O(log \; n)$ time. The overlap removal procedure is very fast, corresponding to less than 2.29% of the total runtime of the proposed TDP technique (as detailed in Section 5.2).

The integration of TDP with other techniques like gate sizing and threshold voltage assignment is essential to achieve timing closure [26]. In that sense, our technique can be easily extended to account for different sizes and/or threshold voltages during the discrete local search by including the options available in the library in line 3 of Algorithm 1.

4.2 Solve LDP

This step is crucial to guarantee the efficiency of our dynamic net-weighting strategy. To accurately update the circuit timing information we implemented an static timing analyzer (STA) that complies with the timing specifications defined in [11]. It also invokes FLUTE [4] to estimate Steiner trees. We adopted the modified subgradient method from [25] to update late and early net-weights (LMs). Therefore, late and early net-weights at each $c_j \in PO$ and each $c_j \in C$ are updated according to (27) and to (28), respectively. After updating the net-weights, they must be distributed to satisfy the flow conservation conditions (Section 3.3). The distribution is performed by traversing the circuit in reverse topological order, visiting each c_j to distribute proportionally the sum of its output net-weights to each input net. Note that such distribution tends to increase the net-weights on critical paths, and therefore the worst negative slack is expected to be minimized.

$$\lambda_j^L = \lambda_j^L \left(\frac{a_j^L}{r_j^L} \right), \lambda_j^E = \lambda_j^E \left(\frac{r_j^E}{a_j^E} \right), \forall j \in \mathcal{PO} \quad (27)$$

$$\lambda_{i,j}^L = \lambda_{i,j}^L \left(\frac{a_i^L + d_{i,j}^L}{a_j^L} \right), \lambda_{i,j}^E = \lambda_{i,j}^E \left(\frac{a_j^E}{a_i^E + d_{i,j}^E} \right), \forall j \in \mathcal{C} \quad (28)$$

The advantage of using Lagrange multipliers as net-weights is that they keep historic information w.r.t. the criticality of each net. Therefore, if a net is historically critical, it keeps a high multiplier even if a slack variation occurs in any iteration, avoiding drastic oscillation between critical and non-critical paths. In addition, LMs indirectly embeds information concerning the number of critical paths passing through a net, which is an essential feature to effectively compress the slack histogram [19]. For instance, if a net influences several critical paths, then its weights incorporate such criticality due to the flow conservation constraints.

5. EXPERIMENTAL RESULTS

This section presents experimental results using the infrastructure provided by the ICCAD 2014 contest (problem B: incremental timing-driven placement) [11]. Our technique

was implemented in C++ and the experiments were performed on a Linux workstation with two CPUs Intel®Xeon®E5-5620 running at 2.4 GHz with 12GB RAM. Section 5.1 details the adopted infrastructure. Section 5.2 analyzes the improvements over the global placer solution provided in [11] and Section 5.3 compares our results with those obtained by the team that achieved the 1st place in the contest.

5.1 Infrastructure

The ICCAD contest infrastructure comprises 7 benchmark circuits, with sizes from 131k to 959k cells [11] (Table 1, column 1). For each benchmark, the contest organizers provided the circuit timing constraints (sdc format), lef and def files containing all relevant physical information, and also an initial solution from a global placer that minimized wirelength and congestion. In addition, two maximum cell displacement constraints (tight and loose) were specified for each benchmark to limit the movements of each cell to a few microns (Manhattan distance) from the initial solution. The infrastructure also includes a cell library containing timing information of cells such as delay and slew characterization coefficients. As stated in [11], the objective is to minimize the total timing violation which includes late and early total negative slacks, as well as late and early worst negative slacks. Another objective metric is to maintain a similar routing congestion from the initial solution. It is measured using the ABU (average bin utilization) metric, which computes the average $\gamma\%$ densest bins in the circuit [10]. A solution is considered legal if: 1) no overlap occurs, 2) standard cells are aligned to rows and sites, 3) macros and fixed blocks were not moved and 4) maximum cell displacement is respected. We used the evaluation scripts provided in the contest infrastructure to validate timing and legality of each solution. As in the contest guidelines, we considered late violations 5 times more important than early violations.

5.2 Empirical Validation

Figure 5 presents late slack histograms at the primary outputs (circuit outputs and input of sequential elements) before and after applying our technique to circuit vga_lcd. One can observe a significant reduction of negative slacks at the primary outputs after optimization. Particularly, the number of primary outputs with negative slack reduced from 2004 to only 2 (i.e., more than 99% of reduction). Besides this, the number of paths with positive slacks between 0 and 1 ns (i.e., potential critical paths) was clearly reduced, showing a consistent histogram compression. Slack compression is highly desirable to minimize the impact of variability [22].

Figure 6 presents placement snapshots with late and early slacks before and after optimizing circuit netcard with our

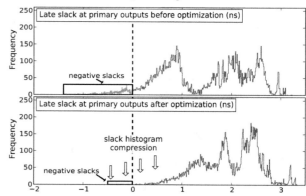

Figure 5: Late slack histogram compression after applying our technique to circuit vga_lcd.

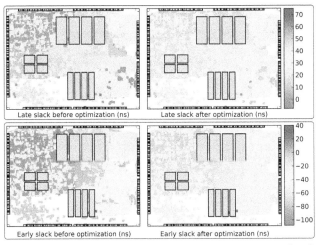

Figure 6: Placement snapshots of *netcard* **for late (top) and early (bottom) slacks.**

technique. These snapshots represent the slack value of each cell through colors (red denotes the worst slacks) except for the large gray rectangles, that represent (fixed) macro blocks. Comparing the late slack snapshots, one can observe that several red cells placed in the upper left corner became orange after optimization. Similar optimization occurred with a few cells in the lower right corner. Particularly, the initial late worst slack of -7.51 ns was improved to 5.88 ns. Analyzing the placement snapshots for early slacks, one can observe important improvements mainly in the upper left corner. Initially, the worst early slack was −108.10, being improved to −75.05. Such improvements are significant mainly because in this circuit early slack violations are more frequent and also more severe than late slack violations. It is worth mentioning that in the final solution cells are not far from their positions from the global placer. This is an important requirement for TDP, since keeping similar placement tends to preserve the wirelength and routability.

Table 1 presents, for each benchmark, the initial solution provided in the contest infrastructure (generated by a global placer) [11], our results and those results from the 1st place place in the contest. Columns 3, 5, 4 and 6 present late and early worst negative slacks (wns) and late and early total negative slacks (tns), respectively. Column 7 gives ABU penalty and column 8 brings the overall placement quality metric that comprises late and early slack improvements and ABU penalty (as defined in the contest [11]). Steiner wirelength (StWL), displacement (obtained / tight constraint) and runtime are given in columns 9 to 11. The bottom lines report the average reduction of our technique when compared to the initial solution and to the 1st place, in which a negative reduction means a worse result. Firstly, we analyze the improvements obtained using our technique over the initial solution.

Late wns and tns: late timing violations are removed for the three largest circuits and significantly reduced for the other ones, achieving improvements on wns and tns of 90%, 99% for *b19* and 88% and 99% for *vga_lcd*. The obtained improvements on *edit_dist* and *matrix_mult* were quite lower, representing reductions on wns and tns of 12%, 61%, 12% and 36%, respectively. Nevertheless, the average wns and tns reductions are 72% and 85%, respectively, showing the potential contribution of the technique to achive timing closure.

Early wns and tns: The average improvements on early wns and tns are 35% and 43%, respectively. Although the

contest guidelines assigned lower importance to early violations (compared to late violations), the initial solutions present significantly more early timing violations than late violations what makes such results remarkable.

ABU penalty, StWL and displacement: The average overfill penalty increase (measured through the ABU metric) is 0.006, meaning an increase of 0.6% of overflowing bins. The average increase in wirelength (computed using FLUTE [4]) is less than 0.1%. In addition, our technique maintains displacements far from those of the tight constraints, what means that cell distribution does not change too much w.r.t the global placement. These results indicate that besides reducing timing violations, our technique preserves the quality of the global placement.

Runtime: for the considered benchmark circuits, solving LRS requires, on average, 33,77% of the runtime, whereas STA requires, on average, 62,11%. The overlap removal and net-weight update procedures take, on average, 0.76% and 3.36%, respectively. A significant portion of STA time is due to estimating Steiner trees (43.32%) which, by its turn, strongly depends on the circuit routing characteristics. This explains the long runtimes to optimize *leon2* and *leon3*. For smaller circuits (< 220k cells), the runtime is less than 8 minutes, whereas for circuit *netcard* (almost 1M cells) the runtime is less than 2.2 hours.

5.3 Comparisons

The comparison of our results with those from the contest 1st team is detailed below.

Late wns and tns: on average, our technique further improves wns and tns by 13.42% and 20.18%, respectively. Particularly, the more expressive reductions are obtained on circuit *vga_lcd*: 50.22% on wns and 89.52% on tns.

Early wns and tns: on average, our technique improves wns and tns by 5.07% and 4.55% , respectively. Particularly, the more expressive reductions are obtained on circuit *leon3*: 11.89% on wns and 23.20% on tns.

ABU penalty and quality: according to Table 1, the improvements obtained in wns and tns increased the ABU penalty when compared to the 1st place, except for circuits *edit_dist*, *matrix_mult* and *vga_lcd*. The average increase of overfill penalty is 0.47%. On the other hand, according to the contest quality metric, the reductions on timing violations have more impact on quality than ABU penalty itself. That is why we obtained an average improvement on quality of 1.28%, achieving 6.04% on *vga_lcd*.

Runtime: Our technique requires shorter runtime to optimize three circuits: *edit_dist*, *matrix_mult* and *netcard*. The longer runtimes to optimize the other ones are mainly due to the circuit routing characteristics. Finally, we highlight that our machine configuration is slightly inferior to that used during the contest evaluation [11].

6. CONCLUSIONS

Slack histogram compression is generally performed by gate sizing and buffer insertion while TDP mainly focuses on minimizing the wns. We proposed a TDP technique that compresses the slack histogram and minimizes the wns. Such a technique is based on a complete LR formulation to minimize late and early tns. The use of LMs as net-weights showed to be effective since they are dynamically updated using an accurate timer and represent historic information about net criticalities. In addition, the flow conservation constraints applied in the formulation increased the net-weights on critical paths.The proposed technique performed discrete local search on each movable cell, followed by an efficient overlap removal procedure. Experimental results

Table 1: Results using timing-driven placement contest benchmarks [11] for the tight displacement constraint. For each circuit, the table presents the metrics from: global placement (initial), our technique and contest 1st team.

benchmark	solution	late wns (s)	late tns (s)	early wns (s)	early tns (s)	ABU (E-2)	Quality	StWL (m)	obt./max. displ.(μm)	runtime (min)
edit_dist	Initial	-8.08E-10	-9.41E-8	-1.45E-9	-3.45E-6	0	—	5.21	—	—
cells: 131k	Ours	-7.15E-10	-3.69E-8	-8.84E-10	-1.64E-6	0	808.73	5.21	16.2 / 30	4.9
macros: 13	1st place	-7.02E-10	-3.37E-8	-8.34E-10	-1.48E-6	0	864.55	5.21	4.8 /30	82.4
matrix_mult	Initial	-4.41E-10	-2.61E-9	-3.59E-10	-1.10E-7	0	—	3.09	—	—
cells: 155k	Ours	-3.90E-10	-1.67E-9	-2.85E-10	-4.38E-8	0	558.23	3.09	6.1 / 30	5.4
macros: 16	1st place	-3.96E-10	-1.72E-9	-2.81E-10	-4.39E-8	0	534.46	3.09	4.8 / 30	39.2
vga_lcd	Initial	-1.33E-9	-6.39E-7	-4.58E-9	-4.75E-5	1.25	—	5.80	—	—
cells: 165k	Ours	-1.64E-10	-2.28E-10	-2.73E-9	-3.02E-5	1.84	1542.33	5.81	0.2 / 10	7.6
macros: 0	1st place	-3.30E-10	-2.17E-9	-3.27E-9	-3.18E-5	2.17	1454.50	5.81	10 / 10	1.5
b19	Initial	-1.16E-9	-1.58E-8	-3.76E-9	-1.15E-5	2.59	—	4.29	—	—
cells: 219k	Ours	-1.17E-10	-2.19E-10	-1.83E-9	-4.06E-6	3.09	1608.46	4.28	0.2 / 20	7.0
macros: 0	1st place	-2.09E-10	-5.31E-10	-1.95E-9	-4.52E-6	2.59	1546.31	4.29	19.8 / 20	0.9
leon3mp	Initial	-7.61E-9	-2.82E-5	-6.85E-8	-3.62E-3	0.78	—	24.20	—	—
cells: 649k	Ours	0	0	-4.76E-8	-2.37E-3	1.71	1584.65	24.33	0.3 / 30	143.3
macros: 0	1st place	0	0	-8.22E-8	-3.09E-3	0.78	1550.51	24.20	3.2 / 30	44.2
leon2	Initial	-1.07E-8	-2.00E-5	-1.25E-7	-1.05E-2	2.45	—	47.86	—	—
cells: 794k	Ours	0	0	-8.06E-8	-8.22E-3	2.92	1571.28	47.96	0.2 / 40	281.5
macros: 0	1st place	0	0	-8.22E-8	-7.80E-3	2.45	1585.57	47.86	3.2 / 40	18.1
netcard	Initial	-7.51E-9	-7.55E-6	-1.08E-7	-7.35E-3	1.13	—	59.48	—	—
cells: 959k	Ours	0	0	-7.51E-8	-5.18E-3	2.84	1566.46	59.45	11.7 / 50	126.5
macros: 12	1st place	0	0	-8.05E-8	-5.77E-3	1.13	1568.42	59.48	6.4 / 50	134.1
Average Red.	Initial	71.55%	85.03%	35.40%	42.72%	-0.60%	—	-0.09%	—	—
Average Red.	1st place	13.42%	20.18%	5.07%	4.55%	-0.47%	1.28%	-0.07%	—	—

showed that the adopted small fixed-size window maintained the accuracy of delay estimates and preserved the placement quality. Moreover, instead of focusing only on cells of a few critical paths, the adopted strategy optimized a large number of cells, which significantly improved the slack histogram and wns.

7. ACKNOWLEDGMENTS

This work was partially supported by CAPES and by CNPq through the grants 550185/2013-5 (PNM), 309047/20-12-9 (PQ) and 303546/2012-3 (PQ).

8. REFERENCES

[1] C. Alpert et al. Placement: hot or not? In *Proc. ICCAD*, pages 283–290, 2012.

[2] W.-K. Chow et al. Cell density-driven detailed placement with displacement constraint. In *Proc. ISPD*, pages 3–10, 2014.

[3] A. Chowdhary et al. How accurately can we model timing in a placement engine? In *Proc. DAC*, pages 801–806, 2005.

[4] C. Chu et al. Flute: Fast lookup table based rectilinear steiner minimal tree algorithm for vlsi design. *TCAD*, 27(1):70–83, 2008.

[5] H. Eisenmann et al. Generic global placement and floorplanning. In *Proc. DAC*, pages 269–274, 1998.

[6] B. Halpin et al. Timing driven placement using physical net constraints. In *Proc. DAC*, pages 780–783, 2001.

[7] T. Hamada et al. Prime: a timing-driven placement tool using a piecewise linear resistive network approach. In *Proc. DAC*, pages 531–536, 1993.

[8] A. B. Kahng et al. An analytic placer for mixed-size placement and timing-driven placement. In *Proc. ICCAD*, pages 565–572, 2004.

[9] A. B. Kahng et al. *VLSI physical design: from graph partitioning to timing closure*, volume 312. 2011.

[10] M.-C. Kim et al. Maple: multilevel adaptive placement for mixed-size designs. In *Proc. ISPD*, pages 193–200, 2012.

[11] M.-C. Kim, J. Hu, and N. Viswanathan. Iccad-2014 cad contest in incremental timing-driven placement and benchmark suite. In *Proc. ICCAD*, pages 361–366, 2014.

[12] T. T. Kong. A novel net weighting algorithm for timing-driven placement. In *Proc. ICCAD*, pages 172–176, 2002.

[13] Z. Li et al. Guiding a physical design closure system to produce easier-to-route designs with more predictable timing. In *Proc. DAC*, pages 465–470, 2012.

[14] T. Luo et al. A new lp based incremental timing driven placement for high performance designs. In *Proc. DAC*, pages 1115–1120, 2006.

[15] I. L. Markov et al. Progress and challenges in vlsi placement research. In *Proc. ICCAD*, pages 275–282, 2012.

[16] M. D. Moffitt et al. Path smoothing via discrete optimization. In *Proc. DAC*, pages 724–727, 2008.

[17] M. M. Ozdal et al. Algorithms for gate sizing and device parameter selection for high-performance designs. *TCAD*, 31(10):1558–1571, 2012.

[18] K. Rajagopal et al. Timing driven force directed placement with physical net constraints. In *Proc. ISPD*, pages 60–66, 2003.

[19] H. Ren et al. Sensitivity guided net weighting for placement-driven synthesis. *TCAD*, 24(5):711–721, 2005.

[20] H. Ren et al. Hippocrates: first-do-no-harm detailed placement. In *Proc. ASP-DAC*, pages 141–146, 2007.

[21] B. M. Riess et al. Speed: Fast and efficient timing driven placement. In *Proc. ISCAS*, pages 377–380, 1995.

[22] D. Sinha et al. Tau 2013 variation aware timing analysis contest. In *Proc. ISPD*, pages 171–178, 2013.

[23] A. Srinivasan et al. Ritual: A performance driven placement algorithm for small cell ics. In *Proc. ICCAD*, pages 48–51, 1991.

[24] W. Swartz and C. Sechen. Timing driven placement for large standard cell circuits. In *Proc. DAC*, pages 211–215, 1995.

[25] H. Tennakoon et al. Nonconvex gate delay modeling and delay optimization. *TCAD*, 27(9):1583–1594, 2008.

[26] N. Viswanathan et al. Itop: integrating timing optimization within placement. In *Proc. ISPD*, pages 83–90, 2010.

Closing the Gap between Global and Detailed Placement: Techniques for Improving Routability

Chun-Kai Wang[1], Chuan-Chia Huang[2], Sean Shih-Ying Liu[1], Ching-Yu Chin[1],
Sheng-Te Hu[1], Wei-Chen Wu[1], Hung-Ming Chen[1]
[1] Institute of Electronics, National Chiao Tung University, Hsinchu, Taiwan
[2] NovaTek Inc., Hsinchu, Taiwan
{oldkai.ee90, chuan.ee96, sniealu, alwaysrain.gr, jim2212001,
sherlock21315}@gmail.com, hmchen@mail.nctu.edu.tw

ABSTRACT

Improving routability during both global and detailed routing stage has become a critical problem in modern VLSI design. In this work, we propose a placement framework that offers a complete coverage solution in considering both global and detailed routing congestion. A placement migration strategy is proposed, which improves detailed routing congestion while preserving the placement integrity that is optimized for global routability. Using the benchmarks released from ISPD2014 Contest, practical design rules in advanced node design are considered in our placement framework. Evaluation on routability of our placement framework is conducted using commercial router provided by the 2014 ISPD Contest organizers. Experimental results show that the proposed methodologies can effectively improve placement solutions for both global and detailed router.

Categories and Subject Descriptors

B.7.2 [**Integrated Circuits**]: Design Aids—*Placement and routing*; J.6 [**COMPUTER-AIDED ENGINEERING**]: Computer-aided design (CAD)

Keywords

routability, placement migration

1. INTRODUCTION

Routability of the design is a critical factor to achieve design closure using minimal area. If the design is unroutable, designer is forced to increase chip area to obtain a routable design. Increase in chip area indicates increase in cost. Thus, improving routability is critical to achieve cost effective design.

[1] This work was supported by the Ministry of Science and Technology of Taiwan by Grant No. MOST 103-2220-E-009-028.

While global routing congestion captures the general routability of the design, routing violations induced by non-default routes and routing blocked pins are unable to identify by global router. Previous works have shown that detailed routing congestion in advanced node design becomes more critical and can be inconsistent with congestion during global routing stage [18]. Additional effort is required during placement stage to consider the detailed routability and design rule constraints.

Prior arts proposed several methods on resolving global routing congestion. The work done in [15, 6, 8, 3, 2] resolves congestion by adjusting cell density through cell inflation. The work done in [8, 6] dynamically controls the target cell density during global placement iteration. In [3], a net based removal algorithm is proposed to reduce congestion. The work done in [5, 4] directly models routing overflow penalty in the nonlinear optimization. In [20], the placer adopted from the SimPL framework [9] expands look ahead region with precise amount of white space to meet routing demand. Based on empirical results from prior arts, cell inflation is effective in reducing local routing congestion and regional density control is effective in reducing global routing congestions.

Several recent works [7, 12, 1] addressed their effort on congestion and design rule violations occurred during detailed routing stage. Conventional congestion-aware placer is unaware of the detailed routing congestion. In advanced node technology, design rule violations often occur around fixed macro blocks and between certain types of adjacent cells.

In terms of modeling routing congestion, recent work done in [12, 6] has proposed several methods to account local net congestion by adjusting global routing edge capacity. In 2014 ISPD Detailed Routing Driven Placement Contest [19], more realistic constraints from advanced node design are included in the contest, which include non-default routing (NDR), predefined power ground stripes, and edge type spacing rules. This requires delicate routing resource modeling to capture routing congestion at detailed routing stage.

In this work, we address global routing congestion using several global routing congestion optimization techniques including history based cell inflation and dynamic target density control in our global placer adopted from the SimPL framework [9]. To optimize placement for better detailed routability and to maintain the integrity of the original placement, we implement an incremental placer adopted from the

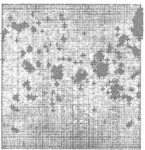

(a) Detailed routing map w/ our placement migration (b) Detailed routing map w/o our placement migration

(c) Cell displacement map w/ our placement migration (d) Cell displacement map w/o our placement migration

Figure 1: The short number of detail routing is reduced after placement migration. (a) and (b) shows detail routing result; (c) and (d) shows cell movement from the end of global placement to the end of detail placement.

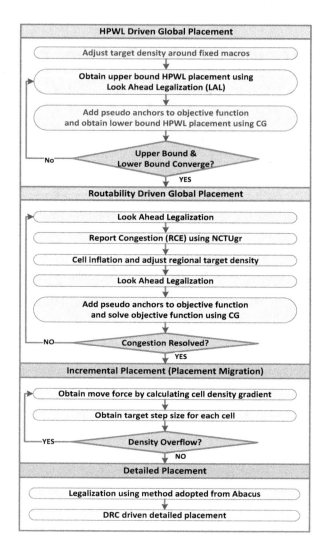

Figure 2: Flow chart of the proposed placement framework

Kraftwerk2 framework [17]. Finally, a DRC-driven detailed placement is performed after incremental placement.

The purpose of our incremental placer follows the concept of placement migration proposed in [14, 13]. In [14], it is shown that placement migration can improve timing and total wirelegnth compared to conventional legalization. The concept of placement migration can also be observed in MAPLE [10] which applies progressive local refinement to mitigate local cell overlapping. This work on applying incremental placer demonstrates similar benefit compared to placement migration. However, the work done in [14] moves cells using diffusion-based method which does not include a wirelength model. On the contrary, our incremental placer is a three force balance system which include a hold force to maintain the integrity of original placement, a net force that models the wirelength and a move force to perturb the placement.

Fig. 1 shows the benefit on applying our incremental placer for placement migration. Fig. 1(a) is the detailed routing congestion map with our placement migration and Fig. 1(b) is the detailed routing congestion map without our placement migration. Regions colored in red indicate severe detailed routing violation, regions colored in yellow indicate moderate detailed routing violation and regions colored in blue indicate no detailed routing violation. It can be observed regions colored in red is greatly reduced with our placement migration.

Fig. 1(c) is the cell displacement map with our placement migration and Fig. 1(d) is the cell displacement map without

our placement migration. Fig. 1(d) finds nearest legalization spot for each cell. Thus, it generates less cell displacement. Although the placement migration generates larger cell displacement, it effectively reduces the disruption of routability induced by legalization.

Fig. 2 is the flow chart of the proposed placement framework. The placement framework consists of four stages. The first stage is a HPWL driven global placer. The second stage optimizes routability of the placed design using NCTUgr [11] for routing congestion estimation. The third stage performs placement migration to reduce the disruption during legalization and maintain the integrity from first stage global placement. The forth stage is a DRC-driven detailed placer that serves to reduce edge type spacing violations.

The contributions of this work are summarized as follows.

- An incremental placer for placement migration is proposed to improve cell relative order and maintain integrity of the original placement. Experimental result shows that with placement migration, detailed routing congestion can be greatly reduced.

- A design rule constraint (DRC) driven detailed placer is proposed to reduce the edge type minimum spacing violation for specific types of cell.

- Routing resource model for non-default routing and the power ground stripes.

The rest of this paper is organized as follows. Section 2 formulates the problem. Section 3 presents our routability driven global placer. Section 4 presents our incremental placer for placement migration. Section 5 presents our DRC-driven detailed placer. Section 6 shows the experimental result of our placement framework on 2014 ISPD Contest Benchmark [19] and Section 7 concludes this work.

2. PROBLEM FORMULATION

Given a netlist $N = (V, E)$ in which V is a set of modules and E is a set of connections of modules. The problem is to place all movable modules on placement site with the following objectives: 1) minimize total detailed routing violations, 2) minimize routed wire length, and 3) minimize total run time.

In 2014 ISPD Contest Placement benchmarks, a given design includes the following files.

- **A technology LEF** file that defines the placement site, available metal layers and routing rules. The routing rules include metal width, metal spacing, end of line rule, and non-default-routing (NDR).

- **A cell LEF** file that defines physical information of modules.

- **A floorplan DEF** file that defines the routing resource occupied power ground rails, fixed I/O ports, fixed modules, and unplaced modules.

- **A Verilog** file that defines the netlist in gate level.

3. ROUTABILITY DRIVEN GLOBAL PLACEMENT

Before global placer begins, the target density adjacent to fixed macros is scaled down using Gaussian Blurring. This prevents cell sliding to thin channels between fixed macro blocks. After target density around fixed macros is configured, a HPWL driven global placer is performed until the upper bound and lower bound of HPWL is converged. Routability optimization begins after HPWL driven global placement. Our routability optimization techniques consist of cell inflation which serves to reduce local routing congestion and regional target density control which serves to reduce global routing congestion.

During global routing stage, the design is partitioned into a 2D global routing tile array (g-cell). Each g-cell has a routing capacity in horizontal and vertical direction. Routing overflow occurs if routing demand of a g-cell exceeds its routing capacity.

Pin density of g-cell is monitored to determine on which circumstance to apply cell inflation and target density control. Congested g-cell with low pin density is considered as global congestion, and target density is adjusted for these g-cells. Algorithm 1 describes our procedure on inflating cells and adjusting target density. Table 1 defines the annotations used in Algorithm 1.

Table 1: Annotations used Algorithm 1

Variable	Definition
g_k	g-cell k
v_i	cell i
Dem(g_k)	Routing Demand of g_k
Cap(g_k)	Routing Capacity of g_k
width(v_i)	Current cell width of v_i
orig_width(v_i)	Original cell width of v_i
pin(g_k)	Pin density in g_k
H-Cap(g_k)	Horizontal routing capacity of g_k
V-Cap(g_k)	Vertical routing capacity of g_k
current_dens(g_k)	Current cell density in g_k
target_dens(g_k)	Target cell density in g_k

Algorithm 1 Cell Inflation and Target Density Control

1: **for** each g-cell g_k **do**
2:   **if** Dem(g_k)/Cap(g_k) > 90% **then**
3:     **for** each cell v_i in g_k **do**
4:       width(v_i) = orig_width(v_i) * $(1 + 0.1\beta)$
5:     **end for**
6:     **if** pin(g_k)<0.3*(H-Cap(g_k)+V-Cap(g_k)) **then**
7:       target_dens(g_k) = current_dens(g_k)*0.9
8:     **end if**
9:   **else**
10:     target_dens(g_k) += (1.0 - current_dens(g_k)) * 0.6
11:   **end if**
12: **end for**

In Algorithm 1, a g-cell is defined as congested if routing demand of a g-cell exceeds 90% of its routing capacity. Each cell in a congested g-cell is inflated by 10% of its original width times β that is the number of times this cell has been inflated. A g-cell is defined as a globally congested g-cell if it is congested and its pin density is less than 30% g-cell capacity. The target densities for these global congested g-cell is scaled down by 0.9. For non-congested g-cell, the target density is increased by scaled up by 0.6 on its current white space.

Look ahead legalization is performed after cell inflation and target density in selected regions is adjusted. Routability of the placement is evaluated using the ACE metric [18] (weighted sum of top 0.5%, 1%, 2%, and 5% congested g-edges) and total routed wire length $rtWL$. When Eq. (1) is satisfied, the placement location will be updated.

$$ACE_{best} - ACE_{new} > \alpha \times (\frac{rtWL_{new}}{rtWL_{best}} - 1)) \qquad (1)$$

Initially, the ACE_{best} and $rtWL_{best}$ are assigned by routing congestion estimation of first iteration. When the condition described in Eq. (1) is satisfied, ACE_{best} and $rtWL_{best}$ are updated with the new placement result. In this work, α is set to 10.

NCTUgr [11] is applied to estimate routing congestion. NCTUgr provides APIs to define size of g-cell, pin blockage and routing mode. In this work, g-cell size is set to twice of the row height, pin blockage is set according to the number of available routing metal layers.

To account for NDR nets, the routing congestion estimation has two steps. In the first step, the routing resource is scaled down by the spacing and width of NDR and only nets belong to NDR are routed. In the second step, the remaining nets are routed using the routing resource that

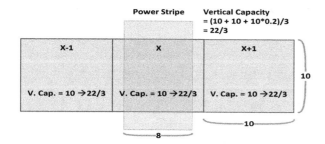

Figure 3: Routing resource model with power stripes

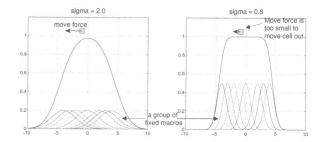

Figure 4: Gaussian superposition in response to different value of *sigma*.

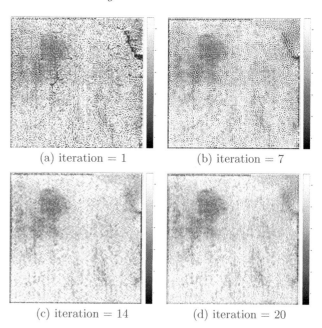

(a) iteration = 1   (b) iteration = 7

(c) iteration = 14   (d) iteration = 20

Figure 5: Cell density of testcase mgc_matrix_multiply during incremental placement. Cell density is gradually smooth during placement migration.

is deducted by the NDR routing resource. In addition, to account for the NDR-pin-access, the cell with NDR pin are inflated by one site so that the spacing is preserved.

When the routing demand of the predefined power stripes is considered, the local regions that g-cells are covered by power stripes will lack of routing resource, and the congestion would be easily generated around. However, it is inefficient to solve this type of congestion in global placement. Since the prior task in global placement is to solve the highly-congested region, and it is usually only few number of nets causing this type of congestion, which may be easily solved by a detail router. Our solution is to evenly deduct routing capacity from n g-cells adjacent to the g-cell overlapped with the power stripe. Fig. 3 illustrates an example of adjust routing capacity with power stripes. In Fig. 3, the original vertical capacity is set to 10 and window size is set to 3. 80% of the vertical routing capacity of the g-cell at the center is occupied by one power stripe. The adjusted vertical capacity takes total routing capacity to subtract occupied capacity by the power stripe and divide to three other g-cells.

4. PLACEMENT MIGRATION

The technique of placement migration is applied to migrate placement solution from global placement to legalization. In this work, we found that detailed routing congestion is improved when placement migration is applied. The Kraftwerk2 placement framework proposed in [17] is adopted as the incremental placer used in this work. The main difference between Kraftwerk2 and this work is how to derive the move force, which effectively smooths the transition from global placement to legalization.

Kraftwerk2's force system includes three forces: net force, hold force, and move force. The net force models the net connection and can be minimized using iterative method. Adding hold force to the force model cancels out the effect of net force so that cells remain in same location. Adding move force to the force model, the force equilibrium model moves cells to new position and placement is incrementally spread out. The force equilibrium system consisting of net force, hold force, and move force preserves the integrity of the original placement and incrementally adjust placement to migrate cell density.

In Kraftwerk2, each move force is modeled by an anchor $\mathring{x}$ as a pseudo net and a pseudo net weight $\mathring{w}$. The anchor position is derived by solving the Poisson equation describe in Eq. (2) in which cells are regarded as charges and the electric field implies the direction of cell spreading. However,

since the primary objective is not the accuracy of the potential surface, any distribution function is suffice to meet the supply-demand constraint. In this work, the surface model is obtained using Gaussian Blurring described in Eq. (3)(4).

$$\mathring{x}(x,y) = -\nabla\Phi(x,y) \tag{2}$$

$$\Phi(x,y) = \sum_{i \in standard} h(x,y) * g(x,y,\sigma_s)$$
$$+ \sum_{i \in fixed} h(x,y) * g(x,y,\sigma_f) \tag{3}$$

$$g(x,y,\sigma) = \frac{1}{2\pi\sigma^2}\exp\left(-\left(\frac{x^2}{2\sigma^2} + \frac{y^2}{2\sigma^2}\right)\right) \tag{4}$$

In terms of image processing, Gaussian blurring is equivalent to the convolution between a Gaussian function $g(x,y,\sigma)$ and a density function $h(x,y)$. The term σ defines the affected range for each unit cell area. In Eq. (3), the fixed macros and the standard cells are separated, and the different σ is applied to remove the overlap that standard cells are illegally placed on fixed macros. To remove such overlap, σ_f is larger than σ_s, or only the overlap near macros boundary will be removed. Fig. 4 illustrates difference in cell density surface model between a large σ_f value and a low σ_f values. After the overlap on fixed macros are removed, σ_f are reduced to be equal to σ_s so that the white space near macro boundary could be utilized.

In our implementation, $h[m,n]$ and $g[i,j]$ are the discrete representation for $h(x,y)$ and $g(x,y)$. The plane is discretized by slicing chip into small bins. The area overlap between each bin and cells are then calculated. Each unit cell area has an amplitude of 1 unit Gaussian distribution. In this work, the bin size is equal to the row height.

$$h[m,n] = \sum_{v \in V} P_v[m,n] \tag{5}$$

$$\Phi_x[m,n] = \sum_i \sum_j h[m-i,n-j] \frac{\partial}{\partial \boldsymbol{x}} g[i,j] \tag{6}$$

$$\Phi_y[m,n] = \sum_i \sum_j h[m-i,n-j] \frac{\partial}{\partial \boldsymbol{y}} g[i,j], \tag{7}$$

$P_v[m,n]$ is the discrete density function contributed by cell v. To derive Φ_x and Φ_y, the convolution between density matrix and Gaussian matrix is performed, and then the anchor of cell located at (x',y') is interpolated by Φ_x and Φ_y. Note that no target density is set in this stage, since the derived anchors are located within local bins, the global density were not changed in our experiment.

The execution time of two dimensional convolution in spatial domain increases quadratically with the size of Gaussian matrix g. The computation complexity is reduced, when convolution is performed in frequency domain. Suppose a $M \times M$ Gaussian matrix and a $N \times N$ density matrix, the complexity is reduced from $O(M^2N^2)$ to $O(N^2 log N^2)$ in frequency domain.

In Kraftwerk2, the pseudo net weight is iteratively adjusted using Eq. (8) in which μ_T is the target step size to control the trade-off between convergence rate and placement quality. However, the target step size is the average movement of all cells that lacks of local view and does not effectively remove local overlaps.

$$\mathring{w}_i^{k+1} = \mathring{w}_i^k \cdot (1 + \tanh(\ln(\mu_T/\mu))) \tag{8}$$

Thus, Eq. (9) is applied to configure the pseudo net weight $\mathring{w}_i^k$ in this work. To prevent large perturbation, the pseudo net weight is set to half of the Bound2Bound (B2B) wirelength model. Compared to the pseudo net weight in Eq. (10) which is applied in the SimPL framework, the net weight is equivalent to the 50th global placement iteration.

$$\mathring{w} = 0.5 \times \frac{1}{|x' - \mathring{x}|} \tag{9}$$

$$\mathring{w}^{k+1} = \frac{0.01 \cdot (1 + \text{iterationNumber})}{|x' - \mathring{x}|}, \tag{10}$$

The incremental placer iteratively spreads out placement density until the maximum iteration is reached. As the iteration number increases, σ_s is gradually decreased so that cells are separated from each other. Larger value of σ_s implies that each cell affects larger region of placement which

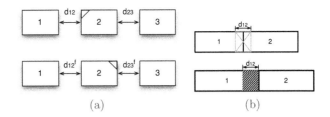

(a)   (b)

Figure 6: Cells are flipped if the spacing between adjacent cells is reduced after flipping. (a) Flipping cell 2. (b) Inflating cell 1 to resolve spacing rule violation.

Table 2: Statistics on ISPD 2014 Detailed Routing-Driven Placement Contest Benchmarks

Benchmarks	Util.	#Cell	#nets	#I/O
Suite A				
mgc_des_perf_1	90%	112644	112878	374
mgc_des_perf_2	85%	112644	112878	374
mgc_edit_dist_1	40%	130661	133223	2574
mgc_edit_dist_2	43%	130661	133223	2574
mgc_pci_bridge_1	84%	30675	30835	361
mgc_pci_bridge_2	85%	30675	30835	361
mgc_fft	83%	32281	33307	3010
mgc_matrix_mult	80%	155325	158527	4802
Suite B				
mgc_superblue_11	44%	925616	935731	27371
mgc_superblue_12	48%	1286948	1293436	5908
mgc_superblue_16	49%	680450	697458	17498

can drive small cell out of fixed macro. A smaller value of σ_s implies that each cell affects smaller region of placement which let cell rearrange its relative order and find nearest white space.

In this work, the maximum incremental placement iteration is set to 20 and the value of σ_s is halved in every 7 iterations. The initial value of σ_s is set to four times of row height. Figure 5 shows the change in cell density for testcase mgc_matrix_multiply during incremental placement. It can be observed that cell density is gradually decreased on each iteration of incremental placement.

5. DRC DRIVEN DETAILED PLACEMENT

After placement migration, cells are legalized using technique adopted from Abacus [16]. A DRC driven detailed placer is initiated to reduce the edge type spacing violations. Cells are examined in pairs on each row from left to right. There are two rounds of examination. In the first round of examination, if a pair of cells violates edge type spacing rule, the width of the left cell is inflated to the minimum width such that spacing rule is satisfied. In the second round of examination, cell is flipped and checked whether the spacing between adjacent cells can be reduced. After examining all adjacent pairs, cells are legalized again. Figure 6 illustrates the cell flipping and cell inflation to resolve edge type spacing rule. In Figure 6(a), cell 2 is flipped if $d_{12} + d_{23} > d_{12}^f + d_{23}^f$. In Figure 6(b), cell 1 and cell 2 have an edge type spacing violation, the width of cell 1 is inflated with the required amount of spacing. Note that the pin blockage due to power stripes was not be dealt in this work.

Table 4: Comparison on placement result of our placement framework with top 3 teams in 2014 ISPD Placement Contest. (Normalized value excludes the unaccepted results)

Benchmark	UW&UC	CUHK	NCTU	[7]	Our	run time (sec)
DP						
mgc_des_perf_1	3.05	3.43	4.08	2.12	4.26	233.99
mgc_des_perf_2	2.85	2.27	1.75	1.55	2.47	228.72
mgc_edit_dist_1	0.99	0.91	0.84	0.03	1.14	363.93
mgc_edit_dist_2	1.06	1.15	1.48	0.03	1.15	365.31
mgc_pci_bridge_1	1.46	1.58	1.51	0.26	1.45	60.41
mgc_pci_bridge_2	1.44	1.62	1.44	0.44	1.62	60.73
mgc_fft	2.04	2.09	2.48	0.96	2.88	72.21
mgc_matrix_mult	1.27	1.22	1.30	0.32	1.43	345.09
mgc_superblue_11	0.55	0.00	0.01	-	0.00	4217.31
mgc_superblue_12	-	-	-	-	0.00	7638.05
mgc_superblue_16	0.04	0.00	0.00	-	0.00	2821.62
Norm.	0.90	0.87	0.91	0.35	1.00	
DR						
mgc_des_perf_1	998.7	421.0	1411.9	296.0	1536.75	
mgc_des_perf_2	19.1	8.5	507.2	3.8	3.75	
mgc_edit_dist_1	3.0	265.5	0.0	23.9	0.0	
mgc_edit_dist_2	120.3	151.0	50.3	209.8	0.0	
mgc_pci_bridge_1	0.0	0.0	0.0	3.9	0.0	
mgc_pci_bridge_2	0.0	0.3	1.5	0.7	0.5	
mgc_fft	105.2	266.6	228.5	331.7	165.2	
mgc_matrix_mult	158.1	1033.4	311.4	182.1	30.95	
mgc_superblue_11	349.8	99.6	349.8	-	232.7	
mgc_superblue_12	-	-	-	-	178.05	
mgc_superblue_16	449.1	21.0	298.4	-	122.25	
Norm.	1.05	1.08	1.51	0.53	1.00	
rtWL (m)						
mgc_des_perf_1	1.838	1.995	2.026	1.820	2.016	
mgc_des_perf_2	1.920	1.972	1.893	1.863	1.952	
mgc_edit_dist_1	4.977	5.417	na	4.854	4.968	
mgc_edit_dist_2	4.695	5.138	5.048	4.858	4.876	
mgc_pci_bridge_1	0.3653	0.3602	0.3688	0.361	0.3709	
mgc_pci_bridge_2	0.3719	0.3704	0.3660	0.352	0.3718	
mgc_fft	0.6516	0.6796	0.6600	0.646	0.6734	
mgc_matrix_mult	3.085	3.133	3.085	3.045	3.073	
mgc_superblue_11	44.54	44.09	45.24	-	44.17	
mgc_superblue_12	-	-	-	-	61.59	
mgc_superblue_16	35.29	38.25	35.89	-	32.88	
Norm.	1.02	1.06	1.10	0.97	1.00	

Table 3: Parameters in the implemented global placement

Benchmarks	p.f.	d.l.	NDR Util.
mgc_des_perf_1	0.15	96%	95%
mgc_des_perf_2	0.15	91%	89%
mgc_edit_dist_1	0.15	51%	42%
mgc_edit_dist_2	0.175	55%	46%
mgc_pci_bridge_1	0.15	96%	95%
mgc_pci_bridge_2	0.15	98%	97%
mgc_fft	0.15	92%	91%
mgc_matrix_mult	0.175	87%	84%
mgc_superblue_11	0.15	70%	53%
mgc_superblue_12	0.15	62%	47%
mgc_superblue_16	0.15	70%	57%

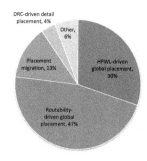

Figure 7: Run time breakdown

6. EXPERIMENTAL RESULTS

In this section, experimental results of our implementations are presented. All of our implementations are implemented using standard C++ language and performed on an Intel Xeon E5620 machine running at 2.4G Hz. Table 2 lists the statistics of the benchmarks used in 2014 ISPD Contest.

The parameters used in the HPWL driven placement are described as follows. For the Gaussian Blurring fixed macros before global placement, the grid size is four times of the row height, and the σ term of Gaussian function is 8. The look ahead legalization has the finest bin area being 64 row height square and the bin aspect-ratio being the average cell width to the row height. Table 3 lists the density limit (d.l.) for look ahead legalization in HPWL driven placement and the pin factor (p.f.) for routing congestion estimation. Note that the density limit considers the inflated cells due to NDR-pin-access, and the utilization after inflating cells due to NDR-pin-access is listed in the last column. The HPWL driven placement is terminated after 45th iteration.

Table 4 compares our results with the top three teams in 2014 ISPD Contest and [7]. Score for each team is collected from the contest website. Every placement result of our placement framework is evaluated by Mentor Graph-

Table 5: Comparison on placement quality without placement migration, force directed placement migration and diffusion-based placement migration

	No PM		Force Directed PM		Diffusion-Based PM	
Bench	rtWL	DR	rtWL	DR	rtWL	DR
mgc_des_perf_1	-	-	2.02	1536.75	2.05	1744.80
mgc_des_perf_2	-	-	1.95	3.75	1.99	13.20
mgc_edit_dist_1	5.00	0.0	4.97	0.0	4.99	0.0
mgc_edit_dist_2	4.92	0.0	4.88	0.0	4.93	0.0
mgc_pci_bridge_1	0.412	0.0	0.371	0.0	0.382	0.0
mgc_pci_bridge_2	0.382	0.5	0.372	0.5	0.378	1.75
mgc_fft	0.680	225.95	0.673	165.2	0.683	250.10
mgc_matrix_mult	3.18	262.05	3.07	30.95	3.15	127.0
Norm.	-	-	1.000	1.000	1.013	1.230

ics OLYMPUS-SOC placement and route tool by submitting the result to the contest server. The contest evaluates placement quality using three metrics. The first metric is the detailed placement (DP) score, which evaluates the displacement of cell from its original input location to its final location, determined by the detailed placer of OLYMPUS-SOC. The second metric is the detailed routing (DR) score, which evaluates the total number of detailed routing violations. Open and short routing violation is penalized by a factor of 1.0, while other routing violations are penalized by a factor of 0.2. The third metrics is the routed wirelength ($rtWL$) from the detailed router.

The contest script first global routes the placement solution. If global routing congestion is higher than a certain threshold, detailed routing will not be performed on the given placement input. The threshold of suite A is that 1.75% g-edge overflow, and the threshold of suite B is that 0.25% g-edge overflow. Lower DP score implies less displacement, lower DR score implies less detailed routing violations and lower $rtWL$ means lower total routed wirelength. The goal is to minimize all three scores.

From Table 4, [7] makes the lowest score among the three metrics but does not report on the case suite of superblue. For all other teams, their DP scores are approximately at the same range. The DP score in mgc_des_perf_1 is slightly higher from our placer. We suspect it is because that this testcase has higher utilization rate for which our placement framework does not perform well. In DR score comparison, we score the least score in 6 out of 11 testcase. Our average routed wire length is similar to UW&UC and is slightly lower than CUHK and NCTU. The normalization value takes the arithmetic mean and normalizes other team's result to our work. The case suite of superblue for [7] and superblue_12 for the top three teams are excluded, since only our placer generates acceptable solution to detailed routing. Figure 7 shows our run time breakdown.

6.1 Placement Migration

Table 5 shows the effectiveness of our incremental placer. Placement solutions without placement migration are compared with two placement migration strategies. The first placement migration strategy (force directed PM) in Table 5 considers HPWL within the force model. The second placement strategy (diffusion-based PM) in Table 5 does not consider HPWL and moves cell based on the gradient of cell density.

Without placement migration, testcase *mgc_des_perf_1* and *mgc_des_perf_2* do not pass the global routing check, which do not proceed to the detailed routing stage. Using both

Table 6: Comparison on placement quality with and without DRC-driven detailed placer

	rtWL		DR	
Benchmark	w/o DRC	w/DRC	w/o DRC	w/DRC
mgc_des_perf_1	2.04	2.02	1377.15	1536.75
mgc_des_perf_2	1.94	1.95	7.4	3.75
mgc_edit_dist_1	4.99	4.97	0.0	0.0
mgc_edit_dist_2	4.90	4.88	0.0	0.0
mgc_pci_bridge_1	0.373	0.371	0.0	0.0
mgc_pci_bridge_2	0.375	0.372	0.0	0.5
mgc_fft	0.676	0.673	208.15	165.2
mgc_matrix_mult	3.09	3.07	31.55	30.95

placement migration strategies, both testcases passed the global routing check. However, considering HPWL within the force model produces placement solution with 1.7% less routing wirelength and 74% less DR score.

6.2 DRC Driven Detailed Placement

Table 6 compares placement solutions with and without DRC-driven detailed placement. DRC-driven detailed placement is more effective on testcases with lower utilization rate. From Table 6, DRC-driven detailed placement improves DR score on 3 out of 8 testcases and 2 out of 8 testcases have worse DR score. The two testcases with worse DR score have utilization rate above 84%.

7. CONCLUSION

In this work, we propose a comprehensive placement solution that resolves routing congestion from global routing stage to detailed routing stage. Optimization techniques for routability across each stage are integrated to one framework. Our placement framework includes a global router for routing congestion estimation, a global placer for routability optimization, an incremental placer to reduce cell density overlaps with better cell relative order, and a detailed placer to reduce design rule violations. Our placement framework considers design constraints in advanced node technology and placement quality is evaluated using commercial place and route tool. Experimental results show that placement migration is effective in reducing detailed routing violation while preserving the integrity of the original placement.

In the future, we are going to investigate the difference between using Gaussian Blurring or electrostatic model to derive the move force in Kraftwerk2's three force system. How to model the complex detailed routing rule, for example of the end-of-line rule, is still a research problem.

8. REFERENCES

[1] X. He, W.-K. Chow, and E. F. Young. Srp: simultaneous routing and placement for congestion refinement. In *Proceedings of the International Symposium on Physical Design*, pages 108–113, 2013.

[2] X. He, T. Huang, W.-K. Chow, J. Kuang, K.-C. Lam, W. Cai, and E. F. Young. Ripple 2.0: High quality routability-driven placement via global router integration. In *Design Automation Conference*, pages 1–6. IEEE, 2013.

[3] X. He, T. Huang, L. Xiao, H. Tian, G. Cui, and E. F. Young. Ripple: an effective routability-driven placer by iterative cell movement. In *Proceedings of the International Conference on Computer-Aided Design*, pages 74–79, 2011.

[4] M.-K. Hsu, Y.-F. Chen, C.-C. Huang, T.-C. Chen, and Y.-W. Chang. Routability-driven placement for hierarchical mixed-size circuit designs. In *Proceedings of the Design Automation Conference*, page 151, 2013.

[5] M.-K. Hsu, S. Chou, T.-H. Lin, and Y.-W. Chang. Routability-driven analytical placement for mixed-size circuit designs. In *Proceedings of the International Conference on Computer-Aided Design*, pages 80–84, 2011.

[6] J. Hu, M.-C. Kim, and I. L. Markov. Taming the complexity of coordinated place and route. In *Design Automation Conference*, page 150, 2013.

[7] A. Kennings, N. K. Darav, and L. Behjat. Detailed placement accounting for technology constraints. In *International Conference on Very Large Scale Integration (VLSI-SoC)*, pages 1–6, 2014.

[8] M.-C. Kim, J. Hu, D.-J. Lee, and I. L. Markov. A SimPLR method for routability-driven placement. In *Proceedings of the International Conference on Computer-Aided Design*, pages 67–73, 2011.

[9] M.-C. Kim, D.-J. Lee, and I. L. Markov. SimPL: an algorithm for placing VLSI circuits. *Communication of the ACM*, 56(6):105–113, June 2013.

[10] M.-C. Kim, N. Viswanathan, C. J. Alpert, I. L. Markov, and S. Ramji. MAPLE: Multilevel Adaptive Placement for Mixed-Size Designs. In *Proceedings of the International Symposium on Physical Design*, pages 193–200, 2012.

[11] W.-H. Liu, W.-C. Kao, Y.-L. Li, and K.-Y. Chao. Multi-threaded collision-aware global routing with bounded-length maze routing. In *Proceedings of the Design Automation Conference*, pages 200–205, 2010.

[12] W.-H. Liu, Y.-L. Li, and C.-K. Koh. A fast maze-free routing congestion estimator with hybrid unilateral monotonic routing. In *Proceedings of the International Conference on Computer-Aided Design*, pages 713–719, 2012.

[13] T. Luo, H. Ren, C. J. Alpert, and D. Z. Pan. Computational geometry based placement migration. In *Proceedings of the International Conference on Computer-Aided Design*, pages 41–47, 2005.

[14] H. Ren, D. Z. Pan, C. J. Alpert, and P. Villarrubia. Diffusion-Based Placement Migration. In *Proceedings of the Design Automation Conference*, pages 515–520, 2005.

[15] J. A. Roy, N. Viswanathan, G.-J. Nam, C. J. Alpert, and I. L. Markov. Crisp: congestion reduction by iterated spreading during placement. In *Proceedings of the International Conference on Computer-Aided Design*, pages 357–362, 2009.

[16] P. Spindler, U. Schlichtmann, and F. M. Johannes. Abacus: fast legalization of standard cell circuits with minimal movement. In *Proceedings of the International Symposium on Physical Design*, pages 47–53, 2008.

[17] P. Spindler, U. Schlichtmann, and F. M. Johannes. Kraftwerk2 - A Fast Force-Directed Quadratic Placement Approach Using an Accurate Net Model. *IEEE Transactions on Computer-Aided Design of Integrated Circuits and Systems*, 27(8):1398–1411, Aug. 2008.

[18] Y. Wei, C. Sze, N. Viswanathan, Z. Li, C. J. Alpert, L. Reddy, A. D. Huber, G. E. Tellez, D. Keller, and S. S. Sapatnekar. Glare: global and local wiring aware routability evaluation. In *Design Automation Conference*, pages 768–773, 2012.

[19] V. Yutsis, I. S. Bustany, D. Chinnery, J. R. Shinnerl, and W.-H. Liu. Ispd 2014 benchmarks with sub-45nm technology rules for detailed-routing-driven placement. In *Proceedings of the International Symposium on Physical Design*, pages 161–168, 2014.

[20] Y. Zhang and C. Chu. Crop: fast and effective congestion refinement of placement. In *Proceedings of the International Conference on Computer-Aided Design*, pages 344–350, 2009.

ISPD 2015 Benchmarks with Fence Regions and Routing Blockages for Detailed-Routing-Driven Placement

Ismail S. Bustany   David Chinnery   Joseph R. Shinnerl   Vladimir Yutsis

Mentor Graphics Corporation
Fremont, California, USA
{Ismail_Bustany, David_Chinnery, Joseph_Shinnerl, Vladimir_Yutsis}@mentor.com

ABSTRACT

The ISPD 2015 placement-contest benchmarks include all the detailed pin, cell, and wire geometry constraints from the 2014 release, plus

(a) added fence regions and placement blockages,
(b) altered netlists including fixed macro blocks,
(c) reduced standard cell area utilization via larger floor plan outlines, and
(d) specified upper limits on local cell-area density.

Compared to the 2014 release, these new constraints add realism and increase the difficulty of producing detail-routable wirelength-driven placements.

Categories and Subject Descriptors

B.7.2 [**Integrated Circuits**]: Design Aids - Placement and Routing; D.2.8 [**Software Engineering**]: Metrics—*complexity measures, performance measures*

General Terms

Algorithms, Design

Keywords

Placement; routability; placement evaluation; global routing; detailed routing; fence regions

1. INTRODUCTION

The challenge of computing placements compatible with increasingly complex design rules enforced in detailed routing was taken up in the 2014 ISPD placement contest [17]. There, contestants from nine universities grappled with realistic constraints such as pin access, edge spacing, end of line, and other non-default rules for routing like double-width vias, for the first time in a publicly released suite of placement benchmarks.

Winning solutions to the contest adapted techniques including detailed-routability enhanced look-ahead legalization [3] and placement migration [15] to produce placements that could be successfully detail-routed by a leading commercial tool [9].

While the ISPD 2014 benchmarks [17] do add important physical detail compared to that in previously released suites [12, 14], they lack the following features commonly seen in real industrial designs: (1) timing constraints, and (2) region placement constraints. Despite being routable, many of the winning placements in ISPD 2014 exhibit significantly higher local cell density than typical industrial solutions. We attribute a large part of this density disparity to the lack of timing constraints in the benchmarks and the resulting absence of a post-route timing-closure design stage including sizing and buffer insertion.

In order to address these shortcomings, the following enhancements have been added to these placement benchmarks for the 2015 ISPD contest:

1. maximum local logic-utilization (cell-density) constraints
2. region placement constraints ("region constraints")
3. diverse standard-cell utilizations ranging from 14.3% to 90.6%
4. placement and routing obstructions added to the Suite A benchmarks.

Although timing constraints are still not explicitly present, the limits on local cell density increase the difficulty of wirelength minimization and anticipate sizing and buffering operations.[1] Region constraints are used to support various design features such as voltage islands [8]. They are also common in top-level floorplans. The geometry of a region may vary from a simple rectangle to a complex, multiple-contour rectilinear shape. In practice, region constraints and large fixed obstructions in close proximity result in placement regions dominated by narrow channels and additional challenges in modeling the wirelength objective and cell density constraints.

In Section 2, we describe the ISPD 2014 detailed routing results and the relevance of global routing in assessing detailed routability. In Section 3, we discuss the importance of placement spreading and maximum utilization constraints. In Section 4, we describe our use of region constraints. The benchmarks are detailed in Section 5. Changes to the scoring for the ISPD 2015 placement contest are described in Section 6. We conclude in Section 7.

---

[1] However, such operations are not part of the contest evaluation.

2. THE ROLE OF GLOBAL ROUTING

A global routing (GR) is typically associated with a grid of global-routing cells called g-cells.[2] The capacity of g-cell edges is calculated from how many available routing tracks cross each edge. The GR edge-overflow percentage is the percentage of g-cell edges where the number of global-routing segments crossing an edge exceeds the edge capacity. Detailed routing (DR) can resolve minor edge overflows, but there will likely be DR violations[3] if there is significant GR congestion in an area, particularly for narrow routing channels between macros, routing blockages, and the floorplan boundary [9].

Several recent papers [16, 14, 17] have drawn attention to large and growing discrepancies between congestion predicted by GR and congestion encountered by DR on the same placement. The discrepancies are often not only in magnitude but also in the location of the congestion. Given the prominent role that GR has traditionally played in physical design, the observed GR-DR discrepancies raise the following questions regarding GR usage.

(1) Can GR be augmented without impairing its run time or scalability in such a way that significant discrepancies with DR are reduced or even eliminated?

(2) Assume GR is useful at coarser modeling stages but misleading at finer ones. As a placement algorithm incrementally increases its modeling resolution, at what point should its use of GR stop?

(3) What is the uncertainty of GR predictions? Specifically,

  (a) On a given placed design, *below* what level of maximum GR edge congestion can we be confident that DR *will* complete with an acceptably small number of violations?

  (b) On a given placed design, *above* what level of maximum GR edge congestion can we be confident that DR will *not* complete with an acceptably small number of violations?

(4) Is it feasible to generate detail-routable placements without *any* use of GR?

Question 1 has been considered in several recent papers [16, 18, 13, 7, 6], which have demonstrated significant reduction in the GR-DR gap but have not eliminated it. The ACE metric [16] introduced at the 2012 DAC placement contest was also used by one of the two winning teams in the ISPD 2014 placement contest. Both of these teams report using GR in global placement but not in legalization or detailed placement [3, 15]; we know of no study investigating whether replacing GR by more precise routability estimation *before* global placement completes can improve final detailed routability.

Questions 3 and 4 are open and do not appear to have simple answers. However, both in industry and in the ISPD 2014 and 2015 placement-contest evaluations (Section 6), a conservative upper limit for GR edge-congestion overflow is used to bail out early on unroutable designs, preventing long run time in DR with low probability of any ultimate success. Results from the ISPD 2014 contest described next suggest

that the uncertainty in this estimated upper limit may be quite substantial and thus support the claim that a GR-free approach to efficient recognition of unroutability may be a better alternative [4].

Figure 1 illustrates how GR edge-congestion values over ISPD 2014 contest placements sometimes fail to show a clear trend in the subsequent number of DR violations. DR violations have been normalized by number of nets in a design, as the benchmarks vary significantly in size. A log scale[4] has been used on the axes to highlight that GR edge-overflow percentage does not correlate well with detailed routing violations.

We would typically consider a design with GR edge overflow of 0.02% or more to be difficult to route [9], but the data in Figure 1 show a wide range of detailed routing scores below 0.15% GR edge overflow. The `mgc_superblue19` design is very difficult to route, despite solutions with GR edge overflow of zero and 0.005%, which respectively had 1,587 and 7,532 detailed routing violations.

Global routing edge overflow does not consider usage of vias between metal layers. However, vias are a limited resource and also use up space that could be used instead by planar routing, and hence can significantly impact detailed routing. GR node congestion is a measure of via usage and planar routing resource usage internal to g-cells.

In particular, for the `mgc_fft_2` design, one solution had zero GR edge congestion but 67 routing violations, whereas another solution with "poor" GR edge overflow of 0.38% actually had only 55 DR violations. As shown in Figure 2, the GR edge overflow and node congestion are worse on both sides of the version of `mgc_fft_2` with even placement spread. However, there are actually more DR violations on the left and top of the version with uneven cell placement. There appears to be only a little GR node congestion at the top of the version of `mgc_fft_2` with even placement spread, but the majority of the DR violations are there. This motivates more careful consideration of GR node congestion or better metrics to identify and address such issues before they cause problems in detailed routing.

Design `mgc_superblue19` is a "blind" benchmark, unseen by the contestants during development of their placers, and not publicly released until after the ISPD 2015 contest.

3. LOCAL CELL-DENSITY CONSTRAINTS

Figure 3 shows global-routing congestion on two different placements of `mgc_superblue11`. The first placement was computed under a uniform-spread constraint equivalent to 65% cell density; the second, under a local cell density constraint of 95%. The second placement might appear unroutable, but, surprisingly, it is not! Some contest placements from the ISPD 2014 contests did complete detailed routing with reasonably low DR violation counts, even with local cell densities near or above 95%. We attribute these results to the use of a wirelength objective coupled with fine-grain design-constraint-aware look-ahead legalization.

Placement constraints on maximum utilization, i.e., local cell density, were imposed in the ISPD 2006 placement contest [10, 11] primarily as a proxy for routability. No routability proxy is needed for the ISPD 2015 placement contest, but there are no timing constraints included in our benchmarks. Realistic placements should still reserve space important for

---

[2] For the ISPD 2015 contest, a global-routing grid of 3x3 standard cell row heights is used.

[3] opens, shorts, blocked pins, insufficient spacing, etc. [17]

[4] The data have been shifted by 0.01 to avoid log(0).

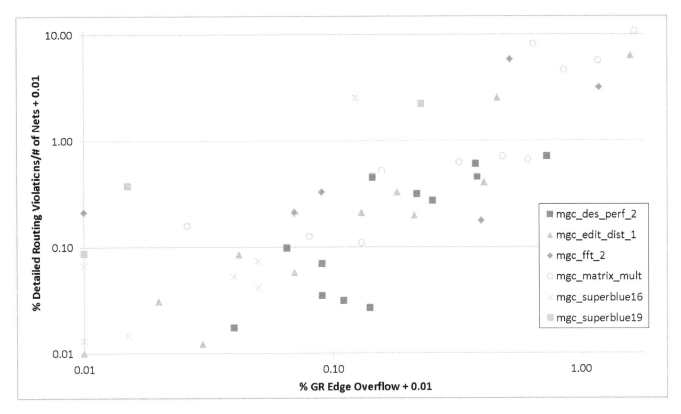

Figure 1: Log-scale DR violation counts normalized by net count vs. GR edge-congestion percentages, over placements from the ISPD 2014 contest.

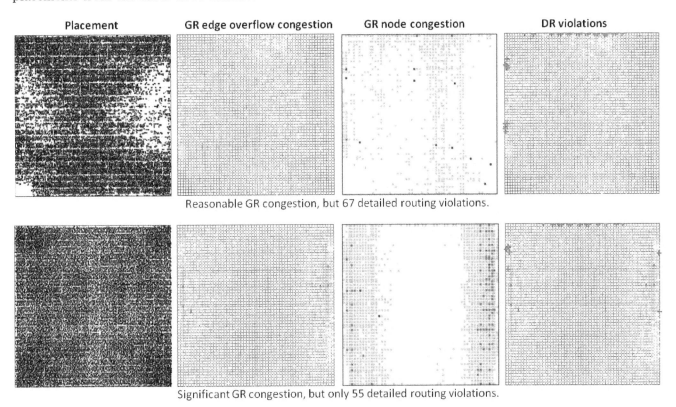

Figure 2: GR edge overflow and node congestion for two different placements of `mgc_fft_2`. The DR violations (red crosses), shown super-imposed on the GR edge overflow congestion map, do not correlate with the GR-congestion hot spots. The algorithm computing the upper placement may have been misled by GR congestion.

significantly worse
routing congestion

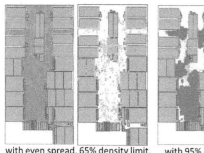 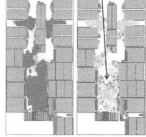

with even spread, 65% density limit,
detail routed wire length 53.6m

with 95% density limit,
detail routed wire length 46.3m

Figure 3: GR congestion maps for placements of mgc_superblue11 at 65% and 95% local cell-density limits.

subsequent timing-optimization operations such as sizing, buffering, and localized netlist remapping.

In the 2015 placement contest, a single local cell-density limit constraint is imposed uniformly on each design, irrespective of any region constraints (Section 4). If any region has a higher area utilization than the limit specified in the local cell-density constraint, the limit will be raised within that region to the region's native area utilization as defined in Section 5.1.

It is emphasized that these maximum-utilization constraints are to be interpreted as soft constraints rather than hard ones. Violations are expected, particularly on high design-utilization test cases where the limit is set to the native design utilization. The scoring penalty in Section 6 is formulated to allow contestants to trade limited violation of this cell-density constraint for significantly improved routability or wirelength.

4. REGION CONSTRAINTS

Placing cells with the same function contiguously in a confined subregion rather than scattering them haphazardly often improves important design characteristics. Region constraints are specified by designers to guide automatic place-and-route tools toward improved performance, power consumption, and/or manufacturability in various ways.

Power domains are used to simplify power/ground distribution and to isolate separate voltage regions. Space may also be reserved for power header/footer cells and always-on cells. Region constraints may be imposed at the block level to reserve whitespace in order to place global repeaters for routing top-level nets across the chip. Clock mesh distribution of clock signals periodically across chip motivates reserving space for the first level of clock buffers and clock gaters that connect to the bottom level of the mesh, in order to reduce clock wire load, which also decreases wire RC delay and hence reduces clock skew. Designers may also specify placement constraints for some datapath cells to improve the datapath placement quality, and for tightly clustering registers to reduce clock wire load and thus decrease clock power.

By definition [1], a *fence* region is *member-hard* and also *non-member-hard*: cells assigned to a fence region must be

placed inside its boundary, and cells not assigned to it must be placed outside that boundary. Some tools support all four possible kinds of region membership based on independent settings of their boolean member-hard and non-member-hard properties. For instance, a region which is neither member-hard nor non-member-hard is sometimes called a *guide* region or *soft* region constraint.

All regions in every test case described here are fence regions. Fence-region constraints are hard constraints. Placements with cells even partially outside their assigned regions' boundaries are inadmissible and are not routed (Section 6).

Regions may overlap spatially in practice, but all distinct regions in the test cases here are defined so as to be spatially disjoint. However, any single region is not required to be contiguous or simply connected: it may consist of multiple spatially disjoint subregions, as shown in Figure 6.

5. BENCHMARKS

The ISPD 2015 test cases have been adapted from the ISPD 2014 test cases by expanding floorplan outlines, creating fixed macros from subnetlists, adding region constraints, and adding upper-limit constaints on local cell density.

5.1 Design utilizations

Design utilization or *area utilization* is the total area of all movable[5] standard cells divided by total available placement area for those standard cells.[6] *Available* area does *not* include the areas of placement obstructions like fixed macros. The test cases in this suite have been deliberately constructed to exhibit widely varying design utilizations. In practice, designs with tens or hundreds of millions of objects are typically partitioned into multiple *block-level* subdesigns or "blocks", which are ultimately reunited in the *top-level* design. Area utilization in each block may be pushed over 80% in order to shrink die size, whereas utilization of "glue logic" in the top level may be left well below 20%. Low utilization in the top level design allows for more aggressive post-placement optimization needed to complete longer timing paths around large obstructions.

5.2 Test case construction

The following scheme has been applied to construct realistic floorplans from some of the Suite A test cases originally without obstructions.

- With all cell sizes held fixed, each floorplan outline is enlarged to attain a distinct target design utilization.
- The outline-enlarged macro-free design is placed and routed in OLYMPUS-SoC.
- Artificial macros are created from spatially localized cell subsets in the placed design as detailed below.
- Fence regions are defined in the placed design by both (a) boundary geometry and (b) cell membership.

Artificial macro construction proceeds as follows.

1. Temporary artificial fence regions are specified in the placed design by boundary geometry and cell members. Each such region has a simple rectangular boundary. A proper subset of cells ("members") inside each

---

[5] As the designs here have no fixed standard cells anyway, we may omit the word "movable."

[6] Tables 1 and 2 also list *total utilization*, i.e., total cell *and* fixed-macro area divided by total chip area.

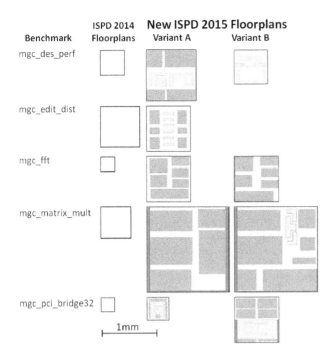

Figure 4: 2015 Suite A Floorplans vs. 2014 Suite A. See Legend in Figure 6.

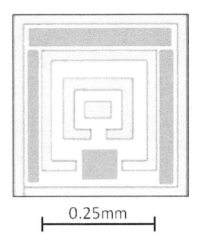

Figure 5: Close-up of mgc_pci_bridge32_a from Suite A. See Legend in Figure 6.

subregion boundary are assigned to the region; all other cells ("non-members") in the netlist are excluded from it.

2. A fresh placement is computed for the design subject to the fence-region constraints.

3. Each fence region is converted to a partition.

4. Each net containing both interior cells and exterior cells of any partition is associated with a single pin on the boundary of the partition.

5. In order to reduce congestion, the pin placement on each partition boundary is recomputed, consistently with the given cell placement.

6. Each partition is converted to a fixed macro with an associated routing blockage obstructing all routing layers over the macro.

Final floorplans for modified Suite A test cases are shown in Figures 4 and 5. Final floorplans for Suite B are shown in Figure 6. Placement blockages have been added to some of the modified Suite A benchmarks to show a common design technique used to avoid routing congestion due to placement of cells in narrow channels between macros and the floorplan boundary. Automating this approach in placement may help improve detailed routability for some designs.

5.3 Test case characteristics

Two separate benchmark suites,[7] A and B, have been adapted from the corresponding 2014 ISPD suites [17] in

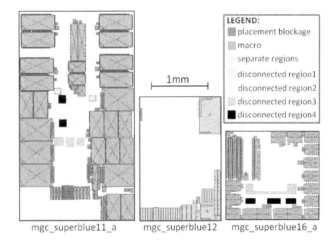

Figure 6: 2015 Suite B Floorplans

---

[7] As of this writing, some specifications of these benchmarks are being adjusted and may still change, to provide an appropriate level of difficulty. Additional test-case variants are also being considered. All such changes and additional test cases, if any, will be collected and posted on the ISPD 2015 contest web site as an addendum to this article.

Table 3: Suite A PG-grid geometry (μm) by layer

	M1	M2	M3	M4	M5
rail width w_r	0.51	0.58	3.50	4.00	4.00
rail spacing s_r	1.49	20.0	14.0	20.0	14.0
track utilization	11%	6%	27%	24%	30 %

Table 4: Suite B PG-grid geometry (μm) by layer

	M2	M3	M4	M5	M6	M7
rail width w_r	0.10	0.86	0.80	0.90	0.90	1.0
rail spacing s_r	9.0	18.0	9.0	18.0	9.0	18.0
track utilization	1%	5%	8%	5%	9%	5%

LEF/DEF format [1]. As in the 2014 benchmarks, all standard-cell rows in each design are the same height. There are no fixed standard cells or movable macros in any of the test cases.

Suite A consists of twelve test cases adapted from benchmarks released by Intel Corporation for the ISPD 2013 discrete cell-sizing contest [12]. All movable objects are standard cells of comparable sizes. Each test case has 5 routing layers, all available for routing on every test case except `mgc_fft_2`, where routing on layer M5 is not allowed. Suite A PG grid geometry is listed in Table 3.

Suite B consists of three test cases adapted from benchmarks released by IBM Corporation for the DAC 2012 placement contest [14]. In contrast to the test cases in Suite A, the test cases in Suite B have many fixed macros and hence more complicated floorplan geometry. Fence regions have been added to `mcg_superblue11a` and `mgc_superblue16a` as shown in Figure 6. Each test case has 8 routing layers, but only `mgc_superblue16` allows routing on all 8; the others restrict routing to layers M1–M7. Suite B power/ground (PG) grid geometry is listed in Table 4. The standard cells in Suite B have been left at their given sizes.

Characteristic physical data and design rules for the benchmarks — cell geometry, pin geometry, routing pitch, routing track density, pin layer assignment, etc. — are unchanged from the ISPD 2014 [17] benchmarks except as noted herein.

Table 1 lists basic statistics for benchmark test cases unchanged from ISPD 2014 except for added limits on local cell density. These relatively unchanged test cases serve to control against overtuning for new benchmark features and facilitate comparisons between the 2014 and 2015 contest entries. Table 2 lists statistics for benchmark test cases revised from ISPD 2014 by resizing floorplan outlines and adding fixed macros and fence regions as described in Section 5.

6. PLACEMENT CONTEST EVALUATION

As in 2014, submitted DEF placement solutions are evaluated in the OLYMPUS-SoC^{TM} place and route system subject to system memory limits and a 24-hour run-time limit. A script is used to check the placed designs for the following invalidating features: cells out of bounds, including region bounds, if any; netlist changes; and movement of fixed objects. Valid placements are legalized and routed in OLYMPUS-SoC.

Each placement's score S is computed as a sum of four category scores: cell legalization displacement, detailed-routing violations, detail-routed wire length, and run time:

$$S = S_{dp} + S_{dr} + S_{wl} + S_{cpu}. \tag{1}$$

All 4 terms except wirelength S_{wl} are evaluated just as in 2014 [17], including normalizing each term to lie in $[0, 25]$. The better the placement, the *lower* the score. An invalid placement receives the worst possible score of $S = 100$.

Detailed routing is not attempted on placements exhibiting excessive GR edge congestion, as described in Question 3b of Section 2. The GR edge-congestion limit is estimated separately for each test case but is typically between 0.05 and 1.0%.

6.1 Adjusted Detail-Routed Wirelength Score

Unscaled score wl_u is simply the final detail-routed wirelength reported by the router. Before normalization, wirelength is penalized by any local maximum-utilization violations as below, following essentially the same formula[8] used in the ISPD 2006 placement contest [10, 11]:

$$\text{WL} = wl_u \left(1 + k f_{of}^2\right), \tag{2}$$

where k is a small constant,[9] and f_{of} is defined over square bins 8×8 standard-cell-row heights each, as follows. Denote the maximum allowed cell density by $d_{\max}$. Let single_bin_area denote the area of one unobstructed bin, i.e., 64 square cell heights. Let free_space(b) denote the total area of bin b *not* occupied by fixed macros or any other placement obstructions. For movable cells c in bin b,

$$\text{overflow}(b) = \left(\sum_{\text{movable } c \in b} \text{area}(c) \right) - \text{free\_space}(b) \times d_{\max},$$

where area(c) denotes the area of the portion of cell c overlapping with bin b. Then

$$\text{total\_overflow} = \sum_{\text{all bins } b} \text{overflow}(b).$$

The final factor f_{of} is then the above total_overflow expressed as a multiple of the minimum number of bins required by the design:

$$f_{of} = \frac{\text{total\_overflow} \times \text{single\_bin\_area} \times d_{\max}}{\displaystyle\sum_{\text{all movable cells } c} \text{area}(c)}$$

On a design with fence regions, the above formulation is applied separately to regions with native cell-area utilizations above $d_{\max}$. The final value of f_{of} used in (2) is then computed as the weighted average of the per-region f_{of} over the regions, using the total cell area of each region as its weight.

The same normalization used in 2014 is then applied to WL. Over all valid placements p on a benchmark with $S_{dp}(p) < 25$, let

$$wl_{med} = \text{the median of the WL}(p).$$
$$wl_{min} = \text{the minimum of the WL}(p).$$

Then

$$S_{wl} = \begin{cases} f_{aff}(\text{WL}) & \text{if WL} < 1.5 \times wl_{med} \\ 25 & \text{if WL} \geq 1.5 \times wl_{med}, \end{cases}$$

---

[8]We use a slightly finer bin grid and a different constant k.
[9]As of this writing, k has yet to be determined.

Table 1: Benchmarks with floorplans unchanged from ISPD 2014

Design	#Macros	#Cells	#Nets	#Fence Regions	#I/O	%Area Utilization Std Cell	Std Cell & Macro	Density Limit %
mgc_des_perf	0	112,644	112,880	0	374	90.6	Same	90.6
mgc_fft	0	32,281	33,307	0	3,010	83.5	Same	83.5
mgc_fft_2	0	32,281	33,307	0	3,010	49.9	Same	65.0
mgc_matrix_mult	0	155,325	158,529	0	4,802	80.2	Same	80.2
mgc_superblue12	89	1,286,948	1,293,436	0	5,908	44.0	57.0	65.0
mgc_superblue19	286	506,097	511,687	0	15,422	52.3	80.7	67.3

Table 2: Benchmarks with floorplans revised from ISPD 2014

Design	#Macros	#Cells	#Nets	#Fence Regions	#I/O	%Area Utilization Std Cell	Std Cell & Macro	Density Limit %
mgc_des_perf_a	4	108,292	115,187	4	374	42.9	71.7	42.9
mgc_des_perf_b	0	112,679	122,951	12	374	49.7	49.7	49.7
mgc_edit_dist_a	6	127,414	134,051	1	2,574	45.5	61.6	45.5
mgc_fft_a	6	30,625	32,090	0	3,010	25.1	74.0	50.0
mgc_fft_b	6	30,625	32,090	0	3,010	28.2	74.0	60.0
mgc_matrix_mult_a	5	149,650	154,286	0	4,802	41.9	76.7	60.0
mgc_matrix_mult_b	7	146,438	154,213	3	4,802	30.9	72.6	60.0
mgc_pci_bridge32_a	4	29,533	34,058	3	361	38.4	40.8	38.4
mgc_pci_bridge32_b	6	28,932	32,546	3	361	14.3	50.6	14.3
mgc_superblue11_a	1,458	925,616	935,731	4	27,371	43.0	73.0	65.0
mgc_superblue16_a	419	680,456	717,046	2	17,498	47.6	73.9	55.0

where f_{aff} denotes simple affine scaling

$$t \to 25 \cdot (t - a)/(b - a)$$

from $[a, b] = [wl_{min}, 1.5 \cdot wl_{med}]$ into $[0, 25]$.

7. CONCLUSION

Region placement constraints are widely used in industry to support voltage regions, datapath placement, and other design features. As floorplan complexity grows, so does the number and complexity of these regions, as does the challenge of producing detail-routable placements following all region constraints.

The ultimate measures of a placement's quality are its timing performance and its detailed routability. While the benchmarks described here still lack timing constraints, their routability and region constraints are reasonably complete. They represent some of the harder design challenges faced by industry in the year 2015 and beyond.

8. ACKNOWLEDGMENTS

We thank the following people for their insight and help: Chuck Alpert, Yao-Wen Chang, Chris Chu, Kevin Corbett, Nima K. Darav, Azadeh Davoodi, Igor Gambarin, John Gilchrist, Andrew B. Kahng, Andrew Kennings, Alex Korshak, Shankar Krishnamoorthy, Wen-Hao Liu, Igor L. Markov, Mustafa Ozdal, Cliff Sze, Liang Tao, Alex Vasquez, Natarajan Viswanathan, Alexander Volkov, Yi Wang, Benny Winefeld, and Evangeline Young.

Professor Evangeline Young and Wing-Kai Chow generously provided their RippleDP detailed placer [2] to the contest. Dr. Wen-Hao Liu generously provided his NCTUgr global router [5] to the contest.

9. REFERENCES

[1] Cadence, Inc. LEF/DEF 5.3 to 5.7 exchange format. 2009. www.si2.org/openeda.si2.org/projects/lefdef.

[2] W. Chow, J. Kuang, X. He, W. Cai, and E. F. Y. Young. Cell density-driven detailed placement with displacement constraint. In *International Symposium on Physical Design, ISPD'14, Petaluma, CA, USA, March 30 - April 02, 2014*, pages 3–10, 2014.

[3] A. A. Kennings, N. K. Darav, and L. Behjat. Detailed placement accounting for technology constraints. In *VLSI-SoC*, pages 1–6, 2014.

[4] W. Liu, T. Chien, and T. Wang. A study on unroutable placement recognition. In *International Symposium on Physical Design, ISPD'14, Petaluma, CA, USA, March 30 - April 02, 2014*, pages 19–26, 2014.

[5] W. Liu, W. Kao, Y. Li, and K. Chao. NCTU-GR 2.0: Multithreaded collision-aware global routing with bounded-length maze routing. *IEEE Trans. on CAD of Integrated Circuits and Systems*, 32(5):709–722, 2013.

[6] W. Liu, C. Koh, and Y. Li. Optimization of placement solutions for routability. In *The 50th Annual Design Automation Conference 2013, DAC '13, Austin, TX, USA, May 29 - June 07, 2013*, page 153, 2013.

[7] W. Liu, Y. Wei, C. C. N. Sze, C. J. Alpert, Z. Li, Y. Li, and N. Viswanathan. Routing congestion estimation with real design constraints. In *The 50th Annual Design Automation Conference 2013, DAC '13, Austin, TX, USA, May 29 - June 07, 2013*, page 92, 2013.

[8] Q. Ma and E. Young. Multivoltage floorplan design. *IEEE Transactions on Computer-Aided Design of Integrated Circuits and Systems*, 29:607 – 617, April 2010.

[9] Mentor Graphics, Inc. Olympus-SoC place and route for advanced node designs. 2015. www.mentor.com/products/ic_nanometer_design/place-route/olympus-soc.

[10] G.-J. Nam. ISPD 2006 placement contest: Benchmark suite and results. In *Proceedings of the 2006 International*

Symposium on Physical Design, pages 167–167, New York, NY, USA, 2006. ACM.

[11] G.-J. Nam and J. Cong. *Modern Circuit Placement: Best Practices and Results.* Springer Publishing Company, Incorporated, 1st edition, 2007.

[12] M. M. Ozdal, C. Amin, A. Ayupov, S. M. Burns, G. R. Wilke, and C. Zhuo. An improved benchmark suite for the ISPD-2013 discrete cell sizing contest. In *Proceedings of the 2013 ACM International Symposium on International Symposium on Physical Design*, pages 168–170, New York, NY, USA, 2013. ACM.

[13] H. Shojaei, A. Davoodi, and J. Linderoth. Planning for local net congestion in global routing. In *Proceedings of the 2013 ACM International Symposium on International Symposium on Physical Design*, pages 85–92, New York, NY, USA, 2013. ACM.

[14] N. Viswanathan, C. Alpert, C. Sze, Z. Li, and Y. Wei. The DAC 2012 routability-driven placement contest and benchmark suite. In *Proceedings of the 49th Annual Design Automation Conference*, pages 774–782, New York, NY, USA, 2012. ACM.

[15] C.-K. Wang, C.-C. Huang, S. S.-Y. Liu, C.-Y. Chin, S.-T. Hu, W.-C. Wu, and H.-M. Chen. Closing the gap between global and detailed placement: Techniques for improving routability. In *Proceedings of the 2015 on International Symposium on Physical Design*, New York, NY, USA, 2015. ACM.

[16] Y. Wei, C. Sze, N. Viswanathan, Z. Li, C. J. Alpert, L. Reddy, A. D. Huber, G. E. Tellez, D. Keller, and S. S. Sapatnekar. Glare: Global and local wiring aware routability evaluation. In *Proceedings of the 49th Annual Design Automation Conference*, pages 768–773, New York, NY, USA, 2012. ACM.

[17] V. Yutsis, I. S. Bustany, D. Chinnery, J. R. Shinnerl, and W.-H. Liu. ISPD 2014 benchmarks with sub-45nm technology rules for detailed-routing-driven placement. In *Proceedings of the 2014 on International Symposium on Physical Design*, ISPD '14, pages 161–168, New York, NY, USA, 2014. ACM.

[18] Y. Zhang and C. Chu. GDRouter: interleaved global routing and detailed routing for ultimate routability. In *Proceedings of the 49th Annual Design Automation Conference*, pages 597–602, New York, NY, USA, 2012. ACM.

FreePDK15: An Open-Source Predictive Process Design Kit for 15nm FinFET Technology

Kirti Bhanushali
North Carolina State University
2410 Campus Shore Drive
Raleigh, NC 27606
knbhanus@ncsu.edu

W. Rhett Davis
North Carolina State University
Campus Box 7911
Raleigh, NC 27605
wdavis@ncsu.edu

ABSTRACT

This paper discusses design rules and layout guidelines for an open source predictive process design kit (PDK) for multi-gate 15nm FinFET devices. Additional design rules are introduced considering process variability, and challenges involved in fabrication beyond 20nm. Particularly, double patterning lithography is assumed and a unique set of design rules are developed for critical dimensions. In order to improve the FinFET layout density, Middle-of-line local interconnect layers are implemented for the FinFET layout. The rules are further validated by running Calibre design-rule checks on Virtuoso layout of an Inverter and NAND4 cells. As part of the validation process, the area of a FreePDK15 inverter was compared to the area of an inverter in 45nm bulk MOS process and the ratio was found to be 1:6. This kit primarily aims to support introduction of sub-20nm FinFET devices into research and universities.

Categories and Subject Descriptors

B.7.1 [**Integrated circuits**]: Types and Design styles—*Advanced technologies, VLSI*; B.7.2 [**Integrated circuits**]: Design aids—*Layout, Graphics, Simulation*

General Terms

Design

Keywords

FinFET; Middle-of-line; Process Design Kit; Design rules; FreePDK15

1. INTRODUCTION

The scaling of bulk MOS technology faces major roadblocks. It is limited by high leakage power, random dopant fluctuations and other short channel effects. However, International Technology Roadmap for Semiconductors (ITRS) predicts the physical length of the transistors to scale down to 16nm by 2016 [3]. Thus multi-gate MOSFETs, FinFETs, have been adopted as an alternative device technology and are anticipated to advance the semiconductor scaling for sub-20nm devices. FinFETs, due to their advanced three dimensional multi-gate geometry accomplish superior control over the channel and thus achieve lower leakage current and an improved short channel performance. Additionally, due to their depleted thin fin structure, they achieve better short channel performance and lower random dopant fluctuation [9].

There is an immmediate need for development of a design flow platform for design and verification of large scale FinFET based integrated circuits. The design flow for these devices has already been developed by the industry, but due to tight control over intellectual property, it is not shared with universities. In order to license these technologies a large investment is required, which is beyond the scope of universities. Thus, it is necessary to develop an open-source predictive process design kit to help students in understanding the complexities of the standard design process during university education. The development of FreePDK15, an open source process design kit, is a step towards achieving a complete predictive process design kit for FinFET devices.

In this paper, a standard FinFET layout is evaluated from the point of view of fabrication and design rules. Fabrication in sub-20nm technology is limited by the standard photo lithography process. Thus, lithographic techniques like double patterning have been adopted, and have been succesfully used for implementation of standard cells in 14nm FinFET technology [8]. This was the primary motivation for developing design rules compatible with double patterning. Furthermore, techniques like use of cut masks and Middle-Of-Line (MOL) layers have been introduced to enhance cell density. This has led to the development of special design rules in addition to the typical design rules. To validate these design rules, layouts of Inverter, NAND4, and their cascaded cells have been designed and their density has been evaluated.

This paper discusses the intermediate steps involved in the development of design rules for FreePDK15. In section II, the layers used for the PDK are discussed. In section III, standard and advanced design rules are presented. In section IV, a standard FinFET layout cell is exhibited along with a discussion on the validation of design rules and section V concludes.

2. FREEPDK15 LAYERS

The layer stack for the FreePDK15 has additional layers to accommodate for the three-dimensional nature of the

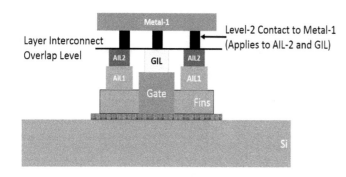

Figure 1: Cross Section of a FinFET device [5]

FinFET device and for intra-device routing. The standard cross-section for a FinFET can be seen in Figure 1. In addition to the standard Back-End-Of-Line (BEOL) layers, and Front-End-Of-Line(FEOL) layers it consists of Middle-Of-Line layers. The BEOL metal layer stack used for connecting the device to the external wiring follows hierarchical scaling used in standard ASIC architecture [2]. It is divided into Metal1 layer, Intermediate metal layers, Semi-global metal layers, and Global metal layers respectively. The active and metal gate form the Front-End-Of-Line(FEOL) layers.

Table 1: MOL layers and their functions

Layer	Purpose
Active Interconnect Layer-1 (AIL1)	Connecting individual fins
Active Interconnect Layer-2 (AIL2)	Connecting AIL-1 to Metal-1 through a via
Gate Interconnect Layer (GIL)	Connecting Gate to Metal1

2.1 Middle-Of-Line layers

The MOL layers are implemented for overcoming electrical resistance concerns and the loss of performance between connected layers[11]. The concept of MOL layers has been around for a long time, however, the primary inspiration behind their use for FreePDK15 comes from [8]. The MOL layers, local interconnect layers IM1 and IM2 [8], are implemented in 14nm bulk FinFET technology and their impact on standard cell parasitics is analyzed in [8]. In addition, MOL layers also help in achieving denser layouts with the provision for connecting internal nets, internal devices as well as providing connection to the power rails. Figure 2 further shows the implementation of these layers for connecting internal nets. The routing for the cells can mostly be handled by MOL layers instead of using contacts to the metal1 layer. The function of all the MOL layers is listed in Table 1.

2.2 Double-patterning of layers

FinFET fabrication at 15nm involves a lot of challenges, particularly from the standpoint of photo-lithography. Since the gate pitch is much smaller, it is very difficult to fabricate devices using the standard 193nm Argon Flouride (ArF) lasers. Additionally, the usage of Extreme Ultra-

Violet (EUV) lithography is held up, as it has not been able to achieve the desired yield for volume production. This has resulted in the introduction of multi-patterning lithography and other resolution enhancement techniques. FreePDK15 allows for the use of Self-Aligned-Double Patterning (SADP) by providing an option for cut masks as well as Litho-Etch-Litho-Etch(LELE) process.

Double patterning lithography (DPL) technique aims to double the pitch density achieved by the single patterning technique. In essence, a layout is decomposed into two masks with different colors each with half the pattern to be printed. In FreePDK15 this is implemented by providing two different colored layers for layers with critical dimensions like lower metal layers and gate layer.

In addition to these layers FreePDK15 also consists of Cut mask/cut layers to remove the unwanted features printed by the previous mask. This helps in printing non-uniform device structures and in overcoming errors due to mask misalignment.

3. DESIGN RULE DEVELOPMENT

The design rules set the basic geometric and connectivity restrictions for a device technology and are thus critical to its development. They ensure sufficient margins against manufacturing process variability and also help the designer to verify the design before it is sent for fabrication. Violations of these rules can result in undesirable operation of the circuits, thus they are critical to the circuit reliability. Furthermore, these design rules are crucial in defining the density of the integrated circuit as non-optimum design rules would result in wastage of the critical design space. Also, with the use of emerging technologies like FinFETs, it is necessary to introduce new sets of design rules to efficiently achieve correct functionality and understand the features of these technologies.

Typically, the number of design rules can vary from few hundreds to thousands. The design rules for FreePDK15 are implemented considering the geometric, electrical and lithographic constraints. They incorporate standard minimum width and spacing rules, along with certain restrictive design rules.

3.1 Standard design rules

Table 2: Standard design rules and their functions

Rule	Function
Minimum width	Defined by the resolution of the lithographic process used, prevents open-circuits.
Minimum Spacing	Ensure electrical isolation between two shapes
Enclosure	Prevent overlay errors due to misalignment of layers
Overlap	Ensure reliability during misalignment of layers
Area	Ensure adhesion and prevent overlay errors

3.2 Advanced design rules

These rules are specific to FinFET layout and double patterning lithography.

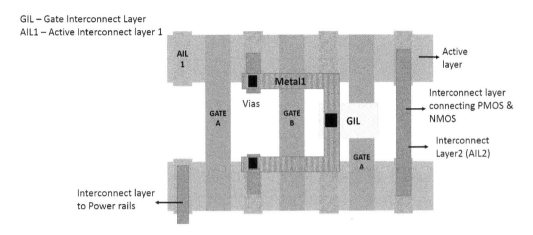

GIL – Gate Interconnect Layer
AIL1 – Active Interconnect layer 1

Figure 2: MOL layers used as interconnects [5]

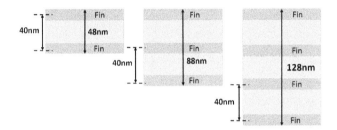

Figure 3: Width quantization of the active layer [5]

3.2.1 Incremental width rule: Active

The incremental width rule is introduced due to the discrete nature of the FinFET width. The total width of a FinFET device is defined by the number of fins in the device and thus can only increase in discrete steps. As it can be seen in Figure 3 the active width can only increment in steps of 40nm, which is the pitch of the active layer.

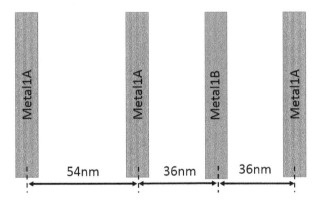

Figure 4: Different pitch rules for different layers [5]

3.2.2 Multi-colored design rules

A distinct feature of device fabrication in the sub-20nm technology is implementation of multi-patterning lithography. In FreePDK15 double patterning lithography(DPL) is assumed. It is thus imperative to use different rules for different colored metal layers. Figure 4 shows that the required minimum pitch between two similar metal layers, Metal-A layers in this case, is bigger than the minimum required pitch between metal layers of different colors, Metal-A and Metal-B in this case.

3.2.3 Restrictive design rules

Restrictive design rules are introduced to maintain the same design methodologies by introducing a new set of restrictions. An example of restrictive design rule is allowing only discrete gate lengths. Another example is restriction of jogs and bends in gate layers as it can result in pinching[6]. However, as this rule causes an increase in the overall area of the layout it is only implemented for critical dimensions.

4. STANDARD FINFET CELL AND DESIGN RULE VALIDATION

The fabrication of a standard FinFET device requires additional fabrication steps due to the three-dimensional thin fin structure. The differences between FinFET fabrication and the planar process is also due to the channel width and use of MOL layers.

4.1 Single FinFET transistor

The layout of a single planar MOS transistor with width W and gate length L is presented in Fig 5.a. The active layer has a direct contact to Metal1 layer for the planar MOS. However, in the layout of a FinFET transistor, contact is established through local interconnect layers. Figure 5.b shows the representation of the FinFET layout drawn in the design tool, however, since the fin width is quantized the device structure on the physical mask looks different and is presented in Fig.5.c.

In order to ensure process uniformity [7] in sub-20nm transistors "dummy" gates are also printed at the end of the Fins as seen in Figure 6. Moreover, GATEA and GATEB have different patterns for double patterning lithography

4.2 Design rule validation

The design rules for FreePDK15 are predictive at best and need further validation. A set of layouts were drawn and a design rule check was performed on them for validating these rules.

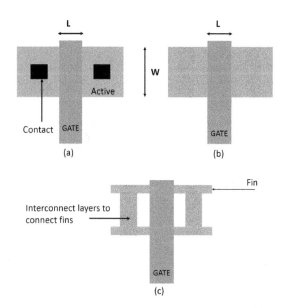

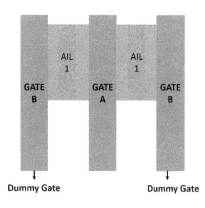

Figure 5: Basic transistor layouts (a) Planar MOS (b) FinFET (c) Physical Mask - FinFET [5]

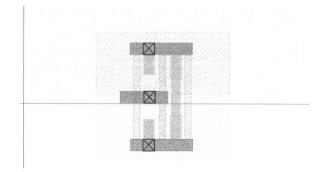

Figure 7: Standard inverter cell-FreePDK15 [5]

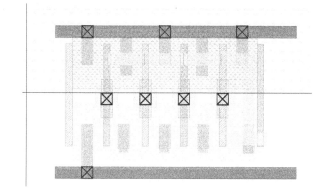

Figure 8: Standard NAND4 cell-FreePDK15 [5]

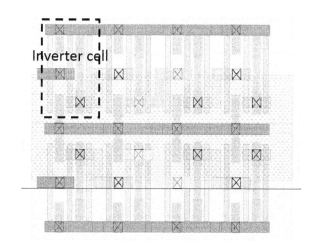

Figure 6: Dummy gates for process uniformity and DPL [5]

4.2.1 Inverter cell

A standard minimum sized FreePDK15 Inverter cell is presented in Figure 7. It uses AIL-2 for connecting the internal nets and power rails. Additionally, GATEA and GATEB are implemented for process uniformity.

4.2.2 NAND4 cell

A standard NAND4 cell shown in Figure 8 consists of double colored metal1 layer for layout density; the design rules were further validated by running design rule checks.

4.2.3 Tiled cells

Tiled Inverter and NAND4 layouts presented in Figure 9 and Figure 10 resp. were also designed for validating the design rules of higher order metal layers.

4.2.4 Layout density comparison

The area of minimum sized FinFET inverter is compared with the standard bulk MOS inverter designed using 45nm bulk FreePDK45 [1] [10] process in order to evaluate the

Figure 9: Tiled Inverter layout-FreePDK15 [5]

layout density of the FinFET process. The layout density in FinFETs does not scale as in bulk MOSFETs. In [4] the layout density for a FinFET design is found to be 1.3 times that for the bulk process at the same process node of 65nm. The primary reason for this can be attributed to the area overhead and width quantization issue in FinFETs.

The area of a standard CMOS bulk technology(FreePDK45) as shown in Figure 11 was compared with the FeePDK Inverter. The area shrink factor of 45nm CMOS inverter to 15nm FinFET inverter was found to be 1/6.

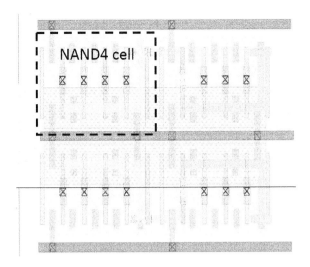

Figure 10: Tiled NAND4 layout-FreePDK15 [5]

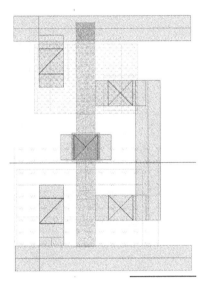

Figure 11: Minimum sized inverter for 45nm bulk CMOS technology(FreePDK45) [5]

5. CONCLUSIONS

FinFET devices are anticipated to continue Moore's Law in the foreseeable future and this requires development of the design flow platform for FinFET based integrated circuit design. These design flows have been developed by the industry but are not shared with the universities and research institutions due to the critical nature of the intellectual property. This has also prevented introduction and extensive research in the area of FinFET based large scale integrated circuits.

FreePDK15 aims to bridge this gap by providing a design flow platform wherein circuits can be designed and verified. Consequently, basic FinFET structures and their fabrication through double patterning lithography process has been analyzed. Additionally, a set of design rules for creating layouts are established for 15nm FinFET based circuits. These design rules are used for designing a basic FinFET cell. The design rules are further validated by designing and evalu-

ating densities of standard Inverter and NAND4 cell. The area for an Inverter designed using FreePDK15 is found to be 1/6th of the area achieved using a standard 45nm bulk MOSFET based Inverter cell.

6. ACKNOWLEDGMENTS

The authors would like to thank Mentor Graphics, since this project would not have been possible without their generous gift of supporting funds and Calibre licenses. The authors would also like to thank Tarek Ramadan, Ahmed Hammed Fathy, Omar El-Sewefy, Ahmed El-Kordy, Hend Wagieh and the team at Mentor Graphics for development of the first set of design rules and their constant support. In addition, the authors would like to thank and acknowledge Alexandre Toniolo at Nangate for clarifying the vision of MOL layers. We would also like to thank Cadence design systems for use of the virtuoso software and Synopsys Inc. for use of Pycell studio.

7. REFERENCES

[1] Webpage for FreePDK45.
www.eda.ncsu.edu/wiki/FreePDK45:Contents.

[2] International Technology Roadmap for Semiconductors report on interconnects - 2011.
http://www.itrs.net/Links/2011ITRS/2011Chapters/2011Interconnect.pdf, 2011.

[3] International Technology Roadmap for Semiconductors tables - 2011. http://www.itrs.net/Links/2011ITRS/Home2011.htm, 2011.

[4] M. Alioto. Analysis and evaluation of layout density of FinFET logic gates. In *Microelectronics (ICM), 2009 International Conference on*, pages 106–109, Dec 2009.

[5] K. Bhanushali. Design Rule Development for FreePDK15: An Open Source Predictive Process Design Kit for 15nm FinFET Devices. diploma thesis, North Carolina State University, Raleigh, NC 27695, May 2014.

[6] W. R. Davis and H. Demircioglu. *Predictive Technology Model for Robust Nanoelectronic Design Integrated Circuits and Systems*, chapter Predictive Process Design Kits, pages 121–140. Springer, 2011.

[7] T. Dillinger. Challenges for FinFET Extraction. In *IEEE Electronic Design Process Symposium,*, April 2013.

[8] P. Schuddinck, M. Badaroglu, M. Stucchi, S. Demuynck, A. Hikavyy, M. Garcia-Bardon, A. Mercha, A. Mallik, T. Chiarella, S. Kubicek, R. Athimulam, N. Collaert, N. Horiguchi, I. Debusschere, A. Thean, L. Altimime, and D. Verkest. Standard cell level parasitics assessment in 20nm BPL and 14nm BFF. In *Electron Devices Meeting (IEDM), 2012 IEEE International*, pages 25.3.1–25.3.4, Dec 2012.

[9] C. Shin, X. Sun, and T.-J. K. Liu. Study of Random-Dopant-Fluctuation (RDF) Effects for the Trigate Bulk MOSFET. *Electron Devices, IEEE Transactions on*, 56(7):1538–1542, July 2009.

[10] J. Stine, I. Castellanos, M. Wood, J. Henson, F. Love, W. Davis, P. Franzon, M. Bucher, S. Basavarajaiah, J. Oh, and R. Jenkal. Freepdk: An Open-Source

Variation-Aware Design Kit. In *Microelectronic Systems Education, 2007. MSE '07. IEEE International Conference on*, pages 173–174, June 2007.

[11] R. Topaloglu. Design with FinFETs: Design rules, patterns, and variability. In *Computer-Aided Design (ICCAD), 2013 IEEE/ACM International Conference on*, pages 569–571, Nov 2013.

Open Cell Library in 15nm FreePDK Technology

Mayler Martins*, Jody Maick Matos*,
Renato P. Ribas and André Reis*
UFRGS, PGMicro/PPGC
Porto Alegre, RS, Brazil
{mayler.martins,
jody.matos,rpribas,andre.reis}@inf.ufrgs.br

Guilherme Schlinker, Lucio Rech and
Jens Michelsen
*Nangate Inc.
Santa Clara, California, USA
{gss,lre,jcm}@nangate.com

ABSTRACT

This paper presents the $15nm$ FinFET-based Open Cell Library (OCL) and describes the challenges in the methodology while designing a standard cell library for such advanced technology node. The $15nm$ OCL is based on a generic predictive state-of-the-art technology node. The proposed cell library is intended to provide access to advanced technology node for universities and other research institutions, in order to design digital integrated circuits and also to develop cell-based design flows, EDA tools and associated algorithms. Developing a $15nm$ standard cell library brings out design challenges which are not present in previous technology nodes. Some of these challenges include double-patterning for both metal and poly layers, a very restrictive set of physical design rules, and the demand for lithography-friendly patterns. This paper discusses the development of the library considering the challenges associated with advanced technology nodes.

Categories and Subject Descriptors

B.7.2 [**Hardware, Integrated Circuits**]: Design Aids;
B.6.3 [**Hardware, Logic Design**]: Design Aids

General Terms

Design, Experimentation, Performance

Keywords

Standard cell Library, FinFET, Predictive Technology, Digital Integrated Circuit, ASIC Design

1. INTRODUCTION

Cell-based design is a widely adopted design methodology in current application-specific integrated circuit (ASIC) and system-on-chip (SOC) designs. This methodology is mainly based on standard cell libraries, which can be roughly defined as collections of basic building blocks that can be used to synthesize circuits. The use of cell libraries offers shorter design time and increases the circuit reliability, in the sense that the design process is less error-prone considering that the cells are pre-designed and verified. Most of cell-based designs rely on commercial cell libraries, which usually have restricted access, specially for advanced nodes. Due to those restrictions, both universities and other institutions have difficulties in having access to the information needed to perform research on EDA and design for advanced technology nodes.

Previous works have presented predictive standard cell libraries for educational and research purposes. In 2008, the open cell library $45nm$ (also known as FreePDK45) was released [26]. Since then, a considerable number of researchers have been using this library [5,8,36] . However, albeit its extensive use, the $45nm$ library does not correspond to a state-of-the-art technology node anymore, since there are new emerging technologies and devices, as FinFETs [15]. Synopsys also offers two generic standard cell libraries (also referred to as educational design kits): the $90nm$ and $32/28nm$ libraries [12,31]. However, Synopsys' initiatives also do not represent state-of-the-art technologies anymore.

Since 2001, the International Technology Roadmap for Semiconductors (ITRS) has pointed out that FinFETs [15] are a promising technology for transistor scaling beyond CMOS limits [17]. Intel started using FinFETs in 2011, with the production of processors in $22nm$ technology [1,16]. Research efforts have been made to enable FinFET technologies, in order to continue the advances both in Moore's law and in Koomey's law [9,11,19–21,27,28,35]. Recent works have also presented predictive technology models for high-performance and low-standby power FinFETs transistors in $20/16/14/10/7nm$ technology nodes [29,30].

In this work, we present the $15nm$ FinFET based Open Cell Library (OCL) and we also describe the challenges in the methodology while designing a standard cell library for an advanced technology node. The $15nm$ OCL is based on a generic $15nm$ predictive state-of-the-art process design kit, the FreePDK15 [4]. The $15nm$ OCL can be downloaded in [24]. The proposed cell library is intended to provide access to advanced technology node for universities and other research institutions, in order to design digital integrated circuits and also to develop cell-based design flows, EDA tools and associated algorithms. Developing a $15nm$ standard cell library brings out design challenges which are not present in previous technology nodes. Some of these challenges include double-patterning for both metal and poly layers, a very restrictive set of physical design rules, and the demand for lithography-friendly patterns. This paper also discusses how the challenges associated to advanced technology nodes have affected the development of OCL.

This paper is organized as follows. In Section 2, the library content is presented. Section 3 discusses the main library characteristics, such as its architecture, design methodology and modeling. Section 5 describes the synthesis results of a public-domain design using the proposed library. In Section 6, future works are discussed. Section 7 outlines the conclusions.

2. LIBRARY CONTENT

In this section, we present the content released in the $15nm$ OCL, describing the set of cells and available views. The usual design flow needs to perform some tasks beyond combinational and sequential synthesis. Examples of these tasks are scan-chain insertion to yield circuit observability, clock tree synthesis and sizing of buffers. The proposed library was thought to be a small (but complete) cell set able to treat all these cell-based design demands.

The proposed library consists of 76 cells, covering 21 unique logic functions that commonly appear in circuits. Sequential cells as flip-flops, scan flops and latches were also included. Other cells include antenna, tie high, tie low, and filler cells.

Most of combinational cells are available in two different drive strengths ($X1$ and $X2$). Driver cells, as inverters and different kinds of buffers (regular, clock and tri-state), are available in a wide range of drive strengths (from $X1$ to $X16$). The list of all available cells and the respective drive strengths are presented in Appendix A, at the end of this paper.

The proposed library is being released with all necessary views to perform the usual tasks involved in commercial flows for integrated circuit design. The available views are presented in Table 1.

3. LIBRARY CHARACTERISTICS AND DESIGN CHALLENGES

This section presents the main characteristics of the proposed library. The following subsections introduce a general overview on its main features, its architecture, design methodology and modeling. Besides the characteristics, we also describe the challenges in the methodology while designing a standard cell library for such advanced technology node. Some fundamentals of the library were defined early, in conjunction with the design rules and fabrication technology definition for the PDK [4]. Details of FreePDK15 predictive technology are beyond the scope of this paper. For a detailed description of the PDK, we refer the reader to [3] and [4].

3.1 Library Overview

The $15nm$ OCL is based on multi-gate FinFET transistors, available in the target FreePDK15 technology [4]. The move from two- to three-dimensional transistors introduces several design challenges, including modeling. Figure 1 illustrates a 3D view of the $15nm$ PDK FinFET device. FinFETs originated in the 90s, when researchers were looking into possible successors to the planar transistor. FinFETs were proposed as a new structure for the FET transistor that would reduce leakage current [15]. FinFET technology takes its name from the fact that the FET structure used

Table 1: List of available views released in the $15nm$ Open Cell Library.

View Name	File Extension	View Description
Technology Library	.lib	Provide logic, timing, power and area information of the cells in the library
Geometric Library	.lef	Provide information about the physical layout of the library in plain text, including design rules and abstract information about the cells
Simulation Library	.v	Provide a behavioral information of the cells for simulation intents
Cell Layouts	.gds	Provide information about planar geometric shapes, text labels, and other layout information in a binary format
Cell Netlists	.spi	Provide an instance-based transistor netlist, representing instances, nets, and some attributes
OpenAccess	.oa	Provide a database containing layouts and netlists

looks like a set of (radiator) fins when viewed. The peculiar gate structure present in a FinFET device provides a better electrical control over the channel, helping to reduce the leakage current and overcoming other short-channel effects. Given the control of the channel by the gate, the leak current is very small, thus reducing considerably the static leakage. This allows the use of lower threshold voltages, which improves the switching frequency and decreases the power consumption. FinFETs can also be implemented with two electrically independent gates, which allow the development of designs with low-power gates [28].

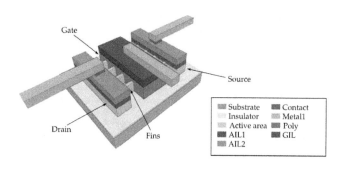

Figure 1: 3D view of the FreePDK $15nm$ transistor

The optical lithography process is an important aspect when designing a 15*nm* FinFET-based standard cell library. The target FreePDK15 technology adopts a double patterning technique as its predictive lithography process [3, 4]. Double patterning is a technique used in the lithography step that defines the features of integrated circuits at advanced process nodes. This technique is applied since the 32*nm* technology node , once enhancement techniques as as Optical Proximity Correction (OPC) were not compensating all diffraction errors and the photoresist started to blur [14]. In this library, the double patterning plays a vital role, both to poly-silicon and metal layers. This is due to the fact that most foundries are still using 193*nm* immersion lithography process [23]. The double patterning also imposes a regular layout, due to the poly-silicon arrangement. The line patterns formed by the regular poly-silicon reduces the number of exposures needed in the lithography process. Among different double patterning techniques, FreePDK15 adopts Self-Aligned Double Patterning (SADP) [2], as it has the lower overlay issues and it is well suited for further scaling [37].

Increasing the overall regularity in the circuit also poses difficulties in the layout. One of them occurs because some cells in the library have transistor networks in which the N-network are not dual to the P-network. In order to generate a valid network respecting the regularity constraints, the cell layout requires the insertion of gaps. In this case, the regular poly layers only controls one (NMOS or PMOS) FinFET, differently from a normal poly gate, which controls a pair of FinFETs. Figure 2 illustrates the layout of the D Flip-

Flop labeled *DFFRNQ_X1*, in which it is possible to identify gaps where the poly layer controls just one FinFET (either PMOS or NMOS).

The very restrictive design rules of FreePDK15 also impose the need for dummy poly gates that do not control any FinFET. The poly layers are required to be repeated at regular intervals. Additionally, only two gate terminals can be placed in neighbor polys (depending on the transistor width). Some cells in the library require more than two gate terminals to be placed in subsequent neighbor poly layers. Due to this reason, one dummy poly layer that is not controlling FinFET transistors has to be inserted to isolate sequences of at most two neighbor gate terminals, in order to respect gate terminal separation design rules. Examples of dummy gates are also illustrated in Figure 2.

3.2 Library Architecture

In order to be used together, as the building blocks of a circuit, cells have to share some common characteristics to constitute a library. These shared characteristics among the cells are thought to allow routing of power rails by abutment, as well as sharing of wells and diffusion regions. The name commonly attributed to this set of standard positions and dimensions to be respected by the cells from a library is the library template. Figure 3 shows the template adopted in the OCL design. Beyond the physical template, the library shared characteristics include naming convention, physical design template, choice of available functions, drive-strength definitions, electrical and physical design guidelines, that some authors define as the library architecture [7]. This

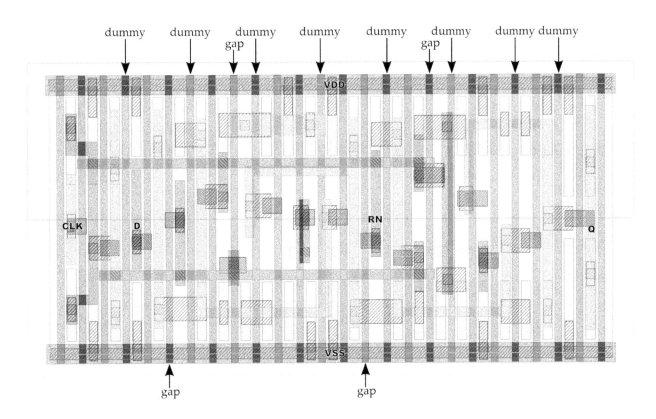

Figure 2: Layout of a D Flip-Flop with asynchronous reset containing 8 dummy gates, 4 gaps and 2 lines of metal2

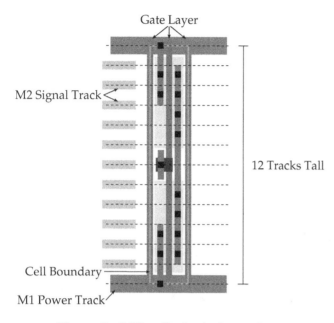

Figure 3: OCL cell physical template.

architectural specification is what distinguishes a standard cell library from a random collection of cells.

The chosen naming convention aims to inform the user about the main characteristics of the cell, while still being simple. For the combinational cells, the format is the name of the logic function and the number of inputs separated by an underscore and the drive strength (e.g. an AND with 4 inputs and drive strength of X2 has the name $AND4\_X2$). The sequential cells have a similar definition. For instance, a scan D Flip-Flop with negated set, Q output and $X1$ drive strength was named $SDFFSNQ\_X1$. For cells that are neither combinational or sequential, the names chosen reflect the role in the library. The drive strength suffix only appears in these cells if it is meaningful.

The OCL cell physical template is illustrated in Figure 3. The developed cells are 12 metal 2 (M2) tracks tall, while the width is variable, but corresponds to an integer number of regular gate layers. This architecture features two wide metal 1 (M1) power tracks and eleven M2 tracks for internal signal routing.

The internal routing of the cells was designed to achieve acceptable levels of resistance and capacitance, while minimizing both cell area and the use of upper levels of metal. An example of adopted measures to minimize levels of resistance and capacitance while routing cells is to use as less as possible the so-called local interconnection layers, such as AIL1, AIL2 and GIL [3, 4]. The levels of resistance and capacitance are minimized when avoiding these layers due to their electrical properties. With relation to avoid upper levels of metal layers, among all 76 released cells, only 6 of them (around 8%) are using M2 for internal routing. There is no M3 being used inside the cells. All interconnection pins are in M1.

3.3 Cell Design Methodology

The library design was performed with the help of Nangate Library Creator [25], considering the device characteristics, design rules and constraints for the $15nm$ predic-

tive technology. This subsection presents details about the methodology applied to design the proposed cells, such as the adopted P/N ratios, the transistor sizing approaches and a detailed description on the applied internal routing methodology.

The correct sizing of a standard cell is achieved by properly setting the number of N-type fins and P-type fins that produce almost equal rise and fall times, being equivalent to the P/N ratio. The P/N ratios were computed based on carrier mobility. In advanced technology nodes, it is possible to enhance the carrier mobility by straining the substrate [34]. This mobility enhancement increases the hole mobility, approximating the current capability of N and P transistors. As this feature can be observed in the $15nm$ technology model applied in this library, [4, 30], the P/N size ratio and fin ratio adopted for single-stage cells is 1.

When considering the transistor sizing, we adopted different approaches for single and multi-stage cells. As the library has less than 100 cells, more time could be invested to optimize each cell individually. The transistor sizing for single-stage cells (NAND, NOR, INV, AOI, OAI) were defined considering the regular layout structure of this technology. The adopted criteria was to increase transistor widths while avoiding transistor folding in order to maximize the cell performance without area drawbacks.

For multi-stage cells, we tried to apply the same single-stage criteria, additionally regarding the internal cell routability. In the cells with simple transistor networks (AND, OR, MUX, XOR, XNOR), performance could be maximized without routability problems. For complex cells, as half-adders, full-adders, and sequential cells, the sizing of each transistor pair was adjusted to yield internal cell routing while avoiding the use of upper levels of metal layers, without sacrificing performance whenever possible. In some layouts, so-called local interconnection layers (such as AIL2) were used to route close connection points in order to prevent metal 2 usage.

4. LIBRARY CHARACTERIZATION

This section presents the timing and power characterizations performed in the proposed library. For both timing and power characterization, we adopted the model of single input switching, where only one input signal switches at a time.

The $15nm$ OCL is characterized with three different timing delay models: (1) Non-Linear Delay Model (NLDM); (2) Effective Current Source Model (ECSM); and (3) Composite Current Source (CCS). In the following, we present a brief overview on these characterization models. Afterwards, details on the $15nm$ OCL timing and power characterization are presented.

4.1 Characterization Models

The Non-Linear Delay Model (NLDM) [18] is a voltage-based model that relies on input signal slopes and output capacitive loads. Such information is obtained from electrical simulations (Spice) and provided through the Liberty file in a look-up table (LUT) format. During the static timing analysis (STA), the gate delay characteristics of each instantiation are provided by these LUTs to compose the critical delay paths. Notice that the timing LUTs must be available for each input-to-output delay arc. A similar procedure based on LUTs is applied to the dynamic power consumption analysis, whereas the static power (leakage) is evaluated for each gate input vector. As rarely the conditions of each gate instantiation match the LUT parameters (input slope and output load), the applied delay value is obtained through the interpolating of weighted average from LUT neighboring values. The gate output capacitive load considered in NLDM is most valid for old technology nodes, where the resistive and inductive effects in interconnection wiring can be neglected. However, the continuous process shrinking has emphasized the resistive behavior of wires impacting the STA accuracy. To overcome such a trouble, the concept of 'effective capacitance' was introduced [13]. However, the NLDM model still fails to consider some non-linearities such as the Miller effect [33]. Part of these challenges are treated by current-based models [10].

The Effective Current Source Model (ECSM) is a current-based model proposed by Cadence [6]. Current sources are able to consider more non-linear transistor switching behaviors. These source models also allow an accurate modeling of interconnections, which are even more complex in nanometer designs. Current sources also have additional granularity to reflect sensitivities like Miller capacitance, input transition times and output load. In ECSM, the concept of LUTs for gate delay characterization with different input slopes and output loads is still applied. However, instead of specific delay values at each LUT position, the gate output voltage waveform is described through a data vector. This waveform is segmented corresponding to the size of the vector and resulting in a trade-off between accuracy and data volume.

The Composite Current Source (CCS), also a current-based model, was proposed by Synopsys [32]. The main difference from ECSM is that the gate output current waveform is characterized instead of the output voltage performed by ECSM. An interesting improvement provided by CCS model was the extension of this kind of modeling to noise and power analysis, besides timing. However, there are still some practical accuracy limitations. Both ECSM voltage and CCS current waveforms are sampled with far fewer points from reference simulator's output, typically 1% to 10% of the reference points.

4.2 Timing Characterization

The $15nm$ OCL presents different characterization results considering these three timing models: NLDM, ECSM and CCS. Each model has five characterization corners: slow, typical, fast, low temperature and a worst case, which considers a low temperature characterization. The OCL also includes a functional library, containing only the cell functionality. All models use a 9x9 LUT dimension for timing. For ECSM, the output voltage waveform is presented in a 3D LUT, with a 9x9 table storing an array with up to 12 values. In the CCS case, the output current waveform is also presented in a 3D LUT, now with a 9x9 table storing an array with up to 17 values for fast and typical corners, while the worst corner has at most 20 values.

Notice that the NLDM is provided for convenience. However, since the OCL is an advanced node library and some discussed effects are not effectively modeled in NLDM, the use of a current-based model is recommended. Using NLDM model might require a large safety margin affecting the overall timing and power estimation.

4.3 Power Characterization

The main objective of a power characterization is to model both leakage and internal power of the standard cells. The leakage (or static power) is the power consumed by the gate when it is not switching. The internal power is related with the short-circuit power consumption and dynamic power of the diffusion capacitors at the output pin of the cell. The overall power consumption is evaluated by summing up the leakage power, internal power, and switching power (consumed when charging and discharging the load capacitance).

The NLDM- and ECSM-based power characterizations have a similar methodology for power characterization. In the OCL characterization for these models, we measure the leakage power by multiplying the supply voltage to the average current flowing out from the Vdd terminal, considering neither input nor output signal transition. The internal power is estimated differently for combinational and sequential cells. When taking combinational cells into account, the internal power is measured by subtracting the switching energy at the load capacitance from the total energy consumption when output signal transits. For sequential cells, we measured the internal power by considering the switching power of output, input and clock pins. The resulting characterizations of both NLDM- and ECSM-based models are presented by the $15nm$ OCL as a 9x9 LUT.

The CCS-based power characterization differs from NLDM- and ECSM-based models. The modelling for power based on CCS characterizations assumes the leakage power as a leakage current. The internal power is modeled as an internal current, which is derived from the dynamic current by subtracting the switching component. This way, we measured the leakage currents with simple DC analysis. The dynamic current is measured with transient analysis, capturing a current waveform for each combination of input transition time and output loads. The resulting dynamic current characterization of the CCS-based model is presented by the $15nm$ OCL as a 9x9 table storing an array with up to 15 values.

5. SYNTHESIS RESULTS

The benchmark chosen as case study in order to evaluate the proposed library is an OpenCore floating point unit [22]. This design implements the four basic arithmetic operations: sum, subtraction, multiplication and division. It respects the IEEE 754 standard for double precision (64 bit) floating point, and has 136 input pins and 70 output pins.

The benchmark was synthesized using a commercial tool. Besides the synthesis, we performed Place & Route. We compared results of the same benchmark using the $45nm$ OCL library. As the $45nm$ OCL has more cells than $15nm$ OCL, the extra cells were removed in order to have a fair comparison. Table 2 shows information about the used libraries and compares the area, delay and power consumption obtained for the circuit synthesized with the two libraries. The reduction column, when applicable, shows the reduction that the $15nm$ OCL circuit presented, compared to the $45nm$ OCL counterpart. The $15nm$ OCL circuit was able to reduce the total area (considering routing) by almost one order of magnitude, when compared to the $45nm$ implementation. The timing results show that the $45nm$ OCL had some difficulties to achieve the timing closure, for a target frequency of $1GHz$. Indeed, the $45nm$ OCL used more than 1500 buffers and inverters than $15nm$ OCL. As the $15nm$

Table 2: Results for OpenCore FPU benchmark

	15nm	45nm	Reduction
Library Characteristics			
Operation Voltage (V)	0.8	1.1	N/A
Operation Frequency (GHz)	1.0	1.0	N/A
Characterization Corner	Typical	Typical	N/A
Area Results			
Total Area (μm^2)	21706.92	211068.87	89.7%
Cell Area (μm^2)	15437.17	68566.29	77.5%
#Cells	31442	36583	14.1%
Timing Results			
Timing Slack (ps)	307.5	0	N/A
Power Results			
Leakage Power (mW)	0.542	1.365	60.3%
Dynamic Power (mW)	37.767	94.919	60.2%
Total Power (mW)	38.309	96.284	60.2%

had some slack, we increased the operation frequency and were able to achieve $5GHz$, for the $15nm$ implementation. Regarding the power consumption, both leakage and dynamic power were reduced to one third, compared against $45nm$ OCL. This reduction is also caused by the smaller operation voltage of $15nm$ compared to $45nm$.

6. FUTURE WORK

The presented library contains a functionally complete set of cells, meaning it can be used to successfully synthesize circuits with commercial flows. As future work, this set can be enhanced. We plan to develop a larger set of combinational cells, including complex cells (e.g. AOI, OAI) with more inputs. A wider set of sequential cells will also be implemented, adding cells with asynchronous inputs, scan chain support and different sizing. For multi-stage cells, the transistor size of first stage can be downsized to consume less power, with no significant drawbacks in cell delay. Another interesting enhancement is the support of different gate-length versions of the library (14, 16 and $20nm$). Finally, libraries characterized with different V_t would be necessary, in order to synthesize circuits aiming low power and/or high performance.

Both layout versus schematic (LVS) and layout parasitic extractions (PEX) files are not yet available. Also, some technology files are missing, such as design rule manual, design rule checking deck, and capacitance tables. These will be included as soon as they are made available by the FreePDK15 alliance.

7. CONCLUSIONS

This paper introduced the $15nm$ FinFET-based Open Cell Library (OCL). The library content, characteristics and characterization were presented. Together with its main characteristics, we also described the challenges in the methodology while designing a standard cell library for such advanced technology node. Some of these challenges include double-patterning for both metal and poly layers, a very restrictive set of physical design rules, and the demand for lithography-friendly patterns. The $15nm$ OCL can be downloaded in [24]. The proposed cell library is intended to provide access to advanced technology node for universities and other research institutions, in order to design digital integrated circuits and also to develop cell-based design flows, EDA tools and associated algorithms. In order to validate the proposed cell library, an OpenCore design using the $15nm$ OCL was successfully synthesized.

8. ACKNOWLEDGEMENTS

The work presented herein has been partially funded by CAPES, by CNPq and by FAPERGS under grant 11/2053-9 (Pronem), by NanGate Inc. and by the European Community's Seventh Framework Programme under grant 248538 - Synaptic.

9. REFERENCES

[1] C. Auth, C. Allen, A. Blattner, et al. A 22nm high performance and low-power CMOS technology featuring fully-depleted tri-gate transistors, self-aligned contacts and high density MIM capacitors. In *Proc. of Symp. on VLSI Tech. (VLSIT)*, 2012.

[2] C. Bencher, Y. Chen, H. Dai, et al. 22nm half-pitch patterning by CVD spacer self alignment double patterning (SADP). In *Proc. of SPIE Advanced Lithography*. Int'l Soc. for Optics and Photonics, 2008.

[3] K. Bhanushali. Design Rule Development for FreePDK15: An Open Source Predictive Process Design Kit for 15nm FinFET Devices. Master's thesis, North Carolina State University.

[4] K. Bhanushali and W. R. Davis. FreePDK15: An Open-Source Predictive Process Design Kit for 15nm FinFET Technology. In *Proc. of Int'l Symp. on Physical Design (ISPD)*, 2015.

[5] S. Bobba, A. Chakraborty, O. Thomas, et al. CELONCEL: Effective design technique for 3-D monolithic integration targeting high performance integrated circuits. In *Proc. of Asia and South Pacific Design Automation Conference (ASP-DAC)*, 2011.

[6] Cadence Design Systems. Effective Current Source Model ECSM. http://www.cadence.com/Alliances/languages/Pages/ecsm.aspx, 2005.

[7] B. Chappell, A. Duncan, K. Ganesh, M. Gunwani, A. Sharma, and M. Swarna. Library architecture

challenges for cell-based design. *Intel Technology Journal*, 8(1), 2004.

[8] E. Y. Chin, C. S. Levy, and A. R. Neureuther. Variability aware timing models at the standard cell level. In *Proc. of SPIE Advanced Lithography*. Inter'l Soc. for Optics and Photonics, 2010.

[9] J.-P. Colinge. Multigate transistors: Pushing Moore's law to the limit. In *Int'l Conf. on Simulation of Semiconductor Processes and Devices (SISPAD)*, 2014.

[10] J. F. Croix and D. Wong. Blade and razor: cell and interconnect delay analysis using current-based models. In *Design Automation Conference, 2003. Proceedings*, pages 386–389. IEEE, 2003.

[11] I. Ferain, C. A. Colinge, and J.-P. Colinge. Multigate transistors as the future of classical metal-oxide-semiconductor field-effect transistors. *Nature*, 479(7373):310–316, 2011.

[12] R. Goldman, K. Bartleson, T. Wood, K. Kranen, C. Cao, V. Melikyan, and G. Markosyan. Synopsys' open educational design kit: capabilities, deployment and future. In *Proc. of Int'l Conf. on Microelectronic Systems Education*, 2009.

[13] M. Hafed, M. Oulmane, and N. C. Rumin. Delay and current estimation in a cmos inverter with an rc load. *Computer-Aided Design of Integrated Circuits and Systems, IEEE Transactions on*, 20(1):80–89, 2001.

[14] T. Honda, Y. Kishikawa, Y. Iwasaki, et al. Influence of resist blur on ultimate resolution of arf immersion lithography. *Journal of Micro/Nanolithography, MEMS, and MOEMS*, 5(4):043004–043004, 2006.

[15] X. Huang, W.-C. Lee, C. Kuo, et al. Sub 50-nm finfet: Pmos. In *Inter'l Electron Devices Meeting (IEDM)*, 1999.

[16] Intel Newsroom. 22nm 3-D Tri-Gate Transistor Technology. http://newsroom.intel.com/docs/DOC-2032.

[17] ITRS. Int'l Tech. Roadmap for Semiconductors. http://www.itrs.net/reports.html, 2013.

[18] P. Ju, E. Handschin, and D. Karlsson. Nonlinear dynamic load modelling: model and parameter estimation. *Power Systems, IEEE Transactions on*, 11(4):1689–1697, 1996.

[19] A. K. Kambham, J. Mody, M. Gilbert, et al. Atom-probe for FinFET dopant characterization. *Ultramicroscopy*, 111(6):535–539, 2011.

[20] J. G. Koomey, S. Berard, M. Sanchez, and H. Wong. Implications of historical trends in the electrical efficiency of computing. *Annals of the History of Computing, IEEE*, 33(3):46–54, 2011.

[21] C.-H. Lin, B. Greene, S. Narasimha, et al. High Performance 14nm SOI FinFET CMOS Technology with 0.0174um2 embedded DRAM and 15 Levels of Cu Metallization. In *Inter'l Electron Devices Meeting (IEDM)*, 2014.

[22] Lundgren, D. Opencores.org. http://opencores.org/project,double_fpu, 2009.

[23] A. Mallik, N. Horiguchi, J. Bömmels, et al. The economic impact of euv lithography on critical process modules. In *SPIE Advanced Lithography*. Int'l Soc. for Optics and Photonics, 2014.

[24] Nangate, Inc. NanGate FreePDK15 Open Cell Library. http://www.nangate.com/?page_id=2328.

[25] Nangate, Inc. NanGate Library Creator. http://www.nangate.com/.

[26] NanGate, Inc. NanGate 45nm Open Cell Library. http://www.nangate.com/?page_id=2325, 2008.

[27] S. Natarajan, M. Agostinelli, S. Akbar, et al. A 14nm Logic Technology Featuring 2nd-Generation FinFET Transistors, Air-Gapped Interconnects, Self-Aligned Double Patterning and a 0.0588um2 SRAM Cell Size. In *Int'l Electron Devices Meeting (IEDM)*, 2014.

[28] M. Rostami and K. Mohanram. Dual-V_{th} Independent-Gate FinFETs for Low Power Logic Circuits. *Trans. on Computer-Aided Design of Integrated Circuits and Systems (TCAD)*, 30(3):337–349, March 2011.

[29] S. Sinha, B. Cline, G. Yeric, V. Chandra, and Y. Cao. Design benchmarking to 7nm with FinFET predictive technology models. In *Proc. of Int'l Symp. on Low Power Electronics and Design (ISLPED)*, 2012.

[30] S. Sinha, G. Yeric, V. Chandra, B. Cline, and Y. Cao. Exploring sub-20nm finfet design with predictive technology models. In *Proc. of Design Automation Conference (DAC)*, 2012.

[31] Synopsys, Inc. Mountain View, CA. http://www.synopsys.com.

[32] Synopsys, Inc. CCS Technology. http://www.synopsys.com/Community/Interoperability /Documents/devforum_pres/2005nov/ CCS_Technical.pdf, 2005.

[33] Synopsys, Inc. CCS timing technical white paper. http://www.opensourceliberty.org/ccspaper/ ccs_timing_wp.pdf, 2006.

[34] S. Thompson, M. Armstrong, C. Auth, et al. A 90-nm logic technology featuring strained-silicon. *Trans. on Electron Devices (TED)*, 51(11):1790–1797, Nov 2004.

[35] E. Vogel. Technology and metrology of new electronic materials and devices. *Nature nanotechnology*, 2(1):25–32, 2007.

[36] J. Zhang, S. Bobba, N. Patil, et al. Carbon nanotube correlation: promising opportunity for CNFET circuit yield enhancement. In *Proc. of Design Automation Conference (DAC)*, 2010.

[37] P. Zimmerman. Double patterning lithography: double the trouble or double the fun? *SPIE Newsroom*, 20, 2009.

APPENDIX

A. LIST OF AVAILABLE CELLS IN THE 15NM OPEN CELL LIBRARY

COMBINATIONAL CELLS			
Cell Name	#In	Boolean Function	Drive Strengths
BUF	1	$O = A$	X1, X2, X4, X8, X12 and X16
INV	1	$O = !A$	X1, X2, X4, X8, X12 and X16
AND2	2	$O = A * B$	X1 and X2
AND3	3	$O = A * B * C$	X1 and X2
AND4	4	$O = A * B * C * D$	X1 and X2
OR2	2	$O = A + B$	X1 and X2
OR3	3	$O = A + B + C$	X1 and X2
OR4	4	$O = A + B + C + D$	X1 and X2
NAND2	2	$O = !(A * B)$	X1 and X2
NAND3	3	$O = !(A * B * C)$	X1 and X2
NAND4	4	$O = !(A * B * C * D)$	X1 and X2
NOR2	2	$O = !(A + B)$	X1 and X2
NOR3	3	$O = !(A + B + C)$	X1 and X2
NOR4	4	$O = !(A + B + C + D)$	X1 and X2
MUX2	3	$O = A * !Sel + B * Sel$	X1
XOR2	2	$O = A \oplus B$	X1
XNOR2	2	$O = !(A \oplus B)$	X1
AOI21	3	$O = !((A * B) + C)$	X1 and X2
AOI22	4	$O = !((A * B) + (C + D))$	X1 and X2
OAI21	3	$O = !((A + B) * C)$	X1 and X2
OAI22	4	$O = !((A + B) * (C + D))$	X1 and X2
FA	3	$S = A \oplus B \oplus Cin, Cout = A \oplus B * Cin + A * B$	X1
HA	2	$S = A \oplus B, Cout = A * B$	X1
SEQUENTIAL CELLS			
Cell Name	#In	Description	Drive Strengths
DFFRNQ	3	D flip-flop with asynchronous !reset	X1
DFFSNQ	3	D flip-flop with asynchronous !set	X1
SDFFRNQ	5	D flip-flop with scan and asynchronous !reset	X1
SDFFSNQ	5	D flip-flop with scan and asynchronous !set	X1
LHQ	2	High enable Latch	X1
ADDITIONAL CELLS			
Cell Name	#In	Description	Drive Strengths
CLKBUF	2	Clock buffer	X1, X2, X4, X8, X12 and X16
TBUF	2	Tri-state buffer	X1, X2, X4, X8, X12 and X16
FILL	-	Filler cell	X1, X2, X4, X8 and X16
CLKGATETST	3	Clock gate with test pin	X1
ANTENNA	-	Antenna cell	-
FILLTIE	-	Cell to tie the wells	-
TIEH	-	Tie-high cell	-
TIEL	-	Tie-low cell	-

Design Rule Management and Its Applications in 15nm FreePDK Technology

Michiel Oostindie
Sage Design Automation
2075 De La Cruz Blvd. #105
Santa Clara, CA USA
+1 408 727-6234
m.oostindie@sage-da.com

Coby Zelnik
Sage Design Automation
2075 De La Cruz Blvd. #105
Santa Clara, CA, USA
+1 408 727-6234
c.zelnik@sage-da.com

Maarten Berkens
Sage Design Automation
2075 De La Cruz Blvd. #105
Santa Clara, CA USA
+1 408 727-6234
m.berkens@sage-da.com

ABSTRACT

This paper reviews the industry practice of using the design rule manual (DRM) for documenting semiconductor manufacturing limitations and how these are translated to design rule check (DRC) decks. The fundamental flaws in the current paradigm are shown as well as the resulting negative impact on the industry. We will then describe a new paradigm to document and manage design rules that eliminates these flaws and closes the loop between design and manufacturing. We will illustrate the talk with application of the methodology for design rule management and checks performed during the development of the Open Cell Library (OCL) as part of the 15nm FreePDK technology.

Categories and Subject Descriptors

B7.1 **[Integrated Circuits]**: Types and Design Styles - *advanced technologies, Standard cells.*

B7.2 **[Integrated Circuits]**: Design Aids - *graphics, verification.*

General Terms

Management, Documentation, Design, Experimentation, Verification.

Keywords

Integrated Circuits; Semiconductor Technology; Design Rules; Design Rule Check; Electronic Design Automation; Physical Design Verification.

1. INTRODUCTION: DESIGN RULES, DRM AND DRC

Design Rules constitute the interface between semiconductor design and manufacturing [1] [2]. Design rules are defined by process technology engineers, as specific geometric constraints on the configuration and distances of the shapes within each layer or between shapes of multiple layers. These constraints reflect the physical fabrication limitations of the process, and keeping the physical design within these constraints ensures that it can be fabricated correctly at the expected yield rate.

The foundry specifications of all its design rules are published in a book that is usually referred to as the Design Rule Manual (DRM). This specification is then being used by the design teams for all physical design and verification tasks. To verify that the design conforms to the rules, designers use Design Rule Check (DRC) tools [3] [4] [5] [6] [7]. These are software tools that run a process-specific program called DRC deck or DRC runset. Unlike the DRM which uses descriptive form to define each design rule, the DRC deck is composed of code in a proprietary tool language that manipulates the design shapes in search of rule violations. The use of such paradigm that separates DRM writing from the internal format to be used in DRC tools causes an overhead for the development of design rules (DRMs) for new design processes and the associated physical design kits (PDKs). For every new process technology, the process and design technologists get together and develop the Design Rule Manual (DRM), which implies these two teams have to perform co-development of the DRM [8] [9]. We propose a new paradigm address the development of design rules using a system that captures design rules formally and establishes a direct and verifiable interface between process limitations and design checks. Such a system will be most useful for agile development of technology process rules and PDK development tasks.

This paper is organized as follows. Section 2 presents the currently used DRC/DRM paradigm, while the associated limitations are presented in Section 3. A new paradigm is presented in Section 4. Section 5 presents iDRM, a tool based on the newly proposed paradigm. The use of iDRM in the development of the 15nm FreePDK Open Cell library is discussed in Section 6. Finally, conclusions are presented in Section 7.

2. TRADITIONAL DRM/DRC PARADIGM

The DRM/DRC pair paradigm has been used for decades, but over time it has exhibited the following inherent characteristics that negatively impact the time and effort it takes to develop process technologies and design enablement kits.

2.1 DRM is informal

The DRM is a hardcopy book or a pdf file. Design rule definitions in the DRM are described using drawings and free-form human language that capture the geometric constraints. Since it uses free language, with no formal semantics and syntax, the rule descriptions might often be unclear, incomplete and ambiguous.

2.2 DRC is based on human interpretation

This problem becomes even more severe as it propagates to the DRC deck. The deck is programmed manually based on the programmer's interpretation of the DRM design rule description.

Following that subjective interpretation, the programmer writes a sequence of low level geometry manipulations that attempt to identify design rule violations and flag them. Since many rules in the DRM are already unclear and ambiguous to begin with, adding subjective interpretation to it and then implementing a code compounds and exacerbates the problem.

2.3 DRC deck correctness and completeness

Today there is no formal way to compare and verify that each piece of code in the DRC deck implementation fully and correctly represents the design rule intent it is supposed to check. It is a difficult problem, because the DRC deck coder has to think about all possible ways to violate the rule and make sure his check code covers them all. This mainly exhibits itself in early version implementations of the DRC deck for a new technology, which often suffer from errors and inaccuracies. Finding such errors and cleaning up the DRC deck code is done through an iterative trial and error process which takes a long time and effort, and even then few errors may remain after a DRC deck is released to designers.

2.4 Different roles and expertise domains

The DRM and DRC deck represent two very different functions, view-points and expertise domains. The DRM is a rule specification written by process technology people for humans. It is descriptive in nature so that designers can understand what configurations and distances are legal and construct the physical design accordingly.

By contrast, the DRC code is a machine code that executes geometric operations on physical design. The DRC code has no notion of what is the allowed rule – it is focused on the negative side, i.e. rule violations, manipulating the design to generate error marker polygons in specific locations where the programmer thinks such errors will manifest themselves.

The DRC programmer is a CAD professional skilled in a specific DRC programming language that manipulates polygons. In most cases the programmer does not know the original design rule exact intent and therefore can misinterpret it or miss some aspects of it. Because of tool or human limitations, in some cases it may be hard to program a complete and accurate check for a specific rule description, and the DRC code may be constructed to check only an approximation of the rule, but not the exact rule intent. Such compromises are hard to detect.

2.5 Advanced node rule complexity

With newer and more advanced process technologies. the above issues have become much more profound and with increasingly negative impact on process ramp-up and design enablement efforts. The number and complexity of design rules has grown exponentially with every technology node since the 40nm node [10]. Advanced lithography limitation, OPC requirements, double patterning, new materials, new layers, and new device structures and constraints have all added new types of rules and complexities that have not existed before. As a result, current commercial technologies use DRMs that hold thousands of design rules and each rule may have multiple variables and conditions. Understanding the exact intent of each and every rule and implementing them correctly in DRC decks have become a very laborious, difficult and error prone task.

3. LIMITATIONS OF CURRENT METHOD

Due to the above mentioned characteristics, using the traditional paradigm has the following disadvantages and limitations. These limitations become more pronounced in the case of PDK and library development at the early stages of a new process offering.

3.1 Double work

Each new rule requires creating both a DRM representation and a DRC deck implementation.

3.2 Consistency

The DRC deck representation is independent of the DRM representation, and the current methodologies cannot ensure consistency between the two.

3.3 Iterations

Due to the inconsistencies the current paradigm requires iterations between programming the DRC deck and the DRM specification.

3.4 No interaction or feedback

The current system is not suitable for quick and interactive design rule exploration and for doing what/if analysis using changing design rules.

3.5 Collaboration

The current system is not suitable for intra-group or inter-group collaboration. For example the library team needs to work closely with the design rule team exploring adding or modifying rules.

4. A NEW PARADIGM

In order to overcome the limitations described in the previous Section, we propose a new paradigm: A system that captures design rules formally and establishes a direct and verifiable interface between process limitations and design checks. Such a system will be most useful for process development and PDK development tasks.

The new system should offer the following qualities and capabilities:

- Enable design rules to be entered and captured by process engineers that are not programmers.

- The captured description should be formal, complete and unambiguous.

- The captured description should be clear and interactive - allowing the user to query certain details and properties This will resolve any problems caused by communication issues between the two groups of DRM development and DRC deck development.

- Executable: The design rule description is machine readable and its representation can be used for a variety of automated tools and tasks. For example, the rule description could generate a correct-by-definition rule check, putting an end to subjective interpretation and error-prone programming. This allows rule developers to immediately try their rule definition on test layout and verify it against their mental intent. It shortens the iteration loop and since all is done by the same person, errors are avoided.

5. THE iDRM SYSTEM

One commercial system that offers the above capabilities is the iDRM (integrated Design Rule Management) platform from Sage Design Automation. The iDRM system includes a graphical design rule editor where the user draws the pattern that describes the design rule, adds arrows marking proximities and distances between shapes, edges or corners, and assigns parameter names to them. e.g. *spacing*, *width*, *gate-pitch*, etc. The user can then add logical expressions and conditions, using these parameters as variables, to express statements that further qualify the patterns that are associated with a design rule.

Once a rule has been captured it serves not only as a clear visual description and documentation, but it also becomes an executable program. The user can run this rule definition on a physical design, and iDRM will scan the layout and will find all locations where a pattern matches the design rule description and for each instance will measure all the parameters used in that definition. Based on the logical expression in the rule, the tool will determine a pass or fail result for each instance. This is the equivalent of a DRC check although no DRC check has been programmed.

iDRM takes this concept a step further with automatic physical design scan and analysis. For each rule instance it finds, the tool will take all the relevant measurements of the parameters that were used in the rule definition. The result of this scan is a complete list of all design rule instances, each with complete information of all the relevant measurements, orientations, etc.

The scan & analysis function can be considered as a superset of a DRC check, where instead of a binary pass/fail result, it provides full resolution measurements and geometrical information for each use of a design rule in the layout. iDRM outputs the results in tables or various graph formats, and the integrated layout viewer provides a one-click hop from each such result entry to the layout location where this specific instance is found.

6. USING IDRM FOR DEVELOPMENT OF THE FREEPDK15 LIBRARY

The FreePDK15 is an open source predictive process design kit for 15nm FinFET technology [11] [12]. It was developed mainly for educational and demonstration purposes, but it includes a set of design rules that were developed to represent the main types of rules seen in actual foundry 14/16nm FinFET technologies. While FreePDK15 technology is not a real process that is used for silicon fabrication in any specific foundry, it does exhibit some of the main innovations of this technology node, e.g. FinFETs, MOL (middle-of-line) interconnect layers, cut layers and double patterning layers.

Our team took part in creating the standard cell library for this PDK and making it design rule correct. We had to start working on the library very early on when the design rules were still being developed. Moreover, the cell and library architecture has also influenced some of the design rules, and so this was a dynamic co-development process. During this co-development process we needed a method to quickly try and explore different rules as well as check them and also add specific library architecture rule checks. We could not rely on traditional DRC decks, since these take longer time to code and verify, and were not fully released at the time of our library development work.

For developing the library we needed to consider the technology design rules of all the FEOL layers, MOL layers and up to M1 and Via1. We drew and defined the rules in iDRM and had immediate DRC checkers for our needs. Any rule modification was automatically turned into an updated and accurate DRC check.

In the next section we'll describe a few design rule implementation examples that illustrate the use of iDRM and this new methodology. The DRM reference for these rules is the FreePDK15 design rule development document published by NCSU [11] [12].

6.1 Rule Example: Enclosure of V0 by AIL2

Via0 (V0) is used to connect active local interconnect layer (AIL2) to Metal1 (M1A) layer. The V0.5 design rule defines the minimum enclosure of V0 by the AIL2 layer [11] [12].

6.1.1 DRM Design Rule Description

Fig. 1 shows how this specific enclosure design rule is defined in the DRM.

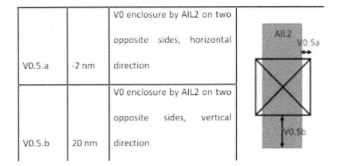

		V0 enclosure by AIL2 on two opposite sides, horizontal direction	
V0.5.a	-2 nm		
V0.5.b	20 nm	V0 enclosure by AIL2 on two opposite sides, vertical direction	

Figure 1: V0.5 rule in the DRM [11]

6.1.2 IDRM Implementation

The rule is captured in iDRM GUI by a similar drawing of the two layers and with similar arrows defining the enclosure distances, as illustrated by Fig. 2. In this implementation we chose to denote the horizontal enclosure distances as **l** (left) and **r** (right), and the vertical ones as **t** (top) and **b** (bottom). To make the rule definition more general, we used parameter names minHorExt and minVertExt that we can populate with any specific values (in this case -2nm and 20nm respectively). The DRCheck statement shown in the right hand section checks that all 4 distances are equal or greater than the respective values.

Once the design rule is captured the user can immediately run it on a physical design and the tool will find every instance of this drawn rule, and for each instance will measure the four distances l,r,t,b and will evaluate the DRCheck expression using these values and determine whether it adheres to the rule or violates it. The tool will highlight all these instances in its integrated viewer. In our case we used a layout consisting of standard cells under development. Fig. 3 shows a clip of the layout with V0.5 instances highlighted by iDRM. Note that all arrows are green indicating no design rule violation was found. This interactive feedback allows the user to immediately review and verify the rule definition and ensure it accurately represent its original intent.

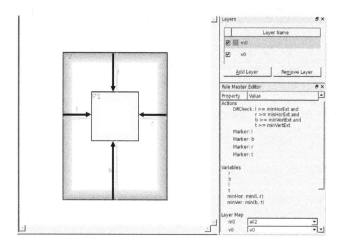

Figure 2: Rule captured in iDRM

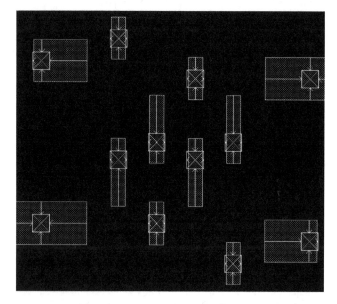

Figure 3: Design rule matches found and evaluated in iDRM

Using its data scan analysis function, iDRM can also provide complete numerical information on all such matches in the design.

Fig. 4 shows a result of using this function. In this case a table format was selected. Each table entry shows a different combination of values measured and their occurrence in the design. Each table entry is linked to its respective locations in the viewer for further review and analysis.

r	b	l	t	/	Occurrence
-0.002	0.02	-0.002	0.02		62984
0.062	0.02	-0.002	0.02		844
0.126	0.02	-0.002	0.02		811
0.06	0.02	0	0.02		59
0.042	0.02	0.018	0.02		252
0.034	0.02	0.026	0.02		51
0.098	0.02	0.026	0.02		19
0.026	0.02	0.034	0.02		12
0.129	0.02	0.035	0.02		18
0.018	0.02	0.042	0.02		199
0.082	0.02	0.042	0.02		199
0	0.02	0.06	0.02		54
-0.002	0.02	0.062	0.02		847
0.062	0.02	0.062	0.02		496
0.042	0.02	0.082	0.02		252
0.026	0.02	0.098	0.02		26
-0.002	0.02	0.126	0.02		691
0.035	0.02	0.129	0.02		28
-0.002	0.021	-0.002	0.02		255
-0.002	0.022	-0.002	0.02		87
-0.002	0.024	-0.002	0.02		39

Variable	Show	Lower	LowVal	Upper	UpVal	Binning	BinVal	Cumulative	Scale
r	☑	☐ Manual	-0.002	☐ Manual	0.129	☐	0.001	☐	☐ %
b	☑	☐ Manual	0.02	☐ Manual	0.221	☐	0.001	☐	☐ %
l	☑	☐ Manual	-0.002	☐ Manual	0.129	☐	0.001	☐	☐ %
t	☑	☐ Manual	0.02	☐ Manual	0.221	☐	0.001	☐	☐ %

Figure 4: Results of using scan analysis function

6.2 Cell Architecture rules

Not all design rules are related strictly to manufacturing. There are types of design rules that emanate from electrical requirements or physical architecture requirements. In the case of a standard cell library development, there is a need for library specific rules. These rules are in place to ensure standard height of all cells, clean abutment between cells, a certain width of the common supply bars, etc. We also used iDRM to define such rules and enforce them. The mechanism to define these rules is similar to the DRM rules and therefore we don't see a need to repeat it here in the same level of detail.

For illustration we have included a screen image of a high level representation of the rules in iDRM, which includes a few cell architecture rules grouped together by the user, as it is shown in Fig. 5. Each specific rule can be expanded upon selection of the hyperlink by the user.

Cell Architecture

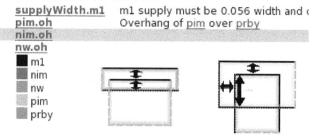

Figure 5: A group of cell architecture rules in iDRM

7. CONCLUSIONS

The current methodologies of defining, documenting and creating checks for design rules are still done manually, lacking automatic verification capabilities and slow to converge. This is particularly problematic during the early development phase of process technology and design enablement kits.

We suggested a new methodology that enables machine readable design rule capture and a single design rule representation for both documentation and check. This eliminates double and triple capturing of design rules and the inherent inconsistencies that are caused by it. It also speeds up the development process and facilitates easy design rule development and exploration.

The iDRM tool is a software platform that implements such new methodology, and we had the opportunity to use it for the development of the freePDK15 library [13] [14], enabling us to capture and use design rule checks when rules were still changing. We showed a few examples that illustrate the use of this methodology and its contribution to fast PDK development.

As a future suggested work, we highlight that iDRM has a distinct function (DRVerify) that generates an exhaustive set of test cases for each captured design rule, which is then used to verify DRC decks. The set includes both pass cases and fail (rule violation) cases that completely cover the design rule expression. We suggest the use of this function to generate test cases for the freePDK15 design rules, so that any commercial DRC deck made for these rules can use these test cases to verify its correctness.

8. ACKNOWLEDGMENTS

We want to thank Prof. Andre Inacio Reis and his team from the Universidade Federal do Rio Grande do Sul, Brazil, for reviewing our work and for their significant contributions to this paper. We also thank Kirti Bhanushali and Prof. Rhett Davis from North Carolina State University for letting us use the FreePDK design rule examples.

9. REFERENCES

[1] Carver Mead and Lynn Conway. *Introduction to VLSI systems*. Vol. 1080. Reading, MA: Addison-Wesley, 1980.

[2] Neil Weste and David Harris. *CMOS VLSI Design: A Circuits and Systems Perspective*. Addison-Wesley; 4 edition, 2010

[3] Y. Z. Liao and C. K. Wong. 1983. *An algorithm to compact a VLSI symbolic layout with mixed constraints*. In Proceedings of the 20th Design Automation Conference (DAC '83). IEEE Press, Piscataway, NJ, USA, 107-112.

[4] Losleben, P.; Thompson, K., "*Topological Analysis for VLSI Circuits*," Design Automation, 1979. 16th Conference on , vol., no., pp.461,473, 25-27 June 1979.

[5] Smith, R.; Joy, R., "*Computer aided design tools for VLSI*," Solid-State Circuits Conference. Digest of Technical Papers. 1980 IEEE International , vol.XXIII, no., pp.193,193, 13-15 Feb. 1980.

[6] Jin-Fuw Lee, "*A new framework of design rules for compaction of VLSI layouts*," Computer-Aided Design of Integrated Circuits and Systems, IEEE Transactions on , vol.7, no.11, pp.1195,1204, Nov 1988.

[7] McGrath, E.J.; Whitney, T., "*Design Integrity and Immunity Checking: A New Look at Layout Verification and Design Rule Checking*," Design Automation, 1980. 17th Conference on , vol., no., pp.263,268, 23-25 June 1980.

[8] Vito Dai ; Jie Yang ; Norma Rodriguez ; Luigi Capodieci; DRC Plus: augmenting standard DRC with pattern matching on 2D geometries. Proc. SPIE 6521, Design for Manufacturability through Design-Process Integration, 65210A (March 28, 2007).

[9] Raina, R.. *What is dfm & dfy and why should i care?* IEEE Test Conference, 2006. ITC'06, pp. 1-9.

[10] Rick Merritt, *Synopsys bullish despite rising chip complexity* Article, EETimes designlines March 26 2013 http://www.eetimes.com/document.asp?doc_id=1280659

[11] Kirti N Bhanushali. May 2014. *Design Rule Development for FreePDK15: An Open Source Predictive Process Design Kit for 15nm FinFET Devices* Thesis, North Carolina State University http://www.lib.ncsu.edu/resolver/1840.16/9519

[12] Kirti Bhanushali and Rhett Davis. "*FreePDK15: An Open-Source Predictive Process Design Kit for 15nm FinFET Technology*", ISPD 2015.

[13] Mayler Martins, Jody Matos, Renato Ribas, Andre Reis, Guilherme Schlinker, Lucio Rech and Jens Michelsen. "*Open Cell Library in 15nm FreePDK Technology*", ISPD 2015.

[14] Jody Matos, Augusto Neutzling, Renato Ribas and Andre Reis. "*A Benchmark Suite to Jointly Consider Logic Synthesis and Physical Design*", ISPD 2015.

A Benchmark Suite to Jointly Consider Logic Synthesis and Physical Design

Jody Maick Matos, Augusto Neutzling, Renato P. Ribas and André Reis
UFRGS, PPGC/PGMicro
Porto Alegre, RS, Brazil
{jody.matos,ansilva,rpribas,andre.reis}@inf.ufrgs.br

ABSTRACT

This paper presents an improved benchmark suite to jointly consider logic synthesis and physical design. Usually, benchmark circuits were provided by the physical design and the logic synthesis communities separately, according to their specific needs. The files provided for each benchmark set were restricted to the views necessary for the community. Additional specifications of design intents are necessary to express optimization goals that can be shared by logic synthesis and physical design communities, as circuits alone do not carry sufficient information to establish a benchmark with a clear optimization goal. In this paper, we describe benchmarks as a set composed of circuits, design intents (constraints), floorplan, target library and technology. Disregarding pieces of information provided for the benchmarks can change the associated criticality and affect the combined or isolated outcome of logic synthesis and physical design. The proposition of this benchmark suite brings attention to the problem of considering adequately the complete context of design intent throughout the flow.

Categories and Subject Descriptors

B.7.2 [**Hardware, Integrated Circuits**]: Design Aids;
B.6.3 [**Hardware, Logic Design**]: Design Aids

General Terms

Algorithms, Design, Experimentation, Performance

Keywords

Logic Synthesis, Physical Design, Benchmarks, Circuit Optimization.

1. INTRODUCTION

In current advanced technologies, the quality of digital VLSI circuits is becoming increasingly dependent on physical layout characteristics. However, significant transforma-

tions and design decisions are performed early in the design flow. For instance, during the technology-independent logic synthesis, the logic network can be iteratively changed when applying factorization, decomposition and extraction algorithms. In current design flow practices, powerful transformations on logic synthesis step are not aware of physical layout characteristics that most influence final performance. A possible origin of this drawback in design flow practices is that they are composed of tools conceived independently, which are invoked in sequence. This reflects the way EDA tools have been historically developed.

In old technologies and, consequently, in early design flows, the main source of circuit delay was the logic gates, disregarding wires. At these days, logic synthesis was determinant for the performance of integrated circuits, as wire delays could be disregarded. In advanced technology nodes, the delay can be significantly changed after place and route, invalidating the performance assumptions made during logic synthesis. A recurrent argument in this sense is that, in current technologies, wire delay is becoming more important than cell delay [1–6]. Disregarding wires in early steps of the synthesis flow is just one example of issues in current design flow practices. Other physical characteristics are also ignored in early steps of synthesis, such as congestion and routability.

The same behavior can also be observed on physical design tools. Even on early steps of physical synthesis, the cells in a mapped netlist are commonly considered as blackboxes, disregarding logic information. Changes in the netlist usually performed by most placement and routing tools are limited to adjust drive strengths, taking time budget into account.

The current situation points the need of more dialog between the logic synthesis and physical design communities. Even benchmarking efforts from both communities reproduce this lack of dialog. From a stand point of the logic synthesis community, academic benchmarks [7–11] are distributed without design constraints, floorplanning data, I/O pin placement and available routing resources description. This way, the logic synthesis academic community is stimulated to disregard physical information. From the point of view of the physical design community, academic benchmarks [12–22] are distributed without information about the logic inside the blocks. This way, the physical design academic community is stimulated to disregard the possibility of logic transformations. As a consequence, the way EDA students are taught tends to keep this strict division among the design flow steps might be limiting the algorithm advances on EDA tools.

In this paper, we propose a set of benchmarks which enables to jointly consider logic synthesis and physical design. The proposed benchmark suite can be downloaded in [23]. From educational and benchmarking standpoints, this benchmark suite is intended to break the barrier between logic synthesis and physical design. The set of benchmarks proposed herein can be used to achieve two major purposes: (1) to consider physical information during the early steps in design flow, which makes possible to perform a draft design closure during logic synthesis; and (2) to regard logic features while handling physical designs, which allows investigations about resynthesis approaches by collapsing/splitting logic cells in such a way to obtain more physical-friendly designs. The initiative presented herein is an early move towards more comprehensive benchmarks, by adding specific files with physical information and timing requirements to existing logic synthesis benchmarks. Much has still to be done, e.g. add larger benchmarks. However, this first initiative identifies the lack of benchmarks that would serve to both logic synthesis community, which attend the International Workshop on Logic and Synthesis (IWLS), and physical design community, which attend the International Symposium on Physical Design (ISPD). This is a first, naive set of benchmarks aiming the use and discussions by both communities, in order to capture a more comprehensive list of requirements for a more complete benchmark suite, which fulfils requirements of logic synthesis and physical design.

The rest of the paper is organized as follows. Section 2 presents a historical perspective considering both logic synthesis, physical design, associated benchmarks and the evolution of technology throughout time. Section 3 makes an analysis of the recent benchmarking efforts from the physical design community. Section 4 discusses a similar analysis on logic synthesis benchmarking efforts. In Section 5, the proposed benchmark suite is described. In Section 6, we present experimental results enabled by using the proposed set of benchmarks. Section 7 discusses the intended future works. Section 8 outlines the conclusions.

2. HISTORICAL PERSPECTIVE

In this section, we try to establish an historical perspective about logic synthesis, physical design and associated benchmarks. Obviously, this historical perspective has also to consider the evolution of technology throughout time, which greatly affects algorithms and benchmarks.

In the beginning of LSI, physical design was made through programmable logic arrays (PLAs) and logic synthesis was performed as two-level logic synthesis. From this time, the first benchmarks for two-level logic synthesis appeared [9].

With the increase of design size, two-level implementations of logic became too costly, and logic designs moved to multi-level logic. At the same time, physical designs become cell based designs, based on placing and routing of standard cells. From this era, combinational [7] and later sequential [8] logic netlists appeared as benchmarks. The first benchmarks for placement were also from this time [24]. The logic synthesis and the physical design communities were distinct and so the used benchmarks were also different. Concurrently, benchmarks were already being discussed to be improved [25]. Also, it was pointed out that empirical com-

parisons through benchmarks were necessary as algorithms were not exact, but heuristic [26].

For early technology nodes, circuit delay was dominated by device delay. As a result, delay estimated while producing logic netlists were sufficiently accurate to estimate final characteristics of a circuit. At this time, wireload models were used to predict routing capacitance parasitics from purely logic netlist descriptions [27] [28] [29].

With circuits scaling down, wiring parasitics introduced during place and route started to dominate circuit delay in intermediate technology nodes. This could be resolved with gain based models, such as logical effort being applied and cells being scaled to a $Cout/Cin$ ratio that allowed to keep delay budgets under control. At this time, it was still possible to maintain logic synthesis and physical design as separate tasks. However, benchmark size became an issue, and an effort was made to obtain larger circuits for logic synthesis benchmarking [30] [11]. The same was made for placement [31], and commercial circuits were donated by companies to be used as benchmarks. However, in order to keep intellectual property, the logic functionality of the cells was not disclosed. This way, placement benchmarks kept on being a set of interconnected black-boxes. Even pin direction (input or output) was not disclosed for the cells. The IWLS05 [11] benchmarks were a quite complete distribution. However, this benchmark suite [11] still missed design intent specification given by design constraints and pin placement.

With further scaling, effects like input signal slope started to affect delay, making simple scaling of cell performances with a gain based model difficult or impossible. Other nonlinear effects such as signal slope and RC effects started to dominate delay.

Currently, we are in a situation where the best solutions at the logic level can be different depending if the logic has to be delivered to neighbour or distant cells. Also, arrival times and input slopes can greatly affect the best mapping solution for a logic sub-circuit. This way, it is important to be able to map logic considering use context, where the use context is imposed by physical design. For this reason, this papers proposes circuit benchmarks where more design context is provided, including design intent specification given by design constraints and pin placement.

3. PHYSICAL DESIGN BENCHMARKS ANALYSIS

In this section, we present a study of the recent benchmarking efforts from the physical design community. The analysed set of benchmarks is limited to ISPD contests, ranging from ISPD'05 to ISPD'15. Following subsections describe an overview about the analysed benchmark suites (grouped by contest subject). After that, the main issues regarding the lack of logic synthesis related information in the benchmarks are presented. For comparison intents, Table 1 presents the distribution information released in the benchmarks.

3.1 Benchmarks Overview

3.1.1 ISPD 2005/2006 (Placement)

The 2005 edition of ISPD contest [12] has focused the placement problem, taking the wire length minimization as primary objective. The main claim is that the weighted wire length minimization provides a general framework for performance and routability optimization in placement. The quality metrics were based on legality and half-perimeter bounding box wire length (HPWL). Neither timing nor congestion metrics were adopted. Eight industrial benchmark circuits were released containing cell instances and interconnections, described in *Bookshelf* format. Circuit sizes range from $211K$ to $2,177K$ objects, considering both movable and fixed objects. In the 2006 edition [13], a different set of benchmarks were distributed, again described in *Bookshelf* format. At this time, routability estimation via density target was included to HPWL quality metric, leading to spreading capability.

3.1.2 ISPD 2007/2008 (Global Routing)

Both 2007 and 2008 editions of ISPD contest [14, 15] addressed the global routing problem. The problem was formulated as a tile-based grid structure superimposed on the chip area. Both 2D and 3D problem instances were considered, requiring single metal layer and multiple metal layers approaches, respectively. Considering these two editions, 16 new global routing benchmarks were released, all derived from ISPD 2005/2006 placement benchmark solutions. The benchmarks were described in Labyrinth format, containing only interconnection and routing resources. The quality of a global routing solution was measured primarily by the total overflow with two tie-breakers: the maximum overflow and the routed wire length.

3.1.3 ISPD 2009/2010 (Clock Network Synthesis)

In the ISPD 2009 edition, a simplified version of the clock network synthesis (CNS) problem was addressed in the contest [16]. The problem was formulated by considering each buffer as a "point", representing both the buffer input and output pins in a single (x, y) coordinate. As a result, two buffers/inverters could not overlap, even when placed at the same point, and wires could not short, even if overlapping each other. Effectively, this also implies participants can use larger buffers/inverters at the same point at the cost

of higher power consumption. The power consumption was estimated by the CV^2f equation, instead of using the *I-V* curve. The distributed benchmark suite was derived from seven IBM microprocessors and high-performance ASIC designs, described in an input/output format specially developed to this contest. The quality of a CNS was evaluated by the clock latency in two SPICE simulations, considering voltage variation and constrained by total power consumption.

Compared to 2009 CNS contest, the 2010 edition [17] has revised rules to better reflect the real problems from the industry. Eight new IBM and Intel microprocessor and high-performance ASIC designs were released, described in the same format of 2009. Instead of clock latency range upon two simulations with different supply voltage settings, the major judging criteria was set to be the total clock power (modeled by capacitance) respecting local clock skew constraints and considering hundreds of simplified Monte Carlo simulations.

3.1.4 ISPD 2011 (Routability-Driven Placement)

Despite the placement problem has already been addressed in 2005 and 2006 editions, these contests were still not addressing a fundamental requirement for placement approaches: the ability to produce routable placements. Based on this claim, the 2011 ISPD contest [18] addressed the routability-driven placement problem. Eight new industrial benchmark circuits were released, with circuit sizes ranging from $483K$ to $1,239K$ objects, considering both movable and fixed objects. An extended version of *Bookshelf* format was adopted, adding new file types with both placement and routing information. After placed, each result were submitted to "golden routers" (released from the contest committee). The quality of final results was measured primarily by a scaled total overflow and running time, taking a scaled tile-to-tile routed wire length metric as tie-breaker.

3.1.5 ISPD 2012/2013 (Discrete Gate Sizing)

The 2012 edition of ISPD contest [19] has focused on dis-

Table 1: Distribution and related file types of both previous benchmarks and the set of benchmarks proposed herein.

	Logic Synthesis Information				Physical Design Information			
	Logic Representation	RTL/Netlist	SDC	LIB	DEF/Bookshelf	LEF/Labyrinth	CNS	SPEF
ISPD'05 [12]					X			
ISPD'06 [13]					X			
ISPD'07 [14]						X		
ISPD'08 [15]						X		
ISPD'09 [16]							X*	
ISPD'10 [17]							X*	
ISPD'11 [18]					X			
ISPD'12 [19]		X	X	X				X
ISPD'13 [20]		X	X	X				X
ISPD'14 [21]		X			X	X		
ISCAS'85 [7]	X	X						
ISCAS'89 [8]	X	X						
ITC'99 [10]	X	X						
IWLS'05 [11]		X		X		X		
Our Benchmark	X	X	X	X	X	X	X	

* Both ISPD'09 and ISPD'10 provide a proper format aiming to solve the Clock Networking Synthesis problem.

crete gate sizing. The problem was formulated in such a way that, by taking a standard cell library, a circuit netlist and the associated timing constraints and interconnect parasitics as inputs, the cell sizes and types suggested for each instance in the netlist should be determined. The interconnect models have lumped capacitance and zero resistance. 14 benchmarks were used for evaluation purposes. They were composed from 7 netlists, derived from IWLS-2005 set of benchmarks [11], using 2 different clock periods for each netlist (fast and slow). Three quality criteria of results were adopted: (1) the number of violations, divided into three different types: negative slack, maximum capacitance and slew; (2) the total leakage power; and (3) the running time. All violations were added together into a single value. Two different rankings were proposed. The first one takes the quality in terms of leakage power as main ranking, with running timing as tie-breaker. In the second one, leakage power and running time were took together. The number of violations was primarily considered for both rankings. For 2013 edition [20], improvements were performed both in the benchmark suite and in the interconnect models utilized. Four new netlists were produced by the contest organizers in order to release more challenging benchmarks. With relation to interconnect models, distributed RC trees (one tree per net) were adopted as improvement.

3.1.6 ISPD 2014/2015 (Detailed-Routing-Driven Placement)

For 2014 and 2015 editions of ISPD contests [21, 22], the placement problem again became addressed. The focus now is detailed-routing-driven approaches. The claim for that is based on recent studies suggesting that academic placement algorithms may lack sufficient awareness of the pin geometry and routing rules to adequately address the challenge of computing routable placements at $28nm$-process technologies and below. The current challenge to placement approaches is the formulation of routability models which (1) provide high enough scale-appropriate accuracy when needed and (2) demand low computational overhead when this accuracy is irrelevant.

In the 2014 edition, two different benchmark suites were released. The first one was adapted from ISPD 2013 gate sizing contest and has rectangular floorplans with no fixed or movable macros. The second one was adapted from DAC 2012 routability-driven placement contest [32] and has more complex floorplans with fixed macros. Both released benchmarks were described with industrial formats. Each benchmark has four files: (1) routing resources, described in a Library Exchange Format (LEF); (2) physical characteristics of the technology library, also in LEF; (3) floorplanning, in a Design Exchange format (DEF); and (4) a gate-level netlist, described in Verilog (V). The placement results were legalized, routed, and scored based on cell legalization perturbations, detail routed wire length, routing violations, and design-rule check (DRC) violations.

For 2015 edition, the detailed-routing-driven placement problem is being extended to a blockage-aware version. This extension is intended to make it applicable to a more realistic setting. For example, more attention should be paid to minimize routed wire-length in the presence of large floorplan blockages and thin placement channels. The design suite in the benchmark set contains eight designs adapted from ISPD 2013 gate-sizing contest. The quality metric is

also being extended by examining the distribution of the cell density map on a 4x4 standard cell grid for placement density.

3.2 Physical Design Benchmark Drawbacks

The physical design benchmarks fail to provide logic information in almost all editions. We refer the reader to Table 1 for a better understanding. Even when this information is provided, as in ISPD 2012/2013 discrete gate sizing contests, neither logic transformations were allowed in the contest nor physical information was provided. In this sense, research works on logic-synthesis-aware physical design are not able to perform experiments by using physical design benchmarks. For example, it has been recently pointed out by some researchers [33] that tangled logic could be less favorable to generate friendly layout than untangled logic. This implies in logical rewriting, which cannot be done on the physical design benchmarks because the logic functionality of leaf blocks is not provided with the benchmarks.

4. LOGIC SYNTHESIS BENCHMARKS ANALYSIS

In this section, we present an overview of the main academic logic synthesis benchmarks. Firstly, we try to summarize the features and main contributions of each benchmark set. After that, we present a discussion addressing benchmark drawbacks, as the lack of floorplanning and routing information. Again, we refer the reader to Table 1, which presents the distribution information released in the analysed benchmarks.

4.1 Benchmarks Overview

4.1.1 ISCAS'85 and ISCAS'89

The ISCAS'85 [7,34] and ISCAS'89 [35] benchmarks were introduced to evaluate combinational and sequential automatic test-pattern generation (ATPG) tools. Despite their initial purpose, they have been used for evaluating the effectiveness of methods in additional areas, including logic synthesis, formal verification, layout synthesis, test field, power estimation and partitioning. The ISCAS'85 suite is composed by 10 combinational circuits, described in a proprietary logic representation format. A translator was distributed together the circuits in order to outputs the benchmark descriptions in other formats. The ISCAS'89 suite provided a new set of benchmarks, composed of sequential circuits and extending the size and complexity of the ISCAS'85 benchmark circuits.

4.1.2 MCNC

The Microelectronics Center of North Carolina (MCNC) benchmark suite was published in IWLS'1991 [9]. It included logic synthesis and optimization benchmark sets from the ISCAS'85 and ISCAS'89 suites, in addition to some other benchmarks collected from industry and academia. The benchmark provided only logic representations, such as BLIF and PLA formats.

4.1.3 ITC'99

The ITC'99 benchmark suite was published in the International Testing Conference (ITC), 1999 [10]. The main contribution of this set was the availability of high-level descriptions, which offer a wide set of test cases for ATPG and logic synthesis environments. The ITC'99 benchmark set consists of 22 VHDL designs collected from the internet and from class work, modified for uniformity and synthesizability. The ITC'99 suite is an improvement of ISCAS'89, since it has more complex circuits than the latter. Larger designs were generated by stitching together smaller designs. For instance, b15 is a subset of 80386 microprocessor, and b17 has three copies of b15. Additionally to the RTL descriptions, the ITCÂt'99 suite includes gate-level EDIF format and stuck-at fault lists.

4.1.4 IWLS'05

The IWLS 2005 benchmark suite contains the ISCAS, MCNC and ITC'99 suites, as well as some OpenCores and a few other designs [11]. All benchmarks were synthesized and mapped to a 180nm library. RTL description and the standard library are provided, as well as the synthesis reports, in order to allows easy exchanging of benchmarks and experimental results in the community.

4.1.5 Altera Benchmarks

An improved benchmarking methodology was proposed in IWLS'07 in partnership with Altera [36]. The methodology consists of a collection of designs associated with a reference compilation flow and experimental results for evaluating logic synthesis and technology mapping algorithms. The initial design set consists of 8 FPGA-based large designs, each containing at least 10,000 4-LUTs. Larger designs in the benchmark set allows to measure running time and memory usage in addition to the traditionally measured properties of new tools, such as area, delay and power consumption. It also enables to follow new trends in design style and characteristics. Designs are available in RTL format and in several types of hierarchical BLIF.

4.2 Logic Synthesis Benchmark Drawbacks

All analysed logic synthesis benchmarks lack some information that is fundamental to determine the final performance of a circuit, for instance: design constraints, floorplanning data, I/O pin placement and a description of available routing resources. In the following, the effect of these factors in the quality of design are described.

4.2.1 Floorplanning Data and I/O Pin Placement

Floorplanning data describes the physical space where the design has to fit. Some crucial information can be obtained in this description, such as the die area which is available in the design. Another valuable information in this way is the I/O pin placement, which may affects the cell placement. Certainly, this information has a huge impact in future steps of the design flow, as routing and clock tree synthesis.

4.2.2 Design Constraints

Design constraints [37] are used to express designer intent for the final circuit. Simple examples of design constraints include arrival times for inputs and required times at outputs. The synthesis tool has to respect design constraints (e.g. required frequency) while minimizing design costs (e.g. area and power). Academic tools for logic synthesis rarely have support for design constraints. For instance, ABC [38]

does not support design constraints. User imposed design constrains can severely change the regions of a circuit that should be optimized, as well as the type of optimization needed. This way, design constraint information awareness is an important step in linking logic and physical design.

4.2.3 Availability of Routing Resources

Logic synthesis tools have recently started to consider metrics for wire congestion. Placement tools are also considering to perform wireplanning together with cell placement. The availability (or the lack thereof) of routing resources can severely change the regions of a circuit that should be optimized, as well as the type of optimization needed. Enabling wire planning during logic synthesis would be of great value for a design flow. Logic synthesis benchmarks provide no information about availability of routing resources such as number of available routing layers and number of available tracks for each layer, as well as the RC characteristics of wires.

5. PROPOSED BENCHMARK SUITE

This section describes the proposed set of benchmarks. We briefly describe the benchmarks intent, the circuits and the complementary files. The designs in the benchmark suite proposed herein are derived from IWLS 2005 benchmarks [11] and Altera benchmarks [36]. However, the addition of files with physical information (e.g pin placement) and timing requirements (e.g. SDC files) makes the benchmark versions very distinct among them. In this sense, all benchmark circuits presented in this paper contain both logic information files (such as RTL descriptions and AIGs) and physical information files (such as floorplanning data, I/O pin placement and available routing resources). We refer the reader to Table 1, which presents the distribution information released in the proposed benchmark suite. The following subsections present a brief description of the main information available in the proposed set of benchmarks. After that, Section 6 presents a brief case study, which makes possible to realize the effect of considering some physical information during logic synthesis.

5.1 Circuits

There are 29 different circuits being released in the benchmark suite proposed herein. A listing of these circuits is presented in Table 2. Notice that the circuits from 05 to 17 are based IWLS 2005 benchmarks [11]. In the same way, circuits from 18 to 29 are derived from Altera benchmarks [36]. The size of the circuits range from 5 to 200,762 instances of cells in a non-optimized mapping.

5.2 AAG Files

The AAG file [39] is an ASCII format for describing and-inverter graphs (AIGs) [40]. Each benchmark follows with an AIG description in this format. This file is commonly used for logic synthesis tasks and AIG is a data structure used in current state-of-the-art logic synthesis tools, like ABC [38].

5.3 DEF Files

The DEF file contains information about the design itself. DEF stands for Design Exchange Format [41]. Our intent in release this file is to provide floorplanning information, as well as I/O pin placements. For each original benchmark

#	Circuit	Inputs	Outputs	# Cell Instances
01	aig4place	6	2	5
02	aig4place2	5	2	4
03	baseTest	4	1	3
04	fullAdder	3	2	7
05	C17	5	2	6
06	C432	36	7	127
07	C499	41	32	386
08	C880	60	26	306
09	C1355	41	32	390
10	C1908	33	25	354
11	C2670	233	139	534
12	C3540	50	22	918
13	C5315	178	123	1323
14	C6288	32	32	1870
15	C7552	207	108	1377
16	i10	257	224	1799
17	b20	32	22	12041
18	oc_aquarius	464	3328	26535
19	oc_cfft_1024x12	52	592	14889
20	oc_cordic_r2p	34	40	16788
21	oc_cordix_p2r	50	32	12565
22	oc_des_perf	121	64	31881
23	oc_ethernet	192	1171	12092
24	oc_fpu	262	280	25591
25	oc_mem_ctrl	115	152	18552
26	oc_video_dct	1903	3528	49982
27	oc_video_jpeg	1720	3450	60573
28	radar20	3292	17732	84343
29	uoft_raytracer	4364	10569	200762

(Table 2), we provide DEF files with different versions of I/O pin placement, including random, left-right, good and bad placements. The goal of these files is to create versions of the benchmarks that allow the users to understand how pin placement affects design flow pratices.

5.4 SDC Files

The SDC file contains information about the design constraints. SDC stands for Synopsys Design Constraints [37]. Our intent in release this file is to provide delay constraints for the benchmarks. We provide fast, slow and average timing constraints in different SDC files. The goal is to create versions of the benchmarks that allow the users to understand how timing requirements affect the area and timing of the benchmarks.

5.5 Verilog Files

The Verilog file contains a logic/structural description of the circuits. This file is provided to have a description acceptable in most design flows.

5.6 LEF and LIB Files

These two files define both the physical and technology libraries following the benchmarks. The LEF file contains information about the layout of the cells in the library, such as the position of the pins inside the cells and routing blocakges. LEF stands for Layout Exchange Format [41]. Our intent releasing this file is to provide a physical library for the benchmarks. The LIB file contains information about the technology library. LIB is the abbreviation for Liberty format [42]. The LIB file provides information about logic, timing, power and area for all the cells available in the library. The availability of a library allows to perform technology mapping as well as to perform place and route of the resulting circuits. We are not distributing neither LEF nor LIB files, since we are releasing the proposed benchmarks considering the NanGate 15nm Open Cell Library (OCL 15nm) [43]. Any usage of the OCL 15nm is under a NanGate license. We refer the reader to [44] to download the library.

6. CASE STUDIES

In this section, we try to demonstrate the effect of considering some physical information during logic synthesis. The experimental results presented in this section were enabled by using the proposed set of benchmarks. The adopted methodology for this experiment can be split in two base cases:

Case A: Traditional logic synthesis

1. Perform a traditional logic synthesis, without taking a DEF file as input;
2. Perform a one-shot place;
3. Perform a one-shot route;
4. Analyse the obtained results.

Case B: Physical-aware logic synthesis

1. Perform a physical-aware logic synthesis, taking additionally a DEF file as input;
2. Perform a one-shot place;
3. Perform a one-shot route;
4. Analyse the obtained results;

The DEF file considered in step A.1 contains only floorplanning information, such as I/O pin placement and the available area for the synthesis. The design we choose for this experiment is *uoft_raytracer* (benchmark #20 in Table 2). These experiments were performed by using a commercial tool. A summary of the obtained results after logic synthesis are presented in Table 3. Notice that the obtained results after logic synthesis are not so different. There are 2% more cells, 7% of area overhead. The main different result is related with power estimation, with 12% of power overhead.

Table 3: Obtained results after logic synthesis.

	Case A	Case B
Target Time	3802 ps	3802 ps
# Cell Instances	133913	137035
Area Estimation	0.527 μm^2	0.565 μm^2
Power Estimation	118.98 mW	133.31 mW

The most valuable results obtained with these experiments rely on the physical design steps. After placing and routing the design in a one-shot non-optimal approach, the design synthesized by the traditional logic synthesis has presented 98791 routing violations. However, following the same one-shot non-optimal approach to place and route the design synthesized by the physical-aware logic synthesis has presented 35149 routing violations, which represents 64.42% of reduction in terms of routing violations.

7. FUTURE WORKS

The presented benchmarks suite contains the necessary information to bring logic synthesis and physical design together. However, much has still to be done. Larger benchmarks need to be distributed, as well as floorplans containing blockages and more realistic design challenges. Benchmarks with different clock regions and power domains are also intended to be added. However, this first initiative identifies the lack of benchmarks that would serve to both logic synthesis and physical design communities.

8. CONCLUSIONS

This paper presented an improved benchmark suite to jointly consider logic synthesis and physical design. The proposed benchmark suite can be downloaded in [23]. In this paper, we described benchmarks as a set composed of circuits, design intents (constraints), floorplan, target library and technology. From educational and benchmarking standpoints, this benchmark suite is provided to allow its use both for logic synthesis and for physical design experiments. The set of benchmarks proposed herein can be used to achieve two major purposes: (1) to consider physical information during the early steps in design flow, which makes possible to perform a draft design closure during logic synthesis; and (2) to regard logic features while handling physical designs, which allows investigations about resynthesis approaches by collapsing/splitting logic cells in such a way to obtain more physical-friendly designs. The main educational message given by this benchmark suite is that the same circuit can become a very different benchmark if design intent (e.g. design constraints (SDC files) or pin placement (DEF files)) is changed.

9. ACKNOWLEDGEMENTS

The work presented herein has been partially funded by CAPES, by CNPq and by FAPERGS under grant 11/2053-9 (Pronem), and the European Community's Seventh Framework Programme under grant 248538 - Synaptic.

10. REFERENCES

[1] Jae-sun Seo, Igor L Markov, Dennis Sylvester, and David Blaauw. On the decreasing significance of large standard cells in technology mapping. In *Proc. of Int'l Conf. on Computer-Aided Design (ICCAD)*, 2008.

[2] T. N. Theis. The future of interconnection technology. *IBM Journal of Research and Development*, 44(3):379–390, 2000.

[3] Kurt Keutzer, A. Richard Newton, and Narendra Shenoy. The future of logic synthesis and physical design in deep-submicron process geometries. In *Proc. of Int'l Symp. on Physical Design (ISPD)*, 1997.

[4] W. Gosti, A. Narayan, R.K. Brayton, and A.L. Sangiovanni-Vincentelli. Wireplanning in logic synthesis. In *Proc. of Int'l Conf. on Computer-Aided Design (ICCAD)*, 1998.

[5] Kai-hui Chang, Igor L. Markov, and Valeria Bertacco. Safe Delay Optimization for Physical Synthesis. In *Proc. of Asia and South Pacific Design Automation Conference (ASP-DAC)*, 2007.

[6] Michael J Flynn, Patrick Hung, and Kevin W Rudd. Deep-Submicron Microprocessor Design Issues. *IEEE Micro*, 19(4), 1999.

[7] David Bryan. The ISCAS'85 benchmark circuits and netlist format. *North Carolina State University*, 1985.

[8] F. Brglez, D. Bryan, and K. Kozminski. Combinational profiles of sequential benchmark circuits. In *Proc. of Int'l Symp. on Circuits and Systems*, 1989.

[9] Saeyang Yang. ACM/SIGDA Benchmarks: Logic Synthesis and Optimization Benchmarks User Guide Version 3.0, 1991.

[10] Fulvio Corno, Matteo Sonza Reorda, and Giovanni Squillero. Rt-level itc'99 benchmarks and first atpg results. *IEEE Design & Test of Computers*, 17(3):44–53, 2000.

[11] Christoph Albrecht. IWLS 2005 Benchmarks. In *Int'l Workshop on Logic & Synthesis (IWLS)*, 2005.

[12] Gi-Joon Nam, Charles J. Alpert, Paul Villarrubia, Bruce Winter, and Mehmet Yildiz. The ISPD2005 Placement Contest and Benchmark Suite. In *Proc. of Int'l Symp. on Physical Design (ISPD)*, 2005.

[13] Gi-Joon Nam. ISPD 2006 Placement Contest: Benchmark Suite and Results. In *Proc. of Int'l Symp. on Physical Design (ISPD)*, 2006.

[14] Gi-Joon Nam, Mehmet Yildiz, David Z. Pan, and Patrick H. Madden. ISPD Placement Contest Updates and ISPD 2007 Global Routing Contest. In *Proc. of Int'l Symp. on Physical Design (ISPD)*, 2007.

[15] Gi-Joon Nam, Cliff Sze, and Mehmet Yildiz. The ISPD Global Routing Benchmark Suite. In *Proc. of Int'l Symp. on Physical Design (ISPD)*, 2008.

[16] Gi-Joon Nam, Cliff Sze, and Mehmet Yildiz. The ISPD Global Routing Benchmark Suite. In *Proc. of Int'l Symp. on Physical Design (ISPD)*, 2009.

[17] C. N. Sze. ISPD 2010 High Performance Clock Network Synthesis Contest: Benchmark Suite and Results. In *Proc. of Int'l Symp. on Physical Design (ISPD)*, 2010.

[18] Natarajan Viswanathan, Charles J. Alpert, Cliff Sze, Zhuo Li, Gi-Joon Nam, and Jarrod A. Roy. The ISPD-2011 Routability-driven Placement Contest and Benchmark Suite. In *Proc. of Int'l Symp. on Physical Design (ISPD)*, 2011.

[19] Muhammet Mustafa Ozdal, Chirayu Amin, Andrey Ayupov, Steven Burns, Gustavo Wilke, and Cheng Zhuo. The ISPD-2012 Discrete Cell Sizing Contest and Benchmark Suite. In *Proc. of Int'l Symp. on Physical Design (ISPD)*, 2012.

[20] M. M. Ozdal, C. Amin, A. Ayupov, S. Burns, G. Wilke, and C. Zhuo. An Improved Benchmark Suite for the ISPD-2013 Discrete Cell Sizing Contest. In *Proc. of Int'l Symp. on Physical Design (ISPD)*, 2013.

[21] Vlad Yutsis, Ismail S. Bustany, David Chinnery, and Joseph Shinnerl. A benchmark suite for the ISPD-2014 detailed routing-driven placement contest. In *Proc of Intl Symp on Physical Design (ISPD)*, 2014.

[22] Ismail S. Bustany, David Chinnery, Joseph R. Shinnerl, and Vladimir Yutsis. ISPD 2015 Benchmarks with Fence Regions and Routing Blockages for Detailed-Routing-Driven Placement. In *Proc. of Int'l Symp. on Physical Design (ISPD)*, 2015.

[23] Jody Matos, Renato Ribas, and Andre Reis. Logic-physical-aware benchmark suite. http://www.inf.ufrgs.br/logics/downloads, 2015.

[24] Bryan Preas. Benchmarks for cell-based layout systems. In *Proc. of Design Automation Conference (DAC)*, 1987.

[25] Krzysztof Koźmiński. Benchmarks for layout synthesis - evolution and current status. In *Proc. of Design Automation Conference (DAC)*, 1991.

[26] Steve Meyer. Using controlled experiments in layout. *ACM SIGDA Newsletter*, 21(1):46–55, 1991.

[27] Carl Sechen. Average interconnection length estimation for random and optimized placements. In *Proc. of Int'l Conf. on Computer-Aided Design (ICCAD)*, 1987.

[28] M. Pedram and B. Preas. Interconnection length estimation for optimized standard cell layouts. In *Proc. of Int'l Conf. on Computer Design: VLSI in Computers and Processors (ICCD)*, 1989.

[29] M. Pedram and B. Preas. Accurate prediction of physical design characteristics for random logic. In *Proc. of Int'l Conf. on Computer Design: VLSI in Computers and Processors (ICCD)*, 1989.

[30] A. Reis, J. Roy, V. Shende, I. Markov, F. Mo, and A. Kuehlmann. IWLS 2003 Focus Group on Benchmarks Presentation. http://www.iwls.org/iwls2003/benchmarks.ppt.

[31] Saurabh N Adya, Mehmet Can Yildiz, Igor L Markov, et al. Benchmarking for large-scale placement and beyond. *Trans. on Computer-Aided Design of Integrated Circuits and Systems (TCAD)*, 23(4), 2004.

[32] N. Viswanathan, C. Alpert, C. Sze, Zhuo Li, and Yaoguang Wei. The DAC 2012 routability-driven placement contest and benchmark suite. In *Proc. Design Automation Conference (DAC)*, 2012.

[33] Tanuj Jindal, Charles J. Alpert, Jiang Hu, Zhuo Li, Gi-Joon Nam, and Charles B. Winn. Detecting tangled logic structures in VLSI netlists. In *Proc of Design Automation Conference (DAC)*, 2010.

[34] Franc Brglez. A neutral netlist of 10 combinational benchmark circuits and a target translation in fortran. In *Proc. of Int'l Symp. on Circuits and Systems (ISCAS)*, 1985.

[35] Franc Brglez, David Bryan, and Krzysztof Kozminski. Combinational profiles of sequential benchmark circuits. In *Proc. of Int'l Symp. on Circuits and Systems (ISCAS)*, 1989.

[36] Joachim Pistorius, Mike Hutton, Alan Mishchenko, and Robert Brayton. Benchmarking method and designs targeting logic synthesis for fpgas. In *Proc. of Int'l Workshop on Logic & Ssynthesis (IWLS)*, 2007.

[37] Synopsys. Synopsys Design Constraints (SDC), 2013.

[38] Berkeley Logic Synthesis and Verification Group. Abc: A system for sequential synthesis and verification. http://www.eecs.berkeley.edu/~alanmi/abc/.

[39] A. Biere. AIGER Format. http://fmv.jku.at/aiger/, 2007.

[40] A. Mishchenko, S. Chatterjee, and R. Brayton. DAG-aware AIG rewriting: a fresh look at combinational logic synthesis. In *Proc. of Design Automation Conference (DAC)*, 2006.

[41] Cadence Inc. LEF/DEF 5.3 to 5.7 exchange format, 2009.

[42] Open Source Liberty. Liberty Specifications and Documentation, 2011.

[43] M. Martins, Jody Matos, Renato Ribas, André Reis, Guilherme Schlinker, Lucio Rech, and Jens Michelsen. Open Cell Library in 15nm FreePDK Technology. In *Proc. of the Int'l Symp. on Physical Design (ISPD)*, 2015.

[44] Nangate Inc. NanGate FreePDK15 Open Cell Library. http://www.nangate.com/?page_id=2328.

Author Index

join today!

SIGDA & ACM

www.acm.org/sigda   www.acm.org

The **ACM Special Interest Group on Design Automation** (SIGDA) has a tradition of more than forty years of supporting conferences and the EDA profession. In addition to sponsoring DAC, SIGDA sponsors ICCAD, DATE, and ASP-DAC, plus approximately 15 smaller symposia and workshops. SIGDA provides a broad array of additional resources to our members, to students and professors, and to the EDA profession in general. SIGDA organizes the University Booth and Ph.D. Forum at DAC and the CADathlon at ICCAD, and funds various scholarships and awards. SIGDA provides its members with full access to SIGDA-sponsored conference proceedings in the ACM Digital Library and the SIGDA E-Newsletter containing information on upcoming conferences and funding opportunities, emailed to SIGDA members twice each month. The SIGDA E-Newsletter also includes *SIGDA News* which highlights the most relevant events in the EDA and semiconductor industry, and the "What is...?" column that brings to the attention of EDA professionals the most recent topics of interest in design automation. For further information on SIGDA's programs and resources, see www.sigda.org.

The **Association for Computing Machinery** (ACM) is an educational and scientific computing society which works to advance computing as a science and a profession. Benefits include subscriptions to *Communications of the ACM*, *MemberNet*, *TechNews* and *CareerNews*, full and unlimited access to online courses and books, discounts on conferences and the option to subscribe to the ACM Digital Library.

❏ SIGDA (ACM Member) . . . . $ 25

❏ SIGDA (ACM Student Member & Non-ACM Student Member). . . . . $ 15

❏ SIGDA (Non-ACM Member). . . . . $ 25

❏ ACM Professional Membership ($99) & SIGDA ($25) $124

❏ ACM Professional Membership ($99) & SIGDA ($25) & ACM Digital Library ($99) $223

❏ ACM Student Membership ($19) & SIGDA ($15) . . . . $ 34

payment information

Name_____

ACM Member #_____

Mailing Address_____

_____

City/State/Province_____

ZIP/Postal Code/Country_____

Email_____

Mobile Phone_____

Fax_____

Credit Card Type: ❏ AMEX   ❏ VISA   ❏ MC

Credit Card #_____

Exp. Date_____

Signature_____

Make check or money order payable to ACM, Inc

ACM accepts U.S. dollars or equivalent in foreign currency. Prices include surface delivery charge. Expedited Air Service, which is a partial air freight delivery service, is available outside North America. Contact ACM for more information.

Mailing List Restriction
ACM occasionally makes its mailing list available to computer-related organizations, educational institutions and sister societies. All email addresses remain strictly confidential. Check one of the following if you wish to restrict the use of your name:

❏ ACM announcements only
❏ ACM and other sister society announcements
❏ ACM subscription and renewal notices only

Questions? Contact:
ACM Headquarters
2 Penn Plaza, Suite 701
New York, NY 10121-0701
voice: 212-626-0500
fax: 212-944-1318
email: acmhelp@acm.org

Remit to:
ACM
General Post Office
P.O. Box 30777
New York, NY 10087-0777

SIGAPP

www.acm.org/joinsigs

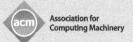

Association for
Computing Machinery

Advancing Computing as a Science & Profession

www.ingramcontent.com/pod-product-compliance
Lightning Source LLC
LaVergne TN
LVHW060140070326
832902LV00018B/2876